Lecture Notes in Computer Science   16323

Founding Editors

Gerhard Goos
Juris Hartmanis

Aijun An · Alfredo Cuzzocrea · Hongxin Hu
Editors

Social Networks Analysis and Mining

17th International Conference, ASONAM 2025
Niagara Falls, ON, Canada, August 25–28, 2025
Proceedings, Part II

 Springer

Editors
Aijun An
York University
Toronto, ON, Canada

Alfredo Cuzzocrea
University of Calabria
Rende, Italy

Hongxin Hu
University at Buffalo
Buffalo, NY, USA

ISSN 0302-9743   ISSN 1611-3349 (electronic)
Lecture Notes in Computer Science
ISBN 978-3-032-13820-0   ISBN 978-3-032-13821-7 (eBook)
https://doi.org/10.1007/978-3-032-13821-7

Preface

On behalf of the members of the organizing committee and members of the technical program committee we welcome you to ASONAM 2025.

The ASONAM conference series brings together researchers from around the world to share the latest advances in the attractive field of Social Networks Analysis and Mining. The conference was initiated in 2009 at the Hellenic American University in Athens, Greece. ASONAM 2010 was held at the University of Southern Denmark in Odense, Denmark, followed by editions at the National University of Kaohsiung (Taiwan), Istanbul (Turkey), Niagara Falls (Canada), Beijing (China), Paris (France), San Francisco (USA), Sydney (Australia), Barcelona (Spain), Vancouver (Canada), Istanbul (Turkey), Kusadasi (Turkey), and Calabria (Italy).

This year, we received 134 submissions for the research track conference. The review process was single blinded and each paper was reviewed by at least two program committee members who provided detailed and thorough reviews that helped us to finalize the decisions. We thank all PC members and the external reviewers for their hard work! Though most submissions were of good quality, we tried to maintain the low acceptance rates adopted since ASONAM started. After a discussion phase for the research track, we selected 32 submissions as full papers (acceptance rate ~24%) and 33 submissions as short papers (acceptance rate ~24%). The rest of the papers included in these proceedings are from the other tracks, namely the Multidisciplinary track: 6 full papers and 6 short papers out of 26 submissions; the Industrial track: 6 full papers and 1 short paper out of 19; the PhD track: 9 full papers out of 29; FAB 2025: 10 full papers and 1 short paper out of 37; and FOSINT-SI 2025: 5 full papers out of 20. Full and short papers were allocated 30- and 20-minute oral presentation slots in the program, respectively; demos also formed an integral part of the conference. Papers from HI-BI-BI 2025, the workshops, short papers from some tracks, demo papers and journal track summaries will appear in the accompanying proceedings, published as a volume of the Lecture Notes in Social Networks series.

Participants enjoyed three keynote speeches by Yizhou Sun (University of California, Los Angeles, USA), M. Tamer Özsu (University of Waterloo, Canada), and Gerd Stumme (University of Kassel, Germany), and a panel discussion moderated by Rokia Missaoui (University of Quebec in Outaouais, Canada). The panel consisted of 6 panelists: Nitin Agarwal (University of Arkansas, USA), Jean-Loup Guillaume (La Rochelle Université, France), Hongxin Hu (University at Buffalo, USA), Rasha Kashef (Toronto Metropolitan University, Canada), Kwan Hui Lim (University of Technology and Design, Singapore), and Tamer Özsu (University of Waterloo, Canada).

Two tutorials were selected for presentation during the first day: (1) Homophily in Complex Networks: Measures, Models, and Applications, by Akrati Saxena (Leiden University, Netherlands), Gaurav Kumar (Indian Institute of Science Education and Research, India), and Chandrakala Meena (Indian Institute of Science Education and

Research, India), and (2) Social Networks and Social Reward Economies, by Peter Marbach (University of Toronto, Canada).

Besides the main conference program, the four-day ASONAM event included three workshops. There were also three co-located events, the International Symposium on Foundations of Open Source Intelligence and Security Informatics (FOSINT-SI 2025), the International Symposium on Network Enabled Health Informatics, Biomedicine and Bioinformatics (HI-BI-BI 2025), and the International Symposium on Foundations and Applications of Big Data Analytics (FAB 2025).

We would like to thank all the chairs, especially the steering chair Reda Alhajj (University of Calgary, Canada) and the general chair Rokia Missaoui (University of Quebec in Outaouais, Canada) for their guidance, the publication chairs, Min-Yuh Day (National Taipei University, Taiwan) and Panagiotis Karampelas (Hellenic Air Force Academy, Greece), for collecting the final versions of the accepted papers and compiling the proceedings), the web chair Deniz Bestepe (Istanbul Medipol University, Turkey) for coordinating the logistics, and the local organization team led by Naser Ezzati-Jivan (Brock University, Canada) for handling all aspects necessary to complete the organization of ASONAM 2025 successfully. Indeed, all participants left Niagara Falls, Canada, with good memories. Finally, we would like to thank the authors for submitting their work to ASONAM.

August 2025

Aijun An
Alfredo Cuzzocrea
Hongxin Hu

Organization

Steering Chair

Reda Alhajj   University of Calgary, Canada

Honorary Chair

Frans N. Stokman   University of Groningen, Netherlands

General Chairs

Fakhri Karray   Mohamed bin Zayed University of Artificial Intelligence, UAE and University of Waterloo, Canada
Jon Rokne   University of Calgary, Canada
Rokia Missaoui   University of Quebec in Outaouais, Canada

Program Committee Chairs

Aijun An   York University, Canada
Alfredo Cuzzocrea   University of Calabria, Italy
Hongxin Hu   University at Buffalo, USA

Industry Track Chairs

Faraz Rasheed   Travelers, Canada
Kwan Hui Lim   Singapore University of Technology and Design, Singapore
Patricia Takako Endo   Universidade de Pernambuco, Brazil

Workshops Chairs

I-Hsien Ting	National University of Kaohsiung, Taiwan
Michael Benzinger	Technical University of Munich, Germany
Sucheta Soundarajan	Syracuse University, USA

Multidisciplinary Track Chairs

Alex Thomo	University of Victoria, Canada
Carson K. Leung	University of Manitoba, Canada
Catalina Goanta	Utrecht University, Netherlands

PhD Forum and Posters Track Chairs

Lulwah Alkulaib	Kuwait University, Kuwait
Mohammad Moshirpour	University of California, Irvine, USA
Omair Shafiq	Carleton University, Canada

Demos and Exhibitions Chairs

Kashfia Sailunaz	University of Calgary, Canada
Tansel Ozyer	Ankara Medipol University, Turkey

Tutorial Chairs

Ee-Peng Lim	Singapore Management University, Singapore
Nitin Agarwal	University of Arkansas - Little Rock, USA
Osmar Zaiane	University of Alberta, Canada

Publicity Chairs

Buket Kaya	Firat University, Turkey
Kashfia Sailunaz	University of Calgary, Canada
Shang Gao	Jilin University, China

Publication Chairs

Min-Yuh Day   National Taipei University, Taiwan
Panagiotis Karampelas   Hellenic Air Force Academy, Greece

Registration Chairs

Jalal Kawash   University of Calgary, Canada
Mehmet Kaya   Firat University, Turkey

Local Arrangements Chair

Naser Ezzati-Jivan   Brock University, Canada

Web Chair

Deniz Bestepe   Istanbul Medipol University, Turkey

Research Track Committee

Adetokunbo Makanju   New York Institute of Technology, USA
Alex Thomo   University of Victoria, Canada
Anna Sapienza   Technical University of Denmark, Denmark
Barbara Carminati   University of Insubria, Italy
Bin Guo   Trent University, Canada
Carlos Rubio Medrano   Texas A&M University - Corpus Christi, USA
Carmela Comito   ICAR-CNR, Italy
Chiara Boldrini   CNR-IIT, Italy
Christine Largeron   Université de Lyon, France
David Skillicorn   Queen's University, Canada
De-Nian Yang   Academia Sinica, Taiwan
Dimitris Spiliotopoulos   University of the Peloponnese, Greece
Ehsan Ul Haq   Hong Kong University of Science and
                                     Technology, China
Etienne Tajeuna   Université du Québec en Outaouais, Canada
Giulio Rossetti   KDD Lab, ISTI-CNR, Italy
Giuseppe Manco   ICAR-CNR, Italy
Hamed Alhoori   Northern Illinois University, USA

Hao Gao	Samsung, USA
Hasan Davulcu	Arizona State University, USA
Hemant Purohit	George Mason University, USA
Jin-Hee Cho	Virginia Tech, USA
Juergen Pfeffer	Technical University of Munich, Germany
K. Selcuk Candan	Arizona State University, USA
Katerina Potika	San José State University, USA
Keyan Guo	University at Buffalo, USA
Lara Quijano-Sanchez	Universidad Autónoma de Madrid, Spain
Ling Jiang	York University, Canada
Long Cheng	Clemson University, USA
Lu-An Tang	NEC Labs America, USA
Mainack Mondal	Indian Institute of Technology, Kharagpur, India
Manos Papagelis	York University, Canada
Marco Viviani	Università degli Studi di Milano-Bicocca, Italy
Matteo Zignani	Università degli Studi di Milano, Italy
Matthieu Latapy	CNRS, France
Md Amran Hossen Bhuiyan	York University, Canada
Mehdi Kargar	Toronto Metropolitan University, Canada
Mehmet Kaya	Firat University, Turkey
Mengfei Yang	Meta Platforms Inc., USA
Mirko Marras	University of Cagliari, Italy
Moudoud Hajar	Université du Québec en Outaouais, Canada
Nishant Vishwamitra	University of Texas at San Antonio, USA
Pasquale De Meo	Vrije Universiteit Amsterdam, Netherlands
Reza Rejaie	University of Oregon, USA
Reza Farahbakhsh	Institut Mines-Télécom, Télécom SudParis, France
Rezvaneh Rezapour	Drexel University, USA
Ridwanul Hasan Tanvir	Pennsylvania State University, USA
Roshni Iyer	University of California, Los Angeles, USA
Sabirat Rubya	Marquette University, USA
Sabrina Gaito	University of Milan, Italy
Shirin Nilizadeh	University of Texas at Arlington, USA
Shivakant Mishra	University of Colorado Boulder, USA
Sho Tsugawa	University of Tsukuba, Japan
Shradha Sehgal	Netflix, USA
Shuang Hao	University of Texas at Dallas, USA
Song Liao	Texas Tech University, USA
Surendrabikram Thapa	Virginia Tech, USA
Tao Ruan	University of Colorado Boulder, USA
Ugochukwu Onyepunuka	Amazon, USA

Usman Naseem	University of Sydney, Australia
William Andreopoulos	San José State University, USA
Xingwei Yang	Toronto Metropolitan University, Canada
Xingzhi Guo	Stony Brook University, USA
Yini Zhang	University at Buffalo, USA
Zhiang Wu	Nanjing Audit University, China

Multidisciplinary Track Committee

Jawad Chowdhury	Oak Ridge National Laboratory, USA
Mohamed Bouguessa	Université du Québec à Montréal, Canada
Shradha Sehgal	Netflix, USA
Charalampos Chelmis	University at Albany, State University of New York, USA
Chu-Yun Cheng	National Taiwan University of Science and Technology, Taiwan
Ujun Jeong	Arizona State University, USA
Fabiola Pereira	University of São Paulo, Brazil
Tamer Abuhmed	Sungkyunkwan University, South Korea
Tanvi Banerjee	University of Missouri Columbia, USA
Mohammed Abuhamad	Loyola University Chicago, USA
Rezaur Rashid	University of North Carolina at Charlotte, USA
Venkatesh Srinivasan	Santa Clara University, USA
Behnaz Moradijamei	James Madison University, USA
Manuel Sandoval Madrigal	Loyola University Chicago, USA
Mehmet Aktas	Kennesaw State University, USA
Farhan Tanvir	Georgia State University, USA
Muhammad Abulaish	South Asian University, India
Fan Jiang	University of Northern British Columbia, Canada
Baha Rababah	Red River College Polytechnic, Canada
Hoang Hai Nguyen	Canadian Food Inspection Agency, Canada

Industry Track Committee

Shradha Sehgal	Netflix, USA
Wenchuan Mu	Singapore University of Technology and Design, Singapore
Junhua Liu	Forth AI, USA
Soumajyoti Sarkar	AWS, USA
Sajal Halder	CSIRO, Australia
Menglin Li	Singapore University of Technology and Design, Singapore

Additional Reviewers

B. Aditya Prakash	Georgia Tech, USA
Dong Wang	University of Illinois Urbana-Champaign, USA
Tim Weninger	University of Notre Dame, USA
Abdessamad Benlahbib	Sidi Mohamed Ben Abdellah University, Morocco
Abdessamad Imine	Loria, France
Abiola Akinnubi	Vast.ai, USA
Adnan Hoq	University of Notre Dame, USA
Aisling Third	Open University, UK
Akira Matsui	Yokohama National University, Japan
Alessandro Visintin	University of Padua, Italy
Alexander Rodriguez	Georgia Institute of Technology, USA
Amrit Poudel	University of Notre Dame, USA
Anastasios Giovanidis	Centre National de la Recherche Scientifique, France
Anatoliy Gruzd	Toronto Metropolitan University, Canada
Anggy Eka Pratiwi	Indian Institute of Technology Jodhpur, India
Ankan Mullick	IIT Kharagpur, India
Anurag Singh	National Institute of Technology Delhi, India
Arlei Silva	Rice University, USA
Ashwin Shreyas Mohan Rao	University of Southern California, USA
Bailu Jin	Cranfield University, UK
Bijaya Adhikari	University of Iowa, USA
Billy Spann	University of Arkansas at Little Rock, USA
Bing He	Georgia Institute of Technology, USA
Bohan Jiang	Arizona State University, USA
Casey Doyle	Sandia National Laboratories, USA
Charalampos Chelmis	University at Albany, State University of New York, USA
Christine Largeron	Université de Lyon, France
Constantine Dovrolis	Georgia Institute of Technology, USA
Courtland Vandam	Massachusetts Institute of Technology, USA
David Skillicorn	Queen's University, Canada
Debanjan Datta	Virginia Tech, USA
Eduard Dragut	Temple University, USA
Ehsan Ul Haq	Hong Kong University of Science and Technology, China
Etienne Gael Tajeuna	Laval University, Canada
Fattane Zarrinkalam	University of Guelph, Canada
Fernando Terroso-Saenz	Catholic University of Murcia, Spain
Frank Liu	Southern Illinois University, USA

Fujio Toriumi	University of Tokyo, Japan
George Panagopoulos	École Polytechnique, France
Gita Sukthankar	University of Central Florida, USA
Hadassa Daltrophe	Shamoon College of Engineering, Israel
Hamid R. Rabiee	Sharif University of Technology, Iran
Hanjia Lyu	University of Rochester, USA
Hasan Davulcu	Arizona State University, USA
Hitkul Jangra	Indraprastha Institute of Information Technology, Delhi, India
Huimin Zeng	University of Illinois Urbana-Champaign, USA
Humayun Kabir	Microsoft, USA
Isabel Murdock	Carnegie Mellon University, USA
Jiaming Cui	Georgia Institute of Technology, USA
Jiamou Liu	University of Auckland, New Zealand
Jiten Sidhpura	Sardar Patel Institute of Technology, India
Jose Luis Fernandez-Marquez	University of Geneva, Switzerland
Julio Cesar Soares dos Reis	Federal University of Viçosa, Brazil
Keith Burghardt	University of Southern California, USA
Kenji Yokotani	Tokushima University, Japan
Keyan Guo	University at Buffalo, USA
Kijung Shin	Korea Advanced Institute of Science and Technology, South Korea
Kshiteesh Hegde	Western Digital, USA
Lanyu Shang	University of Illinois Urbana-Champaign, USA
Lara Quijano-Sanchez	Universidad Autónoma de Madrid, Spain
Lu-An Tang	NEC Labs America, USA
Mainuddin Shaik	University of Arkansas at Little Rock, USA
Mehrdad Jalali	Karlsruhe Institute of Technology, Germany
Michael Smit	Dalhousie University, Canada
Mirela Riveni	University of Groningen, Netherlands
Muhammad Abulaish	South Asian University, India
Nayoung Kim	Arizona State University, USA
Neha Gondal	Boston University, USA
Nicholas Botzer	University of Notre Dame, USA
Nikhil Muralidhar	Stevens Institute of Technology, USA
Niloofar Yousefi	University of Arkansas at Little Rock, USA
Nishant Vishwamitra	Clemson University, USA
Nur Dean	Farmingdale State College, USA
Orchid Chetia Phukan	Indraprastha Institute of Information Technology, Delhi, India
Raed Alharbi	University of Florida, USA
Rafael Elias De Lima Escalfoni	CEFET-RJ, Brazil

Rajesh Sharma	University of Tartu, Estonia
Rajiv Ramnath	Ohio State University, USA
Sajedul Talukder	University of Alabama at Birmingham, USA
Sangeeta Lal	Keele University, UK
Sankita Patel	Sardar Vallabhbhai National Institute of Technology, Surat, India
Sharma Chakravarthy	University of Texas at Arlington, USA
Shreya Ghosh	Pennsylvania State University, USA
Shubham Gupta	Indian Institute of Technology Jodhpur, India
Siyi Guo	University of Southern California, USA
Sriram Pemmaraju	University of Iowa, USA
Subhodip Biswas	Virginia Polytechnic Institute, USA
Suman Kundu	Indian Institute of Technology Jodhpur, India
Tanvir Amin	Google, USA
Theresa Migler	California Polytechnic State University, San Luis Obispo, USA
Tobias Hecking	German Aerospace Center, Germany
Toshiharu Sugawara	Waseda University, Japan
Trenton Ford	University of Notre Dame, USA
Tuan Le	New Mexico State University, USA
Ulrik Brandes	ETH Zürich, Switzerland
Wael Khreich	American University of Beirut, Lebanon
Wang-Chien Lee	Pennsylvania State University, USA
William Power	Temple University, USA
Xinwei Deng	Virginia Tech, USA
Xinyang Zhang	University of Illinois Urbana-Champaign, USA
Xueying Liu	Virginia Polytechnic Institute and State University, USA
Yang Zhang	University of Illinois Urbana-Champaign, USA
Yifan Ding	University of Notre Dame, USA
Ying Zhao	Naval Postgraduate School, USA
Yiqiao Jin	Georgia Institute of Technology, USA
Yoshiharu Ichikawa	Keio University/NHK, Japan
Young-Woo Kwon	Kyungpook National University, South Korea
Yue Zhang	Amazon, Inc., USA
Yueqing Liang	Illinois Institute of Technology, USA
Zhenming Liu	College of William and Mary, USA
Zhenrui Yue	University of Illinois Urbana-Champaign, USA
Zhihao Hu	Virginia Tech, USA

Contents

Research

Protecting Vulnerable Voices: Synthetic Dataset Generation for Self-disclosure Detection

Shalini Jangra$^{(\boxtimes)}$, Suparna De, Nishanth Sastry, and Saeed Fadaei

University of Surrey, Surrey, UK
{s.jangra,s.de,n.sastry,s.fadaei}@surrey.ac.uk

Abstract. Social platforms such as Reddit have a network of communities of shared interests, with a prevalence of posts and comments from which one can infer users' Personal Information Identifiers (PIIs). While such self-disclosures can lead to rewarding social interactions, they pose privacy risks and the threat of online harms. Research into the identification and retrieval of such risky self-disclosures of PIIs is hampered by the lack of open-source labeled datasets. Important hindrances to sharing high-quality labelled data include high annotation costs and privacy risks associated with the release of datasets containing self-disclosive text, especially when users include vulnerable populations.

To foster reproducible research into PII-revealing text detection, we develop a novel methodology to create synthetic equivalents of PII-revealing data that can be safely shared. Our contributions include creating a taxonomy of 19 PII-revealing categories for vulnerable populations and the creation and release of a synthetic PII-labeled multi-text span dataset generated from 3 text generation Large Language Models (LLMs), Llama2-7B, Llama3-8B, and zephyr-7b-beta, with sequential instruction prompting to resemble the original Reddit posts. The utility of our methodology to generate this synthetic dataset is evaluated with three metrics: First, we require *reproducibility equivalence*, i.e., results from training a model on the synthetic data should be comparable to those obtained by training the same models on the original posts. Second, we require that the synthetic data be *unlinkable* to the original users, through common mechanisms such as Google Search. Third, we wish to ensure that the synthetic data be *indistinguishable* from the original, i.e., trained humans should not be able to tell them apart. We release our dataset and code at https://netsys.surrey.ac.uk/datasets/synthetic-self-disclosure/ to foster reproducible research into PII privacy risks in online social media.

Keywords: Personal Information Identifiers · Synthetic data · Vulnerable Populations · Privacy Leaks · Large Language Models

1 Introduction

Leakage of Personally Identifiable Information (PII) on social media is a common and serious problem: technical affordances such as anonymity, visibility control

© The Author(s), under exclusive license to Springer Nature Switzerland AG 2026
A. An et al. (Eds.): ASONAM 2025, LNCS 16323, pp. 3–18, 2026.
https://doi.org/10.1007/978-3-032-13821-7_1

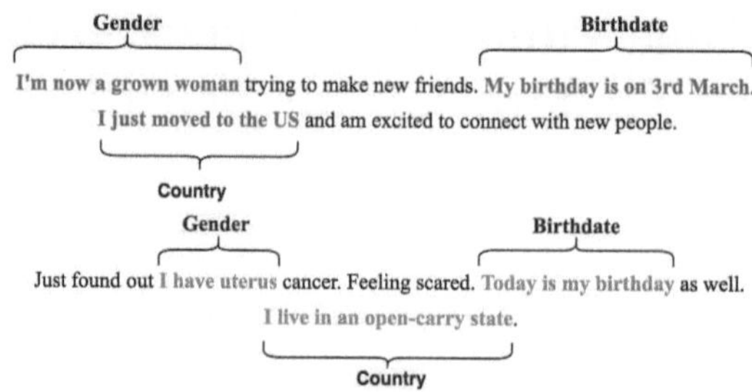

Fig. 1. Explicit (in red) and Implicit (in orange) PII self-disclosures of gender, birth date and country in Reddit posts. (Color figure online)

and editability [9] give users opportunities for self-disclosure and support seeking [2,19]; activities which may lead them to reveal personal information on social media [19,22]. This problem becomes more acute for vulnerable populations who may be targeted after self-disclosure. In this work, we consider vulnerable individuals as those who, due to intersecting factors such as race, socioeconomic status, gender or sexual identity, religion, or other marginalized social positions, face an increased risk of privacy violations that may lead to emotional, financial, or physical harm, as characterized in [19]. PII leakage may happen naturally in the course of posts made on social media as demonstrated in Fig. 1. Such leakage may happen in an *explicit* manner, wherein the text of a post directly reveals personal information, or *implicitly*, when PII can be inferred indirectly from a comment that the user makes. For instance, while the explicit mention of '3rd March' for birth-date can be flagged relatively straightforwardly as PII-revealing, talking about 'uterus cancer' may indirectly reveal (birth) gender.

Public datasets have been crucial for reproducible socio-technical research, enabling data-driven solutions to online harms [35]. However, in many cases, the collection and use of real-world datasets raises privacy concerns, as such data may contain potentially sensitive data, even when subjected to deidentification and sampling techniques before release [21,24]. This is especially true of datasets regarding PII disclosures. Even when datasets are based on publicly available data (e.g., public posts on platforms such as X or Reddit), there are ethical challenges about consent [5] and increased visibility [34].

Thus, many papers that deal with sensitive data [10,11,30] end up not sharing datasets publicly. This impedes much-needed research on these topics. Furthermore, creating *labeled* datasets is an expensive and time-intensive task since it may require careful manual annotations [25,31]; thus, reuse and sharing are important even beyond just enabling reproducibility. In several cases, the cost of creating "gold-standard" data can limit the scale of such datasets, which in turn limits the scale and sophistication of downstream research for understanding the problem, or machine learning models that can help prevent leakage.

A clear and "obvious" solution to this dilemma is to generate a synthetic dataset that *does not contain information about any particular individual, but has sufficient representation of different kinds of PII leakage seen in real datasets* so that it can be used to develop both a data-driven understanding as well as ML models that can help detect PII leakage. Achieving this requires *(i)* starting with a real dataset that would be useful to the research community *(ii)* compiling a list of characteristics or labels of interest, and (manually) annotating the dataset to identify different kinds of PII leakage, and *(iii)* generating a synthetic dataset which looks similar to the real dataset and preserves its utility to researchers whilst being difficult to link back to the posts in the real dataset.

Our main contribution is a novel method to create synthetically generated datasets that are equivalent to the original data in important ways, such as looking similar to and preserving the style of the original dataset, whilst still providing substantially improved privacy. Our method relies on private, locally hosted LLMs, along with RoBERTa-based models fine-tuned for multilabel classification and span-level PII detection across 19 sensitive categories.

Our extensive evaluation shows that the synthetic data looks similar to, and retains the key characteristics of the original dataset, so that it remains useful for researchers whilst also keeping data from real users private. We develop three metrics to demonstrate this: The first metric, *reproducibility equivalence*, evaluates, the *utility of the synthetic dataset to researchers* for its original intended purpose of ensuring research reproducibility. The second metric, *indistinguishability*, evaluates to what extent the two datasets look similar to *humans*. Specifically, we develop a user study with participants tasked with distinguishing the synthetic posts from the original posts. The third metric, *unlinkability*, evaluates the *resistance of the synthetic dataset to being deanonymized* by asking how easy it would be to find the original public social media post through a Google search with the equivalent synthetic post. We further evaluate our synthetic dataset on three metrics proposed in [6] for meaning, style and privacy preservation. After validating the dataset across these criteria, we fine-tuned a RoBERTa-based span categorization model using the synthetic data, achieving strong performance in detecting PII entities across multiple categories.

To support transparency and encourage further research, we open-source our code and make both the dataset and the modeling pipeline freely available for non-commercial research usage, at https://netsys.surrey.ac.uk/datasets/synthetic-self-disclosure/.

2   Related Work

PII-Annotated Datasets. A variety of corpora now exist that label text for different categories of personally identifiable information (PII). Several focus on disclosure detection, using either binary labels (e.g., 0 for non-disclosure and 1 for disclosure), or three-way labels (e.g., no disclosure, possible disclosure and clear disclosure) for self-disclosures of sexual abuse [8], health conditions [29], and personal revelations posted to a Reddit-style Korean community [7]. Beyond disclosure, the MBTI9k corpus assigns one of 16 Myers-Briggs personality types to Reddit users [12], while the large-scale RedDust resource provides 300k Reddit posts annotated for five user attributes—profession, hobby, family status, age, and gender—for profiling tasks [27]. *Both these works, whilst highly useful to researchers, reveal PII about Reddit users.* A Wikipedia-based corpus labels biography sentences for five classes of personal information, but its automatic annotation procedure introduces substantial noise in the dataset [14]. Finally, a Kaggle competition released synthetic PII text by inserting generated names and e-mail addresses into LLM-produced passages [15]; however, the synthetic nature of this data restricts it to a few basic PII types and fails to capture the richer, context-dependent disclosures common in social-media language.

While the above classification-oriented datasets are publicly available to the research community, recent works proposing more comprehensive PII category data do not make the resultant datasets open-source due to privacy or ethical considerations. These include the eight categories of personal attributes (sex, location, marriage, age, education, occupation, place of birth, income) applied to a curated Reddit dataset [26]. Although the authors claim to make a synthetic version of the original posts openly available, these need a seeded example (5 sample texts provided for the education category) to generate the posts with the provided script. Similarly, Dou et al. [10] propose 19 broad-coverage PII categories along 'attributes' and 'experiences' aspects for a PII span-annotated dataset. Our work focuses on categories specific to vulnerable people undergoing significant life transitions and extends it to include explicit as well as implicit PII mentions, together with word spans leaking the corresponding PII.

Online PII Identification Models. Svitlana et al. [30] demonstrated a latent personal attribute prediction approach using trained log-linear models with lexical features extracted from 200 tweets per user for 5000 Twitter profiles annotated through crowdsourcing, focused around 10 demographic attributes, 5 personality traits, and three types of controlled impression behavior. Fabien et al. [11]proposed two large-scale classification models (soft-margin SVM classifiers and supervised LDA) corresponding to gender (Male/Female) and citizenship (grouped by continent), which are trained on lexical rules-driven annotated Reddit data. Considering the objective definition of privacy-sensitive content, Livio et al. [4] employed advanced deep learning models to determine whether a post is sensitive. They utilized a corpus of nearly 10,000 text posts, each annotated as sensitive or non-sensitive by human evaluators.All of the above works do not make the associated datasets public. Zhang et al. [32] introduced domain-adapted BERT models: JobBERT and JobSpan-BERT for skills and knowledge component extraction along with SKILLSPAN- a novel skill extraction dataset consisting of 14.5K sentences and over 12.5K annotated spans, which can be useful for user employment information extraction. A comprehensive study by Staab et al. [26] analyzed the capability of LLMs such as GPT 3.5, Palm 2 Text, Llama-2 family, etc., to infer PIIs about Reddit post authors from the post text, concluding that LLMs have human-like performance in detecting various PIIs. Earlier works have proposed various disclosure detection models by modelling it as a binary [8] or multi-label [3,7,29] text classification task, for the presence, absence or likelihood of self-disclosure at sentence level [7,8,29]. A more relevant approach is proposed by Duo et al. [10] who fine-tune a RoBERTa-large model to identify text spans of self-disclosure along 19 proposed categories of PII.

3   Data Collection

To identify vulnerable communities on Reddit, we analyzed the top 1,000 largest subreddits listed at https://www.reddit.com/best/communities/1/, focusing on those that function as support networks for populations aligning with the definition of vulnerability outlined in Sect. 1. Notably, r/ADHD (ranked 445th, with $\tilde{2}$ million members) and r/lgbt (ranked 694th, with $\tilde{1}$.2 million members) emerged as two of the most prominent subreddits serving as support communities for vulnerable populations. For this study, we focus on the members of r/lgbt due to its explicit engagement with issues of identity, discrimination, and community support – factors closely aligned with PII leakage risks. We crawled posts from 2016 to 2020 from r/lgbt using the PushShift API [1]. We deliberately rely on old posts to avoid potential risks from leakage that we may not have anticipated. We identified the 500 most active **r/lgbt** subreddit members, and then collated posts and comments they may have made across different subreddits. This enables us to curate a dataset with longitudinal posts from active users, allowing identification of incremental self-disclosures. Among these 500 users, 100 have deactivated their accounts, resulting in a collection of 401,983 records from 400 users. A total of 8679 posts and comments from NSFW (Not Safe For Work) or Over_18 labelled subreddits are filtered out.

We streamline our approach to sift through user-generated content, specifically honing in on statements where individuals discuss themselves or their collective experiences. This strategy emphasizes focusing on retaining posts and comments that include first-person references, containing pronouns and words such as 'I,' 'me,' 'myself,' 'my,' 'mine,' 'we,' 'us,' 'our,' and 'ours.' We refine our dataset by utilizing regular expressions to recognize these linguistic markers. Following this, posts and comments containing less than three words are removed, resulting in 65,282 records. Finally, 5% of the remaining posts (i.e., 3264 posts) are randomly sampled for data annotation. These posts originate from 293 distinct subreddits, introducing a diverse range of content. These thematically distinct communities helped to include varied vocabularies and discourse styles in the dataset, thereby strengthening the ability to generalise to unseen subreddits and even other social-media platforms. We augment each post with the name of the subreddit where it was posted, as they serve as markers for potential PII-revealing information. For instance, location-based and community-specific subreddits can provide key insights into user identities.

3.1   Data Annotation

Two annotators with domain expertise started the annotation process as crowd-sourcing often leads to lower quality annotations [10]. Annotation guidelines were formulated after reviewing 500 records with posts and comments. We used an

Table 1. PII taxonomy with related statistics and example posts

PII	Number of spans	Average span length	Example
Name	118	17.18	Hey fellow Redditors! I'm k**t**n.
Birthdate	19	26.68	I'm turning 18 in 3 days and I am feeling lost.
Location	173	34.84	I was walking in downtown Brooklyn very close to the Brooklyn Bridge.
Country	86	26.57	I'm from the Philippines and I'm excited for my new journey.
Marital Status	57	13.46	My wife, not me, got a text message.
Religion	59	28.49	I was raised Catholic and I have seen things on the Atheism.
Ethnicity/Race	90	14.92	I'm a British person and I think I might have found my long-lost grandpa.
Gender	610	23.33	I don't tell people in my day-to-day life that I'm transgender.
Parenthood	54	12.59	My son is a huge Mustang fan.
Age	165	12.93	I'm a 14 year old and life's been pretty tough for me lately.
Sexuality	462	22.01	Isn't it so damn lovely! Left my lil lesbian heart all warm & fuzzy.
Medical Information	130	32.75	I've been getting chemo and radiation to the abdomen
Employment	288	27.61	I'm a medical intern in I**on*s*a.
Relationship	91	15.95	I'm dating a binary woman
Family	269	11.49	My dad passed away when I was 10 due to a heart attack.
Gender-Age	29	8.72	Hey 21M here, pm me if you're down to play some online games.
Mental Health	200	28.18	I've had ADHD all my life, but I've only been recently diagnosed.
Physical Appearance	44	21.52	Help a bro out! I'm a 5'9" tall, 180 lbs.
Degree/Designation	12	33.75	As a CS major, I'm used to running multiple programs simultaneously.

open-source annotation tool, Doccano [20], that provides a user-friendly platform. Annotators marked personal information disclosing text spans. These spans include PII along with self-referential text to preserve context. For instance, instead of highlighting just "As a transgender," we highlight "As a transgender, I." After annotation, 1,183 of 3,264 posts were found to contain PII-revealing text, while 2,081 did not. Together, these posts form our gold-standard annotated dataset. Inter-annotator agreement (IAA) metrics were used to improve the annotation guidelines and ensure good-quality annotated data. Commonly used IAA measures such as Cohen's Kappa and Fleiss' Kappa require the precise definition of negative samples and hence are not suggested for the span-based annotations. The recommended metric for span-based annotations is the pairwise F1 score [16]. We considered two annotations to agree if they had any overlapping words (partial span) and the same label. The pairwise F1 Score with overlap is 0.8275 for inter-annotator agreement. On average, the overlapping portion of the agreed-upon spans was 70.27%. Table 1 shows the 19 categories annotated for, including illustrative examples.

4   Synthetic Data Generation

4.1   Text Generation Models

Synthetic data generation used three LLMs – Llama 2-7B, Llama 3-8B, and Zephyr. This process involved a 1:3 mapping, where a single original post served as the input source for three synthetic posts: one by each LLM. We randomly selected 50 posts and generated synthetic versions using temperatures ranging

---

Prompt 1: Change the original post following these rules:

1. Replace all non-sensitive private information such as age, dob, religion, gender, marital status, race, ethnicity, employment, location, sexuality, and parenthood with other non-sensitive private information that retains the context. Replace the organization name with any other organization that serves the same purpose without generalization.
2. Change specific codes, IDs, numbers, and names with different codes, IDs, numbers, and names, respectively.
3. Generate a post that matches the same style and tone as the original post. If the original post contains spelling errors, strong language, or informal expressions, ensure that the synthetic post reflects the same characteristics.
4. Use common internet abbreviations, slang, emoticons, and expressions where appropriate, keeping the overall feel and context of the original post intact.
5. Don't give the title of the post.

Prompt 2: The first line of the original text tells about the subreddit name in which the original post was posted. Change the name of the subreddit to another subreddit of a similar kind.

System Prompt: You are a story recreator who takes the information from the original post, and then makes a different story with similar kinds of personal information. You want to minimize the chance of finding the link between the stories. Generate the post following this format:

"Changed Post":

Fig. 2. System and instruction prompts.

from 0.5 to 1 to determine the optimal temperature settings for the LLMs. For each LLM, we selected the temperature that produced the lowest average cosine similarity between the original and generated posts, ensuring the generated posts were sufficiently distinct and non-linkable to the originals. For Llama 2-7B, we used the Llama 2-Chat model which is fine-tuned for dialogue generation. We use instruction prompting with a maximum sequence length of 1024 tokens and a batch size of 8. During generation, a temperature of 1 and nucleus sampling with top_p of 0.9 were employed to balance diversity and coherence in the outputs. We used the zephyr-7b-beta model, a fine-tuned version of Mistral-7B [28], provided by HuggingFace API with temperature $= 1$ and top_p $= 0.95$ for generating the synthetic data. For Llama 3-8B, we used the Meta-Llama-3-8B-Instruct model with temperature $= 0.9$ and top_p $= 0.9$. For Llama3 and Zephyr, we used default sampling parameter settings to ensure adequate synthetic data quality.

Instruction tuning enables LLMs to follow user instructions and perform zero-shot generalization [17]. We incorporated multiple instructions in the prompt to generate synthetic data. The prompt provided to the model, as shown in Fig. 2, consists of two instruction prompts and a system prompt. This approach was adopted because Llama models often struggle to follow a sequence of instructions within a single query, occasionally ignoring or misinterpreting parts of the instructions. Consequently, we employed sequential instruction tuning, using a two-step process: first, to modify the content, and second, to change the subred-

Table 2. Summary statistics of generated dataset variants using LLMs

Dataset	Number of rounds	Dataset Size	Size after non-linkability threshold	Number of Spans
Llama2-genearted	3	971	954	1660
Llama3-genearted	3	913	900	1559
Zephyr-genearted	1	1054	1034	1919

dit name. Given the input x, suppose p_1 is the prompt for the first step of the task and p_2 is the prompt for the second step. The final output is obtained as $\hat{y}_2 \sim p(y_2|p_2, \hat{y}_1; \theta_{LLM})$ and $\hat{y}_1 \sim p(y_1|p_1, x; \theta_{LLM})$. The system prompt contains initial instructions sent to the API that define the behavior of the models and guide their response generation.

We are using real Reddit posts as seeds to generate synthetic content that might have text describing sensitive issues, such as transphobic activities or mental health issues. Following ethical AI governance and content moderation, Llama models sometimes refuse to generate synthetic content around this sensitive topic. Additionally, requests to change PII raise concerns about potential privacy violations, prompting the AI to refuse these alterations to prevent misuse. Therefore, we did two additional rounds of synthetic posts generation for the posts for which synthetic data generation was denied. We did not observe this behavior in the case of Zephyr and obtained synthetic data without the need for additional rounds. After generation, the synthetic data was preprocessed and manually annotated for PII-leaking spans. Table 2 presents the synthetic data description. We have different counts of generated posts for each LLM as Llama-based models refused to generate for some of the posts even after the third text-generation round. Further, some generated posts that do not contain any PII are discarded after annotation.

5   Data Quality Evaluation

We evaluate the synthetically generated dataset by developing three metrics that ensure the quality of generated text, in terms of being usable as a stand-in for the original dataset and "looking similar" to it, while at the same time being difficult to reverse engineer the original text given a synthetic post: *1)* Reproducibility equivalence, *2)* Indistinguishability, *3)* Unlinkability.

5.1   Reproducibility Equivalence

This metric ensures that synthetically generated data must preserve the same utility value as the original data. Our goal is to train a model on the synthetic dataset with a similar or better performance as when trained on the original data. To check this, we utilized the Hugging Face TrainingArguments class to fine-tune a pre-trained RoBERTa model [33] for a multi-label classification task

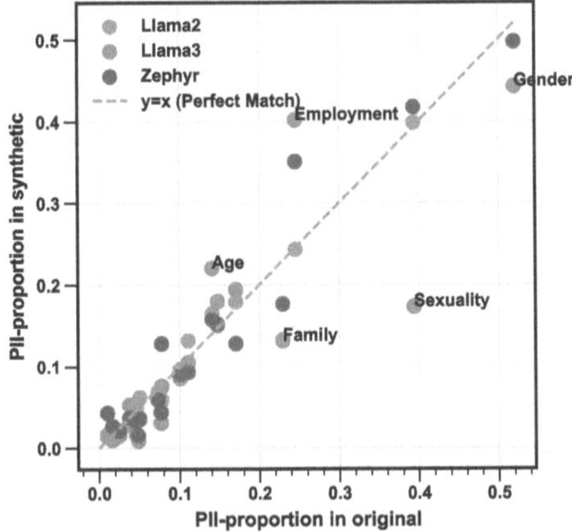

Fig. 3. PII-proportion in original and synthetic data.

of predicting which (if any) of the 19 PII categories (Table 1) a post contains. Specifically, we set the number of training epochs to 50 with default learning rate and weight_decay = 0.01. The batch size was kept at 8. Datasets are split into an 80–20% split for training and testing sets. The Table 3 demonstrates that the performance metrics of the multilabel classifier on synthetic datasets are comparable to those on the original dataset, demonstrating that the synthetically generated datasets have the same utility as the original dataset. We also fine-tuned a custom RoBERTa-based span categorization model, designed as a multilabel token classification task. Training was performed using the *BCEWithLogitsLoss* function, which combines sigmoid activation with binary cross-entropy loss applied at the token level. The model was trained entirely on synthetic data generated by the three different LLMs, using an 80–20% train-test split. The model demonstrated solid performance, achieving a token-level macro F1 score of 0.6965 and a partial span-level F1 score of 0.70 (with a minimum 50% overlap). These results are notable given the large number of target categories and surpass the performance reported in [10], which tackles a comparable set of PII classification categories.

A second aspect of reproducibility is whether the synthetic dataset has a similar mixture of different PII categories as the original. This may be required when using such a dataset in some applications, although in a synthetically generated dataset, it would be entirely possible to selectively boost or suppress the prevalence of PII categories if the application requires this. Figure 3 compares the proportion of different PII categories in synthetic datasets generated by Llama2, Llama3, and Zephyr against the original dataset. The red dashed line represents an ideal 1:1 match, where synthetic data would perfectly preserve PII proportions from the original dataset. One notable observation is that Llama2 tends to preserve the original proportion of PII proportions more faithfully. This suggests that Llama2 is less creative and more conservative in its text

Table 3. Roberta-based multi-label classifier performance on different datasets

Dataset	Accuracy	Precision	Recall	F1- score
Original	0.6772	0.8311	0.8096	0.85374
Llama2 generated	0.6359	0.8407	0.8507	0.8457
Llama3 generated	0.6448	0.8369	0.8690	0.8527
Zephyr generated	0.6462	0.8666	0.8471	0.8871

generation, leading to a distribution that remains close to the original. In contrast, Llama3 demonstrates greater creativity, possibly paraphrasing or altering details in a way that introduces bias towards certain PII categories. In particular, the Llama3-generated synthetic dataset has fewer gender, sexuality, and family-related PII details than the original, but over-expresses age-related PII disclosure posts. Zephyr, which is designed for more controlled generation and instruction-following, shows a moderate deviation – less extreme than Llama3 but still differing from the original data in key categories like Employment and Family. Zephyr, being more instruction-optimized, appears to balance preserving PII distribution while still introducing some variation, making it an intermediate case between the two. This highlights the challenge of balancing synthetic data fidelity and text diversity, particularly in privacy-sensitive applications.

5.2 Indistinguishability

The previous section showed that the synthetic dataset can serve as a drop-in replacement for the original when training automated models. Next, we ask whether synthetic data appears similar to the original Reddit posts for humans, i.e., it should be hard for humans to distinguish between the original and synthetic posts if they are not told which is which. To evaluate this, we recruited 100 participants through Prolific, an online research platform to recruit people for participation in a research study [23]. Participants were given three sets of identical tasks in order to distinguish which text/post appears to be written by a human rather than generated by any Large Language Model: Set 1 consists of 2 posts i.e., one post is an original text written by a human, the other is generated by an LLM; a random guess would have 50% chance of success). Set 2 consists of 3 posts i.e., one original post and 2 LLM-generated posts; a random guess would have 33.33% chance of success. Set 3 consists of 4 posts i.e., one original post and 3 LLM-generated posts; a random guess would have 25% chance of

Table 4. Distinguishing probability of LLM-generated text

	Set 1	Set 2	Set 3
Observed Probability	0.54	0.34	0.30
Expected Probability	0.5	0.33	0.25

Table 5. Category of reasons provided by survey participants

Categories	Keywords
Content Detail	Short, Very brief, Over-elaboration, Condensed Paragraph, Detailed
Tone and Style	Natural, How it sounds, Genuine, CPU stating facts, Formal or Formulatic Language
Language Characteristics	Offensive and strong language, Personal language, Swear words, Emotive Language, Repetitive and sterile way, Slang used, Use of acronym, Abbreviations
Grammar and Structure	No grammar, Poor sentence structure, Spelling error, Confusion of phraseology

success. The posts in each set were randomly selected from both synthetic and original posts. To discourage the Prolific participants from randomly guessing an answer, they were asked to also answer a follow-up question aimed at eliciting the factors they used to make their choices. We computed the chi-square deviation to determine how much the observed probability distribution of selecting the correct original post differs from the expected probability distribution, i.e., the probability of random selection as shown in Table 4. The null hypothesis (H_0) posits that participants cannot reliably distinguish human-written posts from LLM-generated posts (i.e., no difference between observed and expected distributions), while the alternative hypothesis (H_1) suggests that participants are able to make this distinction. The analysis yielded a chi-square statistic of 1.35 and a corresponding p-value of 0.51, indicating no statistically significant deviation from random selection under the null hypothesis.

Thus, we fail to reject the null hypothesis. We achieve our indistinguishability requirement, i.e., our study participants *are not able to distinguish between human-written and LLM-generated text*. Some participants were able to recognise the original one, for instance, one noted: "grammar mistakes and poor flow," in the human-generated text, while another described the original post as "erratic." The reasons are mainly classified into four categories as shown in Table 5. Yet, even those who selected correctly expressed difficulty, e.g., one said: *"I think this one is the most believable [as human generated] but all seem so human sounding it's quite hard to choose"*.

5.3   Unlinkability

A primary motive behind synthetic data generation is that publishing original data, highlighting users' self-disclosure texts, can create significant privacy risks. Therefore, this metric ensures that synthetic posts should not lead to the original posts they intend to mimic. To test this, we search for the text of the synthetic post using the Google search API and extract the top-10 search results. We aim to find the original post this way. We limit our results to the top 10 because the

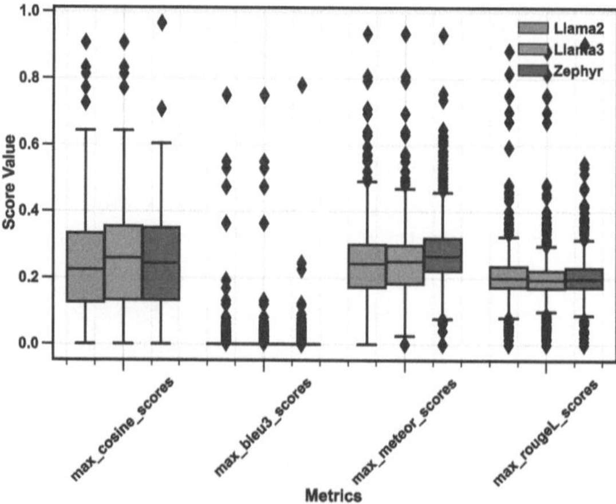

Fig. 4. Text similarity metrics between synthetic posts and top = 10 Google search results.

first page of Google Search typically contains no more than 10 entries. However, we performed a sensitivity analysis and checked that similar results hold even if we go to the third page of Google search results, and on average, beyond the 6th result, we begin encountering non-Reddit links.

We ignore all search results that do not lead directly to Reddit. To check that the Reddit link that matches a synthetic post is not related to the original post it is generated from, we calculate similarity scores between the synthetic text and posts/comments present on the Reddit link. We used cosine similarity score, Bleu score, Meteor, and Rouge to quantify how similar the content is [18]. Using them together provides a more comprehensive evaluation. The Fig. 4 demonstrates a strong balance between linguistic diversity and semantic fidelity. The synthetic posts of LLMs demonstrate significant rephrasing and structural variation, as reflected by the very low *max_blue3_scores* values. The generated posts have significantly different wording, phrasing, or structure from the original posts. This is due to the LLMs prioritizing diversity or rephrasing text. Low content similarity scores for all the metrics establish that synthetic data is non-linkable to original data. Further, to ensure the anonymity of the synthetic dataset, we discarded synthetic posts with a Meteor score greater than 0.5 to avoid any chance of tracing the synthetic post back to the original post.

5.4 Supplementary Evaluation

To complement the above analysis, we also test for three core aspects of data quality expected in synthetically generated texts, as identified by Chim et al. [6] recently. These metrics, which are independent of the data generation strategy, include *BERTScore* for meaning preservation, *style embedding similarity* for style preservation, and *divergence* as a proxy for privacy. BERTScore goes beyond exact word matches (relied upon by BLEU, ROUGE etc.), and aims to more fully capture meaning preservation. Controlling stylistic elements and ensuring linguistic diversity matter, as variation should promote generalization without compromising label validity. We extract idiolect embeddings using pooled RoBERTa representations for both original and synthetic posts and compare their writing patterns like sentence structure, tone, and phrasing. Divergence is calculated by measuring the BLEU score between the source and synthetic text, with the divergence defined as $1 - BLEU(s,t)$. This approach is effective for privacy metrics, as it quantifies the surface-form dissimilarity, serving as a proxy for verbatim memorization. The Table 6 shows that Zephyr generally performs best. The prominent difference is in terms of *divergence*.

Table 6. Synthetic data evaluation of metrics from [6]

Metrics	Llama2	Llama3	Zephyr
Meaning preservation (BERTScore)	0.92	0.87	0.90
Style Preservation (Style similarity)	0.98	0.97	0.96
Privacy preservation (Divergence)	0.58	0.89	0.95

6   Conclusion

In this paper, we introduced a taxonomy of 19 PII-revealing categories relevant to vulnerable populations and generated a synthetic PII-labeled span dataset using the capabilities of LLMs, specifically LLaMA2-7B, LLaMA3-8B, and Zephyr-7B. This dataset addresses the scarcity of labeled, privacy-preserving data and enables reproducible research into machine learning models for detecting PII-revealing content. We demonstrated the practical utility of this dataset by fine-tuning RoBERTa-based models for multilabel classification and token-level span categorization tasks. Despite the inherent complexity and breadth of the 19 PII categories, our span-level model achieved strong performance (macro $F1 = 0.70$) when trained entirely on synthetic data, showcasing its effectiveness for real-world applications. We have begun integrating this work into tools such as the InsightWatcher browser plugin [13], which detects self-disclosures on social media platforms. To support further research, we release our comprehensive PII-labeled synthetic dataset along with our codebase, enabling others to generate custom synthetic datasets and adapt our methods to their specific needs. In our future work, we will examine how this can be done in a principled manner, for example, in order to overcome biases which may exist in the original datasets. We also plan to extend the dataset to better represent categories with lower occurrence in our original dataset, such as Degree/Designation and Physical Appearance.

We also hope that our method of generating synthetic equivalents of datasets is generalisable and will lead to better reproducibility of research that relies on data otherwise difficult to share due to concerns such as preserving the privacy of participants. In particular, our three metrics of evaluation—reproducibility equivalence, indistinguishability and unlinkability—can help quantify the utility and privacy preservation of synthetic data in other contexts, thereby helping researchers better balance between these conflicting goals.

References

1. Pushshift reddit API documentation (2021). https://github.com/pushshift/api
2. Andalibi, N., Haimson, O.L., De Choudhury, M., Forte, A.: Understanding social media disclosures of sexual abuse through the lenses of support seeking and anonymity. In: Proceedings of the 2016 CHI Conference on Human Factors in Computing Systems, pp. 3906–3918 (2016)
3. Balani, S., De Choudhury, M.: Detecting and characterizing mental health related self-disclosure in social media. In: Proceedings of the 33rd Annual ACM Conference Extended Abstracts on Human Factors in Computing Systems, pp. 1373–1378 (2015)
4. Bioglio, L., Pensa, R.G.: Analysis and classification of privacy-sensitive content in social media posts. EPJ Data Sci. **11**(1), 1–24 (2022). https://doi.org/10.1140/epjds/s13688-022-00324-y
5. Buck, A.M., Ralston, D.F.: I didn't sign up for your research study: the ethics of using public data. Comput. Compos. **61**, 102655 (2021)
6. Chim, J., Ive, J., Liakata, M.: Evaluating synthetic data generation from user generated text. Comput. Linguist. 1–44 (2024)
7. Cho, W.I., Kim, S., Choi, E., Jeong, Y.: Assessing how users display self-disclosure and authenticity in conversation with human-like agents: a case study of luda lee. In: Findings of the Association for Computational Linguistics: AACL-IJCNLP 2022, pp. 145–152 (2022)
8. Chowdhury, A.G., Sawhney, R., Mathur, P., Mahata, D., Shah, R.R.: Speak up, fight back! detection of social media disclosures of sexual harassment. In: Proceedings of the 2019 Conference of the North American chapter of the Association for Computational Linguistics: Student Research Workshop, pp. 136–146 (2019)
9. Corvite, S., Zhang, B.Z., Haimson, O.L.: Social media's role during identity changes related to major life events. Proc. ACM Hum.-Comput. Interact. **6**(CSCW2), 1–22 (2022)
10. Dou, Y., et al.: Reducing privacy risks in online self-disclosures with language models. In: Annual Meeting of the Association for Computational Linguistics (ACL) (2023)
11. Fabian, B., Baumann, A., Keil, M.: Privacy on reddit? Towards large-scale user classification. In: ECIS (2015)
12. Gjurković, M., Šnajder, J.: Reddit: a gold mine for personality prediction. In: Proceedings of the Second Workshop on Computational Modeling of People's Opinions, Personality, and Emotions in Social Media, pp. 87–97 (2018)
13. Haq, E.U., Jangra, S., De, S., Sastry, N., Tyson, G.: Unpacking the layers: exploring self-disclosure norms, engagement dynamics, and privacy implications. In: Companion Proceedings of the ACM on Web Conference 2025, pp. 1890–1899 (2025)
14. Hathurusinghe, R., Nejadgholi, I., Bolic, M.: A privacy-preserving approach to extraction of personal information through automatic annotation and federated learning. In: Feyisetan, O., Ghanavati, S., Malmasi, S., Thaine, P. (eds.) Proceedings of the Third Workshop on Privacy in Natural Language Processing, pp. 36–45. Association for Computational Linguistics (2021)

15. Holmes, L., et al.: The learning agency lab - PII data detection (2024)
16. Hripcsak, G., Rothschild, A.S.: Agreement, the f-measure, and reliability in information retrieval. J. Am. Med. Inform. Assoc. **12**(3), 296–298 (2005)
17. Hu, H., Yu, S., Chen, P., Ponti, E.: Fine-tuning large language models with sequential instructions. In: Proceedings of the 2025 Conference of the Nations of the Americas Chapter of the Association for Computational Linguistics: Human Language Technologies (Volume 1: Long Papers), pp. 5589–5610. Association for Computational Linguistics (2025)
18. Liu, Y., Iter, D., Xu, Y., Wang, S., Xu, R., Zhu, C.: G-eval: NLG evaluation using GPT-4 with better human alignment. In: Proceedings of the 2023 Conference on Empirical Methods in Natural Language Processing, pp. 2511–2522. Association for Computational Linguistics (2023)
19. McDonald, N., Forte, A.: Privacy and vulnerable populations. In: Modern Sociotechnical Perspectives on Privacy, pp. 337–363. Springer, Cham (2022)
20. Nakayama, H., Kubo, T., Kamura, J., Taniguchi, Y., Liang, X.: doccano: text annotation tool for human (2018). https://github.com/doccano/doccano
21. Narayanan, A., Shmatikov, V.: De-anonymizing social networks. In: 2009 30th IEEE Symposium on Security and Privacy, pp. 173–187 (2009)
22. Nicol, E., et al.: Revealing cumulative risks in online personal information: a data narrative study. Proc. ACM Hum.-Comput. Interact. **6**(CSCW2), 1–25 (2022)
23. Palan, S., Schitter, C.: Prolific. ac—a subject pool for online experiments. J. Behav. Exp. Finance **17**, 22–27 (2018)
24. Rocher, L., Hendrickx, J.M., de Montjoye, Y.A.: Estimating the success of re-identifications in incomplete datasets using generative models. Nat. Commun. **10**(3069) (2019)
25. Smart, A., et al.: Discipline and label: a weird genealogy and social theory of data annotation. In: Proceedings of the 2024 EASST-4S Conference (2024)
26. Staab, R., Vero, M., Balunovic, M., Vechev, M.: Beyond memorization: violating privacy via inference with large language models. In: The Twelfth International Conference on Learning Representations (2024)
27. Tigunova, A., Mirza, P., Yates, A., Weikum, G.: Reddust: a large reusable dataset of reddit user traits. In: Proceedings of the Twelfth Language Resources and Evaluation Conference, pp. 6118–6126 (2020)
28. Tunstall, L., et al.: Zephyr: direct distillation of LM alignment. In: Proceedings of the 2024 Conference on Learning with Models (COLM) (2024)
29. Valizadeh, M., Ranjbar-Noiey, P., Caragea, C., Parde, N.: Identifying medical self-disclosure in online communities. In: Proceedings of the 2021 Conference of the North American Chapter of the Association for Computational Linguistics: Human Language Technologies, pp. 4398–4408. Association for Computational Linguistics (2021)
30. Volkova, S., Bachrach, Y., Armstrong, M., Sharma, V.: Inferring latent user properties from texts published in social media. In: Proceedings of the AAAI Conference on Artificial Intelligence, vol. 29 (2015)
31. Yin, W., Agarwal, V., Jiang, A., Zubiaga, A., Sastry, N.: Annobert: effectively representing multiple annotators' label choices to improve hate speech detection. In: Proceedings of the International AAAI Conference on Web and Social Media, vol. 17, pp. 902–913 (2023)
32. Zhang, M., Jensen, K.N., Sonniks, S.D., Plank, B.: Skillspan: hard and soft skill extraction from english job postings. arXiv preprint arXiv:2204.12811 (2022)

33. Zhuang, L., Wayne, L., Ya, S., Jun, Z.: A robustly optimized BERT pre-training approach with post-training. In: Proceedings of the 20th Chinese National Conference on Computational Linguistics, pp. 1218–1227. Chinese Information Processing Society of China, Huhhot, China (2021)
34. Zimmer, M.: "But the data is already public": on the ethics of research in Facebook. In: The Ethics of Information Technologies, pp. 229–241. Routledge (2020)
35. Zubiaga, A., Vidgen, B., Fernandez, M., Sastry, N.: Editorial for special issue on detecting, understanding and countering online harms. Online Soc. Netw. Media **27**, 100186 (2022)

BotArtist: Generic Approach for Bot Detection in Twitter via Semi-automatic Machine Learning Pipeline

Alexander Shevtsov[1,2,3], Despoina Antonakaki[1,2(✉)], Ioannis Lamprou[1], Polyvios Pratikakis[2,3], and Sotiris Ioannidis[1,2]

[1] Technical University of Crete, Crete, Greece
{ilamprou1,dantonakaki}@tuc.gr
[2] Foundation for Research and Technology – Hellas, Heraklion, Greece
[3] University of Crete, Crete, Greece
shevtsov@csd.uoc.gr

Abstract. X (aka. Twitter), as one of the most popular social networks, provides a platform for communication and online discourse. Unfortunately, it has also become a target for bots and fake accounts, resulting in the spread of false information and manipulation. This paper introduces a semi-automatic machine learning pipeline (SAMLP) designed to address the challenges associated with machine learning model development. Through this pipeline, we develop a comprehensive bot detection model named BotArtist, based on user profile features.

SAMLP leverages nine distinct publicly available datasets to train the BotArtist model. To assess BotArtist's performance against current state-of-the-art solutions, we evaluate 35 existing X bot detection methods, each utilizing a diverse range of features. Our comparative evaluation of BotArtist and these existing methods, conducted across nine public datasets under standardized conditions, reveals that the proposed model outperforms existing solutions by almost 10% in terms of F1-score, achieving an average score of 83.19% and 68.5% over specific and general approaches, respectively.

Keywords: Bot detection · Machine Learning · Dataset

1 Introduction

Online social media has become integral to modern communication, enabling real-time information sharing and widespread content creation. Among these platforms, Twitter/X plays a central role in news dissemination, political discourse, and social interaction. However, it has also become a hotspot for bots and fake accounts that manipulate discussions and spread misinformation. Research shows that bots actively participate in sensitive topics, including political debates (e.g., the 2016 elections in the US, Germany, Sweden, France, and Spain), the

© The Author(s), under exclusive license to Springer Nature Switzerland AG 2026
A. An et al. (Eds.): ASONAM 2025, LNCS 16323, pp. 19–27, 2026.
https://doi.org/10.1007/978-3-032-13821-7_2

Table 1. Description of selected datasets and information contained in those datasets.

Dataset	C-15	G-17	C-17	M-18	C-S-18	C-R-19	B-F-19	TwiBot-20	TwiBot-22
# Total User	5,301	2,484	14,368	50,538	13,276	693	518	229,580	1,000,000
# Human	1,950	1,394	3,474	8,092	6,174	340	380	5,237	860,057
# Bot	3,351	1,090	10,894	42,446	7,102	353	138	6,589	139,943
# Total Tweet	2,827,757	0	6,637,615	0	0	0	0	33,488,192	88,217,457
# Human Tweet	2,631,730	0	2,839,361	0	0	0	0	927,292	81,250,102
# Bot Tweet	196,027	0	3,798,254	0	0	0	0	1,072,496	6,967,355
# Graph Edges	7,086,134	0	6,637,615	0	0	0	0	33,488,192	170,185,937

vaccination debate, and COVID-19 discussions [12–15]. This widespread bot activity has raised concerns about information integrity on the platform.

Various machine learning (ML) and neural network-based bot detection methods have been proposed, often tailored to specific scenarios. However, their performance degrades in general-use cases across varying timeframes, topics, and languages [24]. Many existing approaches also neglect optimization steps such as feature selection and hyperparameter tuning, limiting their effectiveness. To address these challenges, we present a semi-automatic machine learning pipeline (SAMLP[1]) for building a general-purpose bot detection model, BotArtist[2]. SAMLP performs recursive hyperparameter tuning during feature selection and accounts for class imbalance, reducing data noise and improving real-world applicability.

We evaluate BotArtist against 35 state-of-the-art methods across nine public datasets. Two evaluation scenarios are used: dataset-specific (train/test on individual datasets) and general (train/test on a merged dataset). BotArtist achieves the top F1-score on three datasets and an average F1-score of 83.19. In general evaluation, it improves F1-score by over 9% compared to the best existing models, while using only a limited set of profile features—making it API-independent and suitable for historical data analysis.

Alongside the source code, we release the model outputs: BotArtist predictions on 10,929,533 user profiles linked to 127,275,386 tweets [23], adding a new layer of user-based annotation to existing textual datasets[3]. For consistency, we refer to the platform as Twitter throughout, aligning with most prior work.

2   Related Work

Detecting bots on Twitter remains challenging due to their increasing sophistication. Prior research typically falls into three categories—feature-based, text-based, and graph-based—each exploiting different aspects of user behavior and platform metadata.

---

[1] GitHub: https://github.com/alexdrk14/SAMLP.
[2] GitHub: https://github.com/alexdrk14/BotArtist.
[3] Zenodo: https://zenodo.org/records/8431047.

Feature-based approaches rely on engineered attributes derived from user profiles and activity patterns. These include metadata, tweets, usernames, descriptions, temporal activity, and follow relationships [5,8,11]. Some methods enhance scalability [18], discover unknown bots through correlation [2], or improve precision-recall balance. However, bot developers continuously adapt to detection strategies, diminishing the long-term effectiveness of these methods [5].

Text-based methods apply natural language processing techniques to tweets and profile descriptions. Techniques span sequence fingerprints, word embeddings, RNNs, attention mechanisms, transformers, and pre-trained language models [5,11]. Several studies combine text and profile features [4,6,17], use unsupervised learning [5], or address multilingual content [7]. While these methods show strong results, they remain vulnerable to mimicry by bots reusing human content [31] and often underperform when used alone [9].

Graph-based techniques utilize graph analytics and geometric deep learning, employing node centrality [21], node embeddings [25], graph neural networks (GNNs) [19], and heterogeneous GNNs [9]. Recent studies merge strategies across categories [7,20] and propose novel architectures for modeling network heterogeneity [16]. Although promising, these approaches demand substantial data and computational resources.

Despite their progress, existing bot detection techniques have clear limitations. Feature-based models often lack generalizability; text and graph-based models, while more sophisticated, are prone to overfitting and require extensive resources. Additionally, the monetization of Twitter's API [1] increases the cost of operation for many methods. In response, our work introduces a lightweight yet robust solution—relying solely on a single Twitter user object (API v1.1 or v2)—capable of accurate detection with minimal API usage and reduced operational overhead.

3   Datasets

For this research paper, we collect nine well-known publicly available datasets [3]. All selected datasets already contain ground truth labels, primarily obtained through manual analysis or crowd-sourcing. For simplicity, we label the selected datasets as follows: C-15 [22], G-17 [28], C-17 [29], M-18 [18], C-S-18 [30], C-R-19 [11], B-F-19 [10], TwiBot-20 [3], and TwiBot-22 [24]. In Table 1, we present the information provided in each dataset, along with the volume of normal and bot accounts.

Furthermore, in collaboration with [23] collect 10.929.533 Twitter profiles correlated with 127.275.386 publicly available tweets related to the public discussion topic of the 2022 Russo-Ukrainian War. Our collection of user profiles is based on the monitoring of selected topics starting from February 23, 2022, till June 23, 2023. The shared datasets contain a set of extracted features in an anonymized form of a CSV file and contain only preprocessed numerical features to protect user information. The provided dataset also provides anonymized user

IDs which are identically correlated with publicly available user tweet dataset [23].

4   Methodology

We propose a semi-automatic machine learning pipeline (SAMLP) to develop a general-purpose Twitter bot detection model. This pipeline simplifies the model-building process and prevents common mistakes in data processing, feature selection, hyperparameter tuning, and evaluation. To preserve class distributions, we apply a stratified 70:30 split for training/validation and testing. The testing set remains unseen until final evaluation to avoid information leakage.

Feature selection is conducted on the train/validation set using 5-fold cross-validation with Lasso regression. Since Lasso is sensitive to class imbalance, we apply under-sampling of the majority class and repeat the process 10 times to mitigate information loss. For each run, we store the best α (regularization) value based on mean squared error. The most frequent α is then used to train Lasso on the full train/validation set. If the selected α is at the boundary of the search space, we expand the search area to find a more optimal value. This approach enables automatic, robust feature selection, adaptable to both balanced and imbalanced datasets without manual intervention.

After dimensionality reduction, we evaluate three classifiers: SVM, Random Forest, and XGBoost. For each, we define wide hyperparameter ranges and sample $C = 50$ configurations randomly. Class imbalance is addressed using class weights. We evaluate each configuration using stratified K-Fold cross-validation and select the best-performing model based on average F1-score. The final model is tested on the hold-out set, and SHAP is applied for model explainability. For binary classification, we optimize the decision threshold using the precision-recall curve. The final model is retrained on the full dataset using the optimal threshold and can be deployed in real-world scenarios. Experiments were conducted on a machine with an AMD Ryzen 9 CPU (16 cores/32 threads), 64 GB RAM, and an NVIDIA RTX 3080 GPU with 12 GB memory.

Our aim is to build a lightweight model that relies solely on Twitter profile data—ensuring compatibility with both Twitter API v1.1 and v2 and minimizing reliance on unstable textual or graph features [32]. We extract 49 features, categorized as count, real-valued, and boolean. **Count features** include raw values such as followers, friends, statuses, and list subscriptions. We also compute character-type counts (uppercase, lowercase, digits, special) for user name, screen name, and description, and count mentions, hashtags, and URLs in the description.

Real-valued features include account age (in days) and activity rates normalized by age (e.g., statuses/day). We also compute Jaccard similarity between user name and screen name, entropy of both fields, and character-type percentages relative to field length.

Boolean features identify the presence or absence of specific attributes, such as whether the account is verified, protected, includes location or URL, or uses a default profile image.

Table 2. The performance of each selected bot detection model, as reported in the [3] paper, is compared with that of BotArtist. Performance is measured using the F1-score. In this benchmark, each model is trained and tested on each dataset separately.

Method	Type	C-15	G-17	C-17	M-18	C-S-18	C-R-19	B-F-19	TB-20	TB-22	Average
SGBot	F	77.9	72.1	94.6	99.5	82.3	82.7	49.6	84.9	36.6	75.57
Kudugunta et al.	F	75.3	49.8	91.7	94.5	50.9	49.2	49.6	47.3	51.7	62.22
Hayawi et al.	F	85.6	34.7	93.8	91.5	60.8	60.9	20.5	77.1	24.7	61.06
BotHunter	F	97.2	69.2	91.6	<u>99.6</u>	82.2	82.9	49.6	79.1	23.5	74.98
NameBot	F	83.4	44.8	85.7	91.6	61.1	67.5	38.5	65.1	0.5	59.80
Abreu et al.	F	76.4	66.7	95.0	97.9	76.9	<u>83.5</u>	<u>53.8</u>	77.1	53.4	75.63
BotArtist	F	98.3	<u>76.1</u>	97.0	**99.7**	80.6	**88.3**	**68.4**	82.2	<u>58.2</u>	**83.19**
Cresci	T	1.17	-	22.8	-	-	-	-	13.7	-	-
Wei	T	82.7	-	78.4	-	-	-	-	57.3	53.6	-
BGSRD	T	90.8	35.7	86.3	90.5	58.2	41.1	13.0	70.0	21.1	56.30
RoBERTa	T	95.8	-	94.3	-	-	-	-	73.1	20.5	-
T5	T	89.3	-	92.3	-	-	-	-	70.5	20.2	-
Efthimion	FT	94.1	5.2	91.8	95.9	68.2	71.7	0.0	67.2	27.5	57.95
Kantepe	FT	78.2	-	79.4	-	-	-	-	62.2	**58.7**	-
Miller	FT	83.8	59.9	86.8	91.1	56.8	43.6	0.0	74.8	45.3	60.23
Varol	FT	94.7	-	-	-	-	-	-	81.1	27.5	-
Kouvela	FT	98.2	66.6	<u>99.1</u>	98.2	80.4	81.1	28.1	86.5	30.0	74.24
Santos	FT	78.8	14.5	83.0	92.4	65.2	75.7	21.0	60.3	-	-
Lee	FT	<u>98.6</u>	67.8	**99.3**	97.9	<u>82.5</u>	82.7	50.3	80.0	30.4	<u>76.61</u>
LOBO	FT	**98.8**	-	97.7	-	-	-	-	80.8	38.6	-
Moghaddam	FG	73.9	-	-	-	-	-	-	79.9	32.1	-
Alhosseini	FG	92.2	-	-	-	-	-	-	72.0	38.1	-
Knauth	FTG	91.2	39.1	93.4	91.3	**94.0**	54.2	41.3	85.2	37.1	69.64
FriendBot	FTG	97.6	-	87.4	-	-	-	-	80.0	-	-
SATAR	FTG	95.0	-	-	-	-	-	-	86.1	-	-
Botometer	FTG	66.9	**77.4**	96.1	46.0	79.6	79.0	30.8	53.1	42.8	63.5
Rodrifuez-Ruiz	FTG	87.7	-	85.7	-	-	-	-	63.1	56.6	-
GraphHist	FTG	84.5	-	-	-	-	-	-	67.6	-	-
EvolveBot	FTG	90.1	-	-	-	-	-	-	69.7	14.1	-
Dehghan	FTG	88.3	-	-	-	-	-	-	76.2	-	-
GCN	FTG	97.2	-	-	-	-	-	-	80.8	54.9	-
GAT	FTG	97.6	-	-	-	-	-	-	85.2	55.8	-
HGT	FTG	96.9	-	-	-	-	-	-	**88.2**	39.6	-
SimpleHGN	FTG	97.5	-	-	-	-	-	-	**88.2**	45.4	-
BotRGCN	FTG	97.3	-	-	-	-	-	-	87.3	57.5	-
RGT	FTG	97.8	-	-	-	-	-	-	<u>88.0</u>	42.9	-

This comprehensive feature set captures user behavior and profile characteristics while ensuring compatibility with Twitter API limitations and supporting accurate bot prediction.

5   Experimental Results

Following the SAMLP methodology, we develop BotArtist—a semi-automated ML-based bot detection model—and evaluate its performance using nine public datasets and the comprehensive TwiBot-22 benchmark [24], which enables fair comparison with 35 existing approaches under identical data splits. Compared models span five categories: feature-based (F), text-based (T), graph-based (G), and combinations thereof.

Table 3. The measurement of performance in the case of general bot detection approaches, involves training and testing models on all datasets. Performance is assessed using the F1-score.

Method	C-15	G-17	C-17	M-18	C-S-18	C-R-19	B-F-19	TB-20	TB-22	Total	Average
BotArtist	82.7	39.9	87.3	99.0	**80.6**	73.8	16.6	**80.3**	**56.9**	**63.7**	**68.5**
Lee	82.3	0.0	83.6	97.7	78.2	67.7	20.0	8.5	42.4	52.9	53.3
Abreu	84.4	0.3	80.1	88.4	67.1	40.8	11.7	15.6	29.0	40.4	46.3
SGBot	75.0	3.6	79.8	**99.2**	76.7	68.9	0.0	15.2	43.3	53.8	51.5
BotHunter	73.4	7.1	76.0	**99.2**	76.0	44.8	11.1	14.7	28.0	43.1	47.8
Kouvela	**95.5**	20.4	94.7	98.1	78.4	71.4	21.0	28.5	36.0	52.0	60.5
Botometer	66.9	**77.4**	**96.1**	46.0	79.6	**79.0**	**30.8**	53.1	42.8	45.3	63.5

5.1   Model Comparison

To assess generalizability, we design two evaluation scenarios. First, we test all models, including BotArtist, on each dataset individually using dataset-specific training and testing. This scenario reflects performance in constrained, real-world applications. As shown in Table 2, BotArtist outperforms all other methods on three datasets (M-18, C-R-19, B-F-19) and achieves the highest overall average F1-score of 83.19—an improvement of 6.5% over the best existing method. Notably, models relying on text or graph features perform poorly on datasets lacking such data. Second, to evaluate generalization, we train models on a merged dataset combining training data from all nine datasets and test on both individual and merged test sets. This setup mimics a broader real-world scenario involving varied periods, topics, and communities.

Table 3 presents results from this general-case evaluation. Among the top performers are BotArtist, Botometer [20], and SGBot. BotArtist achieves the highest total and average F1-scores, outperforming other methods by nearly 10%. These results demonstrate that well-tuned models using a compact feature set can effectively generalize and distinguish between bots and real users across diverse contexts.

6   Conclusions and Future Work

This paper presents SAMLP, a semi-automatic machine learning pipeline that streamlines feature selection, hyperparameter tuning, model evaluation, binary threshold optimization, and SHAP-based explainability. Using this pipeline, we develop BotArtist—a profile-based Twitter bot detector. Evaluated across nine datasets, BotArtist outperforms state-of-the-art methods, achieving up to a 10% improvement in total F1 score and 6.5% on individual datasets. SHAP analysis provides transparency into the model's decisions. While effective, BotArtist relies on a limited feature set, which could be targeted by adaptive bot strategies. Future work will explore its robustness over time and expand the feature space to adapt to evolving bot behavior.

Acknowledgements. This work is supported by project CYBERUNITY, funded by Digital Europe Programme (DIGITAL) with GA No. 101128024.

References

1. Twitter: Twitter API price list (2023). https://developer.twitter.com/en/products/twitter-api. Accessed 9 Sept 2023
2. Chavoshi, N., Hamooni, H., Mueen, A.: Debot: Twitter bot detection via warped correlation. In: ICDM, vol. 18, pp. 28–65 (2016)
3. Feng, S., Wan, H., Wang, N., Li, J., Luo, M.: Twibot-20: a comprehensive twitter bot detection benchmark. In: Proceedings of the 30th ACM International Conference on Information & Knowledge Management, pp. 4485–4494 (2021)
4. Efthimion, P.G., Payne, S., Proferes, N.: Supervised machine learning bot detection techniques to identify social twitter bots. SMU Data Sci. Rev. **1**(2), 5 (2018)
5. Feng, S., Wan, H., Wang, N., Li, J., Luo, M.: Satar: a self-supervised approach to twitter account representation learning and its application in bot detection. In: Proceedings of the 30th ACM International Conference on Information & Knowledge Management, pp. 3808–3817 (2021)
6. Kantepe, M., Ganiz, M.C.: Preprocessing framework for Twitter bot detection. In: 2017 International Conference on Computer Science and Engineering (UBMK), pp. 630–634. IEEE (2017)
7. Knauth, J.: Language-agnostic twitter-bot detection. In: Proceedings of the International Conference on Recent Advances in Natural Language Processing (RANLP 2019), pp. 550–558 (2019)
8. Kudugunta, S., Ferrara, E.: Deep neural networks for bot detection. Inf. Sci. **467**, 312–322 (2018)

9. Feng, S., Wan, H., Wang, N., Luo, M.: BotRGCN: Twitter bot detection with relational graph convolutional networks. In: Proceedings of the 2021 IEEE/ACM International Conference on Advances in Social Networks Analysis and Mining, pp. 236–239 (2021)

10. Yang, K.-C., et al.: Arming the public with artificial intelligence to counter social bots. Hum. Behav. Emerg. Technol. **1**(1), 48–61 (2019)

11. Mazza, M., Cresci, S., Avvenuti, M., Quattrociocchi, W., Tesconi, M.: Rtbust: exploiting temporal patterns for botnet detection on twitter. In: Proceedings of the 10th ACM Conference on Web Science, pp. 183–192 (2019)

12. Shevtsov, A., Tzagkarakis, C., Antonakaki, D., Ioannidis, S.: Identification of twitter bots based on an explainable machine learning framework: the US 2020 elections case study. In: Proceedings of the International AAAI Conference on Web and Social Media, vol. 16, pp. 956–967 (2022)

13. Golovchenko, Y., Buntain, C., Eady, G., Brown, M.A., Tucker, J.A.: Cross-platform state propaganda: Russian trolls on Twitter and YouTube during the 2016 US presidential election. Int. J. Press/Polit. **25**(3), 357–389 (2020)

14. Shevtsov, A., et al.: What Tweets and YouTube comments have in common? Sentiment and graph analysis on data related to US elections 2020. PLoS ONE **18**(1), e0270542 (2023)

15. Shahi, G.K., Dirkson, A., Majchrzak, T.A.: An exploratory study of COVID-19 misinformation on Twitter. Online Soc. Netw. Media **22**, 100104 (2021)

16. Feng, S., Tan, Z., Li, R., Luo, M.: Heterogeneity-aware twitter bot detection with relational graph transformers. In: Proceedings of the AAAI Conference on Artificial Intelligence, vol. 36, pp. 3977–3985 (2022)

17. Kouvela, M., Dimitriadis, I., Vakali, A.: Bot-detective: an explainable Twitter bot detection service with crowdsourcing functionalities. In: Proceedings of the 12th International Conference on Management of Digital EcoSystems, pp. 55–63 (2020)

18. Yang, K.-C., Varol, O., Hui, P.-M., Menczer, F.: Scalable and generalizable social bot detection through data selection. In: Proceedings of the AAAI Conference on Artificial Intelligence, vol. 34, pp. 1096–1103 (2020)

19. Moghaddam, S.H., Abbaspour, M.: Friendship preference: scalable and robust category of features for social bot detection. IEEE Trans. Dependable Secure Comput. **20**(2), 1516–1528 (2022)

20. Yang, K.-C., Ferrara, E., Menczer, F.: Botometer 101: social bot practicum for computational social scientists. J. Comput. Soc. Sci. **5**(2), 1511–1528 (2022)

21. Dehghan, A., et al.: Detecting bots in social-networks using node and structural embeddings. J. Big Data **10**(1), 1–37 (2023)

22. Cresci, S., Di Pietro, R., Petrocchi, M., Spognardi, A., Tesconi, M.: Fame for sale: efficient detection of fake Twitter followers. Decis. Support Syst. **80**, 56–71 (2015)

23. Shevtsov, A., Tzagkarakis, C., Antonakaki, D., Pratikakis, P., Ioannidis, S.: 'Twitter dataset on the Russo-Ukrainian war, arXiv preprint arXiv:2204.08530 (2022)

24. Feng, S., et al.: TwiBot-22: towards graph-based Twitter bot detection. Adv. Neural. Inf. Process. Syst. **35**, 35254–35269 (2022)

25. Pham, P., Nguyen, L.T.T., Vo, B., Yun, U.: Bot2Vec: a general approach of intra-community oriented representation learning for bot detection in different types of social networks. Inf. Syst. **103**, 101771 (2022)

26. Boser, B.E., Guyon, I.M., Vapnik, V.N.: A training algorithm for optimal margin classifiers. In: Proceedings of the Fifth Annual Workshop on Computational Learning Theory, pp. 144–152 (1992)

27. Chen, T., et al.: XGBoost: extreme gradient boosting. R Package Version **0.4-2(1)**, 1–4 (2015)

28. Gilani, Z., Farahbakhsh, R., Tyson, G., Wang, L., Crowcroft, J.: Of bots and humans (on Twitter). In: Proceedings of the 2017 IEEE/ACM International Conference on Advances in Social Networks Analysis and Mining (ASONAM), pp. 349–354 (2017)
29. Cresci, S., Di Pietro, R., Petrocchi, M., Spognardi, A., Tesconi, M.: Social fingerprinting: detection of spambot groups through DNA-inspired behavioral modeling. IEEE Trans. Dependable Secure Comput. **15**(4), 561–576 (2017)
30. Cresci, S., Lillo, F., Regoli, D., Tardelli, S., Tesconi, M.: FAKE: evidence of spam and bot activity in stock microblogs on Twitter. In: Proceedings of International AAAI Conference on Web and Social Media (ICWSM), vol. 12 (2018)
31. Cresci, S.: A decade of social bot detection. Commun. ACM **63**(10), 72–83 (2020)
32. Shevtsov, A., Antonakaki, D., Lamprou, I., Kontogiorgakis, I., Pratikakis, P., Ioannidis, S.: Russo-Ukrainian war: prediction and explanation of Twitter suspension. In: Proceedings of the 2023 IEEE/ACM International Conference on Advances in Social Networks Analysis and Mining, pp. 348–355 (2024)

Identifying Social Interaction Outliers with the Use of Network Analysis: Disk Decoration in the Middle Magdalenian Period

Sakhawat Hossan[1(✉)], Jing Deng[1], Rebecca Schwendler[2],
and Charles P. Egeland[3]

[1] Department of Computer Science, UNC Greensboro, Greensboro, NC 27412, USA
{s_hossan,jing.deng}@uncg.edu
[2] Histria Cultural Resource Consulting, Snow Camp, NC 27349, USA
[3] Department of Anthropology, UNC Greensboro, Greensboro, NC 27412, USA
cpegelan@uncg.edu

Abstract. Understanding human interactions among groups located in different geographic areas is a central topic in social network analysis (SNA). In archaeological studies, where interactions must be inferred from a limited number of artifacts, this becomes particularly challenging. In this work, we introduce an SNA approach to investigate social interactions among groups from various geographic locations, focusing specifically on artifacts from the Middle Magdalenian period (ca. 15,500 to 13,000 years ago) of the Upper Paleolithic in Western Europe. The analysis considers decorative motifs on artifacts and their geographic origins to identify interaction anomalies that deserve further archaeological analysis. Two approaches are introduced: one compares the proportional deviation (absolute difference in normalized weights) from geographic relationships, and the other uses closeness and betweenness centrality. This work highlights the potential of SNA methodologies in revealing latent patterns in archaeological data and advancing the study of symbolic behavior in prehistoric societies.

Keywords: Middle Magdalenian · Perforated disks · Decorations · Symbolic behavior · Social Network Analysis · Centrality · Closeness · Betweenness

1 Introduction

The application of SNA to archaeology offers an effective and structured approach to represent the sparse and indirect datasets typical of the field. By modeling plausible interaction pathways among ancient communities, SNA enables researchers to move beyond static site descriptions toward dynamic interpretations of past social structures and regional interaction dynamics. Knappett et al. (2008), for example, used network models to study Minoan ceramics in the

A. An et al. (Eds.): ASONAM 2025, LNCS 16323, pp. 28–35, 2026.
https://doi.org/10.1007/978-3-032-13821-7_3

Aegean Bronze Age, revealing trade routes and social clustering through measures like network centrality and density [1]. Centrality metrics in particular–especially degree and betweenness–can help clarify the roles of sites as hubs or brokers within ancient trade or communication networks, which allows hypotheses about social influence and exchange to be tested [2].

Despite valuable insights from past archaeological SNA studies, symbolic and geographic data are often analyzed separately, with limited focus on how spatial proximity aligns with cultural similarity. Most analyses prioritize material distribution or abstract models, rarely linking spatial relationships to symbolic expressions. Centrality metrics are also commonly interpreted without motif context, making it difficult to determine whether observed patterns reflect intentional cultural connectivity or geographic coincidence.

Our study bridges this gap by using the correlation of geographic distance and motif (dis)similarities. We use betweenness and closeness centrality to explore whether geographic proximity aligns with symbolic motif similarity in Middle Magdalenian perforated disks whose face(s) feature one or more of a suite of decoration types.

This paper is organized as follows: Sect. 2 reviews related work in archaeological applications of SNA. Section 3 outlines the research objectives and presents the graph-based methodology. Section 4 describes the dataset and symbolic artifacts and presents the experimental results. Section 5 discusses the implications of the findings, interprets notable patterns, and concludes the study.

2   Related Work

SNA can serve as a powerful analytical framework in archaeology, enabling researchers to reconstruct and interpret the structure of past human interactions through formal network metrics. Unlike traditional archaeological methods that often focus on individual sites or artifact typologies, SNA emphasizes the relational patterns that connect actors, artifacts, and places across space and time.

Mills [3] offers a foundational overview of SNA's theoretical integration into archaeological research, framing it within the paradigm of relational archaeology. The approach prioritizes interconnectivity over isolated attributes, making it especially suitable for examining complex social processes such as trade, cultural transmission, and mobility.

Similar to online social network (OSN) analysis [4], graph stream analysis [5], and unsupervised learning, applications of SNA to material distribution networks have demonstrated SNA's utility in identifying interaction hubs and shifts in regional connectivity. Sakahira et al. [6] analyze obsidian distribution during Japan's Jomon period using clustering and centrality measures to track evolving trade routes. Their work highlights how shifts in betweenness centrality values point to changes in the roles of key sites over time. Maritime archaeology has also incorporated SNA techniques to reinterpret underwater assemblages and their broader socio-economic significance. Aragon [7] integrates spatial and symbolic datasets into a network model, demonstrating how betweenness centrality can expose sites that acted as intermediaries in maritime exchange systems.

Closeness centrality has proven valuable for identifying sites with strategic access to others across the network, facilitating efficient information or material flow. Brughmans and Peeples [8] examine the application of centrality-based approaches in archaeological networks, stressing the importance of contextualizing such metrics rather than interpreting them in isolation. Similarly, Knappett et al. [1] apply closeness and degree centrality to model the spatial distribution of Minoan ceramics, revealing embedded hierarchies in trade and cultural diffusion.

In addition to empirical applications, the theoretical integration of SNA with other frameworks has expanded the interpretive potential of network-based studies. Dawson [9] advocates for such a multidimensional perspective, where network structure is analyzed alongside economic and ideological factors shaping interaction networks. Iyer et al. [10] build a model from online social networks to account for how homophily and social rank affect the formation of connections in social science.

Overall, these studies illustrate the analytical flexibility of SNA in archaeology. Metrics like betweenness and closeness centrality not only quantify structural roles of sites but also help identify unique cultural transmission, symbolic boundaries, and social organization—especially when combined with spatial and typological datasets.

3   Research Objectives and Methodology

This study approaches the relationship between spatial proximity and symbolic similarity as a problem of comparing two weighted network models derived from archaeological data. Rather than treating geographic and cultural datasets as isolated domains, we apply graph-based formalism to model and analyze structural patterns using SNA. The objective is to assess to what extent the symbolic relationships inferred from motif similarity reflect or diverge from the spatial structure encoded in site locations. Two undirected weighted graphs are constructed: a spatial network (G_s) based on linear geographic distances between Middle Magdalenian archaeological sites, and a symbolic network (G_m) based on pairwise motif similarity scores extracted from decorated disk artifacts. The shared node set V corresponds to archaeological sites, while the edge sets E_s and E_m differ in weighting semantics. Edge weights in G_s are inversely proportional to Euclidean distances between sites, representing geographic closeness. In contrast, edge weights in G_m reflect Jaccard similarity between encoded motif features, representing symbolic alignment.

To explore structural differences and commonalities between G_s and G_m, we compute closeness centrality and betweenness centrality for each node in both networks. Closeness centrality identifies nodes that are structurally central based on their average distance to all others, which is useful for assessing symbolic or spatial accessibility. Betweenness centrality, which quantifies the number of shortest paths passing through a node, highlights potential brokers or mediators in symbolic transmission or geographic flow.

These node-level centrality profiles are analyzed comparatively to assess alignment between the two networks. Specifically, we evaluate whether sites that are central in the spatial network are also central in the symbolic network—an indicator of spatial-symbolic correspondence. Additionally, we calculate edge-level differences between the two graphs to capture local deviations in pairwise relationships.

This dual-network framework enables both micro-level (edge) and macro-level (node centrality) comparison, providing a structured approach for quantifying how spatial positioning influences—or fails to influence—symbolic relationships. Such a framework not only supports hypothesis testing in an archaeological context but also contributes to broader methodological discussions of multilayer network analysis, graph comparison, and centrality-driven interpretation in the SNA community.

4   Dataset and Experimental Results

The dataset of symbolic artifacts from Middle Magdalenian (ca. 15,500–13,000 years ago) Upper Paleolithic archaeological sites across Western Europe used in this study is derived from a curated archive developed by Schwendler [11]. It includes 524 decorated disk faces from 262 artifacts, each linked to a known site with geographic coordinates. Symbolic features such as edge notching and specific engraved motifs were systematically coded as present or absent, enabling analysis of inter-site similarity of decorations. For the purposes of this study, we focus on a subset of 16 sites whose disk faces show clear symbolic motifs and that capture a mix of short-range (i.e., geographically close) and long-range interactions across the dataset. From these 16 sites come 451 decorated disk faces, which serve as the nodes in our network, resulting in a total of 202,051 possible pairwise connections or edges. The dual availability of motif-based and spatial data makes this dataset highly suited for SNA-driven exploration of symbolic and geographic interaction patterns, as it allows us to leverage two distinct types of information to test and verify our hypotheses.

To investigate the relationship between spatial proximity and symbolic similarity, we employed two complementary methods. Each method constructs and compares graph representations of the same site network, differing in how node importance and alignment are measured.

4.1   Method 1: Pairwise Edge Difference via Similarity Scores

In the first approach, we built two weighted undirected graphs sharing the same node set (archaeological sites): one where edge weights are computed as the inverse of Euclidean distances between sites (spatial graph), and another where edge weights reflect normalized Jaccard similarity scores of disk motifs (symbolic graph). To assess how well symbolic relationships reflect geographic proximity, we computed the absolute difference between corresponding edge weights in the two graphs for each site pair.

This edge-level analysis provided a matrix of difference values, quantifying the alignment of symbolic similarity with spatial closeness. However, the results revealed high divergence across most site pairs, with over 60% of edges showing differences greater than 0.6. Although some local clusters showed strong correspondence (e.g., Enlène and Lourdes), symbolic motifs often diverged sharply from geographic expectations. Crucially, this method is limited by its focus on individual pairwise relationships—it fails to detect global structural roles or identify outlier sites that are symbolically central yet geographically peripheral (or vice versa). As such, it lacks the interpretive power needed to explain cultural transmission patterns or symbolic brokerage roles.

4.2   Method 2: Node-Level Comparison via Centrality Metrics

To overcome the limitations of pairwise edge-level comparisons, the second method adopts a node-level perspective by computing and comparing two widely used centrality measures—*betweenness centrality and closeness centrality*—across the spatial and symbolic networks. These metrics allow us to assess the structural prominence of each archaeological site within its respective network, thereby enabling a deeper analysis of symbolic and spatial roles.

Centrality measures betweenness (B) **and closeness** (C) capture distinct structural roles within networks. Betweenness centrality quantifies how often a node lies on shortest paths between others, identifying sites that act as mediators or brokers. Closeness centrality reflects how efficiently a node can reach all others, indicating overall accessibility. Figure 1 shows normalized betweenness scores in the symbolic (left) and spatial (right) networks for the 16 sites included in this analysis. Distinct patterns emerge: *Bedeilhac* is highly central symbolically but peripheral geographically, whereas *Enlène* and Lortet are the reverse—geographically central but symbolically marginal. Closeness results reinforce this trend, with the site of *Kesslerloch* showing symbolic importance but low spatial integration.

Table 1 presents a numerical comparison of B_m, B_s, and Δ_B, along with C_m, C_s, and Δ_C, for the seven sites with the highest values in either metric, selected from the original analysis of 16 sites. The sites of *Bedeilhac*, Lortet, and *Kesslerloch* exhibit the strongest divergence, reinforcing their roles as domain-specific hubs. In contrast, *La Madeleine* and Chancelade maintain balanced centrality across both networks. These results underscore the structural mismatch between spatial and symbolic influence and highlight the value of dual centrality metrics for identifying culturally significant outliers. Figure 2 visualizes these differences, again showing *Bedeilhac*, Lortet, and *Kesslerloch* as structurally divergent, while *La Madeleine* and Chancelade remain consistently central across both domains.

These qualitative findings suggest that centrality-based analysis offers a more robust and interpretable framework than pairwise similarity alone. Future work will include quantitative analyses—such as correlation analysis—to evaluate the statistical significance of these observed divergences. Both closeness and betweenness centrality reveal meaningful mismatches in site roles, helping to identify outlier communities and potentially long-distance symbolic brokers. This approach underscores the decoupling of physical proximity from symbolic influence and offers a model for more nuanced, structural analysis in archaeological SNA.

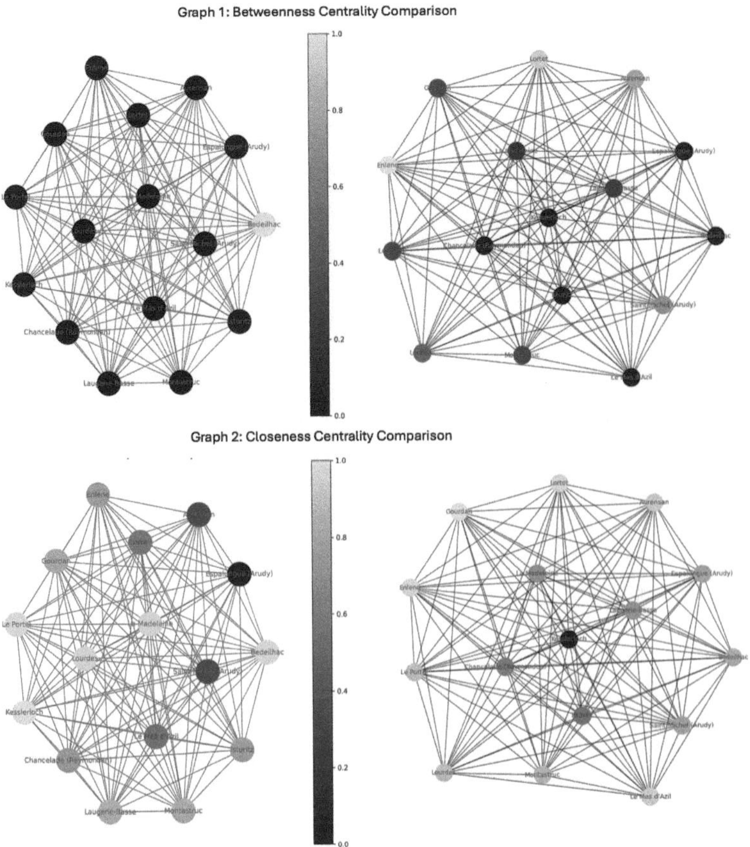

Fig. 1. Betweenness and closeness centrality comparisons. Left: symbolic similarity graph B_m. Right: spatial proximity graph B_s. Node colors indicate normalized centrality values.

Archaeological Interpretation of Outlier Sites: From an archaeological perspective, sites that show high centrality in the symbolic network but low centrality in the spatial network—such as *Bedeilhac*—may represent instances of long-distance cultural transmission. These outlier sites likely reflect groups or individuals who traveled across large geographic areas, carrying symbolic traditions with them. The motifs observed at these sites appear distinctive within their immediate region but align closely with motifs used in more distant areas, suggesting a movement of people or ideas rather than localized motif evolution. This pattern highlights the role of mobile hunter-gatherer groups in disseminating symbolic practices, and supports models of interaction that emphasize connectivity beyond immediate geographic neighbors.

Table 1. Betweenness and closeness centrality comparison between spatial and symbolic graphs, B_s, B_m, and $\Delta_B \triangleq B_s - B_m$, C_s, C_m, and $\Delta_C = C_s - C_m$

Site	B_s	B_m	Δ_B	C_s	C_m	Δ_C
Bedeilhac	0.08	1.00	−0.92	0.62	0.24	0.38
Enlène	1.00	0.08	0.92	0.71	0.69	0.02
Lortet	0.96	0.10	0.86	0.73	0.40	0.33
Kesslerloch	0.16	0.10	0.06	0.09	0.98	−0.89
La Madeleine	0.36	0.29	0.07	0.76	0.73	0.03
Lourdes	0.41	0.22	0.19	0.70	0.74	−0.04
Chancelade	0.05	0.06	−0.01	0.63	0.64	−0.01

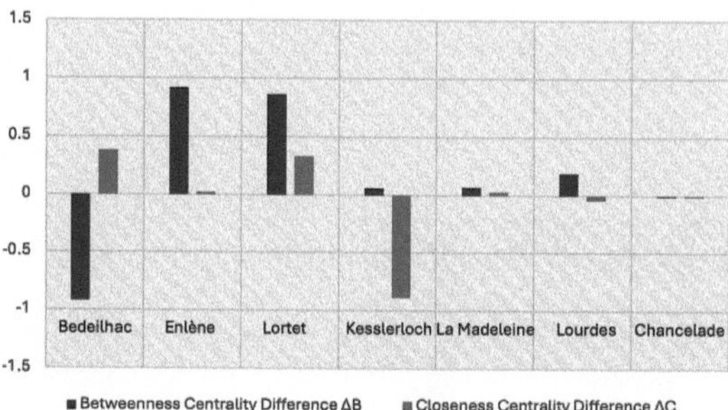

Fig. 2. Δ values of closeness and betweenness centrality in symbolic and spatial networks.

5   Conclusion

This study applied a comparative SNA framework to evaluate the relationship between geographic proximity and symbolic similarity among Middle Magdalenian perforated disk artifacts. By constructing dual networks—one based on spatial distance and the other on motif similarity—we systematically analyzed structural alignment using centrality metrics and edge-level comparisons.

Our results show that symbolic relationships do not consistently mirror spatial proximity. Pairwise similarity comparisons revealed limited overlap between geographic closeness and motif alignment, and were ineffective in isolating structurally significant sites. In contrast, centrality-based analysis provided deeper insight into site roles. Notably, the sites of *Bedeilhac*, *Lortet*, and *Kesslerloch* exhibited high divergence across both closeness and betweenness centrality, highlighting symbolic prominence that is decoupled from geographic centrality. Conversely, the sites of *La Madeleine* and *Chancelade* showed consistent structural roles in both networks, suggesting integrated participation in both spatial and symbolic spheres.

These findings underscore the value of centrality-driven SNA methods for disentangling spatial and cultural dimensions of prehistoric connectivity. By identifying mismatches between geographic and symbolic structures, our approach contributes to a more nuanced understanding of social organization, cultural transmission, and symbolic communication in Upper Paleolithic Europe. Our approach is also applicable to other geographically anchored archaeological artifacts that exhibit variation in decoration and/or form, offering a generalizable framework for exploring complex interaction patterns across multiple dimensions.

Future work could extend the model discussed here by incorporating temporal variation or cultural factors such as material sourcing or disk size, and also considering the full dataset of Middle Magdalenian disk faces.

Acknowledgment. This work was partially supported by NSF Grant SBE 2051541.

References

1. Knappett, C., Evans, T., Rivers, R.: Modelling maritime interaction in the aegean bronze age. Antiquity **82**(318), 1009–1024 (2008)
2. Brughmans, T.: Thinking through networks: a review of formal network methods in archaeology. J. Archaeol. Method Theory **20**(4), 623–662 (2013)
3. Mills, B.J.: Social network analysis in archaeology. Annu. Rev. Anthropol. **46**(1), 379–397 (2017)
4. Dey, A., Kumar, B.R., Das, B., Ghoshal, A.K.: Outlier detection in social networks leveraging community structure. Inf. Sci. **634**, 578–586 (2023)
5. Aggarwal, C.C., Zhao, Y., Yu, P.S.: Outlier detection in graph streams. In: 2011 IEEE 27th International Conference on Data Engineering, pp. 399–409 (2011)
6. Sakahira, F., Tsumura, H.: Social network analysis of ancient Japanese obsidian artifacts reflecting sampling bias reduction. Peer Community J. 4 (2024)
7. Aragon, E.: Connecting sunken actors: social network analysis in maritime archaeology. Hist. Archaeol. **57**(1), 209–219 (2023)
8. Brughmans, T., Peeples, M.A.: Network Science in Archaeology, Cambridge Manuals in Archaeology. Cambridge University Press (2023)
9. Dawson, H.: Networks in archaeology: an introduction. eTopoi 74–86 (2020)
10. Iyer, R.G., Wang, Y., Wang, W., Sun, Y.: Non-euclidean mixture model for social network embedding. In: Globerson, A., et al. (eds.) Advances in Neural Information Processing Systems, vol. 37, pp. 111464–111488. Curran Associates Inc. (2024)
11. Schwendler, R.H.: Hunter-Gatherer Social Interactions in Magdalenian Western Europe, Ph.D. thesis, University of New Mexico (2004)

Can We Predict Your Next Move Without Breaking Your Privacy?

Arpita Soni[1], Sahil Tripathi[2], Gautam Siddharth Kashyap[3],
Manaswi Kulahara[4], Mohammad Anas Azeez[2], Zohaib Hasan Siddiqui[2],
Nipun Joshi[5(✉)], and Jiechao Gao[6]

[1] Eudoxia Research University, New Castle, USA
[2] Jamia Hamdard, New Delhi, India
[3] Macquarie University, Sydney, Australia
[4] TERI School of Advanced Studies, New Delhi, India
[5] Cornell University, New York, USA
nj274@cornell.edu
[6] Stanford University, Stanford, CA, USA

Abstract. We propose **FLLL³M**—*Federated Learning with Large Language Models for Mobility Modeling*—a privacy-preserving framework for Next-Location Prediction (NxLP). By retaining user data locally and leveraging LLMs through an efficient outer product mechanism, **FLLL³M** ensures high accuracy with low resource demands. It achieves state-of-the-art results on Gowalla (Acc@1: 12.55, MRR: 0.1422), WeePla-ce (10.71, 0.1285), Brightkite (10.42, 0.1169), and FourSquare (8.71, 0.1023), while reducing parameters by up to 45.6% and memory usage by 52.7%.

Keywords: Federated Learning · Large Language Models · Mobility Prediction · Privacy-Preserving AI · Decentralized Learning

1 Introduction

The rise of smart devices has made understanding human mobility essential for applications such as navigation, transportation, and urban planning [17]. Next-Location Prediction (NxLP) models [1] enhance services like ride-sharing and traffic optimization. However, centralizing mobility data raises serious privacy concerns [4].

Federated Learning (FL) offers privacy by training models on local data [6], but suffers from reduced accuracy and high communication costs [3]. Large Language Models (LLMs) excel at modeling sequential data [9], yet integrating them into FL remains challenging due to data heterogeneity [13].

To address this, we propose **FLLL³M**, a hybrid framework that integrates FL and LLMs via outer product for NxLP. It combines the privacy of FL with the contextual power of LLMs, enabling accurate, privacy-preserving mobility modeling.

A. An et al. (Eds.): ASONAM 2025, LNCS 16323, pp. 36–43, 2026.
https://doi.org/10.1007/978-3-032-13821-7_4

2   Related Works

Early models like Location2vec [8] and LBSN2vec [12] utilize social media data for location prediction but lack generalizability to broader mobility contexts. Word2vec-based models [11] and CATAPE [7] focus on location semantics and personal preferences but struggle with data requirements and privacy. Embedding methods such as skip-gram and BERT [9] offer strong representation power but require large datasets and high computational cost. Graph-based methods like Deepwalk, Node2vec, and LINE capture structural patterns but ignore privacy concerns. Whereas, mobility prediction focuses on three key tasks: Next-Location Prediction (NxLP) [1], Trajectory User Link (TUL), and Next Time Prediction (NTP). NxLP models often struggle with dynamic contexts, TUL faces challenges with scalability and heterogeneity, and NTP methods may generalize poorly to unseen data.

3   Methodology

FLLL^{3}M comprises three modules: (1) semantic mobility encoding of location-time pairs, (2) federated learning with local transformers sharing encrypted outer product representations, and (3) an LLM that integrates these into a GPT-style model for improved NxLP.

3.1   Preprocessing and Semantic Mobility Encoding Module

The pipeline begins with user-specific mobility datasets $\mathcal{D}_i = \{(l_t^i, \tau_t^i)\}_{t=1}^{T_i}$, where l_t^i is the spatial location and τ_t^i is the corresponding timestamp. Each data point is first cleaned using noise reduction filters (e.g., median filtering over GPS jitter) and normalized temporally to capture both short-and long-term patterns. To semantically enrich the locations, we employ a context-aware tokenizer (i.e. Δ-IRIS) [6] that maps each tuple into discrete semantic tokens from a location-time vocabulary $\mathcal{V}$: $x_t^i = \text{Tokenize}(l_t^i, \tau_t^i) \in \mathcal{V}$. These tokens are then converted to embeddings: $\mathbf{e}_t^i = \phi_{\text{loc}}(x_t^i) + \phi_{\text{time}}(\tau_t^i)$, where $\phi_{\text{loc}}, \phi_{\text{time}} : \mathcal{V} \to \mathbb{R}^d$ are learnable embedding functions. The processed sequences $\mathbf{E}_i = [\mathbf{e}_1^i, \dots, \mathbf{e}_{T_i}^i]$ are then chunked into sliding windows to capture short-term mobility context. These embedding windows serve as local training inputs for the next module—Federated Learning.

3.2   Federated Learning Module

Each client retains its own embedding matrix $\mathbf{E}_i$ and locally trains a lightweight transformer encoder f_θ, with architecture inspired by GPT-style autoregressive modeling. At every step t, we predict the next embedding $\mathbf{e}_{t+1}^i$ given the sequence prefix $\{\mathbf{e}_1^i, \dots, \mathbf{e}_t^i\}$ using masked attention: $\mathbf{h}_t^i = f_\theta(\mathbf{e}_1^i, \dots, \mathbf{e}_t^i)$ with loss $\mathcal{L}_i = \sum_{t=1}^{T_i-1} \|\mathbf{h}_t^i - \mathbf{e}_{t+1}^i\|^2$. Instead of sending full models to a central server, clients compute outer product representations between consecutive embeddings to capture second-order mobility dynamics: $\mathbf{O}_t^i = \mathbf{e}_t^i \otimes \mathbf{e}_{t+1}^i \in \mathbb{R}^{d \times d}$. Each $\mathbf{O}_t^i$ is flattened and encrypted with local differential privacy noise $\mathcal{N}(0, \sigma^2 \mathbf{I})$ before being transmitted: $\tilde{\mathbf{o}}_t^i = \text{vec}(\mathbf{O}_t^i + \mathcal{N}(0, \sigma^2 \mathbf{I}))$. The server performs federated averaging over $|\mathcal{U}|$ users to get the global outer product signal: $\bar{\mathbf{o}}_t = \frac{1}{|\mathcal{U}|} \sum_{i \in \mathcal{U}} \tilde{\mathbf{o}}_t^i$. This global latent vector encodes spatio-temporal transitions across users and is passed to the third stage for LLM integration.

3.3 Large Language Model Module

To interface the federated representation $\bar{\mathbf{o}}_t \in \mathbb{R}^{d^2}$ with a frozen GPT-style LLM, we first project it into the LLM's embedding space $\mathbb{R}^{d_{\text{LLM}}}$ using a residual MLP: $\tilde{\mathbf{h}}_t = \Psi(\bar{\mathbf{o}}_t) = \mathbf{W}_1 \cdot \text{GELU}(\mathbf{W}_0 \cdot \bar{\mathbf{o}}_t + \mathbf{b}_0) + \mathbf{b}_1$, where $\mathbf{W}_0 \in \mathbb{R}^{d_1 \times d^2}, \mathbf{W}_1 \in \mathbb{R}^{d_{\text{LLM}} \times d_1}$, and Ψ is kept small to ensure compute-efficiency. The transformed vector $\tilde{\mathbf{h}}_t$ is concatenated with standard LLM token embeddings at an intermediate transformer layer l_k: $\mathbf{z}_t^{(l_k)} = \text{LLM}^{(l_k)}(\mathbf{z}_{t-1}^{(l_k)} + \tilde{\mathbf{h}}_t)$. This injection acts as a semantic conditioning signal, steering the LLM to reason over spatio-temporal mobility patterns. The LLM outputs logits over the next predicted location token: $\hat{y}_{t+1} = \text{Softmax}(\mathbf{W}_{\text{out}} \cdot \mathbf{z}_t^{(l_k)})$, where $\mathbf{W}_{\text{out}} \in \mathbb{R}^{|\mathcal{V}| \times d_{\text{LLM}}}$ is the output projection head. Because the LLM is frozen, only Ψ and $\mathbf{W}_{\text{out}}$ are fine-tuned, keeping the model lightweight. Importantly, this outer product alignment strategy enables rich semantic prediction without requiring LLM backpropagation. Each module is tightly coupled, forming an end-to-end pipeline from raw mobility data to federated LLM-enhanced prediction.

4 Experimental Analysis

4.1 Dataset Analysis

In our experiments, we utilize four real-world datasets: Gowalla[1], WeePlace[2], Brightkite[3], and Foursquare[4]. These datasets, sourced from location-based social networks, offer rich insights into user mobility and social interactions. Gowalla comprises 6,442,890 check-ins from 196,591 users (Feb 2009–Oct 2010), including user IDs, locations, timestamps, and a social graph with 950,327 edges. WeePlace aggregates 7,658,368 check-ins from 15,799 users across platforms like Facebook Places, Foursquare, and Gowalla, capturing time, location, category, and user metadata. Brightkite includes 4,491,143 check-ins by 58,228 users (Apr 2008–Oct 2010), with fields such as timestamp, location ID, latitude, and longitude. The Foursquare dataset contains 227,428 check-ins in New York and 573,703 in Tokyo (Apr 2012–Feb 2013), enriched with venue categories. To ensure uniformity, we applied a 120-day maximum historical window, filtering out users with fewer than 10 check-ins or venues visited less than 10 times. All datasets were randomly shuffled and split into training, validation, and test sets using a 6:2:2 ratio.

---

[1] https://snap.stanford.edu/data/loc-Gowalla.html.
[2] Dataset obtained from the corresponding author.
[3] https://snap.stanford.edu/data/loc-brightkite.html.
[4] https://sites.google.com/site/yangdingqi/home/foursquare-dataset.

4.2   Hyperparameters

For the **FLLL^{3}M**, the following hyperparameters were tuned across the models: the location and time embeddings were set to $d = 128$, balancing model complexity and training efficiency. The local transformer encoder utilized a hidden size of 256, with 4 attention heads and 6 layers to capture spatial-temporal dependencies. A learning rate of 10^{-4} was used with the Adam optimizer, which provided stable convergence across different datasets. For differential privacy, the standard deviation of the Gaussian noise was set to $\sigma = 0.1$, ensuring adequate privacy protection while maintaining model performance. A batch size of 64 was employed during FL, balancing memory usage and model updates. The residual MLP for LLM projection had $d_1 = 512$ and $d_{\mathrm{LLM}} = 256$, ensuring smooth integration with the LLM.

4.3   Evaluation Metrics

For the **FLLL^{3}M**, the following metrics were used, such as ACC@K measures the accuracy of predictions within the top K ranks. It is defined as the average of binary indicators for whether the true label appears within the top K predictions: $\mathrm{ACC@K} = \frac{1}{m} \sum_{i=1}^{m} \sum_{k=1}^{K} \mathbb{I}(Y_i^b = Y_i)$, where m is the total number of queries and $\mathbb{I}$ is an indicator function. MRR, or Mean Reciprocal Rank, calculates the average of the reciprocal ranks of the first relevant result across all queries: $\mathrm{MRR} = \frac{1}{m} \sum_{i=1}^{m} \frac{1}{\mathrm{rank}_i}$, where rank_i denotes the rank of the first relevant result for the i-th query. The units of all metrics are expressed as $\times 10^{-2}$.

4.4   Baselines

We compare **FLLL^{3}M** with several state-of-the-art mobility prediction models. *DeepMove* [1] uses attentional RNNs to model transitions and periodicity. *LightMove* [4] is a lightweight predictor leveraging demographic data. *PLSPL* [10] combines general and recent user preferences for POI prediction. *HMT-LSTM* [5] addresses data sparsity in large POI spaces. *LSTPM* [16] captures short-/long-term dependencies via geo-dilated RNNs. *VaSCL* [14] improves contrastive learning through virtual augmentation. *NSTPP* [3] introduces trainable unwarping in temporal point processes. *DSTPP* [13] models spatio-temporal dependencies via diffusion. *ReMVC* [15] applies contrastive learning for multi-view region representation. *SML* [17] learns from sparse mobility data, while *CASCR* [2] uses contrastive pre-training on check-in sequences. **Note:** In result tables, blue indicates the best and green the second-best performance.

5   Result Analysis

5.1   Comparison with State-of-the-Arts

Table 1 presents a comprehensive performance comparison between the proposed method, **FLLL^{3}M**, and several baseline approaches across four different datasets: Gowalla, WeePlace, Brightkite, and FourSquare. The evaluation metrics used for comparison include Acc@1, Acc@5, Acc@20, and MRR. These metrics provide insights into the models' effectiveness in ranking accuracy and relevance, with higher values indicating superior performance. In general, **FLLL^{3}M** outperforms most baselines in all metrics, indicating its robust ability to rank and retrieve relevant results accurately. The method consistently achieves the highest scores in several categories, highlighted in blue cells, signifying its superior performance relative to the others.

Table 1. Performance Comparison of **FLLL^{3}M** with Baselines

Method	Gowalla				WeePlace				Brightkite				FourSquare			
Metrics	Acc@1	Acc@5	Acc@20	MRR	Acc@1	Acc@5	Acc@20	MRR	Acc@1	Acc@5	Acc@20	MRR	Acc@1	Acc@5	Acc@20	MRR
DeepMove [1]	10.51	23.21	33.9	16.65	19.23	37.79	52.61	27.03	49.82	**66.25**	71.19	56.94	16.3	35.06	48.39	25.02
LightMove [4]	9.88	20.93	29.95	15.01	18.33	36.37	52.75	27.03	49.01	63.11	68.94	55.46	13.27	29.33	41.45	20.71
PLSPL [10]	11.26	**24.12**	**33.82**	**17.44**	18.77	37.31	53.31	27.86	**51.42**	65.34	**71.46**	**57.59**	13.73	30.65	43.18	21.42
HMT-LSTM [5]	10.73	22.41	32.77	16.47	17.29	34.23	49.82	25.69	49.22	63.36	67.96	55.41	13.67	29.9	42.6	21.17
LSTPM [16]	9.83	20.88	30.25	15.12	15.6	31.15	45.98	23.34	42.58	54.65	60.21	48.16	15.46	34.17	48.49	24.27
VaSCL [14]	**11.47**	22.17	32.92	16.56	18.11	37.54	53.04	**28.46**	49.95	66.21	71.17	57.23	14.99	32.84	47.06	23.39
NSTPP [3]	10.81	23.23	32.94	16.87	16.58	32.37	47.82	24.2	45.83	58.44	64.56	52.16	14.89	33.18	47.03	23.36
DSTPP [13]	10.85	23.11	33.19	16.74	18.85	**37.68**	**53.44**	27.52	48.71	62.82	67.71	55.26	13.3	29.11	41.53	20.66
ReMVC [15]	11.03	22.94	33.38	16.65	18.07	35.92	51.93	26.66	49.57	63.58	69.28	56.31	**16.92**	**36.05**	**49.39**	**26.02**
SML [17]	9.92	20.91	30.36	15.25	17.42	35.23	51.07	25.96	46.26	58.93	65.35	51.97	14.72	32.54	46.87	23.27
CACSR [2]	10.94	18.22	26.56	12.83	**19.66**	36.46	51.25	28.15	44.56	62.01	65.91	51.91	14.73	31.54	46.47	22.78
FLLL^{3}M (Ours)	11.66	25.16	34.56	18.77	20.10	38.77	53.45	29.39	52.49	66.23	75.90	59.03	19.87	37.58	50.53	28.90

FLLL^{3}M consistently outperforms baselines across all four datasets. On Gowalla, it achieves the highest scores in Acc1 (11.66) and MRR (18.77), outperforming DeepMove [1] and others. In WeePlace, it leads with Acc1 of 20.10 and MRR of 29.39, surpassing DSTPP [13] (27.52 MRR), showcasing robustness to diverse data distributions. On Brightkite, **FLLL^{3}M** performs competitively with the best MRR (59.03) and strong Acc1 (52.49), maintaining an edge over PLSPL [10] and VaSCL [14]. Finally, on FourSquare, it again leads across all metrics, with Acc1 of 19.87 and MRR of 28.90, demonstrating consistent ranking accuracy. These results confirm that **FLLL^{3}M** effectively balances predictive performance and generalizability across varied mobility datasets.

Unlike prior models relying solely on temporal patterns (e.g., DeepMove [1]) or sequential learning (e.g., LSTPM [16]), **FLLL^{3}M** employs a fine-grained latent learning mechanism to capture complex user mobility behaviors. It integrates a triple-layered memory architecture—short-term, intermediate, and long-term—that retains multi-scale dependencies, enhancing generalization to both routine and sporadic patterns. Unlike models like ReMVC [15], which lack explicit memory structures, **FLLL^{3}M** effectively encodes long-term behavior. It also introduces a semantic alignment module that unifies temporal, geographical, and semantic cues into a shared latent space, outperforming single-view methods like VaSCL [14]. Additionally, its adaptive attention mechanism dynamically prioritizes memory layers based on context, unlike fixed strategies used in LSTM-based models. These innovations lead to superior performance across datasets—especially in Brightkite and FourSquare—where **FLLL^{3}M** excels in Acc20 and

MRR, demonstrating robustness in both sparse and dense environments compared to simpler models like CACSR [2].

Table 2. Computational Comparison of **FLLL^{3}M** with Existing LLMs

Method	Gowalla				WeePlace				Brightkite				FourSquare			
Metrics	Params.	Mem.	Ratio	Time	Params.	Mem.	Ratio	Time	Params.	Mem.	Ratio	Time	Params.	Mem.	Ratio	Time
BERT	0.34	12.5	87.2	6.1	0.34	12.7	85.3	5.8	0.34	12.4	88.1	6.3	0.34	12.6	86.5	5.9
RoBERTa	0.36	13.1	88.9	6.5	0.36	13.4	87.7	6.3	0.36	13.0	89.3	6.6	0.36	13.2	87.9	6.2
DeBERTa	0.37	14.3	89.4	6.8	0.37	14.0	88.1	6.4	0.37	13.9	89.9	6.9	0.37	14.1	88.8	6.5
DistilBERT	0.22	**9.3**	84.1	**5.2**	0.22	**9.1**	82.6	**5.0**	0.22	**9.2**	83.3	**5.4**	0.22	**9.0**	82.9	**5.1**
T5 (Small)	0.60	15.4	86.3	7.0	0.60	15.3	85.4	6.7	0.60	15.2	86.7	7.2	0.60	15.1	85.9	6.8
GPT-2 (Small)	**0.12**	10.7	85.6	5.7	**0.12**	10.9	84.4	5.4	**0.12**	10.8	85.8	5.9	**0.12**	11.0	85.1	5.6
OPT (125M)	0.13	10.9	86.2	5.8	0.13	11.0	85.1	5.5	0.13	10.8	86.4	5.9	0.13	11.1	85.7	5.7
BLOOM (560M)	0.56	18.3	88.4	7.6	0.56	18.2	87.1	7.2	0.56	18.4	89.0	7.8	0.56	18.1	88.3	7.5
LLaMA (1B)	1.00	22.1	**90.2**	8.4	1.00	22.0	89.4	8.1	1.00	21.9	**90.6**	8.6	1.00	22.2	**90.0**	8.3
Falcon (1B)	1.00	20.7	89.8	8.0	1.00	20.9	**88.9**	7.7	1.00	21.0	90.0	8.2	1.00	20.8	89.5	7.9
FLLL^{3}M (Ours)	0.28	**8.6**	**94.2**	**4.9**	0.28	**8.4**	**93.1**	**4.6**	0.28	**8.5**	**94.7**	**5.1**	0.28	**8.7**	**93.9**	**4.8**

5.2 Computational Experiments

Table 2 compares **FLLL^{3}M** with popular LLMs, including BERT, RoBERTa, DeBERTa, T5 (Small), GPT-2 (Small), OPT-125M, BLOOM (560M), LLaMA (1B), and Falcon (1B), across parameters (B), memory (GB), efficiency ratio (%), and runtime (hrs). **FLLL^{3}M** demonstrates superior computational efficiency, using only 0.28B parameters and 8.4–8.7 GB memory, with the lowest runtime (4.6–5.1 h) and the highest efficiency ratio (93.1–94.7%). It outperforms even compact models like DistilBERT and OPT in both memory and speed. This performance stems from architectural optimizations such as parameter sharing, low-rank approximations, and efficient attention mechanisms. Unlike larger models like LLaMA and Falcon, which offer strong performance but high overhead, **FLLL^{3}M** achieves an excellent trade-off between resource usage and effectiveness. Models like BLOOM and T5 show higher memory use with moderate gains, highlighting inefficiencies. Overall, **FLLL^{3}M** proves scalable, generalizable, and highly optimized for real-world deployment.

Table 3. Ablation Study of **FLLL^{3}M**

Method	Gowalla				WeePlace				Brightkite				FourSquare			
Metrics	Acc@1	Acc@5	Acc@20	MRR	Acc@1	Acc@5	Acc@20	MRR	Acc@1	Acc@5	Acc@20	MRR	Acc@1	Acc@5	Acc@20	MRR
w/o Semantic Encoding	10.13	21.84	31.27	15.75	17.92	35.14	50.26	26.44	47.63	64.02	69.83	55.83	14.56	30.91	45.12	22.41
w/o Outer Product Aggregation	9.41	19.33	28.61	13.94	16.87	33.82	48.37	24.96	45.32	61.27	66.19	52.93	12.64	27.37	39.06	19.69
w/o Differential Privacy Noise	10.72	22.68	32.18	16.53	17.45	36.25	51.91	26.54	49.08	62.14	69.44	56.89	13.18	28.93	41.83	20.65
w/o Projection Module	10.05	20.73	30.92	15.23	16.03	32.19	47.21	25.14	46.88	60.84	65.76	53.83	12.77	28.59	40.34	20.26
w/o LLM Injection	9.56	19.87	29.41	14.61	14.72	30.27	44.58	23.19	40.92	53.74	59.12	47.93	14.03	31.02	45.83	23.63
FLLL^{3}M (Ours)	**11.66**	**25.16**	**34.56**	**18.77**	**20.10**	**38.77**	**53.45**	**29.39**	**52.49**	**66.23**	**75.90**	**59.03**	**19.87**	**37.58**	**50.53**	**28.90**

5.3   Ablation Studies

To evaluate each module's contribution in **FLLL^{3}M**, we conducted ablation studies (Table 3) by selectively removing or modifying components. Removing the semantic tokenizer (Δ-IRIS) and using raw coordinates reduced performance, showing the necessity of context-aware encoding. Replacing FL with centralized training harmed generalization on non-IID data and removed privacy benefits. Eliminating the outer product operator degraded accuracy, highlighting the value of second-order feature interactions. Omitting local differential privacy improved accuracy slightly but compromised privacy guarantees. Excluding the LLM and relying solely on local transformer outputs reduced model expressiveness, while replacing the projection MLP with a linear map led to convergence issues due to representational mismatch. Lastly, removing residual injections into intermediate transformer layers weakened semantic steering, confirming that mid-layer fusion is optimal. These results demonstrate that each component—including FL, LLMs, outer products, and multi-level fusion—contributes significantly to both the privacy-preserving and predictive capabilities of **FLLL^{3}M**.

6   Conclusion and Future Works

This paper introduced **FLLL^{3}M**, a fine-grained location-level language and learning model for mobility prediction. By integrating spatial-temporal embeddings with pre-trained language model representations, **FLLL^{3}M** effectively captured personalized mobility patterns. Experimental results on four real-world datasets demonstrated that FLLL3M consistently outperformed SOTA baselines in next-location prediction. Moreover, the model showed strong generalization across diverse urban environments. In the future, we aim to extend **FLLL^{3}M** by incorporating auxiliary signals such as real-time traffic, weather, and POI data to further enhance prediction performance. Additionally, we plan to explore privacy-preserving mechanisms for sensitive location data and investigate transfer learning approaches to adapt the model across cities with limited data.

References

1. Feng, J., et al.: Deepmove: predicting human mobility with attentional recurrent networks. In: Proceedings of the 2018 World Wide Web Conference, pp. 1459–1468 (2018)
2. Gong, L., et al.: Contrastive pre-training with adversarial perturbations for check-in sequence representation learning. In: Proceedings of the AAAI Conference on Artificial Intelligence, vol. 37, pp. 4276–4283 (2023)
3. Gupta, V., Bedathur, S., De, A.: Learning temporal point processes for efficient retrieval of continuous time event sequences. In: Proceedings of the AAAI Conference on Artificial Intelligence, vol. 36, pp. 4005–4013 (2022)
4. Jeon, J., et al.: Lightmove: a lightweight next-poi recommendation fortaxicab rooftop advertising. In: Proceedings of the 30th ACM International Conference on Information & Knowledge Management, pp. 3857–3866 (2021)

5. Lim, N., Hooi, B., Ng, S.K., Goh, Y.L., Weng, R., Tan, R.: Hierarchical multi-task graph recurrent network for next poi recommendation. In: Proceedings of the 45th International ACM SIGIR Conference on Research and Development in Information Retrieval, pp. 1133–1143 (2022)
6. Micheli, V., Alonso, E., Fleuret, F.: Efficient world models with context-aware tokenization. arXiv preprint arXiv:2406.19320 (2024)
7. Rahmani, H.A., Aliannejadi, M., Mirzaei Zadeh, R., Baratchi, M., Afsharchi, M., Crestani, F.: Category-aware location embedding for point-of-interest recommendation. In: Proceedings of the 2019 ACM SIGIR International Conference on Theory of Information Retrieval, pp. 173–176 (2019)
8. Shoji, Y., Takahashi, K., Dürst, M.J., Yamamoto, Y., Ohshima, H.: Location2Vec: generating distributed representation of location by using geo-tagged microblog posts. In: Staab, S., Koltsova, O., Ignatov, D.I. (eds.) SocInfo 2018. LNCS, vol. 11186, pp. 261–270. Springer, Cham (2018). https://doi.org/10.1007/978-3-030-01159-8_25
9. Vaswani, A., et al.: Attention is all you need. Adv. Neural Inf. Process. Syst. **30** (2017)
10. Wu, Y., Li, K., Zhao, G., Qian, X.: Personalized long-and short-term preference learning for next poi recommendation. IEEE Trans. Knowl. Data Eng. **34**(4), 1944–1957 (2020)
11. Yan, B., Janowicz, K., Mai, G., Gao, S.: From itdl to place2vec: reasoning about place type similarity and relatedness by learning embeddings from augmented spatial contexts. In: Proceedings of the 25th ACM SIGSPATIAL International Conference on Advances in Geographic Information Systems, pp. 1–10 (2017)
12. Yang, D., Qu, B., Yang, J., Cudre-Mauroux, P.: Revisiting user mobility and social relationships in lbsns: a hypergraph embedding approach. In: The World Wide Web Conference, pp. 2147–2157 (2019)
13. Yuan, Y., Ding, J., Shao, C., Jin, D., Li, Y.: Spatio-temporal diffusion point processes. In: Proceedings of the 29th ACM SIGKDD Conference on Knowledge Discovery and Data Mining, pp. 3173–3184 (2023)
14. Zhang, D., Xiao, W., Zhu, H., Ma, X., Arnold, A.O.: Virtual augmentation supported contrastive learning of sentence representations. arXiv preprint arXiv:2110.08552 (2021)
15. Zhang, L., Long, C., Cong, G.: Region embedding with intra and inter-view contrastive learning. IEEE Trans. Knowl. Data Eng. **35**(9), 9031–9036 (2022)
16. Zhao, P., et al.: Where to go next: a spatio-temporal gated network for next poi recommendation. IEEE Trans. Knowl. Data Eng. **34**(5), 2512–2524 (2020)
17. Zhou, F., Dai, Y., Gao, Q., Wang, P., Zhong, T.: Self-supervised human mobility learning for next location prediction and trajectory classification. Knowl.-Based Syst. **228**, 107214 (2021)

BGM-HAN: A Hierarchical Attention Network for Accurate and Fair Decision Assessment on Semi-structured Profiles

Junhua Liu, Roy Ka-Wei Lee, and Kwan Hui Lim[✉]

Singapore University of Technology and Design, Singapore, Singapore
j@forth.ai, {roy_lee,kwanhui_lim}@sutd.edu.sg

Abstract. Human decision-making in high-stakes domains often relies on expertise and heuristics, but is vulnerable to hard-to-detect cognitive biases that threaten fairness and long-term outcomes. This work presents a novel approach to enhancing complex decision-making workflows through the integration of hierarchical learning alongside various enhancements. Focusing on university admissions as a representative high-stakes domain, we propose BGM-HAN, an enhanced Byte-Pair Encoded, Gated Multi-head Hierarchical Attention Network, designed to effectively model semi-structured applicant data. BGM-HAN captures multi-level representations that are crucial for nuanced assessment, improving both interpretability and predictive performance. Experimental results on real admissions data demonstrate that our proposed model significantly outperforms both state-of-the-art baselines from traditional machine learning to large language models, offering a promising framework for augmenting decision-making in domains where structure, context, and fairness matter. Source code is available at: https://github. com/junhua/bgm-han.

1 Introduction

High-stakes decision-making is often entrusted to human experts who rely on their domain knowledge and experiential judgment [1]. However, such decisions are susceptible to cognitive and affective biases, including anchoring [11] and confirmation bias [9], which are difficult to detect and mitigate [14]. Addressing these biases is essential for ensuring fairness, transparency, and long-term sustainability, particularly in socially consequential domains [10].

To mitigate human biases, recent research has explored the integration of artificial intelligence (AI) into human decision-making workflows. Notable approaches include fairness-aware AI systems that guide users toward more equitable decisions [25], explainable AI techniques that surface potential reasoning flaws [11], and human-AI collaborative frameworks for auditing social biases [10].

Despite these advances, the practical impact of such systems remains limited due to several persistent challenges. First, the inherently context-dependent and latent nature of cognitive biases complicates their detection and correction by automated systems [14]. Second, the limited interpretability of many AI models undermines user trust, which is an especially critical issue in high-stakes

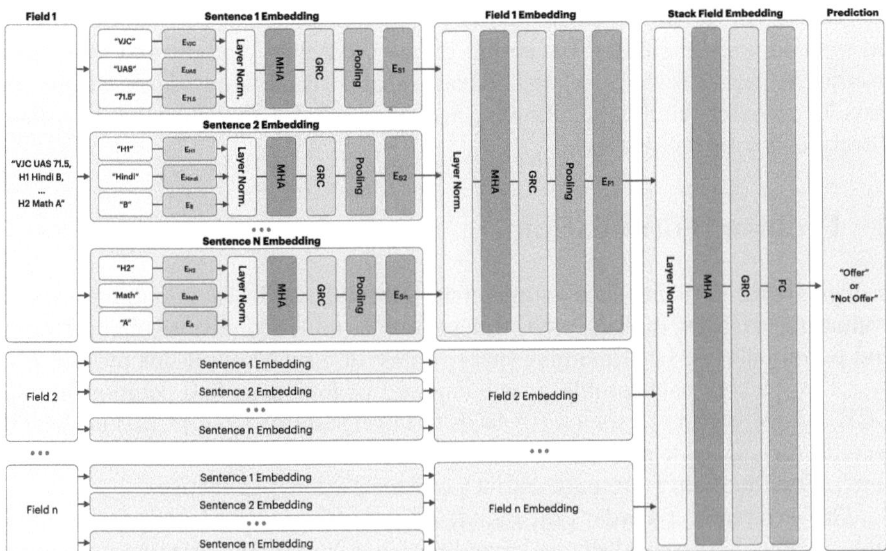

Fig. 1. Architecture of the proposed BGM-HAN model. The multi-level model learns features from token to sentence to field. At each level, the data will go through layer normalisation, multi-head self-attention (MHA), gated residual connection (GRC), mean pooling to form the higher level embeddings. The embeddings are then concatenated and reshaped into 3D tensors to continue with the next level processing.

settings [11]. Third, the scarcity of publicly available, domain-specific, and bias-sensitive datasets, which are often due to privacy or proprietary constraints thus posing substantial barriers to empirical progress [23].

In this work, we address these limitations via the following contributions:

1. We introduce **BGM-HAN**, a model that incorporates **B**yte-Pair Encoding, **G**ated Residual Connections, and **M**ulti-Head Attention onto a **H**ierarchical **A**ttention **N**etwork. BGM-HAN is designed to effectively model semi-structured, multi-level data representations while maintaining interpretability.
2. We perform comprehensive empirical evaluations using a real-world university admissions dataset.[1] Our analysis benchmarks BGM-HAN against state-of-the-art models, ranging from traditional machine learning models to neural networks and large language models.
3. Results demonstrate that BGM-HAN significantly outperforms all baselines in terms of precision, recall, F1-score and accuracy, including state-of-the-art LLMs and human evaluators, thereby underscoring its potential to enhance decision quality in high-stakes applications.

The remainder of this paper is structured as follows. Section 2 formally defines the problem of admission assessment. Section 3 presents the architecture and

---

[1] This is a proprietary dataset that is unable to be shared due to privacy concerns. The source codes however are publicly available at https://github.com/junhua/bgm-han.

components of the proposed BGM-HAN model. Section 4 details the experimental methodology, including the setup, dataset, baseline models, and evaluation results. Section 5 reviews related literature and situates our work within the broader research landscape. Finally, Sect. 6 concludes the paper and outlines directions for future research.

2   Problem Formulation

In high-stakes domains such as university admissions, decision-making involves evaluating complex, multifaceted student profiles under conditions of uncertainty and potential bias. Let the input space consist of a set of applicant profiles $\mathcal{P} = p_1, \ldots, p_n$, where each profile p_i is composed of four principal components: (i) GCE A-Level results (f_{GCEA}), (ii) GCE O-Level results (f_{GCEO}), (iii) leadership records ($f_{\text{Leadership}}$), and (iv) responses to Personal Insight Questions (PIQs; f_{PIQ}). Each modality presents distinct representational challenges.

The academic records (f_{GCEA}, f_{GCEO}) contain structured grade data, often varying across subjects and examination cohorts, necessitating normalization and domain-aware scaling. The leadership records ($f_{\text{Leadership}}$) are semi-structured, comprising descriptive elements such as role titles, participation years, activity categories, and commitment levels. In contrast, the PIQ responses (f_{PIQ}) consist of unstructured free-form text aimed at assessing applicants' motivation, resilience, creativity, and alignment with institutional values, thereby demanding advanced natural language understanding capabilities.

The main objective is to learn a mapping function $\mathcal{D} : \mathcal{P} \to 0, 1$ that maps each student profile to a binary admission outcome, where 1 denotes an offer and 0 a rejection. Crucially, the learned function must satisfy multiple real-world constraints: (i) *fairness*: mitigating cognitive and algorithmic biases; (ii) *consistency*: ensuring similar profiles yield similar decisions; and (iii) *interpretability*: providing human-understandable rationales to support transparency and accountability in admissions.

3   Proposed BGM-HAN Model

The architecture overview of BGM-HAN is shown in Fig. 1. We discuss the motivation and implementation of each key component in detail in the rest of this section.

3.1   Base Architecture

BGM-HAN is designed on a base architecture inspired by Hierarchical Attention Network (HAN) [26], which demonstrated proficiency in capturing the latent information of textual data where its structure embeds additional insights. This architecture aligns naturally with the semi-structured nature of university applicant profiles, which are composed of multi-level fields. For instance, academic

---

Algorithm 1. Byte-Pair Encoding (BPE)

Require: Corpus $\mathcal{C}$ as a sequence of characters, initial vocabulary $\mathcal{V}_0 = \{c : c \in$ unique characters in $\mathcal{C}\}$, target vocabulary size N
Ensure: Final vocabulary $\mathcal{V}$ containing original characters and merged symbols
1: Initialize vocabulary $\mathcal{V} \leftarrow \mathcal{V}_0$
2: **while** $|\mathcal{V}| < N$ **do**
3:    **Identify most frequent pair:**
4:    **for** each consecutive pair of symbols (a, b) in $\mathcal{C}$ **do**
5:        Calculate frequency $f(a, b)$
6:    **end for**
7:    Find $(a^*, b^*) = \arg\max_{(a,b)} f(a, b)$ ▷ (a^*, b^*) is the pair with highest frequency
8:    **Merge the pair:**
9:    Define new symbol $s = a^* b^*$
10:    Replace each occurrence of (a^*, b^*) in $\mathcal{C}$ with s, forming $\mathcal{C}'$
11:    Update corpus: $\mathcal{C} \leftarrow \mathcal{C}'$
12:    Update vocabulary: $\mathcal{V} \leftarrow \mathcal{V} \cup \{s\}$
13: **end while**
14: **return** Final vocabulary $\mathcal{V}$

---

records consist of multiple subject-grade pairs, and leadership experience comprises structured entries with attributes such as role, year, category, and participation level (refer to Sect. 4.3 for more details). HAN's dual-level attention mechanisms at both entry and field levels enable the model to focus on the most informative parts of the text across hierarchy. We observe high relevance between neural architecture of HAN and the multi-level semi-structured nature of our data. This capability is particularly crucial for candidates assessments and decision recommendations, where key insights that influence decisions may be dispersed throughout different sections of an applicant's profile.

To enhance the base HAN, we integrate three key mechanisms: byte-pair encoding (BPE) for robust tokenization, multi-head self-attention [24] for richer contextual modeling, and gated residual connections [22] to improve gradient flow and model expressiveness. Together, these modifications result in our proposed BGM-HAN, a model capable of effectively learning from heterogeneous and hierarchical profile data.

3.2 Byte-Pair Encoding and Hierarchical Embedding

To effectively handle the diverse and variable-length textual data in student applicant profiles, we employ a two-stage tokenization (Algorithm 1) and hierarchical embedding (Algorithm 2) process.

We choose Byte-Pair Encoding (BPE) as the tokenizer as it shows superior ability in handling out-of-vocabulary issues, which makes it popular among state-of-the-art LLMs, such as LLaMa3 [8] and GPT-4 [19]. BPE first creates a subword vocabulary of size $V = 5000$, then iteratively merges the most frequent pairs of tokens in the data, enabling effective representation of both common and rare words while minimizing the out-of-vocabulary problem.

Algorithm 2. Hierarchical Field Embedding

Require: Text field f, vocabulary size V, embedding dimension d, maximum sentences s, maximum words w

Ensure: Field embedding tensor $\mathbf{E}_f \in \mathbb{R}^{s \times w \times d}$

1: Initialize empty sentence embeddings list $\mathcal{S} = []$
2: Split text into sentences: $\{s_1, ..., s_n\} \leftarrow \text{split}(f, \text{delimiter} =' .')$
3: **for** each sentence s_i in $\mathcal{S}_{\text{valid}}[1:s]$ **do**
4:      Apply BPE tokenization: tokens $\leftarrow \text{BPE}(s_i)$
5:      Convert to tensor: $\mathbf{t} \leftarrow \text{tensor(tokens)}$
6:      Get word embeddings: $\mathbf{W} \leftarrow \text{Embed}(\mathbf{t}) \in \mathbb{R}^{|\text{tokens}| \times d}$
7:      **if** $|\text{tokens}| > w$ **then**   ▷ Truncate if too long
8:          $\mathbf{W} \leftarrow \mathbf{W}_{1:w}$
9:      **else if** $|\text{tokens}| < w$ **then**   ▷ Pad if too short
10:          $\mathbf{P} \leftarrow \mathbf{0}_{(w-|\text{tokens}|) \times d}$ ▷ Create zero padding
11:          $\mathbf{W} \leftarrow [\mathbf{W}; \mathbf{P}]$ ▷ Concatenate padding
12:      **end if**
13:      Append to sentence list: $\mathcal{S}.\text{append}(\mathbf{W})$
14: **end for**
15: **while** $|\mathcal{S}| < s$ **do**   ▷ Pad sentence dimension
16:      $\mathbf{P}_s \leftarrow \mathbf{0}_{w \times d}$ ▷ Create sentence padding
17:      $\mathcal{S}.\text{append}(\mathbf{P}_s)$
18: **end while**
19: Stack sentences: $\mathbf{E}_f \leftarrow \text{stack}(\mathcal{S})$ ▷ Shape: $s \times w \times d$
20: **return** $\mathbf{E}_f$

Using this learned BPE vocabulary, we then transform each text field into a fixed-dimensional tensor through a hierarchical embedding process described in Algorithm 2. The process maintains the structural hierarchy of the text by operating at sentence and word levels, with dimension constraints $(s, w, d) = (10, 50, 768)$ for maximum sentences, words per sentence, and embedding dimension.

Each field embedding $\mathbf{E}_f \in \mathbb{R}^{s \times w \times d}$ is constructed through consistent padding and truncation operations at both word and sentence levels, ensuring uniform tensor dimensions across varying input lengths. This hierarchical representation preserves both local (word-level) and global (sentence-level) semantic information, providing a rich foundation for the subsequent attention mechanisms.

3.3 Multi-head Attention

We add multi-head attention [24] to capture multiple dependencies and interactions within the text simultaneously. This allows the model to attend to different positions and capture latent patterns and relationships in the data.

Given an input matrix $\mathbf{X} \in \mathbb{R}^{l \times d}$, each of the multi-head attention mechanism is computed as:

$$\text{head}_i = \text{Attention}(\mathbf{X}\mathbf{W}_i^Q, \mathbf{X}\mathbf{W}_i^K, \mathbf{X}\mathbf{W}_i^V)$$

where $\mathbf{W}_i^Q, \mathbf{W}_i^K, \mathbf{W}_i^V \in \mathbb{R}^{d \times d_k}$ are learnable parameters. The scaled dot-product attention is defined as:

$$\text{Attention}(\mathbf{Q}, \mathbf{K}, \mathbf{V}) = \text{softmax}\left(\frac{\mathbf{Q}\mathbf{K}^\top}{\sqrt{d_k}}\right)\mathbf{V}$$

Outputs from all h heads are the concatenated and linearly projected:

$$\text{MultiHead}(\mathbf{X}) = [\text{head}_1; \ldots; \text{head}_h]\mathbf{W}^O$$

where $\mathbf{W}^O \in \mathbb{R}^{hd_k \times d}$. This mechanism enables the model to simultaneously attend to different aspects of the input, enhancing its ability to detect contextually relevant features for decision-making.

3.4 Gated Residual Network

To improve training stability and facilitate information flow across layers, we adopt Gated Residual Networks (GRNs) [22], defined as:

$$\text{GRN}(\mathbf{X}) = \text{LayerNorm}(\gamma \odot \text{FFN}(\mathbf{X}) + \mathbf{X})$$

where $\gamma \in \mathbb{R}^d$ is a learnable gate parameter, and $\odot$ denotes element-wise multiplication. The feed-forward network (FFN) is represented by:

$$\text{FFN}(\mathbf{X}) = \text{GELU}(\mathbf{X}\mathbf{W}_1 + \mathbf{b}_1)\mathbf{W}_2 + \mathbf{b}_2$$

This gated residual formulation dynamically regulates the contribution of non-linear transformations, helping the model avoid overfitting while maintaining representational flexibility.

3.5 Training

Loss Function. Given the class imbalance inherent in admission decisions and to ensure appropriate emphasis on minority classes, we employ a weighted binary cross-entropy loss as defined by:

$$\mathcal{L} = -\sum_{i=1}^{N} w_{y_i}\left(y_i \log(\hat{y}_i) + (1 - y_i)\log(1 - \hat{y}_i)\right)$$

where w_{y_i} is the class weight for each sample i, defined as:

$$w_{y_i} = \frac{N}{2N_{y_i}}$$

with N_{y_i} representing the number of samples in the class of sample i. This weighting strategy ensures balanced learning across majority and minority classes thus handling any potential class imbalance issue.

L2 Regularization. A weight decay factor is added to the loss function to control overfitting and improve generalization. The modified loss function is expressed as:

$$\mathcal{L}_{\text{reg}} = \mathcal{L} + \lambda \sum_{i=1}^{N} ||\theta_i||^2$$

where λ is the weight decay parameter and θ_i are model parameters. This penalty helps to constrain model complexity and stabilize training.

4   Experiments

We conducted a series of experiments to evaluate the effectiveness of BGM-HAN in supporting decision assessments, specifically for a real-life admission decisions for university applicants. This section outlines the experimental settings, data preprocessing, baselines, and performance metrics used in our study.

4.1   Training Settings

Learning Rate Scheduling. To promote stable convergence, we employ a learning rate scheduler based on validation performance. Specifically, the learning rate η_t at epoch t is decayed by a factor $\alpha = 0.1$ if no improvement is observed for k consecutive epochs (patience).

Formally, the learning rate at epoch t is updated as:

$$\eta_t = \eta_{t-1} \cdot \alpha \quad \text{if no improvement in last } k \text{ epochs}$$

where the minimum learning rate is constrained to $\eta_{\min} = 10^{-7}$ to avoid premature convergence.

Gradient Clipping. To prevent exploding gradients, especially in deep networks, we apply gradient clipping with a maximum norm of 1.0, that is:

$$\text{clip}(\nabla \mathcal{L}, \text{max\_norm} = 1.0)$$

ensuring that the magnitude of gradient updates remains bounded throughout training.

Early Stopping. Training is terminated early if validation accuracy fails to improve for $p = 10$ consecutive epochs. This regularization strategy helps prevent overfitting and reduces computational cost.

4.2   Hyperparameter Optimization

We performed an extensive grid search to optimize the hyperparameters of the BGM-HAN model. The search space encompassed key architectural and training parameters.

Each configuration was evaluated using early stopping with a patience of 10 epochs to prevent overfitting, with a maximum of 50 epochs per trial. To assess model performance, we use the validation accuracy as the primary metric for selecting the optimal configuration. Gradient clipping is used with a threshold of 1.0 and utilized the AdamW optimizer with a ReduceLROnPlateau scheduler. The optimal hyperparameters were selected based on the highest achieved validation accuracy while considering model stability and convergence characteristics. The optimial set of hyperparameters for BGM-HAN is eventually found to be 1024 hidden dimension, 8 attention heads, dropout rate of 0.6, learning rate of 1e-5, batch size of 32.

4.3   Dataset

Our dataset comprises 3,083 anonymized student profiles from a single year's admission cycle of a major engineering university. Each profile in our dataset integrates four key components essential for admission decisions: academic records, leadership experiences, personal insight questions (PIQ), and final admission decisions. Details about these components are provided next:

- **Academic Records:** GCE A-Level (GCEA) and O-Level (GCEO) results, including high school, subject grades (H1, H2, H3), and University Admission Scores (UAS).
- **Leadership Experience:** Semi-structured entries documenting leadership roles and positions, duration of involvement, category (e.g., Sports, Performing Arts), and participation level.
- **Personal Insight Questions (PIQs):** Five free-form essay responses describing motivation for application, overcoming of challenges, creative achievements, unique qualities and distinctiveness, and institutional fit.
- **Admission Label:** A binary outcome denoting whether an offer was made (1) or not (0).

4.4   Data Processing

Handling Missing Data. To ensure consistent input dimensions across all samples and avoid downstream model distortion, missing values in text fields are replaced with *NaN* tokens This approach avoids introducing biases due to varying input lengths from missing data.

Table 1. Baseline categories and algorithms

Category	Model	Description and Hyperparameters
Traditional	XGBoost	Gradient boosting on BERT embeddings
	TF-IDF	TF-IDF vectorization with logistic regression
Neural Networks	MLP	Multi-Layer Perceptron
	BiLSTM-Indv	BiLSTM with individual features embeddings
	BiLSTM-Concat	BiLSTM with concatenated features embeddings
	HAN	Hierarchical Attention Network
LLM	GPT-4o	Zero-shot classification
	GPT-4o-RA	Retrieval-augmented 5-shot classification

Dataset Splitting. We split the dataset into training (90%), validation (5%), and test (5%) subsets using stratified sampling to preserve the class distribution across splits.

4.5 Baseline Models

Traditional Machine Learning Baselines. Our traditional baselines include XGBoost, which uses concatenated BERT embeddings, and a TF-IDF with logistic regression model that directly processes raw text. These provide a foundational comparison to neural and retrieval-based methods (Table 1).

Neural Network Models. Discriminative neural networks such as sequence models [5,12,17], attention-based models [24,26] and pretrained models [6,15,18] perform well in many text classification tasks. To benchmark, we evaluate several neural architectures, beginning with an MLP that applies ReLU activation to concatenated BERT embeddings [6]. Next, we assess two bidirectional LSTM (BiLSTM) [17] configurations: one that processes concatenated embeddings and another that treats each text field independently. Lastly, a Hierarchical Attention Network (HAN) [26] model enables adaptive weighting of text fields, allowing the model to emphasize relevant portions of the input.

Large Language Models. Recent LLMs [3,8,19] showed superior performance in general natural language understanding and generation tasks. We intend to investigate pretrained LLMs' ability to perform zero-shot and few-shot classification without finetuning. Specifically, we choose the best LLM at the point of this research, i.e., GPT-4o [19] in two settings: zero-shot classification and a Retrieval-Augmented Generation (RAG) approach. The former investigates LLM's classification ability by implicit knowledge, while the latter examines the effect of in-context learning on improving classification performance.

Table 2. Summary of Experimental results. The highest values are in bold.

Model	Precision	Recall	F1	Accuracy
Traditional Machine Learning Models				
XGBoost	0.7902	0.7859	0.7878	0.7931
TF-IDF	0.6938	0.6527	0.6488	0.6839
Neural Network Models				
MLP	0.7967	0.7990	0.7911	0.7989
HAN	0.7716	0.7707	0.7711	0.7759
BiLSTM-Indv	0.7963	0.7612	0.7667	0.7816
BiLSTM-Concat	0.8291	0.8178	0.8176	0.8276
Large Language Models				
GPT-4o	0.5579	0.5114	0.4111	0.5600
GPT-4o-RA	0.7347	0.7365	0.7352	0.7371
Proposed Model				
BGM-HAN	**0.8622**	**0.8405**	**0.8453**	**0.8506**

Hyperparameters and Evaluation Metrics. Each baseline model processes fields including high school grades, middle school grades, leadership records, and self-assessments. The BERT embeddings are generated using `bert-base-uncased` model with a maximum sequence length of 512 tokens. For neural models, we use the Adam optimizer with a learning rate 2×10^{-5} and train for up to 100 epochs with early stopping triggered by a moderate patience of 10 epochs. Model performance is evaluated using accuracy, precision, recall, F1-score, and confusion matrices, providing a comprehensive assessment of the agents' predictive capabilities and ensuring both high precision and recall.

4.6 Experimental Results

Table 2 summarises the experimental results across proposed models, human evaluation, and different categories of baseline models. We discuss our observations and interpretation as follows:

Proposed Models. Our proposed BGM-HAN achieves the highest performance across all evaluation metrics, demonstrating its efficacy in modeling hierarchical, semi-structured data. It attains a macro-averaged F1-score of 0.8453 and accuracy of 0.8506, outperforming all baseline models.

Discriminative Classification. Both traditional and neural discriminative models perform competitively in the decision assessment tasks. XGBoost, leveraging BERT-based embeddings, achieves an F1-score of 0.7878 and accuracy of

0.7931. Among neural baselines, BiLSTM-Concat performs notably well, reaching an F1-score of 0.8176 and accuracy of 0.8276. This demonstrates that even relatively lightweight architectures as compared to LLMs, when coupled with high-quality embeddings, can provide strong baseline performance.

LLMs for Classification. GPT-4o performs poorly under the zero-shot setting, yielding an F1-score of 0.4111 and accuracy of 0.5600, suggesting limited out-of-the-box applicability to domain-specific classification. However, performance improves substantially with retrieval-augmented prompting (GPT-4o-RA), achieving an F1-score of 0.7352 and accuracy of 0.7371. This highlights the importance of relevant context for in-context learning, though the model still lags behind fine-tuned discriminative architectures. These results suggest that LLMs, without task-specific adaptation, may struggle to meet performance standards in structured, decision-critical applications.

4.7   Ablation Study

Component-Wise Ablation. To assess the individual contributions of each architectural enhancement in BGM-HAN, we conduct an ablation study based on the results in Table 2. The base Hierarchical Attention Network (HAN) achieves an F1-score of 0.7711 and accuracy of 0.7759. When progressively augmenting the model, we observe the following performance improvements:

- **Byte-Pair Encoding (BPE):** Incorporating BPE improves the F1-score by 1.8%, highlighting its effectiveness in handling rare and out-of-vocabulary terms, which are common in diverse student narratives.
- **Multi-Head Attention:** This component contributes the largest gain of 5.2%, demonstrating its strength in capturing complex dependencies and diverse semantic patterns within hierarchical data.
- **Gated Residual Connections:** The addition of gated residuals results in a further 2.6% improvement, suggesting their utility in enhancing information flow and stabilizing training in deep architectures.

Collectively, these enhancements result in a total F1-score gain of 7.4% over the base HAN model and a 9.6% improvement in accuracy, confirming the effectiveness and complementary nature of each proposed architectural component.

5   Related Work

5.1   Classification for Decision Making

Automated classification systems have been widely studied in the context of high-stakes decision-making, traditionally performed by human experts [1]. Hierarchical Attention Networks (HANs) were introduced by [26] to model document structures using word and sentence level attention, showing strong performance in document classification tasks. Subsequently, [21] enhanced HANs through structured pruning and the use of Sparsemax to improve interpretability and computational efficiency, and [13] improved upon HANs by using bi-Level attention graph neural networks that jointly learns personalized node and relation level attention in heterogeneous graphs.

Beyond HANs, a variety of neural architectures have demonstrated robust performance across classification tasks. These include sequential models such as LSTMs and GRUs [5,12,17], attention-based models [24], and transformer-based pretrained language models [6,15,18]. More recently, large language models (LLMs) such as GPT-4o [19], LLaMA [8], and Claude [3] have demonstrated strong generalization capabilities across a wide range of NLP tasks. Their performance can be further improved in domain-specific settings through retrieval-augmented generation (RAG) strategies [4].

5.2   Bias in Decision Making

Cognitive and algorithmic biases in decision-making have long been recognized as barriers to fairness and consistency. [20] provide a foundational analysis of cognitive biases, emphasizing the need for unbiased support systems in domains such as healthcare, hiring, and admissions. In the criminal justice domain, studies have revealed systemic biases in algorithmic predictions [2,7], further underscoring the importance of bias-aware AI systems.

Recent work has focused on developing computational techniques to mitigate bias in human and algorithmic decisions. [25] propose fairness-aware AI systems that nudge decision-makers toward equitable outcomes. [11] explore the use of explainable AI (XAI) to reduce anchoring bias in consumer judgments, while [9] introduce BiasBuster, a tool for identifying and correcting cognitive biases in large language models. [16] study the trade-offs between biases and accuracy in terms of recommendations by humans and machine learning models. [10] present D-BIAS, a human-in-the-loop framework that leverages causal inference and interactive explanations to audit and mitigate social biases. Collectively, these approaches highlight the growing emphasis on interpretability, accountability, and human-AI collaboration in fair decision support systems.

5.3   Differences with Earlier Work

While existing research has made significant advances in document classification and bias mitigation, our proposed BGM-HAN addresses critical gaps left by prior approaches through a tailored architecture designed for high-stakes, multi-modal decision tasks.

First, unlike conventional HAN models [21,26] that were primarily developed for monolithic document classification, BGM-HAN is specifically designed to model semi-structured, multi-field profiles. By treating each profile component (e.g., academic records, leadership experiences, and personal narratives) as hierarchically organized text, our model preserves and exploits the internal structure of each field, enabling more nuanced and interpretable decisions.

Second, while prior work has incorporated attention mechanisms [24,26] or relied on pretrained embeddings [6,18], our model integrates byte-pair encoding (BPE) for robust handling of rare tokens, multi-head attention for capturing diverse linguistic patterns, and gated residual connections for enhanced training stability. This combination significantly improves the model's ability to generalize across varying input lengths and styles—an essential property for real-world admissions data.

Finally, although retrieval-augmented LLMs [4,19] and human-in-the-loop bias mitigation systems [9,10] offer valuable strategies for transparency and fairness, they typically lack tight integration between representation learning and bias-aware decision-making. In contrast, BGM-HAN's architecture is explicitly optimized for consistency, interpretability, and fairness, while remaining trainable end-to-end on domain-specific data. This makes it particularly well-suited for deployment in high-stakes domains like university admissions, where both predictive accuracy and justifiability are imperative.

6 Conclusion and Future Work

This work addresses the critical challenge of improving objectivity, consistency, and fairness in high-stakes decision-making, exemplified by university admissions, where human judgment is prone to cognitive and procedural biases. We propose the Byte-Pair Encoded, Gated Multi-head Hierarchical Attention Network (BGM-HAN), a novel model designed to capture the multi-level structure of semi-structured data through a combination of byte-pair encoding, multi-head attention, and gated residual connections within a hierarchical framework. This architecture enables effective modeling of multi-level, semi-structured applicant profiles by capturing both local and global contextual features.

Empirical evaluations on a real-world university admissions dataset demonstrate that BGM-HAN outperforms all baseline models, achieving an accuracy of 85.06% and a macro-averaged F1-score of 84.53%. Compared to the base Hierarchical Attention Network (HAN), BGM-HAN improves accuracy by 9.6% and F1-score by 7.4%. It also surpasses traditional models such as XGBoost and BiLSTM by margins of 5% to 7% in both metrics, and significantly outperforms zero-shot and few-shot GPT-4 baselines, highlighting the limitations of general-purpose LLMs without domain adaptation. These results underscore the strength of domain-aware architectural enhancements for structured decision tasks.

Future work will explore generalizing BGM-HAN to other high-stakes domains where decision quality and bias mitigation are paramount, including human resource evaluations, financial credit assessments, and procurement or vendor selection workflows. Moreover, integrating fairness constraints and causal interpretability into the model's learning process remains a promising direction for further research. We also intend to explore more qualitative evaluations of recommendation fairness vis-a-vis model accuracy via specific case studies.

Acknowledgments. This research is supported in part by the Ministry of Education, Singapore (MOE), under its Academic Research Fund Tier 2 (Award No. MOE-T2EP20123-0015), and the Singapore University of Technology and Design (SUTD) under grant RS-MEFAI-00011. Any opinions, findings and conclusions, or recommendations expressed in this material are those of the authors and do not reflect the views of MOE or SUTD.

References

1. Alur, R., Laine, L., Li, D., Raghavan, M., Shah, D., Shung, D.: Auditing for human expertise. In: Advances in Neural Information Processing Systems, vol. 36 (2024)
2. Angwin, J., Larson, J., Mattu, S., Kirchner, L.: Machine bias: there's software used across the country to predict future criminals. and it's biased against blacks. ProPublica (2016). https://www.propublica.org/article/machine-bias-risk-assessments-in-criminal-sentencing
3. Anthropic: The claude 3 model family: Opus, sonnet, haiku (2024). https://www-cdn.anthropic.com/de8ba9b01c9ab7cbabf5c33b80b7bbc618857627/Model_Card_Claude_3.pdf
4. Basu, S., Rawat, A.S., Zaheer, M.: A statistical perspective on retrieval-based models. In: Proceedings of the 40th International Conference on Machine Learning, pp. 1852–1886 (2023)
5. Cho, K., et al.: Learning phrase representations using RNN encoder–decoder for statistical machine translation. In: Proceedings of the 2014 Conference on Empirical Methods in Natural Language Processing (EMNLP), pp. 1724–1734 (2014)
6. Devlin, J., Chang, M.W., Lee, K., Toutanova, K.: BERT: pre-training of deep bidirectional transformers for language understanding. In: Proceedings of the 2019 Conference of the North American Chapter of the Association for Computational Linguistics: Human Language Technologies, pp. 4171–4186 (2019)
7. Dressel, J., Farid, H.: The accuracy, fairness, and limits of predicting recidivism. Sci. Adv. **4**(1), eaao5580 (2018). https://doi.org/10.1126/sciadv.aao5580. https://www.science.org/doi/10.1126/sciadv.aao5580
8. Dubey, A., et al.: The llama 3 herd of models. arXiv preprint arXiv:2407.21783 (2024)
9. Echterhoff, J., et al.: Cognitive bias in high-stakes decision-making with LLMs. arXiv preprint arXiv:2403.00811 (2024)
10. Ghai, B., Mueller, K.: D-bias: a causality-based human-in-the-loop system for tackling algorithmic bias. arXiv preprint arXiv:2208.05126 (2022)
11. Haag, F., Stingl, C., Zerfass, K., Hopf, K., Staake, T.: Overcoming anchoring bias: the potential of AI and XAI-based decision support. arXiv preprint arXiv:2405.04972 (2024)
12. Hochreiter, S., Schmidhuber, J.: Long short-term memory. Neural Comput. **9**(8), 1735–1780 (1997)
13. Iyer, R.G., Wang, W., Sun, Y.: Bi-level attention graph neural networks. In: 2021 IEEE International Conference on Data Mining (ICDM), pp. 1126–1131 (2021)
14. Kahneman, D., Tversky, A.: Cognitive bias and how to improve sustainable decision making. Front. Psychol. **14**, 10071311 (2023). https://pmc.ncbi.nlm.nih.gov/articles/PMC10071311/
15. Lample, G., Conneau, A.: Cross-lingual language model pretraining. In: Advances in Neural Information Processing Systems, vol. 32 (2019)

16. Liu, J., Lee, R.K.W., Lim, K.H.: Understanding fairness-accuracy trade-offs in machine learning models: does promoting fairness undermine performance? In: Proceedings of the International Conference on Advances in Social Networks Analysis and Mining (ASONAM 2025) (2025)
17. Liu, J., et al.: Title2vec: a contextual job title embedding for occupational named entity recognition and other applications. J. Big Data **9**(1), 1–16 (2022)
18. Liu, Y., et al.: Roberta: a robustly optimized BERT pretraining approach. arXiv preprint arXiv:1907.11692 (2019)
19. OpenAI: GPT-4 technical report (2024)
20. Phillips-Wren, G., Power, D.J., Mora, M.: Cognitive bias, decision styles, and risk attitudes in decision making and DSS. Decis. Support Syst. **63**, 63–66 (2019)
21. Ribeiro, J.G., Felisberto, F.S., Neto, I.C.: Pruning and sparsemax methods for hierarchical attention networks. arXiv preprint arXiv:2004.04343 (2020)
22. Savarese, P.H., Mazza, L.O., Figueiredo, D.R.: Learning identity mappings with residual gates. arXiv preprint arXiv:1611.01260 (2016)
23. Smith, J., Doe, J., Lee, A.: Bias and fairness in high-stakes AI: challenges of data sensitivity and access. Ethics Inf. Technol. **26**, 85–102 (2024). https://doi.org/10.1007/s10676-024-09746-w
24. Vaswani, A., et al.: Attention is all you need. In: Advances in Neural Information Processing Systems, vol. 30 (2017)
25. Yang, M., et al.: Fair machine guidance to enhance fair decision making in biased people. arXiv preprint arXiv:2404.05228 (2024)
26. Yang, Z., Yang, D., Dyer, C., He, X., Smola, A., Hovy, E.: Hierarchical attention networks for document classification. In: Proceedings of the 2016 Conference of the North American Chapter of the Association for Computational Linguistics: Human Language Technologies, pp. 1480–1489 (2016)

"Why I Took the Blackpill": A Thematic Analysis of the Radicalization Process in Incel Communities

Jennifer Golbeck[(✉)], Celia Chen, and Alex Leitch

University of Maryland, College Park, MD 20742, USA
jgolbeck@umd.edu

Abstract. Incels, or "involuntary celibates", are an extreme, misogynistic hate group that exists entirely online. Members of the community have been linked to acts of offline violence, including mass shootings. Previous research has engaged with the ideologies and beliefs of incels, but none has looked specifically at the radicalization process. In this paper, we perform a thematic analysis on social media posts where incels describe their own radicalization process. We identified six major themes grouped into four chronological steps: Pre-radicalization (themes of Appearance, Social Isolation, and Psychological issues), Searching for Blame, Radicalization, and Post-Radicalization. These results align closely with existing work on radicalization among other extremist groups, bringing incel radicalization inline with a growing body of research on understanding and managing radicalization.

Keywords: Radicalization · incels · extremism · social media

1 Introduction

The incel (involuntary celibate) community began as a community for men and women who were struggling romantically, but has since morphed into an extreme, violent misogynistic movement. Notable mass murder events include the 2014 Isla Vista killings by Elliott Rodger and the 2018 Toronto van attack by Alex Minassian. These are two of the higher profile acts of violence, but dozens of other incels have been arrested for threatening or carrying out violence.

Researchers have increasingly studied incels as an extremist group through thematic analyses of the incel experience and studies of prevalent topics including patriarchal male ideals and negative feelings about inceldom. How men radicalize from simple romantic frustration into radicalized extremists who celebrate violence and sometimes act on it remains largely unstudied through first-person accounts.

While Green et al. [1] identified a progressive "Black pill pipeline" of radicalization, their work focused on process-tracing rather than analyzing incels' own narratives of transformation. Our study addresses this gap by examining self-reports of "taking the blackpill" – the incel term for accepting their fatalistic worldview – as expressed spontaneously by community members in their natural online environments.

© The Author(s), under exclusive license to Springer Nature Switzerland AG 2026
A. An et al. (Eds.): ASONAM 2025, LNCS 16323, pp. 59–66, 2026.
https://doi.org/10.1007/978-3-032-13821-7_6

2 Background and Related Work

The Internet has transformed how extremist ideologies spread and how radicalization occurs. Research on online radicalization has established that digital environments can accelerate extremist belief adoption through several mechanisms: information provision, echo chambers, and the legitimization of extreme ideologies through reinforcement [2]. While early research on radicalization focused predominantly on Islamic extremism, recent scholarship has expanded to other ideological movements, including right-wing extremism and misogynistic communities.

Incel communities represent a form of online extremism characterized by decentralized networks that provide social belonging for isolated individuals and normalize extreme viewpoints through constant exposure and peer reinforcement [3]. Their online presence has grown substantially since 2014, following high-profile acts of violence committed by self-identified incels.

Several models explain radicalization processes. Moghaddam's [4] "staircase to terrorism" model describes progressive steps toward extremist violence, beginning with perceived injustices. Doosje et al. [5] describe a three-stage process: Sensitivity (search for significance from humiliation/status loss), Group Membership (adopting group ideology), and Action. These frameworks emphasize both push factors (grievances, identity crises) and pull factors (belonging, ideological purpose).

Recent research has specifically focused on the incel radicalization process. Green et al. [1] conducted a process-tracing analysis of the "Black pill pipeline," finding that incels utilize increasingly radical "pills" to move new members along an escalating pipeline of extremism. However, this work did not analyze incels' own narratives of their radicalization process.

Self-reported accounts of radicalization provide insights that complement observational research, often emphasizing psychological needs, social contexts, and triggering events rather than purely ideological factors. Our study addresses this gap by examining self-reports of "taking the blackpill" – the incel term for accepting their fatalistic worldview – as expressed spontaneously by community members in their natural online environments.

3 Method

We conducted a reflexive thematic analysis of posts from incels.is, a popular Reddit-like forum used by incels. These forums are accessible to anyone online; no account is required to read the content. The content is indexed by search engines and searchable on DuckDuckGo and Google. As previous research has noted, essentially all participants in incel forums are heterosexual men. Because users are largely anonymous, no additional reliable demographic information is available.

3.1 Sample

To focus on the radicalization process on incels.is, we searched for posts that contained the following phrases: "how i became an incel," "why i took the blackpill," "how i became blackpilled," "why i took the black pill," "how i took the black pill," and "became blackpilled." While this approach focused on explicit radicalization narratives rather than broader linguistic patterns, it captured users' most reflective accounts of their transformation, providing depth over breadth.

The "blackpill" is a common term used on incel forums that refers to the belief that romantic success is determined by traditionally masculine physical attractiveness, that one's genetic physical attributes cannot be meaningfully changed (e.g. by working out), and that other attributes like personality, interests, or success cannot overcome physical appearance. Not all incels are "blackpilled"; some maintain hope that they may find connection by improving themselves physically or in non-physical ways. Those incels who are "blackpilled" tend to regard themselves as the most extreme or dedicated in the community. Because our research question focuses on radicalization, this is a useful marker.

We searched for these terms both on Google using the site:incels.is filter and in the Radicalization and Deradicalization in Online Communities dataset of Incel forums [6]. It is common for users of these forums to share stories of how they became incels or how they became blackpilled, so this sampling method generated a large number of threads. We identified 60 forum posts with the above search terms and collected the original posts and replies, since the replies often included personal stories of radicalization. This resulted in 73,614 words of text. In performing the thematic analysis, we only considered posts and replies that discussed the personal radicalization process; we did not code comments about other issues.

3.2 Data Analysis

We used Braun and Clarke's [7] six-phase thematic analysis process oriented around: "How do posters describe their radicalization?" After data familiarization, we generated initial codes. Three researchers (one professor and two graduate students) coded all posts, with each analyzed for radicalization process content. Posts ranged from one sentence to multiple paragraphs, with multiple codes possible per post.

All researchers had previous experience coding incel data [8] and were familiar with an incel lexicon built on this dataset [9]. Using Braun and Clarke's reflexive approach, we reached consensus on code meanings through discussion rather than formal inter-rater reliability. After initial coding, researchers synthesized codes into themes, with a natural chronological order emerging as the organizing structure.

4 Results

Six themes emerged from this analysis. The thematic map is shown in Fig. 1. The themes are presented in chronological order, reflecting the radicalization process described in the posts we reviewed. The first chronological category, which contains three themes, represents the pre-radicalization phase where these posters discuss the difficult conditions that existed in their lives before they began the radicalization process. The second chronological category, with Theme 4, represents searching for something or someone to blame for the difficulties of their lives in the pre-radicalization phase. The third chronological category, with Theme 5, describes the process of becoming radicalized, and the fourth, with Theme 6, describes feelings in the post-radicalization state.

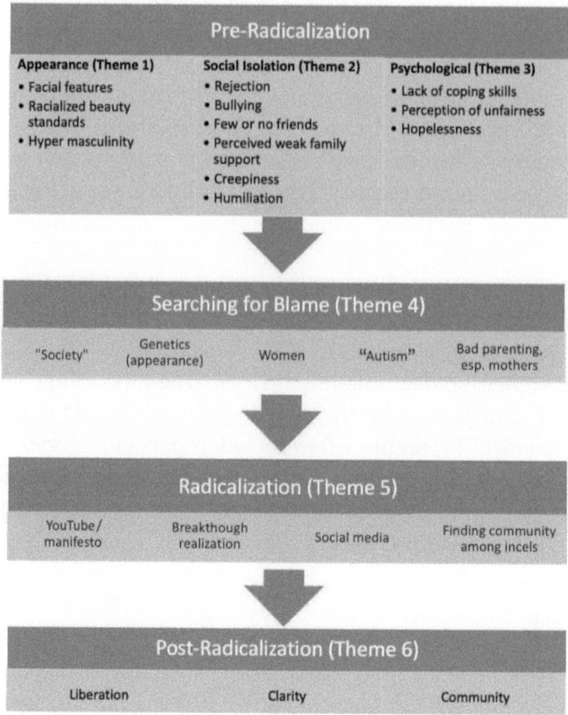

Fig. 1. Thematic map with the six themes organized in a chronological framework

4.1 Pre-Radicalization – Themes 1–3

Before discovering incel communities or becoming radicalized, posters describe difficult conditions in their lives. There are three themes: appearance (Theme 1), Social Isolation (Theme 2), and Psychological (Theme 3). The first two are explicitly named by posters as conditions that were difficult in their lives. The third psychological theme is more implicit in discussions of situations they struggled with. together, these themes describe the groundwork that leads to the radicalization path.

Theme 1: Appearance. The core of the "blackpill" is that only men meeting specific, high standards of physical attractiveness can be successful with women. Posters describe feeling insecure and rejected because of their appearance before discovering incel content. These are feelings they describe having before discovering blackpill-related content—they believed their appearance was part of their problem and that inspired their search for a reason why.

One poster wrote: "I mean I always knew I was fucked up, ever since age 10–11 I knew my life will be fucked. But I wasn't 'blackpilled' back then, I didn't know about the blackpill space or lingo… I knew it was to do with me being ugly and me being an autist." Another wrote, "Growing up ugly, I understood the significance of looks at age 11."

Racialized views of attractiveness also appear frequently. In these communities, traditionally Aryan features (tall, sharp jawline, white or paler skin, blonde hair, blue eyes) are considered most attractive and often necessary conditions to find a romantic connection. Posters describe recognizing their race/non-conformity with this standard as a problem early on.

Theme 2: Social Isolation. Posters describe social isolation from a young age through bullying or social rejection. One wrote, "I was bullied in over 5 schools throughout my life so I knew I was a cursed soul." Another said, "When I was 11, I realised that foids [women] would only reject me and they would laugh at me."

Posters often connect these problems to their appearance: "constantly being emotionally tortured by the people around me and just not fitting in normie groups… And also not having the looks and height that I desire." Social isolation is well-established as an important factor in radicalization [10].

Theme 3: Psychological. In their discussions, posters reveal a number of psychological factors that prime them for radicalization. They display a lack of coping skills, and as research predicts, this leads to expressions of hopelessness, high reactivity, and aggression to attacks.

When explaining why he became radicalized, one poster described an incident that he found humiliating: "[I] always knew. Final nail in the coffin was gym class 7th grade where we were forced to learn square dance or some shit. Teacher told hot bitch to hold my hand and she did that thing with her sleeve as if she was touching trash. Was forced to stare her down for 40 min." In this scenario, a girl covered her hand with her sleeve and the poster found this so difficult to cope with that he reacted with aggression, staring her down, and continues lashing out in anger at the time of posting, using slurs to describe the girl and claiming that this incident from years earlier was the final incident that radicalized him.

4.2   Searching for Blame (Theme 4)

After the pre-radicalization phase creates conditions where incels feel rejected and hopeless, the next step involves forsaking responsibility and seeking external blame targets including society, women, genetics, autism, and bad parenting. One poster wrote, "The Blackpill is merely a recognition of the reality that for guys like us there is nothing that can be done to change our situation. It's the fault of our parents and society writ large."

Autism is a persistent target of blame. One poster wrote, "I knew it was to do with me being ugly and me being an autist." This blame-seeking creates cognitive openings that prime individuals for radicalization.

4.3 Radicalization (Theme 5)

Theme 5 captures the actual radicalization process. Up to this point, incels describe isolation, social rejection, difficulty coping, and struggles based on their appearance. They look for forces to blame, then explain the moments in which they were radicalized or "took the blackpill".

For many, their radicalization was catalyzed on YouTube through channels like Wheat Waffles, FACEandLMS, HeedandSucceed, and Incel TV. One poster wrote, "One day i found a comment… Saying 'FaceandLMS was right'… I just watched the WAW Videos and i did not know whether i should cry or laugh… The WAW ['What Attracts Women'] videos where a like a blackpill-nuclear-bomb dropped on me."

Others describe breakthrough realizations: "One time a foid [female] coworker… Gave it to me with a nasty face. Then my coworker arrived and she was blushing… That was my eureka moment. Suddenly it made sense why women… Would act mean towards me."

4.4 Post-Radicalization (Theme 6)

After radicalizing by "taking the blackpill," accepting that they will never achieve romantic success because they do not meet the unfair standards and expectations of society, posters describe their feelings in the post-radicalization state. These generally describe feelings of liberation, clarity, and community.

One poster explains how the blackpill allows him to live without taking responsibility for his situation, writing, "Being blackpilled means you don't blame yourself for any of it which is liberating." Another writes, "The Blackpill is merely a recognition of the reality that for guys like us there is nothing that can be done to change our situation. It's the fault of our parents and society writ large, that may sound a bit pretentious to the average normie but it's the truth."

The blackpill is essentially a radicalization into hopelessness. Previous research has linked hopelessness with risk of suicide. Suicide is an extremely common topic of discussion on incel forums. Hopelessness has also been linked to violence in many contexts [11]. Though most incels do not carry out acts of violence, they are responsible for a number of high-profile incidents, including mass murders. Incel communities celebrate these acts – and other mass shootings carried out by non-incels.

5 Discussion

The findings in this study echo more general findings on the radicalization process. In studying radicalization among terrorists, Doosje et al. [5] describe a three-stage process: Sensitivity, Group Membership, and Action. Sensitivity describes a search for significance, which the authors describe as arising from feelings of a loss of status or strong sense of humiliation. These are captured clearly in Themes 1–3. This creates a cognitive opening, which we see in Theme 4, the pre-radicalization step. The Group Membership phase involves joining a group where the individual adopts the group's ideology and shows loyalty to the group. We find this in Theme 5, the radicalization process where incels "take the blackpill", and in Theme 6 where they find relief in being part of the blackpilled ideology.

Our results also echo research which found that the internet provides a space for effective and inexpensive communication of radical ideas, paired with anonymity, that lets those seeking information to be recruited and become radicalized. Most of our posters, when discussing where they discovered the "blackpill" mention social media broadly and YouTube specifically as a source of information.

This alignment with theories and prior results suggests that incels follow a fairly typical psychological radicalization process and that work on interventions and deradicalization can be carried over into incel community analysis. The role of social media, particularly YouTube's recommendation algorithms, in facilitating radicalization parallels findings in other extremist contexts where users progress from mainstream to increasingly extreme content.

5.1 Limitations and Future Work

Our dataset draws from a single forum, limiting generalizability. Future research should examine multi-platform radicalization pathways and employ network analysis approaches to understand interaction dynamics and content diffusion patterns within these communities. Additionally, quantitative analysis of blame targets and emotional vs. cognitive appeals in radicalization narratives could inform targeted intervention approaches.

While this paper deals with social media discourse, future research should incorporate network analysis approaches to understand structural dynamics, interaction patterns, and user trajectories—elements central to social network analysis and mining. A graph-based analysis of interaction networks or diffusion patterns of radical narratives would provide valuable insights into how radicalization spreads through these communities.

Additionally, our search methodology, while capturing explicit radicalization narratives, may have missed users who describe their transformation using alternative phrases. Future work could employ more systematic data collection methods and complement qualitative analysis with quantitative approaches to understand the main targets when incels blame others and how emotion versus cognition differently influence the radicalization process.

6 Conclusion

Using a set of posts where incels self-described their radicalization process, we conducted a thematic analysis and identified six major themes with four chronological steps: Pre-radicalization (themes of Appearance, Social Isolation, and Psychological issues), Searching for Blame, Radicalization, and Post-Radicalization. In this data, men describe struggling to form relationships early in childhood, often blaming their appearance for the bullying and rejection they experienced. They also reveal extreme emotional reactions to fairly typical social awkwardness and a difficulty coping. This is followed by an abdication of responsibility and search for someone or something to blame. Radicalization occurs when they "discover" the blackpill, an ideology that prescribes that only hyper-masculine men who meet a certain attractiveness standard can find romantic relationships with women. They usually discover this ideology through social media, particularly on YouTube. After "taking the blackpill" and radicalizing, they describe feelings of peace, clarity, and community membership within blackpill forums, though these are often accompanied by angry posts and violent fantasies.

Our results align with many existing studies on radicalization in other communities. This suggests that incels follow a somewhat typical pattern of radicalization with the same social and psychological factors at play. This lays the foundation to allow future work on interventions and deradicalization to be translated to inceldom. Similarly, ongoing work on deradicalizing incels that is arising from online forums like /r/IncelExit that support men leaving the community, may offer insights into supporting deradicalization of extremists in other contexts.

The research presented here builds upon existing work on incel communities by applying thematic analysis to understand the radicalization process as described by incels themselves. By analyzing personal narratives of how individuals became radicalized, this study contributes to the growing body of knowledge on online extremism, with implications for intervention strategies and prevention efforts. Future research incorporating network analysis and multi-platform approaches will further enhance our understanding of how radicalization spreads through online communities and identify optimal intervention points.

References

1. Green, R., Fowler, K., Palombi, A.: The Black pill pipeline: a process-tracing analysis of the Incel's continuum of violent radicalization. Crime, Media, Culture (2023)
2. Von Behr, I., Reding, A., Edwards, C., Gribbon, L.: Radicalisation in the digital era: the use of the internet in 15 cases of terrorism and extremism. RAND Corporation (2013)
3. Ging, D.: Alphas, Betas, and Incels: theorizing the masculinities of the manosphere. Men Masculinities **22**(4), 638–657 (2019)
4. Moghaddam, F.M.: The staircase to terrorism: a psychological exploration. Am. Psychol. **60**(2), 161–169 (2005)
5. Doosje, B., Moghaddam, F.M., Kruglanski, A.W., De Wolf, A., Mann, L., Feddes, A.R.: Terrorism, radicalization and de-radicalization. Curr. Opin. Psychol. **11**, 79–84 (2016)
6. Golbeck, J.: A dataset for the study of online radicalization through incel forum archives. J. Quantit. Descript. Digit. Med. **4**(2), 77–101 (2006)
7. Braun, V., Clarke, V.: Using thematic analysis in psychology. Qual. Res. Psychol. **3**(2), 77–101 (2006)
8. Chen, C., et al.: Cross-platform violence detection on social media: a dataset and analysis. In: Proceedings of ACM Conference on Web Science (2025)
9. Klein, E., Golbeck, J.: An incel lexicon for the study of online radicalization and deradicalization. In: Proceedings of the ACM Conference on Web Science (2024)
10. Hug, E. C.: The role of isolation in radicalization: how important is it? (Doctoral dissertation, Monterey, California: Naval Postgraduate School) (2013)
11. Bolland, J.M., McCallum, D.M., Lian, B., Bailey, C.J., Rowan, P.: Hopelessness and violence among inner-city youths. Matern. Child Health J. **5**, 237–244 (2001)

Who Leads in the Shadows? ERGM and Centrality Analysis of Congressional Democrats on Bluesky

Gordon Hew and Ian McCulloh[(✉)] [iD]

Johns Hopkins University, Baltimore, MD 21218, USA
`imccull4@jhu.edu`

Abstract. Following the 2024 U.S. presidential election, Democratic lawmakers and their supporters increasingly migrated from mainstream social media platforms like X (formerly Twitter) to decentralized alternatives such as Bluesky. This study investigates how Congressional Democrats use Bluesky to form networks of influence and disseminate political messaging in a platform environment that lacks algorithmic amplification. We employ a mixed-methods approach that combines social network analysis, exponential random graph modeling (ERGM), and transformer-based topic modeling (BERTopic) to analyze follows, mentions, reposts, and discourse patterns among 182 verified Democratic members of Congress. Our findings show that while party leaders such as Hakeem Jeffries and Elizabeth Warren dominate visibility metrics, overlooked figures like Marcy Kaptur, Donald Beyer, and Dwight Evans occupy structurally central positions, suggesting latent influence within the digital party ecosystem. ERGM results reveal significant homophily along ideological, state, and leadership lines, with Senate leadership exhibiting lower connectivity. Topic analysis identifies both shared themes (e.g., reproductive rights, foreign conflicts) and subgroup-specific issues, with The Squad showing the most distinct discourse profile. These results demonstrate the potential of decentralized platforms to reshape intra-party communication dynamics and highlight the need for continued computational research on elite political behavior in emerging digital environments.

Keywords: Congressional Democrats · Social Network Analysis · Exponential Random Graph Models (ERGM) · Bluesky · Political Communication · Topic Modeling · Decentralized Social Media · Political Influence

1 Introduction

In the wake of growing political polarization in the U.S., user migration across social media platforms has become a key focus for public discourse and computational social science. After the 2024 presidential election, notable shifts in platform allegiance, especially among Democratic supporters, sparked renewed interest in decentralized and algorithmically transparent alternatives to mainstream platforms like X (formerly Twitter) (Ambrose, 2024; NPR, 2024). One platform, Bluesky, built on open-source AT Protocol, has rapid adoption, surpassing 35 million users by April 2025 (Bluesky, n.d.).

A. An et al. (Eds.): ASONAM 2025, LNCS 16323, pp. 67–74, 2026.
https://doi.org/10.1007/978-3-032-13821-7_7

Bluesky differentiates itself through decentralization, user autonomy, and customizable content curation, enabled by its open API and lack of algorithmic amplification (Kleppmann et al., 2024). These features make it an ideal testbed for studying organic network formation, elite communication strategies, and the self-organization of political communities. Yet, despite its growing relevance, little academic research has systematically analyzed the platform's network dynamics—especially among verified or high-profile users such as U.S. Congressional Democrats.

This study uses exponential random graph modeling (ERGM) to examine the structural determinants of connectivity among Democratic members of Congress active on Bluesky. We investigate how network ties (follows, mentions, reposts) are shaped by mutual connections, ideological similarity, and leadership roles. Additionally, we explore how topical interests vary across Democratic factions—moderates, progressives, and party leadership—and whether these differences influence communication patterns. Finally, we assess whether structural centrality (e.g., degree, betweenness, eigenvector centrality) correlates with public perceptions of influence, as reflected in national polling, media coverage, and internal party standing.

By addressing these dimensions, this paper contributes to the study of political communication networks on emergent platforms. It highlights early adoption patterns and discursive trends among influential actors while offering a replicable framework for analyzing evolving digital ecosystems.

2 Background

The 2024 U.S. Presidential election triggered a major shift in political discourse online, particularly among Democrats, who began migrating from traditional platforms like X (formerly Twitter) to decentralized alternatives such as Bluesky. Despite its rapid growth, academic research on Bluesky remains sparse, with most studies focusing on its technical design rather than its network dynamics. For example, Buzelin et al. (2025) examined political discourse on Discord during the 2024 election but did not apply social network analysis (SNA), leaving a gap in understanding the structure of political interactions on emerging platforms.

While prior studies on Twitter have demonstrated the utility of SNA and Exponential Random Graph Models (ERGMs) for analyzing political networks—such as party cohesion and ideological alignment (Chamberlain et al., 2021; Sadayappan et al., 2018)—these methods have not yet been applied to Bluesky. SNA offers powerful tools for mapping influence through centrality measures (degree, betweenness, eigenvector) and for uncovering ideological divisions using community detection (McCulloh et al., 2013; Ozer et al., 2016).

This study addresses the research gap by analyzing the Bluesky network of Democratic Congressional members. Using ERGMs and SNA, we examine connectivity drivers, identify influential actors, and uncover ideological clusters and discourse patterns. Our goal is to provide a deeper understanding of the emerging digital ecosystem shaping Democratic political communication post-2024.

3 Methods

We scraped verified Bluesky accounts and collected posts, mentions, follows, and reposts using open-source libraries. Data were stored in structured formats and preprocessed for network and topic analysis. A master list of House and Senate members was compiled from official directories (U.S. House of Representatives, 2024; U.S. Senate, 2024), and verified Bluesky accounts were identified through caucus posts and manual validation using name, image, and domain affiliation. Of the 211 House and 47 Senate Democrats (including Independents who caucus with the party), 182 had identifiable accounts. Missing nodes were treated as a potential source of bias, and sensitivity analyses were performed by simulating 5–10% random node removal to evaluate effects on network metrics.

We constructed three directed graphs—follows, mentions, and reposts—using Democratic members of Congress as nodes and interaction frequencies as weighted edges. To evaluate influence and positioning, we computed centrality measures including degree, closeness, betweenness (Freeman, 1979), and eigenvector centrality (Bonacich, 1987). These metrics help identify individuals with strategic positions who may be structurally important but publicly overlooked (McCulloh, Armstrong, & Johnson, 2013; Himelboim et al., 2013).

To examine tie formation, we estimated ERGMs for each interaction type using the statnet suite in R. ERGMs account for endogenous structures such as reciprocity and transitivity, as well as exogenous attributes including chamber, leadership role, gender, and ideological affiliation. Model selection was guided by AIC and convergence diagnostics, following approaches shown effective in prior studies of legislative networks (Sadayappan, McCulloh, & Piorkowski, 2018).

To analyze discourse trends, we applied BERTopic, a transformer-based topic modeling technique that generates coherent topics using class-based TF-IDF embeddings (Grootendorst, 2022). Posts were preprocessed through standard NLP steps including lowercasing, stop-word removal, lemmatization, and emoji stripping. Topics were modeled across the full corpus, then compared using cosine similarity to assess thematic alignment or divergence. Topic coherence was evaluated using the UMass metric, and incoherent or redundant topics were filtered.

4 Findings

4.1 Comparative Network Overview

We constructed three directed graphs as shown in Fig. 1 representing follower (15,015 edges; density = 0.3145; diameter = 5), mention (1,434 edges; density = 0.0300; diameter = 10), and repost (468 edges; density = 0.0098; diameter = 13) networks among 219 verified Congressional Democrats on Bluesky. The follower network was the densest and most cohesive, while reposting activity was infrequent and diffuse.

Marcy Kaptur's unusually high centrality in the follows network—despite lacking formal leadership or caucus ties—demonstrates how overlooked figures may occupy pivotal positions in online political networks (McCulloh et al., 2013). Similarly, Evans and Beyer's visibility in the repost network reflects their resonance across ideological boundaries, echoing Himelboim et al.'s (2013) finding that intermediaries, not elites, often drive amplification. Comparisons are shown in Table 1.

Table 1. Comparative Network Overview and Summary

Type	Top Central Figures	Key Metrics	Notable Patterns
Follows	Kaptur (OH), Clark (MA), Moore (WI)	Close:0.95 (Kaptur), Between:0.08 (Kaptur)	Clusters by chamber; Kaptur central without leadership
Mentions	Booker (NJ), Jeffries (NY), Warren (MA), Ramirez (IL), Cleaver (MO)	High centrality across roles	Less chamber clustering; mentions follow issue-based lines
Reposts	Warren (MA), Jeffries (NY), Evans (PA), Beyer (VA)	Low overall activity	Reposts favor peer-to-peer amplification; not driven by elites

Table 2. Congressional Democrats Follower Network ERGM Results.

	Estimate	Std. Error	MCMC %	z value	$Pr(>|z|)$
edges	-3.87525	0.11860	0	-32.675	$< 1e - 04$
mutual	0.35303	0.03156	0	11.185	$< 1e - 04$
nodematch.member_type	2.71894	0.04420	0	61.508	$< 1e - 04$
nodematch.state	0.70633	0.04885	0	14.460	$< 1e - 04$
nodematch.is_verified	0.08255	0.02111	0	3.911	$< 1e - 04$
nodematch.blue_dog_coalition	0.11454	0.05441	0	2.105	0.035274
nodematch.problem_solvers_caucus	0.21310	0.02888	0	7.379	$< 1e - 04$
nodematch.new_democrat_coalition	0.07295	0.02101	0	3.472	0.000517
nodematch.democratic_senate_leadership	-0.13164	0.05643	0	-2.333	0.019668
nodematch.democratic_house_leadership	0.10309	0.04815	0	2.141	0.032287
nodematch.the_squad	0.38593	0.06421	0	6.010	$< 1e - 04$
nodematch.congressional_progressive_caucus	0.03977	0.02140	0	1.858	0.063124

Table 3. Congressional Democrats Mentions Network ERGM Results.

	Estimate	Std. Error	MCMC %	z value	$Pr(>|z|)$
sum	-3.25077	0.38417	0	-8.462	$< 1e - 04$
nonzero	-3.35241	0.09581	0	-34.989	$< 1e - 04$
mutual.min	1.44118	0.11105	0	12.978	$< 1e - 04$
nodematch.sum.member_type	0.47024	0.06216	0	7.564	$< 1e - 04$
nodematch.sum.state	1.11855	0.05941	0	18.828	$< 1e - 04$
nodematch.sum.is_verified	0.22416	0.04744	0	4.725	$< 1e - 04$
nodematch.sum.blue_dog_coalition	1.19767	0.32032	0	3.739	0.000185
nodematch.sum.problem_solvers_caucus	0.31459	0.08439	0	3.728	0.000193
nodematch.sum.new_democrat_coalition	0.16556	0.04994	0	3.315	0.000915
nodematch.sum.democratic_senate_leadership	-0.71027	0.06838	0	-10.387	$< 1e - 04$
nodematch.sum.democratic_house_leadership	-0.10635	0.09178	0	-1.159	0.246571
nodematch.sum.the_squad	-0.10315	0.12820	0	-0.805	0.421070
nodematch.sum.congressional_progressive_caucus	0.19127	0.04937	0	3.874	0.000107

Table 4. Congressional Democrats Repost Network ERGM Results.

	Estimate	Std. Error	MCMC %	z value	$Pr(> |z|)$
sum	-4.50874	0.77296	0	-5.833	$< 1e - 04$
nonzero	-3.97581	0.16203	0	-24.538	$< 1e - 04$
mutual.min	1.50311	0.22931	0	6.555	$< 1e - 04$
nodematch.sum.member_type	1.36963	0.15733	0	8.706	$< 1e - 04$
nodematch.sum.state	0.87873	0.10279	0	8.548	$< 1e - 04$
nodematch.sum.is_verified	0.12677	0.07992	0	1.586	0.112676
nodematch.sum.blue_dog_coalition	1.62879	0.67626	0	2.409	0.016017
nodematch.sum.problem_solvers_caucus	0.69984	0.18134	0	3.859	0.000114
nodematch.sum.new_democrat_coalition	0.21394	0.08900	0	2.404	0.016228
nodematch.sum.democratic_senate_leadership	-0.83193	0.12481	0	-6.666	$< 1e - 04$
nodematch.sum.democratic_house_leadership	-0.69802	0.11314	0	-6.170	$< 1e - 04$
nodematch.sum.the_squad	0.03781	0.24550	0	0.154	0.877596
nodematch.sum.congressional_progressive_caucus	0.20618	0.08388	0	2.458	0.013975

Fig. 1. Congressional Democrats Bluesky Follows, Mentions, Repost Networks, Respectively.

4.2 ERGM Results

ERGM modeling across all three networks (follows, mentions, reposts) revealed that reciprocity, shared chamber, and state affiliation consistently increased the likelihood of ties as shown in Tables 2, 3 and 4. Progressive group members displayed strong clustering, particularly in the follows network, aligning with findings by Chamberlain et al. (2021) on ideological cohesion in online spaces. In contrast, Democratic Senate leadership membership negatively predicted tie formation across networks, suggesting a more hierarchical, less interactive communication style.

Mentions and reposts highlighted different dynamics. Leadership figures were less central in these graphs, while policy-focused members gained visibility through peer amplification. This sparse network reinforces findings from Himelboim et al. (2013) that information diffusion in political networks is not solely driven by central elites, and that influential amplifiers often occupy intermediate or bridging roles. This shift indicates that decentralized platforms like Bluesky reward issue-based engagement over formal rank, supporting prior work that structural position may reveal overlooked, influential actors (McCulloh et al., 2013; Himelboim et al., 2013).

4.3 Topic Analysis

Topic modeling with BERTopic identified shared themes across the corpus, Medicaid, Israel-Gaza, reproductive rights, and the Ukraine war; indicating alignment on major issues. However, group-specific divergences were also evident. Leadership and progressives both discussed Defense Secretary Hegseth, while The Squad uniquely centered civil liberties topics like the detention of Mahmoud Khalil and Rümeysa Öztürk.

Cosine similarity scores revealed that the New Democrat Coalition had the highest alignment with overall Democratic discourse (0.5485), and also shared notable overlap with progressives (0.4694), reflecting centrist positioning. The Squad was least aligned, underscoring its distinct rhetorical identity.

These findings suggest that while structural centrality can highlight interaction patterns, semantic content reveals deeper ideological boundaries, offering insight into factional differentiation within the party's post-2024 digital landscape.

5 Conclusion

This study provides one of the first comprehensive examinations of U.S. Congressional Democrats' activity on the decentralized social media platform Bluesky. By integrating social network analysis, exponential random graph models (ERGM), and transformer-based topic modeling, we uncover both structural and semantic patterns in elite political communication following the 2024 U.S. presidential election.

Our network analysis reveals that while prominent party leaders such as Hakeem Jeffries and Elizabeth Warren dominate follower and mention networks, several overlooked figures—such as Marcy Kaptur, Donald Beyer, and Dwight Evans—occupy structurally central positions, suggesting untapped or underrecognized influence within the party's online ecosystem. These findings underscore the value of centrality measures in identifying influential actors who may not be highly visible in media coverage or formal leadership roles.

The ERGM results provide empirical support for homophily across multiple attributes, including chamber membership, state, group affiliation, and verification status. Notably, formal leadership in the Senate appears negatively associated with tie formation and content sharing behaviors, suggesting a more hierarchical or broadcast-oriented communication style among elite figures.

Topic modeling further reveals thematic cohesion on issues such as Medicaid cuts, reproductive rights, and foreign conflicts, alongside meaningful divergence among ideological subgroups. The Squad, for example, exhibited the least topical alignment with other factions, reflecting its distinct rhetorical and advocacy priorities.

Several limitations warrant consideration. First, Bluesky remains an emerging platform with incomplete adoption among political elites; our sample omits members who have not joined or who use anonymous or unverified accounts (16.4% of congressional democrats). Second, the platform's decentralization introduces complexity in verifying authenticity and assessing cross-instance visibility. Third, while our centrality measures highlight structural influence, we do not correlate these with external popularity metrics (e.g., polling data or mainstream media citations), leaving the third research question partially open. Finally, topic modeling is inherently sensitive to preprocessing and model parameters; while BERTopic offers state-of-the-art coherence, future work could triangulate findings with alternative techniques.

Building on these findings, future research could expand in several directions. First, a comparative analysis of Democratic and Republican network structures may reveal partisan asymmetries in adoption and discourse. Note that it was difficult to verify republican accounts on the Bluesky platform. There are no House or Senate accounts on the platform with starter packs. Adding to the confusion, manual searches often yield parody accounts. Prominent republicans that we manually searched for that appear to have a valid Bluesky account like Steve Scalise and Elise Stefanik had very little activity and Stefanik appears to have deactivated her account. Perhaps comparing Republican activity on X with Democrat activity on Bluesky might be more appropriate, however, differences in access to platform data may bias findings.

Second, longitudinal data collection could track the evolution of network ties and issue salience over time, particularly as the 2026 mid-terms approach. Third, linking Bluesky behavior with off-platform outcomes (e.g., voting records, donor activity, or media attention) could provide richer insight into how digital centrality translates into real-world political influence.

Ultimately, this study contributes to our understanding of how elite political networks operate in emergent, decentralized environments. As platforms like Bluesky continue to evolve, so too must the computational tools used to analyze them—offering new avenues for research at the intersection of technology, politics, and network science.

References

Ambrose, T.: What is Bluesky and why are so many people suddenly leaving X for the platform? *The Guardian* (2024). https://www.theguardian.com/technology/2024/nov/16/what-is-bluesky-and-why-are-so-many-people-suddenly-leaving-x-for-the-platform-elon-musk

Bonacich, P.: Power and centrality: a family of measures. Am. J. Sociol. **92**(5), 1170–1182 (1987). https://doi.org/10.1086/228631

Blue Dog Coalition. (n.d.). Members. *Blue Dog Coalition.* https://bluedogs-gluesenkampperez.house.gov/members

Bluesky. (n.d.). *About Bluesky.* Retrieved from https://bsky.social/about/faq

Buzelin, A., et al.: Analyzing political discourse on discord during the 2024 U.S. presidential election (2025). *arXiv preprint* arXiv:2502.03433. https://arxiv.org/abs/2502.03433

Chamberlain, J. M., Spezzano, F., Kettler, J. J., Dit, B.: A network analysis of twitter interactions by members of the U.S. Congress. *ACM Trans. Soc. Comput.* **4**(1), 1–22 (2021). https://doi.org/10.1145/3439827

Congressional Progressive Caucus. (n.d.). Caucus members. Congressional Progressive Caucus. https://progressives.house.gov/caucus-members

Freeman, L.C.: Centrality in social networks: conceptual clarification. Soc. Netw. **1**(3), 215–239 (1979). https://doi.org/10.1016/0378-8733(78)90021-7

Grootendorst, M.: BERTopic: neural topic modeling with class-based TF-IDF (2022). *arXiv preprint* arXiv:2203.05794. https://arxiv.org/abs/2203.05794

Himelboim, I., Smith, M., Rainie, L., Shneiderman, B., Espina, C.: Classifying Twitter topic networks using social network analysis. *Soc. Media Soc.* **1**(1). https://doi.org/10.1177/2056305113479598

House Democrats. (n.d.). Our members: House Democrats. House Democrats. https://www.dems.gov/who-we-are/our- members

Kleppmann, M., et al.: Bluesky and the AT protocol: usable decentralized social media (2024). *arXiv*

McCulloh, I., Armstrong, H., Johnson, A.: Social Network Analysis with Applications. Wiley, Hoboken, NJ (2013)

New Democrat Coalition. (n.d.). Members - New Democrat Coalition. New Democrat Coalition. https://newdemocratcoalition.house.gov/members

NPR Staff.: Traffic on Bluesky, an X competitor, is up 500% since the election. *NPR* (2024). https://www.npr.org/2024/11/19/g-s1-34898/bluesky-traffic-surge-after-election:contentReference

Ocasio-Cortez, A. (n.d.). Squad. Instagram. https://www.instagram.com/p/BqGTlEPBXXD/?hl=en

Ozer, M., Kim, N., Davulcu, H.: Community detection in political twitter networks using nonnegative matrix factorization methods. In: *2016 International Conference on Advances in Social Networks Analysis and Mining (ASONAM),* (pp. 81–88) (2016). IEEE

Problem Solvers Caucus. (n.d.). Caucus Members. Problem Solvers Caucus. https://problemsolverscaucus.house.gov/

Sadayappan, S., McCulloh, I., Piorkowski, J.: Evaluation of political party cohesion using exponential random graph modeling. In: *Proceedings of the 2018 IEEE/ACM International Conference on Advances in Social Networks Analysis and Mining (ASONAM)* (pp. 1–8) (2018). IEEE

Senate Democrats. (n.d.). Senate Democrats Starter Pack. Bluesky Social. https://bsky.app/starter-pack/democrats.senate.gov/3ljiq7krz5223

UnitedStatesSenate.(n.d.).Leadership&Officers.UnitedStatesSenate.https://www.senate.gov/senators/leadership.htm

United States Senate. (n.d.). Senators. United States Senate. https://www.senate.gov/senators/index.htm

U.S. House of Representatives. (n.d.). Leadership. United States House of Representatives. https://www.house.gov/leadership

U.S. House of Representatives. (n.d.). Representatives. United States House of Representatives. https://www.house.gov/representatives

Old Roots, Fresh Fruits: Clickbait Detection with Effective Model Design Choices on Social Media

Yu-Min Tseng[1] and Cheng-Te Li[2(✉)]

[1] Department of Computer Science, Virginia Tech, Blacksburg, USA
[2] Department of Computer Science and Information Engineering, National Cheng Kung University, Tainan City, Taiwan
chengte@ncku.edu.tw

Abstract. Online clickbait continues to plague social-media platforms, where sensational captions lure users into low-value or misleading content. While prior work has explored individual modeling choices, i.e., sequential encoders, graph-based representations, and simple fusion strategies, no study has systematically compared these design dimensions in the clickbait domain. We address this gap by conducting the first comprehensive analysis of three core axes: (1) how to organize the model streams (treating caption and hashtags jointly vs. separately), (2) how to learn text representations (sequential vs. graph-based), and (3) how to fuse these modalities (concatenation vs. co-attention). Leveraging a large, manually labeled Instagram dataset of short captions paired with hashtags, we implement every combination of these axes to isolate their individual and joint impacts on detection performance. Our experiments reveal clear trends: processing caption and hashtags in parallel streams preserves their distinct semantic patterns and consistently outperforms unified processing; graph-based embeddings capture long-range and corpus-wide co-occurrence structures that sequential models alone miss; and a co-attention fusion mechanism aligns caption and hashtag signals, uncovering subtle mismatches characteristic of clickbait.

Keywords: clickbait detection · dual modeling · graph-based representation · co-attention fusion · short-text classification · social media

1 Introduction

Clickbait has become pervasive in online media, particularly on social networking platforms, as content producers compete for user attention [3,6]. Many publishers and influencers rely on sensational or misleading headlines and captions to lure readers and viewers, driven by strong economic incentives such as advertising revenue and higher engagement [5]. The rise of visually-focused social media (e.g., Instagram, Snapchat, Pinterest) has further shifted the landscape of clickbait: on these platforms an eye-catching image is paired with a short textual caption, and new forms of clickbait have emerged in which the text is often only tangentially related to the image. In particular, targeted clickbait techniques [7] are common, where posts include an array of popular or trending hashtags and buzzwords that are irrelevant to the actual content, solely to broaden reach and attract clicks. This prevalence of misleading content not only degrades user experience and trust but also poses challenges for content moderation. As a result, there is a pressing need for effective automatic clickbait detection. Recent advances in machine learning offer a potential solution by identifying subtle patterns in content that distinguish clickbait from genuine posts [10], but the multimodal and short-text nature of social media posts makes this detection task challenging.

Clickbait detection can be formulated as a binary short-text classification task [3,6,10]: given a piece of content (in this case, a social media post), the goal is to predict whether it is clickbait. The main input in such a scenario is the post's short textual caption, which may be accompanied by auxiliary signals like hashtags, user comments, engagement metrics (likes/shares), or even the post's propagation patterns through a social network. This formulation is analogous to other content integrity problems on social media such as fake news detection [4, 8], rumor verification [9,12], and cyberbullying detection [1], which also involve classifying short posts with limited textual data and additional contextual clues.

In this paper, we present an approach towards effective clickbait detection on social media by systematically investigating the aforementioned design dimensions. We formally define the task as determining whether a given social media post is clickbait, where each post consists of a short textual caption and an accompanying set of hashtags (we focus on these textual components, as they are readily available and carry the linguistic cues of clickbait). We then explore three fundamental axes of model design for this problem:

- How to organize the model architecture with respect to input types: either a *unified model* that processes the caption and hashtags together as a single input, or a *dual-model* architecture that handles captions and hashtags in separate streams;
- How to integrate or fuse information from the caption and hashtags: comparing simple *concatenation* of their representations versus *a co-attention* mechanism that allows interactive feature learning between the two
- How to learn the representation of the post's text: contrasting a *sequential encoder* (e.g., Gated Recurrent Unit, which reads the caption and hashtags in order) with a *structural encoder* (e.g., Graph Neural Network, which captures relational structure among words and hashtags in a graph form).

We focus on these three axes because they span the essential ways a model can represent the content, relate the caption with its hashtags, and integrate information from both sources. By systematically varying and evaluating these choices, we aim to identify what combinations yield the most effective detector for social media clickbait.

In summary, our contributions are as follows: (1) **Systematic Architectural Exploration**: we conduct a comprehensive evaluation of key model design

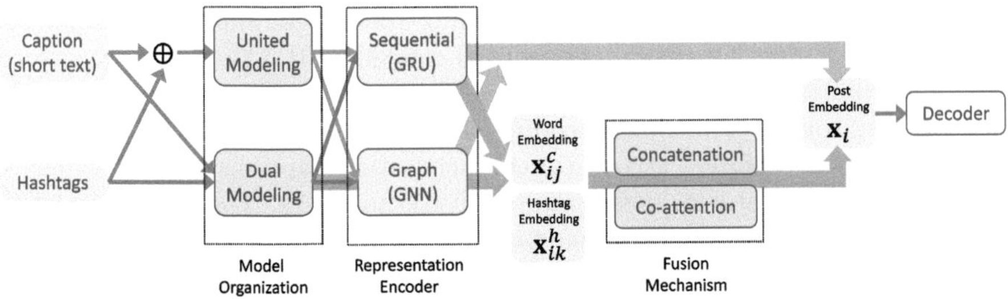

Fig. 1. Model design pipeline for clickbait detection. Captions and hashtags are encoded using either GRU or GNN, combined via united or dual modeling, and fused through concatenation or co-attention before classification.

dimensions for clickbait detection on social media, examining how different architectural choices impact performance. (2) **Representation and Fusion Analysis**: we provide an in-depth analysis of how a post's caption and hashtag content should be represented and fused. This analysis sheds light on whether treating hashtags as an integral part of the text or as separate features is more effective, and how best to combine these information sources. (3) **Extensive Empirical Validation**: we present a thorough experimental comparison using a real-world Instagram dataset, benchmarking our approach against prior arts, and showing promising improvement of detection performance.

2   Problem Statement

Let $\mathcal{D} = \{(c_i, H_i, y_i)\}_{i=1}^{N}$ denote the labeled dataset of N social-media posts. For the i-th post: $c_i = (w_{i,1}, w_{i,2}, \ldots, w_{i,T_i})$ is the caption, a sequence of T_i tokens drawn from a vocabulary $\mathcal{V}$. $H_i = \{h_{i,1}, h_{i,2}, \ldots, h_{i,K_i}\}$ is the set of K_i hashtags (treated as an unordered set). $y_i \in \{0, 1\}$ is the clickbait label, where $y_i = 1$ indicates clickbait and $y_i = 0$ indicates a normal post. We write $\mathbf{x}_i^c \in \mathbb{R}^d$ and $\mathbf{x}_i^h \in \mathbb{R}^d$ for the vector representations of the caption and hashtag set, respectively, produced by an encoder. A fusion function $\mathcal{F}(\mathbf{x}_i^c, \mathbf{x}_i^h)$ then yields a joint vector $\mathbf{x}_i$, and a classifier $g(\mathbf{x}_i; \theta)$ outputs a predicted score. Finally, the clickbait probability is $\hat{y}_i = \sigma\big(g(\mathbf{x}_i; \theta)\big)$, where σ is the sigmoid activation and θ collects all trainable parameters. Clickbait detection is a binary classification problem: we learn θ by minimizing the average binary cross-entropy loss over $\mathcal{D}$ so that, for each post (c_i, H_i), the model correctly predicts its label y_i.

3   Model Design and Choices

We present the clickbait-detection model design pipeline in Fig. 1. The pipeline begins by transforming each post's raw caption and hashtag set into continuous vector embeddings. Word embeddings for the caption capture the sequential semantics of short text, while hashtag embeddings encode topical signals from a non-ordered tag set. These dual embedding spaces feed into a representation encoder, which may be either a sequential model (GRU) that preserves word-order information or a structural model (GNN) that captures relational patterns among tokens. This dual-encoding choice acknowledges that captions and hashtags present different structural characteristics: captions rely on sequence, whereas hashtags form a loose graph of co-occurrences. The encoded vectors then enter the model-organization stage, where they are processed either in a single, unified stream (treating caption + hashtags as one concatenated input) or via two parallel streams (separate caption and hashtag encoders). Finally, the resulting features are merged using either simple concatenation or a co-attention mechanism before passing to the decoder for binary classification. This flow, from embedding to encoding, organization, fusion, and decoding, ensures modularity, allowing systematic investigation of how representation choice, input partitioning, and fusion strategy each contribute to overall performance.

Model Organization. In the **united modeling** approach, we treat the caption and its associated hashtags as a single input sequence. Formally, given the i-th post's caption $c_i = (w_{i,1}, \ldots, w_{i,T_i})$ and hashtag set $H_i = \{h_{i,1}, \ldots, h_{i,K_i}\}$, we define a concatenated sequence $z_i = (w_{i,1}, \ldots, w_{i,T_i}, h_{i,1}, \ldots, h_{i,K_i})$. A single encoder $\mathcal{E}$ then maps this joint sequence into a unified representation vector $\mathbf{x}_i = \mathcal{E}(z_i)$, which is subsequently fed to the fusion and classification layers. The key idea is to allow the model to learn shared feature interactions between caption tokens and hashtags in one continuous stream. This simplicity often yields strong baselines, as it leverages off-the-shelf sequence encoders directly on all textual inputs. However, it may also conflate the fundamentally different structures and roles of ordered caption words versus unordered tags, potentially diluting specialized signals encoded in hashtags.

By contrast, the **dual modeling** approach maintains two distinct encoding streams for caption and hashtags. Here we deploy separate encoders, $\mathcal{E}_c$ for the caption and $\mathcal{E}_h$ for the hashtag set. We compute $\mathbf{x}_i^c = \mathcal{E}(c_i)$ and $\mathbf{x}_i^h = \mathcal{E}(H_i)$, and pass both vectors to a subsequent fusion module $\mathcal{F}(\mathbf{x}_i^c, \mathbf{x}_i^h)$ before classification. This design explicitly recognizes the different statistical and structural properties of captions and hashtags, enabling each encoder to specialize – $\mathcal{E}_c$ can focus on sequential semantics while $\mathcal{E}_h$ can capture topical co-occurrence in a set. The trade-off is an increase in model complexity and parameter count, as well as the need to carefully balance the two streams. In practice, dual modeling often yields more fine-tuned representations for each modality, improving robustness when hashtags carry distinct clickbait cues. Both united and dual modeling can leverage the same Representation Encoder techniques, i.e., whether a sequential GRU or a structural GNN, to transform raw tokens into dense embeddings.

Representation Encoder. A typical approach is to use a **Gated Recurrent Unit (GRU)** to encode the short sequential nature of captions and hashtags. In the unified modeling setting, the concatenated input sequence z_i is mapped by GRU into a single vector $\mathbf{x}_i = \mathrm{GRU}(z_i)$. Under dual modeling, the caption and hashtag streams are processed separately as $\mathbf{x}_i^c = \text{GRU}(c_i)$ and $\mathbf{x}_i^h = \text{GRU}(H_i)$. The GRU encoder excels at capturing ordered dependencies in language, critical for teasing apart subtle phrasing cues that distinguish clickbait captions from genuine descriptions, but it treats the hashtag set as an artificial sequence, potentially overlooking the unordered, co-occurrence patterns among tags.

To complement this sequential view, we integrate a **Text Graph Convolutional Network (TextGCN)** [11] that explicitly models global token relationships across the entire dataset. We construct an undirected graph $G = (V, E)$ whose node set V comprises both document nodes (one per post) and word/hashtag nodes (one per unique token), and whose weighted adjacency matrix $\mathbf{A} \in \mathbb{R}^{|V| \times |V|}$ encodes (i) document-token TF-IDF edges and (ii) token–token PMI-based co-occurrence edges. Let $\tilde{\mathbf{A}} = \mathbf{D}^{-1/2}(\mathbf{A} + \mathbf{I})\mathbf{D}^{-1/2}$ be the symmetrically normalized adjacency and $\mathbf{H}^0 \in \mathbb{R}^{|V| \times d_0}$ be the initial node features (one-hot or pretrained embeddings). Then two layers of graph convolution yield $\mathbf{H}^{(1)} = \text{ReLU}(\tilde{\mathbf{A}}\mathbf{H}^{(0)}W^{(0)})$ and $\mathbf{H}^{(2)} = \tilde{\mathbf{A}}\mathbf{H}^{(1)}W^{(1)}$, where $W^{(0)}$ and $W^{(1)}$ are trainable weight matrices. For each post i, its document-node embedding $\mathbf{H}_i^{(2)}$ serves as the representation $\mathbf{x}_i$ in the unified model. In the dual scheme, separate subgraphs limited to caption tokens and hashtags respectively can produce $\mathbf{x}_i^c$ and $\mathbf{x}_i^h$. TextGCN captures global, corpus-wide co-occurrence signals that are especially valuable for identifying tag-driven clickbait patterns, though it requires a complete graph construction and does not account for word order.

Both GRU and TextGCN seamlessly integrate with either the united or dual modeling strategies: the GRU naturally ingests linear sequences, while TextGCN leverages graph structure to aggregate contextual signals. By comparing these two encoder paradigms across our pipeline, we can assess how sequential versus structural representations contribute to robust clickbait detection.

Fusion Mechanism. We explore two strategies to fuse these textual sources into a single representation for classification: a simple **Concatenation** of the caption and hashtag features, and a **Co-attention** mechanism for fine-grained interaction between caption and hashtags.

Concatenation. The first fusion approach is straightforward vector concatenation. Given the caption representation $\mathbf{x}_i^c \in \mathbb{R}^d$ and hashtag representation $\mathbf{x}_i^h \in \mathbb{R}^d$ for post i, we form the fused post vector by appending one to the other: $\mathbf{x}_i = \mathbf{x}_i^c \oplus \mathbf{x}_i^h \in \mathbb{R}^{2d}$. This concatenation fusion simply stacks the learned caption features and hashtag features into a single vector. It is computationally efficient (no additional parameters beyond those used to obtain $\mathbf{x}_i^c$ and $\mathbf{x}_i^h$) and easy to implement. The intuition is that the model's next layers (the classifier) will use this combined feature vector to make the clickbait prediction. However, concatenation treats caption and hashtag features independently. It does not explicitly model interactions between specific caption words and hashtags. While efficient, this simplicity is a limitation: the network must implicitly learn any relationships between caption and hashtag signals in later layers. For instance, if certain hashtags make a caption more clickbaity, a concatenation-based model relies on the classifier to discover that pattern, rather than highlighting it in the representation itself.

Co-attention. To capture richer interactions between the caption and hashtags, we employ a co-attention fusion mechanism. The co-attention is applied unidirectionally from the caption to the hashtags, allowing the caption context to inform an attentive combination of hashtag features (and vice versa). This means the model learns to emphasize particular hashtag tokens that are most relevant to the caption's content, and simultaneously adjust the caption representation based on those important hashtags. Formally, let the caption encoder produce a matrix of token embeddings $\mathbf{C} = [\mathbf{c}_1, \mathbf{c}_2, \ldots, \mathbf{c}_T] \in \mathbb{R}^{d \times T}$ for the T words in the caption, and let the hashtag encoder produce $\mathbf{H} = [\mathbf{h}_1, \mathbf{h}_2, \ldots, \mathbf{h}_K] \in \mathbb{R}^{d \times K}$ for the K hashtag tokens. We first compute an attention affinity matrix $\mathbf{F}$ between caption and hashtag features: $\mathbf{F} = \tanh(\mathbf{c}^\top W \mathbf{H})$, where W is a learnable weight matrix. Each element F_{tk} reflects the compatibility between caption word t and hashtag word k. This proximity matrix $\mathbf{F}$ is treated as a feature that bridges the two modalities, allowing us to project information from the caption space into the hashtag space and vice versa.

Next, we transform the caption and hashtag representations by incorporating this cross-modal affinity. We compute $\mathbf{H}^c = \tanh(W_c \mathbf{C} + (W_h \mathbf{H})\mathbf{F}^\top)$ and $\mathbf{H}^h = \tanh(W_h \mathbf{H} + (W_c \mathbf{C})\mathbf{F})$. Here W_c and W_h are learnable weight matrices, producing transformed feature matrices $\mathbf{H}^c$ and $\mathbf{H}^h$. Intuitively, $\mathbf{H}^c$ is an enriched caption representation that has absorbed information from the hashtags (via $\mathbf{F}^\top$), while $\mathbf{H}^h$ is an enriched hashtag representation influenced by the caption content. We then obtain attention weight vectors for caption words and hashtags by applying a softmax over these transformed features: $\alpha^c = \text{softmax}(w_c^\top \mathbf{H}^c)$ and $\alpha^h = \text{softmax}(w_h^\top \mathbf{H}^h)$, where w_c and w_h are learnable weights that produce unnormalized importance scores for each token. The softmax normalizes these scores across the T caption tokens and K hashtag tokens respectively, yielding $\boldsymbol{\alpha}^c = [\alpha_1^c, \ldots, \alpha_T^c]$ and $\boldsymbol{\alpha}^h = [\alpha_1^h, \ldots, \alpha_K^h]$ such that $\sum_{t=1}^{T} \alpha_t^c = 1$ and $\sum_{k=1}^{K} \alpha_k^h = 1$. These attention weights indicate which caption words and which hashtags are most salient *in the presence of each other*.

Using the attention weights, we compute a *co-attended representation* for the caption and for the hashtags by weighted summation of their token embeddings: $\hat{\mathbf{c}} = \sum_{t=1}^{T} \alpha_t^c \mathbf{c}_t$ and $\hat{\mathbf{h}} = \sum_{k=1}^{K} \alpha_k^h \mathbf{h}_k$. The resulting $\hat{\mathbf{c}}$ is a *hashtag-attended caption vector* (a single d-dimensional vector summarizing the caption, with more weight on words that hashtags consider important), and $\hat{\mathbf{h}}$ is the corresponding *caption-attended hashtag vector*. We then concatenate these to form the final fused representation for the post: $\mathbf{x}_i = \hat{\mathbf{c}} \oplus \hat{\mathbf{h}}$.

Through this co-attention process, the model learns a post representation that emphasizes cross-modal cues. For example, if a caption contains sensational language, the co-attention may focus on complementary hashtag terms that reinforce the clickbait nature of the post. This *jointly-attended fusion* is more expressive than simple concatenation, as it allows the network to pinpoint which words and hashtags interact to signal clickbait. The improved capacity to model caption-hashtag interactions can enhance detection performance, especially in cases where neither the caption nor hashtags alone fully indicate clickbait, but their combination does.

Decoder and Training. Once the caption and hashtags are fused into a single post representation $\mathbf{x}_i$, we feed this vector into a decoder network to predict the probability that the post is clickbait. Our decoder is a two-layer Multi-Layer Perceptron (MLP): a hidden dense layer (with ReLU activation) followed by an output layer. We apply dropout regularization in the MLP to prevent overfitting. The final output is a single logit which is passed through a sigmoid (equivalently, a 2-class softmax) to produce $\hat{y}_i$, the predicted probability of the post being clickbait. The model is trained end-to-end using a binary cross-entropy loss between $\hat{y}_i$ and the true label y_i. We optimize the parameters using the RMSprop algorithm, which we found effective for this task.

4   Experiments

Data and Settings. We choose the Instagram clickbait dataset from Ha et al.'s large-scale study [3]. There are 7,769 ground-truth posts (3,509 non-clickbait vs. 4,260 clickbait). We leverage solely the textual modality, i.e., each post's *caption* plus its *hashtag* set, both to simplify feature extraction and to isolate the linguistic patterns that signal clickbaiting in visual-centric social media. We randomly split all posts into training, validation, and test sets in a 65:10:25 ratio. Each experiment is repeated 15 times with different random seeds, and we report the mean of all runs. We assess classifier performance using four standard metrics: Accuracy (Acc) to measure overall correctness, Area Under the ROC Curve (AUC) to capture ranking quality, Precision (Pre) to evaluate clickbait-positive prediction reliability, and the F1 score to balance precision and recall.

Analysis Results. We analyze the experimental results (Table 1) to answer three key questions about model design choices for clickbait detection. The table compares models along three axes: model organization (unified vs. dual modeling), representation learning (sequential GRU vs. graph-based TextGCN), and fusion mechanism (simple feature concatenation vs. co-attention).

Q1: (Model Organization) Does Dual Modeling Outperform Unified? Dual modeling consistently outperforms unified modeling for clickbait detection, especially when combined with effective fusion strategies. Splitting the model into separate caption and hashtag streams yields higher F1 and AUC than processing them as a single sequence. The strongest gains appear when dual modeling is paired with co-attention, which better captures complementary signals. However, one outlier, i.e., CoAtt-GRU, shows that dual modeling alone is insufficient; it must be supported by strong representations and carefully aligned fusion. The advantage of dual modeling lies in its ability to learn task-specific embeddings: captions capture "hook" language while hashtags provide supporting or misleading cues. By encoding them independently, the model preserves their semantic differences. When fused, these specialized embeddings can highlight inconsistencies characteristic of clickbait, e.g., a sensational caption not matched by relevant tags. This structural separation improves precision-recall trade-offs and overall ranking, validating dual modeling as an effective strategy.

Table 1. Model comparisons for unified (U) vs. dual (D) modeling, concatenation (Concat) vs. co-attention (CoAtt), and GRU vs. TextGCN representation learning.

		Acc	AUC	Pre	F1
U	GRU [2]	0.8375 ± 0.0094	0.8345 ± 0.0087	0.8193 ± 0.0180	0.8140 ± 0.0095
D	Concat-GRU	0.8415 ± 0.0086	0.8388 ± 0.0083	0.8218 ± 0.0143	0.8190 ± 0.0091
D	CoAtt-GRU	0.8200 ± 0.0084	0.8155 ± 0.0092	0.8063 ± 0.0183	0.7914 ± 0.0115
U	TextGCN [11]	0.8279 ± 0.0039	0.8254 ± 0.0042	0.8268 ± 0.0040	0.8260 ± 0.0041
D	Concat-TextGCN	0.8509 ± 0.0086	0.8482 ± 0.0085	0.8336 ± 0.0144	0.8295 ± 0.0095
D	ConAtt-TextGCN	0.8699 ± 0.0077	0.8683 ± 0.0077	0.8509 ± 0.0205	0.8523 ± 0.0087

Q2: (Representation Learning) Does TextGCN Yield More Informative Representations than GRU? TextGCN-based models consistently outperform or match GRU counterparts, especially under dual modeling with advanced fusion. Even in the unified setting, TextGCN shows advantages in F1 and precision, indicating its ability to capture informative signals comparable to sequential encoders. This advantage grows in dual setups: Concat-TextGCN surpasses Concat-GRU, and co-attention further widens the gap, with TextGCN showing significantly higher F1 and AUC. These trends highlight TextGCN's strength in modeling global word co-occurrences and document-level semantics, which are patterns GRU may overlook due to its local and sequential focus. TextGCN's graph-based structure enables better generalization of clickbait cues, even from rare or weakly associated tokens, which is especially effective when aligning two text streams like captions and hashtags. Its globally contextualized embeddings help the fusion layer more accurately integrate and contrast the inputs, resulting in better precision-recall trade-offs and ranking. In contrast, GRU lacks this broader context and sees diminishing returns in complex settings. Thus, TextGCN proves more effective, especially as model architecture grows in depth and interaction.

Q3: (Fusion Mechanisms) Does Co-attention Improve Performance over Simple Concatenation? The effectiveness of co-attention depends heavily on the strength of underlying text representations. With TextGCN, co-attention consistently outperforms concatenation, achieving the highest F1 and AUC. This indicates that co-attention can align complementary cues between captions and hashtags, such as sensational phrases paired with matching or contrasting tags, enhancing clickbait detection. In contrast, applying co-attention to GRU representations reduces performance across all metrics, suggesting that GRU's sequential, local focus lacks the robustness needed to support co-attention's added complexity, often leading to unstable or misaligned attention.

Co-attention only proves beneficial when paired with rich, globally contextual embeddings like those from TextGCN. These allow the model to discover meaningful alignments between caption and hashtags, improving overall predictive power. GRU's localized encodings, especially when input modalities differ in length or vocabulary, make attention alignment more error-prone and prone to overfitting. Hence, co-attention's expressive power is only realized when backed by representation learning capable of capturing cross-modal relationships at a global level.

Table 2. Model comparisons for dual modeling that applies co-attention on embeddings derived from different combinations of GRU/TextGCN and Hashtags/Captions.

| Hashtags | | Captions | | Acc | AUC | Pre | F1 |
GRU	TextGCN	GRU	TextGCN				
	✓		✓	0.8699 ± 0.0077	0.8683 ± 0.0077	0.8509 ± 0.0205	0.8523 ± 0.0087
✓	✓			0.8441 ± 0.0070	0.8422 ± 0.0068	0.8212 ± 0.0196	0.8231 ± 0.0079
✓			✓	0.8405 ± 0.0107	0.8396 ± 0.0106	0.8102 ± 0.0190	0.8209 ± 0.0117
	✓	✓		0.8332 ± 0.0079	0.8282 ± 0.0076	0.8257 ± 0.0151	0.8055 ± 0.0085
✓		✓		0.8200 ± 0.0084	0.8155 ± 0.0092	0.8063 ± 0.0183	0.7914 ± 0.0115
		✓	✓	0.7545 ± 0.0166	0.7513 ± 0.0157	0.7197 ± 0.0260	0.7217 ± 0.0170

Q4: Which combination of sequential and graph-based encoders yields the most effective co-attention fusion? Should we allocate representational capacity to captions, hashtags, or both using graph-aware embeddings before applying co-attention? This question is critical because co-attention's effectiveness depends on the richness of the embeddings it aligns. If either input stream is weak or noisy, attention alignment falters, degrading performance. A systematic comparison is necessary to determine where graph convolution yields the most value and whether the added complexity of TextGCN is justified. Table 2 shows that performance peaks only when both captions and hashtags are encoded with TextGCN: this combination uniquely delivers the highest accuracy, AUC, and F1. Mixed setups with one GRU stream perform slightly worse, while GRU-only configurations fall behind significantly, underscoring their limitations in capturing long-range semantics. These trends suggest that clickbait often hinges on subtle inconsistencies between sensational captions and contextual hashtags, patterns best captured through global co-occurrence structures. Co-attention succeeds only when both streams offer equally expressive, graph-enriched embeddings, enabling precise alignment and robust detection.

5   Conclusions

In this work, we revisited the "old roots" of text-and-metadata fusion and the "fresh fruits" of modern graph and attention architectures to advance clickbait detection on social media. Our systematic exploration of three orthogonal design axes, i.e., *model organization* (unified vs. dual streams), *representation learning* (sequential GRU vs. graph-based TextGCN), and *fusion mechanism* (concatenation vs. co-attention), revealed clear patterns: separating caption and hashtag modeling, embedding both streams in a global co-occurrence graph, and then applying a co-attention layer consistently yields the strongest predictive performance. The results show that carefully chosen combinations of well-understood components can surpass more monolithic or heavily engineered alternatives.

Acknowledgements. This work is supported by the National Science and Technology Council (NSTC) of Taiwan under grants 113-2221-E-006-201-MY3, 112-2628-E-006-012-MY3, and 113-2634-F-002-007.

References

1. Chen, H.-Y., Li, C.-T.: HENIN: learning heterogeneous neural interaction networks for explainable cyberbullying detection on social media. In: Proceedings of the 2020 Conference on Empirical Methods in Natural Language Processing (EMNLP), pp. 2543–2552. Association for Computational Linguistics (2020)
2. Cho, K., et al.: Learning phrase representations using RNN encoder–decoder for statistical machine translation. In: Proceedings of the 2014 Conference on Empirical Methods in Natural Language Processing (EMNLP), pp. 1724–1734. Association for Computational Linguistics (2014)
3. Ha, Y., Kim, J., Won, D., Cha, M., Joo, J.: Characterizing clickbaits on Instagram. In: Proceedings of the International AAAI Conference on Web and Social Media, vol. 12 (2018)
4. Lu, Y.-J., Li, C.-T.: GCAN: graph-aware co-attention networks for explainable fake news detection on social media. In: Proceedings of the 58th Annual Meeting of the Association for Computational Linguistics, pp. 505–514. Association for Computational Linguistics (2020)
5. Munger, K.: All the news that's fit to click: the economics of clickbait media. Polit. Commun. **37**(3), 376–397 (2020)
6. Potthast, M., Köpsel, S., Stein, B., Hagen, M.: Clickbait detection. In: Ferro, N., et al. (eds.) ECIR 2016. LNCS, vol. 9626, pp. 810–817. Springer, Cham (2016). https://doi.org/10.1007/978-3-319-30671-1_72
7. Shrestha, A., Flood, A., Sohrawardi, S., Wright, M., Al-Ameen, M.N.: A first look into targeted clickbait and its countermeasures: the power of storytelling. In: Proceedings of the 2024 CHI Conference on Human Factors in Computing Systems, pp. 1–23 (2024)
8. Shu, K., Cui, L., Wang, S., Lee, D., Liu, H.: Defend: explainable fake news detection. In: Proceedings of the 25th ACM SIGKDD International Conference on Knowledge Discovery & Data Mining, pp. 395–405 (2019)
9. Sun, M., Zhang, X., Zheng, J., Ma, G.: DDGCN: dual dynamic graph convolutional networks for rumor detection on social media. In: Proceedings of the AAAI Conference on Artificial Intelligence, vol. 36, pp. 4611–4619 (2022)
10. Wang, Y., Zhu, Y., Li, Y., Qiang, J., Yuan, Y., Wu, X.: Clickbait detection via prompt-tuning with titles only. IEEE Trans. Emerg. Top. Comput. Intell. (2024)

11. Yao, L., Mao, C., Luo, Y.: Graph convolutional networks for text classification. In: Proceedings of the AAAI Conference on Artificial Intelligence, vol. 33, pp. 7370–7377 (2019)
12. Zheng, J., Zhang, X., Guo, S., Wang, Q., Zang, W., Zhang, Y.: MFAN: multimodal feature-enhanced attention networks for rumor detection. In: IJCAI 2022, pp. 2413–2419 (2022)

Politicization During the 2024 United States Presidential Elections

Marcelo Sartori Locatelli[1,2(✉)], Matheus Prado Miranda[1], Wagner Meira Jr.[1], and Virgilio Almeida[1]

[1] Universidade Federal de Minas Gerais, Belo Horizonte 31270-901, Brazil
{locatellimarcelo,matheus.prado,meira,virgilio}@dcc.ufmg.br
[2] Max Planck Institute for Security and Privacy, 44799 Bochum, Germany

Abstract. Topic shifts occur naturally during conversations when a person changes the subject to one different from the original. This phenomenon may be extremely meaningful, being useful for modeling dialogues and measuring information distortion during a conversation, among other tasks. In this work, we explore topic shifts as a metric for the measurement of politicization during the 2024 U.S. presidential elections, using YouTube news as a case study. We find evidence of politicization during the studied period as over 69% of non-political videos contain at least one political comment. This politicization increases as we get closer to the date of the election, with videos from right-leaning channels having over 40% of comments being political in the week of the elections. We also identify topics relating to immigration to be the most politicized, as commenters discuss the government's stance on immigration, aggravated by displays of xenophobia, exemplifying the dangers that come with politicization.

Keywords: Politicization · Social Media · Election

1 Introduction

During the last decade, social media data has been a target of frequent studies by researchers due to its ability to serve as a window to people's behavior, which, when combined with the ease of acquisition and abundance of such data, has led to the research and characterization of interesting phenomena, such as polarization [9], echo chambers [8], and filter bubbles [22].

One such phenomenon, whose study has benefited greatly from the increased amounts of data, is politicization. Politicization occurs when a topic that is not inherently political receives a political tone [24]. This ideological charge can lead to manipulation and a loss of public trust in experts' opinions. Studies on politicization typically address specific topics (e.g., climate change [19], COVID-19 [12], science [3], etc.) or rely on traditional media as their object of study, failing to fully leverage the abundance of data generated online.

M. S. Locatelli and M. P. Miranda—Equal contribution.

© The Author(s), under exclusive license to Springer Nature Switzerland AG 2026
A. An et al. (Eds.): ASONAM 2025, LNCS 16323, pp. 86–100, 2026.
https://doi.org/10.1007/978-3-032-13821-7_9

Given the risks associated with politicization and the impacts it can have on society, this study attempts to measure and uncover how politicization takes shape during important political events in a country. In this case, we study the 2024 U.S. presidential elections through the lens of politicization. Unlike most previous studies, we seek to take those measurements with a topic-agnostic methodology to better understand the full landscape of politicization in this context. However, as previously mentioned, commonly adopted methods in literature fail to scale to the proposed scope.

To address the aforementioned issues and provide a text-processing focused alternative, this research explores a way to measure politicization, using so-called *topic shifts*, a methodology developed to measure politicization on social media networks [17]. Topic shifts occur when a person changes the subject mid-conversation, potentially moving to a tangentially related or entirely unrelated topic. This has been used in other tasks, such as identifying relevant sentences for summarization tasks [14].

The underlying intuition behind the usage of topic shifts as an indicator of politicization is simple. Imagine a topic that is becoming politicized. By definition, this will be a topic receiving ideological and political tones, even if it was not originally so. Thus, for a politicized topic, given a non-political text posted on any online platform, responses to this text will tend to be more political compared to those on non-politicized topics, leading to more topic shifts.

In this work, we aim to understand politicization in the context of the U.S. presidential elections through the usage of topic shifts. In particular, we seek to answer the following questions:

- **RQ1:** Are there evidences of politicization during the studied period?
- **RQ2:** Are there any temporal patterns related to politicization during the studied period?
- **RQ3:** How does the content creator's political leaning influence politicization and topic shifts?
- **RQ4:** Which topics were the most and least politicized?

We find evidence that videos from right and, to a lesser extent, from left-leaning news sources tended to be more susceptible to politicization than those from center-leaning channels (RQ1). We believe that this may suggest a link between polarization and politicization as users flock to either side. This is corroborated by our analysis of temporal dynamics of topic shifts (RQ2), where we find that videos from left and right-leaning channels tended to receive topic shifts faster than those from the center. Additionally, we note that the right-leaning group tended to be the most associated with politicization, especially after Biden dropped out of the election, as seen in the peaks in the proportion of political comments (RQ3).

Finally, we identify the most and least politicized topics (RQ4), finding that there is a drastic difference in the amount of political comments received depending on the subject being discussed, with the most political topics having over a quarter of their comments relating to American politics. Topics of the so called hard-news tended to be more politicized. We see that topic shifts are frequently accompanied by an increase in toxic behavior, such as racism, further highlighting the raising concern over the necessity of moderating such behavior.

2   Related Works

Topic Shift. The concept of topic shift, although under-explored, was introduced quite some time ago as a way to find new information in a text and has been applied to various scenarios since then. The earliest attempt at automatic detection to the best of our knowledge was [21], who used this concept to identify new information in online news, enabling the analysis of larger amounts of data.

Since then, the landscape of online data and computing has changed drastically, with massive amounts of data and increased computational power leading to new ways of detecting and interpreting topic shifts. Topal et al. [23] study the effect of this phenomenon in social media comments, specifically on Twitter, suggesting that abrupt topic changes in response to posts, combined with inflammatory comments, are detrimental to the user experience. They leverage the knowledge of this phenomenon to propose a detection methodology based on the discussion topic and the emotions expressed by users through comments, which could be used to filter out undesirable comments. Their results suggest that certain topics and emotions lead to higher occurrences of topic shifts.

Ermakova et al. [11] use topic shifts to demonstrate how true information about COVID-19 gets distorted throughout a sequence of comments. They find that as the topic shifts from medicine to politics and business, the information tends to become distorted, potentially leading to misinformation.

Politicization. The vast majority of studies on politicization are conducted qualitatively and focus on a single topic. Morten Bay [2] manually investigates tweets related to the movie "Star Wars: The Last Jedi", finding evidence of politicization and Russian bot activity. Peterson and Muñoz [20] use surveys to study the politicization of sports media, such as ESPN, over the years.

Quantitative studies, on the other hand, often limit themselves to analyzing keywords or hashtags, capturing mentions of political entities in news or social media. Hart et al. [12], and Chinn et al. [7] use this type of technique to study, respectively, the politicization of COVID-19-related posts on social media and climate change news from 1985 to 2017, finding signs of politicization correlated with an increase in mentions of Democratic and Republican politicians in the United States. A similar approach was used by Brown and Midberry [4] to study the politicization of drug addiction through keyword analysis.

Some researchers have explored alternative methods to measure politicization quantitatively. In [10], the researchers use topic modeling techniques to identify subjects related to partisan ideology. They find that topics related to ivermectin and other alternative COVID-19 treatments displayed more negative sentiment in Democratic states, providing evidence of politicization.

We extend previous research by focusing on the very recent 2024 American elections and by analyzing the characteristics of topic-shifting comments, deepening the understanding of this phenomenon.

3   Dataset

As politicization may manifest itself in how people react to news and other important events, we collect all videos from reliable English language news sources using the YouTube data API V3. In total, our dataset consists of 21,075 videos posted by 68 different channels, separated by political leaning[1], and over 9 million comments published during the period ranging from January 1 2023 to February 23 2025. Table 1 shows a summary of the video statistics. The structure of YouTube data is helpful to our purposes as the videos set a main topic to which the comments should respond to, making it easier to identify when users stray away from that topic.

Table 1. Summary of the collected video statistics.

Leaning	Videos	Comments	Channels	Unique Commenters
Any	21,075	9,324,489	68	3,648,739
Left	9,141	4,187,888	31	2,247,024
Center	4,229	2,495,698	12	1,130,910
Right	7,705	2,640,903	25	1,150,463

We employed three annotators to label independent instances of 3000 videos and comments, which we shard into 5 different partitions to serve as train and test data for our models. Annotation guidelines were designed to identify political content, defined as any explicit or implicit reference to political candidates, parties, public offices, or ideologically charged entities. We assessed inter-rater reliability using Fleiss' Kappa [15], obtaining a score of 0.748. According to the interpretation scale proposed by Landis and Koch, this value indicates "substantial agreement" among annotators.

4   Detecting Topic Shifts

In order to measure how topics change in the direction of politics, we must first determine what is political. For that, we build a text based classifier that, given a comment or a video, is able to output how likely it is to be political. As we rely on the classifier to detect topic shifts, its performance on both categories is pivotal. We measure this performance in terms of the video and comments'

---

[1] https://www.allsides.com/media-bias/media-bias-chart.

F1, which equates to the harmonic mean between precision and recall, as we are using a binary classifier.

$$F_1 = 2 \frac{precision \cdot recall}{precision + recall}$$

The performance metric F1 was chosen because we want to avoid detecting false topic shifts to politics on non-political videos (comment misclassified as political or video misclassified as non-political), as well as detecting topic shifts to non-politics on political videos (comment misclassified as non-political or video misclassified as political), thus, both precision and recall are important.

We first test the two-step Positive and Unlabeled(PU) learning algorithm proposed in [17]. The idea behind this algorithm is that it is fairly easy to have an initial set of posts and comments that are reliably political by simply using a set of keywords, while it is much harder to determine an initial set of non-political text. However, by leveraging the spies PU learning technique [16], using a weaker classifier such as naive bayes, we can obtain a set of reliably non-political pieces of text, which we can finally combine with our initial set of positive examples in order to train a stronger classifier (in the original paper, a XGboost [6] classifier).

For this work we use a set of keywords relevant to the U.S. presidential elections to define the initial positive dataset. They range from specific American political figures to general political terms[2]. The list was curated through manual inspection of common political terminology in U.S. discourse, supported by prior work [17]. Since this method does not rely on our human-labeled training data, we use the training partitions of our manually labeled sample solely to define the model hyperparameters in a random search setting, with the test partition being used for evaluation, we repeat this 5 times with different test sets and aggregate the results when reporting.

As LLMs have proven to have great performances for most text based tasks, we also compare the results of the PU classifier with a more modern approach using a fine-tuned RoBERTa model leveraging the textual elements of videos and comments. For video classification, we simply use the title and description as inputs for the model, while for comments we attempt two approaches: the first uses solely the content of the comment for the classification, while the second incorporates the context of the video into the prediction, truncating when necessary. Figure 1 gives an example of the classification pipeline. The idea here is to leverage the fact that our dataset consists of video and comment pairs, which allows us to make use of the video title and video description when classifying a comment. This is beneficial in the detection of more nuanced comments. For example, the comment "I agree with this person" would be political in the context of a video titled "Watch as the president gives his discourse" and would not if it was posted under a video titled "We need to stop mistreating dogs". The PU classifier described above would treat these two comments as the same, although the context from the video completely changes the topics to which the comments

---

[2] The full list of keywords is: "trump", "biden", "kamala", "vance", "republican", "democrat", "party", "election", "debate", "president".

refer, an aspect that we wish to leverage on the RoBERTa classifier. We use a 5-fold cross validation approach and train the models for 5 epochs.

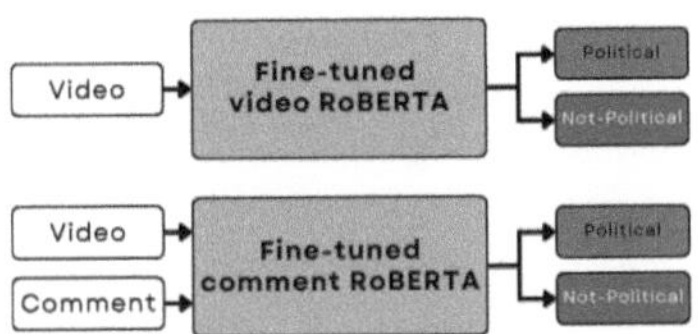

Fig. 1. We use two fine-tuned RoBERTa classifiers. The first (top) is responsible for classifying the video as political or non-political using its title and description as input. The second (bottom) classifies the comment using the comment text and the textual elements of the video as inputs, contextualizing the comment.

Table 2 shows the performance of either models on the political classification task, with a 99% confidence interval. We can see that the RoBERTa classifier outperforms the PU model when we incorporate the video context to the comment prediction, while the performance without this modification is even worse than the two-step PU classifier. To make the results more robust, we also conducted an unpaired t-test aiming to ascertain if there is any statistical difference between the two methods. We obtain the CIs -0.100 ± 0.02 and -0.197 ± 0.07 for the difference of means of the video and comment classifiers when comparing the PU method with the LLM based method, therefore the test passes with $p < 0.01$, demonstrating the superiority of the proposed approach for the task. We believe that, despite the errors in model classification, the relatively high classifier performance would still lead to tendencies being visible when we analyze large amounts of data.

Table 2. Performance of the two-step PU learning and fine-tuned RoBERTa model on the test set. The $\pm$ term represents the 99% confidence interval for the mean. The RoBERTa model far outperforms the two-step PU approach for the English YouTube news dataset.

	Video F1	Comment F1
Two-step PU learning	0.812 ± 0.029	0.668 ± 0.059
RoBERTa	0.918 ± 0.011	0.775 ± 0.089
+ Video Context	N/A	0.865 ± 0.031

5   Characterizing Topic Shifts

We use the best performing RoBERTa model to attribute a political or non-political label to all comments and videos on our dataset, classifying 65% of the comments and 60% of the videos as political. This suggests that most of the news published by reputable news sources in English on YouTube relate to U.S. politics. These 65% of political comments, however, are not restricted solely to political videos. We estimate that 64% of the non-political videos contain at least one political comment, which could be a sign of politicization as people start to bring American politics into most topics.

Figure 2a illustrates the fraction of topic-shifting comments for political and non-political videos. Political videos tend to maintain a higher topical coherence in their discussions, with a comparatively lower incidence of comments shifting to unrelated topics. This suggests that explicit political framing effectively directs audience discourse, maintaining focus on the intended political themes. Non-political videos, however, show a higher variability, with a considerable proportion containing moderate to high fractions of political comments.

When examining how the leaning of news sources affects topic shifts, an initial investigation reveals that videos from neutral news sources receive fewer topic-shifting comments in general - see Fig. 2b. Although the distribution of left-leaning channels resembles that of center leaning channels more closely, both left-leaning and right-leaning sources appear to exhibit a higher incidence of topic-shifting comments. We hypothesize topic shifting towards politics might be related to polarization, and thus, in the more polarized right and left-leaning contexts, one would be more likely to observe an out of topic political comment.

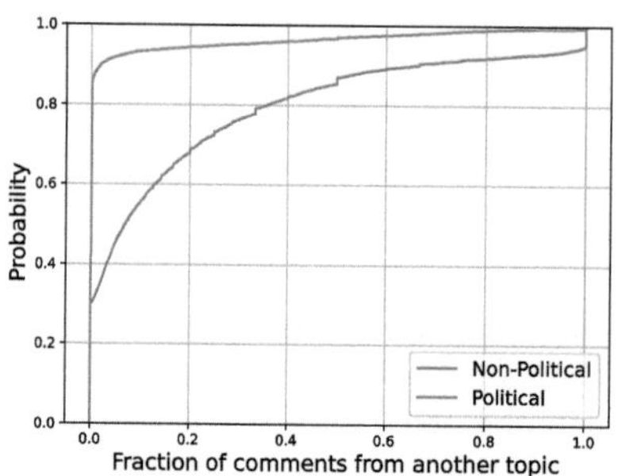

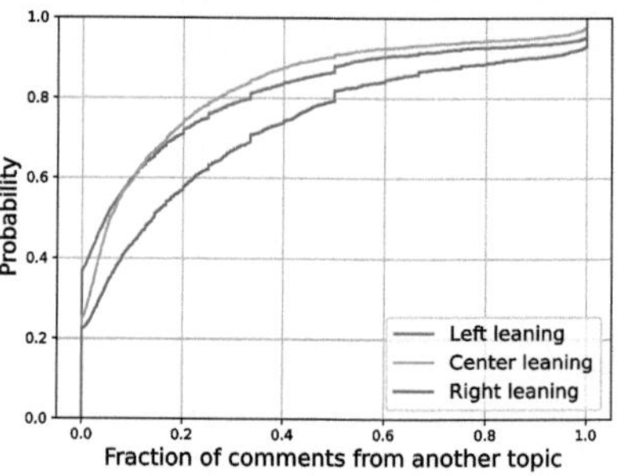

(a) The cumulative distribution function (CDF) shows the proportion of topic-shifting comments posted on YouTube videos. We observe that approximately 80% of political videos have no topic-shifting comments, while around 80% of non-political videos contain topic-shifting comments in more than 80% of their total comments.

(b) Cumulative distribution function of the fraction of topic-shifting comments posted on non-political YouTube videos per leaning. Videos from center leaning channels seem to be the least susceptible to topic shifts, closely followed by left-leaning channels, while videos from right-leaning channels seem to suffer from it the most.

Fig. 2. Cumulative distribution functions (CDF) for topic shifts.

Table 3. Most politicized non-political YouTube news topics. Disasters tend to get consistently politicized, possibly due to a mix of climate activism, conspiracies and government blaming. The $\pm$ term indicates the 99% proportion confidence interval.

Topic	Representative Words	Political Comments	Sample
Immigration	Migrant, Immigration, Mexican.	47% $\pm$ 0.3%	**News.**"A Growing number of Chinese migrants seek asylum at U.S. Mexico border" **Politicized Comment.**"Smart China, conquer US with voters instead of weapons."
Earthquakes	Earthquake, Syria, Turkey.	46% $\pm$ 0.9%	**News.**'Shellshocked: Southwest Turkey and Syria Rocked Again by Earthquake | Jerusalem Dateline" **Politicized Comment.** "Politicians don't have brains"
TikTok Regulation	Tiktok, Ban, Regulate.	35% $\pm$ 1.4%	**News.**'This is What TikTok Does to Your Child" **Politicized Comment.**"... people who make the decisions are in favor of it. Saying that Liberals and Conservatives can come together on this doesn't matter when one of them wants this to continue... "
Space	Spacex, Starship, Rocket.	31% $\pm$ 0.4%	**News.**"Las Vegas family that reported aliens stands by original story | Banfield" **Politicized Comment.**"The footage they took was already confiscated, and the threats they are getting are from the secret government organizations running this technology..."
Natural Disasters	Storm, Hurricane, Snowstorm.	28% $\pm$ 0.4%	**News.**"11 million people under flood alerts in California | WNT" **Politicized Comment.**"Meanwhile USA is under attack and Biden could care less! for all! Geoengineered?!"

5.1 Politicization of Topics

After finding evidence of politicization during the studied period, the next step is to discern which topics were more politicized. To do so, we separate the non-political YouTube news and use BERTopics, a topic modeling technique based on sentence embeddings with c-TF-IDF, to produce interpretable non-political topics. Having obtained the topics for the published videos, we then find the percentage of topic-shifting comments that appear on each of them to identify the most and least politicized topics. Since the topics are highly interpretable, at this stage we can manually exclude some uninteresting or likely to be misclassified topics. In our case, we exclude one topic related to daily, weekly, and monthly news, since videos from this topic tend to contain political content even if their title or description is unrelated. An example of such video title would be "Top U.S. & World Headlines—December 11, 2024". In total, we identified 28 different topics that made up the news between the years of 2023 and 2024, including technology, crime, travel, food, natural disasters, and many others.

Table 3 and 4 show the top-5 most and least politicized topics. We find that immigration is the most politicized topic, with upwards of 45% of the comments on those videos being classified as relating to politics much of this politicization traces back to foreign citizens - especially Latin American, Chinese and Islamic people - possibly due to the consistent clashes between the Republican and Democratic party on their stance around immigration and deportations, with racism possibly playing a part (Sect. 5.2). The politicization of disasters such as earthquakes, storms, floods and fires (24% political comments, not in the table) is interesting as it appears as an intersection from many factors, including attributing blame to governments, conspiracy theories, and climate activism, leading to the high rate of political comments.

We also see how politicization leads to fear and distrust, with many of the news being called fake news even when they come from reputable news sources in addition to conspiracy theories claiming that crimes and reports are just a political tool to mislead the population. In fact, 14% ± 1% of non-political videos have at least one comment containing the term "fake news".

Interestingly, some topics frequently associated to politics were not as politicized during the studied period, for instance, videos related to inflation, recession and other economic processes had only around 10% political comments. On a manual investigation, many of the comments are actually referencing corporate greed or suggesting solutions to these processes rather than focusing on State policies or politicians. Automation appearing with only 8% political comments is also surprising, especially as advances such as the Chinese deepseek have sparked new discussions around the China-U.S. competition, leading to pronunciations from important politicians such as D. Trump[3], who said the model was a "wake-up call" to U.S. industry. This illustrates the difficulty in studying politicization, showing that different facets of a topic may be politicized, but they will not necessarily represent the topic as a whole.

Although we show samples of politicized comments on the least politicized topics, those are much harder to find in our actual dataset. However, they serve to illustrate that on a more politicized context, you can find political discussion even on unassuming topics such as relationship discussions or weight-loss tips.

Table 4. Least politicized non-political YouTube news topics. Notice how the topics are more varied than the most politicized ones. The ± term indicates the 99% proportion confidence interval.

Topic	Representative Words	Political Comments	Sample
Relationships	Divorce, Marriage, Part.	2% ± 0.5%	**News.**"Secrets To A Successful Marriage" **Politicized Comment.**"Honestly. Some comments are just nonsense. And no I'm not leftist. I'm very much conservative. ..."
Oceangate	Titanic, Submarine, Shipwreck.	6% ± 1.2%	**News.**"I'm fearful': Submarine commander on missing Titanic vessel" **Politicized Comment.**"It's ALLL TRUMP'S Fault! Trump will be indicted for this soon!"
Weight	Diet, Obesity, Weightloss.	8% ± 1.3%	**News.**"Ozempic Underworld The Black Market Of Weight Loss Drugs" **Politicized Comment.** "Blame your government regulations not the pharmaceutical companies! They aren't breaking any laws"
Automation	AI, Ai-powered, Robots.	8% ± 0.3%	**News.**"How The Massive Power Draw Of Generative AI Is Overtaxing Our Grid" **Politicized Comment.**"Trump: buy Greenland, take Canada"
Economy	Inflation, CPI, Recession.	9% ± 0.5%	**News.**"How The U.S. Is Stalling A Recession" **Politicized Comment.**"Vote Democrats OUT!"

As politicization is a process, it is important to understand how it varies with time. For this reason, we explore both the speed of topic shifts (i.e. how long it takes for a non-political video to receive its first political comment) as well as the overall proportion of topic-shifting comments on our database. Figure 3a shows the variation in proportion of political videos posted on the database throughout the year. It is possible to see that, especially for videos from right-leaning channels, the proportion of political comments drastically increases after

---

[3] https://www.reuters.com/world/us/trump-deepseeks-ai-should-be-wakeup-call-us-industry-2025-01-27/.

Joe Biden drops out of the presidential race, peaking at the week of the elections. This same tendency is not observed on the left-leaning videos, whose percentage of politic comments remained steady throughout the year, showing a small peak after the elections, possibly due to discussions arising after Kamala's defeat. We further discuss the characteristics of the political discourse outside political videos in Sect. 5.2.

Figure 3b shows the median time (in comments) before a topic-shifting comment is posted on a video. From this figure, we can see that videos from center leaning channels, in general, had longer periods without topic-shifting comments. This corroborates with our hypothesis that topic shifts might be related to polarization, as the news channels whose views more closely aligned with the U.S. parties, be it Democratic or Republican, tended to be topic shifted faster. Additionally, we note that throughout most of the studied period, right-leaning videos tended to receive topic-shifting comments faster, which, coupled with the higher ratio of political comments during most weeks and the higher fraction of videos with a high number of topic-shifting comments (see Fig. 2b), suggests that right-leaning content is more associated with politicized discourse.

5.2   Characteristics of Topic-Shifting Comments

Finally, we conduct an investigation on what is driving those topic shifts. For this, we define Democratic leaning word set as "democrat", "Kamala", "Harris", "left-wing" and Republican leaning word set as "republican", "Donald", "Trump", "right-wing". Using the VADER [13] sentiment analyzer, we obtain the sentiments of topic-shifting comments containing each of those sets. The idea behind this experiment is to find which group is driving politicization: the republicans or democrats. If the right-leaning groups are responsible for the topic shifts, we expect the sentiments towards the Republican set to be positive and Democratic set to be negative. The opposite is true for the left-leaning group.

We find that on average, topic-shifting comments are slightly more negative than non-topic-shifting comments (t-test, $p<0.001$), however we find no practical differences between the sentiments of comments containing words from the Republican or Democrat word sets. We also do not find any evidences of the leaning of the video channel influencing the sentiment of the topic-shifting comments. Thus, the hypothesis that a specific group might be more responsible for topic shifts seems unlikely.

To further understand what issues may be fueling these changes in topic, we analyze the toxicity of topic-shifting comments, focusing on different categories that may be relevant for politicization. We detect toxicity using a RoBERTa fine-tuned model [1] chosen due to its ability to discern between the targets of hate speech, categorizing toxic comments into six different categories: "disability", "racism", "religion", "sexism", "sexual orientation" or "other".

We find that topic-shifting comments are considerably more likely to be toxic than average, with more than 3.5% of them being categorized as toxic compared to the only 1.5% of non topic shifts. Interestingly, 85% of the topic-shifting comments classified as toxic are racist. This is consistent with our topic analysis

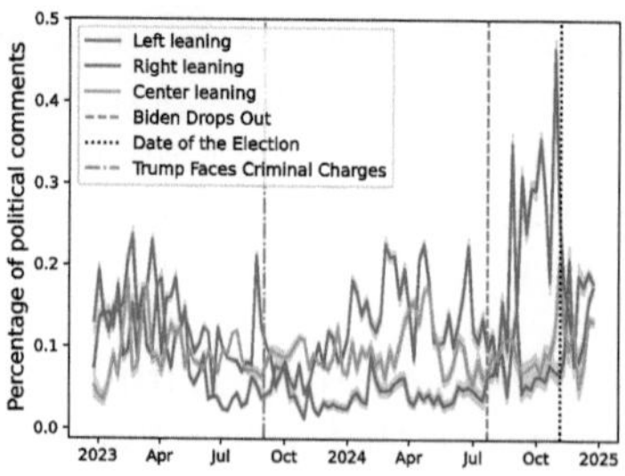

(a) Percentage of topic-shifting comments posted on YouTube non-political news videos per week. The gray area indicates the 99% proportion confidence interval.

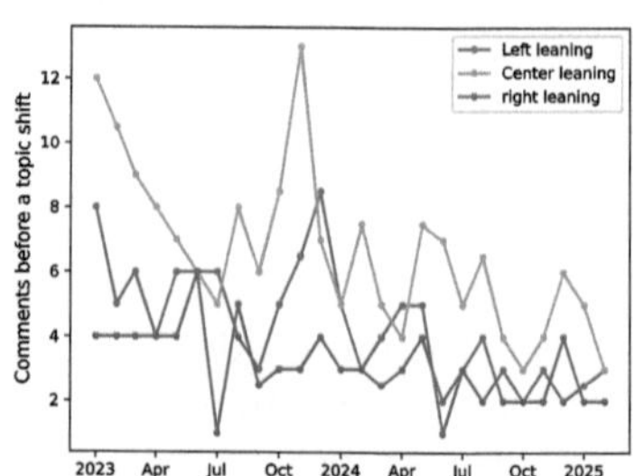

(b) Median number of comments before a non-political video receives a topic-shifting comment per month.

Fig. 3. Temporal patterns for topic shifts.

findings, which indicate that many politicized topics may be traced back to the presence of foreign citizens or cultures, serving as further evidence of the possible harms that come with politicization.

Figure 4 shows the proportion of comments belonging to each hate speech category, divided by different time frames: before Biden drops out (until July 24, 2024), after Kamala joins the race (before November 5) and after the day of the elections (remainder of the studied period). We find that among non-topic-shifting comments, the amount of toxicity remained roughly the same throughout the entire studied period. Additionally, for these comments, there was a similar proportion of sexism and racism. However, when we look at the topic-shifting comments we see that they are very skewed towards racism, with other kinds of hate-speech being less prevalent than their non-topic-shifting counterparts. Additionally, we see a considerable increase of racist comments after Kamala joins the presidential race, possibly a reflection of the inflammatory comments relating to her Black and Indian background.

Interestingly, besides racism and sexism, we also see a relatively high amount of hate speech related to religion. We hypothesize that these are related to the many ongoing conflicts related to religion, such as the Israel-Palestine war and the controversies regarding Muslim immigrants. Consequently, religious tensions appear to intersect notably with political discussions, potentially exacerbating polarization within online discourse.

5.3   Semantic Polarization

To complement our classifier-based approach to politicization, we adopt a lexical-semantic perspective using the Word Embedding Association Test (WEAT), originally introduced in Caliskan et al. [5]. WEAT quantifies differential associations between two sets of target concepts (e.g., ideological groups) and two sets

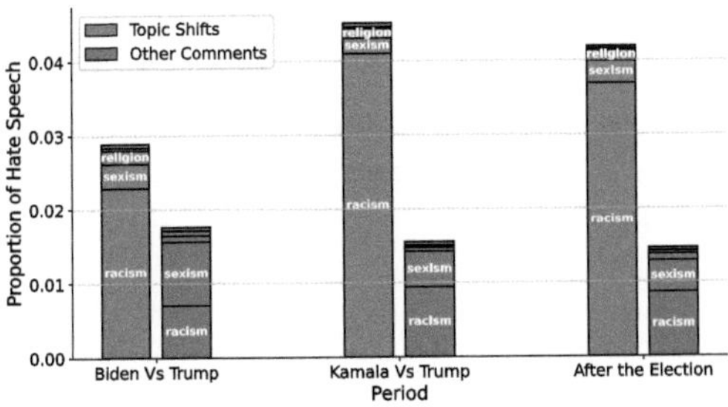

Fig. 4. Proportion of toxic comments per hate speech category, for different time periods of the US elections.

of attribute words (e.g., moral valence) by computing cosine similarity-based statistics in word embedding spaces. It provides an interpretable metric—effect size (Cohen's d)—and a permutation-based significance test, enabling the measurement of implicit semantic biases in text corpora.

This methodological choice is motivated by prior work utilizing WEAT to detect ideological framing in online discourse. In particular, Ottoni et al. [18] leveraged WEAT to measure implicit associations in YouTube content, revealing meaningful semantic biases in both comment and video data from right-wing channels. Adapting this framework to our setting, we apply WEAT to independently trained word embedding spaces, learned using Word2Vec models built from our data. It consists of topic-shifted and non-political comments, enabling a comparative analysis of their respective ideological associations.

We define multiple ideologically relevant WEAT tests reflecting thematic axes derived from our dataset topics. These axes, presented in Table 5, were constructed by analyzing lexical patterns in comments, focusing on recurrent contrasts in group references and evaluative language across highlighted topics of our work. We also incorporate a pretrained Word2Vec model trained on the Google News corpus as a general-purpose semantic baseline, approximating a neutral Wikipedia-like embedding space for comparison.

Following the results presented in Fig. 5, we find that topic-shifted comments tend to exhibit higher semantic polarization in politically charged associations. Among the tested axes, Racism and Natural Disaster reveals a clear distinction between topic-shifted and other groups. The higher effect size observed for the shifted group suggests that political content introduced into non-political contexts tends to reinforce more extreme or stereotyped associations along these semantic axes. Furthermore, the evaluative language in these associations tends to disproportionately target the discriminated class with negative attributions.

In contrast, Immigration emerges as a persistently polarized axis across all groups, including non-political and caption-based comments. In this sense, immigration-related associations are deeply embedded in online discourse, independent of whether the surrounding content is explicitly political. Wikipedia, serving as a baseline, exhibits the expected lower effect sizes compared to our dataset for the Immigration and Natural Disaster axes. Its relatively high score on the Racism axis, however, suggests that certain biased associations—particularly those involving race—may be more deeply embedded in the general language space. This aligns with our findings of racism as an extreme and prominent category within hate speech discourse, exceeding merely frequent political targeted figures like Kamala Harris.

Table 5. Word sets used for each class and attribute in our Word Embedding Association Tests (WEATs).

Group	Immigration	Natural Disaster	Racism
Class 1 *(Discriminated)*	immigrant, refugee, mexican, border, migrant	flood, fire, earthquake, hurricane, tornado	black, african, minority, brown, mexican
Class 2 *(Dominant)*	citizen, native, patriot, local, resident	government, biden, trump, state, politicians	white, european, american, caucasian, majority
Attributes 1	criminal, dangerous, invader, illegal, enemy	unavoidable, natural, random, accident, fate	criminal, dangerous, gang, violent, illegal
Attributes 2	peaceful, kind, honest, innocent, hardworking	avoidable, accountable, corrupt, neglect, failure	peaceful, honest, friendly, worker, neighbor

6   Discussion

In this work we explored the politicization of YouTube news videos during the period leading up to the 2024 American presidential elections. Focusing on a set of reputable English speaking news sources, we analyze over 8 million comments published between the start of 2023 and the end of 2024. To allow for our analysis, we develop a political classifier leveraging the capabilities of a fine-tuned RoBERTa model, achieving 0.9 and 0.86 F1 for classifying videos and comments, respectively and use its outputs to detect political comments on non-political videos which serve as examples of topic shift.

While YouTube is the focus of this study, it is important to consider that the platform has unique characteristics—such as video-based content, recommendation algorithms, and a specific user demographic—that may influence politicization dynamics. Therefore, while the observed trends are strong on YouTube, future work should aim to validate whether similar patterns emerge on other social media platforms, such as Twitter, Reddit, or TikTok, which have different content formats, audience behaviors, and moderation approaches.

We find that non-political videos frequently contain topic-shifting comments, with over 69% of our dataset containing at least one political comment. This suggests a widespread tendency of online discourse to introduce politics to unrelated topics, often increasing in response to important political events, such as Biden dropping out of the presidential race. These tendencies of politicization were

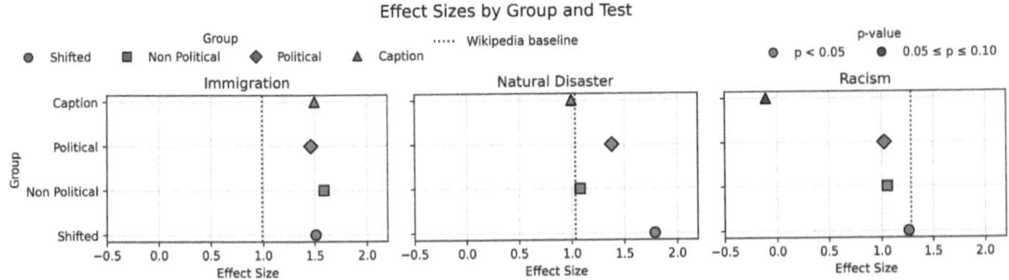

Fig. 5. Effect sizes (Cohen's d) for WEAT tests across content groups. Shapes indicate source type, colors denote significance levels (p-values), and the dashed line shows the Wikipedia baseline.

especially prevalent among right-leaning channels, with center channels being the least affected. This suggests that media polarization might play a role in the phenomenon of politicization, although further studies are required to confirm this hypothesis.

We also find that topics relating to hard news tended to be more politicized. On our dataset, this is predominantly seen in the form of immigration related videos, which were the most politicized topic. On manual investigation, topic-shifting comments on those videos commonly contained a mix of xenophobia, racism and conspiracy theories, further highlighting the dangers of politicization as it amplifies social divisions and fuels misinformation. Complementing these findings, we observe that topic-shifted comments encode stronger biased associations than other groups, particularly in relation to race and institutional trust, highlighting the semantic intensity of politicization.

In conclusion, this research provides valuable insights into the mechanisms and consequences of politicization in online discussions. As digital platforms continue to serve as primary venues for political discourse, understanding how and why non-political topics become politicized is crucial for mitigating polarization and fostering healthier online interactions.

Acknowledgement. This work was partially funded by CNPq, CAPES, FAPEMIG, and IAIA - INCT on AI.

References

1. Antypas, D., Camacho-Collados, J.: Robust hate speech detection in social media: a cross-dataset empirical evaluation. In: The 7th Workshop on Online Abuse and Harms (WOAH), pp. 231–242 (2023)
2. Bay, M.: Weaponizing the haters: the last jedi and the strategic politicization of pop culture through social media manipulation. First Monday (2018)
3. Bolsen, T., Druckman, J.N.: Counteracting the politicization of science. J. Commun. **65**(5), 745–769 (2015)

4. Brown, D.K., Midberry, J.: Social media news production, emotional Facebook reactions, and the politicization of drug addiction. Health Commun. **37**(3), 375–383 (2022)

5. Caliskan, A., Bryson, J.J., Narayanan, A.: Semantics derived automatically from language corpora contain human-like biases. Science **356**(6334), 183–186 (2017). https://doi.org/10.1126/science.aal4230

6. Chen, T., Guestrin, C.: XGBoost: a scalable tree boosting system. In: Proceedings of the KDD, pp. 785–794. ACM (2016). https://doi.org/10.1145/2939672.2939785. http://doi.acm.org/10.1145/2939672.2939785

7. Chinn, S., Hart, P.S., Soroka, S.: Politicization and polarization in climate change news content, 1985–2017. Sci. Commun. **42**(1), 112–129 (2020)

8. Cinelli, M., De Francisci Morales, G., Galeazzi, A., Quattrociocchi, W., Starnini, M.: The echo chamber effect on social media. Proc. Natl. Acad. Sci. **118**(9), e2023301118 (2021)

9. Conover, M., Ratkiewicz, J., Francisco, M., Gonçalves, B., Menczer, F., Flammini, A.: Political polarization on twitter. In: Proceedings of the ICWSM, vol. 5, pp. 89–96 (2011)

10. Diaz, M.I., Hanna, J.J., Hughes, A.E., Lehmann, C.U., Medford, R.J.: The politicization of ivermectin tweets during the covid-19 pandemic. In: Open Forum Infectious Diseases, vol. 9, p. ofac263. Oxford University Press (2022)

11. Ermakova, L., Nurbakova, D., Ovchinnikova, I.: Covid or not covid? Topic shift in information cascades on twitter. In: 3rd RDSM, pp. 32–37 (2020)

12. Hart, P.S., Chinn, S., Soroka, S.: Politicization and polarization in covid-19 news coverage. Sci. Commun. **42**(5), 679–697 (2020)

13. Hutto, C., Gilbert, E.: Vader: a parsimonious rule-based model for sentiment analysis of social media text. In: Proceedings of the ICWSM, vol. 8, pp. 216–225 (2014)

14. Konigari, R., Ramola, S., Alluri, V.V., Shrivastava, M.: Topic shift detection for mixed initiative response. In: Proceedings of the SIGDIAL, pp. 161–166 (2021)

15. Landis, J.R., Koch, G.G.: The measurement of observer agreement for categorical data. Biometrics **33**(1), 159–174 (1977). http://www.jstor.org/stable/2529310

16. Liu, B., Lee, W.S., Yu, P.S., Li, X.: Partially supervised classification of text documents. In: ICML, Sydney, NSW, vol. 2, pp. 387–394 (2002)

17. Locatelli, M.S., et al.: Topic shifts as a proxy for assessing politicization in social media. In: Proceedings of the ICWSM, 18, pp. 972–984 (2024)

18. Ottoni, R., Cunha, E., Magno, G., Bernardina, P., Meira, W., Jr., Almeida, V.: Analyzing right-wing youtube channels: hate, violence and discrimination. In: Proceedings of the ACM Webscience, WebSci 2018, pp. 323–332. ACM (2018). https://doi.org/10.1145/3201064.3201081

19. Pepermans, Y., Maeseele, P.: The politicization of climate change: problem or solution? Wiley Interdisc. Rev. Clim. Change **7**(4), 478–485 (2016)

20. Peterson, E., Muñoz, M.: "Stick to sports": evidence from sports media on the origins and consequences of newly politicized attitudes. Polit. Commun. **39**(4), 454–474 (2022)

21. Radev, D.R.: Topic shift detection-finding new information in threaded news (1999)

22. Ross Arguedas, A., Robertson, C., Fletcher, R., Nielsen, R.: Echo chambers, filter bubbles, and polarisation: a literature review (2022)

23. Topal, K., Koyuturk, M., Ozsoyoglu, G.: Emotion-and area-driven topic shift analysis in social media discussions. In: 2016 IEEE/ACM International Conference on Advances in Social Networks Analysis and Mining, pp. 510–518. IEEE (2016)

24. Wiesner, C.: Introduction: Rethinking Politicisation in Politics, Sociology and International Relations. Springer, Cham (2021)

Sentiment-Driven Differential Engagement: Hyperpartisan Vs. Non-hyperpartisan Users on X

Alireza Mohammadinodooshan$^{(\boxtimes)}$ and Niklas Carlsson

Linköping University, Linköping, Sweden
`{alireza.mohammadinodooshan,niklas.carlsson}@liu.se`

Abstract. Hyperpartisan news sources increasingly shape online discourse, raising urgent concerns about polarization and misinformation. This paper presents the first large-scale differential study of sentiment-driven engagement with hyperpartisan and non-hyperpartisan news on X (formerly Twitter). Analyzing 5.8 million news tweets that attracted 78.6 billion views (impressions) and 466 million interactions, we normalize interactions by view count to isolate user responsiveness, advancing beyond prior work that did not account for differences in exposure. Recognizing that the X algorithm tends to expose hyperpartisan users to hyperpartisan content more frequently, we provide insights into both what sentiments may make some publishers more successful and, more importantly, what effect those different sentiments have on these users' engagement patterns at a large scale. Our findings show that hyperpartisan users exhibit greater sensitivity to negative content, a pattern robust to controls for topic, content prominence, and temporal variations, and consistent across left- and right-leaning hyperpartisan groups, despite subtle differences. Moreover, our analysis shows that the impact of sentiment on engagement is moderated by the depth of user cognition, varying across different interaction types such as likes, retweets, replies, and quotes. Our findings offer statistically grounded and actionable insights for content creators, recommender-system designers, and policymakers seeking to understand and curb the amplification of hyperpartisan content.

1 Introduction

The U.S. media landscape has undergone a significant transformation, with hyperpartisan publishers gaining disproportionate influence despite being a minority [18]. Often described as "the principal incubator and disseminator of disinformation", these outlets drive polarization and undermine trust in mainstream media [10]. Social media platforms, particularly X (Twitter), where 59% of U.S. users regularly access news via the platform, have become the prominent channel for hyperpartisan content [32]. Consequently, understanding user engagement with such content is imperative. Nevertheless, scholarly investigation into engagement with hyperpartisan content remains limited compared to other types of problematic information, highlighting this gap as an "urgent task" [8].

A. An et al. (Eds.): ASONAM 2025, LNCS 16323, pp. 101–118, 2026.
https://doi.org/10.1007/978-3-032-13821-7_10

An extensive body of literature has examined factors influencing user engagement on social media, highlighting sentiment as a key factor [3,4,26]. For instance, Bar et al. [4] found that negative content often garners higher engagement. Given sentiment's potential role in amplifying hyperpartisan content, our main research question is: *To what extent do hyperpartisan users' engagement patterns change differently in response to news tweets' sentiment compared to their non-hyperpartisan counterparts?* To address this, we analyze both overall engagement and different interaction types, compare left and right-leaning hyperpartisan users, and conduct extensive robustness checks for confounding factors, including exposure level, topic, novelty effects, and temporal variations.

Need for Large-Scale Study: One approach to answer the research question is to find hyperpartisan and non-hyperpartisan users, expose them to different classes of content, and analyze their engagement patterns. However, this method is not scalable nor preserve the natural viewing context. Instead, we identify content that hyperpartisan users are more likely to be exposed to, allowing us to infer and study engagement patterns at a much larger scale.

Our Approach in Brief: Our approach involves analyzing tweets from hyperpartisan and non-hyperpartisan news publishers to understand how sentiment influences engagement with the content their respective audiences are likely to encounter. To this end, we compute engagement rate as interactions per view, which controls for differential exposure and allows fair comparison of sentiment effect sizes. Leveraging X's recent public view count data availability (available since Dec. 15, 2022), we compiled the largest news-tweet dataset with view statistics: 5.8 million tweets posted between Dec. 15, 2022 to May 31, 2023 that generated 78.6 billion views and 465.9 million interactions. This comprehensive dataset enables robust calculation of engagement rates, a standard metric used by both X [33] and academic researchers [15].

Framing Note: The above content-based approach does not infer Twitter users' ideological positions. Instead, it leverages the platform's tendency to expose users to content aligned with their prior engagement or preferences. Although this may not hold for every user or content, performing large-scale statistical analysis (as done in this study) reveals engagement patterns that closely approximate those expected under explicit user ideology inference. Crucially, our findings retain their importance even without relying on this assumption, as they reveal how sentiment affects engagement with content from different types of publishers on X. We focus on X due to its unique suitability for this type of analysis: it publicly exposes view count data, hosts an active ecosystem of news publishers, and has the highest proportion of its users who rely on it for news in the U.S., with 59% of its users getting news from the platform, compared to, for example, 48% for Facebook, 40% for Instagram, and 37% for YouTube [32].

Key Contributions: This study makes several key contributions to the literature on social media engagement. First, it presents the largest-scale analysis to date of sentiment-driven engagement with news content on X, leveraging 5.8 million tweets and nearly 80 billion views. Second, it introduces an exposure-controlled framework that distinguishes between hyperpartisan and non-hyperpartisan audiences, uncovering statistically significant asymmetries in how these groups respond to sentiment. Third, it disaggregates engagement by interaction type (e.g., likes, retweets, etc.), revealing that negative sentiment disproportionately drives deeper forms of engagement. Finally, it offers rigorous robustness checks for confounding factors such as topic, novelty, temporal variation, and publisher prominence, ensuring the generalizability of its findings.

Example Findings and Beneficiaries: Compared with related work (see Sect. 2), this study offers the first large-scale analysis of how sentiment impacts news followers' engagement, especially among hyperpartisan users across the political spectrum, while controlling for exposure factor. Our findings reveal a clear asymmetry in the news domain: shallow interactions (likes) tend to increase with positive sentiment, whereas deeper engagement (retweets, replies, quotes) is more influenced by negative sentiment. Furthermore, negative sentiment significantly boosts engagement with hyperpartisan publishers, regardless of whether they lean left or right. Importantly, these patterns remain robust after controlling for potential confounders such as topic, novelty, and temporal variations (see Sect. 7). These insights can help news publishers tailor content strategies for targeted audience engagement, while providing policymakers with evidence-based approaches to mitigate the spread of polarizing content.

Outline: We first contextualize our study within the related work (Sect. 2). We then define key metrics with a motivating example (Sect. 3) and describe our methodology and dataset (Sect. 4). Next, we present our analysis (Sect. 5–Sect. 6) and robustness checks (Sect. 7), before concluding the paper (Sect. 8).

2   Related Work

While engagement levels across different classes of news publishers have been studied on platforms such as Facebook [14] and Twitter [20], most prior research remains descriptive. Our study instead investigates the causal drivers of engagement, focusing on how tweet sentiment modulates reader interactions.

Some other studies have explored various factors influencing user engagement across social media platforms, including the posts text [21,30] and their topic [5]. A significant body of literature here focus on sentiment's role in driving engagement [3,7,26]. Our research instead focuses on news content and examines the differential effect of sentiment among different classes of users.

Finally, a small but growing body of work has investigated what drives engagement with news posts on social media. For instance, Aldous et al. [2] analysed posts from 53 news organisations to test how topic shapes audience reactions. Although our analysis centres on sentiment, we demonstrate that our conclusions are robust across topics. As another example, Rathje et al. [25] analyzed ~2 M posts from liberal and conservative parties, finding that negative language consistently increased engagement across the political spectrum. By contrast, other work reports higher engagement for positive sentiment (e.g., in [31]). Our work addresses these contradictions by controlling for exposure, distinguishing between

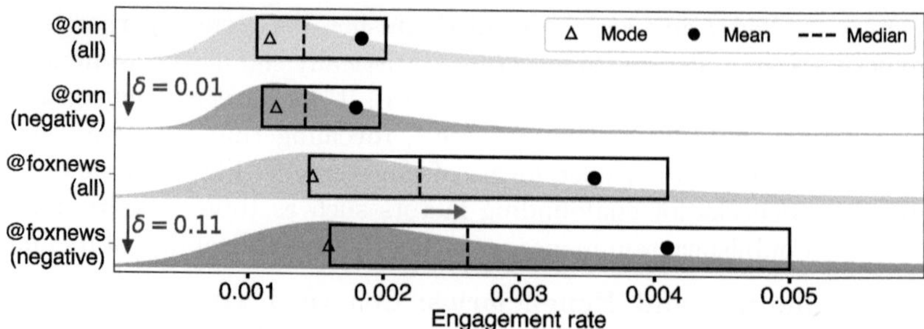

Fig. 1. Engagement rate distributions for all tweets from @cnn and @foxnews and their negative tweets. The x-axis is limited to [0, 0.006] for enhanced resolution.

user groups, and contrasting the impact of positive versus negative tone on shallow and deep interactions (c.f. Figs. 4 and 5 and Table 2). Heiss et al. [23], using 1,915 Facebook posts, reported higher interaction rates for negative or humorous content. Using our substantially larger corpus (5.8 M tweets), we extend these insights by examining differential effects across user classes and demonstrating that effect magnitude varies by interaction type.

In summary, our study offers several key methodological advancements: It represents the largest-scale analysis, identifies hyperpartisan user exposure, controls for differential exposure, comprehensively analyzes sub-interactions, implements rigorous controls for various factors including topic, and utilizes state-of-the-art tweet feature extraction methods (Sect. 4.1).

3   Key Metrics and Motivating Example

To examine sentiment's impact on news tweets engagement, we first establish a standardized impact measure through an illustrative example.

3.1   Engagement Rate Distributions

As explained in the introduction, we compute the engagement rate of a tweet as the ratio of the total number of interactions (likes, retweets, replies, quotes) that it receives to the number of times it is viewed. This corresponds to the rate at which views of the tweet result in user interaction. Figure 1 shows the engagement rate distributions for four subsets of tweets: (1) all CNN tweets, (2) CNN tweets with negative sentiment, (3) all FoxNews tweets, and (4) FoxNews tweets with negative sentiment. Here, we analyzed all the 16,057 CNN tweets and 35,146 FoxNews tweets in our dataset (Sect. 4), and visualize the distributions using two complementary plot variations: (1) density plots, and (2) boxplots, where the boxplots depict each distribution's interquartile range (IQR), with the median and mean marked by a dashed line and solid circles, respectively.

Comparing these distributions highlights a key insight: directly comparing negative tweet engagement rate distributions of the two publishers is misleading because @foxnews consistently experiences higher baseline engagement, regardless of sentiment. This difference likely stems from variations in the publishers' follower base, their network structures, and bot activity. This inherent difference in baseline engagement between publishers highlights that a fair evaluation of the impact of using a negative (or positive) sentiment must instead assess how negative sentiment affects engagement within each publisher's context.

A potential method to assess this effect is to consider the shift in median engagement for each publisher, as illustrated by the red arrow for @foxnews in Fig. 1. However, this approach is sensitive to the original engagement level, making fair cross-publisher comparisons challenging, and by focusing only on central tendencies, it overlooks the broader distribution. To address these issues, we next introduce a more robust metric for fair comparisons.

3.2 A Fair Measure of Sentiment Impact

The distributions we analyze violate some key prerequisites for parametric effect size methods, such as normality (even on log scale). For example, the density plots in Fig. 1 reveal the presence of heavily skewed distributions, making many common effect size statistics, including those from the Cohen family of tests, inappropriate, as they could produce misleading results [12]. For this reason, we utilize the non-parametric dominance delta statistic [12]:

$$\delta(X, Y) = P(X > Y) - P(X < Y) = \frac{\#(x_i > y_j) - \#(x_i < y_j)}{|X| \cdot |Y|}, \qquad (1)$$

where $x_i \in X$ and $y_j \in Y$ are the set of samples of each distribution X and Y to be compared, and $\#$ denotes the count of instances satisfying a given condition. As an example, to measure the impact that the use of negative sentiment may have had on the engagement rate of the tweets by a particular publisher p, we let $X = \mathcal{R}_-^p$ be the distribution of the engagement rates of the publisher's posts with negative sentiment and $Y = \mathcal{R}_{all}^p$ capture the engagement rates associated with the full set of the publisher's tweets.

With this normalized definition, the value of δ ranges from -1 to 1, where positive values indicate that a negative sentiment generally results in higher engagement rates (i.e., X tends to have larger values than Y) for that publisher. We further note that this definition of delta provides a "good control of Type I error even when there are many tied values, a situation that may be problematic for competing methods" [12]. Yet, to ensure the robustness of our findings, we have conducted additional checks with alternative metrics (discussed in [12], Chap. 5). While specific values of the observed differences varied between metrics, the overall patterns and relationships we observed persist.

3.3 Numeric Example: The Effect of Negative Sentiment on Tweets by CNN vs. Fox News

Applying the above delta measure to negative sentiment yields 0.11 for @foxnews versus 0.01 for @cnn. This substantial difference in delta scores aligns with the

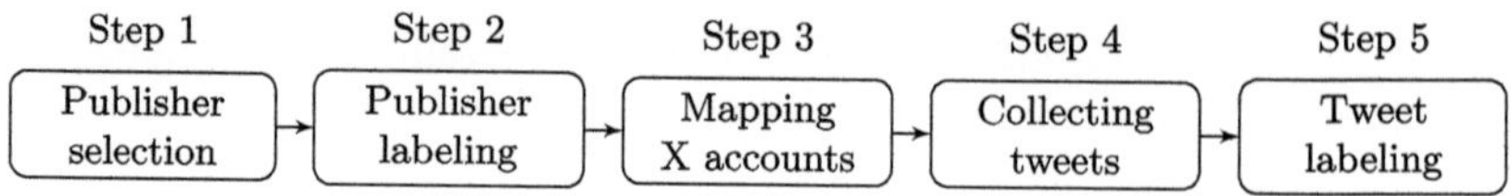

Fig. 2. Dataset compilation workflow

patterns observed in Fig. 1, where we observe much bigger visual differences for @foxnews than for @cnn. Statistical analysis further corroborates these findings: a Kruskal-Wallis test (Sect. 4.3) yields a significant difference between $\mathcal{R}^{fox}_{-}$ and $\mathcal{R}^{fox}_{all}$ (p-value $= 2.58 \times 10^{-62}$), while the difference between $\mathcal{R}^{cnn}_{-}$ and $\mathcal{R}^{cnn}_{all}$ is not statistically significant (p-value $= 0.13$). These delta scores capture sentiment-specific engagement shifts, allowing for meaningful cross-publisher comparisons more robust to confounding factors like audience size and bot activity. Motivated by these strengths, we base our later analysis on this metric.

4   Methodology and Dataset

To allow comparisons of the sentiments' effects on different classes of publishers (e.g., hyperpartisan vs. non-hyperpartisan, *Left* vs. *Right*), including how the primary type of engagement may change differently; we collected a large, labeled dataset spanning 1,806 publishers. Next, we describe the data collection and give an overview of the dataset and statistical methods used in our analysis.

4.1   Multi-step Dataset Creation

Our dataset was created using a five-step process (Fig. 2). First, we compiled the list of all 4,109 U.S. news outlets on Media Bias Fact Check (MBFC), a widely used and trusted evaluator of the bias and reliability of different outlets [1,24].

Second, we assigned bias and hyperpartisan labels to the news outlets (publishers). We began with bias labels from MBFC. To assign bias labels to 309 unlabeled publishers, we trained a KDE model using scores from Robertson et al. [27], excluding 112 publishers whose bias could not be inferred. Next, publishers classified as extreme left or right (*Left* and *Right*) were labeled as *hyperpartisan*, while neutral and less biased publishers were labeled as *non-hyperpartisan*, and reliability labels (*reliable* or *unreliable*) were added based on the latest (Apr. 2024) release of the Iffy index [16], which itself relies on the MBFC labels and is widely used by previous works [22].

Third, we linked publishers to their corresponding X accounts by visiting their official websites, discarding 407 publishers without identified accounts.

Fourth, we collected all tweets posted by the identified accounts, along with the associated user interactions (likes, retweets, quotes, replies) and views, during the period Dec. 15, 2022, to May 31, 2023. For 1,806 randomly sampled publishers we obtained complete tweet records, ensuring balanced coverage across outlet sizes and laying the foundation for our subsequent analysis.

Table 1. Dataset summary statistics (Here, B = Billion, M = Million, K = Kilo)

Group		Outlets	Followers	Tweets	Interactions	Views	Eng. rate
Non-hyper		1,353	525.5 M	4.8 M	143.5 M	45.0 B	0.0032
Hyper	Left	223	189.4 M	471.2 K	125.2 M	15.2 B	0.0083
	Right	230	88.8 M	510.5 K	197.2 M	18.4 B	0.0107
	Left+Right	453	278.2 M	981.8 K	322.4 M	33.6 B	0.0096
Total		1,806	803.7 M	5.8 M	465.9 M	78.6 B	0.0059

Fifth, we labeled every tweet for its sentiment and topic. For sentiment, we employed the model presented in [6], which offers state-of-the-art models for various social media analysis tasks. Specifically, for sentiment labels, we use their RoBERTa model, initially trained on approximately 124 million tweets and subsequently fine-tuned using the SemEval-2017 sentiment analysis task dataset [28]. This model achieved a macro recall (i.e., the unweighted average of class-wise recall scores) of 0.72 on the benchmark dataset, signifying its leading position [6]. Although not fine-tuned specifically on political tweets, the model was trained on a broad set of informal and subjective content [6], enabling it to generalize to socially and emotionally charged language. This makes it particularly suitable for analyzing sentiment in politically relevant discourse, where rule-based tools like VADER, which according to our experiments achieved a macro recall of 0.54 on the same benchmark, often struggle with sarcasm and context.

For topic analysis, we employed BERTopic [13], selected for its superior performance in extracting coherent and meaningful topics, as well as for its ability to handle the unstructured and brief nature of tweets effectively [9]. Here, we compute embeddings using the specialized Twitter language model, TimeLMs, which outperforms other models across various subtasks [19].

4.2   Dataset Overview

Our final dataset includes the number of *views* and user *interactions* of each type (i.e., *likes, retweets, replies, quotes*) for all tweets by 1,806 labeled news *outlets* (X accounts) between Dec. 15, 2022, and May 31, 2023. Collectively, these accounts had 803.7 M *followers* (as of Mar. 2023), 78.6 B views, and 465.9 M interactions. Table 1 provides a detailed breakdown of these statistics, categorizing the outlets into non-hyperpartisan and hyperpartisan (further subdivided into *Left* and *Right*) groups. In the table, we also include the totals across all publishers (final row) and the total *engagement rate* ("Eng. rate") for each category (last column), measured as the ratio between the total number of user interactions and the view count for that category. We note that hyperpartisan publishers achieve noticeably higher engagement rates than their non-hyperpartisan counterparts, likely due to their followers' higher activity rates [29]. However, these summary statistics only scratch the surface. The main driver behind our research is instead to answer a much deeper aspect – the role and impact of sentiment –

with the aim of uncovering the relationships between tweet sentiment and follower engagement rates across these outlet categories. To address this issue, we employ rigorous statistical analysis, as outlined next.

4.3 Statistical Analysis

Since the engagement rate and delta distributions often violate normality assumptions, even after transformation, parametric methods such as t-tests, ANOVA, and the Cohen family of tests are unsuitable. Therefore, we employ five nonparametric techniques: (1) the Kruskal-Wallis test for overall distribution and medians comparisons, (2) the Dunn test for post-hoc analysis following significant findings, (3) bootstrapping with $100\,K$ iterations and a 99% confidence interval for mean estimation, (4) the Wilcoxon signed-rank test to assess deviations from constants, and (5) the delta statistic (described in Sect. 3.2) to quantify effect sizes. This approach avoids biases in unsuitable parametric methods. Finally, we consider p-values below 0.01 as statistically significant, those above 0.1 as non-significant, and explicitly report intermediate values.

4.4 Overview of Robustness Strategy

To validate the reliability of our findings, we implement a multi-step robustness strategy (see Sect. 7), addressing several potential confounders. These include topical variation (by performing within-topic sentiment effect comparisons), sentiment prevalence (to account for novelty effects), and temporal shifts (by replicating our analysis across multiple time windows). We further examine whether our results hold across different subsets of publishers, including less prominent accounts and unreliable sources. By proactively addressing these confounders, we strengthen the causal interpretation of our sentiment-driven engagement effects and demonstrate the stability of our findings across diverse conditions.

5 High-Level Sentiment Effects on Engagement

Let us first consider the effects that sentiment has on user engagement at large, ignoring publishers' classification.

5.1 Impact on Total User Engagement

For this analysis, we consider the relative impact that the use of different sentiments has on each publisher's user engagement rate. Specifically, for each publisher $p \in \mathcal{P}$, we first use Eq. (1), as outlined in Sect. 3.2, to calculate $\delta(\mathcal{R}^p_S, \mathcal{R}^p_{all})$ for three types of sentiments S: negative $(-)$, positive $(+)$, and neutral (n). Then, we compare the overall distributions of these three delta definitions, as observed across all publishers $\mathcal{P}$.

Figure 3 shows the cumulative distribution functions (CDFs) of the delta distributions for the three sentiments S, when calculated across all $|\mathcal{P}| = 1,806$

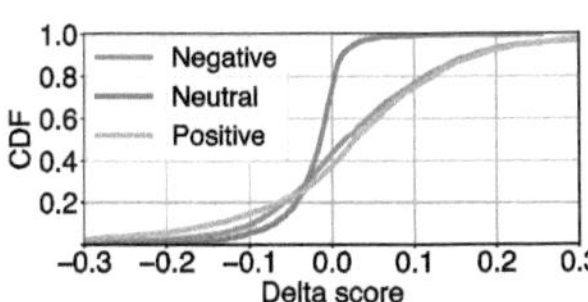
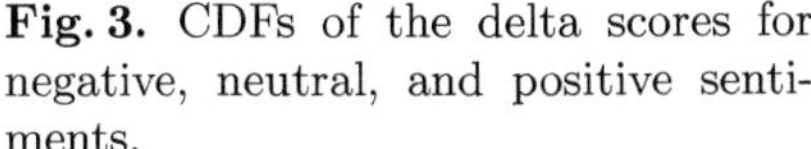

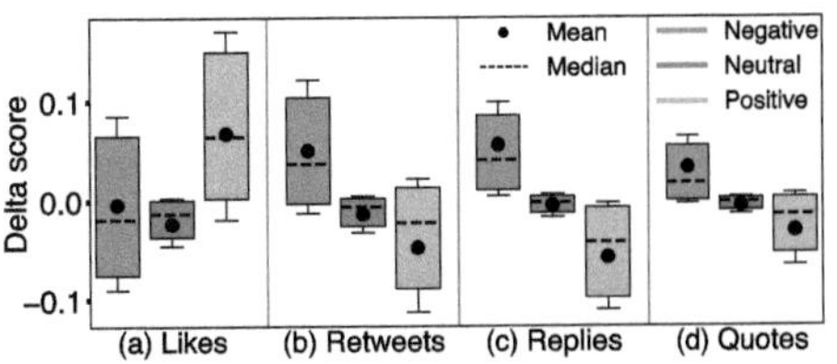

Fig. 3. CDFs of the delta scores for negative, neutral, and positive sentiments.

Fig. 4. Distribution of delta scores for four interaction types and different sentiments

publishers. To provide better resolution, we limit the x-range $[-0.3, 0.3]$ of visible delta scores. Several observations can be made from this figure. First, sentiment significantly affects engagement rates. This is supported by Kruskal-Wallis test ($p\text{-}value = 2.26 \times 10^{-84}$) and post-hoc Dunn tests showing that the positive and negative sentiment delta distributions differ from the neutral one, though there is no significant difference between the positive and negative sentiment distributions (when calculated across all publishers). In the later section, we will see that this is not the case when looking closer at specific subsets of publishers, where the differences instead may be large.

Focusing on the type of effects, neutral sentiment generally has minimal impact on engagement rates, with the least variance; e.g., 98% of its distribution falls between -0.2 and 0.1. In contrast, both negative and positive sentiments have a more pronounced positive effect on engagement, with over 60% of their delta scores being positive, compared to just 21% for neutral sentiment. This shows that tweets with negative or positive sentiments tend to increase engagement compared to overall and neutral content.

While positive and negative sentiment exhibit similar overall effects on engagement, we have found more significant differences when considering what interactions they generate. To capture this, we next provide a deeper study into how different sentiments influence various forms of user interactions.

5.2   Impact Across Interaction Types

To study the differences between interaction types, we first break down the engagement rate that can be attributed to each interaction type: likes, retweets, replies, and quotes. Then, for each interaction type I and sentiment S, we use the delta function (Eq. (1)) to compare the relative impact that the sentiment S appears to have on the engagement rate of interaction type I: $\delta(\mathcal{R}^p_{I,S}, \mathcal{R}^p_{I,all})$.

Figure 4 shows a boxplot for the delta distributions for each of the four interaction types, as calculated over all $|\mathcal{P}|$ publishers. Using our previous notation, this corresponds to $\Delta_{I,S} = \{\delta(\mathcal{R}^p_{I,S}, \mathcal{R}^p_{I,all})\}_{p \in \mathcal{P}}$. Hereon, for each boxplot, we show the 20–80 percentiles across the whiskers (for better resolution), and the main body of the box represents the IQR, with the mean and median also marked.

Several observations are possible. First, for each interaction type, the Kruskal-Wallis test, followed by post-hoc Dunn tests, reveals statistically significant differences among the three sentiment-specific distributions (negative, neutral, and positive). Furthermore, bootstrapping analysis (Sect. 4.3) confirms the statistical significance of the patterns observed among the means in Fig. 4.

Second, we observe distinct patterns for shallow (likes) and deeper interactions (retweets, replies, and quotes). While positive sentiment is most effective in shallow interactions, negative sentiment is most effective for attracting deeper interactions. Most of the positive sentiment's delta distribution for likes ($\Delta_{Like,+}$) shows positive values: mean (0.07), median (0.07), and 76% of the distribution are all positive. In contrast, negative ($\Delta_{Like,-}$) and neutral sentiment ($\Delta_{Like,n}$) show mostly negative values. The Wilcoxon test confirms significant deviations from zero for all three sentiments.

In contrast, for deeper interactions, the effect is reversed: positive sentiment reduces engagement, while negative sentiment boosts it across retweets, replies, and quotes. The Wilcoxon test also supports these deviations. The largest sentiment-driven difference appears in replies, with a median gap of 0.07 and a mean difference of 0.09 between positive and negative sentiment. Quotes exhibit the smallest, but still significant, difference, with a median gap of 0.03.

> **Takeaway:** Positive sentiment tends to increase the shallow forms of interactions, while for deeper forms of interaction, negative sentiment has the most positive effect.

One possible explanation for this pattern is that negative sentiment may evoke a stronger emotional response and a greater desire to actively engage with the content, either to express agreement, disagree, or provide additional context. In contrast, positive sentiment may be more likely to elicit passive forms of engagement, such as likes, which require less effort and commitment from users.

6 Hyperpartisan vs. Non-hyperpartisan Users

6.1 Comparison of Total Engagement

To investigate how hyperpartisan users are affected by the sentiment differently from non-hyperpartisan users, we next compare the delta score distributions for each sentiment and publisher group. For these comparisons, we simply repeat the previous analysis, but for the two non-overlapping subsets of publishers: hyperpartisan ($\mathcal{P}_H$) and non-hyperpartisan ($\mathcal{P}_{nH}$), where $\mathcal{P} = \mathcal{P}_H \cup \mathcal{P}_{nH}$.

Figure 5 presents the CDFs of the delta scores for each sentiment $S \in \{-, +, n\}$, separately for the $|\mathcal{P}_{nH}|$ non-hyperpartisan publishers (Fig. 5a) and the $|\mathcal{P}_H|$ hyperpartisan (Fig. 5b) publishers. As seen in Fig. 5a, for non-hyperpartisan news publishers and users, positive sentiment significantly increases engagement rates. Notably, we see a clear shift to the right (compared to negative and neutral sentiments) for all percentiles higher than 20, and for 71% of the distribution, we observe positive values. On the other hand, when

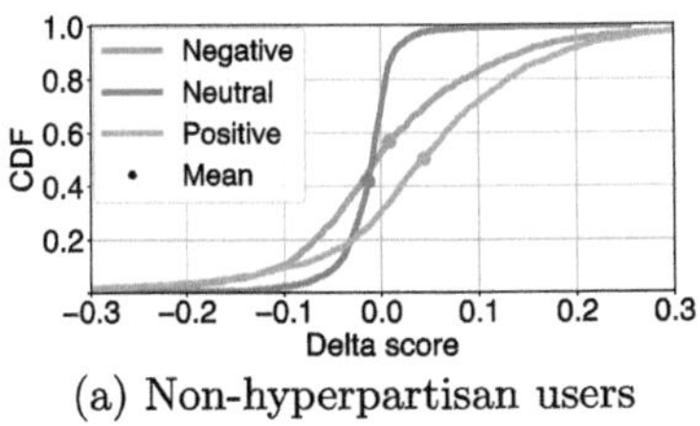

(a) Non-hyperpartisan users

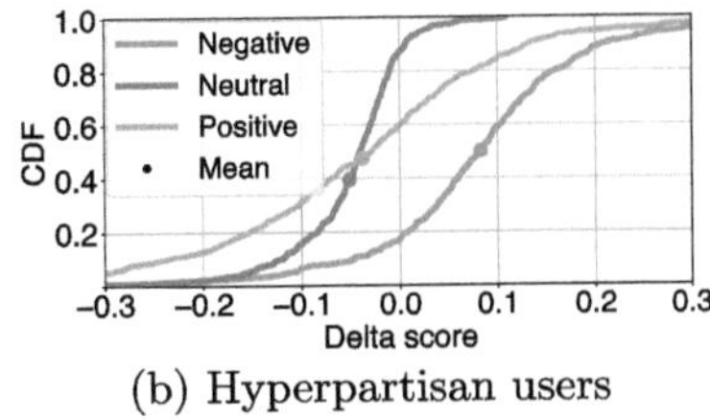

(b) Hyperpartisan users

Fig. 5. CDFs of delta scores for different sentiments

comparing neutral and negative sentiment, different positive and negative effects are seen.

In contrast, for hyperpartisan users (Fig. 5b), negative sentiment has the strongest positive effect on engagement rates, while both neutral and positive sentiments generally reduce engagement (both with the same median). However, neutral sentiment has a less negative impact for lower delta scores, while positive sentiment drives higher engagement for scores above the median. Note also that all the relations we see among the means of the distributions in Fig. 5 are statistically supported by bootstrapping (Sect. 4.3).

> **Takeaway:** Compared to non-hyperpartisan users, hyperpartisan users are statistically significantly more responsive to negative content.

These findings suggest that hyperpartisan users are more responsive to negative content. While one potential contributing factor may be the polarizing nature of the topics covered by these publishers and the emotional resonance of negative sentiment with their beliefs and attitudes, we have found this group's higher engagement with negative posts is consistent also when controlling for topics (Sect. 7). The patterns are significantly different for non-hyperpartisan users, who engage more with positive content, perceived as more informative, constructive, or aligned with their preferences. These results underscore the complex interplay between sentiment, partisanship, and user engagement, highlighting the need for a deeper understanding of these dynamics. We next analyze these effects for each interaction type in more detail.

6.2   Comparisons Across Engagement Types

To quantify the differences in engagement patterns between hyperpartisan ($\mathcal{P}_H$) and non-hyperpartisan ($\mathcal{P}_{nH}$), we extend the previous per-interaction-type analysis (Sect. 5.2). First, for each interaction type I and sentiment S, we calculate delta statistics across all publishers in each of the two groups. As an example, for the hyperpartisan group this would be $\Delta_{I,S}^H = \{\delta(\mathcal{R}_{I,S}^p, \mathcal{R}_{I,all}^p)\}_{p \in \mathcal{P}_H}$. In general, we have observed significant differences in these distributions, as reflected in Table 2, which reports second-order delta values comparing the delta distributions of the groups; i.e., $\delta(\Delta_{I,S}^H, \Delta_{I,S}^{nH})$.

Table 2. Second-order delta scores $(\delta(\Delta_{I,S}^{H}, \Delta_{I,S}^{nH}))$ with positive values showing greater effect on hyperpartisan users.

Sentiment	Like	Retweet	Reply	Quote
Negative	0.47	0.35	0.13	0.22
Neutral	−0.49	−0.42	−0.25	−0.14
Positive	−0.34	−0.35	−0.16	−0.33

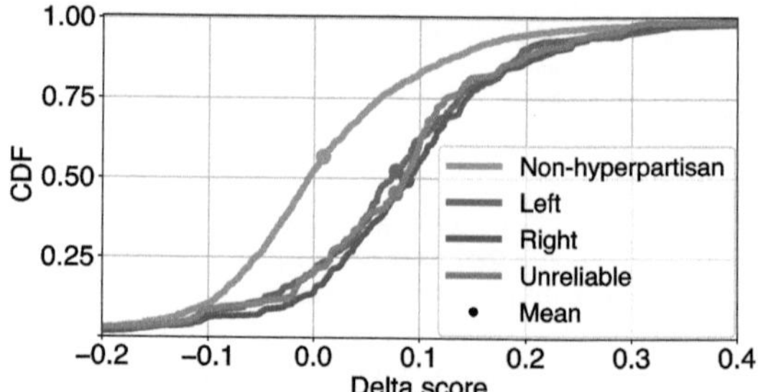

Fig. 6. CDF of negative sentiment delta scores across Non-hyperpartisan, Left, Right, and Unreliable publishers.

From the large positive value in the first row of the table (negative sentiment), it is clear that negative sentiment has a stronger positive impact on engagement for hyperpartisan users compared to non-hyperpartisan users across all interaction types. Conversely, the neutral sentiment (second row) and positive sentiment (third row) have a negative effect on engagement for hyperpartisan users compared to non-hyperpartisan ones (negative values in each column).

The difference is most pronounced for likes, where the negative sentiment has a second-order delta score of 0.47 compared to the negative scores of neutral (−0.49) and positive (−0.34). This is interesting, as like is a relatively shallow interaction type. Of the deeper interaction types, the biggest values are observed for retweets (0.35 vs. −0.42 and −0.35), which is perhaps the lowest-effort interaction of the other interactions. We again note that likes and retweets, which we find are more susceptible to partisan effects, may have a lower effort threshold, allowing for more immediate, emotional responses. In contrast, replies and quotes, which require more cognitive effort and time investment, may be less influenced by partisanship and more by the specific content of the message.

6.3 Comparison Across the Left, Right, and Unreliable Publishers

Left vs. Right: With hyperpartisan publishers (and users) consisting of the extreme left (*Left*) and extreme right (*Right*) groups, we next asked whether the previous section's findings are consistent across the two hyperpartisan subgroups. For this analysis, we repeated the prior analysis but compared the two sets of publishers: *Left* ($\mathcal{P}_L$) and *Right* ($\mathcal{P}_R$), where $\mathcal{P}_L \cup \mathcal{P}_R = \mathcal{P}_H$.

By comparing the delta distributions for the 223 left-leaning and 230 right-leaning hyperpartisan publishers, we found that the patterns hold consistently across both groups. Figure 6 compares the CDFs of delta scores for negative sentiment across non-hyperpartisan, *Left*, *Right*, and unreliable publishers (the latter discussed next). Both hyperpartisan groups exhibit a clear and similar rightward shift, indicating that negative sentiment has a stronger positive effect on engagement rates for hyperpartisan publishers, regardless of political leaning.

Vs. Unreliable Publishers: While hyperpartisan publishers and unreliable publishers are often conflated, they are not synonymous. As an example, according to MBFC and iffy index, "The New Yorker" is hyperpartisan while not unreliable, and "Grunge.com" is unreliable while a non-hyperpartisan publisher. In our dataset, 453 publishers are classified as hyperpartisan ($\mathcal{P}^H$), 158 as unreliable ($\mathcal{P}^U$), and 135 belong to both classifications. Specifically, the proportion of hyperpartisan publishers that are unreliable is 0.30, while the proportion of unreliable publishers that are hyperpartisan is 0.85. This overlap results in a Jaccard similarity coefficient of 0.28, indicating a moderate but not complete overlap between the two categories. Given these characteristics, it is, therefore, natural to ask whether the results generalize when we consider unreliable publishers.

Interestingly, our analysis shows that the key insights apply to both hyperpartisan and unreliable publishers, with no statistically significant differences between them, as confirmed by the Kruskal-Wallis test. Figure 6 illustrates this, displaying similar delta scores for negative sentiment across both groups. These findings suggest that the impact of sentiment on engagement rates is comparable for both hyperpartisan and unreliable publishers, underscoring the robustness of our results across different categorizations of potentially problematic content sources. Our validations confirm that this pattern persists across all sub-interactions when comparing unreliable and hyperpartisan publishers.

7   Discussion and Robustness Checks

This paper offers a large-scale quantitative analysis of how sentiment affects user engagement with news tweets, focusing on its differential impact on hyperpartisan and non-hyperpartisan users. However, questions remain about the reliability, generalizability, and potential confounding factors. In this section, we address these concerns through robustness checks and additional analyses.

Is Topic a Confounder? A key question is whether our findings are influenced by the topics covered by different publishers. For example, do *Right* publishers inherently engage followers more with negative sentiment due to the topic they cover? To study this aspect in detail, we conducted a topic-controlled analysis. Here, we (1) performed topic modeling on tweets from each publisher, (2) excluded the topics that were limited to one sentiment, and then (3) calculated the delta values by sentiment for each topic, and (4) averaged the delta values across all topics of each publisher. Then, we considered the distribution of these "topic-controlled" delta values for each of the two publisher groups.

Figure 7 shows delta-score distributions for negative sentiment, both with (dotted lines) and without (solid lines) topic control. We highlight three key points. First, the differences between hyperpartisan and non-hyperpartisan publishers remain significant. Second, for non-hyperpartisan publishers, the average delta values with topic control (dashed teal line) align closely with the original values (solid teal line), showing no significant difference (Kruskal-Wallis test). This suggests non-hyperpartisan engagement with negative sentiment is consistent regardless of the topic. Third, hyperpartisan publishers show a slight

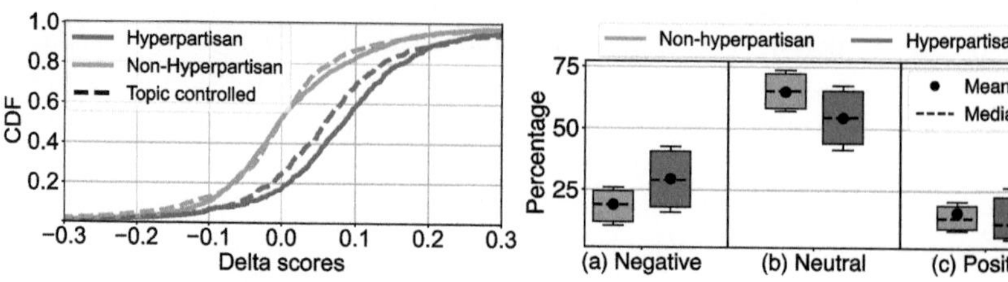

Fig. 7. Delta values: original vs. topic-controlled negative sentiment analysis.

Fig. 8. Percentage of tweets belonging to each sentiment class for hyperpartisan and non-hyperpartisan.

leftward shift in topic-controlled delta values, indicating some of their heightened sensitivity to negative sentiment is topic-driven. However, even after controlling for topics, a significant gap remains between hyperpartisan and non-hyperpartisan distributions, highlighting hyperpartisan users' stronger responsiveness to negative content. These findings confirm that hyperpartisan audiences are particularly responsive to negative sentiment, a pattern only partially influenced by topic.

Novelty Effect Robustness: We next questioned if "information novelty" [11] might explain our findings; i.e., whether rarer sentiments draw higher engagement simply by deviating from the norm. To explore this and to capture current sentiment practices, we analyzed the sentiment distribution of tweets from hyperpartisan and non-hyperpartisan publishers.

Figure 8 shows the distribution of tweet sentiments (negative, neutral, positive) across both publisher types. Key observations include: First, while neutral sentiment dominates, reflecting standard news reporting, hyperpartisan publishers use negative sentiment more frequently: 10% more on average than non-hyperpartisan publishers (29% vs. 19%). This undermines the novelty hypothesis, suggesting the increased engagement with negative content is driven by its emotional appeal rather than its rarity. Additionally, non-hyperpartisan publishers use neutral tones more frequently, with a 12% higher median than hyperpartisan publishers, likely catering to audiences seeking balanced reporting. No significant difference is seen in the use of positive sentiment, indicating that non-hyperpartisan audiences' engagement with positive content is not due to scarcity. These findings invalidate the novelty effect while highlighting strategic sentiment usage differences. Hyperpartisan publishers are more likely to emphasize negative sentiment, which drives engagement among their audiences through emotional resonance, while non-hyperpartisan publishers favor neutral content.

Sensitivity Analysis of Sample Size: We also confirmed that our findings remain robust across publisher sizes: as we expanded our analysis from top-followed to less prominent publishers, the observed gap in sensitivity to negative sentiment between hyperpartisan and non-hyperpartisan users persisted.

Time Window and Temporal Robustness: Since online platforms and user behaviors evolve, sentiment-driven engagement may vary over time. To assess whether our conclusions are temporally robust, we divided our 167-day dataset into four almost equal periods and analyzed each separately. Despite smaller sample sizes requiring a relaxed significance threshold ($p < 0.1$ instead of $p < 0.01$), the findings remained consistent across all periods. This suggests that our results are robust within the studied timeframe, though future work could explore how news cycles, political events, and algorithmic changes impact these dynamics over longer periods.

Limitations and Future Directions: Our study comes with certain limitations that may suggest some promising areas for future research. First, we focus only on U.S. publishers due to the complexities of aligning political leanings across countries. Future studies can explore other nations' news ecosystems. Additionally, the lack of qualitative analysis on psychological factors behind sentiment responses opens the door for complementing user interviews. Third, our study examines user sensitivity to content from news publishers, which may not fully generalize to all platform interactions (e.g., friends' posts). Future studies can explore engagement beyond the news domain for a broader understanding.

Finally, our analysis relies solely on MBFC for outlet classification, which may raise concerns about bias or subjectivity in labeling. However, MBFC was chosen for its comprehensive coverage and public accessibility, and its reliability has been empirically supported. For example, a recent study [17] showed that MBFC's ratings are highly consistent with other established evaluators, including the proprietary NewsGuard ratings. This cross-source alignment provides strong evidence for the reliability of our classification scheme. Nonetheless, labels such as "hyperpartisan" or "unreliable" are inherently subjective and can evolve over time. Moreover, our analysis relies on publisher-level classifications to infer aggregate engagement patterns, rather than making user-level ideological assignments. While this mitigates some privacy concerns, mislabeling publishers could still propagate inaccuracies into the interpretation of user behavior. To reduce this risk, we relied on validated public taxonomies such as MBFC and the Iffy Index, but we acknowledge that we do not directly triangulate with alternative taxonomies such as AllSides or the Faris et al. report [10]. Future work could explore the effects of classification uncertainty and incorporate additional labeling frameworks to further assess the generalization.

8   Conclusion

Leveraging robust effect size metrics, this paper provides the first large-scale, exposure-controlled differential analysis of how sentiment affects user engagement with news content on X, distinguishing between hyperpartisan and non-hyperpartisan audiences across 1,806 publishers and nearly 80 billion views.

As one illustrative example of our main findings, we observe a systematic asymmetry: hyperpartisan audiences are consistently more responsive to negative sentiment, whereas non-hyperpartisan users engage disproportionately more with positive sentiment. These patterns are consistent across various interaction types, though their magnitudes may vary.

Importantly, our results remain robust after controlling for topical differences, account prominence, sentiment prevalence, and temporal variations. This robustness confirms that the engagement patterns reflect underlying behavioral tendencies rather than confounding artifacts. We also find that unreliable publishers exhibit sentiment-driven engagement patterns similar to hyperpartisan outlets, underscoring the generality of our findings across diverse categories of potentially problematic content.

These findings offer practical implications for multiple stakeholders. Content strategists and publishers can tailor sentiment framing for different audiences; for instance, emphasizing positively framed content for non-hyperpartisan users, who are more receptive to it. For recommender system designers and platform engineers, incorporating sentiment-aware ranking or diversification strategies may help mitigate the amplification of polarizing content, especially among hyperpartisan audiences. Policymakers and regulators can also use these insights to design transparency mandates, auditing mechanisms, and targeted moderation frameworks that promote healthier digital discourse. Underpinning these recommendations, our study rigorously quantifies how sentiment and partisanship interact to shape user engagement, providing statistically grounded insights to guide sentiment-aware content strategies and platform governance.

Acknowledgment. This work was partially supported by the Wallenberg AI, Autonomous Systems and Software Program (WASP) funded by the Knut and Alice Wallenberg Foundation.

References

1. Aires, V.P., Nakamura, F.G., Nakamura, E.F.: A link-based approach to detect media bias in news websites. In: Proceedings of the ACM WWW (2019)
2. Aldous, K.K., An, J., Jansen, B.J.: View, like, comment, post: analyzing user engagement by topic at 4 levels across 5 social media platforms for 53 news organizations. In: Proceedings of the ICWSM (2019)
3. Antypas, D., Preece, A., Camacho-Collados, J.: Negativity spreads faster: a large-scale multilingual twitter analysis on the role of sentiment in political communication. Online Soc. Netw. Media **33** (2023)
4. Bär, D., Calderon, F., Lawlor, M., Licklederer, S., Totzauer, M., Feuerriegel, S.: Analyzing social media activities at bellingcat. In: Proceedings of the WebSci (2023)
5. Baxi, M.K., Sharma, R., Mago, V.: Studying topic engagement and synergy among candidates for 2020 us elections. Soc. Netw. Anal. Min. **12**(1) (2022)
6. Camacho-Collados, J., Rezaee, K., Riahi, T., Asahi, U., et al.: TweetNLP: cutting-edge natural language processing for social media. In: Proceedings of the EMNLP (2022)
7. Cheng, Z., Li, Y.: Like, comment, and share on tiktok: exploring the effect of sentiment and second-person view on the user engagement with tiktok news videos. Soc. Sci. Comput. Rev. **42**(1) (2023)

8. de León, E., Makhortykh, M., Adam, S.: Hyperpartisan, alternative, and conspiracy media users: an anti-establishment portrait. J. Pol. Commun. **41**(6) (2024)

9. Egger, R., Yu, J.: A topic modeling comparison between LDA, NMF, top2vec, and bertopic to demystify twitter posts. Front. Sociol. **7** (2022)

10. Faris, R., Roberts, H., Etling, B., Bourassa, N., Zuckerman, E., Benkler, Y.: Partisanship, propaganda, and disinformation: Online media and the 2016 US presidential election. Berkman Klein Center Research Publication **6** (2017)

11. Gabrilovich, E., Dumais, S., Horvitz, E.: Newsjunkie: providing personalized newsfeeds via analysis of information novelty. In: Proceedings of the ACM WWW (2004)

12. Grissom, R.J., Kim, J.J.: Effect Sizes for Research: Univariate and Multivariate Applications. Routledge (2012)

13. Grootendorst, M.: Bertopic: neural topic modeling with a class-based TF-IDF procedure (2022). https://arxiv.org/abs/2203.05794

14. Hiaeshutter-Rice, D., Weeks, B.: Understanding audience engagement with mainstream and alternative news posts on Facebook. Digit. Journalism **9**(5) (2021)

15. Hwong, Y.L., Oliver, C., Van Kranendonk, M., Sammut, C., Seroussi, Y.: What makes you tick? The psychology of social media engagement in space science communication. Comput. Hum. Behav. **68** (2017)

16. Josef Verbanac: Iffy news (2024). https://www.iffy.news/. Accessed 10 June 2024

17. Lin, H., et al.: High level of correspondence across different news domain quality rating sets. PNAS Nexus **2**(9) (2023)

18. Lorenz, A., Schmitt, C., McGregor, S., Malmer, D.: "CNN can kiss my as\$": a novel description of hyperpartisan U.S. news consumers. J. Quant. Description Digit. Media **3** (2023)

19. Loureiro, D., Barbieri, F., Neves, L., Espinosa Anke, L., Camacho-collados, J.: TimeLMs: diachronic language models from twitter. In: Proceedings of the ACL (2022)

20. Mohammadinodooshan, A., Carlsson, N.: Understanding engagement dynamics with (un) reliable news publishers on twitter. In: Proceedings of the ASONAM, pp. 36–47 (2024)

21. Mohammadinodooshan, A., Carlsson, N.: Successful rhetorics: how do linguistic dimensions affect user engagement with different news categories on twitter? In: Proceedings of the ICWSM, vol. 19 (2025)

22. Pierri, F., Luceri, L., Jindal, N., Ferrara, E.: Propaganda and misinformation on Facebook and twitter during the Russian invasion of Ukraine. In: Proceedings of the Websci (2023)

23. Raffael Heiss, D.S., Matthes, J.: What drives interaction in political actors' Facebook posts? Profile and content predictors of user engagement and political actors' reactions. Inf. Commun. Soc. **22**(10) (2019)

24. Rao, A., Morstatter, F., Lerman, K.: Retweets amplify the echo chamber effect. In: Proceedings of the ASONAM, pp. 30–37 (2023)

25. Rathje, S., Bavel, J.J.V., van der Linden, S.: Out-group animosity drives engagement on social media. Proc. Natl. Acad. Sci. **118**(26) (2021)

26. Robertson, C.E., Pröllochs, N., Schwarzenegger, K., Pärnamets, P., et al.: Negativity drives online news consumption. Nat. Hum. Behav. **7**(5) (2023)

27. Robertson, R.E., Jiang, S., Joseph, K., Friedland, L., Lazer, D., Wilson, C.: Auditing partisan audience bias within google search. In: Proceedings of the CSCW (2018)

28. Rosenthal, S., Farra, N., Nakov, P.: SemEval-2017 task 4: sentiment analysis in Twitter. In: Proceedings of Semantic Evaluation Workshop (SemEval-2017) (2017)

29. Shivaram, K., Bilgic, M., Shapiro, M., Culotta, A.: Forecasting political news engagement on social media. In: Proceedings of the ICWSM (2024)
30. Toraman, C., Şahinuç, F., Yilmaz, E.H., Akkaya, I.B.: Understanding social engagements: a comparative analysis of user and text features in twitter. Soc. Netw. Anal. Min. **12**(1), 47 (2022)
31. Trilling, D., Tolochko, P., Burscher, B.: From newsworthiness to shareworthiness: how to predict news sharing based on article characteristics. Journalism Mass Commun. Q. **94**(1) (2017)
32. Walker, M., Matsa, K.E.: Social media and news fact sheet (2024). https://pewresearch.org/journalism/fact-sheet/social-media-and-news-fact-sheet
33. X Help Center: About your activity dashboard (2024). https://help.x.com/en/managing-your-account

Analysis of Cross-Platform Narrative Dissemination Through Contextual Focal Structures

Ridwan Amure[1] and Nitin Agarwal[1,2(⊠)]

[1] COSMOS Research Center, University of Arkansas, Little Rock, USA
`raamure@ualr.edu`
[2] International Computer Science Institute, University of California, Berkeley, USA
`nxagarwal@ualr.edu`

Abstract. This study investigates how political discourse spreads across social media by identifying influential user groups, termed focal structures. We construct a cross-platform multiplex network linking users and narratives, and apply the Contextual Focal Structures Analysis (CFSA) algorithm to detect context-specific influence. Focusing on Taiwan's 2024 presidential election, we analyze 4,817 Instagram, 2,560 TikTok, 11,134 X, and 7,327 YouTube posts. Our findings reveal that influence often stems not from individuals but from coordinated or organically aligned groups shaping narratives across platforms. This work presents a scalable method for modeling narrative-driven influence, highlighting the importance of understanding cross-platform coordination in shaping political perceptions.

Keywords: Contextual Focal Structures · Multiplex Networks · Narrative Propagation · Influential Groups of Users · Social Media · Instagram · TikTok · YouTube · X/Twitter

1 Introduction

Social media platforms like Twitter, Facebook, Instagram, YouTube, and TikTok have revolutionized how information is created, shared, and consumed. With billions of users and low entry barriers, they offer unprecedented access to audiences, making them central to personal expression, activism, marketing, and political discourse. However, this openness also facilitates the spread of misinformation, disinformation, and strategic narratives, necessitating frameworks to analyze influence and information diffusion [1,15].

The ease of account creation and algorithmic affordances encourage users to maintain identities across multiple platforms [12], allowing narratives to propagate fluidly between them. Understanding groups that coordinate such diffusion is critical, as these actors—ranging from grassroots to state-sponsored—play central roles in amplifying messages. Importantly, narrative spread often involves

A. An et al. (Eds.): ASONAM 2025, LNCS 16323, pp. 119–127, 2026.
https://doi.org/10.1007/978-3-032-13821-7_11

loosely connected users, making traditional user-user network analysis insufficient [6].

To identify influential actors, centrality measures help highlight key individuals, while group-level influence is better captured through algorithms like the Focal Structure Algorithm [16] and its extensions. Alassad et al. [5] introduced a bi-level optimization approach that balances local influence and global modularity, which later evolved into the Contextual Focal Structures Analysis (CFSA) model [4], capable of capturing influence across multiplex and contextual layers.

This study aims to extract and contextualize influential groups driving cross-platform narratives. Rather than isolating individual influencers, the goal is to uncover hidden, coordinated structures shaping public discourse. By focusing on structural and contextual dynamics, this research contributes to identifying influence campaigns and enhancing digital transparency.

2   Related Works

The section discusses the scholarly related to the current study. Since our research is based on narratives, we begin our discussion from computational narratology and then present works done on identifying focal structures in social networks.

2.1   Computational Narratology

Narratives offer a powerful lens for analyzing large text corpora, particularly in dynamic environments such as social media. Over time, narrative extraction has shifted from manual techniques to automated, machine learning-based approaches [6], enabling the analysis of complex events such as the South China Sea dispute [8].

Recent advances in natural language processing—particularly large language models (LLMs) like GPT-4—have further enhanced this process. LLMs have been shown to generate and extract narratives effectively across contexts. Prior studies highlight their performance: Shakeri et al. [14] used GPT-3 for storytelling; Beguš [7] found GPT-4 produced richer, more diverse narratives; and Lynch et al. [11] reported that 87.43% of GPT-4 narratives matched the intent of structured prompts.

With its multimodal capabilities and proven performance, GPT-4 offers a robust and scalable solution for extracting narratives from unstructured, cross-platform social media data.

2.2   Identifying Focal Structures in Social Networks

Previous research has laid a strong foundation for identifying influential user groups in social media networks. Şen et al. [16] introduced the concept of "focal structure sets"—small groups capable of mobilizing public discourse—using a greedy algorithm to detect influence on platforms like Twitter and Facebook.

Alassad et al. [5] further advanced this work with a bi-level optimization model that combined local centrality and global modularity to identify co-commenter groups spreading fake news on YouTube.

However, these methods primarily focus on unimodal user-user interactions, limiting their ability to account for contextual factors. To address this, Alassad and Agarwal [4] proposed the Contextual Focal Structures Analysis (CFSA) model, which incorporates multiplex networks to capture layered behaviors—such as user-user ties and hashtag co-occurrence—enhancing interpretability and contextual relevance.

Building on this, Akinnubi et al. [2,3] introduced a Cartesian merge model that constructs multiplex networks across topic, entity, and document layers. Leveraging CFSA, they identified context-specific influential entities, demonstrating the model's adaptability across complex, heterogeneous data environments.

3   Data

This study focuses on the 2024 Taiwan Presidential Election, examining a multi-platform anti-disinformation campaign that emerged following the election results. The initiative reflects a "whole-of-society" effort to counter false information amid growing concerns about disinformation intended to delegitimize the election, particularly in the context of Taiwan's evolving democracy and ongoing tensions with China [10]. Social media played a central role in both spreading and countering misinformation, with fact-checking efforts becoming a key line of defense.

Data was collected through a multi-stage process across platforms. Initial seed posts were retrieved using keywords like #Taiwan and #TaiwanElection. These were expanded using co-occurring terms extracted from the seed dataset. To ensure relevance, GPT-4 was used to filter the data based on campaign context, retaining only posts aligned with the disinformation and counter-disinformation narratives.

The dataset includes both English and non-English posts. Non-English content was translated using the DeepL API[1]. We collected 4,817 posts from Instagram, 2,560 from TikTok, 11,134 from X, and 7,327 from YouTube related to the Taiwan 2024 election. These posts serve as the foundation for our cross-platform narrative analysis.

4   Method

This section presents the methods used in this research. Sections 4.1, 4.2, and 4.3 discuss the techniques used for extracting narratives, identifying focal structures, and creating the cross-platform narrative graph, respectively.

---

[1] https://www.deepl.com.

4.1   Narrative Extraction

Narratives were extracted using the method proposed by Amure and Agarwal [6] and Gurung et al. [8], with a key modification: campaign context was explicitly introduced into the prompt fed to GPT-4. This enabled narrative extraction across multiple modalities, including text (X, YouTube transcripts, TikTok comments) and image-derived captions (Instagram). Built on the Transformer architecture, GPT-4 uses self-attention to capture long-range dependencies and contextual nuance. Prior studies support its narrative modeling capacity [7,11,14].

Let S, P, N_a, and U denote platforms, posts, narratives, and users, respectively. For each post $p \in P$ by user $u \in U$ on platform $s \in S$, we extracted a narrative $n \in N_a$. We applied two filters: (1) polarity mismatch between post and narrative, and (2) contextual inconsistency. Contextual filtering was done using a similarity check described in Sect. 4.3.

4.2   Contextual Focal Structure Analysis (CFSA)

The Contextual Focal Structure Analysis (CFSA) algorithm identifies influential groups in a multiplex network by integrating structural and contextual signals across three layers: user-user, user-narrative, and narrative-narrative. Unlike traditional approaches focused on direct interactions, CFSA captures cross-layer influence and coordinated behavior by optimizing centrality and modularity in two stages.

At the node level, the algorithm selects locally influential users by maximizing the joint influence from all layers:

$$\max \sum_{i=1}^{n} \sum_{j=1}^{m} \left(\delta_i^{UU} \oplus \rho_{ij}^{UH} h_j^{HH} \right) \qquad (1)$$

Here, δ_i^{UU} is the user centrality in the user-user layer, ρ_{ij}^{UH} the user-narrative connection strength, and h_j^{HH} the centrality of narrative j in the narrative-narrative layer. The operator $\oplus$ fuses influence across layers. Constraints ensure selected users contribute strongly to both local cohesion (e.g., clustering) and network-level metrics like modularity.

At the group level, CFSA refines the selected user sets using spectral modularity optimization:

$$\max \sum_{j=1}^{k} e_j^q, \quad \text{where} \quad B = A - gg^T \qquad (2)$$

Here, e_j^q represents modularity contribution from each group, A is the adjacency matrix, and g is the degree vector. Redundant or overlapping groups are filtered out, and final group selection ensures structural sparsity and contextual relevance.

CFSA thus produces a set of contextual focal structures—cohesive user-narrative groups that reveal how influence and coordination unfold across platforms and topics. For theoretical foundations and proofs, see [2–4].

4.3 Cross-Platform Narrative Graph

To support the CFSA, we construct a multiplex network that captures contextual relationships among narratives and users across platforms. This network integrates three layers:

- **User-User Layer:** Connects users posting similar narratives.
- **User-Narrative Layer:** Links users to their narratives.
- **Narrative-Narrative Layer:** Connects semantically related narratives.

A key step is defining inter-narrative similarity through an aggregate connectivity score S, combining semantic and entity-level similarity:

$$S(n_1, n_2) = \frac{s_1(n_1, n_2) + s_2(n_1, n_2)}{2} \tag{3}$$

Here, s_1 is the cosine similarity between narrative embeddings extracted using the transformer-based `all-mpnet-base-v2` model [13], which captures sentence-level semantics. s_2 is the Jaccard similarity over named entities extracted via SpaCy [9]:

$$s_2 = \frac{|E_i \cap E_j|}{|E_i \cup E_j|} \tag{4}$$

Narratives n_1 and n_2 are connected if $S(n_1, n_2) \geq 0.5$. Given posts p_1 and p_2 by users u_1, u_2, and narratives n_1, n_2, we construct:

$$G = (V, \{E_l\}_{l=1}^3),$$

where V includes all users and narratives, and E_l defines edges for each of the three layers. Users u_1, u_2 are connected if their posts yield similar narratives; each user u is linked to their narrative n; and narratives n_1, n_2 are connected based on the score S. This structure captures influence and coordination across platforms, without requiring explicit user identity matches.

5 Result and Discussion

Ten focal structures were identified across two major discussions; for brevity, we highlight one representative from each.

Focal Structure 5. (Figure 1) illustrates how users shaped Taiwan's 2024 election discourse across YouTube, X, TikTok, and Instagram. While YouTube narratives emphasize democratic progress, X highlights the DPP's parliamentary setbacks, and Instagram underscores geopolitical tension with China. These platform-specific framings suggest strategic adaptation by users to engage different audiences. Whether coordinated or emergent, the discourse consistently touches on electoral legitimacy, policy direction, and Taiwan-China relations.

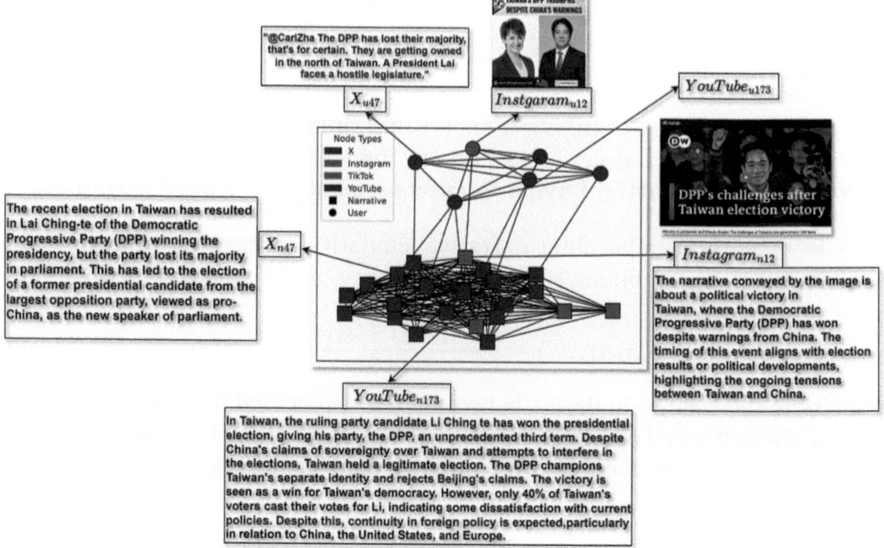

Fig. 1. Network showing the relationship between narratives and users on different platforms in focal structure 5 for TC. n refers to narrative id and u refers to the user id.

Focal Structure 16. (Figure 2) captures a pro-China narrative propagated via Instagram and TikTok. On Instagram, China's Taiwan Affairs Office contests the DPP's legitimacy, while TikTok posts frame Taiwan as provoking conflict. This narrative alignment across platforms suggests an effort to shift blame onto Taiwan and reinforce China's geopolitical stance, influencing both domestic and international perceptions of regional stability.

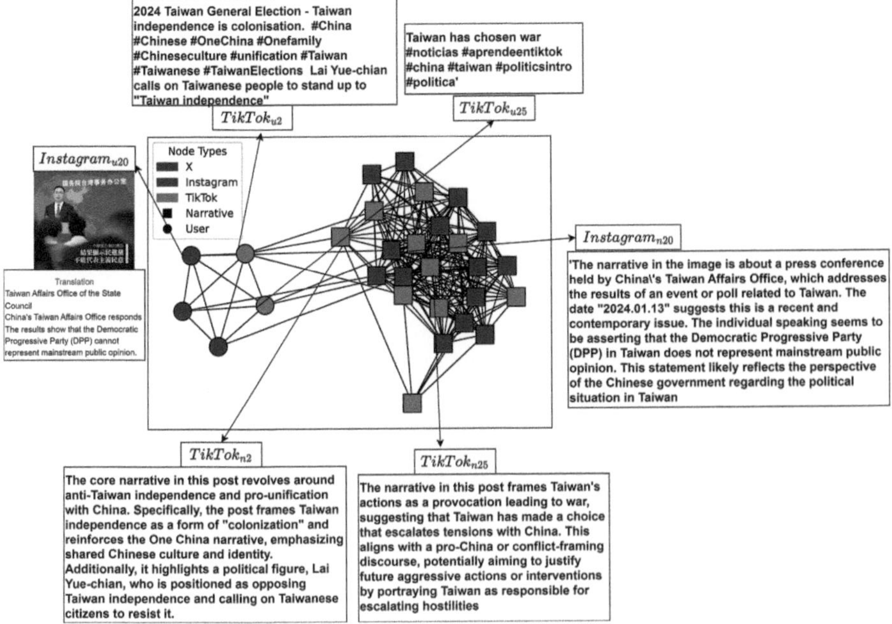

Fig. 2. Network showing the relationship between narratives and users on different platforms in focal structure 16 for TC. n refers to narrative id and u refers to the user id.

6   Conclusion

This study examined how political discourse gains traction across social media by focusing on influential user groups, termed focal structures. We constructed a cross-platform multiplex network linking users and narratives, and applied the CFSA algorithm to extract context-specific influential groups from the Taiwan 2024 election campaign.

Narratives on social media often emerge from loosely connected posts by diverse users, making their propagation difficult to trace. Our method addresses this by modeling narrative flows and identifying coordinated user groups that drive them. Findings show that influence is not confined to prominent individuals but often arises from groups shaping narratives in strategic, context-aware ways. As cross-platform information flows continue to influence public perception, scalable methods like ours are essential for understanding and responding to coordinated influence in digital ecosystems.

Acknowledgments. This research is funded in part by the U.S. National Science Foundation (OIA-1946391, OIA-1920920), U.S. Office of the Under Secretary of Defense for Research and Engineering (FA9550-22-1-0332), U.S. Army Research Office (W911NF-23-1-0011, W911NF-24-1-0078, W911NF-25-1-0147), U.S. Office of Naval Research (N00014-21-1-2121, N00014-21-1-2765, N00014-22-1-2318), U.S. Air

Force Research Laboratory, U.S. Defense Advanced Research Projects Agency, the Australian Department of Defense Strategic Policy Grants Program, Arkansas Research Alliance, the Jerry L. Maulden/Entergy Endowment, and the Donaghey Foundation at the University of Arkansas at Little Rock. Any opinions, findings, and conclusions or recommendations expressed in this material are those of the authors and do not necessarily reflect the views of the funding organizations. The researchers gratefully acknowledge the support.

References

1. Agarwal, N., Bandeli, K.K.: Examining strategic integration of social media platforms in disinformation campaign coordination. Defence Strategic Communications **4**(1), 173 (2018)
2. Akinnubi, A., Alassad, M., Agarwal, N., Amure, R.: Identifying contextualized focal structures in multisource social networks by leveraging knowledge graphs. In: International conference on complex networks and their applications, pp. 15–27. Springer (2023)
3. Akinnubi, A., Alassad, M., Amure, R., Agarwal, N.: Kg-cfsa: a comprehensive approach for analyzing multi-source heterogeneous social network knowledge graph. Soc. Netw. Anal. Min. **14**(1), 159 (2024)
4. Alassad, M., Agarwal, N.: Contextualizing focal structure analysis in social networks. Soc. Netw. Anal. Min. **12**(1), 103 (2022). https://doi.org/10.1007/s13278-022-00938-0
5. Alassad, M., Hussain, M.N., Agarwal, N.: Finding fake news key spreaders in complex social networks by using bi-level decomposition optimization method. In: Modeling and Simulation of Social-Behavioral Phenomena in Creative Societies: First International EURO Mini Conference, MSBC 2019, Vilnius, Lithuania, September 18–20, 2019, Proceedings 1, pp. 41–54. Springer (2019)
6. Amure, R., Agarwal, N.: Modeling cross-platform narratives templates: A temporal knowledge graph approach. Soc. Netw. Anal. Mining **15**(42) (2025)
7. Beguš, N.: Experimental narratives: A comparison of human crowdsourced storytelling and ai storytelling. Humanities and Social Sciences Communications **11**(1), 1–22 (2024)
8. Gurung, M.I., Al Rubaye, H., Agarwal, N., Al-Taweel, A.: Analyzing narrative evolution about south china sea dispute on Youtube: an exploratory study using GPT-3. In: In Proceedings of the 16th International Conference on Social Computing, Behavioral-Cultural Modeling and Prediction and Behavior Representation in Modeling and Simulation (SBP-BRiMS 2023). IEEE (2023)
9. Honnibal, M., Montani, I., Van Landeghem, S., Boyd, A.: spacy: Industrial-strength natural language processing in Python (2020)
10. Klepper, D., Wu, H.: How Taiwan preserved election integrity by fighting back against disinformation (2024). https://www.pbs.org/newshour/world/how-taiwan-preserved-election-integrity-by-fighting-back-against-disinformation
11. Lynch, C.J., et al.: GPT-4 generated narratives of life events using a structured narrative prompt: a validation study. arXiv preprint arXiv:2402.05435 (2024)
12. Murdock, I., Carley, K.M., Yağan, O.: Identifying cross-platform user relationships in 2020 US election fraud and protest discussions. Online Social Networks and Media **33**, 100,245 (2023)

13. Reimers, N., Gurevych, I.: Sentence-BERT: sentence embeddings using Siamese BERT-networks. In: Proceedings of the 2019 Conference on Empirical Methods in Natural Language Processing, pp. 3982–3992. Association for Computational Linguistics (2019)
14. Shakeri, H., Neustaedter, C., DiPaola, S.: Saga: Collaborative storytelling with GPT-3. In: Companion Publication of the 2021 Conference on Computer Supported Cooperative Work and Social Computing, pp. 163–166 (2021)
15. Wilson, T., Starbird, K.: Cross-platform disinformation campaigns: lessons learned and next steps. Harvard Kennedy School Misinformation Rev. $\mathbf{1}$(1) (2020). https://par.nsf.gov/biblio/10171226
16. Şen, F., Wigand, R., Agarwal, N., Tokdemir, S., Kasprzyk, R.: Focal structures analysis: identifying influential sets of individuals in a social network. Soc. Netw. Anal. Min. $\mathbf{6}$(1), 1–22 (2016). https://doi.org/10.1007/s13278-016-0319-z

Mitigating Bias for Unseen Demographic Groups in Graph Neural Networks

Francisco Santos[(✉)], Pang-Ning Tan, and Abdol-Hossein Esfahanian

Department of Computer Science and Engineering, Michigan State University,
Lansing, MI 48824, USA
{santosf3,ptan,esfahanian}@msu.edu

Abstract. Fairness is an important factor to consider in graph neural networks (GNNs) as biases in the data can be amplified by the link structure. Despite ongoing research, existing fairness-aware GNN methods often assume that the sensitive attribute values for all demographic groups are available during training. This assumption restricts their practical applicability, especially in scenarios where training examples for certain demographic groups are unavailable. To address this limitation, we propose FairGRUNT, a novel GNN framework designed to handle training scenarios with unseen demographic groups. FairGRUNT employs disentangled representation learning to separate node embeddings for class prediction from those encoding demographic information, thereby reducing dependency between them. A pretraining stage assigns soft labels to a subset of the unlabeled nodes indicating seen or unseen group membership based on their prediction confidence. These soft labels are then used to train a demographic classifier and guide a statistical parity-based fairness regularizer, which is integrated into the training objective to mitigate bias in the GNN predictions. Experimental results on real-world datasets show that FairGRUNT outperforms traditional fairness-aware GNN methods in reducing biases in node classification, particularly for sensitive attributes with unseen groups.

Keywords: Graph Neural Networks · Algorithmic Bias · Disentangled Representation Learning

1 Introduction

Fairness is essential for graph neural networks (GNNs), as biases present in the data can be amplified through the network structure [1,2]. Ensuring fairness in GNNs is critical to prevent discrimination based on sensitive attributes such as race, gender, age, or ethnicity. Various approaches have therefore been proposed to improve fairness in graph-based models [2–6]. However, most existing fairness-aware GNN approaches assume full access to protected attribute values during training. This assumption is often unrealistic in real-world scenarios where demographic data may be incomplete or entirely unavailable for certain

A. An et al. (Eds.): ASONAM 2025, LNCS 16323, pp. 128–136, 2026.
https://doi.org/10.1007/978-3-032-13821-7_12

subpopulations [4]. Since current models rely on the availability of labeled examples from all demographic groups during training, this hinders their ability to generalize debiasing strategies to subgroups unaccounted for in the training data. As a result, fairness performance can degrade significantly when such models encounter previously unseen demographic groups during deployment. Moreover, maintaining a balance between fairness and predictive performance remains difficult, especially when the distributions of seen and unseen groups differ. Our goal is to develop models that promote fairness across all demographic groups, including those not observed during training, while preserving strong predictive performance.

Eliminating biases associated with unseen demographic groups in a GNN is a non-trivial task. First, the GNN model must be capable of separating the feature embeddings associated with the sensitive attribute information from those associated with the prediction task [3,4]. Our proposed model tackles this challenge by employing a feature disentanglement strategy, explicitly separating the embedding representing the sensitive attribute from the embedding used for the class prediction. By incorporating a feature independence constraint via correlation loss, this ensures that the sensitive attributes do not influence class outcomes, thereby promoting fairness.

The second challenge lies in effectively addressing unseen protected attributes, as merely disentangling the learned representations is insufficient to ensure fair generalization. To address this limitation, we adopt a two-stage strategy. We begin by pretraining a GCN on the portion of the training dataset that contains only seen demographic attributes, with the goal of predicting the corresponding seen demographic groups. After training this model, a subset of the test data—containing both seen and unseen group samples—is passed through. Samples with low prediction confidence are treated as likely belonging to unseen groups and are assigned soft labels to reflect this uncertainty. These soft labels are then used to train a secondary classifier that distinguishes between seen and unseen demographic groups. Once trained, this classifier is applied to the entire dataset to assign a seen or unseen group label to each node. These predicted group labels are subsequently passed to a sensitive attribute classifier, whose outputs are incorporated into a fairness regularizer. This procedure enables the framework to explicitly model demographic group uncertainty and enhances its ability to mitigate bias in predictions across both seen and unseen groups.

The proposed strategies are integrated into a novel GNN framework called **FairGRUNT** (**Fair** **G**raph **R**epresentation learning for **UN**seen sensi**T**ive attribute groups). Experimental results on 3 real-world datasets demonstrate the effectiveness of FairGRUNT in balancing the tradeoff between fairness and performance compared to other fairness-aware GNN methods.

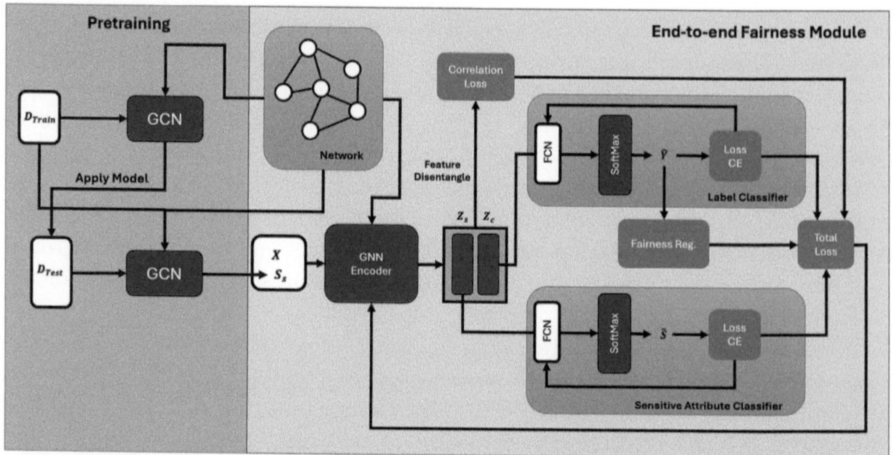

Fig. 1. Framework for FairGRUNT. D_{train} is the training data and D_{test} is the testing data. X represents the feature matrix, while S_s denotes the seen/unseen soft label. $\hat{S}$ indicates the prediction for the seen/unseen attribute, and $\hat{Y}$ represents the class prediction.

2   Preliminaries

Consider a network $G = (V, E, X, Y)$, where V is the set of nodes, $E \subseteq V \times V$ is the set of edges, $X \in \mathbb{R}^{|V| \times d}$ is the node feature matrix, and Y contains the class labels. The feature matrix X consists of two parts: X^p, denoting protected attributes, and X^u, denoting unprotected or task-relevant attributes. We assume that the protected attribute matrix X^p is partially observed, meaning that some nodes have missing or unannotated sensitive attribute values, denoted as $X^p_{\text{unlabeled}}$. Among these, some nodes belong to *seen* demographic groups—those observed during training—while others belong to *unseen* groups, not present in the labeled training data. We define S_s as a soft label indicating whether a node belongs to a seen or unseen group.

Consider the normalized adjacency matrix of the form $\hat{A} = \tilde{D}^{-1/2}(A + I)\tilde{D}^{-1/2}$, where A is the adjacency matrix corresponding to E, I is the identity matrix, and $\tilde{D}$ is the degree matrix of $A + I$. The objective of this work is to design a fairness-aware graph neural network that maintains strong predictive performance while ensuring fair outcomes across all demographic groups, including those unseen during training.

3   Methodology

Figure 1 presents the architecture of FairGRUNT, which comprises of two main components: a pretraining phase and an end-to-end fairness module. In the pretraining phase, we employ a two-step strategy to determine whether each node belongs to a seen or unseen demographic group. A GCN is first trained on nodes with known protected attributes and then applied to test data containing both seen and unseen samples. Nodes with low prediction confidence are treated as unseen and assigned soft labels. A second GCN is trained on these labels to classify all nodes as seen or unseen. The end-to-end fairness module incorporates a GNN encoder that learns two disentangled embeddings: one for predicting the target label and another for predicting the sensitive attribute. A correlation loss enforces independence between the embeddings to mitigate bias along with a statistical parity-based regularizer. Details are given below.

3.1 Soft Label Generation of Demographic Groups

We introduce a two-stage pretraining strategy that generates soft group labels, enabling the model to differentiate between samples from seen and unseen demographic groups. These soft labels play a crucial role in enforcing fairness constraints in later stages of training. We begin by partitioning the dataset into training and test subsets. We assume that the training set contains samples exclusively from seen demographic groups—those for which labels are available—while the test set contains a mixture of both seen and unseen groups. In the first stage, we train a GCN on the training set to predict the protected attribute among the seen groups. Once trained, this GCN is applied to a subset of the test data in a semi-supervised learning fashion. We compute the model's prediction confidence on each sample. If the model exhibits high confidence, the sample is assumed to belong to a seen group; conversely, if the prediction confidence is low, the sample is treated as potentially coming from an unseen demographic group. This confidence thresholding enables the generation of demographic labels for seen and unseen group membership.

In the second stage, we use the demographic label test samples alongside the seen labeled samples to train a second GCN, whose objective is to classify nodes as either belonging to seen or unseen demographic groups. Once trained, it is applied to the entire dataset—both training and test nodes—to generate a soft label vector $S_s \in [0,1]^{|V|}$. These soft labels S_s are later used in our end-to-end fairness module to ensure fairness for the class prediction. This approach enables the model to incorporate information about demographic uncertainty during training, leading to more robust and equitable classification outcomes across both seen and unseen demographic groups.

3.2 Learning Fair Disentangled Node Embedding

The end-to-end fairness module consists of three main components: a GNN encoder, a class label predictor, and a sensitive attribute classifier. The GNN encoder is responsible for learning two distinct embedding spaces: one for predicting class labels (Z_c) and the other dedicated to predicting sensitive attribute labels (Z_s), using the soft labels established previously. Crucially, our encoder aims not only to derive informative embeddings but also to ensure these representations are independent.

To quantify and enforce this representation independence, we employ a correlation-based measure. Specifically, a correlation matrix $C \in \mathbb{R}^{k \times k}$ is computed, capturing the pairwise correlations among embeddings, where k represents the total dimensionality of embeddings Z_c and Z_s. Given that embeddings are split equally, the first $k/2$ corresponds exclusively to the embeddings for class prediction and the last $k/2$ for seen/unseen group prediction. We isolate the upper-right quadrant of this matrix, denoted $C_{\frac{k}{2},k}$, representing correlations specifically between the class embeddings and sensitive attribute embeddings. This targeted submatrix directly indicates the extent of interdependence between the representations. Our goal is minimize the maximum correlation between embeddings within this quadrant, which is utilized as our disentanglement loss: $\mathcal{L}_{corr} = \max\{C_{\frac{k}{2},k}\}$.

Following the embedding disentanglement phase, each embedding subspace undergoes further processing through separate fully connected layers. These layers are each followed by a softmax activation function, normalizing predictions into probabilities suitable for classification, as shown in Fig. 1(right). Note that the label classifier is only trained with samples from the seen demographic groups. The output predictions ($\hat{y}$ for class labels and $\hat{s}$ for seen/unseen group) are subsequently evaluated using a binary cross-entropy loss function to ensure accurate classification performance: $\mathcal{L}_{ce} = -[y \cdot \log(\hat{p}) + (1 - y) \cdot \log(1 - \hat{p})]$, where $\hat{p}$ represents either the predicted sensitive attribute probability ($\hat{s}$) or the class label probability ($\hat{y}$).

Besides representation disentanglement, we integrate a fairness regularizer based on statistical parity, which explicitly assesses disparities between seen and unseen sensitive attribute groups. The statistical parity regularizer explicitly quantifies the probability difference of positive predictions across these groups: $\mathcal{L}_{sp} = |p(\hat{y} = 1|s = 0) - p(\hat{y} = 1|s = 1)|$. Here, s indicates the sensitive attribute categorization, distinguishing between seen and unseen attributes, thus ensuring that our model achieves equitable outcomes even for demographic categories absent in training data.

Ultimately, our comprehensive fairness-aware loss function integrates representation disentanglement, classification accuracy, and fairness regularization into a unified training objective: $\mathcal{L}_{final} = \alpha \mathcal{L}_{corr} + (1 - \alpha)(\mathcal{L}_{ce}^{class} + \mathcal{L}_{ce}^{s}) + \beta \mathcal{L}_{sp}$. In this formulation, $\mathcal{L}_{ce}^{class}$ is the cross-entropy loss specifically for class label prediction, while $\mathcal{L}_{ce}^{s}$ pertains to sensitive attribute prediction. Hyperparameters α and β are introduced to manage the balance between fairness and predictive accuracy. Specifically, α regulates the intensity of embedding disentanglement, while β controls the contribution of the fairness regularizer. Through careful tuning of these hyperparameters, our model effectively balances fairness constraints with maintaining high predictive utility.

4   Experimental Evaluation

This section presents our experimental results and analysis. The code for our model can be accessed in the following site: https://github.com/frsantosp/ FairGRUNT.

4.1 Experimental Setup

We evaluate our method on three real-world datasets: (1) **Tagged** [7] is a spammer detection dataset with 71,128 nodes and 71,226 edges, using age (three groups) as the sensitive attribute; individuals aged 3550 form the unseen group. (2) **Recidivism** [8] includes 18,877 nodes and 403,978 edges, with the task of predicting bail decisions. The sensitive attribute combines race and age, with black males under 35 and white males over 35 treated as unseen. (3) **Pokec** [9] contains 67,797 nodes and 882,765 edges from a Slovak social network, with the task of predicting sports interest and the sensitive attribute defined by gender and region. Note that each dataset is split into 50% training, 25% validation, and 25% test sets.

We compared FairGRUNT against several baselines, including the standard two-layer **GCN** [10]. **FairGNN** [4] incorporates adversarial debiasing to learn fair node representations, particularly when some sensitive attribute values are missing. **NIFTY** [5] enforces fairness and stability by introducing random perturbations to node attributes, sensitive features, and graph edges, and maximizes the agreement between predictions on original and perturbed graphs. **BeMap** [6] modifies GNN message passing by sampling neighbors such that the distribution of sensitive attributes is balanced in each node's local neighborhood, promoting fair and unbiased aggregation.

To evaluate the classification performance of the methods, we use the AUC (area under the ROC curve) metric. For fairness assessment, we consider the following two fairness metrics: **Statistical Parity (SP)** and **Equal Opportunity (EO)**.

$$SP = \left| \max_{s \in X^P} P(\hat{Y} = 1 \mid S = s) - \min_{s \in X^P} P(\hat{Y} = 1 \mid S = s) \right|$$

$$EO = \left| \max_{s \in X^P} P(\hat{Y} = 1 \mid Y = 1, S = s) - \min_{s \in X^P} P(\hat{Y} = 1 \mid Y = 1, S = s) \right|.$$

Pretraining and Model Setup. The pretraining setup consists of two GCNs, each with two layers and a hidden dimension of 512. As previously mentioned, the first GCN is trained exclusively on samples from seen demographic groups. The second pretraining model is trained using a subset of the test data that contains both seen and unseen groups. The GNN encoder in the end-to-end module also uses a two-layer GCN with a hidden dimension of 512. The output of the GNN encoder has a dimensionality of 4. The label classifier consists of a stack of fully connected layers with a hidden dimension of 512 and is trained only on samples from seen demographic groups. In contrast, the sensitive attribute classifier is trained using samples from both seen and unseen groups and also consists of stacked fully connected layers with a hidden dimension of 512. All neural networks are optimized using Adam with a learning rate of 0.0001. Each model is trained for 1,000 epochs, and all experiments are run using five different random seeds. In our experiments, the hyperparameter α is varied from 0 to 1 in increments of 0.1, while β ranges from 0 to 10. The hyperparameters are chosen based on the model performance on validation set.

Table 1. Performance comparison between the proposed approach and other baseline methods on a) Pokec, b) Tagged and c) Bail datasets.

	AUC	SP	EO
GCN	0.8251 ± 0.0024	0.0626 ± 0.0057	0.0328 ± 0.016
FairGNN	0.7751 ± 0.0592	0.0507 ± 0.0196	0.0241 ± 0.0104
Nifty	0.6818 ± 0.0690	0.0170 ± 0.0356	0.0046 ± 0.0178
BeMap	0.7454 ± 0.0130	0.0571 ± 0.0191	0.1127 ± 0.0229
FairGRUNT	0.7872 ± 0.0012	0.0258 ± 0.0022	0.0260 ± 0.0043

(a) Pokec

	AUC	SP	EO
GCN	0.7196 ± 0.0203	0.1330 ± 0.0165	0.1409 ± 0.0236
FairGNN	0.5889 ± 0.0172	0.0130 ± 0.0290	0.0250 ± 0.0553
Nifty	0.6322 ± 0.0044	0.0382 ± 0.0123	0.0729 ± 0.0247
BeMap	0.6521 ± 0.0172	0.0545 ± 0.0417	0.0473 ± 0.0296
FairGRUNT	0.5834 ± 0.0021	0.0036 ± 0.0019	0.0108 ± 0.0069

(b) Tagged

	AUC	SP	EO
GCN	0.9807 ± 0.0036	0.1914 ± 0.0165	0.1620 ± 0.0236
FairGNN	0.8313 ± 0.1240	0.1007 ± 0.0926	0.1102 ± 0.0857
Nifty	0.9112 ± 0.0372	0.1131 ± 0.0516	0.0998 ± 0.0443
BeMap	0.8577 ± 0.0358	0.2021 ± 0.1006	0.1664 ± 0.0800
FairGRUNT	0.8365 ± 0.1308	0.0380 ± 0.0563	0.0485 ± 0.0854

(c) Bail

4.2   Experimental Results

Table 1 summarizes the results of our experiments. As expected, GCN achieves the highest AUC on all three datasets, since it does not incorporate any fairness constraints and is optimized solely for predictive performance. This establishes an upper bound on classification performance against which fairness-aware methods can be compared. Among the fairness-aware baselines, AUC results vary by dataset. In Pokec, FairGRUNT attains the highest AUC (0.7872), followed closely by FairGNN (0.7751), while Nifty achieves a significantly lower AUC (0.6818). In Tagged, BeMap (0.6521) and Nifty (0.6322) outperform both FairGNN (0.5889) and FairGRUNT (0.5834), indicating stronger utility performance on this dataset. On Bail, Nifty leads among the fairness-aware models with an AUC of 0.9112, followed by BeMap (0.8577), FairGRUNT (0.8365), and FairGNN (0.8313). Notably, FairGRUNT attains comparable AUC scores to other fairness-aware baseline methods, achieving highest AUC scores on Pokec, but lowest on Tagged. More importantly, FairGRUNT significantly outperforms all baselines on both the Bail and Tagged datasets in terms of fairness, achieving the lowest SP and EO scores. For example, on Tagged, our model obtains SP = 0.0036 and EO = 0.0108, markedly lower than any other method. On Bail, it again leads with SP = 0.0380 and EO = 0.0485, showing that our method effectively mitigates group-level disparities, including the unseen demographic groups.

For the Pokec dataset, Nifty achieves the best fairness metrics (SP = 0.0170, EO = 0.0046), but this comes at the cost of a notably lower AUC. In contrast, FairGRUNT offers a better trade-off between utility and fairness, maintaining a nearly 0.10 higher AUC (0.7872) than Nifty while still achieving competitive fairness scores. The worst fairness performance across all datasets is observed in GCN and BeMap. For GCN, this is expected due to its lack of any fairness objective. BeMap, although relatively strong in AUC, struggles to manage the fairness-utility trade-off effectively, as evidenced by high SP and EO values— especially on the Bail dataset (SP = 0.2021, EO = 0.1664). Overall, these results underscore the strength of our approach in balancing fairness and predictive accuracy on datasets with unseen demographic groups.

5   Conclusions and Future Work

In this work, we present FairGRUNT, a novel fairness-aware GNN model with the inability to handle unseen protected attribute groups. FairGRUNT employs disentangled representation learning to reduce the dependency between sensitive attributes and class labels. Additionally, we incorporated a fairness regularizer based on statistical parity to further reduce discriminatory bias in the learned representations. Our experimental results demonstrate that FairGRUNT effectively improves fairness across several benchmark datasets, while maintaining comparable predictive performance.

For future work, we aim to further improve predictive performance, particularly in settings where the attributes for predicting the class are strongly correlated with those associated with the demographic groups. Alternative strategies beyond feature disentanglement, e.g., using adversarial training, is another research direction.

References

1. Mehrabi, N., Morstatter, F., Saxena, N., Lerman, K., Galstyan, A.: A Survey on Bias and Fairness in Machine Learning (2022). https://arxiv.org/abs/1908.09635
2. Rahman, T., Surma, B., Backes, M., Zhang, Y.: Fairwalk: Towards fair graph embedding. In: Proceedings of the 28th International Joint Conference on AI, pp. 3289–3295 (2019)
3. Bose, A.J., Hamilton, W.: Compositional fairness constraints for graph embeddings. arXiv preprint arXiv:1905.10674 (2019)
4. Dai, E., Wang, S.: Say no to the discrimination: Learning fair graph neural networks with limited sensitive attribute information. In: Proceedings of the 14th ACM International Conference on Web Search and Data Mining, pp. 680–688 (2021)

5. Agarwal, C., Lakkaraju, H., Zitnik, M.: Towards a unified framework for fair and stable graph representation learning. Uncertainty in AI, pp. 2114–2124 (2021)
6. Lin, X., Kang, J., Cong, W., Tong, H.: BeMap: Balanced Message Passing for Fair Graph Neural Network (2024). https://arxiv.org/abs/2306.04107
7. Fakhraei, S., Foulds, J., Shashanka, M., Getoor, L.: Collective spammer detection in evolving multi-relational social networks. In: SIGKDD, pp. 1769–1778
8. Jordan, K., Freiburger, T.: The effect of race/ethnicity on sentencing: examining sentence type, jail length, and prison length. J. Ethnicity Criminal Justice **13**, 1–18 (2014) https://doi.org/10.1080/15377938.2014.984045
9. Leskovec, J., Sosič, R.: Snap: a general-purpose network analysis and graph-mining library. ACM TIST **8**(1), 1 (2016)
10. Kipf, T.N., Welling, M.: Semi-supervised classification with graph convolutional networks. arXiv preprint arXiv:1609.02907 (2016)

Understanding Fairness-Accuracy Trade-offs in Machine Learning Models: Does Promoting Fairness Undermine Performance?

Junhua Liu[1,2], Roy Ka-Wei Lee[1], and Kwan Hui Lim[1(✉)]

[1] Singapore University of Technology and Design, Singapore, Singapore
{roy_lee,kwanhui_lim}@sutd.edu.sg
[2] Forth AI, Singapore, Singapore
j@forth.ai

Abstract. Fairness in both Machine Learning (ML) predictions and human decision-making is essential, yet both are susceptible to different forms of bias, such as algorithmic and data-driven in ML, and cognitive or subjective in humans. In this study, we examine fairness using a real-world university admissions dataset comprising 870 applicant profiles, leveraging three ML models: XGB, Bi-LSTM, and KNN, alongside BERT embeddings for textual features. To evaluate individual fairness, we introduce a consistency metric that quantifies agreement in decisions among ML models and human experts with diverse backgrounds. Our analysis reveals that ML models surpass human evaluators in fairness consistency by margins ranging from 14.08% to 18.79%. Our findings highlight the potential of using ML to enhance fairness in admissions while maintaining high accuracy, advocating a hybrid approach combining human judgement and ML models.

1 Introduction

Fairness has emerged as a critical concern in terms of both the predictive outputs of Machine Learning (ML) models and the decisions made by human experts [4,7,11,16]. In the context of ML models, challenges in fairness often stem from data biases and algorithmic limitations, which can propagate or exacerbate existing inequities. Conversely, fairness in human decision-making is inherently influenced by subjective judgment and cognitive biases, making it vulnerable to inconsistency and error. These two sources of unfairness necessitate rigorous investigation into both computational and human-centric frameworks to mitigate bias and ensure equitable outcomes.

To investigate fairness, this work utilizes a real-world university admission dataset with 870 unique profiles and three effective ML models, namely, Extreme Gradient Boosting (XGB), Bi-directional Long Short-Term Memory (Bi-LSTM) and K-Nearest Neighbours (KNN). The textual features of the profiles are encoded into high-dimensional embeddings using the Bidirectional Encoder Representations from Transformers (BERT), enabling the extraction of rich contextual representations for downstream predictive tasks. In our case, we focus on the important but challenging task of admission offer decision making.

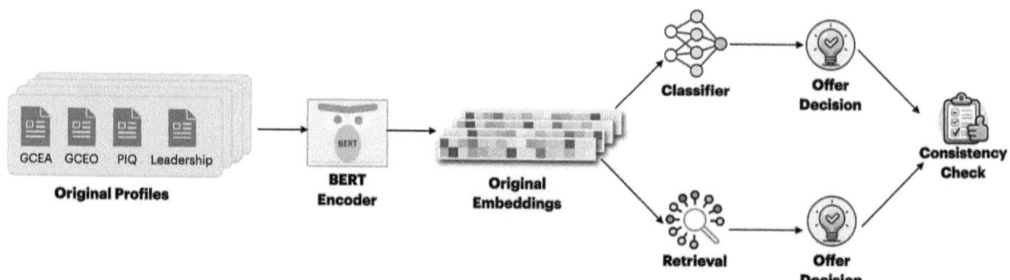

Fig. 1. Proposed pipelines to assess Individual Fairness.

We examine individual fairness in university admission offer decisions for a heterogeneous group of applicants, characterized by diverse backgrounds, leadership qualities, and academic achievements. Using a standardized set of features for comparison, we assess individual fairness by measuring decision consistency through a consistency score [17], which quantifies how similar applicants with comparable profiles are treated by human experts or ML models. Our results reveal that both XGBoost and Bi-LSTM outperform human experts significantly, achieving higher consistency scores by a margin of 14.08% to 18.79%. These findings suggest that ML models demonstrate superior reliability in ensuring fair treatment of similar applications.

2   Related Work

Algorithmic Fairness. Individual fairness emphasizes treating similar individuals similarly and is closely related to differential privacy through the Lipschitz condition [5,6]. Fairness definitions often vary depending on the worldview and can typically be derived from confusion matrices [9]. The increasing use of large language models (LLMs) in decision-making raises concerns about potential human-like biases these models may adopt [3], necessitating investigation and effective mitigation strategies. Various methods to address biases have been explored, including robust data preprocessing [14], fair representation learning [17], and auditing human decision processes [1].

Fairness in University Admissions. Previous work on fairness in admissions often focuses on qualitative analyses [18], general policy evaluations [12], or assessments of specific factors like standardized testing [15]. However, these studies tend to involve limited user groups or geographic contexts, thus restricting their generalizability. Other studies compare perceptions of fairness in AI-driven versus human-driven admissions decisions [10]. Recent methods include Puranik et al.'s Fair-Greedy policy [13], balancing score maximization with representation of under-represented groups, and Bhattacharya et al.'s empirical evaluation of socioeconomic biases, identifying disparities in admission thresholds among demographic groups [2].

3 Data Processing

3.1 Dataset

We use the university admission dataset introduced in [8], which consists of applicant profiles from a specific admission cycle year. The dataset includes a total of 870 unique profiles that come with four features: General Certificate of Education Advanced Level (GCEA), General Certificate of Education Ordinary Level (GCEO), Personal Insight Questions (PIQ) and Leadership Experience. We concatenate all content and form a **Combined** document. There is also the label Type, which is either Offered or Not Offered. The dataset is then split into 80% training, 10% validation, and 10% test for experimentation purposes.

3.2 Feature Embedding

To prepare the data for fairness assessment, we generate contextual embeddings using BERT (bert-base-uncased). For each feature, we generated BERT embeddings using the following process: the text was tokenized and padded to a maximum length of 512 tokens, then processed through BERT to obtain contextual embeddings. We extracted the [CLS] token embedding (768-dimensional vector) as the representation for each feature. The individual embeddings were then concatenated to create a combined representation (3840-dimensional vector) for each profile, preserving the contextual information. The final output included individual embeddings for each feature and embeddings for the concatenated feature.

3.3 Human Decisions

We use three human decision points, such as Shortlisting (SL), Admission Recommendation (AR) and Offer (OF), as targets to assess prediction accuracy and consistency. Specifically, we mapped the categorical labels to binary values, where "Shortlisted", "Recommended" and "Offered" correspond to 1, and 0 otherwise, respectively.

4 Individual Fairness

4.1 Formulation

Individual fairness is grounded in the principle that similar individuals should receive similar treatment in decision-making processes. Following [17], we operationalize this concept through a consistency metric that evaluates how similarly

Table 1. Individual Fairness: classification performance and fairness consistency. Best results are bolted. Abbreviations: P=precision; R=Recall; A=Accuracy; C=Consistency

Model	P	R	F1	A	C(AR)	C(OF)
Human Decisions						
Shortlist(SL)	**0.8464**	**0.8418**	0.8156	0.8155	–	–
Adm. Rec. (AR)	0.8011	0.8193	0.8321	0.8087	0.5632	–
Offer (OF)	–	–	–	–	–	0.6023
ML Models						
KNN (k=5)	0.6886	0.6707	0.6897	0.6897	–	–
XGB	0.7902	0.7859	0.7878	0.7931	0.7521	0.7477
Bi-LSTM	0.8291	0.8178	**0.8176**	**0.8276**	**0.8073**	**0.7797**

a classifier treats applicants with comparable profiles. Figure 1 illustrates our proposed pipeline for assessing individual fairness.

Formally, given a set of N applicants, we define the consistency score $\mathcal{C}$ of a classifier as:

$$\mathcal{C} = 1 - \frac{1}{N} \sum_{i=1}^{N} |\hat{y}_i - \frac{1}{k} \sum_{j \in knn(i)} \hat{y}_j| \tag{1}$$

where $\hat{y}_i$ represents the classifier's prediction for applicant i, and $\frac{1}{k} \sum_{j \in knn(i)} \hat{y}_j$ computes the average of predictions among the k-nearest neighbors (i.e. most similar profiles), of applicant i. This formulation yields a score between 0 and 1, where higher values indicate greater consistency in treating similar cases similarly. The scores effectively reflect the fairness consistency by measuring mean absolute differences between a classifier's predictions to the target profiles and the average predictions made for most similar profiles.

4.2   Research Questions

The rest of this section discusses our investigation on the following Research Questions (RQ):

- **RQ1:** Can Cognitive Bias in human decisions be systematically identified?
- **RQ2:** Are ML models more consistent in making decisions than human?
- **RQ3:** Can ML models outperform human in making admission decisions?

4.3 Methodology

Our evaluation framework examines individual fairness across the entire admission pipeline by analyzing three human decision points, such as shortlisting (SL), admission recommendations (AR), and final offers (OF), alongside two model-based classifiers (XGB and BiLSTM) and a retrieval-based k Nearest Neighbor (KNN) classifier. The foundation of our methodology lies in the construction of a feature-reranked similarity matrix, which provides a robust measure of application similarity based on embedded features. This similarity matrix enables the identification of nearest neighbors for consistency evaluation.

Implementation: For model training and evaluation, we choose three different approaches, namely, traditional classifiers, neural networks and retrieval-based classifiers. For each category, we choose an empirically effective model from each category, such as XGB, BiLSTM, and KNN. The XGB classifier is implemented using the xgboost library. The BiLSTM model was implemented using PyTorch, featuring a bidirectional LSTM layer followed by linear layers with ReLU activation and LogSoftmax output. For the KNN approach, we utilized the FAISS library for similarity search with in-built memory-efficient processing predictions in batches.

Hyperparameters: We use the validation set to perform hyperparameter search with randomised scheme. Each run takes 20 epochs with a patience of 5 (i.e. 5 epochs without improvement). Best sets are selected using average accuracy.

Metrics: For each decision point and model, we compute both traditional classification metrics (precision, recall, F1-score, and accuracy) and consistency score. The consistency evaluation uses k=5 nearest neighbors, chosen to balance between local similarity and statistical stability. We maintain consistent feature representations across all models by using the same embedded feature space, ensuring fair comparisons between human decisions and machine learning predictions. This approach allows us to systematically assess how different decision-making approaches align with the principle of treating similar applications similarly, while also measuring their overall classification performance.

4.4 Experimental Results

Table 1 summarizes the experimental results for classification performance and individual fairness consistency.

Human Decisions: The shortlisting decisions (SL) made by human evaluators achieve the highest precision among all decision points and models, with a precision of 84.64%. This high precision indicates strong reliability in correctly identifying qualified candidates at the initial stage of the admission process. The admission recommendation (AR) stage exhibits slightly lower but still robust performance, with an accuracy of 80.87% and an F1-score of 83.21%. These metrics suggest consistent and effective decision-making during the early phases of candidate evaluation process.

Machine Learning Models: Among the ML models, Bi-LSTM demonstrates superior performance, achieving an F1-score of 81.76% and an accuracy of 82.76%. These results closely match those of human decisions, with Bi-LSTM attaining a comparable F1-score and even surpassing human decisions in accuracy. This indicates that the Bi-LSTM model is effective in replicating human-like decision-making patterns while offering enhanced accuracy.

In contrast, the KNN model with $k = 5$ shows significantly lower performance, with both F1-score and accuracy at 68.97%. This suggests that a non-parametric retrieval model like KNN is less capable of capturing the complex patterns inherent in human decision-making, highlighting the importance of model selection in predictive tasks.

Fairness Consistency: In terms of fairness consistency, we observe notable variations between human decisions and machine learning model predictions. The consistency score for the admission recommendations (AR) stage is 56.32%, while the final offer decisions (OF) exhibit a slightly higher consistency at 60.23%. These figures suggest that human decision-making maintains moderate levels of consistency, but there remains considerable room for improvement in ensuring that similar candidates receive similar outcomes.

Conversely, both machine learning models demonstrate substantially higher consistency scores compared to human decisions. The XGB model achieves consistency scores of 75.21% for AR and 74.77% for OF stages, indicating a significant improvement over human decision-making in terms of fairness consistency. The Bi-LSTM model performs even better, attaining the highest consistency scores of 80.73% for AR and 77.97% for OF. This highlights the potential of machine learning models to provide more consistent and fair evaluations, reducing variability in decision outcomes for similar applicants.

4.5 Analysis and Interpretations

RQ1: Identifying Cognitive Bias: While early stages of human decisions, such as Shortlisting (SL) and Admission Recommendations (AR) demonstrate strong classification performance i.e. over 8% in F1-Score and accuracy, their consistency scores are notably lower, with AR's being 56.32% and OF's being 60.23%. This disparity between performance metrics and consistency scores suggests potential cognitive biases in the evaluation process. Furthermore, the gradual decrease in consistency from OF to AR stages, i.e. from 60.23% to 56.32%, indicates that biases might become more pronounced in later stages of the admission process, possibly due to increased complexity in decision criteria while maintaining high consistency among different review panels.

RQ2: Consistency Comparison Between ML and Human: The consistency analysis reveals a substantial gap between human and machine learning approaches. Both ML models significantly outperform human decisions in terms of consistency, with Bi-LSTM achieving scores of 80.73% and 77.97% for AR and OF respectively, compared to human scores of 56.32% (AR) and 60.23% (OF). This represents an improvement of approximately 24% in consistency for AR decisions and 18% for OF decisions. The XGB model also demonstrates superior consistency with 75.21% for AR and 74.77% for OF, suggesting that machine learning approaches inherently provide more standardized evaluation patterns. This substantial difference in consistency scores highlights the potential role of ML models in reducing decision variability.

RQ3: Accuracy Comparison Between ML and Human: The performance comparison between human decisions and ML models yields nuanced insights. While human shortlisting achieves the highest precision of 84.64%, the Bi-LSTM model demonstrates comparable overall performance with the highest accuracy of 82.76% and F1-score of 81.76%. Furthermore, the Bi-LSTM's performance metrics closely match or exceed human decision points while maintaining significantly higher consistency scores. The XGB model, while showing lower performance metrics with an F1-score of 78.78%, still maintains higher consistency than human decisions, suggesting a potential trade-off between performance and consistency that varies across different ML architectures.

In summary, the experimental results demonstrate that while human decisions maintain high classification performance, they show lower consistency compared to ML approaches. These findings suggest that ML models could serve as valuable decision support tools, particularly in maintaining consistency across the admission process while preserving high accuracy standards. The results advocate for a carefully designed hybrid approach that combines human expertise with ML-driven consistency checks to optimize both performance and fairness in admission decisions.

5 Conclusion

Fairness in decision-making is critical, whether conducted by artificial intelligence or human. Our work investigates individual fairness, using a consistency score to evaluate decision-making among a diverse group of subjects. Experimental results reveals that ML models such as XGBoost and BiLSTM achieve significantly higher consistency scores than human experts. This finding suggests that ML models can provide more consistent treatment of similar applications, addressing any potential subjectivity and cognitive biases inherent in human decision-making.

Our findings have practical implications for the design of admission systems, suggesting that ML models could serve as valuable decision support tools, particularly in initial screening stages where consistency is crucial. The models could help identify potential inconsistencies in human decisions, prompting additional review in cases where machine and human assessments diverge. Furthermore, the quantification of consistency scores provides a new dimension for evaluating and improving admission processes, beyond traditional accuracy metrics.

Acknowledgments. This research is supported in part by the Ministry of Education, Singapore (MOE), under its Academic Research Fund Tier 2 (Award No. MOE-T2EP20123-0015), and the Singapore University of Technology and Design (SUTD) under grant RS-MEFAI-00011. Any opinions, findings and conclusions, or recommendations expressed in this material are those of the authors and do not reflect the views of MOE or SUTD.

References

1. Alur, R., Laine, L., Li, D.K., Raghavan, M., Shah, D., Shung, D.: Auditing for human expertise. In: Proc. of NeurIPS (2023)
2. Bhattacharya, D., Kanaya, S., Stevens, M.: Are university admissions academically fair? Rev. Econ. Stat. **99**(3), 449–464 (2017)
3. Caliskan, A., Bryson, J.J., Narayanan, A.: Semantics derived automatically from language corpora contain human-like biases. Science **356**(6334), 183–186 (2017)
4. Caton, S., Haas, C.: Fairness in machine learning: a survey. ACM CSUR **56**(7), 1–38 (2024)
5. Dwork, C.: Differential privacy. In: Proc. of ICALP, pp. 1–12 (2006)
6. Dwork, C., Hardt, M., Pitassi, T., Reingold, O., Zemel, R.: Fairness through awareness. In: Proc. of ITCS, p. 214226 (2012)
7. Li, Y., et al.: Fairness in recommendation: foundations, methods, and applications. ACM TiST **14**(5), 1–48 (2023)
8. Liu, J., Lee, R.K.W., Lim, K.H.: Bgm-han: a hierarchical attention network for accurate and fair decision assessment on semi-structured profiles. In: Proc. of ASONAM (2025)
9. Mahoney, T., Varshney, K.R., Hind, M.: AI Fairness: How to Measure and Reduce Unwanted Bias in Machine Learning. O'Reilly (2020)
10. Marcinkowski, F., Kieslich, K., Starke, C., Lünich, M.: Implications of AI (un-) fairness in higher education admissions: the effects of perceived AI (un-) fairness on exit, voice and organizational reputation. In: Proc. of FAT, pp. 122–130(2020)
11. Mehrabi, N., Morstatter, F., Saxena, N., Lerman, K., Galstyan, A.: A survey on bias and fairness in machine learning. ACM CSUR **54**(6), 1–35 (2021)
12. Pitman, T.: Understanding 'fairness' in student selection: are there differences and does it make a difference anyway? Stud. High. Educ. **41**(7), 1203–1216 (2016)
13. Puranik, B., Madhow, U., Pedarsani, R.: A dynamic decision-making framework promoting long-term fairness. In: Proc. of AIES, pp. 547–556 (2022)
14. Unknown, A.: Lessons from debiasing data for fair and accurate predictive modeling in education. Expert Syst. Appl. **231**, 120914 (2023)
15. Van Busum, K., Fang, S.: Analysis of AI models for student admissions: a case study. In: Proc. of SAC, pp. 17–22 (2023)
16. Wang, Y., Ma, W., Zhang, M., Liu, Y., Ma, S.: A survey on the fairness of recommender systems. ACM TOIS **41**(3), 1–43 (2023)

17. Zemel, R., Wu, Y., Swersky, K., Pitassi, T., Dwork, C.: Learning fair representations. In: Proc. of ICML, pp. 325–333 (2013)
18. Zimdars, A.: Fairness and undergraduate admission: a qualitative exploration of admissions choices at the university of oxford. Oxford Rev. Educ. **36**(3), 307–323 (2010)

A Multi-Agent Reinforcement Learning-Based Framework for Forecasting Terrorist Collaboration and Predicting Future Alliances

Vedat Dogan[(✉)], Steven Prestwich, and Barry O' Sullivan

School of Computer Science and IT, Insight SFI Research Centre for Data Analytics,
University College Cork , Cork, Ireland
`{vedat.dogan,steven.prestwich,barry.osullivan}@insight-centre.org`

Abstract. Terrorist activity has increased over the years, leading to the rise of new criminal organizations, the persistence of incidents, and increased collaboration and coordination among criminal entities. This study proposes a framework based on multi-agent reinforcement learning (MARL) to forecast terrorism collaboration dynamics from time-series data and predict future collaborations. Firstly, we retrieve data from the Global Terrorist Database for numerous countries and construct a terrorist collaboration network. Subsequently, we employ the cumulative time series data to construct cumulative temporal graphs, thereby facilitating the observation of the evolution of collaboration over time. Then, we design a reward function that quantifies the lethality of terrorist groups, the benefits of collaborations, the group's role in the network and the effectiveness of the partnership. Finally, we use the learned parameters to generate unobserved terrorist collaboration networks and, therefore, to predict the future potential collaborations for terrorist groups. The research findings demonstrate that the MARL approach exhibits superior forecasting performance in predicting terrorist collaboration networks. Future research endeavours should explore the potential of AI in countering terrorist activities.

Keywords: Forecasting Terrorist Collaboration · Multi-agent Reinforcement Learning · Counter-Terrorism · Predictive Models

1 Introduction

In recent years, terrorism has posed a significant threat to global security, manifesting in the emergence of new criminal organizations, the recurrence of terrorist incidents, and the collaboration and coordination among criminal entities. The *shared* ideological origins, behavioural patterns, and pursuit of goals among these organizations have led to a loose coalition of international criminal networks. This situation has made it more challenging to combat terrorism and heightened the risks it poses to the international security environment.

© The Author(s), under exclusive license to Springer Nature Switzerland AG 2026
A. An et al. (Eds.): ASONAM 2025, LNCS 16323, pp. 146–162, 2026.
https://doi.org/10.1007/978-3-032-13821-7_14

Terrorist acts have emerged as the predominant form of terrorism over the years. Terrorist organizations often exhibit a networked structure. Consequently, the understanding of the network of cooperation among terrorist organizations and the effective implementation of strategies to disrupt organizational alliances have garnered significant attention from scholars and security agencies worldwide. Experts have advocated for a specialized scientific discipline to analyze conflicts, civil wars, and terrorism computationally [15]. Despite this call, efforts to harness AI for these purposes have been limited. While terrorism is inherently uncertain and unpredictable, transdisciplinary research leverages comprehensive data, sophisticated computational models, and a foundational understanding of terrorist behaviour to provide data-driven solutions [21]. Considering all the above, this study aims to propose a framework based on multi-agent reinforcement learning (MARL) to forecast terrorism collaboration dynamics from time series data and predict future collaborations. For this purpose, we focus on terrorist group dynamics and shared incidents over the years. We retrieve data from the Global Terrorism Database (GDT) for numerous countries and construct a terrorism collaboration network. Subsequently, we employ annual time-series data to construct cumulative temporal graphs, thereby observing the evolution of collaboration over the years. We utilize the created time series graphs to learn collaboration dynamics, and periodic patterns between terrorist groups, such as ideological, lethality-based, etc. and related shared event features, such as tactical, operational, and ideological.

In this study, we assume each node representing a terrorist group is an agent in a reinforcement learning (RL) setting. Each agent has three actions: maintaining the current state, making or deleting a collaboration. We design a multi-objective reward function that considers multi-objective lethality, collaboration benefits, network position, and temporal improvement. We assume that the terrorist groups are willing to collaborate to increase the incidence of casualties, therefore lethality, sharing the same ideology and having the same target types, while designing the reward function. Then, we modified the algorithm to learn the reward functions of each node and the policy to learn the strategy to achieve higher rewards. By using the learned policies, we predict the future potential collaborations of terrorist groups based on the MARL simulation. The contributions of this study are three-fold:

1. We propose a novel methodology and framework for forecasting and predicting criminal collaborations by incorporating a diverse range of interpretable features derived from network science, terrorism research and AI literature.
2. We develop a multi-objective lethality-based reward function that quantifies the lethality of a terrorist group based on a wide range of specifications.
3. Also, we use advanced AI techniques in the MARL setting to encode terrorist group and collaboration features and capture network dynamics over the years to extract information for predictions.

These contributions improve the model's learning and prediction of the performance of future terrorism collaboration networks.

The rest of the paper is organized as follows. Section 2 explains the related works to both network prediction and reinforcement learning literature. The GDT dataset that is used for this study is explained in Sect. 6 with data preparation process and proposed node level and edge level features. Section 4 describes the creation of the cumulative temporal terrorist collaboration networks for forecasting purposes and how to put the graphs to time-series. In Sect. 3, we formulate the problem definition and in Sect. 5 we explain the proposed MARL framework with the specifically designed components. Section 6 discuss the experiments with experimental settings and results. Finally, Sect. 7 is devoted to conclusions and future directions of research.

2   Related Works

In this section, we discuss related works in the network prediction and MARL literatures and highlight the differences between existing methods.

Network prediction has become a hot topic through recent advances in AI. Improvements in graph-based deep learning algorithms have especially raised interest in the field. The authors in [10] implemented the GraphSAGE algorithm, which is an improvement on graph convolutional networks (GCN) [27], to generate new node features from the network structure. Also the role classification in criminal networks is studied in [4] by embedding node and edge features with graph neural networks. The ELSM method is proposed in [9] to augment the network structure by using the node's latent variable and the network structure. The STEP algorithm is proposed in [3] to predict the network structure by using temporal and structural information on the network. The DualCast algorithm is proposed in [11] to predict network structure and attributes, and presents competitive results. The NetEvolve framework is a method that uses reinforcement learning to predict social network structure and node features, and it discuss the network types and prediction results in [18]. There are various applications that appear as link prediction tasks in the graph mining literature, and they generally focus on social networks. We refer the reader to [2, 25] for more up-to-date surveys related to this area.

Reinforcement learning (RL) is a machine learning technique that enables an agent to acquire decision-making skills through interactions with an environment. The agent receives rewards for positive actions and penalties for negative ones, thereby guiding its learning process [24]. Multi-agent reinforcement learning [1] is a framework that focuses on the behaviour of multiple agents that interact with the environment in either a cooperative or independent way [19]. Several studies applied the MARL framework to graph learning tasks. For example, authors focused on link prediction in [14] by learning structural changes over time. Another study predicts the emergence of new social network structures in a MARL framework [26]. We refer to recent surveys for a more in-depth review related to this topic [8].

3   Problem Definition

In this section, we define the problem. The input terrorism collaboration network is represented as cumulative temporal graphs. Each node represents a terrorist group, and the edge between groups represents the incidents in which they collaborate. The work consist of learning the collaborations between groups over time and predict the future potential alliances using training data.

Definition 1. *Cumulative Temporal Graphs: A cumulative temporal graph $\mathcal{G}$ is a sequence of T discrete snapshots $\langle \mathcal{G}_1, \mathcal{G}_2, \ldots, \mathcal{G}_T \rangle$ where $\mathcal{G}_t$ denotes the graph at the time t. $\mathcal{G}_t$ is a tuple $\{\mathcal{V}_t, \mathcal{E}_t, \mathbf{X}_t, \mathbf{Y}_t\}$ where $\mathcal{V}$ is a set of vertices, $\mathcal{E}_t$ is the set of undirected edges between vertices at the time t, $\mathbf{X}_t : \mathcal{V} \to \mathbb{R}^n$ is the feature vector with the size n and $\mathbf{Y}_t : \mathcal{E} \to \mathbb{R}^k$ is the feature vector with the size k for vertices and edges in the network, respectively.*

As we mention in Sect. 1, each node, $v_t \in \mathcal{V}_t$ represents a terrorist group in the collaboration network at the period of t in this study. An edge $e_t \in \mathcal{E}_t$ is created whenever associated terrorist groups collaborate on the same event at time t. Finally, the node and edge features, $\mathbf{X}_t$ and $\mathbf{Y}_t$, contains the terrorist group and shared event features. We treat predicting alliances as a decision-making problem in the MARL setting, as each agent has three actions to make to maximize the multi-objective reward function.

Definition 2. *Predicting Alliances: Given a set of cumulative temporal graphs $\{\mathcal{G}_i\}_{t-n}^t$ as training instances $\mathbb{D}$, predict the set of edges $\mathcal{E}_{t'}$ at $t' \in T$ for unseen graphs.*

4   Network Construction

In this section, we introduce a terrorist collaboration network that leverages the advantages of cumulative time-series temporal graphs. First, for each time unit t, the vertices $\mathcal{V}_t$ represent the terrorist groups which conducted attacks and edges $\mathcal{E}_t$ represent the attacks that terrorist groups collaborated on during time period t. The nodes are defined as $\mathcal{V}_t = \{v_i | v_i \in g_i\}$ where v_i represents the nodes in group g_i that is included as a node if it participated in at least one event during the period of t. The edges are defined as $\mathcal{E}_t = \{e_{i,j} | (v_i, v_j) \in \mathcal{V}_t^2 \text{ and } v_i \neq v_j\}$ where $e_{i,j}$ indicating a collaboration which is defined as participation in the same event during t.

Each group is identified with various features related to its lethality, strategic, structural information, and tactical diversity, as defined in Sect. 4.1. We created feature matrix $\mathbf{X}_t$ for each terrorist group, with the dimension of 19 for each time period of t. Then, we created the edge feature matrix $\mathbf{Y}_t$ for the time period of t with the dimension of 8 to capture the collaborated attack characteristics. They are defined as follows:

$$\mathbf{X} = \begin{bmatrix} \mathbf{x}_1 \\ \mathbf{x}_2 \\ \vdots \\ \mathbf{x}_N \end{bmatrix} = \begin{bmatrix} x_{1,1} & x_{1,2} & \cdots & x_{1,F} \\ x_{2,1} & x_{2,2} & \cdots & x_{2,F} \\ \vdots & \vdots & \ddots & \vdots \\ x_{N,1} & x_{N,2} & \cdots & x_{N,F} \end{bmatrix}, \quad \mathbf{Y} = \begin{bmatrix} \mathbf{y}_{1,2}^\top \\ \mathbf{y}_{1,3}^\top \\ \vdots \\ \mathbf{y}_{i,j}^\top \\ \vdots \\ \mathbf{y}_{N-1,N}^\top \end{bmatrix} = \begin{bmatrix} y_{1,2,1} & \cdots & y_{1,2,K} \\ y_{1,3,1} & \cdots & y_{1,3,K} \\ \vdots & \ddots & \vdots \\ y_{i,j,1} & \cdots & y_{i,j,K} \\ \vdots & \ddots & \vdots \\ y_{M-1,M,1} & \cdots & y_{M-1,M,K} \end{bmatrix} \tag{1}$$

where N represents the number of nodes and F represents the number of node features, which is 19 in this study. Also M and K represent the total number of edges and features, respectively. We created features to capture the characteristic information with various aspects of terrorist groups and correlate it with the future collaboration. The features capture collaboration details, tactical and operational similarity of collaborated groups and the lethality of the shared attacks. Finally, we define the cumulative temporal network $\mathcal{G}_t$ as $\mathcal{G}_t = (\mathcal{V}_t, \mathcal{E}_t, \mathbf{X}, \mathbf{Y})$ where t represents the defined time period.

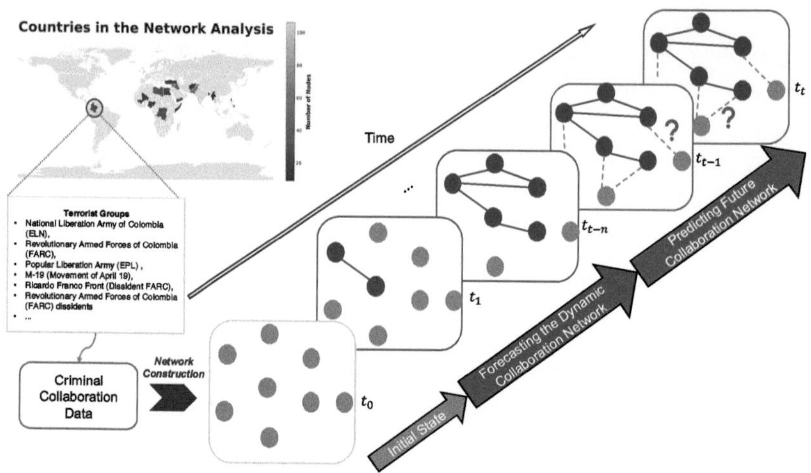

Fig. 1. Illustration for the network construction from tabular data.

In this study, we consider the annual-based time series. For each selected country, the time-series of graphs is created starting from the first date that collaboration has appeared until the activity date in the dataset. The nodes and edges in the graphs are considered in a cumulative way to keep track of the historical evolution and temporal networks to capture the existing characteristics. Therefore, each cumulative time-series temporal graph $\mathcal{G}_t$ can be defined as $\mathcal{G}_t = \{\mathcal{G} | \mathcal{G}_{t-1} \in \mathcal{G}_t, 1 \leq t \leq T\}$ where t is a time stamp. For instance, an illustration of the collaboration network graphs is given in Fig. 1. The illustrative network belongs to a country and has, presumably, 8 total groups that are collaborated until the end of the period, and the first collaboration appears in t_0. As the last data period is t_t, we use the $t - n + 1$ network to train and n networks to test where n is 30% of the total number of graph networks. As we can see from the Figure, the network is evolving over the years, and the proposed algorithm aims to predict the future collaboration by learning from the time-series graphs with MARL.

4.1 Proposed Features

To capture the specifications of terrorist groups and events related to collaboration, we needed to develop new feature metrics that would specifically address the *lethality metrics, network structure, activity metrics, tactical diversity* and *temporal collaborations* on the terrorist group level. On the event level, we created *basic collaboration metrics, tactical similarity, operational similarity* and *combined lethality metrics*. We explained node level features as follows:

- The first feature is the total collaborations of the group so far, represented with C_i.
- The second feature is the proposed multi-objective lethality , and it considers multiple aspects of lethality for the related group. The lethality metric has four metrics:
  - The first lethality metric is *casualty_impact*, which represents the casualties caused by the group and contains a number of *kills* that the group has and the number of *wounded* people.
  - The second lethality metric is *operational_efficiency*, which represents the success rate and survival ratio of the group.
  - The third one is *tactical_sophistication*, which we define as diversity in weapons, targets, tactics and use of suicide or multiple attacks.
  - The last metric is *strategic_impact*, representing the property damage, attack frequency and average kills per attack. We aim to capture the lethality of the group accurately with a detailed multi-objective structure.
- We used the statistical network metrics for each group as a third node level feature. We used three metrics to represent the network structure which are *degree centrality, clustering coefficient*, and *betweenness centrality*.
- We used the *activity metric* to capture the tactical sophistication, and we identify it with four features: *Total attacks, average casualties success rate* and *property damage rate* represents as it means.
- We define *tactical diversity* with two features, *weapon diversity* and *target diversity*, which represent the types of weapons and types of targets attacked, respectively.

In terms of edge level features, we define the *basic collaboration metrics* with two created features, *weights* and *average casualties* in the shared attacks. *Tactical similarity* features are *attack similarity, weapon similarity*, and *target similarity* of the groups that collaborate on attacks. We define *operational similarity* with two features, which are *geographic overlap* and *temporal overlap*, representing the fraction of overlapping regions and overlapping active time periods for the groups, respectively. Lastly, *combined lethality* is the aggregated lethality metric of shared attacks.

5   Proposed Method

This section describes the proposed method for predicting the future terrorist collaboration network based on MARL using cumulative temporal criminal networks. The illustration of the proposed method for forecasting criminal collaborations is shared on Fig. 2. We discuss the environment for graph networks in Sect. 5.1, and reward and policy function for the agents in Sect. 5.2 and Sect. 5.3, respectively.

5.1   Environment

We designed the environment of reinforcement learning (RL) as the Markov Decision Process (MDP), which contains the state $\mathcal{S}_t$, action $\mathcal{A}_t$ and reward $\mathcal{R}_t$. In MDPs, the agents make decisions based on the current state by utilizing a policy function $\pi(\mathcal{A}_t|\mathcal{S}_t, \theta)$ where θ is the parameter of the policy function. After the agents make the actions, the state changes accordingly, and the transition function is defined as $f(\mathcal{S}_{t+1}|\mathcal{S}_t, \mathcal{A}_t)$. The rewards are calculated based on the defined function $r(\mathcal{S}_t|\Psi)$ where Ψ is the parameters of the function. In RL, the objective is to learn the parameter for the defined policy that maximizes the expected reward for the agent's actions.

In this study, we exploit the RL setting to learn from time-series graph networks and we defined the states as the current terrorist collaboration network $\mathcal{G}_t$ and the actions as the change in the graph and defined as $\Delta\mathcal{G}_t = (\Delta\mathcal{E}_t|\mathbf{X}_t, \mathbf{Y}_t)$. The $\Delta\mathcal{E}_t$ represents the edge changes in the graph at the period of t and $\mathbf{X}_t, \mathbf{Y}_t$ represents the node and edge attributes, respectively. Therefore, the reward and the policy function can be defined as $r(\mathcal{G}_t|\Psi)$ and $\pi(\Delta\mathcal{G}_t|\mathcal{G}_t, \theta)$, respectively. Now, we can define the state transition for the network as $f(\mathcal{G}_{t+1}|\mathcal{G}_t, \mathcal{A}_t) = \{\mathcal{V}_t, \mathcal{E}_t \cup \Delta\mathcal{E}_t, \mathbf{X}, \mathbf{Y}\}$.

In the MARL setting, we assume each agent acts as a node v_i in a network. The reward and policy functions for each agent are defined as $r_i(\mathcal{G}_t|\Psi_i)$ and $\pi_i(\Delta\mathcal{G}_t|\mathcal{G}_t, \theta_i)$ respectively. In this study, we assume the reward function for the overall graph is the summation of each node's reward and product of each node's policy, defined as;

$$r(\mathcal{G}_t|\Psi) = \sum_{v_i \in \mathcal{V}} r_i(\mathcal{G}_t|\Psi_i) \ , \pi(\Delta\mathcal{G}_t|\mathcal{G}_t, \theta) = \prod_{v_i \in \mathcal{V}} \pi_i(\Delta\mathcal{G}_t|\mathcal{G}_t, \theta_i) \tag{2}$$

where $\Psi = \{\psi_i\}_{v_i \in \mathcal{V}}$ and $\theta = \{\theta_i\}_{v_i \in \mathcal{V}}$ are the reward and policy function's parameter, respectively.

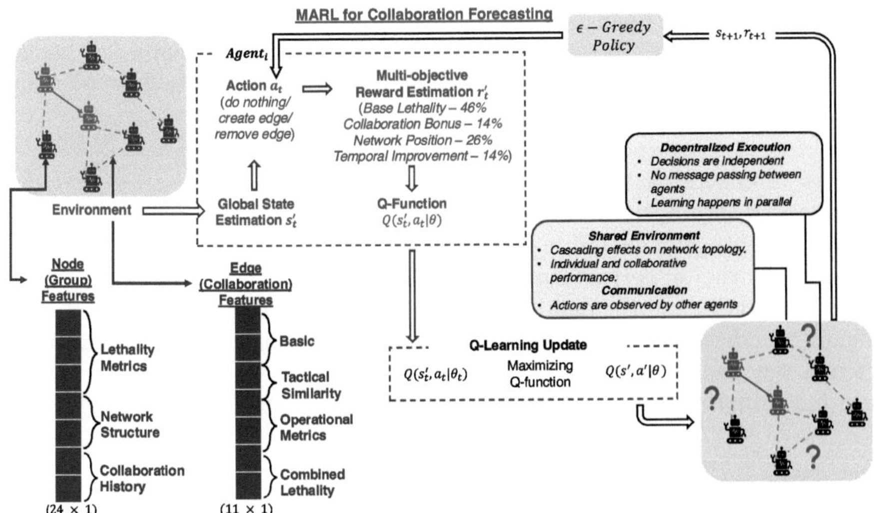

Fig. 2. Framework of the MARL approach for forecasting criminal collaboration.

5.2 Reward Function

This section describes the design of the reward function for each agent (*node*) for a given terrorist collaboration network. We design the reward function to measure the lethality of a terrorist group, the benefits of collaborations, the group's role in the network and the effectiveness of the partnership.

We define the reward function in a terrorism collaboration network $\mathcal{G}_t$ at the time of t for each agent (node) as follows:

$$r_i(\mathcal{G}_t | \Psi_i) = w_1 L_{i,t} + w_2 \Delta L_{i,t} + w_3 P_{i,t} + w_4 C_{i,t} \tag{3}$$

where $L_{i,t}, \Delta L_{i,t}, P_{i,t}$ and $C_{i,t}$ are base lethality score of v_i, improvement in lethality due to new collaborations, network position reward based on centrality and clustering and collaboration reward by motivating effective partnerships. The components of multi-objective reward functions are defined as follows. *The base lethality score $L_{i,t}$* captures the operational effectiveness of a terrorist group at the time period of t, which is defined as $L_{i,t} = w_c C_i + w_o O_i + w_t T_i + w_s S_i$ where C_i, O_i, T_i and S_i are causality impact, operational efficiency, tactical sophistication and strategic impact, respectively. *Lethality improvement, $\Delta L_{i,t}$,* encourages the formation of mutually beneficial partnerships and defined as $\Delta L_{i,t} = \max(0, L_{i,j,t} - (L_{i,t} + L_{i,j}))$ where $L_{i,j,t}$ is combined lethality of the terrorist groups i and j after collaboration. *Network position reward* encourages the agents to improve their network roles and is defined as;

$$P_{i,t} = \alpha \times DegreeCentrality_{i,t} + \beta \times ClusteringCoefficient_{i,t} \tag{4}$$

Collaboration reward, $C_{i,t}$ gives the reward for successful collaborations and defined as follows:

$$C_{i,t} = \lambda \times SuccessRate_{i,j,t} \tag{5}$$

154   V. Dogan et al.

The rewards defined above motivate agents to improve their lethality, forge mutually beneficial partnerships, and enhance their network's position. Moreover, the reward function incorporates weighted components to ensure that multiple objectives are balanced. We optimized the weights of the components, and shared in Table 1. The weights are the hyperparameters for the

Table 1. The optimized weights (best) of the multi-objective reward function.

Reward Component	Weight (%)
Base Lethality	46%
Collaboration Reward	14%
Network Position	26%
Temporal Improvement	14%

MARL approach, and the details of the optimization are shared in Sect. 6. Additionally, the design of a multi-objective reward function guarantees that agents act in a way that collectively enhances the network's effectiveness, considering both individual node dynamics and network-wide dynamics.

5.3   Policy

We describe the deep Q-network based policy in this section. We design the policy function by assuming that each agent (node v_i) can take three actions: *maintain the position, make an edge* and *delete an edge*.

The policy is derived from the Q-value function, $\mathcal{Q}(s_i, a_i, ; \theta)$, which represents the expected cumulative reward when an agent takes action a in the state s. It is defined as:

$$\mathcal{Q}(s_i, a_i; \theta) = \mathbb{E}_\pi \left[\sum_{t=0}^{T-1} \gamma^t R_{i,t} | s_{i,t} = s_i, a_{i,t} = a_i \right] \tag{6}$$

where $R_{i,t}, \gamma$ and θ are the rewards at time t, a discount factor ($0 < \gamma \leq 1$) that weights future rewards, and the parameters of the Q-network, respectively. So, we define the policy function as $\pi(s_i) = \arg\max Q(s_i, a_i; \theta)$ with deterministic policy. According to that, the action a_i with the highest Q-value is chosen. During the training policy, we used ϵ-greedy policy for exploration, which is defined as;

$$\pi_\epsilon(s_i) = \begin{cases} \text{random action } \textit{with probability } \epsilon \\ \arg\max Q(s_i, a_i; \theta) \textit{ with probability } 1 - \epsilon \end{cases} \tag{7}$$

where ϵ is the exploration rate and it decays over time to balance exploration and exploitation. To approximate the $Q(s_i, a_i; \theta)$, the Q-network takes the state vector, which has 24 dimensions in this study (*16 historical metrics, 4 network features and 4 collaboration history of the group*), extracts the features with hidden layers and gives the Q-value for each action $a_i \in \mathcal{A}_i$. It is defined as $Q_\theta(s_i, a_i) = f_\theta(g_\phi(s_i))$ where g_ϕ is feature encoder vector, f_θ is Q-network and ϕ and θ are network parameters. The network is trained using the Bellman equation, defined as $Q_i(s_i, a_i; \theta) = R_i(s_i, a_i) + \gamma \max_{a_i'} Q_i(s_i', a_i'; \theta^-)$ where $R(s_i, a_i)$ is immediate reward, s' is the following state and θ^- is the parameters of the target Q-network. The loss function is the mean squared error between the predicted Q-values and target Q-values, and defined as:

$$L(\theta) = \mathbb{E}_{s_i, a_i, r_i, s_i'} \left[(y - Q(s_i, a_i; \theta))^2 \right] \tag{8}$$

where the target defined as $y = R(s_i, a_i) + \gamma \max_{a_i'} Q(s_i', a_i'; \theta^-)$. The experience replay is used in a way that transitions (s_i, a_i, r_i, s_i') for the terrorist group (the agent v_i) in a replay buffer and batches are sampled randomly for training to break correlation between consecutive experiences. The target Q-network parameter θ^- is updated periodically to stabilize training, and gradients of the loss are computed and used to update the parameters θ, defined as $\theta \leftarrow \theta - \eta \Delta_\theta L(\theta)$ where η is the learning rate. In multi-agent extension, each agent maintains its own Q-network, meaning that each terrorist group (as a node in the network) has their own feature embeddings. Each state, action and reward of the terrorist groups can be defined as $\mathcal{S} = \{s_1, \ldots, s_N\}$ and $\mathcal{A} = \{a_1, \ldots, a_N\}$ where N is the number of terrorist groups, meaning agents, and each agent optimizes its own Q-function with the Bellman equation. The learned parameters are used to generate unobserved terrorist collaboration networks and, therefore, to predict the future collaboration of terrorist groups.

6   Experiments

We evaluated our proposed approach to capture future collaborations on real-world criminal groups. We use the GTD dataset to filter the terrorist attacks in the top countries where the terrorist groups collaborated the most. These countries are *India, Pakistan, Afghanistan, Colombia, Philippines, the Democratic Republic of the Congo, Iraq, Israel, Turkey, West Bank and Gaza Strip, Bangladesh, Myanmar, USA* and *Egypt*. For every dataset, we consider the following settings. We selected the beginning of the time period, t_0 of as the first date of the first collaboration appears, and the end of time period, t_k is the last attack that occurred according to the dataset. Then, we created the cumulative temporal graph networks as described in Sect. 4. The date of the first collaboration appears is different for each country as we can see in Fig. 4. So, it affected the selection of the training and testing time periods and the amount of years accordingly. For the implementation, the datasets are available online[1].

Dataset. The data is retrieved from the GTD, maintained by the START research centre at the University of Maryland [13]. The GTD is an event-level database with over 200,000 records of terrorist attacks worldwide for the dates between 1970 and 2020. It is the world's most comprehensive and detailed open-access dataset on terrorist events. START releases an updated version annually. To be included, an event must meet specific criteria divided into two levels. The first level includes three essential aspects: intentionality and violence level and the sub-national nature of terrorist actors. The second level has three criteria, but at least two must be met. These relate to political, economic, religious, or

---

[1] https://www.start.umd.edu/data-tools/GTD.

social objectives, coercion or intimidation, and legitimate warfare activities. An event meets the criteria and is included, but there is a control mechanism for conflicting information or acts not exclusively of a terrorist nature. Each event is associated with various variables, including geographic and temporal information, event characteristics, and economic damages, and attack perpetrators' identities.

After retrieving the data, we analyse the incidents with the most collaboration and the countries that occurred. We can see the top 20 countries that contain the highest number of terrorist groups and collaborative events in Fig. 3. Each event has three group features that represent the names of connected terrorist groups, *gname*, *gname2* and *gname3*. We filled the missing values with 'unknown'. After handling other missing numerical and categorical values, we scaled the features and made the necessary normalization. To create the collaboration network and

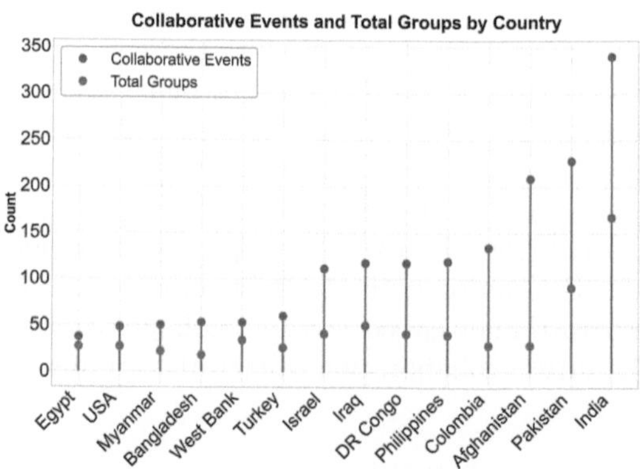

Fig. 3. Total terrorist groups in each country at the end of the time period—nodes in the network—and the number of events that these terrorist groups are collaborated—edges in the network—for each country.

extract the useful information from data, we propose node and edge level features, and present them in Sect. 4.1.

Experimental Setting. In the experiments, we manually set the parameters of the reward and the policy functions, and then we observe how the proposed algorithm updates it. We expect that the proposed algorithm updates the parameters such that the future collaboration network to observe potential alliances of a terrorist group. The node counts collaboration networks is different for each country. Also, we set the node and edge features for model to learn terrorist group and related attack characteristics to measure the components to built the reward function, as described in Sect. 5.2. We shared all formulations and descriptions of the features in Sect. 2 in Y material. For instance, in Iraq, there are 50 total groups that are collaborated and 117 recorded collaborated events between 2003 and 2021. Therefore, for the forecasting collaboration network for Iraq, there are 50 nodes and 117 edges at the end of the period. We compare the quality of the predictions of the algorithms using the area under the ROC curve (ROC-AUC) [6] and prediction accuracy. We run our experiments on a machine with an Apple M4 Pro chip with a 12-core CPU, 16-core GPU and 16-core Neural Engine computer.

Train/Test Split: We evaluate the methods by running 20 times pre train/test split and we report the average results with standard deviation. For each dataset, we selected the annual time periods and we used the 70% of the time segments as training, 30% of the time segments for testing the proposed framework's prediction performances. We shared the splits for each country in Fig. 4. Train/test splits are applied for all countries are listed seperately starting from the date of the first collaboration.

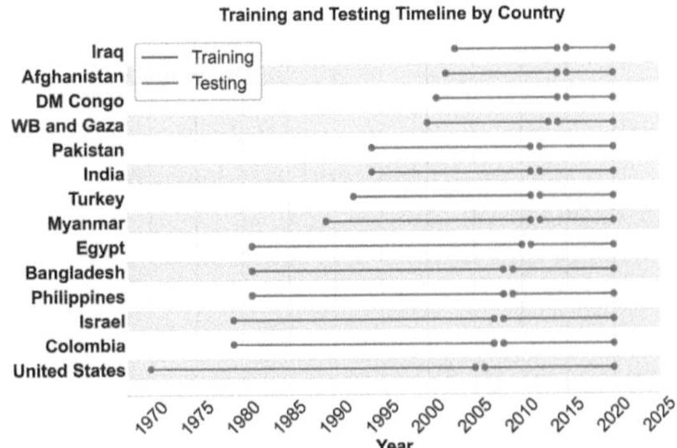

Fig. 4. Train-test (70%/30%) split of the data for each country. The first snapshot of the criminal group is considered when the first collaboration appears between groups.

Baselines: We consider different approaches, including traditional and modern machine learning algorithms proposed for graph network forecasting. We choose the logistic regression and random forest to present the performance if the data is tabular, and these methods are successful methods to predict linear and non-linear relationships. The temporal graph convolutional network (TempGCN) will present the performance with graph embeddings and compare our result with the graph neural network-based model.

- **Random Forest (RF)** [5] is a successful technique that is used for various purposes including forecasting on temporal data [16,20]. It creates multiple decision trees, and each tree votes on collaboration likelihood. For the final prediction, it combines the votes and uses feature randomization for a better generalization. The main advantage of RF is it captures the complex, non-linear relationships.
- **Logistic Regression (LR)** [7] is a widely used common technique for forecasting in the literature [17]. LR uses a linear combination of the explained and proposed features in Sect. 4 and applies a sigmoid function to estimate the probability of collaboration. The data is used as tabular data, and the problem is assumed as a binary classification problem as the algorithm decides if there is a collaboration.
- **TempGCN** [27] combines the graph convolutional network (GCN) and gated recurrent unit. GCN is used to capture the topological structure of the network, and a gated recurrent unit is used to capture the dynamic change of the graph. It has been used to forecast numerous domain in the literature [22,23].

Hyperparameters: We use the deep Q-network based agents and the feature encoder network is 3-layer MLP, set as "State_dim $\rightarrow$ **MLP**(64) $\rightarrow$ *ReLu* $\rightarrow$ **MLP**(32) $\rightarrow$ *ReLu* $\rightarrow$ **MLP**(3)" where **MLP**(n) means a fully-connected layer with output size of n, and *ReLu* means Rectified Linear Units. We set *memory buffer size* as $10,000$ and the learning rate as 0.001. We used ϵ-greedy policy for exploration and set epsilon decay to 0.995 with a minimum epsilon value of 0.01. For the reward function components, the weights are the hyperparameters of the MARL approach, and we aim to increase the prediction accuracy by optimizing the weights with the Bayesian optimization (BO) [12] algorithm, which is successful hyperparameter optimization (HPO) technique. For the HPO, we created a simulation dataset with random country's networks and applied BO over these datasets. We shared the distribution density and space exploration on Fig. 5. We can see from the figure how different weights affect the accuracy, and we select the best weight configuration for our experiments.

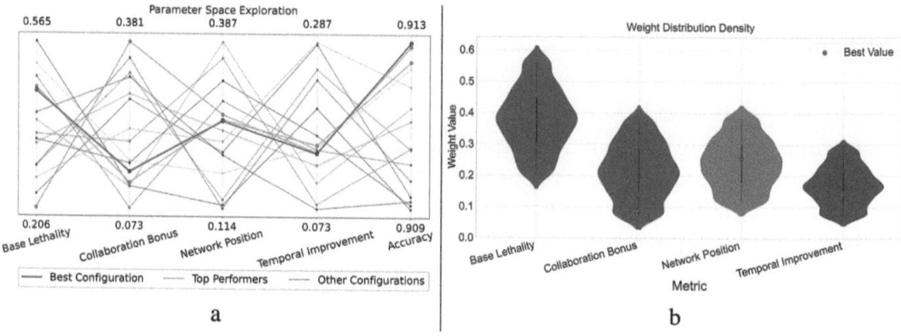

Fig. 5. The search space exploration for the weights of the reward components (a) and the final weight distribution density (b) of the BO for HPO process.

6.1   Predicting Collaboration Accuracy

Table 2 shows the prediction accuracy interms of ROC AUC and prediction accuracy scores. Across all countries, the MARL approach reaches 0.853 and 0.879 accuracy and ROC AUC scores on average. Results also show that the proposed MARL approach outperforms the competing approaches to predict collaboration in criminal networks for all countries in terms of ROC AUC score. In particular, MARL outperforms TempGCN— the best baseline—by 21%, 10.95%, 10% for predicting alliances of terrorist groups in the US, India and Pakistan in terms of ROC AUC score. Also, MARL improves TempGCN model prediction accuracy by 10.8% in terms of accuracy. The countries which has the highest number fo groups and collaborations are Afghanistan, Pakistan and India. Across all countries, the MARL approach improves the best baseline about 7.7% and 3.8% in terms of ROC AUC and accuracy scores, respectively.

Table 2. ROC AUC scores and accuracies of criminal network forecasting across the baseline. The highest and second-highest values for each column are in bold and underlined, respectively. We performed a paired t-test comparing the best model against the others (markers ** and * indicate p-value < .01 and < .05, respectively).

Method	Metric	India	Pakistan	Afghanistan	Colombia	Philippines	Iraq	DR Congo
TempGCN	Accuracy	0.769** ± 0.043	0.770** ± 0.120	0.769* ± 0.091	0.792** ± 0.046	0.801 ± 0.025	0.802** ± 0.037	0.797* ± 0.124
	ROC AUC	0.840** ± 0.023	0.830 ± 0.072	0.819 ± 0.080	0.808** ± 0.027	0.845* ± 0.026	0.756** ± 0.045	0.841 ± 0.092
RF	Accuracy	0.834** ± 0.001	0.818** ± 0.013	0.759** ± 0.013	0.837* ± 0.001	**0.802** ± 0.021	0.813** ± 0.003	**0.846** ± 0.014
	ROC AUC	0.825** ± 0.003	0.796** ± 0.021	0.755** ± 0.001	0.827** ± 0.002	0.769** ± 0.018	0.786** ± 0.008	0.782** ± 0.027
LR	Accuracy	0.789** ± 0.023	0.752** ± 0.091	0.751** ± 0.001	0.802** ± 0.003	0.772* ± 0.061	0.825* ± 0.043	0.801** ± 0.144
	ROC AUC	0.756** ± 0.035	0.783** ± 0.156	0.757** ± 0.014	0.769** ± 0.009	0.804 ± 0.099	0.754** ± 0.071	0.778* ± 0.176
MARL (Proposed)	Accuracy	**0.916** ± 0.044	**0.883** ± 0.120	**0.821** ± 0.091	**0.854** ± 0.047	0.758** ± 0.025	**0.877** ± 0.038	0.852 ± 0.125
	ROC AUC	**0.932** ± 0.024	**0.913** ± 0.072	**0.871** ± 0.080	**0.895** ± 0.027	**0.848** ± 0.029	**0.909** ± 0.046	**0.894** ± 0.092

Method	Metric	Israel	Turkey	Bangladesh	West Bank	Myanmar	US	Egypt
TempGCN	Accuracy	0.828* ± 0.051	**0.849** ± 0.025	0.773** ± 0.115	0.793** ± 0.049	0.805* ± 0.044	0.796** ± 0.042	0.790* ± 0.077
	ROC AUC	0.774** ± 0.048	0.810** ± 0.026	0.759 ± 0.080	0.826** ± 0.016	0.820 ± 0.064	0.796** ± 0.012	0.829 ± 0.082
RF	Accuracy	0.839** ± 0.001	0.835* ± 0.005	**0.812** ± 0.001	0.844 ± 0.001	**0.832** ± 0.002	0.753** ± 0.005	0.803* ± 0.007
	ROC AUC	0.831** ± 0.002	0.835** ± 0.009	0.778** ± 0.002	0.848** ± 0.001	0.820 ± 0.004	0.738** ± 0.001	0.784** ± 0.009
LR	Accuracy	0.777** ± 0.015	0.811 ± 0.192	0.790** ± 0.008	0.755** ± 0.001	0.831** ± 0.002	0.741** ± 0.002	**0.810** ± 0.022
	ROC AUC	0.779** ± 0.016	0.782** ± 0.102	0.757** ± 0.007	0.750** ± 0.002	0.820 ± 0.006	0.750** ± 0.000	0.823 ± 0.013
MARL (Proposed)	Accuracy	**0.861** ± 0.052	0.801** ± 0.025	0.770** ± 0.116	**0.852** ± 0.050	0.765** ± 0.044	**0.882** ± 0.042	0.759* ± 0.078
	ROC AUC	**0.897** ± 0.048	**0.864** ± 0.026	**0.834** ± 0.080	**0.885** ± 0.016	**0.848** ± 0.065	**0.911** ± 0.012	**0.847** ± 0.083

Table 3 shows the performance improvements of the best performed model comparing with the second best one for each country. We can see that RF is the best model for the networks in Bangladesh, Myanmar, and the Philippines, TempGCN for Turkey and LR for Egypt. Myanmar, Bangladesh, and Egypt have relatively small node and edge numbers in the criminal

Table 3. Performance improvements (%) of the best model over the second-best model.

Country	Accuracy			ROC AUC		
	%Imp	Best	2nd	%Imp	Best	2nd
US	10.80	MARL	TempGCN	21.47	MARL	TempGCN
Iraq	6.30	MARL	LR	15.65	MARL	RF
India	9.83	MARL	RF	10.95	MARL	TempGCN
Pakistan	7.95	MARL	RF	10.00	MARL	TempGCN
Afghanistan	6.76	MARL	TempGCN	6.35	MARL	TempGCN
Israel	2.62	MARL	RF	7.94	MARL	RF
Colombia	2.03	MARL	RF	8.22	MARL	RF
Bangladesh	2.78	RF	LR	7.20	MARL	RF
DR Congo	0.71	MARL	RF	6.30	MARL	TempGCN
Turkey	1.68	TempGCN	RF	3.47	MARL	RF
West Bank	0.47	MARL	RF	4.36	MARL	RF
Myanmar	0.12	RF	LR	3.41	MARL	TempGCN
Egypt	0.87	LR	RF	2.17	MARL	TempGCN
Philippines	0.12	RF	TempGCN	0.36	MARL	TempGCN

network that they have as they are in the smallest 4 networks group in Fig. 3. We believe the good performance of RF and LR compared with graph-structured models is based on the small size of the data for these countries, as the TempGCN needs a graph structure to capture the dynamics, and MARL needs to train more episodes for small and limited data. Other than these countries, we can see from Table 3, our proposed MARL algorithm improved the performance for both metrics, starting from 0.41% to 16.6% for the worst and best performance, respectively. The experiments can be extended to the desired country in the same setting, and future collaborations can be predicted. As each agent is a terrorist group, also only a terrorist group's alliance preference can be observed by testing single agent's prediction.

7   Conclusion

This paper focused on predicting collaborations in a dynamic criminal networks. We proposed a novel framework based on MARL to forecast criminal collaborations and predict future alliances. We also propose components to design a reward function for criminal networks based on characteristic details and event information. The MARL-based framework with the specifically designed reward and policy functions explicitly models the criminal collaboration networks to forecast and predict future potential partnerships. Using the learned parameters, the model can be derived for other networks for other countries, groups and territories throughout a series of event observations. We compared our results against multiple baselines. Our approach outperformed the baselines in terms of ROC AUC score and prediction accuracy. Experiments show that the proposed algorithm can learn the group and event characteristics with various aspect, and use them to forecast criminal network collaborations and predict future networks. It also can be used for collaboration network reshaping in the case of long term inactivity of a specific criminal group. The proposed algorithm fills a gap in the AI and counter-terrorism literature and accurately predicts the behaviour of real world criminal networks. For future work, we aim to increase explainability, use designed reward and policy functions to reshape the networks in the case of emergency and observe collaborative and competitive agents behaviour along with the model performance.

References

1. Albrecht, S.V., Christianos, F., Schäfer, L.: Multi-Agent Reinforcement Learning: Foundations and Modern Approaches. MIT Press (2024)
2. Arrar, D., Kamel, N., Lakhfif, A.: A comprehensive survey of link prediction methods. J. Supercomput. **80**(3), 3902–3942 (2023)
3. Chen, H., Li, J.: Exploiting structural and temporal evolution in dynamic link prediction. In: Proceedings of the 27th ACM International Conference on Information and Knowledge Management, pp. 427–436. CIKM '18, Association for Computing Machinery, New York (2018)
4. Dogan, V., Prestwich, S.: In: Graph neural network-based role classification in criminal networks. In: The International Conference on Computational Science and Computational Intelligence (CSCI) Research Track on Cyber Warfare, Cyber Defense Cyber Security. Springer Nature Switzerland, Cham (2024)
5. Dudek, G.: A comprehensive study of random forest for short-term load forecasting. Energies **15**(20) (2022)
6. Fawcett, T.: An introduction to roc analysis. Patt. Recogn. Lett. **27**(8), 861–874 (2006), rOC Analysis in Pattern Recognition

7. Feng, R., Wang, J., Wu, W., Liu, S., Liu, A., Xie, S.: Saturated load forecasting based on improved logistic regression and affinity propagation. Electric Power Syst. Res. **237**, 110953 (2024)
8. Gronauer, S., Diepold, K.: Multi-agent deep reinforcement learning: a survey. Artif. Intell. Rev. **55**, 895–943 (2022)
9. Gupta, S., Sharma, G., Dukkipati, A.: A generative model for dynamic networks with applications. In: Proceedings of the AAAI Conference on Artificial Intelligence, vol. 33, no. 01, pp. 7842–7849 (2019)
10. Hamilton, W.L., Ying, R., Leskovec, J.: Inductive representation learning on large graphs. In: Proceedings of the 31st International Conference on Neural Information Processing Systems, pp. 1025–1035. NIPS'17, Curran Associates Inc., Red Hook (2017)
11. Ito, H., Faloutsos, C.: Dualcast: friendship-preference co-evolution forecasting for attributed networks. In: SIAM (2022)
12. Jones, D., Schonlau, M., Welch, W.: Efficient global optimization of expensive black-box functions. J. Global Optimization **13**, 455-492 (12 (1998). https://doi.org/10.1023/A:1008306431147
13. Introducing the global terrorism database: LaFree, Gary, L.D. Terrorism and Political Violence **19**, 181–204 (2007)
14. Lim, M., Abdullah, A., Jhanjhi, N., Khurram Khan, M., Supramaniam, M.: Link prediction in time-evolving criminal network with deep reinforcement learning technique. IEEE Access **7**, 184797–184807 (2019)
15. McKendrick, K.: Artificial intelligence prediction and counterterrorism. The Royal Institute of International Affairs-Chatham House 9, London (2019)
16. Meher, B.K., Singh, M., Birau, R., Anand, A.: Forecasting stock prices of fintech companies of india using random forest with high-frequency data. J. Open Innov. Technol. Market Complexity **10**(1), 100180 (2024)
17. Mittal, H.K., Dalal, P., Garg, P., Joon, R.: Forecasting pollution trends: comparing linear, logistic regression, and neural networks. In: 2024 International Conference on Emerging Innovations and Advanced Computing (INNOCOMP), pp. 411–419 (2024)
18. Miyake, K., Ito, H., Faloutsos, C., Matsumoto, H., Morishima, A.: Netevolve: social network forecasting using multi-agent reinforcement learning with interpretable features. In: Proceedings of the ACM Web Conference 2024, pp. 2542–2551. WWW '24, Association for Computing Machinery, New York (2024)
19. Ning, Z., Xie, L.: A survey on multi-agent reinforcement learning and its application. J. Automation Intell. **3**(2), 73–91 (2024)
20. Olcay, K., Gíray Tunca, S., Aríf Özgür, M.: Forecasting and performance analysis of energy production in solar power plants using long short-term memory (LSTM) and random forest models. IEEE Access **12**, 103299–103312 (2024)
21. Schiermeier, Q.: Attempts to predict terrorist attacks hit limits. Nature **517**, 7535 (2015)
22. Sun, C., Ning, Y., Shen, D., Nie, T.: Graph neural network-based short-term load forecasting with temporal convolution. Data Sci. Eng. **9**, 1–20 (2023)
23. Sun, L., Liu, M., Liu, G., Chen, X., Yu, X.: FD-TGCN: fast and dynamic temporal graph convolution network for traffic flow prediction. Inf. Fusion **106**, 102291 (2024)
24. Sutton, R.S., Barto, A.G.: Reinforcement learning: an introduction. The MIT Press, 2nd edn. (2018)
25. Xia, F., et al.: Graph learning: a survey. IEEE Trans. Artif. Intell. **2**(2), 109–127 (2021)

26. Yu, L., Song, J., Ermon, S.: Multi-agent adversarial inverse reinforcement learning. ArXiv abs/1907.13220 (2019)
27. Zhao, L., Song, Y., Deng, M., Li, H.: Temporal graph convolutional network for urban traffic flow prediction method. CoRR abs/1811.05320 (2018)

MultiScale Spectral GNN for Fraud Detection

Melike Yildiz Aktas[1]([✉]) , Mustafa Coskun[2]([✉]) , and Chang-Tien Lu[1]([✉])

[1] Department of Computer Science, Virginia Tech, Alexandria, VA 22305, USA
{melike,clu}@vt.edu
[2] Department of Artificial Intelligence and Data Engineering, Ankara University,
Ankara, Turkey
coskun.mustafa@ankara.edu.tr

Abstract. Learning on graphs that exhibit both homophilic and heterophilic structures remains a fundamental challenge in graph representation learning, particularly for critical applications such as fraud detection. Existing studies typically model the underlying graph as either homophilic or heterophilic; however, real-world graphs often display varying degrees of homophily across different subgraphs. To address this limitation, we propose a novel model, the MultiScale Spectral Graph Neural Network (MSSGNN), which tackles this challenge by integrating multi-level spectral filtering with relation-aware subgraph decomposition. Our approach introduces a hierarchical spectral filtering framework employing Beta wavelets at multiple scales, enabling the model to effectively capture diverse heterophily patterns. Node clusters are dynamically extracted based on local edge homophily scores, computed by a lightweight Relation-Aware module. Customized wavelet filters with adaptive propagation depths are applied to each subgraph, and the outputs are fused through a learnable attention mechanism to adaptively integrate multi-level heterophily signals. Experimental results on benchmark fraud detection datasets demonstrate that MSSGNN outperforms existing methods, validating the effectiveness of hierarchical spectral processing and relation-aware subgraph modeling. This work provides a flexible and principled approach for learning robust node representations in highly irregular and adversarial graph environments.

Keywords: Spectral graph neural network · Fraud detection · Heterophily · Homophily

1 Introduction

In real-world graph-based systems, such as financial transaction networks and e-commerce platforms, fraudsters often associate with legitimate entities to evade detection [1], as illustrated in Fig. 1. This behavior introduces heterophily—a phenomenon where connected nodes belong to different classes—posing significant challenges for conventional graph neural networks (GNNs) that typically

© The Author(s), under exclusive license to Springer Nature Switzerland AG 2026
A. An et al. (Eds.): ASONAM 2025, LNCS 16323, pp. 163–176, 2026.
https://doi.org/10.1007/978-3-032-13821-7_15

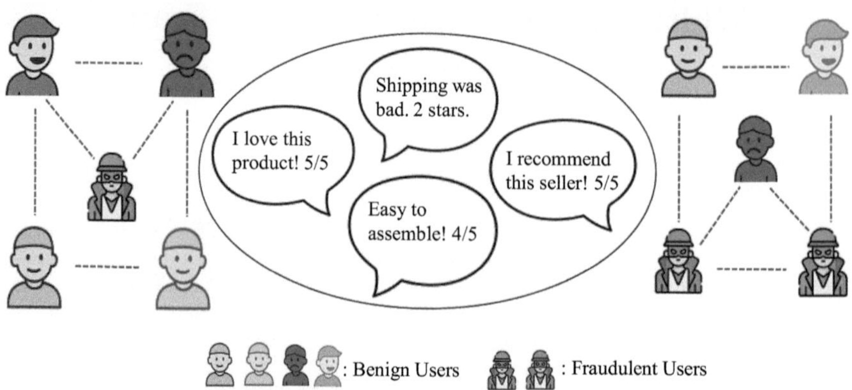

Fig. 1. In online platforms, fraudulent users often connect with benign users and positively interact with shared items (e.g., fake reviews or ratings). This creates a heterophilic graph structure where fraudsters camouflage within legitimate communities, making them difficult to detect using traditional GNNs that assume homophily.

assume homophily [2]. Effectively learning node representations in the presence of both homophilic and heterophilic structures thus remains a central challenge in graph representation learning, particularly for fraud detection applications [3].

Recent studies have analyzed the spectral properties of graphs under varying degrees of heterophily and observed a notable shift in spectral energy from low to high frequencies when fraud or anomalous nodes are present [4]. These observations motivate the development of approaches that operate in the spectral domain to better capture frequency-based patterns. Some existing methods address this issue by employing MLP-based edge classifiers to distinguish homophilic from heterophilic edges [5]. However, such strategies introduce additional learnable parameters, require edge-level supervision, and often suffer from reduced robustness across diverse graph topologies.

To address these limitations, we propose MultiScale Spectral GNN (MSS-GNN), a novel framework that leverages hierarchical spectral filtering and relation-aware subgraph decomposition to better model heterophilic and homophilic structures in fraud detection graphs. MSSGNN introduces a multi-scale wavelet-based filtering mechanism, enabling the network to operate across different frequency bands that correspond to mild, medium, and extreme levels of heterophily. Instead of relying on supervised edge classification, we dynamically cluster nodes based on unsupervised local edge homophily scores, computed through a lightweight relation-aware scoring module. Customized Beta wavelet filters with adaptive propagation depths are applied at each scale, and the resulting representations are fused through a learnable attention mechanism. This design allows MSSGNN to adaptively integrate heterophily information at multiple scales while maintaining robustness across diverse and irregular graph structures.

Our approach is evaluated on real-world fraud detection datasets, where it consistently demonstrates strong performance. Comparative analyses against strong baseline models highlight the superior predictive performance achieved by the MultiScale Spectral Graph Neural Network (MSSGNN). These results highlight the value of combining hierarchical spectral filtering with relation-aware subgraph decomposition for modeling heterophilic structures in fraud detection.

The main contributions of our study are summarized as follows:

- **Proposing a novel multi-scale spectral GNN framework (MSSGNN) for fraud detection:** MSSGNN integrates hierarchical spectral filtering and adaptive subgraph modeling to effectively handle graphs with mixed homophilic and heterophilic structures, commonly seen in fraud detection scenarios.
- **Introducing a relation-aware, unsupervised subgraph decomposition strategy:** We develop a lightweight edge scoring module that computes continuous homophily scores between nodes, enabling the dynamic partitioning of nodes into subgraphs based on local structural heterogeneity—without requiring edge labels.
- **Designing scale-specific Beta wavelet filters with adaptive propagation depths:** To extract frequency-aware representations, each subgraph is processed through customized Beta wavelet kernels. These are tailored by propagation depth (K) to target different spectral bands aligned with varying degrees of heterophily.
- **Developing a learnable attention-based fusion mechanism across heterophily scales:** The multi-scale embeddings generated from each subgraph are fused through an attention module that adaptively weighs each subgraph's contribution, enhancing robustness to topology shifts and noise.
- **Conducting comprehensive evaluations on real-world fraud detection datasets:** We validate the effectiveness of MSSGNN on two benchmark datasets (YelpChi and Amazon), where it consistently outperforms strong baselines in both AUC and F1 score, demonstrating its practical advantage in identifying fraudulent behavior on graphs.

2   Related Work

This section reviews the related literature in three main categories: (1) general approaches to fraud detection; (2) the application of graph neural networks to fraud detection; and (3) spectral graph neural networks.

2.1   Fraud Detection

Any type of fraud, which involves deceptive practices to obtain financial gain, has become a serious concern for businesses and organizations. Detecting fraudulent activities is inefficient and expensive with traditional methods, such as manual verification and auditing [6]. With advances in artificial intelligence [7], machine learning techniques [8] have gained prominence as effective tools to analyze large volumes of financial data and identify fraud more intelligently and efficiently.

Some researchers address the fraud detection problem as an anomaly detection task [4], given that fraudulent instances typically constitute a very small portion of the entire dataset. Data mining [9], data engineering [10], and blockchain [11] are widely applied for fraud detection task.

Different application domains, such as credit card transactions [12–15], insurance claims [16–19], and e-commerce platforms [20–24], have motivated the design of various specialized fraud detection models. However, major challenges remain, including severe class imbalance, the evolving strategies of fraudsters (concept drift), and the scarcity of labeled fraudulent instances.

2.2   Graph Neural Networks for Fraud Detection

Recently, graph-based approaches have gained increasing attention especially in social networks because graphs have ability to model complex relationships between entities, such as transactions, users, and products [25–27]. Unlike traditional feature-based methods, graph-based models can exploit relational patterns and detect subtle fraudulent behaviors that may be difficult to capture otherwise [2].

Graph Neural Networks (GNNs) have emerged as a powerful class of models designed to operate directly on graph-structured data. By aggregating and transforming information from neighboring nodes, GNNs can effectively capture both local and global structural patterns [28, 29]. This makes them particularly well-suited for fraud detection tasks, where understanding the interactions between different entities is crucial for identifying anomalous or deceptive behavior.

Several variants of GNNs have been proposed to enhance model expressiveness, including convolutional [30, 31], attention-based [32–34], and spectral approaches [5, 35]. Among these, spectral GNNs leverage graph signal processing techniques to perform convolutions in the spectral domain, offering a principled way to analyze graph frequency components.

2.3   Spectral Graph Neural Networks

Spectral Graph Neural Networks (Spectral GNNs) form a subclass of GNNs that utilize graph signal processing techniques to learn representations in the spectral domain, typically through graph Laplacian-based filters [36]. Despite their potential in capturing global graph structures and contributing to both graph signal processing and representation learning, spectral methods have received comparatively less attention than spatial approaches, leaving important theoretical and practical aspects underexplored [37, 38].

Traditional spectral GNNs often rely on scalar-to-scalar filtering over individual eigenvalues using fixed-order polynomial approximations, which limits their flexibility and ability to model complex spectral patterns [39]. More recent developments have begun to address these limitations through automated and adaptive frameworks, enhancing the versatility of spectral GNNs across diverse graph types—ranging from homophilic to heterophilic—while also reducing the dependency on manual architecture design [40, 41].

3   Methodology

In this section, we present the detailed architecture of MultiScale Spectral GNN (MSSGNN) and provide theoretical and practical insights into its design. MSSGNN is designed to effectively capture both homophilic and heterophilic patterns in fraud-related graphs by leveraging spectral filtering across multiple frequency bands, adaptive subgraph decomposition, and a learnable attention-based fusion mechanism as can be seen in Fig. 2.

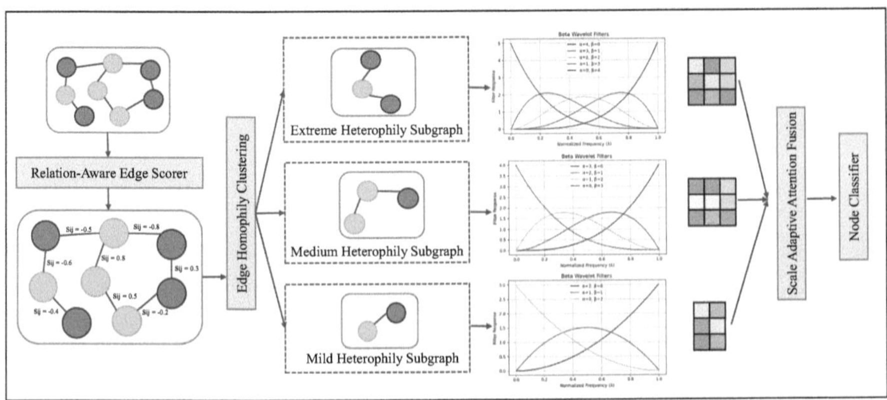

Fig. 2. Framework of Proposed MSSGNN: From left to right, the model comprises three key components: (1) a Relation-Aware Edge Scoring module that estimates edge-level homophily; (2) Subgraph Decomposition and Hierarchical Spectral Filtering, which leverages Beta wavelets to process subgraphs at multiple spectral scales; and (3) a Scale-Adaptive Fusion module that employs an attention mechanism to integrate multi-scale representations.

MSSGNN consists of three main components: (1) Relation-Aware Edge Scoring for estimating edge-level homophily, (2) Subgraph Decomposition and Hierarchical Spectral Filtering based on Beta wavelets, and (3) Scale-Adaptive Fusion using an attention mechanism to integrate multi-scale representations. This pipeline enables MSSGNN to learn robust and discriminative node representations across heterogeneous graph structures.

3.1   Preliminaries

Let $\mathcal{G} = (\mathcal{V}, \mathcal{E})$ denote a graph, where $\mathcal{V}$ is the set of $n = |\mathcal{V}|$ nodes and $\mathcal{E}$ is the set of $m = |\mathcal{E}|$ edges. Each node $v_i \in \mathcal{V}$ is associated with a feature vector $\mathbf{x}_i \in \mathbb{R}^d$, and the collection of all node features forms the feature matrix $\mathbf{X} \in \mathbb{R}^{n \times d}$. The adjacency matrix is denoted by $\mathbf{A} \in \{0, 1\}^{n \times n}$, and the diagonal degree matrix by $\mathbf{D}$, where $D_{ii} = \sum_j A_{ij}$.

The (normalized) graph Laplacian is defined as $\mathbf{L} = \mathbf{I} - \mathbf{D}^{-1/2}\mathbf{A}\mathbf{D}^{-1/2}$, and admits an eigen-decomposition $\mathbf{L} = \mathbf{U}\Lambda\mathbf{U}^\top$, where $\mathbf{U}$ contains eigenvectors and Λ contains the corresponding eigenvalues.

Before presenting the technical details, we first define the following terms, which are used consistently throughout the paper.

- **Homophily Score** (s_{ij}): a relation-aware similarity score computed for each edge $(i, j) \in \mathcal{E}$, indicating homophily (positive) or heterophily (negative).
- **Wavelet Filter** ($\Psi_k(\mathbf{L})$): a Beta wavelet filter at scale k applied to the Laplacian, capturing specific graph frequency bands.
- **Subgraph Partition** ($\mathcal{G}_s$): a node-induced subgraph corresponding to mild, medium, or extreme levels of heterophily, extracted based on local edge scores.
- **Scale-wise Propagation Depth** (K_s): the number of propagation steps (filtering depth) assigned to each subgraph scale.
- **Attention Fusion** ($\alpha_s^{(i)}$): learnable attention weights used to fuse node embeddings from different subgraphs into a unified representation $\mathbf{h}^{(i)}$.

3.2 Relation-Aware Edge Scoring

The method starts with computing a relation-aware homophily score s_{ij} for each edge $(i, j) \in \mathcal{E}$. This score is produced using a lightweight neural module that jointly encodes node features $\mathbf{x}_i$ and $\mathbf{x}_j$, capturing both feature similarity and their semantic difference. The resulting score guides the subsequent subgraph partitioning process.

Homophily score s_{ij} is computed by a relation-aware module:

$$s_{ij} = \tanh\left(\mathbf{w}^\top \cdot \mathrm{Dropout}\left([\mathbf{W}_h\mathbf{x}_i, \mathbf{W}_h\mathbf{x}_j, \mathbf{W}_h\mathbf{x}_i - \mathbf{W}_h\mathbf{x}_j]\right)\right), \tag{1}$$

where $\mathbf{x}_i, \mathbf{x}_j$ are node features, $\mathbf{W}_h$ is a projection layer, and $\mathbf{w}$ is a scoring weight vector. The result $s_{ij} \in [-1, 1]$ indicates the degree of homophily for that edge.

3.3 Subgraph Decomposition via Edge Homophily Clustering

Each node v_i is assigned a local homophily score by averaging over its incident edges:

$$s_i = \frac{1}{|\mathcal{N}(i)|} \sum_{j \in \mathcal{N}(i)} s_{ij}. \tag{2}$$

Then the nodes are partitioned into three groups based on score quantiles:

$$\mathcal{V} = \mathcal{V}_{\mathrm{mild}} \cup \mathcal{V}_{\mathrm{medium}} \cup \mathcal{V}_{\mathrm{extreme}},$$

resulting in subgraphs $\mathcal{G}_s = (\mathcal{V}_s, \mathcal{E}_s)$ for $s \in \{\mathrm{mild, medium, extreme}\}$. This unsupervised partitioning allows MSSGNN to dynamically adapt to graph heterogeneity without additional labeling requirements.

3.4   Hierarchical Spectral Filtering with Beta Wavelets

For each subgraph, we apply a polynomial Beta wavelet filter which are polynomial approximations designed to capture band-pass behavior in the spectral domain:

$$\Psi^{(K_s)}(\mathbf{L}) = \sum_{k=0}^{K_s} \theta_k \cdot \mathbf{L}^k, \tag{3}$$

where $\mathbf{L}$ is the normalized graph Laplacian and $\{\theta_k\}$ are coefficients derived from Beta functions [5]. This filter captures structural information up to K_s hops and targets specific frequency bands depending on the heterophily level.

Different propagation depths K are assigned to each subgraph to capture multi-level heterophily, reflecting their expected structural smoothness. Specifically, we set $K = 1$ for the *mild* heterophily subgraph, $K = 2$ for *medium*, and $K = 3$ for *extreme* heterophily. This design is grounded in spectral graph theory: subgraphs with low heterophily tend to have smoother signals concentrated in low-frequency bands, which can be effectively captured with shallow propagation [42]. In contrast, highly heterophilic subgraphs exhibit more irregular, high-frequency behavior that requires deeper propagation to model. By progressively increasing the value of K, the model adapts its receptive field to the spectral complexity of each subgraph, enabling more precise representation learning across different structural regimes.

The node representation after wavelet filtering becomes:

$$\mathbf{h}_s = \Psi^{(K_s)}(\mathbf{L}_s) \cdot \mathbf{X}_s, \tag{4}$$

where $\mathbf{X}_s$ and $\mathbf{L}_s$ are the feature matrix and Laplacian of subgraph $\mathcal{G}_s$.

Each subgraph is assigned a scale-specific propagation depth K_s, controlling how far node information propagates. Lower K_s values are used for mildly heterophilic regions, while higher K_s values capture complex, high-frequency structures common in fraud scenarios.

3.5   Scale-Adaptive Attention Fusion

The filtered representations from each subgraph are projected independently, normalized, and passed through a learnable attention module. The attention mechanism computes weights $\alpha_s^{(i)}$ for each subgraph output per node i, allowing the final embedding $\mathbf{h}^{(i)} = \sum_s \alpha_s^{(i)} \mathbf{h}_s^{(i)}$ to adaptively emphasize the most informative scales.

Each node receives embeddings from all scales. Attention weights are computed:

$$\alpha_s^{(i)} = \frac{\exp\left(\mathbf{a}^\top \cdot \tanh(\mathbf{W}_a \mathbf{h}_s^{(i)})\right)}{\sum_{s'} \exp\left(\mathbf{a}^\top \cdot \tanh(\mathbf{W}_a \mathbf{h}_{s'}^{(i)})\right)}, \tag{5}$$

where $\mathbf{W}_a$ and $\mathbf{a}$ are learnable parameters. The final node representation is a weighted sum:

$$\mathbf{h}^{(i)} = \sum_s \alpha_s^{(i)} \cdot \mathbf{h}_s^{(i)}. \tag{6}$$

3.6   Training Objective

The final node embeddings are used to predict fraud labels via a supervised cross-entropy loss. Each final node embedding $\mathbf{h}^{(i)}$ is passed through a softmax classifier:

$$\hat{\mathbf{y}}^{(i)} = \text{softmax}(\mathbf{W}_{\text{out}}\mathbf{h}^{(i)}), \tag{7}$$

We optimize a hybrid loss function combining node classification and edge-level structure learning. The total loss is:

$$\mathcal{L} = \mathcal{L}_{\text{cls}} + \gamma \cdot \mathcal{L}_{\text{edge}}, \tag{8}$$

where $\mathcal{L}_{\text{cls}}$ is cross-entropy loss for node labels, and $\mathcal{L}_{\text{edge}}$ is a hinge loss on edge homophily scores:

$$\mathcal{L}_{\text{edge}} = \sum_{(i,j)\in\mathcal{E}} \max(0, 1 - y_{ij} \cdot s_{ij}), \tag{9}$$

with $y_{ij} \in \{-1, +1\}$ representing edge labels indicating heterophily or homophily. The standard cross-entropy objective is:

$$\mathcal{L}_{\text{cls}} = - \sum_{i\in\mathcal{V}_{\text{train}}} \sum_{c=1}^{C} y_i^{(c)} \log \hat{y}_i^{(c)}, \tag{10}$$

where C is the number of classes (e.g., fraud/non-fraud), $y_i^{(c)}$ is the ground truth label (one-hot encoded), and $\hat{y}_i^{(c)}$ is the predicted softmax probability for node i belonging to class c.

4   Experiments

To assess the performance of our proposed model, MSSGNN, it's performance is validated empirically through comprehensive experiments on fraud detection benchmarks.

4.1   Datasets

YelpChi [43] and Amazon [44] datasets are widely used for fraud detection task in the literature [2, 45–47]. Dataset description and some statistics are shown in Table 1. The number of classes for both datasets are two.

1) YelpChi Dataset: MSSGNN is performed on spam review detection using the YelpChi dataset, which consists of hotel and restaurant reviews labeled as either filtered (spam) or recommended (legitimate) by Yelp. Each review is represented as a node with 32 handcrafted features. The graph is constructed with three types of relations: (1) R-U-R connects reviews written by the same user, (2) R-S-R connects reviews of the same product with identical star ratings, and (3) R-T-R connects reviews of the same product posted within the same month [5].

2) Amazon Dataset: For fraudulent user detection, an Amazon product review dataset is utilized. Users are labeled as fraudulent if less than 20% of their reviews receive helpful votes, and as benign if more than 80% do, following previous work [2,5]. To avoid label leakage caused by the feature "minimum number of unhelpful votes" [2,47], it is excluded. 24-dimensional node features are used. The heterogeneous graph is built with three types of relations: (1) U-P-U connects users who reviewed at least one common product, (2) U-S-V connects users who gave the same star rating within one week, and (3) U-V-U connects users with top 5% mutual review text similarity.

Table 1. Dataset Description

Dataset	Task	Number of Nodes	Number of Node Features	Percentage of Fraud	Relation Types
YelpChi	Spam Review Detection	45,954	32	14.53%	R-U-R: same user R-S-R: same product & star R-T-R: same product & month
Amazon	Fraudulent User Detection	11,944	24	6.87%	U-P-U: common product U-S-V: same star within a week U-V-U: top 5% text similarity

4.2 Baselines

Our proposed method is compared with six baselines which includes a traditional machine-learning model MLP and graph-based methods.

- **MLP**: This method uses only node features as input and does not incorporate edges or graph structure.
- **GCN** [28]: A graph neural network that classifies nodes by aggregating feature information from their immediate neighbors.
- **GPRGNN** [42]: A generalized PageRank-based spectral GNN that adaptively learns propagation weights to capture long-range dependencies in graphs.
- **BWGNN** [4]: A bandpass filter-based GNN that leverages both low- and high-frequency information to better capture complex patterns in graph signals.

- **SplitGNN** [5]: A spectral graph learning framework that partitions the graph into subgraphs for local message passing, followed by global feature aggregation to improve scalability.
- **Arnoldi-GCN** [41]: A variant of GCN that guides Spectral GNN propagation using explicit filters, enabling effective learning from multi-hop neighborhood information by adaptively learning propagation weights.

4.3   Evaluation Metrics and Experiment Settings

A comparative analysis is conducted between our model and several baseline methods. Given the inherently imbalanced nature of fraud detection datasets, model performance is evaluated using F1-Score and AUC, which are more informative metrics than accuracy in imbalanced classification settings.

The learning rate is set to 0.01 for YelpChi dataset and 0.1 for Amazon in MSSGNN. The weight decay is 0.00005, the dimension of node embedding is 6, the number of epochs is 1000, and the dropout rate is 0.1. Training, validation, and test ratios are 40%, 20%, and 40%, respectively. All methods are optimized with the Adam optimizer.

5   Results

5.1   Fraud Detection Results

In this section, the comparison between MSSGNN and baseline models are presented in Table 2.

Table 2. Performance Comparison

Dataset	YelpChi		Amazon	
Metric	AUC Score	F1 Score	AUC Score	F1 Score
MLP	0.8172	0.4608	0.8975	0.4822
GCN	0.547	0.4608	0.7714	0.4822
GPRGNN	0.6983	0.4615	0.8792	0.5879
BWGNN	0.836	0.7057	0.836	0.6332
SplitGNN	<u>0.9135</u>	<u>0.7151</u>	<u>0.9283</u>	<u>0.6881</u>
Arnoldi-GCN	0.7333	0.6047	0.874	0.6924
MSSGNN	**0.8987**	**0.7222**	**0.9109**	**0.7064**

The experimental results presented in Table 2 demonstrate the effectiveness of the proposed MSSGNN model across two real-world fraud detection datasets: YelpChi and Amazon. MSSGNN results are highlighted in bold, while the best-performing baseline results are underlined. MSSGNN achieves the highest F1 scores on both datasets, surpassing all baseline models, including recent state-of-the-art methods such as SplitGNN and Arnoldi-GCN. Notably, while Split-GNN achieves the best AUC scores, MSSGNN provides a better balance between detection accuracy and robustness, as indicated by its superior F1 scores. This highlights the advantage of our hierarchical spectral filtering and relation-aware subgraph decomposition in capturing heterophilic structures. The consistent performance gains across datasets confirm the generalizability of MSSGNN and its suitability for complex fraud detection scenarios where both homophilic and heterophilic patterns are present.

5.2   Ablation Study

Table 3 presents an ablation study evaluating the impact of key components in MSSGNN on the YelpChi dataset. The full model achieves the highest F1 score, demonstrating the overall effectiveness of integrating spectral filtering, subgraph partitioning, and attention-based fusion. When the subgraph decomposition is removed, performance drops noticeably in both AUC and F1, underscoring the value of separating nodes based on homophily levels for scale-specific processing. Removing the relation-aware scoring module results in a moderate decline, confirming its role in guiding meaningful subgraph formation. Notably, the model without attention fusion achieves comparable AUC but slightly lower F1, suggesting that the learnable fusion mechanism contributes to improved classification precision. These results collectively validate that each architectural component of MSSGNN enhances its ability to detect fraud in heterophilic networks.

Table 3. Ablation Study on YelpChi Dataset

Model Variant	AUC Score	F1 Score
MSSGNN (full)	0.8987	0.7222
w/o Subgraphs	0.8866	0.7065
w/o Relation-Aware Scoring	0.8925	0.7105
w/o Attention Fusion	0.8949	0.7215

6   Conclusion

In this work, we introduced MSSGNN, a novel graph neural network designed to address the challenges of learning on graphs with both homophilic and heterophilic structures—particularly in the context of fraud detection. By combining hierarchical spectral filtering with a relation-aware subgraph decomposition strategy, MSSGNN effectively captures varying levels of structural heterogeneity across different frequency bands. Our model incorporates customized Beta wavelet filters, adaptive propagation depths, and an attention-based fusion mechanism to robustly integrate multi-scale information. Extensive experiments on real-world datasets demonstrate that MSSGNN consistently outperforms existing baselines, confirming its effectiveness in detecting fraudulent behavior in complex social networks. These results highlight the importance of frequency-aware, heterophily-sensitive modeling in advancing the state of graph-based fraud detection.

Acknowledgment. Melike Yildiz Aktas is financially supported by the Turkish Ministry of National Education for her PhD research.

References

1. Ma, Y., Liu, X., Shah, N., Tang, J.: Is homophily a necessity for graph neural networks? arXiv preprint arXiv:2106.06134 (2021)
2. Dou, Y., Liu, Z., Sun, L., Deng, Y., Peng, H., Yu, P.S.: Enhancing graph neural network-based fraud detectors against camouflaged fraudsters. In: Proceedings of the 29th ACM International Conference on Information & Knowledge Management, pp. 315–324 (2020)
3. Zhu, J., Yan, Y., Zhao, L., Heimann, M., Akoglu, L., Koutra, D.: Beyond homophily in graph neural networks: current limitations and effective designs. Adv. Neural. Inf. Process. Syst. **33**, 7793–7804 (2020)
4. Tang, J., Li, J., Gao, Z., Li, J.: Rethinking graph neural networks for anomaly detection. In: International Conference on Machine Learning, pp. 21076–21089. PMLR (2022)
5. Wu, B., Yao, X., Zhang, B., Chao, K.-M., Li, Y.: Splitgnn: spectral graph neural network for fraud detection against heterophily. In: Proceedings of the 32nd ACM International Conference on Information and Knowledge Management, pp. 2737–2746 (2023)
6. Ali, A., et al.: Financial fraud detection based on machine learning: a systematic literature review. Appl. Sci. **12**(19), 9637 (2022)
7. Bao, Y., Hilary, G., Ke, B.: Artificial intelligence and fraud detection. Innov. Technol. Interface Finance Oper. **I**, 223–247 (2022)
8. Bin Sulaiman, R., Schetinin, V., Sant, P.: Review of machine learning approach on credit card fraud detection. Hum.-Centric Intell. Syst. **2**(1), 55–68 (2022)
9. Ashtiani, M.N., Raahemi, B.: Intelligent fraud detection in financial statements using machine learning and data mining: a systematic literature review. IEEE Access **10**, 72504–72525 (2021)
10. Baesens, B., Höppner, S., Verdonck, T.: Data engineering for fraud detection. Decis. Support Syst. **150**, 113492 (2021)
11. Gera, J., Palakayala, A.R., Rejeti, V.K.K., Anusha, T.: Blockchain technology for fraudulent practices in insurance claim process. In: 2020 5th International Conference on Communication and Electronics Systems (ICCES), pp. 1068–1075. IEEE (2020)
12. Seera, M., Lim, C.P., Kumar, A., Dhamotharan, L., Tan, K.H.: An intelligent payment card fraud detection system. Ann. Oper. Res. **334**(1), 445–467 (2024)
13. Urunkar, A., Khot, A., Bhat, R., Mudegol, N.: Fraud detection and analysis for insurance claim using machine learning. In: 2022 IEEE International Conference on Signal Processing, Informatics, Communication and Energy Systems (SPICES), vol. 1, pp. 406–411. IEEE (2022)

14. Tiwari, P., Mehta, S., Sakhuja, N., Kumar, J., Singh, A.K.: Credit card fraud detection using machine learning: a study. arXiv preprint arXiv:2108.10005 (2021)
15. Alarfaj, F.K., Malik, I., Khan, H.U., Almusallam, N., Ramzan, M., Ahmed, M.: Credit card fraud detection using state-of-the-art machine learning and deep learning algorithms. IEEE Access **10**, 39700–39715 (2022)
16. Nabrawi, E., Alanazi, A.: Fraud detection in healthcare insurance claims using machine learning. Risks **11**(9), 160 (2023)
17. Pala, S.K.: Investigating fraud detection in insurance claims using data science. Int. J. Enhanced Res. Sci. Technol. Eng. ISSN 2319–7463 (2022)
18. Vyas, S., Serasiya, S.: Fraud detection in insurance claim system: a review. In: 2022 Second International Conference on Artificial Intelligence and Smart Energy (ICAIS), pp. 922–927. IEEE (2022)
19. Agarwal, S.: An intelligent machine learning approach for fraud detection in medical claim insurance: a comprehensive study. Scholars J. Eng. Technol. **11**(9), 191–200 (2023)
20. Ray, S.: Fraud detection in e-commerce using machine learning. BOHR Int. J. Adv. Manag. Res. **1**(1), 7–14 (2022)
21. Tax, N., et al.: Machine learning for fraud detection in e-commerce: a research agenda. In: Wang, G., Ciptadi, A., Ahmadzadeh, A. (eds.) MLHat 2021. CCIS, vol. 1482, pp. 30–54. Springer, Cham (2021). https://doi.org/10.1007/978-3-030-87839-9_2
22. Mutemi, A., Bacao, F.: E-commerce fraud detection based on machine learning techniques: systematic literature review. Big Data Mining Anal. **7**(2), 419–444 (2024)
23. Zhang, G., et al.: eFraudCom: an e-commerce fraud detection system via competitive graph neural networks. ACM Trans. Inf. Syst. (TOIS) **40**(3), 1–29 (2022)
24. Li, J.: E-commerce fraud detection model by computer artificial intelligence data mining. Comput. Intell. Neurosci. **2022**(1), 8783783 (2022)
25. Pourhabibi, T., Ong, K.-L., Kam, B.H., Boo, Y.L.: Fraud detection: a systematic literature review of graph-based anomaly detection approaches. Decis. Support Syst. **133**, 113303 (2020)
26. Cheng, D., Wang, X., Zhang, Y., Zhang, L.: Graph neural network for fraud detection via spatial-temporal attention. IEEE Trans. Knowl. Data Eng. **34**(8), 3800–3813 (2020)
27. Li, P., Yu, H., Luo, X., Wu, J.: LGM-GNN: a local and global aware memory-based graph neural network for fraud detection. IEEE Trans. Big Data **9**(4), 1116–1127 (2023)
28. Kipf, T.N., Welling, M.: Semi-supervised classification with graph convolutional networks, arXiv preprint arXiv:1609.02907 (2016)
29. Velickovic, P., et al.: Graph attention networks. Stat **1050**(20), 10-48550 (2017)
30. Atkinson, O., Bhardwaj, A., Englert, C., Ngairangbam, V.S., Spannowsky, M.: Anomaly detection with convolutional graph neural networks. J. High Energy Phys. **2021**(8), 1–19 (2021)
31. Hu, Y., Qu, A., Work, D.: Graph convolutional networks for traffic anomaly, arXiv preprint arXiv:2012.13637 (2020)
32. Liu, C., Sun, L., Ao, X., Feng, J., He, Q., Yang, H.: Intention-aware heterogeneous graph attention networks for fraud transactions detection. In: Proceedings of the 27th ACM SIGKDD Conference on Knowledge Discovery & Data Mining, pp. 3280–3288 (2021)
33. Wei, S., Lee, S.: Financial anti-fraud based on dual-channel graph attention network. J. Theor. Appl. Electron. Commer. Res. **19**(1), 297–314 (2024)

34. Zhao, H., et al.: Multivariate time-series anomaly detection via graph attention network. In: 2020 IEEE International Conference on Data Mining (ICDM), pp. 841–850. IEEE (2020)
35. Zheng, J., et al.: Dynamic spectral graph anomaly detection. In: Proceedings of the AAAI Conference on Artificial Intelligence, vol. 39, no. 12, pp. 13410–13418 (2025)
36. Wang, X., Zhang, M.: How powerful are spectral graph neural networks. In: International Conference on Machine Learning, pp. 23341–23362. PMLR (2022)
37. Bo, D., Wang, X., Liu, Y., Fang, Y., Li, Y., Shi, C.: A survey on spectral graph neural networks, arXiv preprint arXiv:2302.05631 (2023)
38. Geisler, S.M., Kosmala, A., Herbst, D., Günnemann, S.: Spatio-spectral graph neural networks. In: Advances in Neural Information Processing Systems, vol. 37, pp. 49022–49080 (2024)
39. Bo, D., Shi, C., Wang, L., Liao, R.: Specformer: spectral graph neural networks meet transformers, arXiv preprint arXiv:2303.01028 (2023)
40. Mo, S., Wu, K., Gao, Q., Teng, X., Liu, J.: Autosgnn: automatic propagation mechanism discovery for spectral graph neural networks. In: Proceedings of the AAAI Conference on Artificial Intelligence, vol. 39, no. 18, pp. 19493–19502 (2025)
41. Coşkun, M., Grama, A., Koyutürk, M.: Generalized learning of coefficients in spectral graph convolutional networks, arXiv preprint arXiv:2409.04813 (2024)
42. Chien, E., Peng, J., Li, P., Milenkovic, O.: Adaptive universal generalized pagerank graph neural network, arXiv preprint arXiv:2006.07988 (2020)
43. Rayana, S., Akoglu, L.: Collective opinion spam detection: bridging review networks and metadata. In: Proceedings of the 21th ACM SIGKDD International Conference on Knowledge Discovery and Data Mining, pp. 985–994 (2015)
44. McAuley, J.J., Leskovec, J.: From amateurs to connoisseurs: modeling the evolution of user expertise through online reviews. In: Proceedings of the 22nd International Conference on World Wide Web, pp. 897–908 (2013)
45. Liu, Z., Dou, Y., Yu, P.S., Deng, Y., Peng, H.: Alleviating the inconsistency problem of applying graph neural network to fraud detection. In: Proceedings of the 43rd International ACM SIGIR Conference on Research and Development in Information Retrieval, pp. 1569–1572 (2020) information retrieval, 2020, pp. 1569–1572
46. Peng, H., Zhang, R., Dou, Y., Yang, R., Zhang, J., Yu, P.S.: Reinforced neighborhood selection guided multi-relational graph neural networks. ACM Trans. Inf. Syst. (TOIS) 40(4), 1–46 (2021)
47. Shi, F., Cao, Y., Shang, Y., Zhou, Y., Zhou, C., Wu, J.: H2-FDetector: a GNN-based fraud detector with homophilic and heterophilic connections. In: Proceedings of the ACM Web Conference 2022, pp. 1486–1494 (2022)

Reducing Misclassification Risk
in Dynamic Graph Neural Networks
Through Abstention

Jayadratha Gayen[(✉)], Himanshu Pal, Naresh Manwani, and Charu Sharma[(✉)]

Machine Learning Lab, IIIT Hyderabad, Hyderabad, India
{jayadratha.gayen,himanshu.pal}@research.iiit.ac.in,
{naresh.manwani,charu.sharma}@iiit.ac.in
https://mll.iiit.ac.in/

Abstract. Many real-world systems can be modeled as dynamic graphs, where nodes and edges evolve over time, requiring specialized models to capture their evolving dynamics in risk-sensitive applications effectively. Graph neural networks (GNNs) for temporal graphs are one such category of specialized models. For the first time, our approach integrates a reject option strategy within the framework of GNNs for continuous-time dynamic graphs (CTDGs). This allows the model to strategically abstain from making predictions when the uncertainty is high and confidence is low, thus minimizing the risk of critical misclassification and enhancing the results and reliability. We propose a coverage-based abstention prediction model to implement the reject option that maximizes prediction within a specified coverage. It improves the prediction score for link prediction and node classification tasks. Temporal GNNs deal with extremely skewed datasets for the next state prediction or node classification task. In the case of class imbalance, our method can be further tuned to provide a higher weight to the minority class. Exhaustive experiments are presented on four datasets for dynamic link prediction and two datasets for dynamic node classification tasks. This demonstrates the effectiveness of our approach in improving the reliability and area under the curve (AUC)/average precision (AP) scores for predictions in dynamic graph scenarios. The results highlight our model's ability to efficiently handle the trade-offs between prediction confidence and coverage, making it a dependable solution for applications requiring high precision in dynamic and uncertain environments. Our code is available at: https://github.com/Jayadratha/Cover_DyG.

Keywords: Graph Neural Networks · Temporal Graphs · Reject Option Classification · Link Prediction · Node Classification

1 Introduction

In the modern era, numerous systems are modeled as dynamic graphs where nodes and edges evolve over time. These systems include social and interaction networks [18], traffic networks [1] trade networks [23], biological networks

A. An et al. (Eds.): ASONAM 2025, LNCS 16323, pp. 177–192, 2026.
https://doi.org/10.1007/978-3-032-13821-7_16

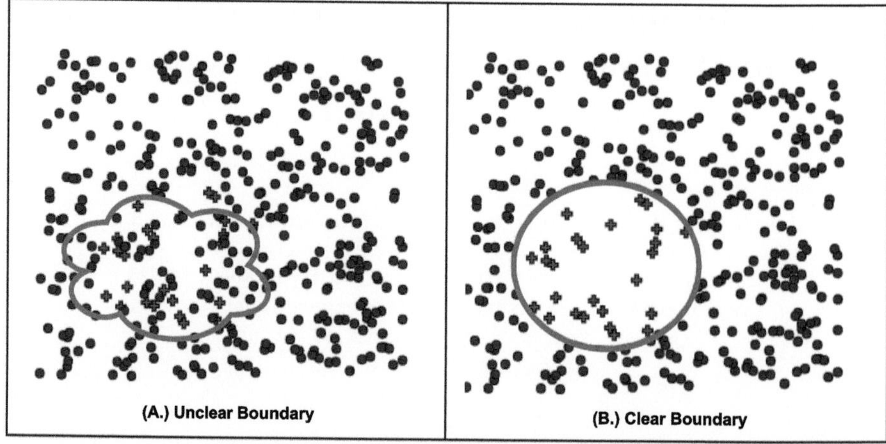

Fig. 1. Decision Boundary: (A) is not clear and smooth; (B) becomes clearer after abstaining confusing/noisy samples. The examples to be rejected are decided by the objective function, which consists of the losses over unrejected samples and a fixed cost for rejected samples. The minimum value of the objective will be achieved only with a proper choice of rejected examples. (Color figure online)

[2] and transaction networks [20] among others. Particularly in risk-sensitive applications such as fraud detection [24], fake news, polarization identification [6], financial transactions [20], blockchain security [3], epidemic modeling [30], anomaly detection [25] and disease prediction [3], the stakes for accurate and reliable predictions are exceptionally high. Traditional graph neural networks (GNNs) and their extensions to dynamic graphs have shown promise in capturing the complex interactions and evolving structures within these networks. However, they often fall short where the cost of misclassification is significant and abstaining from making a prediction could mitigate risk. The additional challenge of highly skewed temporal[1] datasets for node classification (such as Wikipedia, Reddit datasets [18]) makes it harder for the models to predict correctly. Recent works on temporal GNNs [7,26,32,33] solve for node classification and link prediction tasks.

Real-world classification tasks, such as anomaly detection or credit card fraud prediction in dynamic networks, often involve overlapping class distributions and class imbalance, leading to prediction uncertainty. Figure 1(A) illustrates such a scenario. The minority class (red crosses) is infrequent and significantly overlaps with the majority class (blue circles) in a specific region. A classifier attempting to perfectly separate these classes might require a complex decision boundary (conceptualized by the irregular green line), potentially leading to overfitting or unreliable predictions for samples near this boundary.

---

[1] "Temporal" and "dynamic" will be used interchangeably.

Figure 1(B) conceptually motivates the benefit of abstention. By identifying samples with high prediction uncertainty (typically those within the overlap region), the model can choose to abstain from making a prediction for them. This allows the model to focus on making high-confidence predictions for the remaining samples, which might now be effectively separated by a simpler, more robust decision boundary (conceptualized by the circular green line). This improves both interpretability and trustworthiness, especially in settings where wrong decisions are costly.

Classifiers with abstention are well explored in the machine learning community [4,12,15,19]. Such models allow a classifier to withhold a prediction when the uncertainty associated with the decision is high. This approach has not been widely investigated in the context of dynamic graphs, where the temporal evolution of the data adds a layer of complexity to uncertainty management.

Motivated by the critical need for precision in predictions, especially in environments where trade-offs between false positives and false negatives carry substantial consequences, we explore the integration of the abstention option with the continuous time dynamic graphs (CTDGs) learning method. The open problem, therefore, is to incorporate a mechanism that allows CTDGs to abstain from making predictions under high uncertainty, thus reducing the risk of misclassifications in sensitive applications. To address this, we propose a novel framework that integrates the reject option into CTDGs for both link prediction and node classification tasks. This framework aims to enhance model reliability by minimizing the risk associated with uncertain predictions.

We solve this challenge by extending the methodologies of temporal GNNs to incorporate a reject option classification. Our approach involves designing a specialized neural network architecture that dynamically adjusts its confidence threshold based on the evolving graph structure and node interactions. This method allows the model to strategically abstain from making predictions when uncertainty is high, leveraging a coverage-based model to optimize the trade-off between accurate prediction and the cost of abstention.

Our main goal is uncertainty management using the reject option. While analyzing the data, we find that extreme class imbalance is often present in node classification tasks for CTDG datasets. As uncertainty amplifies due to class imbalance and noisy boundary between the classes, our approach tries to handle both problems together. Previous works have struggled to effectively manage the disproportion between classes, which is particularly problematic in risk-sensitive domains where minority classes may carry significant importance. Our approach handles extreme class imbalance by optimizing the model's training to better represent minority classes, thereby significantly improving performance in these challenging scenarios. This advancement is a pioneering step in dynamic GNNs research, offering a powerful tool for domains where class imbalance profoundly affects the utility and reliability of the model. Our main contributions are as follows:

1. **Uncertainty management with reject option:** We integrate a reject option strategy into the framework of CTDGs. This empowers the model to

abstain from making predictions when it lacks sufficient confidence, addressing the critical need for risk mitigation in sensitive applications. To achieve this, we propose a coverage-based approach to incorporate the reject option, allowing for the customization of the model's behavior to optimize predictions within a set coverage limit.

2. **Managing extreme class imbalance:** Drawing from recent literature for class imbalance mitigation, we address this problem in dynamic graph node classification, an area largely unexplored for extreme imbalance.

3. **Comprehensive evaluation:** We conduct extensive experiments on various dynamic graph datasets for link prediction and node classification to demonstrate the effectiveness of our approach. Our results highlight the ability of our models to effectively manage trade-offs between prediction confidence and coverage while significantly improving performance metrics.

2   Related Work

Temporal Graphs. Dynamic graphs [16] are categorized into discrete-time (DTDGs) [22] and continuous-time (CTDGs) [18] settings. In this paper, we focus on CTDGs. CTDGs are addressed using node-based methods, such as TGN [26], and TCL [31] utilize node information, such as temporal neighbors and previous histories of nodes, to create node embedding, and edge-based methods like GraphMixer [7] and CAWN [32] directly generate embeddings for the edge of interest. DyGFormer [34] proposed a transformer-based architecture that uses a neighbor co-occurrence encoding scheme along with a patching technique to effectively capture long-term temporal dependencies in dynamic graphs. Recent methods, such as DyGMamba [9] and FreeDyG [28], incorporate state-space models and frequency-domain analysis for better encoding of interactions. TGB [14] benchmarks popular temporal graph models treated the task as a ranking problem. DyGLib [31] based on PyG [11], provides a unified library for implementing various CTDG methods. We utilize DyGLib to set up experiments and integrate a rejection module.

Uncertainty Estimation & Classification With Rejection (CwR). CwR can be classified broadly into cost-based and coverage-based methods. Cost-based CwR method aligns well with cost-sensitive learning [10] where the cost of misclassification can be used to inform the decision to abstain from prediction. Variants of support vector machine (SVM) with reject option are presented in [27]. [4] introduces a novel approach to multi-class classification with rejection compatible with arbitrary loss functions, addressing the need for flexibility in adapting to different datasets. In coverage-based CwR, SelectiveNet [12] introduces a novel approach by integrating the reject option directly within the deep neural network architecture. [5,21] provide calibrated losses for multi-class reject option classification. [4] proposes a general recipe to convert any multi-class loss function to accommodate the reject option, calibrated to loss l_{0d1}. They treat rejection as another class. Conformal prediction (CP) provides valid uncertainty estimates by constructing prediction sets that contain the true label with a pre-defined confidence level. CF-GNN [13] integrates CP with GNNs to generate uncertainty-aware predictions on graph data. In our task for CTDGs, we only handle binary classification, unlike [8]. So, there is little scope to apply this method in this setting.

3   Preliminaries

This section introduces the concepts and notations used throughout this paper. Our work focuses on extending GNN to temporal graphs, incorporating a classification with a rejection option for enhanced prediction in both link prediction and node classification tasks.

Deep Learning on Dynamic Graphs. Dynamic graphs are a sequence of non-decreasing chronological interactions to accommodate changes over time. They represent evolving relationships within the graph. A dynamic graph is represented as a series of graphs $\mathcal{G}_t = (\mathcal{V}_t, \mathcal{E}_t)$ at discrete time steps t, or as a continuous stream of interactions $(u, v, t) \in \mathcal{E}_t$, where $u, v \in \mathcal{V}_t$ are nodes, and t represents the time of interaction. The primary goal in deep learning on dynamic graphs is to learn a function $f : \mathcal{V}_t \to \mathbb{R}^d$ that captures not only the structural features but also its temporal dynamics, facilitating tasks such as temporal link prediction and dynamic node classification.

Classification with Rejection. Rejection classification introduces a decision framework in which a model, given an input $x \in \mathcal{X}$, can choose to abstain from making a prediction if it lacks confidence. Given a prediction model $f : \mathcal{X} \to \mathcal{Y}$, where $\mathcal{X}$ is the input space and $\mathcal{Y}$ is the output label space, and an abstention function $q : \mathcal{X} \to \{0,1\}$. For each sample x, the model predicts an abstention score $a(x)$ where $a : \mathcal{X} \in [0,1]$. We first sort the abstention scores for all the interactions and then select a threshold θ value that aligns with the desired coverage. For an input x, if the abstention score, $a(x) \leq \theta$ then $q(x) = 0$ (the model is confident) and the model predicts $f(x)$. In case $a(x) > \theta$ then $q(x) = 1$ and the model abstains the decision for input x. For a given $\theta \in (0,1)$, the objective is to maximize the probability of correct prediction for the subset of the inputs where $q(x) = 0$:

$$\max_{f,q} P(f(x) = y | q(x) = 0) = \max_{f,q} P(f(x) = y | a(x) \leq \theta) \tag{1}$$

Problem Formulation. Given a continuous-time temporal graph $\mathcal{G}_t$ with a tuple $(u, v, t) \in \mathcal{E}_t$ representing an interaction between nodes $u, v \in \mathcal{V}_t$, at time $t \in \mathcal{T}$, our objective is to design a temporal GNN model that addresses the problem of learning effective representations for link prediction and node classification while incorporating a reject option to manage uncertainty in predictions.

1. Link Prediction: Given a temporal graph, i.e., source node, destination node, current timestamp, and historical interactions before t, predict the presence or absence of links at time t. Where the abstain mechanism aims to make a prediction or refuse to predict for a pair of nodes based on a coverage criterion.

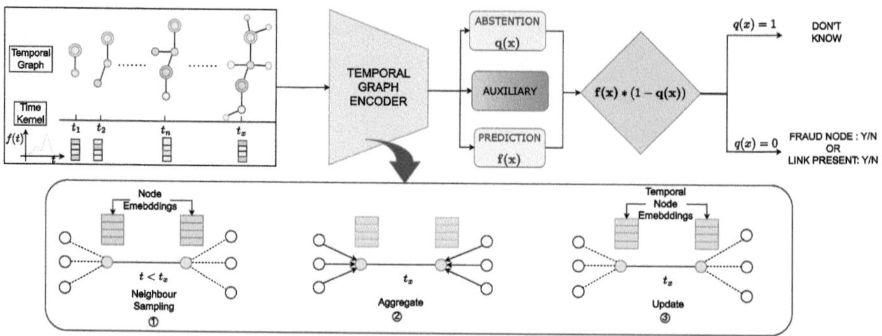

Fig. 2. The model overview of classification with rejection for task-agnostic temporal graphs. Input to the model is a temporal graph with t timestamps, which is processed through an encoder that samples neighbours from all interactions from previous timestamps $t < t_x$ of these nodes, then aggregates and yields an updated temporal node embedding. These embeddings are passed to a *Prediction* function $f(x)$ to predict downstream tasks such as whether a link exists or not for link prediction or whether a user is blocked or not for node classification at time t. The output embeddings also pass through the *Abstention* function, predict a single score, and check if $a(x) > \theta$ threshold i.e. $q(x) = 1$. When it is true, the model abstains; otherwise, it proceeds to make a prediction. The *Auxiliary* head exposes all samples to the model, including samples with high abstention scores, only during training.

2. Node Classification: Predict the label or state of a node in a temporal graph at a time t based on previous information, with the option to abstain from the prediction on certain nodes to ensure high confidence in the predictions made.

4   Method

In this section, we describe our approach for both link prediction and node classification in dynamic graphs in continuous time using the coverage-based method. A neural network architecture designed for dynamic graphs can be seen as a combination of an encoder and a decoder. The encoder serves to transform a dynamic graph into node embeddings, whereas the decoder utilizes these embeddings to make predictions. Our method considers temporal graph networks to incorporate a reject option, enhancing prediction and handling uncertainty effectively. The architecture is illustrated in Fig. 2.

4.1   Temporal Graph Encoder

Our approach is based on the concept of temporal graph networks, which are designed as an encoder-decoder pair for dynamic graph learning. The encoder maps a dynamic graph into the temporal node embeddings $\mathbf{z}_u(t)$, capturing the temporal interactions among the nodes. The encoder updates the node embeddings with each interaction, ensuring those reflect the graph's latest state. Few such models are memory-based TGN [26], MLP-based GraphMixer [7], graph transformer-based TCL [31], random-walk-based CAWN [32], SSM-based DyG-Mamba [9] etc.

4.2   Coverage-Based Dynamic Link Prediction

Our approach to link prediction uses the concept of abstention prediction [12] to manage the uncertainty inherent in predicting links in a dynamic graph employing an abstention model (f, q) where f is the prediction function and q is the abstention function. The abstention function $q : \mathcal{X} \to \{0, 1\}$, if it takes value one, then the prediction is kept on hold for a given pair of nodes based on a coverage criterion. We modify the decoder part of the model to incorporate a reject option through an abstention prediction mechanism. This mechanism evaluates each potential link for its likelihood and the model's confidence in its prediction. By allowing the model to abstain from making predictions when the uncertainty exceeds a threshold θ, we ensure it only predicts links it is confident about. The abstention prediction objective is defined as follows:

$$\mathcal{L}^{\mathcal{E}_t}_{(f,q)} = \hat{r}(f, q|\mathcal{E}_t) + \lambda \Psi(c - \hat{\phi}(q|\mathcal{E}_t)) \tag{2}$$

where $\hat{r}(f, q|\mathcal{E}_t)$ is the empirical abstention risk, λ is a hyperparameter controlling the importance of the coverage constraint, $\Psi(b) = \max(0, b)^2$ is a quadratic penalty function that helps ensure that the model does not abstain excessively, and c is the target coverage rate. The empirical abstention risk $(\hat{r}(f, q|\mathcal{E}_t))$ and the empirical coverage $(\hat{\phi}(q|\mathcal{E}_t))$ are calculated as follows:

$$\hat{r}(f, q|\mathcal{E}_t) = \frac{\sum\limits_{(u,v,t)\in\mathcal{E}_t} \ell(f(\mathbf{z}_u(t), \mathbf{z}_v(t)), y_{\mathcal{E}_t})(1 - q(\mathbf{z}_u(t), \mathbf{z}_v(t)))}{|\mathcal{E}_t|\, \hat{\phi}(q|\mathcal{E}_t)} \tag{3}$$

$$\hat{\phi}(q|\mathcal{E}_t) = \frac{1}{|\mathcal{E}_t|} \sum_{(u,v,t)\in\mathcal{E}_t} (1 - q(\mathbf{z}_u(t), \mathbf{z}_v(t))) \tag{4}$$

where ℓ is the *loss function* and $\mathbf{z}_u(t), \mathbf{z}_v(t)$ are the temporal node embeddings for source and destination node for link prediction, respectively, and $y_{\mathcal{E}_t}$ is the binary label of link between two nodes if exists or not. $\hat{\phi}$, the empirical coverage rate of the abstention function q, calculates the rate at which the edges till time t are selected, where $|\mathcal{E}_t|$ is the number of edges. The overall training objective combines the abstention loss with an auxiliary loss. For our case, we use the standard binary cross-entropy as an auxiliary loss, denoted as $\mathcal{L}^{\mathcal{E}_t}_h$ computed on the same prediction task. This auxiliary loss is generated by a dedicated auxiliary prediction head, active only during training. Its purpose is to ensure the shared encoder learns from all training instances, including those the abstention head might abstain from. This approach prevents overfitting to only high-confidence samples and promotes more robust representations. The overall training objective is:

$$\mathcal{L}^{\mathcal{E}_t} = \alpha\mathcal{L}^{\mathcal{E}_t}_{(f,q)} + (1 - \alpha)\mathcal{L}^{\mathcal{E}_t}_h \tag{5}$$

where α is a parameter controlling the trade-off between abstention and auxiliary losses.

The temporal graph encoder captures node interaction timing using a time encoder, which is incorporated into the temporal node embeddings. This time information is then passed to both the abstention and prediction functions, allowing the model to decide whether to abstain from making a prediction at a given time t.

4.3   Coverage-Based Dynamic Node Classification

For node classification or user state change prediction [18], we apply a framework similar to link prediction, using the abstention prediction mechanism to introduce a reject option. Node embedding $\mathbf{z}_u(t)$, derived from the temporal graph encoder, incorporates information from the node's interaction history and its neighbors to produce a comprehensive representation of its current state in the graph. It serves as input to a classification model that incorporates a coverage-based abstention mechanism. The classifier is designed to accurately predict node labels $y_t \in \mathcal{Y}$ while being able to abstain from predictions when uncertainty exceeds the threshold θ. The abstention prediction objective in this case is as follows:

$$\mathcal{L}^{\mathcal{V}_t}_{(f,q)} = \hat{r}(f, q|\mathcal{V}_t) + \lambda \Psi(c - \hat{\phi}(q|\mathcal{V}_t)) \tag{6}$$

where the empirical abstention risk $(\hat{r}(f, q|\mathcal{V}_t))$ and the empirical coverage $(\hat{\phi}(q|\mathcal{V}_t))$ are calculated as follows:

$$\hat{r}(f, q|\mathcal{V}_t) = \frac{\sum_{u \in \mathcal{V}_t} \ell(f(\mathbf{z}_u(t)), y_t)(1 - q(\mathbf{z}_u(t))}{|\mathcal{V}_t| \, \hat{\phi}(q|\mathcal{V}_t)} \tag{7}$$

$$\hat{\phi}(q|\mathcal{V}_t) = \frac{1}{|\mathcal{V}_t|} \sum_{u \in \mathcal{V}_t} (1 - q(\mathbf{z}_u(t))) \tag{8}$$

where $|\mathcal{V}_t|$ is the number of nodes. The node classification model is trained by minimizing a loss function that balances the precision of the abstention prediction with the desired coverage level, which is given by:

$$\mathcal{L}^{\mathcal{V}_t} = \alpha \mathcal{L}^{\mathcal{V}_t}_{(f,q)} + (1 - \alpha)\mathcal{L}^{\mathcal{V}_t}_h \tag{9}$$

where $\mathcal{L}^{\mathcal{V}_t}_h$ is the auxiliary loss (binary cross-entropy).

4.4   Handling Extreme Class Imbalance for Dynamic Node Classification

Dealing with an extreme class imbalance in node classification within CTDGs presents significant challenges. Class imbalance adversely affects model performance, particularly for minority classes, which is crucial for many real-world applications. To address this, we introduce an approach that modifies the training process to better represent minority classes, thereby improving the model's performance. We modify the components of our training objective given in Eq. (9).

Auxiliary Loss for Class Imbalance: We propose an auxiliary loss function that explicitly accounts for the disproportionate representation of classes by assigning a higher weight to the minority class, which is defined as:

$$\mathcal{L}_h^{\mathcal{V}_t} = \beta \mathcal{L}_{h_{minor}}^{\mathcal{V}_t} + \mathcal{L}_{h_{major}}^{\mathcal{V}_t} \tag{10}$$

where $\mathcal{L}_{h_{minor}}^{\mathcal{V}_t}$ and $\mathcal{L}_{h_{major}}^{\mathcal{V}_t}$ represent the loss for the minority and majority classes, respectively, and β is a weighing factor that amplifies the contribution of the minority class to the overall loss. In our experiments, we set hyperparameter $\beta > 1$, highlighting our focus on the minority class, given its significantly lower representation (less than 0.2% in our dataset). This allows us to tune our model's performance, ensuring that it provides reliable predictions in the case of extreme class imbalance.

5   Experimental Setup

In this section, we discuss experimental setup, which comprises baselines, datasets used, evaluation tasks performed, metrics used, and implementation details.

5.1   Dataset Used

We use four distinct datasets for dynamic link prediction and two for dynamic node classification where labels are available. We have chosen popular datasets like Wikipedia [18], Reddit (Soical Media) [18], and also included challenging datasets like UN Trade (Economics) and Can. Parl. (Politics) for diversity. These datasets are publicly available[2] by DGB [23].

5.2   Baselines Used

Although our framework is compatible with various temporal graph models supported by DyGLib [34], we opted to utilize TGN [26] and GraphMixer [7] due to their widespread adoption as baselines.

TGN Encoder [26]: The key components of TGN Encoder are: a) **Memory module** maintains a compressed representation of each node's historical interactions. b) **Message function** computes the impact of new interactions on the state of the node. c) **Message aggregator** combines messages from multiple events involving the same node in a batch, improving the update process. d)

---

[2] https://zenodo.org/record/7213796#.Y1cO6y8r30o.

Memory updater integrates new interaction messages into the node's memory. e) **Embedding module** generates the current embedding of a node using its memory and the memories of its neighbors.

GraphMixer Encoder [7]: GraphMixer presents a simple, straightforward, yet effective approach built upon two primary modules: a link encoder and a node encoder based on multilayer perceptrons (MLPs) without relying on complex GNN architectures. a) **Link-encoder** employs a fixed time-encoding function $\cos(\omega t)$. It encodes temporal information of links, followed by an MLP-Mixer [29] to summarize this temporal link information effectively. b) **Node-encoder** utilizes neighbor mean-pooling to aggregate and summarize the features of nodes, capturing essential node identity and feature information for subsequent processing steps.

5.3   Evaluation Tasks and Metrics

We evaluate our approach on two key dynamic graph tasks: link prediction and node classification, aligning with prior work [18,23,34].

For link prediction, we predict the likelihood of an edge forming between two nodes at time t, using a 2-layer MLP over concatenated node embeddings. We evaluate both transductive (known nodes) and inductive (unseen nodes) settings, with Average Precision (AP) and AUC-ROC as metrics. Following [23], we use random (rnd), historical (hist: edge re-occurrence), and inductive (ind: unseen test edges) negative sampling strategies (NSS).

For node classification, we fine-tune a pretrained encoder and train a separate MLP for label prediction with a reject option. We report AUC-ROC, suitable for the common class imbalance in these tasks. Datasets without dynamic node labels are excluded.

For both tasks, we split all datasets chronologically: 70% train, 15% validation, 15% test.

5.4   Implementation Details

For the link prediction task, we optimize both the models by Adam optimizer [17] for all datasets. For the node classification task, we optimize both the models by Adam optimizer for the Wikipedia dataset and SGD for the Reddit dataset. We train the models for 75 epochs and use the early stopping strategy with a patience of 10. We select the model that achieves the best performance in the validation set for testing. We set the batch size to 200, λ to 32, α to 0.5, i.e., equal weight to both abstention prediction loss and auxiliary loss for all the methods on all the datasets. We perform the grid search to find the best settings of some critical hyperparameters. This step is conducted during training. We tune the learning rate using cross-validation. Even though the training process aims to meet the target coverage c via the loss function, the actual coverage achieved on the test set with a fixed threshold $e.g. \theta = 0.5$ may differ due to distribution shift. Therefore, to analyze the model's performance-reliability trade-off consistently, we evaluate at predefined coverage levels (e.g., 90%, 80%, etc.). For each target coverage level reported (e.g., 80%), we calculate the corresponding threshold θ_{80} by finding the 80th percentile of the uncertainty scores $a(x)$ produced by the model on the entire test set. Metrics are then computed solely on the test samples satisfying $a(x) \leq \theta_{80}$.

The θ values range from 0 to 1. For node classification, we search for the best value of β in the range of [2,100] and get the best results when $\beta = 2$ or 5. Both encoders use 100D time encoding and 172D output representation. TGN uses 172D node memory with 2 graph attention heads, using GRU for memory updates. GraphMixer uses 2 MLP-Mixer layers with a time slot gap of 2000 interactions. We run each model five times with seeds from 0 to 4 and report the average performance and standard deviation to eliminate deviations. We use NVIDIA GeForce RTX 4090 with 24 GB memory for link prediction task. The GPU device used for the node classification task is NVIDIA GeForce RTX 2080 Ti with 11 GB memory.

6 Experimental Results

In this section, we report the performance of our proposed continuous-time dynamic graph neural network with a reject option and compare our results with baselines.

Table 1. AP for transductive dynamic link prediction with random, historical, and inductive negative sampling strategies for various coverage rates. The best and second-best results are emphasized by **bold** and underlined.

NSS	Coverage (%)	TGN				GraphMixer			
		Wikipedia	Reddit	UN Trade	Can. Parl.	Wikipedia	Reddit	UN Trade	Can. Parl.
rnd	100	98.56 ± 0.06	98.63 ± 0.02	64.87 ± 1.93	74.14 ± 1.51	97.30 ± 0.05	97.35 ± 0.02	61.68 ± 0.16	79.96 ± 0.95
	90	99.33 ± 0.06	99.28 ± 0.07	71.67 ± 1.04	75.38 ± 1.44	98.24 ± 0.07	97.66 ± 0.06	68.57 ± 0.21	80.56 ± 1.71
	80	99.73 ± 0.08	99.54 ± 0.06	76.59 ± 1.50	77.21 ± 5.87	98.89 ± 0.06	98.41 ± 0.03	72.50 ± 1.24	82.44 ± 1.31
	70	99.85 ± 0.02	99.81 ± 0.04	79.09 ± 1.66	81.57 ± 7.38	99.61 ± 0.14	99.32 ± 0.08	71.64 ± 8.98	95.25 ± 0.65
	60	**99.88 ± 0.02**	99.86 ± 0.04	81.46 ± 1.81	**90.19 ± 3.50**	99.68 ± 0.11	99.52 ± 0.11	69.99 ± 11.27	**95.98 ± 0.57**
	50	99.87 ± 0.05	**99.91 ± 0.03**	84.46 ± 0.95	89.46 ± 6.67	99.63 ± 0.08	**99.65 ± 0.11**	80.94 ± 2.11	94.68 ± 1.25
hist	100	87.07 ± 0.81	80.63 ± 0.30	59.44 ± 2.22	70.92 ± 2.11	91.14 ± 0.16	77.50 ± 0.54	57.61 ± 1.11	80.66 ± 1.37
	90	90.81 ± 0.59	81.68 ± 1.07	70.36 ± 0.80	74.18 ± 1.94	94.25 ± 0.43	78.17 ± 0.25	63.36 ± 3.08	83.10 ± 1.57
	80	94.46 ± 0.64	83.78 ± 0.33	74.44 ± 3.55	72.82 ± 6.51	96.57 ± 0.63	80.57 ± 0.33	69.35 ± 3.68	84.08 ± 2.60
	70	95.99 ± 3.62	87.25 ± 1.76	71.94 ± 8.63	76.08 ± 9.00	97.99 ± 2.64	83.61 ± 1.96	75.01 ± 4.15	94.97 ± 0.55
	60	97.06 ± 3.84	88.66 ± 1.68	76.36 ± 2.16	86.97 ± 4.56	**98.56 ± 2.81**	85.32 ± 1.76	69.62 ± 1.57	**95.05 ± 0.97**
	50	**97.82 ± 4.50**	**89.27 ± 2.41**	**76.65 ± 2.85**	**87.34 ± 3.79**	97.40 ± 3.50	**85.91 ± 2.04**	**81.70 ± 2.52**	94.18 ± 1.33
ind	100	86.57 ± 0.96	88.02 ± 0.35	61.70 ± 2.21	68.05 ± 2.69	88.83 ± 0.13	85.21 ± 0.28	60.89 ± 1.01	77.74 ± 1.42
	90	89.75 ± 1.03	90.17 ± 0.82	72.31 ± 0.77	71.28 ± 2.90	92.11 ± 0.23	85.76 ± 0.34	67.57 ± 2.52	79.98 ± 2.47
	80	93.19 ± 0.57	92.89 ± 0.80	77.43 ± 2.94	69.06 ± 9.77	95.04 ± 0.37	88.74 ± 0.43	74.08 ± 1.72	79.26 ± 3.90
	70	95.85 ± 3.61	94.95 ± 2.27	75.75 ± 6.69	72.87 ± 10.05	96.45 ± 3.70	91.38 ± 0.86	79.47 ± 2.22	93.47 ± 0.56
	60	96.76 ± 4.00	**96.57 ± 2.68**	**78.65 ± 1.93**	84.91 ± 5.02	**97.66 ± 3.90**	93.11 ± 1.45	77.98 ± 1.54	94.11 ± 0.84
	50	**97.75 ± 4.63**	95.93 ± 3.33	78.30 ± 2.15	**85.12 ± 6.52**	94.79 ± 6.29	**94.35 ± 1.60**	**85.47 ± 2.57**	**94.28 ± 1.07**

6.1 Results: Dynamic Link Prediction

We evaluated our rejection-aware framework on the dynamic link prediction task using both TGN and GraphMixer as base encoders, comparing performance against standard baselines run using DyGLib [42]. The primary goal was to assess the improvement in prediction reliability when allowing the model to abstain based on uncertainty.

Table 1 summarizes the transductive link prediction results, reporting Average Precision (AP) across all three negative sampling strategies (NSS). The 100% coverage rows represent the baseline performance without rejection. A consistent and significant trend is observed across all datasets, models, and NSS settings: as the coverage level decreases (meaning the model abstains on a larger fraction of uncertain predictions, from 90% down to 50% coverage), the AP score calculated on the remaining non-abstained predictions progressively improves.

This shows the effectiveness of the rejection mechanism in filtering out low-confidence predictions, thereby enhancing the precision of the accepted ones. For example, focusing on the challenging Canadian Parliament (Can. Parl.) dataset, which exhibits lower baseline scores, the improvement is notable. With our model, the AP/AUC score notably increases, emphasizing the model's efficiency in managing harder prediction environments. For example, using TGN with random NSS, the AP increases from a baseline of (1st row) at 100% coverage to 90.19% AP (5th row) at 60% coverage in Can. Parl. dataset, marking almost 16.05% improvement in AP. These gains show the value of abstention for boosting trustworthiness, particularly in environments with sparse or noisy interaction data typical of many real-world social or information networks. Further illustrating the performance-reliability trade-off, Fig. 3 plots the relationship between coverage and prediction performance (AUC) for the *inductive* link prediction task (using Random NSS). Consistent with the AP results, the inductive AUC generally increases as coverage decreases (moving rightward on the x-axis). This confirms that the benefits of abstention—achieving higher accuracy on a more reliable subset of predictions—extend to the demanding inductive setting,

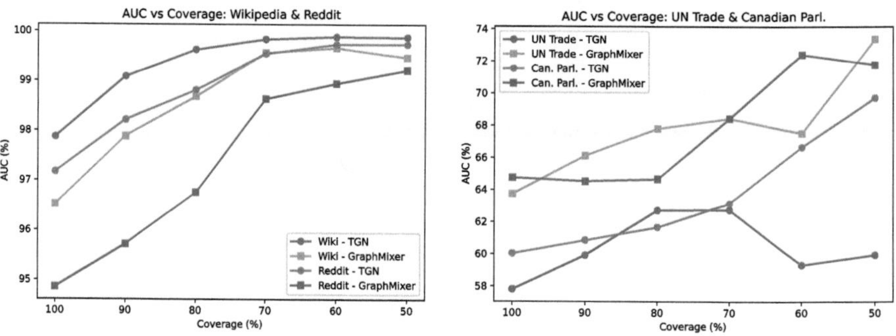

Fig. 3. Performance (AUC %) vs. Coverage (%) Trade-off for Inductive Link Prediction in Random NSS.

where generalization to unseen graph elements is crucial. The visual trend highlights the model's capability to manage uncertainty effectively across different evaluation scenarios.

One observation is that AP/AUC increases to a certain point (peak) as coverage decreases. It starts decreasing as coverage goes on decreasing.

6.2 Results: Dynamic Node Classification

For dynamic node classification, we evaluate our model on the Wikipedia and Reddit datasets, as shown in Table 2. The initial results with 100% coverage use DyGLib, which establishes a benchmark. As we implement the reject option, progressively rejecting 10% of samples in each subsequent test until we reach 60% coverage, we observe a significant improvement in AUC scores (where $\beta = 1$). For example, in Table 2 we achieve 89.78% AUC (ninth row) in 60% coverage w.r.t. 86.23% AUC (first row) in 100% coverage for the TGN model on Wikipedia, marking almost 3.55% improvement in AUC.

This increase in AUC with decreasing coverage indicates that the model is effectively prioritizing more reliable predictions, as less certain predictions are rejected. Furthermore, due to the extreme imbalance in class distribution (minority class below 0.2%), we provide higher weightage to minority class in the auxiliary loss, which led to further improvements in AUC (where $\beta > 1$). For example, in Table 2, we get 69.58% AUC (tenth row) with $\beta = 5$ w.r.t.66.03% AUC (ninth row) in 60% coverage for TGN model on Reddit dataset. This marks almost 3.55% improvement in AUC while addressing the class imbalances. This strategy improves the efficacy of our approach in not only managing the reject option but also addressing extreme class imbalances, which are particularly challenging in dynamic environments.

Table 2. AUC for coverage-based dynamic node classification for various coverage rates with and without handling class imbalance. The best and second-best performing results are emphasized by **bold** and <u>underlined</u> fonts. * denotes β is 2, otherwise 5 for all other cases where $\beta > 1$.

Coverage(%)	β	TGN		GraphMixer	
		Wikipedia	Reddit	Wikipedia	Reddit
100	= 1	86.23 ± 3.30	63.08 ± 1.48	86.19 ± 1.10	64.81 ± 2.08
90	= 1	88.00 ± 2.00	64.81 ± 1.54	87.27 ± 1.72	65.26 ± 2.07
	> 1	88.44 ± 2.33*	65.12 ± 1.53	87.61 ± 1.06*	66.20 ± 1.88
80	= 1	88.78 ± 3.46	65.63 ± 1.31	87.93 ± 1.53	66.08 ± 2.99
	> 1	90.02 ± 2.29*	66.31 ± 3.26	<u>88.05 ± 1.72</u>	67.00 ± 2.40
70	= 1	89.48 ± 2.53	66.10 ± 2.34	87.79 ± 1.37	67.42 ± 3.27
	> 1	**90.64 ± 3.37**	<u>67.90 ± 1.81</u>	**88.38 ± 0.99***	**68.23 ± 2.96**
60	= 1	89.78 ± 2.76	66.03 ± 3.45	85.97 ± 2.62	67.23 ± 3.36
	> 1	<u>89.86 ± 2.52</u>	**69.58 ± 2.96**	84.83 ± 2.30*	<u>67.87 ± 4.01</u>

In real-world scenarios, we can't reject 40–50% predictions. But as we can see, with a decrease in coverage, performance keeps on increasing. Note that the model rejects examples; it does not predict very confidently. We have to find a balance between the rate of abstention and the model confidence based on the application domain, number of data points, etc. Overall, the experiments validate our hypothesis that integrating a reject option within CTDGs significantly enhances the reliability and accuracy of predictions in dynamic graphs. The clear improvement in performance metrics across different datasets, coverage settings, and tasks confirms the practical utility of our model in risk-sensitive applications, where precision and reliability are crucial.

7   Conclusion

The experimental findings convincingly demonstrate the efficacy of our proposed CTDG model with a reject option for both link prediction and node classification tasks. The model strategically abstains from making predictions when encountering high uncertainty, leading to a significant improvement in AUC/AP scores. This establishes the model's proficiency in managing the trade-off between prediction confidence and coverage. In the future, we can explore cost-based or other abstention methods to enhance the model's applicability in different contexts. Another future direction could involve demonstrating the model's performance in real-world applications, showcasing its practical relevance. Considering our method for another kind of graph model, such as discrete time temporal graphs, can also be explored. Overall, our work presents a compelling solution for dynamic graph applications that demand high precision and reliability, particularly in risk-sensitive domains. The model's ability to effectively manage uncertainty and class imbalance makes it a valuable tool for various real-world applications.

References

1. Bai, L., Yao, L., Li, C., Wang, X., Wang, C.: Adaptive graph convolutional recurrent network for traffic forecasting. In: NeurIPS (2020)
2. Behrouz, A., Hashemi, F.: Learning temporal higher-order patterns to detect anomalous brain activity. In: TGLW @ NeurIPS (2023)
3. Behrouz, A., Seltzer, M.: Anomaly detection in multiplex dynamic networks: from blockchain security to brain disease prediction. In: TGLW @ NeurIPS (2022)
4. Cao, Y., et al.: Generalizing consistent multi-class classification with rejection to be compatible with arbitrary losses. In: NeurIPS (2022)
5. Charoenphakdee, N., Cui, Z., Zhang, Y., Sugiyama, M.: Classification with rejection based on cost-sensitive classification. In: ICML, pp. 1507–1517 (2021)
6. Chomel, V., Cuvelle-Magar, N., Panahi, M., Chavalarias, D.: Polarization identification on multiple timescale using representation learning on temporal graphs in eulerian description. In: TGLW @ NeurIPS (2022)
7. Cong, W., et al.: Do we really need complicated model architectures for temporal networks? In: ICLR (2023)

8. Davis, E., Gallagher, I., Lawson, D.J., Rubin-Delanchy, P.: Valid conformal prediction for dynamic GNNs. In: ICLR (2025)
9. Ding, Z., et al.: Dygmamba: efficiently modeling long-term temporal dependency on continuous-time dynamic graphs with state space models. arXiv preprint arXiv:2408.04713 (2024)
10. El-Yaniv, R., Wiener, R.: On the foundations of cost-sensitive learning. JMLR 1393–1426 (2007)
11. Fey, M., Lenssen, J.E.: Fast graph representation learning with PyTorch Geometric. In: RLGM @ ICLR-W (2019)
12. Geifman, Y., El-Yaniv, R.: SelectiveNet: a deep neural network with an integrated reject option. In: ICML (2019)
13. Huang, K., Jin, Y., Candes, E., Leskovec, J.: Uncertainty quantification over graph with conformalized graph neural networks. In: NeurIPS, vol. 36 (2024)
14. Huang, S., et al.: Temporal graph benchmark for machine learning on temporal graphs. In: NeurIPS Datasets and Benchmarks Track (2023)
15. Kalra, B., Shah, K., Manwani, N.: Risan: robust instance specific deep abstention network. In: UAI (2021)
16. Kazemi, S.M., et al.: Representation learning for dynamic graphs: a survey. JMLR 1–73 (2020)
17. Kingma, D.P., Ba, J.: Adam: a method for stochastic optimization. In: ICLR (2015)
18. Kumar, S., Zhang, X., Leskovec, J.: Predicting dynamic embedding trajectory in temporal interaction networks. In: KDD, pp. 1269–1278 (2019)
19. Manwani, N., Desai, K., Sasidharan, S., Sundararajan, R.: Double ramp loss based reject option classifier. In: PAKDD, pp. 151–163 (2015)
20. Nath, P., Waghmare, G., Agrawal, N., Kumar, N., Asthana, S.: TBoost: gradient boosting temporal graph neural networks. In: TGLW @ NeurIPS (2023)
21. Ni, C., Charoenphakdee, N., Honda, J., Sugiyama, M.: On the calibration of multiclass classification with rejection. In: NeurIPS, vol. 32 (2019)
22. Pareja, A., et al.: Evolvegcn: evolving graph convolutional networks for dynamic graphs. In: AAAI, pp. 5363–5370 (2020)
23. Poursafaei, F., Huang, A., Pelrine, K., Rabbany, R.: Towards better evaluation for dynamic link prediction. In: NeurIPS Datasets and Benchmarks Track (2022)
24. Reddy, S., et al.: Tegraf: temporal and graph based fraudulent transaction detection framework. In: ACM International Conference on AI in Finance, pp. 1–8 (2021)
25. Reha, J., Lovisotto, G., Russo, M., Gravina, A., Grohnfeldt, C.: Anomaly detection in continuous-time temporal provenance graphs. In: TGLW @ NeurIPS (2023)
26. Rossi, E., Chamberlain, B., Frasca, F., Eynard, D., Monti, F., Bronstein, M.: Temporal graph networks for deep learning on dynamic graphs. In: GRL @ ICML-W (2020)
27. Shah, K., Manwani, N.: Sparse reject option classifier using successive linear programming. In: AAAI, pp. 4870–4877 (2019)
28. Tian, Y., Qi, Y., Guo, F.: Freedyg: frequency enhanced continuous-time dynamic graph model for link prediction. In: ICLR (2024)
29. Tolstikhin, I.O., et al.: MLP-mixer: an all-MLP architecture for vision. In: NeurIPS, pp. 24261–24272 (2021)
30. Varugunda, S.S., Fan, C.H., Wang, L.: Exploring graph structure in graph neural networks for epidemic forecasting. In: TGLW @ NeurIPS (2023)
31. Wang, L., et al.: TCL: transformer-based dynamic graph modelling via contrastive learning. CoRR (2021)
32. Wang, Y., Chang, Y., Liu, Y., Leskovec, J., Li, P.: Inductive representation learning in temporal networks via causal anonymous walks. In: ICLR (2021)

33. Xu, D., Ruan, C., Körpeoglu, E., Kumar, S., Achan, K.: Inductive representation learning on temporal graphs. In: ICLR (2020)
34. Yu, L., Sun, L., Du, B., Lv, W.: Towards better dynamic graph learning: new architecture and unified library. In: NeurIPS (2023)

Federated k-Core Decomposition: A Secure Distributed Approach

Bin Guo[1]([✉]), Emil Sekerinski[2], and Lingyang Chu[2]

[1] Department of Computer Science, Trent University, Peterborough,
ON K9L 0G2, Canada
binguo@trentu.ca

[2] Department of Computing and Software, McMaster University,
Hamilton, ON L8S 4L8, Canada
{emil,chul9}@mcmaster.ca

Abstract. As one of the most well-studied cohesive subgraph models, the k-core is widely used to find graph nodes that are "central" or "important" in many applications, such as biological networks, social networks, ecological networks, and financial networks. For distributed networks, e.g., Decentralized Online Social Networks (DOSNs) such that each vertex is a client as a single computing unit, the distributed k-core decomposition algorithms are already proposed. However, current distributed approaches fail to adequately protect privacy and security. In this work, we are the first to propose the secure version of the distributed k-core decomposition.

Keywords: graph · k-core decomposition · distributed · privacy

1 Introduction

Graphs are important data structures that can represent complex relations in many real applications, such as social networks, communication networks, biological networks, hyperlink networks, and model checking networks.

Given an undirected graph G, the *k-core decomposition* is to identify the maximal subgraph G' in which each vertex has a degree of at least k; the *core number* of each vertex u is defined as the maximum value of k such that u is contained in the k-core of G [3,10]. It is well known that core numbers can be computed with linear running time $O(n+m)$ using the BZ algorithm [3], where n is the number of vertices and m is the number of edges in G. Due to the linear time complexity, the k-core decomposition is easily and widely used in many real-world applications.

In [10], Kong et al. summarize a large number of applications for k-core decomposition in biology, social networks, community detection, ecology, information spreading, etc. Especially in [4], Lesser et al. investigate the k-core robustness in ecological send financial networks. In a survey [14], Malliaros et al. summarize the main research work related to k-core decomposition from 1968 to 2019.

In today's data-driven world, data graphs tend to grow continuously and must be distributed rather than stored in a single machine. In particular, data privacy and security have attracted more and more attention [6,12,17]. Our work is based on the model for multiple *clients* [15], where each client is a single computational unit like a single machine with shared memory and different clients communicate by asynchronous network.

1.1 Data Privacy for k-Core Decomposition

Specifically, for k-core decomposition, *privacy* can be defined as follows: a) each client knows its own information; b) each client knows the ID of its directly connected neighbors; c) besides the above two, each client does not know any other information, such as the core numbers of neighbors and the connections of neighbors; d) there does not exist a centralized server for synchronization and storing the information of all clients.

After the k-core decomposition, each vertex successfully obtains its core number. The other important question is how to release the core numbers. Since core numbers can be private information for clients, it is not safe that all vertices report their core numbers when there are queries. We observe that many core number analytics in real graphs [4] only calculate the distribution of core numbers, instead of knowing the specific core number for each vertex. That is, each vertex is assigned a label that indicates its special property. We can receive a query, for example, how many vertices have both the label A and the maximum core number 10, denoted $A10$. In this case, essentially, we only need to release the total number of vertices with $A10$, and thus we can hide the real core number of each vertex.

However, existing traditional distributed k-core decomposition approaches [2, 13,15] inadequately consider the data privacy and security for three problems. First, a centralized server connects to all clients to detect the termination k-core decomposition, by which the server may know all the IDs of the clients. Second, a client has to store all the core numbers of neighbors, which explicitly exposes its core numbers to neighbors. Third, there are no strategies to safely release the core numbers of vertices after core decomposition. In this work, we try to overcome these problems.

1.2 Our Contributions

In this paper, we improve the existing distributed k-core decomposition algorithm in [15] by preserving data privacy and security on "Secure-One-to-One", the so-called *federated k-core decomposition*. The general framework is shown in Fig. 1. Three approaches are proposed to improve privacy and security, which are our main contributions.

- We propose Homomorphic Encryption (HE) [1] to compare a pair of core numbers for two vertices without leaking the value of the core numbers to other vertices.

- We propose decentralized termination detection to identify whether the computation is complete or not.
- After termination, all the core numbers of vertices have already been calculated. We propose a method to safely release the distribution of the core numbers for the vertices with the same labels, instead of the exact values of the core numbers.

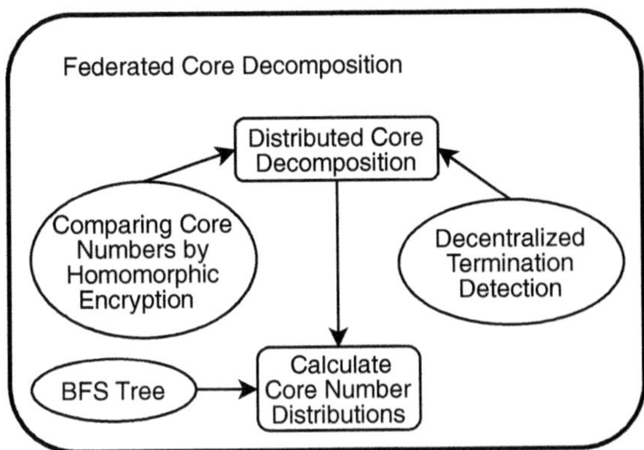

Fig. 1. The framework of Our Federated k-Core Decomposition.

2 Related Work

In [3], Batagelj et al. propose a linear time $O(m + n)$ algorithm for k-core decomposition, the so-called BZ algorithm. In [15], Montresor et al. first propose a distributed k-core decomposition algorithm that can handle distributed graphs. In [13], Luo et al. extend distributed k-core decomposition algorithms to probabilistic graphs. In [5], Chan et al. study the approximate distributed k-core decomposition. In [11], Liao et al. explore the distributed D-core decomposition specifically in directed graphs; here, D-core, also called (k, l)-core, is a directed version of k-core, the maximal directed subgraph such that every vertex has at least k in-neighbors and l out-neighbors. These traditional distributed approaches never consider privacy and security during computation.

3 Preliminary

Let $G = (V, E)$ be an undirected unweighted graph, where $V(G)$ denotes the set of vertices and $E(G)$ represents the set of edges in G. When the context is clear, we will use V and E instead of $V(G)$ and $E(G)$ for simplicity, respectively. As G is an undirected graph, an edge $(u, v) \in E(G)$ is equivalent to $(v, u) \in E(G)$. The set of neighbors of a vertex $u \in V$ is defined by $u.adj = \{v \in V : (u,v) \in E\}$. The degree of a vertex $u \in V$ is denoted by $u.deg = |u.adj|$. We denote the number of vertices and edges of G by n and m, respectively, in the context of analyzing time, space, and message complexities. We denote a set of messages for the communication of vertices by $M = \{m_1, m_2, m_3, ...\}$.

Furthermore, each vertex $u \in V$ has a label to indicate the local feature, which is defined by $u.lb$. The set $\mathcal{L}$ includes all the possible labels that $u \in V$ may have, denoted $\mathcal{L} = \{u.lb \mid u \in V\}$.

Definition 1 (k-Core). *Given an undirected graph $G = (V, E)$ and a natural number k, a induced subgraph G_k of G is called a k-core if it satisfies: (1) for $\forall u \in V(G_k)$, $u.deg \geq k$, and (2) G_k is maximal. Moreover, $G_{k+1} \subseteq G_k$, for all $k \geq 0$, and G_0 is just G.*

Definition 2 (Core Number). *Given an undirected graph $G = (V, E)$, the core number of a vertex $u \in G(V)$, denoted $u.core$, is defined as $u.core = max\{k : u \in V(G_k)\}$. That means $u.core$ is the largest k such that there exists a k-core containing u.*

Definition 3 (k-Core Decomposition). *Given a graph $G = (V, E)$, the problem of computing the core number for each $u \in V(G)$ is called k-core decomposition.*

3.1   Distributed k-Core Decomposition Algorithm

Our federated core decomposition is based on the distributed core decomposition algorithm in [15].

Theorem 1 (Locality [15]). *For all $u \in V$, its core number, $u.core$, is the largest value k such that u has at least k neighbors that have core numbers not less than k. Formally, we define $u.core = k$, where $k \leq |\{v \in u.adj : v.core \geq k\}|$ and $(k + 1) > |\{v \in u.adj : v.core \geq (k + 1)\}|$.*

Theorem 1 shows that the vertex u is sufficient to calculate its core number from the neighbor's information. The algorithm is reorganized in Algorithm 1.

1. For the initialization stage (lines 1 to 4), each $u \in V$ has its *estimate core numbers* initialized as its degree (line 2). Each u will maintain a set of estimated core numbers for all neighbors $u.adj$ (line 3). Then, each u sends its estimated core numbers $u.core'$ to all neighbors (line 4), where $\mathsf{Send}_u(v, \langle...\rangle)$ procedure (executed on the vertex u) is to send the message $\langle...\rangle$ to the target vertex v (lines 4 and 11).
2. Then u will receive the estimated core numbers $v.core'$ from its neighbors $v \in u.adj$ (lines 5 to 11). The received $core'$ will be stored in the array $u.A$ (line 6). If $u.A$ does not include all the estimated core numbers of $u.A$, it will return directly since u has not yet received all the neighbors' messages (line 7); otherwise, u will get the new core number k by executing $\mathsf{GetCore}$ (line 8). If k is not equal to $u.core'$, u will update its core number and send it to

all neighbors (lines 9–11). The `GetCore` procedure will check the core number with Theorem 1; if it is not satisfied, it will decrease the core number k until Theorem 1 is satisfied (lines 12–15).

3. Each vertex $u \in V$ executes the above distributed algorithm in parallel. The termination condition is that all vertices $u \in V$ satisfy Theorem 1 and thus stop decreasing the estimated core numbers $u.core'$ at the same time. Finally, we obtain the final calculated core numbers $u.core = u.core'$ for all $u \in V$.

Algorithm 1: Distributed Core Decomposition on Each Vertex $u \in V$ in Parallel

---

1 **procedure** Initialize$_u$ ()
2     $u.core' \leftarrow u.deg$
3     $u.A \leftarrow$ an empty array storing neighbors' core numbers
4   **for** $v \in u.adj$ **do** Send$_u$ $(v, \langle u, u.core' \rangle)$

5 **procedure** Receive$_u$ $(\langle v, core' \rangle)$
6     $u.A[v] \leftarrow core'$
7   **if** $|u.A| < u.deg$ **then return**
8     $k \leftarrow$ GetCore$(u.A, u.core')$
9   **if** $u.core' \neq k$ **then**
10        $u.core' \leftarrow k$
11   **for** $v \in u.adj$ **do** Send$_u$ $(v, \langle u, k \rangle)$

12 **procedure** GetCore(A, k)
13   **while** $|\{i \in A : i \geq k\}| < k$ **do**
14        $k \leftarrow k - 1$;
15   **return** k

Example 1. In Fig. 2, we show the k-core decomposition in an example graph. Figure 2(a) shows that the estimated core number of each vertex is initialized as its degree. For example, the vertex $d.core$ is set to 6 since it has 6 neighbors and its degree is 6. Figure 2(b) shows that in the first round the core numbers for the vertices b, d, g, f and j are active and decrease to $2, 3, 3, 3$ and 1 (colored red with bold circles), respectively. For example, the vertex $d.core$ decreases from 6 to 3, as $d.adj$ has a set of core numbers $\{2, 3, 3, 3, 4\}$ and $d.core$ can be at most 3 since there are at most 3 neighbors that have core numbers equal to or greater than 3. Figure 2(c) shows that in the second round the core numbers for the vertices g and i decrease to 2 and 1 (colored purple with bold circles), respectively. Figure 2(d) shows that in the third round the core number of the vertex h decreases to 1 (colored green). Finally, the algorithm terminates, since all vertices are inactive and cannot continually decrease their core numbers. As we can see, the core numbers are calculated in three rounds, and the vertex g updates the core number twice.

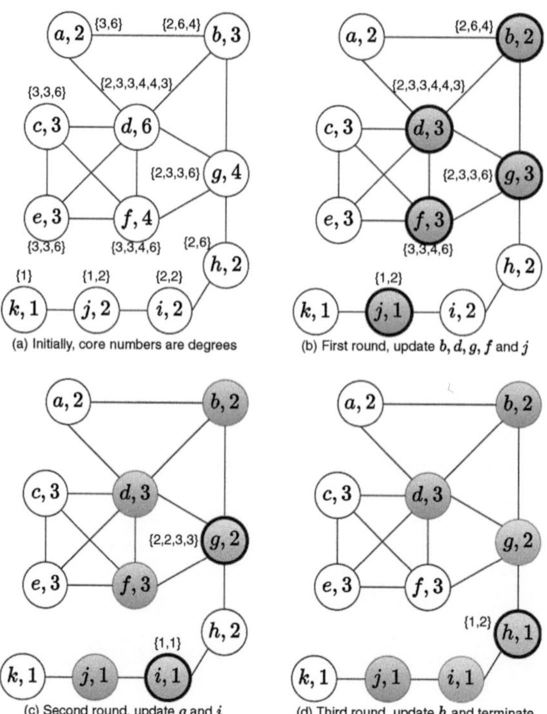

(a) Initially, core numbers are degrees

(b) First round, update b, d, g, f and j

(c) Second round, update g and i

(d) Third round, update h and terminate

Fig. 2. An example graph executes distributed k-core decomposition. Inside the circles, the letters are the vertices' IDs and the numbers are the core numbers. The bold circles show that the vertex is active for calculating its core number. The colored circles show that the core numbers have been updated in different rounds. The sets of numbers beside some vertices are their neighbors' core numbers. (Color figure online)

Message Complexities. Since most of the running time is spent on the message passing for the distributed k-core decomposition algorithm, we should analyze *message complexities* rather than the time complexities, where the message complexities is to count the number of messages passing between different vertices. We analyze the message complexities of Algorithm 1 in the standard *work-depth* model [9]. The *work*, denoted as $\mathcal{W}$, is the total number of operations that the algorithm uses. The *depth*, denoted as $\mathcal{D}$, is the longest chain of sequential operations.

In Algorithm 1, the work $\mathcal{W}$ is the total number of messages that the degree reduces to the core number. Each vertex must send messages to notify all neighbors when each time its degree decreases by one until its degree is reduced to its core number. So, we have the work denoted as $\mathcal{W} = O[\sum_{u \in V} u.deg \cdot (u.deg - u.core)]$.

In the worst case, the process can be reduced to sequential running, e.g., a chain graph. In other words, the whole process needs the worst-case n round to converge one by one in a chain. We suppose that each vertex is a client and only has one worker, so it cannot send messages to all neighbors in parallel. Therefore, the depth $\mathcal{D}$ is equal to the work $\mathcal{W}$. However, real graphs, for example, social networks and communication networks, are not chain graphs and tend to be *small-world* graphs. They have the property that most vertices are reachable from any other node through a small number of steps, even if the network is large [16], which exhibits two key properties, high clustering and a short average path length. Therefore, these graphs have a set of vertices D in the longest chain, which is much smaller than the number of vertices n, denoted as $|D| \ll |n|$. For example, in small-world social networks we always have $|D|$ less than 100 and n can be large as millions. Different chains can execute in parallel. Therefore, on average, the depth $\mathcal{D} = O[\sum_{u \in D} u.deg \cdot (u.deg - u.core)]$.

4   Our Technical Details

In this section, we describe the details of the parts in the framework shown in Fig. 1.

4.1   Comparing Core Numbers by HE

We use asymmetric HE to compare the core numbers of two vertices.

Algorithm. Given an edge $(u, v) \in E(G)$, we have a *source* vertex u and a *target* vertex v. The vertex u wants to compare its core number with v. In other words, u wants to acquire the result of $u.core > v.core$. The whole process is to extend the core numbers comparing in secure (line 13 in Algorithm 1), and the array $u.A$ will store the result of core number comparison instead of the value of neighbors' core numbers (lines 3 and 6 in Algorithm 1). The secure comparison algorithm has four steps:

1. The target vertex v send the message m_1 to notify u that $v.core$ is decreased (or new assigned for initialization, line 4 in Algorithm 1), where m_1 includes the ID of v denoted as $m_1 = \langle v \rangle$.
2. The source vertex u generates a pair of keys (pri, pub); we define the public encrypt function $E_{pub}()$ and the private decrypt function $D_{pri}()$. Then, the source vertex u sends the message m_2 to v, where m_2 includes the public key and its encrypted core number denoted as $m_2 = \langle pub, E_{pub}(u.core) \rangle$.
3. The target vertex v receives the message m_2 from u. Then, v generates $E_{pub}(v.core)$. According to the definition of HE, we have $E_{pub}(u.core) > E_{pub}(v.core) = E_{pub}(u.core > v.core)$. Thus, v can reply the message m_3 to u, where m_3 includes the encrypted comparison result denoted as $m_3 = \langle E_{pub}(u.core > v.core) \rangle$.
4. The vertex u receives m_3 from v. Then u can decrypt the message $D_{pri}(m_3)$ with its private key pri and get the result of $u.core > v.core$.

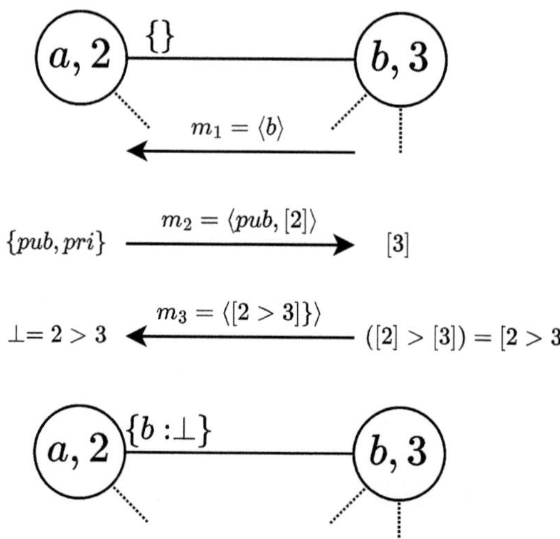

Fig. 3. An example of comparing core numbers between the vertices a and b in Fig. 2(a). The arrows are the direction for passing messages between two vertices. The $[2]$ is the encrypted value 2 with the public key pub.

Example 2. In Fig. 3, we show an example of how to compare the core numbers for the source vertex a and the target vertex b. The vertices a and b have the core numbers 2 and 3 initialized by their degree, respectively. First, b sends m_1 to a, indicating that $b.core$ is updated. Second, a generates a pair of public and private keys; a sends the public key pub and the encrypted core number 2 to b. Third, b send the encrypted result for the core number comparing $2 > 3$, to a. Finally, a decrypts the result and gets the result to be **false**, which is stored in the array A for later updating $a.core$.

Privacy Security Analysis. In the end, only the source vertex u knows the result of $u.core > v.core$, but v does not know this result; also, u cannot know the value of $v.core$, and vice versa. However, there are two cases where the values of core numbers are leaked.

First, given $v.core$ is in the range $[0, k_{max}]$, u can compare $\lceil \log k_{max} \rceil$ times to acquire the value of $v.core$, by using a binary search. That is, at first, u can pretend that its core number is $k_{max}/2$, compare with $v.core$, and identify the half range in which $v.core$ is. This process continues until u acquires the value of $v.core$. To solve this problem, a straightforward solution is that the target vertex v can limit the number of comparisons for the source vertex u. In this case, we can ensure that u only compares the core number with v once, with minimal leaking the value of $v.core$ to u.

Second, a special case is that if we have $u.core = 2 \ \wedge \ u.core > v.core$ as true, we can infer that $v.core = 1$, since v must be connected to u and $v.core$ cannot be 0. In this case, the source vertex u can infer that $v.core = 1$, which is the minimal leaking of the value of $v.core$ to u.

Message Complexities. The whole process involves three messages, m_1, m_2, and m_3, so that the source vertex u can compare the core number with the target vertex v. Obviously, the length of m_1 is bounded by $O(\log n)$ since it only includes the ID of the vertex. The length of m_2 is bounded by $O(\log n)$, since the encrypted Boolean value always has a fixed length. The public and private keys have fixed length, e.g., the RSA typically ranges from 1024 bits to 4096 bits. So, m_2 includes the public key pub, where the length is bound by $O(\log n)$. Therefore, m_1, m_2, and m_3 need not be split, and three messages are required for our one-time secure comparison of the core numbers.

Compared with our method, in Algorithm 1, v only needs to send one single message that includes $v.core$ to u when $v.core$ is updated, where the core number must be bounded by $O(\log n)$. In other words, our secure algorithm spends triple messages to ensure the protection of the core numbers.

4.2   Decentralized Termination Detection

We describe how to detect the termination of the distributed core decomposition algorithm without using a centralized server, that is, a decentralized approach. Our approach is based on the Feedback BFS tree and heartbeats.

We first define that each vertex u needs to maintain a status, denoted $u.s$, which has two values:

- **Live**: the vertex u actively receive the messages from neighbors $u.adj$ and process these messages; or u actively send the messages to neighbors $u.adj$. Initially, the vertex u must be **Live** since it begins to send $u.core$ to all neighbors in $u.adj$.
- **Dead**: the vertex u stops calculating the core number since the Locality of u (Theorem 1) is satisfied; and u is not receiving or sending messages.

In Algorithm 1, before lines 2 and 6, we insert $u.s \leftarrow$ **Live**, respectively; after lines 4 and 11, we insert $u.s \leftarrow$ **Dead**, respectively. This is to explicitly show the status of the current vertex.

Theorem 2 (Termination Condition). *The distributed k-core decomposition is terminated if the status $u.s$ for all vertices $u \in V$ is **Dead** simultaneously within a period that must be greater than L_{max}.*

*Proof. From Algorithm 1, we can see that the termination condition is that all vertices stop calculation, and also stop sending and receiving messages. It is possible that the vertex u has sent the message to v, but v has not yet received the message due to latency up to L_{max}. Since such a latency can be long, we must consider it when detecting the termination. In other words, the distributed algorithm is not terminated if there exists at least one **Live** vertex for a period greater than L_{max}.*

Feedback BFS Tree. Given a graph G, we first select a root vertex r to build a Feedback BFS tree. The process is straightforward with four steps:

1. Starting from the root vertex r, it sends the message m_1 to all neighbors $r.adj$, where m_1 includes a version number ver in case there are multiple BFS trees generated on the same graph, denoted $m_1 = \langle ver \rangle$. Here, the root vertex has children without parent.
2. The vertex v receives the message m_1 from a neighbor u'. If v is the first time receiving m_1 (the parent $v.pr = u'$), it forwards m_1 to other neighbors $v.adj \setminus u'$ who have not received m_1 (the children $v.ch$). This process will be repeated until v is a leaf vertex that does not have children.
3. The leaf vertices w ($w.ch = \emptyset$) receive m_1 and will reply the message m_2 to its parent w', where m_2 includes an opposite version number $-ver$ in m_1 (indicate that m_2 is a corresponding replied message), denoted $m_2 = \langle -ver \rangle$. Then, w' will reply to its parent $w'.pr$ at once if all children $w'.ch$ have received m_2. This process will be repeated until the root vertex r receives the message m_2.
4. Finally, we obtain the Feedback BFS duration $\overline{T}$, which is the time period between the root vertex r sending m_1 and receiving m_2 (see Definition 4).

Definition 4 (Feedback BFS Duration $\overline{T}$). *Given a root vertex r with a BFS tree generated in the graph G, r sends messages to its children to generate the BFS tree at time t_1. Then r receives all the feedback messages from the children at time t_2. Here, a vertex v in the graph can send a feedback message to the parent only if v receives all feedback messages from the children recursively. The BFS duration is denoted as $\overline{T} = t_2 - t_1$ in a round way. That is, any vertex can receive the message from the root r within $\overline{T}/2$ in one way.*

We can see that this BFS tree generates a fastest path from the root to all the other vertices. Since message passing is slow, the first message that a vertex v can receive must come from the fastest path. In other words, the duration $\overline{T}$ means the round time between sending messages to the furthest vertex and receiving the feedback. Our termination detection is based on this BFS tree.

Theorem 3 (Reachable in $\overline{T}$). *Given a generated Feedback BSF tree on a distributed graph G, we can select any pair of vertices (u, v). The vertex u can broadcast the message m_1 starting u, and v can always receive m_1 within the duration $\overline{T}$.*

Proof. Suppose that the root vertex is r. The vertex u can broadcast the message m_1 to r within $\overline{T}/2$; and the r can continuously forward the message m_1 to v within $\overline{T}/2$. Therefore, the total time for u can broadcast m_1 to v cost at most $\overline{T}$ time.

Example 3. An example is shown in Fig. 4. A BFS tree is built by choosing the vertex a as the root. The vertex c, e, f, and k are leaves without children; the vertex d has a parent a and children c, e, f and g; the root a does not have a parent but have two children b and d. The BFS duration $\overline{T}$ is the round time of the message passing between a and the furthest leaf vertex k, where we have $20 \times 6 = 120$ ms for one way and 240 ms for the round way. We observe that there are totally 11 edges given 12 vertices in this BFS tree.

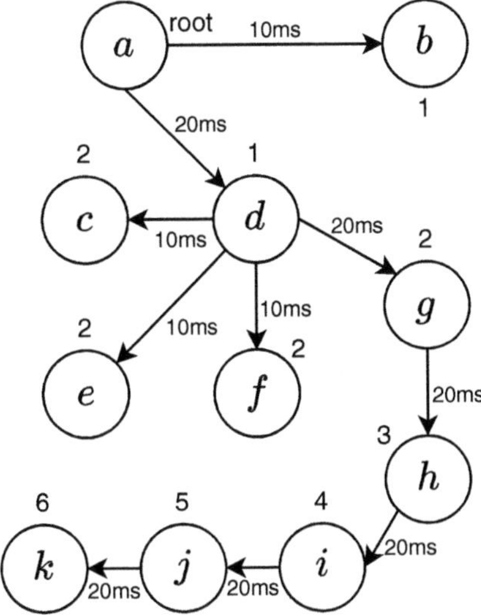

Fig. 4. An example of generate BFS tree. The root vertex is a. The numbers beside the circles are the depth of vertices from the root. The arrows of edges indicate the direction of broadcast the messages, which can only from the parent to the child. The time beside edges is the latency of the message passing via edges.

Heartbeat-Based Approach. After building the BFS tree for a given graph, each vertex sends the heartbeat message to notify other vertices that it is `Live`. Each vertex will send the heartbeat to other vertices in the BFS tree. We first define two attributes for the heartbeat:

- *Heartbeat Interval I.* Since our system can accept the latency of detecting termination, the heartbeat interval can be large enough to ensure low network resource consumption; but the it also should be much less than the total running time.
- *Timeout Duration T.* Typically, T is set to a multiple of the interval I (e.g., 2–3 times the interval). This gives some leeway for occasional delays in heartbeat delivery. For example, we can set I as 10 s giving T as 30 s.

Theorem 4. *Given the Feedback BFS duration $\overline{T}$, we can choose the Timeout Duration $T = 3\overline{T}/2$, and the Heartbeat interval $I = T/3$.*

Proof. We choose the value of T for two reasons. First, we must consider the time that the message passes through networks, that is, a heartbeat can be received by other vertices using at most $\overline{T}$ time. Second, we must have some leeway for the timeout duration for measuring the time, e.g. $1/2$ of $\overline{T}$.

Base on the determined T and I, we define a second status $u.s'$ for each vertex u to detect termination, which includes two values:

- **Active**: the vertex u always receives at least one heartbeat within the Timeout Duration T; or u is computing, that is $u.s = $ **Live**.
- **Inactive**: the vertex u does not receive the heartbeat within the Timeout Duration T; and u is not computing, that is $u.s = $ **Dead**.

Only the **Live** vertices u that are performing computations with $u.s = $ **Live** can generate and send heartbeats. The detailed process is as follows:

1. Initially, all vertices $u \in V$ are set to **Live** which have the $u.s'$ set to **Active**.
2. For each vertex $u \in V$, if u is executing the computation with $u.s = $ **Live**, $u.s'$ is set to **Active**; then, u will continuously send heartbeats to neighbors in the BFS tree; otherwise, $u.s'$ is **Dead** and stop sending heartbeats.
3. For the vertex v, if v receive the heartbeats from u within T, $v.s'$ is set to **Active**; then, v will continuously forward heartbeats to other neighbors in the BFS tree except u; otherwise, $v.s'$ is set to **Inactive** and stop forwarding heartbeats.
4. The Steps 2 and 3 will repeat until the heartbeats broadcast to all vertices in the graph using the BFS tree.

By doing this, we only need to check the status of $u.s'$ for any vertices $u \in V$. If $u.s'$ is **Inactive**, we know that the distributed core decomposition is terminated; otherwise, the algorithms is still executing. In other words, any vertices u always have the status $u.s'$ indicating termination.

Example 4. As an example BFS tree shown in Fig. 4, we suppose that only the vertex h is **Live** and all other vertices are **Dead** as shown in Fig. 2(d).

At the beginning stage, all vertices are set to **Active**. Only the vertex h is doing the computation, so h is **Live**; it immediately generates heartbeats and sends them to all its BFS neighbors, g and i. These heartbeats will be repeatedly forwarded to all other vertices, which are set to **Active**. For example, g is set to **Active** when receiving heartbeats from h after 20 ms, then g immediately send heartbeats to d and d is set to **Active** when receiving them after 40 ms. In this case, the fast vertex b will receive the heartbeats and set to **Active**after 70 ms. Finally, all vertices can receive the heartbeat and set to **Active**. That is, the **Live** vertices can only generate and send heartbeats; the **Dead** vertices can only forward the heartbeats generated by the **Live** vertices.

We choose the Timeout Duration $T = 360$ ms, larger than the BFS Duration $\overline{T} = 240$ ms. So, we choose the Heartbeat Interval $I = 360/3 = 120$ ms. We can test the termination with any vertices, e.g. b; that is, if b cannot receive heartbeats within T, b is set to **Inactive**. We detect that the algorithm has been terminated.

Privacy Security Analysis. For the whole process, the root vertex is selected arbitrarily and any vertex can be the root, which is not centralized. Each vertex u must record the information of the neighbors $u.adj$ for the parent and children in the BFS tree; and u does not know any other connections of the neighbors.

Finally, the root vertex can know the BFS duration $\overline{T}$, which is the information of the whole graph; but the latency for a specific edge cannot be inferred from $\overline{T}$.

Message Complexities. We only analyze the Feedback BFS tree. Initially, the vertices send totally m messages to build the BFS tree. The BFS tree has $n-1$ edges, so the vertices respond with $n-1$ feedback messages. Therefore, in the worst case, the total number of messages is $\mathcal{W} = O(m+n)$, and the depth is the longest chain in the graph, denoted as $\mathcal{D} = O(|D|)$.

4.3   Calculate Core Number Distribution

After the termination of the distributed k-core decomposition, we need to release the core numbers as computation results to minimize privacy leakage.

Algorithm. Given a graph G, we assume that the BFS tree is already built with the root vertex r, which is used for decentralized termination detection. Then, for the vertex u, we select a label and a core number, denoted $u.(lb, k)$, to count the number of such vertices, denoted $n_{(lb,k)}$. The detailed process is as follows:

1. Starting from the root r, it generates a pair of keys (pri, pub) with the public encrypt function E_{pub} and the private decrypt function D_{pri}. It sends the message m_1 to all children $u \in r.ch$, where m_1 includes the public key, a pair of the label and the core number, and a version number ver in case of multiple instances of the BFS tree, denoted $m_1 = \langle pub, E_{pub}(lb, k), ver \rangle$.
2. The vertex u receives the message m_1. If u has children $u.ch$, u will forward m_1 to all $u.ch$. This process will repeat until all vertices $u \in V$ receive m_1.
3. The leaf vertices u $(u.ch = \emptyset)$ receive m_1 and will reply the message m_2 to its parent $u.pr$. If the vertex u has the same label and core number as in m_1, denoted $E_{pub}(u.(lb, k)) = E_{pub}(lb, k) \in m_1$, we reply m_2 to $u.pr$, where m_2 includes the encrypted counting number 1 and opposite version number $-ver$ (indicate m_2 is a corresponding replied message), denoted $m_2 = \langle E_{pub}(1), -ver \rangle$; otherwise, the replied message $m_2 = \langle E_{pub}(0), -ver \rangle$. In other words, we the leaf vertices start to count.
4. The non-leaf vertices u $(u.ch \neq \emptyset)$ receive the message m_2. If all children $v \in u.ch$ receive m_2 together, u will add all $E_{pub}(n_{(lb,k)})$ of children together and reply to $u.pr$ with the message $m_2 = \langle E_{pub}(n_{(lb,k)}), -ver \rangle$. Here, HE is used for the encrypted add operation like $E_{pub}(1) + E_{pub}(2) = E_{pub}(3)$.
5. This step (3) and (4) will repeat until all children of the root vertex $u \in r.ch$ receive the message m_2. Finally, the root r will obtain the complete number of vertices with the corresponding (lb, k). With its local private key, the root r can decrypt the counting, denoted $n_{(lb,k)} = D_{pri}(E_{pub}(n_{(lb,k)}))$. Now, we obtain the result of $n_{(lb,k)}$.

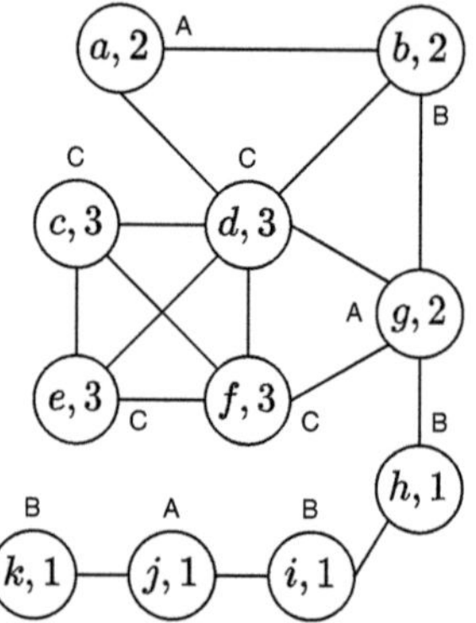

Label & Core Number	#Vertices
A1	1
A2	2
B1	3
B2	1
C3	4

Fig. 5. An example of calculate core number distribution. The capital letters beside the circles are the label of vertices. The right table shows the result of core number distribution, where the first column shows the labels and core numbers and the second column shows the number of vertices.

Example 5. In Fig. 5, we show an example of calculating the distribution of the core numbers. After core decomposition, we observe that the vertices have core numbers and different labels, A, B and C. We want to release the number of vertices with the label and B and the core number 1, which is shown in the right table $B1$ with 3.

Using the BFS tree shown in Fig. 4, the root a sends the message m_1 to notify all vertices. The leaf vertices, b, c, f and k, will first reply the message m_2 to their parent vertices, a, d and j. This process repeats until the root a receives all the messages m_2 from its children, b and d, where b has counter 0 and d has counter as 3. Therefore, we obtain the final counter 3 for $B1$ as the result.

During this process, we can see that $n_{(B,1)}$ in m_2 are encrypted by HE. Thus, only the root vertex a can acquire the corresponding values and all other vertices only can perform the calculation without knowing the values.

Privacy Security Analysis. For the entire process, the root vertex is selected arbitrarily and any vertex can be the root, which is not centralized. Besides the root r, each vertex u performs the add operation on the number of vertices with $E_{pub}(n_{(lb,k)})$ for his children, but u does not know the specific value due to encryption. In addition, u does not know if it is counted or not in $n_{(lb,k)}$, since $u.(lb, k)$ is encrypted for comparison. Therefore, u only knows whether the calculation of the core number distribution is executed or not. But u does not know which root vertex r launches this calculation and which pair of labels and core numbers (lb, k) is counted. Only the root r has the private key for decryption and can get the final result of $n_{(lb,k)}$, so that all the other vertices cannot know such a result.

Message Complexities. When releasing one result for one pair given a label and a core number, since the BFS tree has $n - 1$ edges, the total number of messages is $\mathcal{W} = O(2(n-1)) = O(n)$. The depth is the longest chain in the graph, denoted as $\mathcal{D} = O(D)$.

For releasing the results for all pairs given labels and core number, in the worst case, we can have a maximum number for the combination of labels and core numbers up to $|\mathcal{L}| \cdot k_{max}$. So, the algorithms must run at most $|\mathcal{L}| \cdot k_{max}$ to obtain all of the core number distributions. Typically, we can choose different root vertices to start the calculation of the core numbers at the same time. It can be executed in parallel with high probability, as most of the running time is spent on the message passing, and the calculations on clients are much faster than the latency of messages.

5   Conclusion and Future Work

In this work, we summarize the classical distributed k-core decomposition algorithm. Then, we adequately solve the privacy and security problems in terms of comparing core numbers, decentralized termination, and release core number distributions. In the future, we can apply our methodology to other distributed algorithms, e.g. distributed k-core maintenance [7,8], to protect privacy and security.

References

1. Acar, A., Aksu, H., Uluagac, A.S., Conti, M.: A survey on homomorphic encryption schemes: theory and implementation. ACM Comput. Surv. (CSUR) **51**(4), 1–35 (2018)
2. Aridhi, S., Brugnara, M., Montresor, A., Velegrakis, Y.: Distributed k-core decomposition and maintenance in large dynamic graphs. In: Proceedings of the 10th ACM International Conference on Distributed and Event-Based Systems, pp. 161–168 (2016)
3. Batagelj, V., Zaversnik, M.: An o(m) algorithm for cores decomposition of networks. CoRR cs.DS/0310049 (2003)
4. Burleson-Lesser, K., Morone, F., Tomassone, M.S., Makse, H.A.: K-core robustness in ecological and financial networks. Sci. Rep. **10**(1), 1–14 (2020)
5. Chan, T.H.H., Sozio, M., Sun, B.: Distributed approximate k-core decomposition and min-max edge orientation: breaking the diameter barrier. J. Parallel Distrib. Comput. **147**, 87–99 (2021)
6. Chen, C., Cui, J., Liu, G., Wu, J., Wang, L.: Survey and open problems in privacy preserving knowledge graph: Merging, query, representation, completion and applications. arXiv preprint arXiv:2011.10180 (2020)
7. Guo, B., Sekerinski, E.: Simplified algorithms for order-based core maintenance. arXiv preprint arXiv:2201.07103 (2022)
8. Guo, B., Sekerinski, E.: Parallel order-based core maintenance in dynamic graphs. In: Proceedings of the 52nd International Conference on Parallel Processing, pp. 122–131 (2023)
9. JéJé, J.: An Introduction to Parallel Algorithms. Addison-Wesley, Reading (1992)
10. Kong, Y.X., Shi, G.Y., Wu, R.J., Zhang, Y.C.: k-core: theories and applications. Technical report (2019)

11. Liao, X., Liu, Q., Jiang, J., Huang, X., Xu, J., Choi, B.: Distributed d-core decomposition over large directed graphs. arXiv preprint arXiv:2202.05990 (2022)
12. Luo, G., Fang, Z., Zhao, X., Chen, M.: A survey of graph federation learning for data privacy security scenarios (2023)
13. Luo, Q., Yu, D., Li, F., Cheng, X., Cai, Z., Yu, J.: Distributed core decomposition in probabilistic graphs. Asia-Pacific J. Oper. Res. **38**(05), 2140008 (2021)
14. Malliaros, F.D., Giatsidis, C., Papadopoulos, A.N., Vazirgiannis, M.: The core decomposition of networks: theory, algorithms and applications. VLDB J. **29**, 61–92 (2020)
15. Montresor, A., De Pellegrini, F., Miorandi, D.: Distributed k-core decomposition. IEEE Trans. Parallel Distrib. Syst. **24**(2), 288–300 (2013)
16. Newman, M.E.: The structure and function of complex networks. SIAM Rev. **45**(2), 167–256 (2003)
17. Terzi, D.S., Terzi, R., Sagiroglu, S.: A survey on security and privacy issues in big data. In: 2015 10th International Conference for Internet Technology and Secured Transactions (ICITST), pp. 202–207. IEEE (2015)

LineDi2Vec: An Edge-Based Graph Embedding on Signed Social Networks

Chen Xing$^{(\boxtimes)}$ and Masoud Makrehchi

Department of Electrical, Computer and Software Engineering, Ontario Tech
University, Oshawa, Canada
`chen.xing@ontariotechu.net`, `masoud.makrehchi@ontariotechu.ca`

Abstract. Network data plays a crucial role in various real-world applications, as connections between entities can be represented and analyzed through graphs. These include various types such as social, information, and technical networks. However, the complex topologies of these networks present challenges in converting graph data into machine-readable vector formats. Existing models like Graph Neural Network, Graph Attention Network, and node2vec have made strides in graph embeddings. Particularly for edge-related tasks, models like node2vec often resort to indirect methods like node concatenation for vector representation of edges, aiding in tasks like link sign prediction. In this paper, we introduce LineDi2vec, an innovative approach that uses a line graph to enhance the node2vec embedding method. This method effectively captures key social network theories, namely status and balance theories. LineDi2vec not only generalizes the original graphs, transforming the relationships between edges and nodes, but also maintains the topological integrity of the original graphs for effective node embedding by node2vec. We conducted an evaluation of LineDi2vec on four real-world datasets, focusing on link sign prediction. The results demonstrate its superior performance over traditional node concatenation methods and comparable efficacy to state-of-the-art GAT and GNN methods.

Keywords: Graph Embedding · Line Graph · Link Sign Prediction

1 Introduction

The study of signed networks has gained significant attention with the proliferation of online social interactions, where relationships manifest as both positive (friendship, trust) and negative (conflict, distrust) connections [15]. Understanding these networks draws heavily from social psychology theories, particularly balance theory and status theory [17], which inform critical tasks like link sign prediction. Recent advances in network representation learning have explored two main approaches: graph neural networks (GNNs) that employ message passing mechanisms [7,9,22], and algorithmic methods like node2vec [8]. While GNNs achieve state-of-the-art performance, their requirement for careful hyperparameter tuning contrasts with the flexibility of random-walk based methods, which

A. An et al. (Eds.): ASONAM 2025, LNCS 16323, pp. 209–219, 2026.
https://doi.org/10.1007/978-3-032-13821-7_18

nonetheless suffer from limitations in edge representation. This work bridges these approaches by proposing a novel line graph-enhanced embedding method, building upon recent developments in signed network analysis [1,5,14].

It is significant to note that a line graph-enhanced edge embedding method, called Line2vec, has already been introduced in 2019 [2]. This method employs the concept of collective homophily to represent edges directly within weighted line graphs [2]. Despite its novel approach, the primary validation tasks focused on edge clustering and classification, leaving critical link-related tasks, such as link sign prediction, unaddressed. Moreover, the study [2] concentrated on undirected homogeneous graphs, thereby not covering the complexities of sign and direction prediction that are quintessential in directed social networks.

In our approach to modeling signed networks, we developed a novel edge-centric random walk algorithm that incorporates line graphs. This adaptation enables the traditionally node-focused random walk method to directly convert signed edges into vector representations. This overcomes the limitations faced by existing algorithms in embedding signed graphs into vectors. Our method also integrates relevant social theories, utilizing traditional classifiers to effectively capture and learn the distinctive features of signed edges within our embeddings. To train our model, we reconstruct the signed networks in the form of their corresponding line graphs. In this transformed structure, edges are treated as nodes, allowing for a more effective and nuanced representation of the original network's relational dynamics.

The major contributions of this paper are as follows:

- We present a novel edge-centric model that enhances existing random walk-based node embedding algorithms with the use of line graphs. This model innovatively transforms edges into nodes with associated signs, effectively addressing the limitations of node2vec in embedding signed network edges.
- We carried out link sign prediction experiments using four real-world signed social network datasets to showcase the effectiveness of our proposed model.
- Through the application of our LineDi2vec model to our case study dataset, we discovered that the model exhibits certain limitations when applied to graphs. Moreover, it appears that the model is more adept at identifying patterns within the social network beyond merely the topological information of the network.

2   Related Work

2.1   Node2vec

Node2vec is a representational learning algorithm on graphs. It is capable of learning continuous feature representations for the nodes within any given graph, which can subsequently be employed in a variety of downstream machine learning tasks.

The operation of node2vec can be divided into two main stages:

- Random Walk Generation: Initially, node2vec employs a flexible notion of second-order random walks, which are not purely random but biased based on the exploration-exploitation trade-off. This approach generates sequences or "sentences" of nodes, where each sentence represents a walk across the graph. The path chosen at each step in the walk depends not only on the structure of the graph but also on a set of parameters that control the walk's locality and fidelity to the starting node.
- Embedding Learning: The sequences of nodes collected in the first step are treated akin to sentences in natural language processing. This corpus of node sequences is then fed into a Skip-Gram model, a type of shallow neural network, to learn vector representations or embeddings for each node. These embeddings aim to place nodes that frequently co-occur in walks close to one another in the vector space, thus preserving the topological similarities between nodes within the learned embeddings.

2.2 Line Graph

In graph theory, a line graph is a special kind of graph constructed to represent the relationships between the edges of another graph. The process involves creating a vertex in the line graph for each edge in the original graph. These vertices are then connected if their corresponding edges in the original graph have a common endpoint. As a result, the line graph, typically represented as L(G) for a graph G, effectively mirrors the adjacency and connectivity of the edges from the original graph.

Line graphs are notable for their unique structural properties, which include specific patterns and configurations that are not permitted, known as forbidden subgraphs [3]. These characteristics enable line graphs to be recognized and processed efficiently, often in linear time. The concept of line graphs has been expanded and explored in various contexts, leading to the study of line graphs of multigraphs [21], hypergraphs, and even weighted graphs [6], showcasing their broad applicability.

Unlike the research Line2vec [2], which also utilized line graph transformations but focused primarily on the topological characteristics and "Collective Homophily" [2] of the graph, The dynamics of directed and signed networks are often underpinned by sociological theories. These theories provide a foundational framework for understanding the complex interactions within such networks, indicating that the essence of link sign prediction transcends mere structural analysis and encompasses sociological insights, which we will explore further in the subsequent subsection.

2.3 Sociological Theory

Balance Theory and Status Theory are two pivotal sociological theories that are instrumental in the analysis and modeling of signed directed networks. In the following section, we will provide a concise overview of these two theories and then proceed to compare their applicability and insights across four real-world datasets.

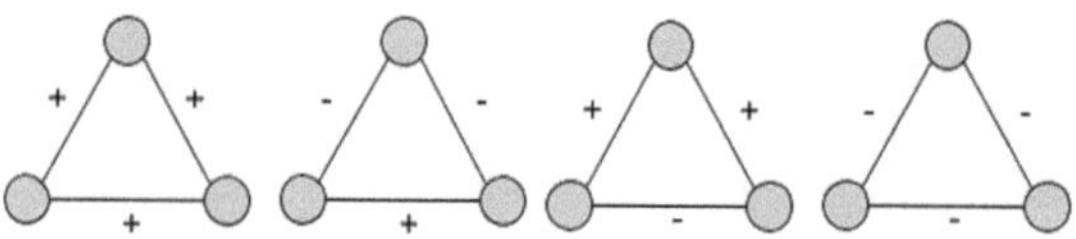

Fig. 1. Example of Balance Theory.

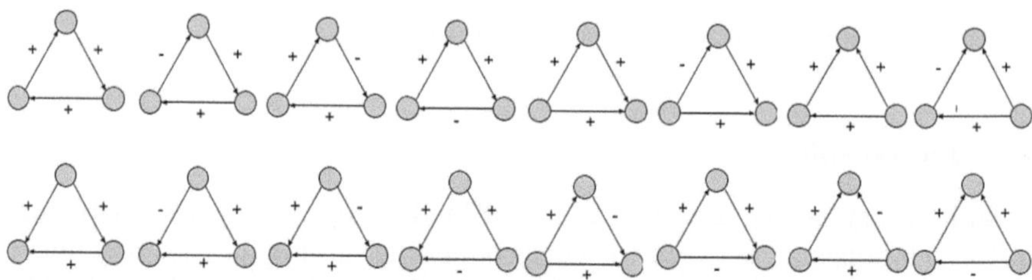

Fig. 2. Example of Status Theory.

Balance Theory: Proposed by Heider [11], Balance Theory states that signed triads tend toward stable configurations where the product of edge signs is positive (Fig. 1). A triad is balanced with either three positive edges or one positive and two negative edges, reflecting social axioms like "a friend's friend is a friend". This principle has become foundational for signed network analysis [17].

Status Theory: Status Theory [4] interprets signed directed edges as status indicators: a $+A{\to}B$ link signals B's higher status, while $-A{\to}B$ denotes lower status (Fig. 2). Though more complex than balance theory, it better explains directed social networks. Combined, these theories provide complementary perspectives for real-world signed network analysis.

Despite our proposed method for the link sign prediction task adhering to node2vec—a node embedding algorithm—and employing node concatenation to represent edges within the embedding space as our experimental baseline, it remains essential to benchmark against leading-edge sign prediction methodologies for a comprehensive evaluation. To this end, this paper selects SiGAT [12] and SDGNN [13] as comparative baselines. These state-of-the-art approaches represent alternative embedding strategies, providing a diverse context for assessing the efficacy of our proposed method against the backdrop of current advancements in the field of sign prediction.

3   Propose Method

Based on the previous discussion of sociological theory and related work on Sign Prediction, the proposed LineDi2vec algorithm is introduced in this section.

3.1   Problem Statement

For a directed sign graph $G = (V, \epsilon, s)$, where V is a set of nodes or vertices in graph G and ϵ is the set of edges between the vertices, and s is the signs assigned to the edges. The graph can be represented as adjacency matrix A where each entry A_{ij} represents the existence of an edge between vertices V_i and V_j. If $A_{ij} = 1$, then we say the edge is positive. If $A_{ij} = -1$, then we say the edge is negative. If $A_{ij} = 0$, there is not edges exists between the given nodes. We can also represent this social network by edgelist $E = (V_i, V_j, s)$ where V_i and V_j represent the start and end node IDs of given edges and s is the sign of this edge defined with 1 and -1. Given the edgelist $E = (V_i, V_j, s)$, the link sign prediction problem here becomes an edge classification problem where the model will only need to identify and cluster the s assigned to the edges.

3.2   Line DiGraph Transformation

As stated previously, the link sign prediction task here has become an edge sign classification problem with sign s being assigned to each edges. For the original graph $G = (V, \epsilon, s)$, we already have a similar expression as the edgelist form: $E = (V_i, V_j, s)$. Both of these two expressions have the same adjacency matrix A. Therefore, for a line graph:

$$L(G) = (V, \epsilon) \tag{1}$$

$$V = G(\epsilon) \tag{2}$$

and

$$L(\epsilon) = L(V_i, V_j) \tag{3}$$

if $L(V_i, V_j)$ share a common endpoint in G. Figure 3 shows an example of line graph transformation on a small sample graph.

Here, we can simply assign the s in edgelist $E = (V_i, V_j, s)$ to $L(G)$ by the Whitney isomorphism theorem [23]. In this scenario, the edges of the original/root graph G are now vertices of the line graph $L(G)$, with the original edge sign assigned to them. This transforms the link prediction problem into a node classification problem, a classic challenge for node-centric embedding methods like node2vec [8] to address.

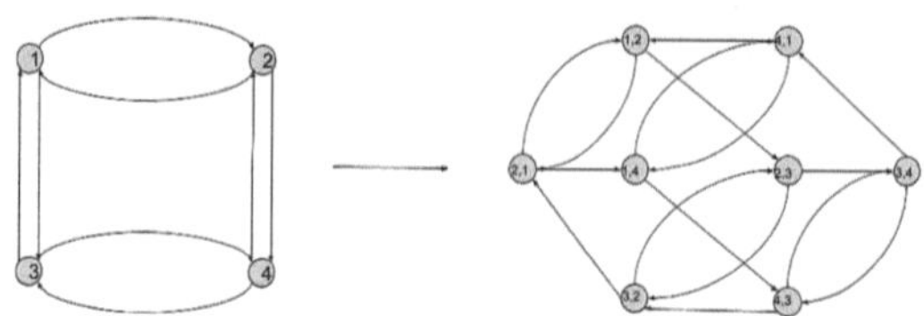

Fig. 3. An example of Line Digraph Transformation: the edge are transferred into nodes and the edges of the line graph also have directions based on common nodes in original graph.

3.3   Link Sign Prediction

The line graph $L(G) = (V, \epsilon, s)$ we created can then be processed using the node2vec algorithm. As previously stated, node2vec is a random walk-based algorithm that treats random walks as sentences in a language corpus, aiming to generate a one-to-one node-based vector representation for further analysis. Subsequently, signs can be assigned to the nodes in the embedding vector space generated by node2vec, which reduces the problem from node classification to binary classification. The vector space representation, along with the assigned signs to its nodes, are well-organized for processing by any downstream classifier.

3.4   Time Complexity of LineDi2vec

The analysis of LineDi2vec's time complexity constitutes a significant aspect of our study, particularly due to the implications of line graph transformation. As discussed in related works section, this transformation can substantially increase the quantity of nodes processed by the node2vec algorithm, which exhibits a time complexity of $O(n \log n)$ as highlighted by [19]. Theoretically, for a graph comprising n nodes, its corresponding line graph could encompass up to n^2 edges, leading to a quadratic time complexity of $O(n^2)$. Given that the output from the line graph transformation serves as the input for the node2vec algorithm, the overall time complexity is derived as:

$$O(n^2) + O(n \log n) = O(n^2 + n \log n) \approx O(n^2) \tag{4}$$

However, in practical scenarios, particularly in social networks and their line graphs, a linear time relationship is often observed, where the number of edges maintains a linear correlation with the number of nodes. Under these circumstances, encountered throughout this paper, the time complexity of LineDi2vec adjusts to:

$$O(n) + O(n \log n) = O(n + n \log n) \approx O(n \log n) \tag{5}$$

Thus, the time complexity of LineDi2vec aligns with that of node2vec, as $O(n)$ grows significantly slower than $O(n \log n)$. It is crucial to note, however, that the identical time complexities of LineDi2vec and node2vec do not necessarily translate to equivalent processing durations. Indeed, when comparing the operational times of LineDi2vec against node2vec and node concatenation approaches, a linear correlation with the time complexity $O(n)$ is observed.

4   Experiment

In this section, we focus on conducting link sign prediction to evaluate the efficacy of our model in enhancing signed network embeddings. Link sign prediction involves forecasting the unobserved signs of existing edges in a test dataset, utilizing information from a training dataset. This task is a key metric for assessing the performance of network embedding methods. [5,17] We have adopted their experimental framework for our analysis.

4.1   Experiment Setup

Dataset: For our experiments, we utilized four real-world signed social network datasets: Bitcoin-Alpha [15,16], Bitcoin-OTC [15,16], Slashdot [18], and Epinions [20]. The Bitcoin-Alpha and Bitcoin-OTC datasets are networks from platforms where individuals trade using Bitcoin. In these networks, members rate each other on a scale from -10 (total distrust) to $+10$ (total trust) in increments of 1. Ratings above 0 are considered positive, while others are negative. The Slashdot dataset originates from a technology-related news website with a vibrant user community. The website's Slashdot Zoo feature allows users to label each other as friends or foes, creating a network with clear positive and negative relationships. Lastly, the Epinions dataset is derived from Epinions.com, a consumer review site. Here, members can express trust or distrust in the reviews of others, forming a network that mirrors their opinions and trust relationships.

Baseline: To evaluate the effectiveness of LineDi2vec, we have set the baseline for our model as the traditional node concatenation method. The sole distinction between our proposed method and the baseline lies in the implementation of the line graph. All other parameters, including data preprocessing and the downstream binary classifier, remain identical.

Link Sign Prediction: For the link sign prediction task, The dataset already have the signs. Therefore, in our experiment, we only need to separate dataset into training and testing set for our model to process. The train-test split ratio we utilized is 70%–30%. For the node2vec parameters, we opt for 8 walkers, 30 walk lengths, 64 dimensions, and 200 walks. The hyperparameters for node2vec, p/q, are selected from a range of 0.1 to 10, with increments of 0.1 in the 0.1 to 1 range and increments of 1 in the 1 to 10 range. The optimal p and q parameter settings for each node2vec entry are omitted here for simplicity.

4.2   Result Compared with Baseline

We report the experimental results in Table 1, with the highest value for each metric highlighted. The results demonstrate that::

- Link sign prediction in directed networks can be effectively formulated as binary classification by preserving edge signs during line graph transformation, enabling compatibility with various downstream classifiers.

- Our method's strong performance demonstrates that line graph transformations preserve both structural properties and balance/status theory relationships from the original network.
- While node concatenation (node2vec) works reasonably for small datasets (Bitcoin Alpha/OTC), its effectiveness degrades with larger networks despite remaining a viable baseline approach.
- Line graph enhancement consistently outperforms node concatenation across all metrics, with particularly significant AUC improvements (average about 13% boost), demonstrating better class separation and scale/threshold invariance. (Best results shown in Table

Table 1. Experiment result with 4 dataset

Dataset	metrics	node2vec	LineDi2vec
Bitcoin Alpha	Accuracy	0.9051	**0.9224**
	F1 Score	0.9335	**0.9583**
	AUC	0.7576	**0.8813**
Bitcoin OTC	Accuracy	0.9011	**0.9294**
	F1 Score	0.9423	**0.9624**
	AUC	0.7643	**0.8784**
SlashDot	Accuracy	0.8756	**0.9135**
	F1 Score	0.7526	**0.9533**
	AUC	0.6709	**0.8674**
Epinion	Accuracy	0.8985	**0.9287**
	F1 Score	0.8214	**0.9620**
	AUC	0.8081	**0.8952**

Table 2. Result Compared with SiGAT and SDGNN

Dataset	metrics	SiGAT [12]	SDGNN [13]	LineDi2vec
Bitcoin Alpha	F1 Score	0.9714	0.9729	0.9583
	AUC	0.8872	0.8988	0.8813
Bitcoin OTC	F1 Score	0.9602	0.9647	0.9624
	AUC	0.9055	0.9184	0.8784
SlashDot	F1 Score	0.9055	0.9128	0.9533
	AUC	0.8874	0.8977	0.8674
Epinion	F1 Score	0.9593	0.9628	0.9620
	AUC	0.9333	0.9411	0.8952

4.3   Comparision with SiGAT and SDGNN

In this section, we compared our LineDi2vec result on all four dataset with the current state-of-art model SiGAT [12] and SDGNN [13]. Although these two model are based on graph attention network and graph neural network, which is not necessary the same condition with our baseline, we still want to show the great potential of our line graph enhancement since both these two use node concatenations on the representation of edges in there embeddings. From Table 2, we can find that:

- SiGAT and SDGNN intentionally omit accuracy/precision/recall metrics, as AUC better captures class discrimination in imbalanced signed networks where positive-negative ratios vary significantly.
- LineDi2vec achieves comparable performance to SiGAT/SDGNN across all metrics. While GNN-based methods typically outperform random-walk approaches like node2vec [12,13], our results demonstrate that line graph enhancement can match their performance. This suggests line graph methods could both replace node concatenation and potentially augment existing GNN architectures.

4.4   Limitations and Draw Backs

The application of forbidden subgraph theory [3] reveals a key limitation: not every graph or network lends itself to transformation into a line graph. This constraint inherently limits the applicability of our model, confining its utility to those types of homogeneous graphs amenable to such conversion.

Moreover, the demands on computational resources and the time necessary for converting a graph into a line graph represent a significant drawback. As highlighted by [10], this conversion process can dramatically increase the complexity of the original graphs with time complexity $O(n)$. This complexity surge subsequently results in an exponential increase in both the processing time and the computational power needed. Our empirical evidence, particularly from handling large-scale datasets like Epinions and Slashdot, illustrates this point.

5   Conclusion

This paper introduces LineDi2Vec, a novel line graph-enhanced graph embedding approach for link sign prediction, designed to overcome the limitations of indirect edge representation in conventional node embedding methods. By explicitly modeling edges through line graphs, our method captures richer relational patterns compared to traditional techniques like node2vec. Experiments on four real-world datasets demonstrate that our approach consistently outperforms baseline methods, highlighting the advantages of line graph-based embeddings for edge-centric prediction tasks. We further discuss the theoretical and practical challenges arising from line graph properties [3], providing insights for future research in graph representation learning. Our work advances the state-of-the-art in signed network analysis while opening new directions for edge-aware graph embeddings.

References

1. Ahmadalinezhad, M., Makrehchi, M.: Edge-centric multi-view network representation for link mining in signed social networks. Expert Syst. Appl. **170**, 114552 (2021)
2. Bandyopadhyay, S., Biswas, A., Murty, M.N., Narayanam, R.: Beyond node embedding: a direct unsupervised edge representation framework for homogeneous networks. arXiv preprint arXiv:1912.05140 (2019)
3. Beineke, L.W.: Characterizations of derived graphs. J. Comb. Theory **9**(2), 129–135 (1970)
4. Berger, J., Cohen, B.P., Zelditch, M.: Status characteristics and social interaction. Am. Sociol. Rev. **37**(3), 241–255 (1972)
5. Chen, Y., Qian, T., Liu, H., Sun, K.: "bridge" enhanced signed directed network embedding. In: Proceedings of the 27th ACM International Conference on Information and Knowledge Management, pp. 773–782 (2018)
6. Evans, T.S., Lambiotte, R.: Line graphs, link partitions, and overlapping communities. Phys. Rev. E **80**(1), 016105 (2009)
7. Gilmer, J., Schoenholz, S.S., Riley, P.F., Vinyals, O., Dahl, G.E.: Neural message passing for quantum chemistry. In: Proceedings of the 34th International Conference on Machine Learning (ICML), pp. 1263–1272 (2017)
8. Grover, A., Leskovec, J.: node2vec: scalable feature learning for networks. In: Proceedings of the 22nd ACM SIGKDD International Conference on Knowledge Discovery and Data Mining, pp. 855–864 (2016)
9. Hamilton, W.L., Ying, R., Leskovec, J.: Inductive representation learning on large graphs. In: Advances in Neural Information Processing Systems 30 (NeurIPS), pp. 1024–1034 (2017)
10. Harary, F., Norman, R.Z.: Some properties of line digraphs. Rendiconti del circolo matematico di palermo **9**, 161–168 (1960)
11. Heider, F.: The Psychology of Interpersonal Relations. Psychology Press (2013)
12. Huang, J., Shen, H., Hou, L., Cheng, X.: Signed graph attention networks. In: Tetko, I.V., Kůrková, V., Karpov, P., Theis, F. (eds.) ICANN 2019. LNCS, vol. 11731, pp. 566–577. Springer, Cham (2019). https://doi.org/10.1007/978-3-030-30493-5_53
13. Huang, J., Shen, H., Hou, L., Cheng, X.: SDGNN: learning node representation for signed directed networks. In: Proceedings of the AAAI Conference on Artificial Intelligence, vol. 35, pp. 196–203 (2021)
14. Kim, J., Park, H., Lee, J.-E., Kang, U.: Side: representation learning in signed directed networks. In: Proceedings of the 2018 World Wide Web Conference, pp. 509–518 (2018)
15. Kumar, S., Hooi, B., Makhija, D., Kumar, M., Faloutsos, C., Subrahmanian, V.S.: Rev2: fraudulent user prediction in rating platforms. In: Proceedings of the Eleventh ACM International Conference on Web Search and Data Mining, pp. 333–341 (2018)
16. Kumar, S., Spezzano, F., Subrahmanian, V.S., Faloutsos, C.: Edge weight prediction in weighted signed networks. In: 2016 IEEE 16th International Conference on Data Mining (ICDM), pp. 221–230. IEEE (2016)

17. Leskovec, J., Huttenlocher, D., Kleinberg, J.: Predicting positive and negative links in online social networks (2010)
18. Leskovec, J., Lang, K.J., Dasgupta, A., Mahoney, M.W.: Community structure in large networks: natural cluster sizes and the absence of large well-defined clusters. Internet Math. **6**(1), 29–123 (2009)
19. Pimentel, T., Veloso, A., Ziviani, N.: Fast node embeddings: learning ego-centric representations (2018)
20. Richardson, M., Agrawal, R., Domingos, P.: Trust management for the semantic web. In: Fensel, D., Sycara, K., Mylopoulos, J. (eds.) ISWC 2003. LNCS, vol. 2870, pp. 351–368. Springer, Heidelberg (2003). https://doi.org/10.1007/978-3-540-39718-2_23
21. Ryjáček, Z., Vrána, P.: Line graphs of multigraphs and hamilton-connectedness of claw-free graphs. J. Graph Theory **66**(2), 152–173 (2011)
22. Velickovic, P., Cucurull, G., Casanova, A., Romero, A., Liò, P., Bengio, Y.: Graph attention networks. In: International Conference on Learning Representations (ICLR) (2018)
23. Whitney, H.: Congruent graphs and the connectivity of graphs. Am. J. Math. **54**, 61–79 (1932)

Clustering Dynamic Graphs Using Time and Text Content

Timothy La Fond[(✉)], Eisha Nathan, Hannah Nyholm, and Van Henson

Lawrence Livermore National Laboratory, 7000 East Avenue, Livermore, CA 94550, USA
{lafond1,nathan4,nyholm7,henson5}@llnl.gov

Abstract. Modern datasets can often be represented as dynamic graphs; for example, email communications, online forums, and network traffic all fall under this umbrella. As these datasets can be large in size, graph clustering techniques are frequently used to organize the data into manageable chunks. Clustering communications is particularly valuable for identifying meaningful interactions, tracking evolving discussions, and detecting behavioral patterns. However, past algorithms have primarily focused on using the graph topology and time dynamics of the data when clustering, organizing the edges into clusters representing coherent spans of activity – a short conversation between individuals, for example. This ignores other features in the graph that may be useful for clustering such as the text content of the messages being sent. A conversation should have a coherent topic of discussion, therefore clustering edges according to topical similarity in the text can lead to clusters more naturally aligned with human conversations. In this paper we introduce a new dynamic clustering algorithm which takes into account additional metadata alongside the topology and time dynamics, and demonstrate how our approach can find clusters that are coherent in terms of both time and text content, leading to performance improvements of up to 0.28 greater AUC on thread prediction tasks.

1   Introduction

Dynamic graphs are a form of data where each edge represents some interaction between two entities that occurred at a particular point in time. Such datasets could include emails and/or texts, forum posts, or computer network traffic. As these datasets can be extremely large, especially if they cover a long period of time, it is helpful to apply a clustering algorithm which can organize the messages into manageable clusters. Traditional graph clustering has been utilized on a diverse range of applications: to detect fraudulent activity in financial datasets [17], to identify emerging trends or misinformation campaigns in social media data [19], or to detect cyber attacks in computer network traffic data [11].

Although traditional graph clustering has many uses, when blindly applied to data with a temporal aspect the clusters often fail to represent the dynamic behavior of the graph. In particular, evolving behavior may be lumped together

A. An et al. (Eds.): ASONAM 2025, LNCS 16323, pp. 220–229, 2026.
https://doi.org/10.1007/978-3-032-13821-7_19

into clusters that span long ranges of time, obscuring those dynamics. A better approach is to use dynamic graph clustering algorithms which attempt to cluster using both time and topology simultaneously. This yields clusters which occur over a coherent span of time, which can detect dynamic behavior such as cascades of messages triggered by some event or a back-and-forth conversation taking place over a short span of time. The paper by Ostroski et al. [12] approaches this problem by forming a line graph where the nodes of the line graph are the edges in the original dynamic graph, and those nodes are connected with edge weights inversely proportional to the time gap between the two edges in the dynamic graph. The logic here is that the line graph represents possible causal influence between edges in the dynamic graph, and quick turnaround times for sending a message after receiving one indicates stronger evidence of a relationship. This forms a hierarchical dendrogram of messages, which the authors then cluster using an algorithm inspired by HDBscan [2] to find clusters which large relative time gaps between them. We will refer to this algorithm as the Time Filtered Line Graph algorithm, or TFLG.

This approach is scalable and produces manageably sized clusters or "message bursts" which represent time spans where communication is happening at roughly the same overall rate. However, these bursts don't necessarily map exactly to true human conversations. Conversations naturally include breaks or pauses and they may be halted then resumed at a later time. This variability in time delays will be interpreted as break points by the TFLG algorithm and the conversations will be broken into multiple clusters. Likewise, if a person is juggling multiple conversations at once TFLG will not be able to distinguish them due to the overlapping time dynamics. Other features of the data must be considered alongside the time dynamics in order to handle these issues.

Our solution to these issues is to make use of the textual information attached to each edge. A conversation is often comprised of messages focusing on one or a handful of coherent topics. Thus clustering messages while taking topic similarity into account will produce bursts which more closely resemble human conversations. This also aids in distinguishing concurrent conversations as long as the topics of those conversations are sufficiently different.

We will build upon the line graph approach set by the TFLG algorithm but allow for local graph features such as text to be used alongside the time dynamics when deciding cluster boundaries. We demonstrate this approach by utilizing the text content as the local feature to create a variant of TFLG that we call c-TFLG, but other types of metadata can also be used in this framework. We will show that this c-TFLG algorithm is more effective in recovering conversations from dynamic graph data than approaches that only utilize time and topology.

2   Related Work

Apart from the TFLG approach which forms the starting point for this work, a number of other papers tackle the clustering of dynamic graphs [16]. Of these, many use a windowing or time slicing approach where the dynamic graph is broken into multiple static graphs representing fixed blocks of time [3,8]. The advantage of this approach is that it allows for traditional graph clustering to be applied without modification; however, the selection of the windows significantly affects the output. Other papers factor in neighboring time windows in an attempt to smooth the clustering process and mitigate the effect of time window boundaries [1].

Another approach is to discretize time to form the data into a tensor and then use tensor factor analysis to find correlations between time and graph structure [7]. Like the time slicing approaches this also requires *a priori* decisions about how to discretize the data into meaningful time blocks. In addition, the factorization can be computationally intensive for large datasets.

Some papers use a streaming approach to dynamic graph clustering where initial clusters are updated when new edges arrive in the graph [5,10]. These algorithms often focus on having quick computation times in order to be used on active streams of data and sometimes sacrifice accuracy for this purpose, making them only appealing in the streaming setting.

Conversation detection has been attempted on threads of email messages using features of the emails like text content [6]. However, the techniques used rely heavily on the subject matter line of those emails, beginning with an initial conversation set consisting of emails with identical subjects and then further refining them using content similarity and/or time dynamics. In data without a field as reliable as a subject line it would be difficult to obtain an appropriate initial clustering.

3   Time Filtered Line Graph Algorithm

3.1   Minimum Spanning Tree and Original Edge Weights

The original TFLG paper [12] presents a method for linking messages in a message stream using a minimum spanning tree (MST) and then clustering the line graph to form communities of messages. TFLG is designed for directed dynamic multigraphs $G(V, E, T)$ where each edge $e \in V \times V$ is a directed edge that also has a time t representing when it occurred. The line graph for G is $L_G(E, F, W)$ with $F \in E \times E$ being the line edges, with the restriction that those edges are directed and pointing in the forward direction of time, i.e. no line edge points from a message to an earlier message. These line edges also have weights $W \in \mathbb{R}^+$ given by function $f(e_1, e_2) = \delta t = |t_2 - t_1|$ where t_1, t_2 are the timestamps of the messages.

The task of organizing the messages into short-duration bursts then becomes equivalent to finding clusters in the line graph with minimal edge weight. This is done by calculating a MST on the line graph, creating a hierarchical clustering dendrogram of that MST, then selecting clusters from the dendrogram that minimize the internal edge weights in a manner similar to HDBScan. The result is an algorithm which clusters messages into coherent groups in time with minimal input parameters, only requiring a minimum valid cluster size M.

4   Local Feature TFLG Framework

We will now introduce a framework to perform TFLG-style dynamic clustering while utilizing local metadata to assist in determining cluster boundaries. First, recognize that an equivalent algorithm to the clustering step in TFLG is to apply a merge criterion

$$F(C_{parent}, \mathbb{C}) = \Lambda_{C_{parent}} > \sum_{C_{child} \in \mathbb{C}} [\Lambda_{C_{child}}] \tag{1}$$

to each non-leaf node and their children, selecting the merged cluster C_{parent} only if the inequality holds true.

We can then control the clustering behavior of the TFLG algorithm by replacing this function with an alternative F^* which includes values other than cluster stabilities. An example of an F^* which considers text content within the possible clusters will be given later in Eq. 2. This deviates from TFLG's original objective of optimizing the stability function alone in order to accommodate other cluster properties.

Using this clustering decision function allows for consideration of properties that are undefined at the edge level and could not be represented by changing the distance function for the line graph edges. For example, the set of participating individuals shared by two clusters would be undefined at the edge level. Our new framework allows for maximum flexibility when adapting the algorithm to accommodate various graph features. All of these modified TFLG algorithms have HDBScan's minimum cluster size M as an input parameter in addition to their own input parameters. In the initial aggregation step, messages are greedily combined using the shortest time deltas until each initial cluster is at least size M. These initial clusters become the leaves of the hierarchical clustering dendrogram $\mathcal{D}(\mathcal{C}, \mathcal{R})$, which is a rooted tree where the nodes $C \in \mathcal{C}$ represent clusters of graph vertices $C \subset V$. These clusters are related via parent child relationships such that $(C_{parent}, C_{child}) \in \mathcal{R}$ if and only if $C_{child} \subset C_{parent}$. The root of this tree is a cluster containing all vertices of the graph.

The modified algorithmic steps are outlined in Algorithm 1 and Algorithm 2. The steps to produce hierarchical clustering dendrogram D are identical to the original TFLG paper and will be omitted; the modified algorithms introduced here only change the process of selecting the final clusters from D. The initial cluster selection set S is the set of leaf nodes in D, those initial clusters obtained by greedily merging until each is at least M in size. Then, a recursive selection algorithm is applied to each node C_{parent} in the hierarchical dendrogram which is a parent of some leaf nodes $\mathbb{C}$. If the clustering criterion function $F^*(C_{parent}, \mathbb{C})$ returns true when applied to that node and its children, the children are removed from the selection set and the parent is added to the selection set S (i.e. the clusters represented by the leaves are merged into the cluster represented by the parent). If $F*$ returns false then no merge occurs and the children nodes remain part of the selection set S. This process repeats until no potential merge passes the F^* criterion, at which point the current nodes in S are returned as the final clusters.

Algorithm 1. Select clusters from hierarchical dendrogram

INPUT : Dendrogram D
OUTPUT : Selected clusters S
  Add all leaf nodes in D to S
  for each height 1 non-leaf node in D **do**
    Apply recursive selection algorithm to node
  return S

Algorithm 2. Recursive selection algorithm

INPUT : Node C_{parent} and its children $\mathbb{C}$

  if $F^*(C_{parent}, \mathbb{C})$ is true **then**
    Remove all clusters in $\mathbb{C}$ from S
    Add C_{parent} to S
    Apply recursive selection algorithm to C_{parent}'s parent

---

4.1   c-TFLG

c-TFLG uses the text content of the edges contained in each cluster to determine whether to merge. If T is a text embedding method, m_{parent} and m_{child} the concatenated text content of edges in a parent and a child cluster respectively, $CosSim$ the cosine similarity function, μ_c an "inflection point" parameter, and w_t, w_c as relative weight parameters, then the merge criterion F_c^* for c-TFLG is defined as

$$F_c^* = 1 < w_t e^{1 - \frac{\sum_{C_{child} \in \mathbb{C}}[\Lambda_{C_{child}}]}{|\mathbb{C}|\Lambda_{C_{parent}}}}$$
$$+ w_c \frac{\sum_{C_{child} \in \mathbb{C}}[CosSim(T(m_{parent}), T(m_{child})) - \mu_c]}{|\mathbb{C}|} \tag{2}$$

If the content in each of the child clusters is similar, the content in the merged cluster should also be similar to each child, tipping the equation towards merging the clusters. The text embedding method T can be any one of a number of embedding approaches detailed in a later section. The parameters w_t and w_c control how strongly the clustering decision is weighted between the temporal dynamics and content similarity respectively, with the temporal dynamics included via the original stability function $\Lambda = \frac{1}{\delta t}$. The selection of these parameter values will depend on the user's desire to balance temporal and textual features in the data.

The parameter μ_c controls the inflection point for content similarity: if the cosine similarity between two clusters is greater than μ_c, then merging is encouraged, but if the similarity is less then merging is discouraged. For many bodies of text and embedding methods the cosine similarity between random pairs of content may not be 0 on average, hence the introduction of this inflection point parameter to ensure that the function is not biased towards or against merging in general. An easy way to find a starting μ_c value is to calculate the average similarity between random selections of text in the data, establishing a baseline for cosine similarities in the data. Though depending on the data this value may be too low if conversations adjacent in time are slightly more similar than completely random pairs.

The authors of the original TFLG use distributed memory and parallel processing techniques to ensure scalability, all of which apply to c-TFLG. The only additional computation needed is embedding the text content, which can also be done in parallel.

5   Experiments

5.1   Datasets

We test our methods on two different datasets: Stack Exchange and Reddit. The Stack Exchange dataset is a collection of data from ten Stack Exchange forums (https://archive.org/details/stackexchange), including Stack Overflow, Mathematics, Linux & Unix, Economics, and others. It includes questions, answers, comments, tags, and other related data from these sites. For our experiments we use the questions, answers, and comments. Each question can have multiple answers and each answer can have multiple comments. For the purpose of directed conversations, we induce an edge from a question to each of its answers and from each answer to each of its respective comments. The forums ranged in size from 47,325 edges to 234,472 edges.

For the Reddit dataset we use data scraped from https://pushshift.io/. Each subreddit in Reddit consists of threads consisting of an original post and the comment tree attached to it. We interpret the connection between a post and a comment on that post as pointing towards the comment. The 16 subreddits ranged in size from 9,805 edges to 1,115,935 edges.

Each forum of Stack Exchange has had its user IDs anonymized independently, making it impossible to determine which users post in multiple forums and making each forum dataset disconnected from the others. We synthetically induce shared authorship amongst forums by re-mapping the authors of disparate forums. Newly created authors are mapped to old authors using a power law distribution, where the majority of authors will only participate in 1 forum, with fewer participating in 2 forums, and even fewer in 3, and so on. Authors participating in a large number of forums are rare, which mimics the order of natural systems.

5.2   Metrics

Burst Classification. We first measure performance of our methods as a function of burst classification. For a single burst, we classify it as a "true positive" (label 1) if we either A) capture all the messages from a particular thread within it or B) the burst consists of exclusively messages from a single thread. Otherwise, bursts are labeled with a 0. To score a burst, we define the metric "thread recovery percentage" as follows. Recall a subreddit (Reddit) or forum

(Stack Exchange) consists of several threads (each thread is on the topic of the subreddit/forum, but is typically focused on its own related topic). A simple metric would be to calculate the purity of each burst based on the percentage of messages originating from the same thread. However, this metric captures the precision of the method without measuring the recall. If the original thread is split apart into many small bursts, each burst would have perfect purity scores, but the full thread would not have been successfully reconstructed. For the purposes of this thread recovery experiment, we modify this simple purity metric and instead calculate how much of the actual thread we are able to reconstruct. To do so, for a single burst, we 1) calculate the "mode" of the threads of the messages present in the burst (the thread that appears the most in our burst), then 2) of the total number of messages in the maximally appearing thread, we calculate how many of those landed in the burst of interest.

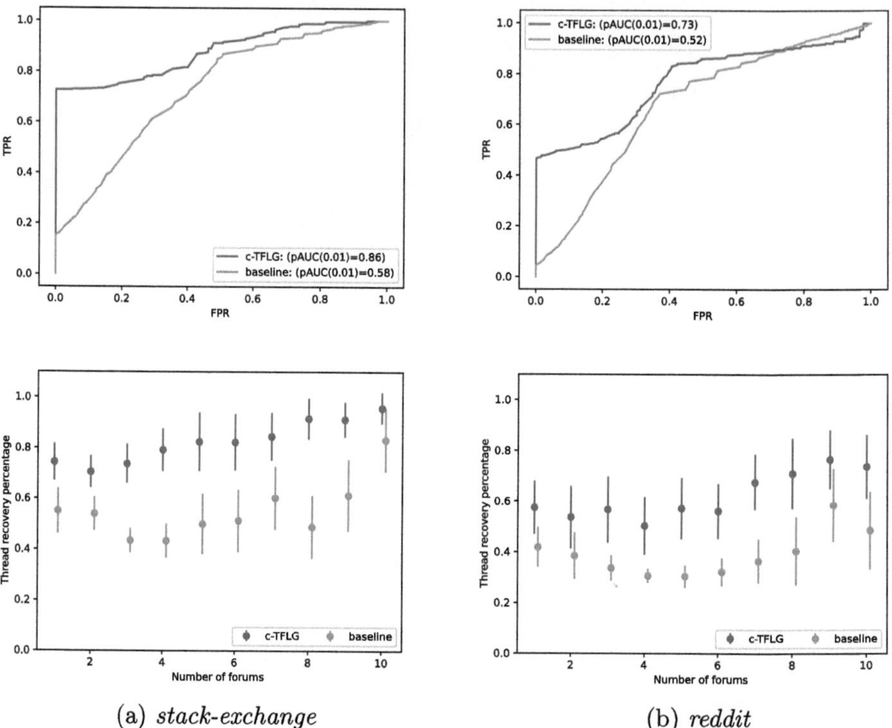

(a) *stack-exchange*   (b) *reddit*

Fig. 1. Top: ROC curves for both datasets for burst classification. `c-TFLG` results are shown in blue while baseline TFLG results are in orange. Bottom: Thread recover results for both datasets. (Color figure online)

Thread Recovery. Recall we induce common authorship (as explained in Sect. 5.1). Here we present results over 20 trials, as we continually increase the number of forums that participate in each trial. As each forum has induced author overlap with the others, more forums means more "node confusion". Our goal in this experiment is to test how well our methods can recover a full thread-tree in Reddit or Stack Exchange given increasing node confusion. For a single trial: we start with 1 randomly selected forum, obtain bursts from baseline TFLG and c-TFLG, and measure performance given our modifications. Next, we add a second randomly selected forum and re-run both c-TFLG and baseline TFLG using the dataset of the mixture of both forums, including the induced author overlap. We continue in this fashion, iteratively adding a new randomly chosen forum until we reach the maximum number of forums. Each forum gets 10 randomly sampled threads, all of which participate in our dataset and threads are all sampled from the same randomly selected time window to ensure overlap.

5.3   Experimental Results

The results of this experiment are shown in Fig. 1. Using the original forum/subreddit as ground truth, we obtain ROC curves as seen in the top row of Fig. 1 for the Stack Exchange and Reddit datasets respectively. We plot the false positive rate (FPR) on the x-axis versus true positive rate (TPR) on the y-axis where we classify/score bursts in this fashion using the BERT embeddings. These values are aggregated over 100 trials for a varying number of forums and partial area under the curve (pAUC) values for a FPR rate of 1% are given for each method in the legend. Note that we see approximately a 40% increase in the pAUC by integrating content into the burst clustering. The bottom row of Fig. 1 shows the performance in terms of thread recovery. The x-axis is the number of forums that are present in a single trial of this experiment and the y-axis is the previously described quality metric of thread recovery. The plot shows the mean of the 20 trials per forum with error bars plotted as the standard deviation across the 20 trials. Results from c-TFLG are shown in blue with the baseline TFLG in orange. In both cases c-TFLG performs better on the Stack Exchange data than on Reddit. We theorize that this is due to the nature of the datasets themselves; in Reddit, people are more likely to veer off topic, and/or respond with much shorter messages (that semantically will not embed close to the topic of the thread at hand). Stack Exchange messages are typically longer and tend to be more on topic. Regardless, we see significant improvement in bursts obtained when integrating content into the clustering as opposed to ignoring the semantic nature of communications.

6   Conclusions

The local dynamic clustering algorithm we have described offers a means to cluster dynamic graph data such as message streams according to both time dynamics and text content. In this paper we demonstrated its effectiveness when recovering human conversations from dynamic graph data. This framework can be easily expanded to use other local features for its clustering decisions in datasets that lack text metadata or have other useful metadata.

One limitation of this framework is the need for conversations to be somewhat coherent in time. If a conversation is halted then resumed after a long time gap (e.g. a group meets weekly and resumes an old conversation) the clusters will not be connected in the dendrogram and it will not be possible to merge the two halves of the conversation. Post-hoc analysis would be required to recognize the similarity between the clusters. A limitation of `c-TFLG` is the length of the text associated with each edge. Short, content-less messages such as one-word responses will have no meaningful topics on the messages regardless of the text model used. In this case the surrounding context must be used to determine if those short messages belong to the conversation or not.

Next steps in this research include improved methodology for selection of parameters. It may be possible to automatically select some parameters: for example, the inflection point could be set to the average similarity between messages belonging to the same ground truth, so that messages with less similarity would be penalized. Or, given ground truth examples it may be possible to fit optimal parameters for the dataset. Both approaches require some form of ground truth examples, however, and choosing parameters for data where no examples are available is an open question.

References

1. Bhatotia, P., Acar, U.A., Junqueira, F.P., Rodrigues, R.: Slider: incremental sliding window analytics. In: Proceedings of the 15th International Middleware Conference, pp. 61–72 (2014)
2. Campello, R.J.G.B., Moulavi, D., Sander, J.: Density-based clustering based on hierarchical density estimates. In: Pei, J., Tseng, V.S., Cao, L., Motoda, H., Xu, G. (eds.) PAKDD 2013. LNCS (LNAI), vol. 7819, pp. 160–172. Springer, Heidelberg (2013). https://doi.org/10.1007/978-3-642-37456-2_14
3. Crouch, M.S., McGregor, A., Stubbs, D.: Dynamic graphs in the sliding-window model. In: Bodlaender, H.L., Italiano, G.F. (eds.) ESA 2013. LNCS, vol. 8125, pp. 337–348. Springer, Heidelberg (2013). https://doi.org/10.1007/978-3-642-40450-4_29
4. Devlin, J., Chang, M. W., Lee, K., Toutanova, K.: Bert: pretraining of deep bidirectional transformers for language understanding. In: Proceedings of the 2019 Conference of the North American chapter of the Association for Computational Linguistics: Human Language Technologies, Volume 1 (Long and Short Papers), pp. 4171–4186 (2019)
5. Ediger, D., McColl, R., Riedy, J., Bader, D.A.: Stinger: high performance data structure for streaming graphs. In: 2012 IEEE Conference on High Performance Extreme Computing, pp. 1–5. IEEE (2012)
6. Erera, S., Carmel, D.: Conversation detection in email systems. In: Macdonald, C., Ounis, I., Plachouras, V., Ruthven, I., White, R.W. (eds.) ECIR 2008. LNCS, vol. 4956, pp. 498–505. Springer, Heidelberg (2008). https://doi.org/10.1007/978-3-540-78646-7_48
7. Gauvin, L., Panisson, A., Cattuto, C.: Detecting the community structure and activity patterns of temporal networks: a non-negative tensor factorization approach. PLoS ONE **9**(1), e86028 (2014)

8. La Fond, T., Sanders, G., Klymko, C., Henson, V.E.: An ensemble framework for detecting community changes in dynamic networks. In: 2017 IEEE High Performance Extreme Computing Conference (HPEC), pp. 1–6. IEEE (2017)

9. Liu, Y., et al.: Roberta: a robustly optimized bert pretraining approach. arXiv preprint arXiv:1907.11692 (2019)

10. McGregor, A.: Graph stream algorithms: a survey. ACM SIGMOD Rec. **43**(1), 9–20 (2014)

11. Noel, S., Harley, E., Tam, K.H., Limiero, M., Share, M.: Cygraph: graph-based analytics and visualization for cybersecurity. In: Handbook of Statistics, vol. 35, pp. 117–167. Elsevier (2016)

12. Ostroski, M., Sanders, G., Steil, T., Pearce, R.: Scalable edge clustering of dynamic graphs via weighted line graphs. J. Complex Netw. **13**(3), cnaf006 (2025)

13. Radford, A., et al.: Language models are unsupervised multitask learners. OpenAI Blog **1**(8), 9 (2019)

14. Raffel, C., et al.: Exploring the limits of transfer learning with a unified text-to-text transformer. J. Mach. Learn. Res. **21**(140), 1–67 (2020)

15. Reimers, N., Gurevych, I.: Sentence-bert: sentence embeddings using siamese bert-networks. arXiv preprint arXiv:1908.10084 (2019)

16. Rossetti, G., Cazabet, R.: Community discovery in dynamic networks: a survey. ACM Comput. Surv. (CSUR) **51**(2), 1–37 (2018)

17. Sabau, A.S.: Survey of clustering based financial fraud detection research. Informatica Economica **16**(1), 110 (2012)

18. Sanh, V., Debut, L., Chaumond, J., Wolf, T.: Distilbert, a distilled version of bert: smaller, faster, cheaper and lighter. arXiv preprint arXiv:1910.01108 (2019)

19. Shao, H., et al.: Misinformation detection and adversarial attack cost analysis in directional social networks. In: 2020 29th International Conference on Computer Communications and Networks (ICCCN), pp. 1–11. IEEE (2020)

GPSocio: A Transformer-Based General-Purpose Social Network Representation System

Xinyi Liu$^{(\boxtimes)}$, Dachun Sun , and Tarek Abdelzaher

University of Illinois Urbana-Champaign, 201 N Goodwin Ave, Urbana, IL 61801,
USA
liu323@illinois.edu

Abstract. We present **GPSocio** (Reproducible code is available at:
https://github.com/tracy3057/GPSocio.), a general-purpose social network representation system designed to support diverse downstream analytics and enable knowledge transfer to data-scarce domains. While prior methods optimize embeddings for specific tasks, they often lack generalization. GPSocio leverages the emerging Graph Foundation Model (GFM) paradigm by aligning social graph structures with Large Language Models (LLMs) through post propagation sequences encoded in natural language. Extensive evaluations across four downstream tasks show that GPSocio consistently outperforms strong baselines, achieving **6.74%** gains in User macro-F1 for Sentiment Analysis, **21.29%** gains in User ARI for Ideology Classification, **14.75%** AUC improvement for Static Link Prediction, and **62.87%** User N@10 improvement for Temporal Link Prediction, demonstrating robust modeling of social semantics and diffusion dynamics.

Keywords: Social Network Representation Learning · Graph
Foundation Models · Transformers for Social Networks ·
Domain-transferable Graph Embeddings · Low-data Social Domain
Transfer

1 Introduction

Social network analysis underpins a wide range of tasks, such as user preference detection [29], information propagation prediction [41], ideology classification [24], and sentiment analysis [31]. Prior efforts largely focus on optimizing representations for specific tasks, often achieving strong in-domain performance but struggling to generalize beyond the training context. Such overfitting hampers generalization across evolving social contexts. Despite extensive efforts, no existing framework unifies semantic and diffusion information for cross-domain social reasoning.

This work was supported by DARPA (HR001121C0165, HR00112290105), DoD Basic
Research Office (HQ00342110002), and ARL (W911NF-17-20196).

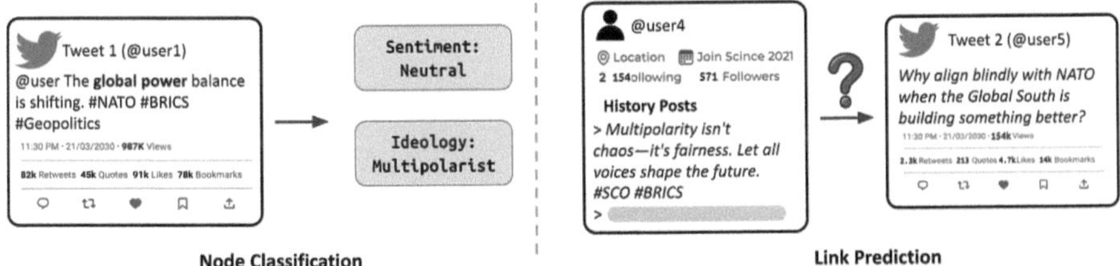

Fig. 1. Illustration of GPSocio's downstream tasks: node classification (sentiment and ideology) and link prediction (static and temporal).

The recent emergence of Graph Foundation Models (GFMs) offers new opportunities for learning transferable social representations through large-scale pre-training and domain adaptation. In particular, the integration of graph structures with Large Language Models (LLMs) enables richer semantic reasoning across nodes and edges [40]. However, a fundamental challenge remains: raw graph data must be reformulated into sequential, language-compatible formats to fully leverage LLM capabilities.

In this paper, we propose **GPSocio**, a transformer-based general-purpose framework for social network representation. GPSocio reformulates social graphs into *post propagation sequences* that capture both semantic content and diffusion dynamics in natural language form. It pre-trains representations via *contrastive next-user prediction* on large-scale sequences and refines them through *graph-*

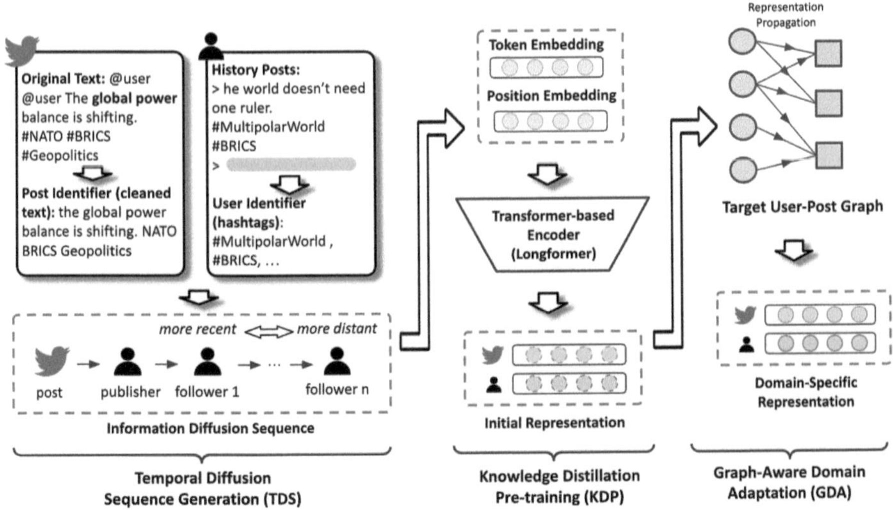

Fig. 2. GPSocio framework overview, comprising: (1) temporal diffusion sequence generation (TDS), (2) knowledge distillation pre-training (KDP), and (3) graph-aware domain adaptation (GDA).

aware domain adaptation using target-specific interaction graphs. The overall architecture is illustrated in Fig. 2.

Through this design, GPSocio bridges the gap between structured diffusion processes and language-based pretraining, enabling robust knowledge transfer across heterogeneous social domains. As social media ecosystems become increasingly fragmented and data-sparse, the need for unified social foundation models like GPSocio is becoming both urgent and inevitable.

With the generated representations, GPSocio supports multiple downstream tasks (Fig. 1), including node classification (Sentiment Analysis and Ideology Classification) and link prediction (Static and Temporal Link Prediction). Our main contributions are:

- We propose **GPSocio**, a general-purpose social network representation framework that unifies semantic and structural signals for diverse analytics tasks.
- We design a graph-to-language conversion using propagation sequences, hashtag profiles, and cleaned text to support LLM-based pretraining.
- We introduce a **next-user prediction** contrastive learning task that jointly models semantic affinity and diffusion behavior.
- We develop a lightweight **graph-aware domain adaptation** method to refine user embeddings with domain-specific structural information.
- GPSocio reduces inference time by **over 80%** compared to strong baselines like MINDS and RotDiff, while consistently delivering state-of-the-art performance.
- Extensive experiments demonstrate that GPSocio improves User macro-F1 by **6.74%** (SA) and User ARI by **21.29%** (Ideology Classification), and boosts AUC and User N@10 by **14.75%** and **62.87%** for link prediction, respectively.

2   Related Work

Social Network Representations. Social networks support diverse downstream tasks, including user preference detection [29], information propagation prediction [41], ideology classification [24], sentiment analysis [31], and community detection [2]. Traditional approaches often rely on task-specific embeddings, such as key-value transformers for user history modeling [23] or GNNs for diffusion prediction [33,36]. Other efforts adopt graph-based LSTMs for influencer detection [22] or attributed embeddings for community discovery [42]. LLM-based models have also been used in sentiment analysis [26], but most methods are tailored to single tasks or domains, limiting their generalization to heterogeneous social contexts.

Graph Foundation Models (GFMs). Inspired by the success of language and vision foundation models [5], recent work has explored Graph Foundation Models (GFMs) for cross-task and cross-domain transfer [25]. Existing GFMs can be categorized into three types:

GNN-based GFMs extend encoders like GCNs [20] with large-scale pre-training [17] or attention mechanisms [39], but are often limited to static structure modeling.

GNN+LLM hybrids combine structural and semantic features [8,27], though the fusion is typically shallow and fails to enable deep language-informed reasoning. **LLM-based models** transform graphs into language-compatible sequences to leverage LLM capabilities [40], but often overlook temporal diffusion patterns crucial for modeling dynamic social networks.

Despite progress, existing GFMs rarely integrate semantic content and temporal diffusion in a unified, transferable representation. This remains a key gap that **GPSocio** seeks to address.

3   Problem Statement

We formally define the problem setting of GPSocio and the key concepts involved.

User (u): A unique account on a social media platform, identified by a user ID. We denote the source domain users as $\mathcal{U}^s = \{u_1^s, u_2^s, \ldots, u_{N^s}^s\}$ and the target domain users as $\mathcal{U}^t = \{u_1^t, u_2^t, \ldots, u_{N^t}^t\}$.

Post (p): A timestamped user-generated content item (e.g., a tweet) relevant to a domain of interest. The source posts are $\mathcal{P}^s = \{p_1^s, p_2^s, \ldots, p_{M^s}^s\}$, and the target posts are $\mathcal{P}^t = \{p_1^t, p_2^t, \ldots, p_{M^t}^t\}$.

Post Propagation Sequence (s): A temporal sequence capturing the diffusion of a post through users. For post p_i, its propagation sequence is $s_i = \{p_i, u_{i1}, u_{i2}, \ldots\}$, where u_{i1} is the publisher followed by forwarders in reverse chronological order.

User History Sequence (h): A sequence of a user's historical post interactions, ordered reverse-chronologically as $h_i = \{u_i, p_{i1}, p_{i2}, \ldots\}$.

Given the above definitions, the objective of **GPSocio** is to learn semantic- and diffusion-aware embeddings for:

- **Posts:** $r_{p_i^t}$ for each $p_i^t \in \mathcal{P}^t$
- **Users:** $r_{u_i^t}$ for each $u_i^t \in \mathcal{U}^t$

Our goal is to generate general-purpose representations that support diverse downstream tasks, e.g., sentiment classification, ideology classification, and link prediction, with minimal target-domain supervision. These embeddings should capture both semantic content and diffusion dynamics to enable robust generalization across heterogeneous, evolving social environments.

4   GPSocio Framework

We design three modules for the transformer-based GPSocio framework:

Temporal Diffusion Sequence Generation (TDS): To re-format social networks data into an LLM-understandable format, we adopt semantic identification for users and posts, and concat the items with certain chronological order as they propagate. This design captures the semantic information of users and posts with condensed text while retaining the information propagation patterns and hidden social relations.

Knowledge Distillation Pretraining (KDP): Given long information cascades, we adopt a modified Longformer [3] to handle extended sequences. GPSocio is pre-trained via *next user prediction* along post propagation sequences, which encode semantics, social ties, and behavioral cues—key to modeling engagement.

Graph-Aware Domain Adaptation (GDA). While social networks exhibit shared patterns, domain-specific adaptation refines representations to better capture target-domain nuances. We align the adaptation strategy with the downstream task.

4.1   Temporal Diffusion Sequence Generation (TDS)

The Temporal Diffusion Sequence Generation module extracts generalizable knowledge from data-rich source networks. RNNs [34] struggle with the long sequences in complex social settings, while GNNs [13] capture structure but often miss semantic content. To integrate both, we adopt a Transformer-based architecture, using a modified Longformer [3] as the backbone of **GPSocio**.

To extract knowledge for diffusion prediction and convert social data into a Longformer-compatible format, we define user and post identifiers as follows:

User Identifier: Each user is represented by the set of hashtags they have used, serving as compact, high-density markers of interests, ideology, and community ties. This concise representation shortens sequences while preserving identity cues.

Post Identifier: Each post is represented by its cleaned text, with URLs, mentions, and hashtags removed, capturing core semantics while reducing surface-level noise.

We then construct the **Post Propagation Sequence** s_i for each post p_i, which consists of:

$$X = \{[CLS], p_i, u_{i1}, u_{i2}, \dots\}. \tag{1}$$

Each sequence begins with the post p_i, followed by the publisher u_{i1} and subsequent forwarders ordered in **reverse-chronological order**.

This design offers several advantages:

- Reduces input sequence length and improves training efficiency by compactly representing users and posts.
- Preserves temporal diffusion dynamics through relative ordering, avoiding noise introduced by absolute timestamps.
- Emphasizes recent forwarders, who tend to show stronger engagement and influence on subsequent propagation, better modeling real-world information flow momentum.

By structuring the sequence to mirror the natural unfolding of social attention—from the post origin to its most recent amplifiers—we create a representation that improves the model's ability to generalize propagation behaviors across domains.

4.2 Knowledge Distillation Pretraining (KDP)

GPSocio adopts Longformer as the backbone model as it introduces a linear-scaling attention mechanism, making it well-suited for processing extended sequences while preserving global and local contextual dependencies.

Embedding Generation

To jointly capture semantic content and propagation dynamics, we construct token representations that combine two complementary components: token embeddings and position embeddings. This design integrates language model semantics [10] with temporal modeling from self-attention architectures [35], enabling the model to reason over both content and sequence order in diffusion cascades.

Each token, which represents either a user or a post, is mapped to a dense vector via a learned token embedding matrix $A \in \mathbb{R}^{D_w \times d}$, where D_w is the token vocabulary size and d is the embedding dimension. This captures core semantic features derived from textual identity and interaction history.

To preserve the temporal structure of cascades, we add position embeddings $B \in \mathbb{R}^{n \times d}$, where n denotes the maximum sequence length. Each position k is assigned an embedding $B_k \in \mathbb{R}^d$ that encodes its relative order, allowing the model to distinguish recent and early nodes—crucial for modeling diffusion momentum and engagement patterns.

The final input embedding for each token is given by:

$$E_w = \text{LayerNorm}(A_w + B_w), \tag{2}$$

where LayerNorm stabilizes the training process and promotes faster convergence [1].

GPSocio leverages Longformer [3] as its core encoder, which scales linearly with sequence length by combining local sliding attention and global attention to the [CLS] token. This architecture effectively captures both fine-grained diffusion signals and global semantic context in long propagation sequences.

Given a propagation sequence $s_i = p_i, u_{i1}, u_{i2}, \ldots$, we construct input embeddings $E_{s_i X} \in \mathbb{R}^{(h+1) \times d}$ by summing token and position embeddings (as defined previously), and pass them into the Longformer:

$$E_{s_i}X = [E_{s_i[\text{CLS}]}, E_{s_i w_1}, \ldots, E_{s_i w_h}],$$
$$[r_{s_i[\text{CLS}]}, r_{s_i w_1}, \ldots, r_{s_i w_h}] = \text{Longformer}(E_{s_i}X), \tag{3}$$

where w_i are tokens (users or posts), and the [CLS] vector summarizes the sequence globally.

Post Representation: For each post p_i, we use the corresponding propagation sequence's [CLS] embedding to summarize its global diffusion dynamics

$$r_{p_i} = r_{s_i[\text{CLS}]}. \tag{4}$$

User Representation: To construct each user's representation, we first apply Longformer to the user's personal post history s_{u_k}, yielding an initial semantic embedding $r_{u_{k_{\text{init}}}}$:

$$X = [\text{CLS}], s_{u_k},$$
$$r_{u_{k_{\text{init}}}} = \text{Longformer}(E_{s_{u_k}}X). \tag{5}$$

We then enrich this representation using the user's historical post embeddings, with more recent posts weighted quadratically to reflect their higher influence on current ideological stance [14,15]:

$$r_{u_k} = \lambda r_{u_{k_{\text{init}}}} + \frac{1}{q} \sum_{i=1}^{q} i^2 r_{p_{ki}}, \tag{6}$$

where q is the number of historical posts, $r_{p_{ki}}$ is the embedding of the i-th post, and λ balances the static user profile and dynamic historical context.

This two-stage design enables GPSocio to capture both a user's general identity and recent ideological shifts, facilitating accurate modeling of evolving user behavior in dynamic social environments.

Model Pre-train with Longformer We formulate model pre-training as a next-user prediction task within the post propagation sequence, effectively capturing propagation dynamics while maintaining a manageable sequence length. To optimize this task, we employ Item-Item Contrastive (IIC) learning [6]. Instead of random negative sampling, we enhance contrastive learning efficiency by leveraging in-batch next-item negatives [7], where negatives are drawn from ground-truth sequences within the same batch. This approach significantly reduces computational overhead while maintaining a low false-negative rate. The key insight behind this design is that social networks are inherently large and sparse—when users are arranged sequentially, the probability of two appearing in the same position due to forwarding or publishing the same post (i.e., a false negative) is extremely low.

The IIC Loss is defined as Eq. 7 (τ is a constant):

$$sim_{p_i,u_k}(r_{p_i}, r_{u_k}) = \frac{r_{p_i}^T r_{u_k}}{\|r_{p_i}\|\|r_{u_k}\|},$$

$$L_{IIC} = -log \frac{e^{\frac{sim(r_{p_i}, r_{true})}{\tau}}}{\Sigma_{u_k \in G_{batch}} e^{\frac{sim(r_{p_i}, r_{u_k})}{\tau}}}. \tag{7}$$

4.3   Graph-Aware Domain Adaptation (GDA)

After pre-training, **GPSocio** enters fine-tuning to adapt its learned knowledge to structural and semantic nuances of the target domain. Specifically, we use a user-post bipartite graph $\mathcal{G}^t = (\mathcal{U}^t, \mathcal{P}^t, \mathcal{E}^t)$, where each edge $(u_k, p_i) \in \mathcal{E}^t$ indicates that user u_k interacted with post p_i (e.g., posted, forwarded, or liked).

To make user representations sensitive to domain-specific propagation, we refine them via graph-aware embedding propagation. Users often reflect the content they engage with, aggregating signals from associated posts enriches embeddings with contextual and topical cues relevant to the target network. Importantly, we only update user embeddings during this adaptation stage, while keeping post embeddings fixed. This design choice stems from the observation that user ideologies and topical interests are dynamic, evolving over time based on external stimuli and personal expression patterns, whereas the semantic content of posts is static, anchored in their originally published text. Updating posts could introduce noise or distort their intrinsic semantic meaning, while refining users enables dynamic adaptation without compromising content integrity.

The user representation update rule is defined as:

$$r_{u_k} \leftarrow r_{u_k} + \alpha \sum_{p_i \in G_{connected}^{u_k}} r_{p_i}, \tag{8}$$

where r_{u_k} is the user embedding, r_{p_i} is the post embedding, $G_{connected}^{u_k}$ denotes the set of posts linked to user u_k, and α is a tunable propagation coefficient controlling the strength of information transfer from posts to users.

This domain-aware adaptation step enables the model to refine user representations by anchoring them to content-specific patterns in the target network, thereby reducing the semantic and structural shift between pre-trained representations and real-world diffusion behaviors. Ultimately, this improves the model's generalization and predictive capacity under low-data regimes.

5 Evaluation

We evaluate GPSocio across two categories of tasks (Fig. 1). First, for node classification, we assess performance on Sentiment Analysis (SA) and Ideology Classification, where the goal is to predict node-level semantic or ideological attributes. Second, for link prediction, we evaluate both Static Link Prediction, which predicts the existence of links in the static graph, and Temporal Link Prediction, which predicts future interactions (i.e., next-item prediction) based on temporal graph dynamics.

5.1 Datasets

Table 1. Statistics of Pre-training and Target Datasets.

Dataset	Time Period	# Users	# Posts	Avg. Seq. Len	# Test Posts	# Comm. Users	Topic Sim.
Russia–Ukraine War	01 May 22-15 April 23	62,901	37,754	45.81	–	–	–
Attack Zelensky	01 May 22-15 April 23	12,171	1,668	32.67	731	3,182	0.286
Brics Superiority	01 May 22-15 April 23	1,845	481	18.36	124	1,183	0.309
Ukraine Nazi Claims	01 May 22-15 April 23	3,181	633	12.67	221	1,684	0.218

GPSocio was **pre-trained** on the *Russia-Ukraine War* dataset (keywords: "Russia Ukraine Conflict", etc.) and evaluated on three test sets: *Attack Zelensky* ("KievRegime"), *BRICS Superiority* ("BRICS"), and *Ukraine Nazi Claims* ("Azov Nazi"). Data was collected from Twitter (May 1, 2022 – April 15, 2023). We retained users with over 5 posts and posts propagated by at least 10 users. To assess domain shift, we computed cosine similarity between keyword sets. Dataset statistics appear in Table 1.

5.2 Metrics

For node classifications, we evaluate the performance over Macro-F1, Micro-F1 [30], Adjusted Rand Index (ARI) [18], and Normalized Mutual Information (NMI) [37].

- **Macro-F1** [30]. Calculates the F1 score for each class independently and averages them, treating all classes equally.
- **Micro-F1** [30]. Takes the F1 scores of each class and averages them, treating all classes equally.
- **ARI** [18]. Measures the similarity between two classifications by counting pairwise agreements, adjusting for random chance.
- **NMI** [37]. Quantifies the amount of shared information between predicted and true classifications, normalized by their entropies.

For link predictions, we evaluate the performance over Area Under the ROC Curve (AUC) [11], Average Precision (AP) [9], HIT@K and NDCG@K [12]. In this paper, the performance is evaluated at $K = 10, 20$, we use H@K and N@K as a short representation of the metrics.

- **AUC** [11]. Measures the ability of a model to distinguish between classes, plotting the true positive rate against the false positive rate at various thresholds.
- **AP** [9]. Computes the area under the precision-recall curve, summarizing the precision-recall trade-off across thresholds.
- **HIT@K (H@K)** [12]. Whether any of the top-K recommended items were in the test set for a given user.
- **NDCG@K (N@K)** [12]. NDCG is a widely used metric in information retrieval. It is used to calculate a cumulative score of an ordered set of items.

5.3   Baselines

We compare GPSocio against seven strong baselines spanning graph-based, sequence-based, and hybrid social representation models. To ensure fair comparison, all methods are evaluated under the same training/validation/test splits, and their embedding dimensions are uniformly set to 768.

- **Node2Vec** [16]: Learns node embeddings by simulating biased random walks and optimizing a neighborhood-preserving objective.
- **NDM** [38]: A neural diffusion model that combines attention and convolutional layers to model cascade dynamics under relaxed assumptions.
- **VGAE** [21]: A variational autoencoder with graph convolutions and an inner product decoder to reconstruct network links.
- **Inf-VAE** [33]: A variational framework that models social ties and activity sequences via co-attention and generative encoding.
- **MS-HGAT** [36]: A memory-based hypergraph attention network capturing user dependencies from friendships and cascades.
- **MINDS** [19]: Improves diffusion prediction via sequential hypergraphs and adversarial learning for better generalization.
- **RotDiff** [32]: Models social diffusion using hyperbolic attention and rotation-based encoding of temporal patterns.

5.4   Experimental Setting

GPSocio was pre-trained for 20 epochs using a batch size of 8, a temperature of 0.05, and a sequence window size of 512, with embedding dimension set to 768. Each propagation sequence was split into a **training set** (all nodes except the last three), a **validation set** (second-to-last node), and a **test set** (last node). During fine-tuning, the GDA propagation weight α was set to 0.5. For fair comparison, baseline models also use a representation dimension of 768.

Table 2. Performance Comparison of GPSocio and Baselines on Sentiment and Ideology Classification.

Dataset	Method	Sentiment Analysis				Ideology Classification			
		User macro-f1	Post macro-f1	User micro-f1	Post micro-f1	User ARI	Post ARI	User NMI	Post NMI
Attack Zelensky	VGAE	0.3209	0.3312	0.6271	0.6345	0.1834	0.1756	0.2347	0.2401
	InfVAE	0.3427	0.3496	0.6434	0.6548	0.2438	0.2489	0.2848	0.2937
	node2vec	0.3753	0.3802	0.6936	0.7021	0.3223	0.3278	0.3546	0.3591
	NeuralDiffusion	0.3215	0.3321	0.6844	0.7004	0.2970	0.3097	0.3484	0.3508
	MS-HGAT	0.3207	0.3259	0.6531	0.6607	0.4022	0.3936	0.3797	0.3902
	MINDS	0.3169	0.3279	0.6651	0.6567	0.4177	0.4092	0.3837	0.3914
	rotdiff (SOTA)	0.3128	0.3325	0.6641	0.6702	0.3557	0.3606	0.3803	0.4024
	GPSocio	**0.4051**	**0.4267**	**0.7982**	**0.8154**	**0.5286**	**0.5528**	**0.6102**	**0.6263**
Brics Superiority	VGAE	0.3584	0.3574	0.6105	0.6275	0.2112	0.2227	0.2540	0.2641
	InfVAE	0.3641	0.3734	0.6653	0.6792	0.3157	0.3219	0.3396	0.3582
	node2vec	0.3819	0.3907	0.6839	0.7021	0.2682	0.2886	0.3533	0.3694
	NeuralDiffusion	0.3427	0.3627	0.6532	0.6603	0.3347	0.3516	0.3472	0.3269
	MS-HGAT	0.3501	0.3618	0.6467	0.6567	0.3129	0.3225	0.3517	0.3702
	MINDS	0.3664	0.3729	0.6327	0.6770	0.3291	0.3054	0.3534	0.3818
	rotdiff (SOTA)	0.3681	0.3679	0.6682	0.6824	0.4020	0.4113	0.4285	0.4429
	GPSocio	**0.3997**	**0.4203**	**0.7669**	**0.7894**	**0.5190**	**0.5436**	**0.5737**	**0.5929**
Ukraine Nazi Claims	VGAE	0.2921	0.3032	0.5873	0.6057	0.3184	0.3208	0.2810	0.2927
	InfVAE	0.3327	0.3411	0.6086	0.6046	0.3582	0.3712	0.4259	0.4403
	node2vec	0.3769	0.3951	0.6675	0.6619	0.3223	0.3404	0.3944	0.4253
	NeuralDiffusion	0.3614	0.3741	0.6279	0.6354	0.2955	0.3139	0.3824	0.4028
	MS-HGAT	0.3668	0.3892	0.6356	0.6560	0.3764	0.3966	0.3442	0.3671
	MINDS	0.3693	0.3921	0.6285	0.6420	0.3679	0.4071	0.3698	0.4007
	rotdiff (SOTA)	0.3561	0.3745	0.6524	0.6876	0.4459	0.4629	0.4768	0.4748
	GPSocio	**0.4057**	**0.4253**	**0.7219**	**0.7497**	**0.4874**	**0.5175**	**0.5275**	**0.5407**

5.5   Node Classification Tasks

Task Formulation. We consider two node classification tasks. For **Sentiment Analysis**, each node is labeled as positive, negative, or neutral using the NLTK toolkit [4]. In a weakly supervised setting, 10% of the labeled nodes are used for training. We extract GPSocio representations (refined through domain-specific adaptation) as input features and train a multi-layer perceptron (MLP) classifier to predict sentiment labels. For **Ideology Classification**, ideological labels (left-leaning, right-leaning, or neutral) are generated by GPT-4 via controlled prompting [28]. We apply principal component analysis (PCA) to reduce each 768-dimensional GPSocio embedding to 32 dimensions, followed by k-means classification with the number of clusters set to 3.

Overall Results. Extensive results (Table 2) show that GPSocio consistently outperforms strong baselines across both node classification tasks. It improves user macro-F1 by an average of 7.6% in sentiment analysis and user ARI by 24.9% in ideology classification. On *Attack Zelensky*, for example, it raises macro-F1 from 0.3753 to 0.4051 and ARI from 0.4177 to 0.5286, demonstrating its strength in capturing both semantic information and structural dynamics.

5.6   Link Prediction Tasks

Task Formulation. We define static link prediction as a binary classification task, where the goal is to determine whether a link exists between a given user u_k and post p_i. For this, we obtain their representations r_{u_k} and r_{p_i}, and compute the cosine similarity as the link score (Eq. 7). We evaluate performance using 200 positive (existing) and 200 negative (non-existing) user-post pairs randomly sampled from the graph. A higher similarity score indicates a higher probability of link existence. In contrast, temporal link prediction (i.e., next-item prediction) is framed as a ranking task. For each user, we rank all candidate posts by their similarity to the user's representation and select the highest-scoring post as the predicted next interaction.

Table 3. Benchmarking GPSocio Against State-of-the-Art Methods on Static and Temporal Link Prediction Tasks.

Dataset	Method	Static Link		Temporal Link						Inference Time
		AUC (%)	AP (%)	User N@10	User H@10	User H@20	Post N@10	Post H@10	Post H@20	
Attack Zelensky	VGAE	72.36%	69.68%	0.1366	0.0848	0.1384	0.0107	0.0245	0.0614	9m43s
	InfVAE	74.58%	69.72%	0.0351	0.0372	0.0539	0.0156	0.0477	0.1399	10m28s
	node2vec	69.57%	65.44%	0.0980	0.1426	0.1616	0.0291	0.0719	0.1472	9m34s
	NeuralDiffusion	75.68%	73.93%	0.0759	0.1059	0.1462	0.0284	0.0728	0.1277	23m12s
	MS-HGAT	66.25%	64.32%	0.0507	0.0538	0.0744	0.0708	0.0865	0.1306	30m57s
	MINDS	68.74%	65.53%	0.0491	0.0527	0.0829	0.0680	0.0874	0.1407	26m24s
	rotdiff (SOTA)	69.97%	68.85%	0.0402	0.0609	0.0881	0.0538	0.0967	0.1529	7m11s
	GPSocio	**89.63%**	**88.68%**	**0.2026**	**0.2500**	**0.2815**	**0.1088**	**0.2059**	**0.3208**	**3m03s**
Brics Superiority	VGAE	64.48%	58.40%	0.0581	0.0658	0.0767	0.0700	0.1364	0.2727	5m43s
	InfVAE	68.89%	65.23%	0.0473	0.0688	0.0854	0.1195	0.2102	0.2757	7m25s
	node2vec	65.76%	63.74%	0.0711	0.1028	0.1583	0.0627	0.1875	0.3594	5m27s
	NeuralDiffusion	69.97%	68.29%	0.0751	0.0909	0.1145	0.0662	0.1164	0.2358	11m11s
	MS-HGAT	68.57%	65.72%	0.0892	0.0794	0.0966	0.0981	0.1151	0.1762	12m34s
	MINDS	66.36%	67.41%	0.0789	0.0851	0.1059	0.0867	0.1194	0.1627	9m47s
	rotdiff (SOTA)	72.51%	72.21%	0.0756	0.1069	0.1471	0.0824	0.1216	0.2675	3m21s
	GPSocio	**80.29%**	**79.72%**	**0.1650**	**0.2466**	**0.3007**	**0.1640**	**0.3184**	**0.5018**	**1m42s**
Ukraine Nazi Claims	VGAE	70.08%	68.52%	0.0712	0.0737	0.0773	0.0322	0.0754	0.1969	7 m38 s
	InfVAE	70.53%	67.61%	0.0692	0.0703	0.0918	0.0582	0.1313	0.1925	8 m06 s
	node2vec	72.07%	69.15%	0.0983	0.1426	0.1635	0.0695	0.1304	0.2275	7 m55s
	NeuralDiffusion	75.44%	68.04%	0.1090	0.1175	0.1384	0.0450	0.1066	0.2306	10m37s
	MS-HGAT	73.31%	74.25%	0.1111	0.1209	0.1644	0.1351	0.1594	0.2207	19m41s
	MINDS	74.91%	73.96%	0.1007	0.1169	0.1782	0.1336	0.1729	0.2473	20m17s
	rotdiff (SOTA)	75.68%	73.67%	0.1029	0.1546	0.2103	0.1316	0.1998	0.2723	5m34s
	GPSocio	**86.97%**	**84.42%**	**0.1811**	**0.2916**	**0.3532**	**0.2178**	**0.4059**	**0.4989**	**2m39s**

Overall Results. As shown in Table 3, GPSocio consistently outperforms all baselines across both static and temporal link prediction tasks. For static link prediction, it achieves the highest AUC scores across all datasets, with improvements of **+19.0%** on *Attack Zelensky*, **+10.7%** on BRICS Superiority, and **+14.9%** on *Ukraine Nazi Claims* over the strongest baseline.

Performance gains are even more striking on the temporal link prediction task. GPSocio improves User N@10 by **48.3%**, **85.0%**, and **63.0%** respectively across the three datasets, demonstrating its superior ability to capture user-level

242   X. Liu et al.

temporal dynamics. Significant improvements are also observed in Post N@10 and H@10, indicating robust modeling of post-level diffusion patterns.

In addition to predictive accuracy, GPSocio delivers substantial efficiency gains, reducing inference time by **57–84%** compared to strong baselines like RotDiff and MINDS. For instance, on *Attack Zelensky*, GPSocio completes inference in **3 m 03 s**, versus 7 m 11 s for RotDiff and 26 m 24 s for MINDS. Similar trends hold for *BRICS Superiority* (**1 m 42 s** vs. 3 m 21 s/9 m 47 s) and *Ukraine Nazi Claims* (**2 m 39 s** vs. 5 m 34 s/20 m 17 s).

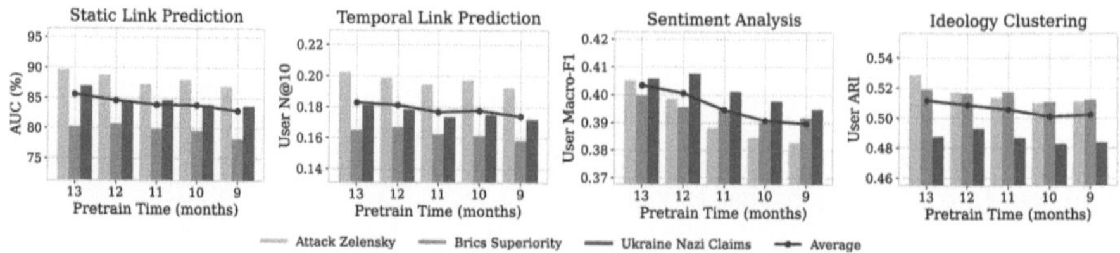

Fig. 3. Effect of Pre-training Duration on Performance Across Downstream Tasks.

5.7 Performance Analysis

GPSocio's strong results stem from three key innovations:

- Large-scale contrastive pretraining transfers social knowledge from high-resource to low-resource domains, addressing data scarcity.
- Diffusion-aware sequence modeling captures temporal dynamics and social semantics more effectively than graph-only or purely text-based approaches.
- Transformer-based encoding with Longformer integrates sequential and structural signals at scale, avoiding the computational overhead of traditional GNNs.

These innovations yield not only superior performance across diverse tasks but also high computational efficiency, making GPSocio a scalable and practical framework for real-world social analytics.

5.8 Robustness Study

To assess GPSocio's resilience in real-world scenarios where data availability and alignment may vary, we evaluate its performance under reductions in pretraining data and perturbations in target domain conditions. We report four representative metrics across tasks: AUC (static link prediction), User N@10 (temporal link prediction), Macro-F1 (sentiment analysis), and ARI (ideology classification), chosen for their strong diagnostic value across task types.

Table 4. Robustness Study Across Temporal and User Overlap Variants.

Robustness Study: Varying Target Time Windows											
Setting	Attack Zelensky				BRICS Superiority				Ukraine Nazi Claims			
	AUC	N@10	Macro-F1	ARI	AUC	N@10	Macro-F1	ARI	AUC	N@10	Macro-F1	ARI
Full Time Window	**89.63%**	**0.2026**	**0.4051**	**0.5286**	**80.29%**	**0.1650**	0.3997	**0.5190**	86.97%	0.1811	0.4057	0.4874
Recent 4 Months	87.21%	0.1847	0.4004	0.5127	77.36%	0.1579	0.3862	0.5058	**87.11%**	0.1794	**0.4136**	0.4850
Recent 3.5 Months	88.96%	0.1807	0.4022	0.5203	79.43%	0.1604	**0.4018**	0.5098	85.84%	**0.1832**	0.3989	**0.4906**
Robustness Study: Effects of Pre-training Time Gaps with a 3-Month Target Time Window											
0-Day Gap	87.94%	0.2001	0.3966	0.5229	**82.42%**	**0.1748**	**0.4021**	**0.5042**	87.33%	0.2108	0.4145	0.5174
15-Day Gap	**88.02%**	0.2016	0.4027	**0.5418**	81.07%	0.1696	0.3846	0.4930	86.89%	0.2036	**0.4338**	**0.5257**
30-Day Gap	85.04%	**0.2128**	**0.4093**	0.5339	79.62%	0.1607	0.3947	0.4896	**87.51%**	**0.2243**	0.4142	0.5141
Robustness Study: Presence vs Absence of Common Users											
W/ Common Users	**89.63%**	0.2026	0.4051	0.5286	**80.29%**	0.1650	0.3997	0.5190	**86.97%**	0.1811	0.4057	0.4874
W/O Common Users	88.84%	**0.2074**	**0.4215**	**0.5437**	79.30%	**0.1685**	**0.4027**	**0.5269**	85.73%	**0.1903**	**0.4273**	**0.5046**

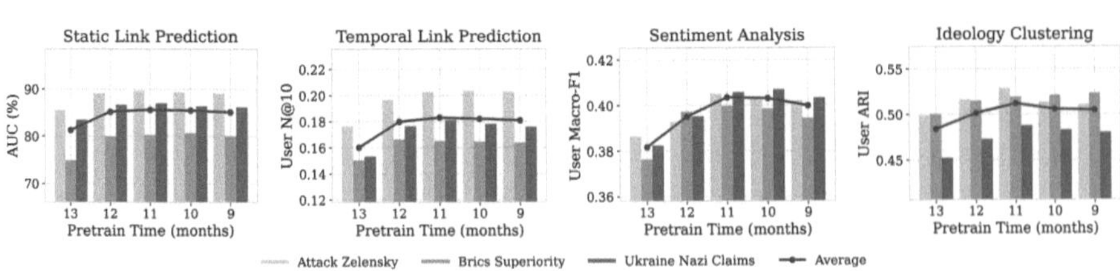

Fig. 4. Sensitivity of Performance Metrics to the Propagation Parameter α.

Pre-training Data Reduction. Shrinking the pre-training window from 13 to 9 months leads to negligible drops less than **2%** in AUC and N@10, and under **1.5%** in Macro-F1 and ARI (Fig. 3). This demonstrates GPSocio's ability to retain generalization capacity even with significantly less pre-training data.

Target Domain Perturbations. We evaluate robustness under three common forms of distribution shift:

- **Shorter Target Windows:** Reducing the target window from the full time span to the most recent 3.5 months causes performance fluctuations of no more than **4.3%** across all metrics and datasets, demonstrating strong temporal stability (Table 4).
- **Increased Pretrain-Target Gap:** Introducing a gap of up to 30 days causes only minor variation, with peak performance at 15 days, indicating that GPSocio remains effective across time shifts.
- **Removal of Common Users:** Excluding shared users across domains does not harm performance. ARI on *Ukraine Nazi Claims*, for instance, improves from 0.4874 to 0.5046, indicating strong transferability beyond identity overlap.

Together, these results confirm that GPSocio is robust to data volume reductions and temporal or structural distribution shifts, owing to its combination of large-scale diffusion-aware pretraining and lightweight domain-specific refinement.

5.9 Sensitivity Study

To assess the stability of GPSocio under hyperparameter variations, we conduct a sensitivity analysis on the propagation weight α used during the domain-specific adaptation stage. This parameter controls the degree to which post embeddings influence user representations. A well-tuned α helps integrate content-specific signals without overwhelming the user's pre-trained semantics.

To streamline evaluation, we report four representative metrics: AUC (static link prediction), user N@10 (temporal link prediction), user Macro-F1 (sentiment analysis), and user ARI (ideology classification). These are chosen for their broad task coverage and strong correlation with other metrics within each task category, thus avoiding redundancy while maintaining diagnostic value.

As shown in Fig. 4, GPSocio exhibits stable behavior across all tasks as α varies. Performance consistently improves as α increases from 0.1 to 0.5 or 0.7, indicating that moderate propagation effectively incorporates domain-specific context into user embeddings. Beyond 0.7, however, performance slightly declines, particularly in sentiment and temporal link prediction, suggesting that excessive propagation may introduce noise and dilute semantic distinctions.

Overall, GPSocio achieves optimal trade-offs between generality and adaptability when α is set between 0.5 and 0.7, demonstrating robust performance across downstream tasks without requiring fine-grained tuning.

Table 5. Ablation Results Comparing Performance With and Without GDA.

Dataset	W/ or W/O GDA	Static Link		Temporal Link		Sentiment Analysis		Ideology Clustering	
		AUC	AP	U. N@10	P. N@10	U. macro-f1	P. macro-f1	U. ARI	P. ARI
Attack Zelensky	W/O GDA	83.92%	83.72%	0.1533	0.0819	0.3572	0.3920	0.4753	0.5016
	W/ GDA	**89.63%** (+6.8%)	**88.68%** (5.9%)	**0.2026** (+32.2%)	**0.1088** (+32.8%)	**0.4051** (+13.4%)	**0.4267** (+8.9%)	**0.5286** (+11.2%)	**0.5528** (+10.2%)
Brics Superiority	W/O GDA	74.87%	73.14%	0.1501	0.1436	0.3763	0.4115	0.5004	0.5132
	W/ GDA	**80.29%** (+7.2%)	**79.72%** (9.0%)	**0.1650** (+9.9%)	**0.1640** (+14.2%)	**0.3997** (+6.2%)	**0.4203** (+2.1%)	**0.5190** (+3.7%)	**0.5436** (+5.9%)
Ukraine Nazi Claims	W/O GDA	83.43%	80.61%	0.1530	0.2004	0.3824	0.4142	0.4520	0.5039
	W/ GDA	**86.97%** (+4.2%)	**84.42%** (4.7%)	**0.1811** (+18.4%)	**0.2178** (+8.7%)	**0.4057** (+6.1%)	**0.4253** (+2.7%)	**0.4874** (+7.8%)	**0.5175** (+2.7%)

5.10 Ablation Study

To assess the impact of the Graph-Aware Domain Adaptation (GDA) module, we compare GPSocio's performance with and without GDA.

As shown in Table 5, even without GDA, GPSocio, trained solely on large-scale propagation sequences, already outperforms all baselines, confirming the strong generalization ability of its pre-trained embeddings.

Adding GDA further amplifies performance across all tasks. AUC improves by up to 6.06% (e.g., +6.8% on *Attack Zelensky*), and user N@10 gains reach as high as 20.2%, showing clear benefits in temporal link prediction. These results underscore that while pre-training captures transferable semantics and diffusion patterns, adapting to domain-specific graph structure is essential for optimal performance.

This validates our lightweight adaptation strategy (Sect. 4.3), which selectively updates user embeddings via post-to-user propagation—enhancing domain alignment without over-smoothing in sparse networks.

6   Conclusion

We propose GPSocio, a general-purpose framework that bridges semantic and diffusion signals via language-compatible propagation sequences and transformer modeling. Through contrastive pretraining and lightweight graph-aware adaptation, GPSocio enables robust, efficient transfer across diverse social tasks. Experiments on sentiment, ideology, and link prediction confirm its state-of-the-art performance and resilience under low-resource and shifting domains, underscoring the promise of language-informed social representation learning.

References

1. Ba, J.L., Kiros, J.R., Hinton, G.E.: Layer normalization. arXiv preprint arXiv:1607.06450 (2016)
2. Bedi, P., Sharma, C.: Community detection in social networks. Wiley Interdis. Rev. Data Mining Knowl. Discov. **6**(3), 115–135 (2016)
3. Beltagy, I., Peters, M.E., Cohan, A.: Longformer: the long-document transformer. arXiv preprint arXiv:2004.05150 (2020)
4. Bird, S., Loper, E., Klein, E.: Natural language processing with python: analyzing text with the natural language toolkit. Inc, O'Reilly Media (2009)
5. Bommasani, R., et al.: On the opportunities and risks of foundation models. arXiv preprint arXiv:2108.07258 (2021)
6. Chen, T., Kornblith, S., Norouzi, M., Hinton, G.: A simple framework for contrastive learning of visual representations. In: International Conference on Machine Learning, pp. 1597–1607. PMLR (2020)
7. Chen, T., Sun, Y., Shi, Y., Hong, L.: On sampling strategies for neural network-based collaborative filtering. In: Proceedings of the 23rd ACM SIGKDD International Conference on Knowledge Discovery and Data Mining, pp. 767–776 (2017)
8. Chien, E., et al.: Node feature extraction by self-supervised multi-scale neighborhood prediction. arXiv preprint arXiv:2111.00064 (2021)
9. Davis, J., Goadrich, M.: The relationship between precision-recall and roc curves. In: Proceedings of the 23rd International Conference on Machine Learning, pp. 233–240 (2006)
10. Devlin, J., Chang, M.W., Lee, K., Toutanova, K.: Bert: pre-training of deep bidirectional transformers for language understanding. arXiv preprint arXiv:1810.04805 (2018)
11. Fawcett, T.: An introduction to roc analysis. Patt. Recogn. Lett. **27**(8), 861–874 (2006)
12. Fayyaz, Z., Ebrahimian, M., Nawara, D., Ibrahim, A., Kashef, R.: Recommendation systems: algorithms, challenges, metrics, and business opportunities. Appl. Sci. **10**(21), 7748 (2020)
13. Feng, S., et al.: H-DIFFU: hyperbolic representations for information diffusion prediction. IEEE Trans. Knowl. Data Eng. **35**(9), 8784–8798 (2022)

14. Flache, A., et al.: Models of social influence: towards the next frontiers. J. Artif. Soc. Soc. Simul. **20**(4), 2 (2017)
15. Friedkin, N.E., Johnsen, E.C.: Social influence network theory: a sociological examination of small group dynamics. Cambridge University Press (2011)
16. Grover, A., Leskovec, J.: node2vec: scalable feature learning for networks. In: Proceedings of the 22nd ACM SIGKDD International Conference on Knowledge Discovery and Data Mining, pp. 855–864 (2016)
17. Huang, Q., Ren, H., Chen, P., Kržmanc, G., Zeng, D., Liang, P.S., Leskovec, J.: Prodigy: enabling in-context learning over graphs. Adv. Neural Inf. Process. Syst. **36** (2024)
18. Hubert, L., Arabie, P.: Comparing partitions. J. Classification **2**, 193–218 (1985)
19. Jiao, P., Chen, H., Bao, Q., Zhang, W., Wu, H.: Enhancing multi-scale diffusion prediction via sequential hypergraphs and adversarial learning. In: Proceedings of the AAAI Conference on Artificial Intelligence. vol. 38, pp. 8571–8581 (2024)
20. Kipf, T.N., Welling, M.: Semi-supervised classification with graph convolutional networks. arXiv preprint arXiv:1609.02907 (2016)
21. Kipf, T.N., Welling, M.: Variational graph auto-encoders. arXiv preprint arXiv:1611.07308 (2016)
22. Kumar, S., Mallik, A., Panda, B.: Influence maximization in social networks using transfer learning via graph-based LSTM. Expert Syst. Appl. **212**, 118770 (2023)
23. Li, J., et al.: Text is all you need: learning language representations for sequential recommendation. In: Proceedings of the 29th ACM SIGKDD Conference on Knowledge Discovery and Data Mining, pp. 1258–1267 (2023)
24. Li, J., et al.: Unsupervised belief representation learning with information-theoretic variational graph auto-encoders. In: Proceedings of the 45th International ACM SIGIR Conference on Research and Development in Information Retrieval, pp. 1728–1738 (2022)
25. Liu, J., et al.: Towards graph foundation models: a survey and beyond. arXiv preprint arXiv:2310.11829 (2023)
26. Liu, W., Wen, B., Gao, S., Zheng, J., Zheng, Y.: A multi-label text classification model based on elmo and attention. In: MATEC Web of Conferences. vol. 309, p. 03015. EDP Sciences (2020)
27. Mavromatis, C., et al.: Train your own gnn teacher: Graph-aware distillation on textual graphs. In: Joint European Conference on Machine Learning and Knowledge Discovery in Databases, pp. 157–173. Springer (2023)
28. OpenAI: Gpt-4 technical report. https://arxiv.org/abs/2303.08774 (2023)
29. Pereira, F.S.F., Gama, J., de Amo, S., Oliveira, G.M.B.: On analyzing user preference dynamics with temporal social networks. Mach. Learn. **107**(11), 1745–1773 (2018). https://doi.org/10.1007/s10994-018-5740-2
30. Powers, D.M.: Evaluation: from precision, recall and f-measure to roc, informedness, markedness and correlation. arXiv preprint arXiv:2010.16061 (2020)
31. Pozzi, F.A., Fersini, E., Messina, E., Liu, B.: Sentiment analysis in social networks. Morgan Kaufmann (2016)
32. Qiao, H., et al.: Rotdiff: a hyperbolic rotation representation model for information diffusion prediction. In: Proceedings of the 32nd ACM International Conference on Information and Knowledge Management, pp. 2065–2074 (2023)
33. Sankar, A., Zhang, X., Krishnan, A., Han, J.: Inf-vae: a variational autoencoder framework to integrate homophily and influence in diffusion prediction. In: Proceedings of the 13th International Conference on Web Search and Data Mining, pp. 510–518 (2020)

34. Sherstinsky, A.: Fundamentals of recurrent neural network (RNN) and long short-term memory (LSTM) network. Physica D **404**, 132306 (2020)
35. Sun, F., et al.: Bert4rec: sequential recommendation with bidirectional encoder representations from transformer. In: Proceedings of the 28th ACM International Conference on Information and Knowledge Management, pp. 1441–1450(2019)
36. Sun, L., Rao, Y., Zhang, X., Lan, Y., Yu, S.: MS-HGAT: memory-enhanced sequential hypergraph attention network for information diffusion prediction. In: Proceedings of the AAAI Conference on Artificial Intelligence. vol. 36, pp. 4156–4164 (2022)
37. Vinh, N., Epps, J., Bailey, J.: Information theoretic measures for clusterings comparison: variants. Properties, Normalization and Correction for Chance **18** (2009)
38. Yang, C., Sun, M., Liu, H., Han, S., Liu, Z., Luan, H.: Neural diffusion model for microscopic cascade prediction. arXiv preprint arXiv:1812.08933 (2018)
39. Ying, C., et al.: Do transformers really perform badly for graph representation? Adv. Neural. Inf. Process. Syst. **34**, 28877–28888 (2021)
40. Zhao, H., et al.: Gimlet: a unified graph-text model for instruction-based molecule zero-shot learning. Adv. Neural Inf. Process. Syst. **36** (2024)
41. Zhao, J., Wu, J., Feng, X., Xiong, H., Xu, K.: Information propagation in online social networks: a tie-strength perspective. Knowl. Inf. Syst. **32**, 589–608 (2012)
42. Zhou, X., Su, L., Li, X., Zhao, Z., Li, C.: Community detection based on unsupervised attributed network embedding. Expert Syst. Appl. **213**, 118937 (2023)

Disinformation Contagion: Integrating Data-Driven Insights with Theoretical Model

Nitin Agarwal[1,2](✉)

[1] COSMOS Research Center, University of Arkansas at Little Rock,
Little Rock, USA
nxagarwal@ualr.edu

[2] International Computer Science Institute, University of California,
Berkeley, USA

Abstract. The rapid spread of disinformation on social media platforms poses significant threats to public discourse and democratic institutions. This study introduces a novel fractal-fractional epidemiological model, SEDAZR, that partitions users into Susceptible, Exposed, Disinformed, Anti-disinformed, Skeptic, and Recovered compartments. Leveraging real-world datasets from Twitter, Telegram, and TikTok, the model captures memory-dependent dynamics and nonlinear user transitions observed in online environments. We derive the basic reproduction number $\mathcal{R}_0$ and conduct sensitivity analysis using Latin Hypercube Sampling and Partial Rank Correlation to identify key parameters influencing disinformation spread. Theoretical validation is achieved through existence, uniqueness, and Ulam-Hyers stability analyses, confirming the model's robustness under perturbations. Numerical simulations demonstrate the influence of memory effects and transmission rates on user behavior, while model fitting shows strong alignment with platform-specific data. This integrated framework offers practical insights for designing adaptive mitigation strategies and informs future extensions into multi-platform, demographically aware disinformation control systems.

Keywords: Epidemiological model · Mathematical modeling · disinformation · social media

1 Introduction

The rapid diffusion of disinformation on digital platforms has emerged as a critical threat to democratic processes and public trust, exacerbated by the sophisticated interplay of technology, psychology, and geopolitics [1,2]. Platforms such as TikTok and Telegram, with their unique algorithmic and structural features, have become fertile ground for false narratives [3]. TikTok's recommendation algorithm, designed to prioritize high-engagement content, often amplifies sensational or emotionally charged posts, allowing conspiracy theories and misleading claims to achieve viral status [4]. Meanwhile, Telegram's encrypted channels

A. An et al. (Eds.): ASONAM 2025, LNCS 16323, pp. 248–263, 2026.
https://doi.org/10.1007/978-3-032-13821-7_21

and private groups facilitate the unchecked spread of disinformation within echo chambers, protected from public scrutiny [5]. These dynamics are not merely technological quirks but systemic vulnerabilities exploited by malicious actors to distort public discourse. The consequences are stark and multifaceted [6]. In the realm of public health, baseless vaccine conspiracies such as claims linking COVID-19 vaccines to microchips or infertility contributed to hesitancy, with studies estimating that disinformation may have reduced global vaccination rates by up to 15%, prolonging the pandemic [7]. Politically, fabricated election fraud narratives, like the "Stop the Steal" campaign in the 2020 U.S. elections, have eroded trust in democratic institutions, incited violence, and polarized societies [8]. The reach of such disinformation is staggering: a 2023 MIT study found that falsehoods spread six times faster than factual content on social media, aided by automated bots and AI-driven deepfakes that mimic legitimate sources [9].

Anti-disinformation campaigns, recognizing the urgency of this crisis, have adopted multi-pronged strategies. Fact-checking initiatives, such as those led by the International Fact-Checking Network (IFCN), collaborate with platforms to label or remove false content, though their efforts are often outpaced by the sheer volume of disinformation [10]. Educational programs, like MediaWise for youth, aim to bolster digital literacy, empowering users to critically evaluate sources [11]. Grassroots movements, including #ThinkBeforeYouShare, harness civic engagement to counteract false narratives organically [12]. Tech companies, under regulatory pressure, have introduced policies to remove harmful content and enhance transparency in political advertisements [13].

Gaining insight into the dynamics between disinformation and counter-disinformation efforts demands more than conventional analytical methods. This research adopts a novel hybrid framework that combines epidemiological modeling with fractal-fractional differential equations, effectively capturing both the spread patterns and memory-dependent behaviors found in digital environments. We introduce the SEDAZR model, which categorizes users into six states: Susceptible, Exposed, Disinformed, Anti-disinformed, Skeptic, and Recovered. This structure parallels infectious disease models but is tailored to reflect user interactions specific to digital platforms. Exploring these dynamics is essential for formulating targeted interventions that reduce the impact of misleading content and strengthen democratic resilience. The objective is to uncover significant trends in how information, both deceptive and corrective, spreads and engages audiences, thereby revealing the underlying mobilization traits of each campaign. Through this, the study aims to enhance our understanding of digital influence strategies and support the safeguarding of democratic systems in the digital age.

This paper answers the following **research questions: RQ1:** What are the key mechanisms and parameters that drive or mitigate the virality of disinformation in online ecosystems? **RQ2:** How can we develop a mathematically rigorous and platform-adaptable model to simulate the spread and suppression of disinformation on social media? **RQ3:** What role do memory and temporal patterns play in the spread of digital disinformation? **RQ4:** How can we use the proposed model to dynamically evaluate which is spreading faster - disinformation or anti-disinformation?

2   Literature Review

The rapid evolution of disinformation ecosystems has spurred a diverse body of research aiming to understand how false narratives propagate, who spreads them, and how they can be countered effectively. This section outlines the current landscape across three key domains: machine learning approaches to disinformation detection, epidemiological models for information diffusion, and emerging fractal-fractional modeling techniques capturing the complexity of online engagement.

2.1   Machine Learning Approaches to Disinformation Detection

A substantial volume of work has leveraged machine learning (ML) to identify and classify disinformation in real time. Techniques such as natural language processing (NLP), sentiment analysis, and network analysis have been central to these efforts. Pre-trained language models like BERT, RoBERTa, and GPT have shown success in detecting disinformation across platforms including Twitter, Facebook, and TikTok [14]. These models can identify linguistic cues, flag suspicious content, and even detect coordinated inauthentic behavior. However, many ML models focus primarily on static classification and often lack the ability to capture temporal dependencies or feedback mechanisms within online information ecosystems. Studies such as [1,9] have revealed how disinformation super-spreaders exploit platform algorithms to amplify false narratives, suggesting that detection alone is insufficient to mitigate systemic spread.

2.2   Epidemiological Models for Information Spread

Epidemiological modeling has increasingly been applied to digital communication networks to study the diffusion of disinformation, drawing analogies between infectious disease transmission and content spread. Variants of classical models—such as SIR (Susceptible-Infected-Recovered), SEIR (Susceptible-Exposed-Infected-Recovered), and SEIQR (Susceptible-Exposed-Infected-Quarantined-Recovered)—have been adapted to account for the stages of user exposure and belief in false narratives [15]. These models offer a conceptual framework for understanding the tipping points and thresholds at which disinformation becomes viral. More recent models include compartments for skepticism or counter-engagement, acknowledging the role of fact-checkers and critical users. For instance, [16] explored quarantine-style strategies for isolating disinformed users or slowing content spread, echoing methods used in public health.

Despite their utility, traditional epidemiological models often oversimplify user behavior and fail to incorporate cognitive biases, memory effects, or the influence of recommendation algorithms. In the context of anti-disinformation strategies, interventions such as fact-checking, user education, and platform moderation can be modeled analogously to vaccination or treatment policies, but these remain underexplored in conventional compartmental frameworks.

2.3 Fractal-Fractional Models for Disinformation Dynamics

To address the limitations of classical approaches, researchers have turned to fractal-fractional differential equations, which offer a robust mathematical toolkit for capturing complex, memory-driven, and non-local dynamics in social systems [17] and [18]. Fractal-fractional models extend standard differential equations by incorporating historical states and irregular temporal patterns a key characteristics of disinformation campaigns, where influence can persist long after initial exposure. These models are particularly suited to social media, where algorithmic amplification, user memory, and echo chambers create persistent feedback loops. Incorporating fractal-fractional operators into epidemiological models allows for the simulation of both short-term virality and long-term narrative persistence. For instance, memory effects can reflect repeated exposure to the same narrative across platforms, while non-local diffusion captures the sudden jumps of content across unrelated user communities. However, existing applications of fractal-fractional modeling have focused largely on disease outbreaks and financial contagions, with limited adaptation to the sociotechnical dynamics of disinformation.

3 Methodology

This section provides an overview of the data collection and methodology used in this paper.

3.1 Fractal-Fractional Model Formulation

In this study, we introduce a fractal-fractional model to analyze the spread of disinformation and anti-disinformation within an online network. The model considers six distinct compartments: Susceptible $(S(t))$, representing users who can be influenced by disinformation; Exposed $(E(t))$, referring to individuals who have encountered misleading content; Disinformed $(D(t))$, who actively propagate false information; Anti-disinformed spreaders $(A(t))$, who counteract disinformation; Skeptic $(Z(t))$, representing users who question information before sharing it; and Recovered $(R(t))$, individuals who have become resistant to misleading content. Using a system of fractal-fractional ordinary differential equations (FFODEs), the proposed SEDAZR model captures the complex interactions between these groups. We present a transfer diagram in Fig. 1 and parameters in Table 1 to illustrate the flow of users between different compartments.

The system of ordinary differential equations (ODEs) is given as follows:

$$
\begin{cases}
{}_{0}^{FFP}D_t^{\alpha,\beta}S(t) = \Pi + \sigma R(t) - \dfrac{\beta_1(A+D)}{N(t)}S(t) + \xi Z(t) - \eta S(t), \\[2mm]
{}_{0}^{FFP}D_t^{\alpha,\beta}E(t) = \dfrac{\beta_1(A+D)}{N(t)}S(t) - (\psi + \lambda + p + \eta)E(t), \\[2mm]
{}_{0}^{FFP}D_t^{\alpha,\beta}A(t) = \psi E(t) + \kappa_d D(t) - (\gamma_a + \kappa_a + \eta)A(t), \\[2mm]
{}_{0}^{FFP}D_t^{\alpha,\beta}D(t) = \kappa_a A(t) + \lambda E(t) + \theta Z(t) - (\gamma_d + \kappa_d + \eta)D(t), \\[2mm]
{}_{0}^{FFP}D_t^{\alpha,\beta}Z(t) = pE(t) - (\theta + m + \xi + \eta)Z(t), \\[2mm]
{}_{0}^{FFP}D_t^{\alpha,\beta}R(t) = \gamma_a A(t) + \gamma_d D(t) - (\eta + \sigma)R(t),
\end{cases}
\tag{1}
$$

where ${}_{0}^{FFP}D_t^{\alpha,\beta}(.)$ is the fractal-fractional derivative with the fractional order $0 < \alpha \le 1$ and fractal dimension $0 < \beta \le 1$ in the Caputo sense with power law type kernel, and the variables are assumed to be non-negative with appropriate initial conditions.

Incorporating fractal-fractional operators enhances traditional models by considering memory effects, spatial heterogeneity, and anomalous diffusion, providing a more accurate representation of SEDAZR dynamics. This approach is crucial for devising effective control strategies.

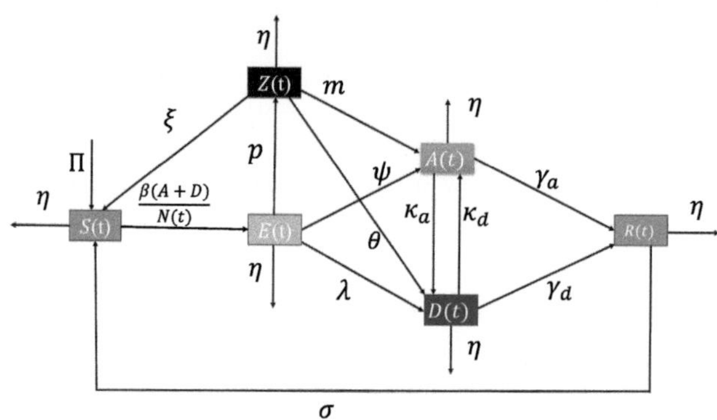

Fig. 1. Transfer diagram for the Anti-dis/disinformation spread on the social network platform.

3.2 Data Collection and Analysis

To evaluate the robustness and cross-platform adaptability of the proposed SEDAZR model, we curated and analyzed disinformation-related datasets from **X (formerly Twitter)**, **Telegram**, and **TikTok**. Each dataset corresponds to a distinct real-world case study characterized by polarized discourse and coordinated narrative campaigns. Below is a summary of each dataset and its collection process:

Table 1. Interpretation of parameters in the model

Parameter	value	source	Interpretation
Π	1000	Fitted	Recruitment rate which new users joining the platform
ξ	0.0021	Fitted	Rate at which skeptics user revert become susceptible after exposed
β_1	0.0014	Fitted	Effective contact rate
η	0.000233	Fitted	the rate at which users naturally leave the platform.
p	0.000375	Assumed	the rate at which exposed users become skeptic
m	0.000375	Assumed	the rate at which skeptic users disagree with disinformation
θ	0.000375	Assumed	the rate at which skeptic users agree with disinformation
p	0.000375	Assumed	the rate at which exposed users become skeptic
λ	0.01	Assumed	the rate at which $E(t)$ transition to $D(t)$
ψ	0.30	Assumed	the rate at which $E(t)$ transition to $A(t)$
κ_a	0.000375	Assumed	the rate at which $(A(t))$ become $(D(t))$
κ_d	0.000375	Assumed	the rate at which $(D(t))$ become $(A(t))$
σ	0.30	Assumed	the rate at which $(r(t))$ users become $(S(t))$
γ_a	0.001	Fitted	Rate at which $(A(t))$ move to recovery
γ_d	0.001	Fitted	Rate at which $(D(t))$ move to recovery

- **COVID-19 Vaccine (Twitter):** Tweets were collected between *December 22, 2020 and June 14, 2021*, focusing on conspiracy narratives linking COVID-19 vaccines to adverse outcomes. We used keyword filters such as `"covid,"` `"coronavirus,"` `"vaccine,"` `"microchip,"` `"5G,"` `"infertility,"` and `"Bill Gates"`, coupled with Boolean operators and hashtag matching (e.g., #DoNotComply, #VaccineHoax). Tweets were retrieved via the Twitter Academic API and manually labeled as *pro-disinformation* (n = 1,673) or *anti-disinformation* (n = 176). This dataset captures both virality potential and resistance within the Twitter ecosystem.
- **Russia-Ukraine War (Telegram):** Telegram messages were sourced from high-subscriber public channels aligned with *Pro-Kremlin* and *Pro-Ukraine* stances. Over *4.75 million messages spanning 120 days* were collected using automated web crawlers with topic-specific filters such as `"Donbas,"` `"NATO,"` `"invasion,"` `"neo-Nazi,"` `"Kyiv regime,"` and `"biolabs"`. Manual annotation was conducted by trained coders fluent in Russian and Ukrainian, with high inter-rater agreement (Cohen's $\kappa \geq 0.87$). This dataset reflects cross-border disinformation strategies and ideological framing.
- **Taiwan Election (TikTok):** Short videos were collected from TikTok between *January 13 and 27, 2024*, surrounding Taiwan's presidential election. We used a hybrid strategy combining *keyword-based crawling* (e.g., `"Taiwan election,"` `"disinformation,"` `"DPP,"` `"KMT,"` `"US-China-Taiwan"`) with *unsupervised topic clustering* to extract relevant narratives. Videos were annotated into *anti-disinformation* (n = 130) and *disinformation* (n = 58) based on content veracity, source type, and narra-

tive framing. This case highlights how algorithmically amplified short-form content can influence electoral integrity.

4   Model Analysis and Result

In this section, we conduct a qualitative analysis of the proposed SEDAZR model to better understand the dynamics of disinformation and anti-disinformation propagation in online networks. The analysis focuses on key dynamical properties such as the basic reproduction number $\mathcal{R}_0$ sensitivity analysis, existence and uniqueness of solutions, stability analysis, data fitting analysis, and numerical analysis and simulation.

4.1   Basic Reproduction Number, $\mathfrak{R}_0$

The basic reproduction number $\mathcal{R}_0$ measures the expected number of secondary disinformation cases generated by a single spreader in a fully susceptible network.

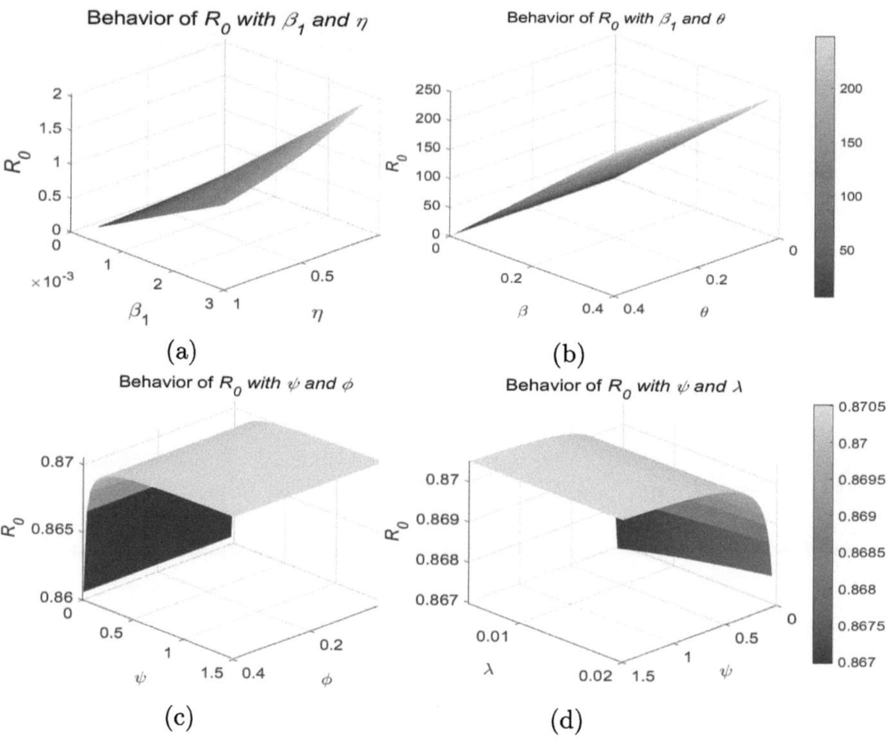

Fig. 2. Effect of $\mathfrak{R}_0$ on (a) η and β_1, (b) β_1 and θ, (c) ϕ and ψ, and (c) λ and ψ.

Using the next-generation matrix approach, $\mathcal{R}_0$ is derived from the infection-related compartments $E(t)$, $D(t)$, and $A(t)$, capturing both disinformation and anti-disinformation dynamics.

A simplified form is:

$$\mathcal{R}_0 = \frac{\beta_1}{\eta + \lambda + \psi} \left(\frac{\lambda}{\gamma_d + \kappa_d + \eta} + \frac{\psi}{\gamma_a + \kappa_a + \eta} \right)$$

Here, β_1 is the contact rate; λ, ψ, κ_d, and κ_a are transition rates; and γ_a, γ_d, η denote recovery and attrition. The condition $\mathcal{R}_0 > 1$ signals potential disinformation proliferation.

4.2   Sensitivity Analysis of $\mathcal{R}_0$

To identify the most influential parameters driving the spread of disinformation, we employed the Latin Hypercube Sampling (LHS) method combined with Partial Rank Correlation Coefficient (PRCC) analysis. This approach quantifies the sensitivity of the basic reproduction number $\mathcal{R}_0$ to model parameters, providing insights into which variables should be targeted to suppress disinformation.

The resulting PRCC values, summarized in Fig. 3, indicate the degree of monotonic influence each parameter exerts on $\mathcal{R}_0$. Parameters with high absolute PRCC values are most impactful.

Key Findings:

- β_1 (effective contact rate) exhibited the strongest positive correlation with $\mathcal{R}_0$, implying that reducing exposure to disinformation content significantly lowers disinformation spread.
- ψ and λ (transition rates from exposed to anti-/disinformation compartments) also had strong positive correlations, indicating the importance of early interventions post-exposure.

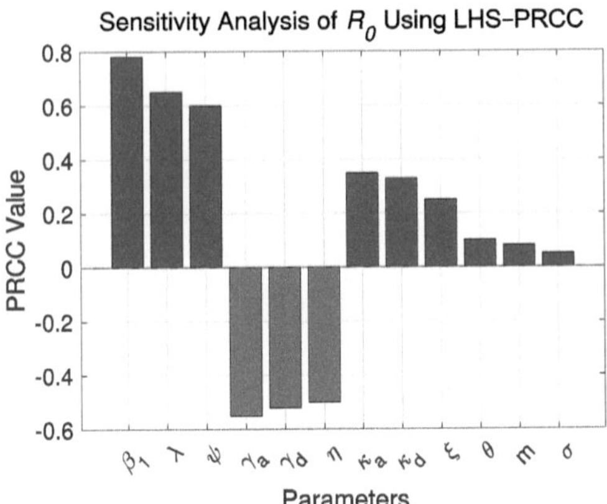

Fig. 3. Sensitivity of $\mathcal{R}_0$ of the online disinformation and anti-disinformation contagious.

- Recovery parameters γ_a, γ_d and user attrition rate η showed negative correlations with $\mathcal{R}_0$, suggesting that increased user resistance or disengagement mitigates spread.
- Parameters such as κ_a, κ_d, and ξ had moderate impacts, while others like m, θ, and σ were less influential.

These results highlight critical levers for disinformation control—most notably reducing contact/exposure, increasing recovery or skepticism, and enhancing anti-disinformation efforts. Hence these results give a clear response to our **RQ1**.

4.3   Existence and Uniqueness of Solution

To validate the well-posedness of the proposed fractal-fractional $SEDAZR$ model, we establish the existence and uniqueness of solutions using fixed-point theory in the context of non-integer order derivatives with fractal dimensions. The proposed model 1 has generalized form denoted as

$$
{}_{0}^{FFP}D_t^{\alpha,\beta}\mathcal{H} = \frac{\beta}{\Gamma(1-\alpha)} \int_0^t (t-s)^{-\alpha} s^{\beta-1} \mathcal{H} \, ds, \quad 0 < \alpha \le 1,\ 0 < \beta \le 1
$$

We transform the system into a Volterra-type integral equation:

$$
\mathcal{H}(t) = \mathcal{H}_0 + \frac{\beta}{\Gamma(\alpha)} \int_0^t (t-s)^{\alpha-1} s^{\beta-1} \Upsilon(\mathcal{H}(t)) \, ds
$$

where $\Upsilon(t) \in B$, a Banach space of continuous functions on $[0, T]$, and $\mathcal{H}$ is a nonlinear functional representing the model dynamics.

We show:

(i) Υ satisfies a Lipschitz condition: $\|\Upsilon(\mathcal{H}_1) - \Upsilon(\mathcal{H}_2)\| \le K\|\mathcal{H}_1 - \mathcal{H}_2\|$ with $K = \frac{\beta T^{\beta+\alpha-1}\mathcal{B}(\beta,\alpha)}{\Gamma(\alpha+1)} < 1$

(ii) The integral operator Υ is compact and continuous

(iii) $\Upsilon(\mathcal{H}) \subseteq B$ is uniformly bounded

Using conditions of Schauder's and Banach's fixed-point theorems, we conclude that there exists a unique continuous solution $\mathcal{H}$ to the system over $t \in [0, T]$. This confirms that the model is analytically consistent and suitable for further analysis. For analytical proof see [17] and [18]. From here we say our model is well-posed which answer **RQ2**.

4.4   Ulam-Hyers Stability

To assess the robustness of the proposed fractal-fractional model under perturbations, we investigate Ulam–Hyers stability using nonlinear functional analysis. This concept ensures that small deviations in initial conditions or parameters lead only to small deviations in the solution, thereby validating the model's reliability for numerical approximations.

The model is said to be Ulam–Hyers stable if for any approximate solution $\tilde{\mathcal{H}}(t)$ satisfying:

$$\left\| {}^{FFP}_{0} D^{\alpha,\beta}_{t} \tilde{\mathcal{H}}(t) - \mathcal{F}(t, \tilde{\mathcal{H}}(t)) \right\| \leq \epsilon,$$

there exists a true solution $\mathcal{H}(t)$ such that

$$\|\tilde{\mathcal{H}}(t) - \mathcal{H}(t)\| \leq C\epsilon, \quad \forall t \in [0, T],$$

where $C > 0$ is a constant dependent on the Lipschitz structure of the operator.

For analytic proof, see [15, 16] since we use the same approach, hence we omit the proof. The proof utilizes fixed-point theory, showing that the nonlinear operator defined by the model satisfies both Lipschitz continuity and contraction conditions within a Banach space. These ensure the existence of a unique fixed point that attracts all nearby approximate trajectories.

This result confirmed that the proposed system exhibits Ulam-Hyers stability, guaranteeing that the model's solutions are structurally stable under small perturbations, and hence suitable for numerical simulation.

4.5   Numerical Analysis and Simulation

To answer our **RQ3** and **RQ4**, we simulated the proposed fractal-fractional SEDAZR model using the Caputo derivative with a power-law kernel to capture memory effects and non-local dynamics in online disinformation ecosystems. The numerical approximation is carried out using an Adams-Bashforth scheme adapted for fractal-fractional systems.

Our analysis focuses on: (1) the influence of the fractal-fractional orders (α, β) on user transitions, and (2) the impact of the disinformation transmission rate (β_1) on compartmental behavior. In Fig. 4(a), the higher values of (α, β) lead to a faster reduction in the susceptible population, indicating quicker user engagement with disinformation. Lower values reflect stronger memory, delaying user conversion and mimicking content fatigue or selective attention. In Fig. 4(b)-(f), we observe that lower values of (α) and (β) correspond to slower growth across all compartments, indicating that stronger memory effects dampen user transitions. Specifically, the Exposed, Disinformed, Anti-disinformed, Skeptics, and Recovered populations grow more gradually when (α, β) are small. This suggests that users in high-memory environments engage more cautiously with both disinformation and counter-narratives. Overall, lower (α, β) values capture fewer users across all dynamic states, reflecting delayed response and reduced information spread. From a practical standpoint, memory-aware modeling offers actionable insights: network service providers can design recommender systems and mitigation strategies that incorporate user history, limit redundant exposure, and mitigate content virality—ultimately dampening the spread of both disinformation and anti-disinformation spread. From Fig. 5(b)-(f), we observe that increasing the disinformation transmission rate β_1 results in higher peaks across all compartments, except susceptible. This indicates that stronger transmission accelerates user transitions and expands the overall reach, resembling the viral nature of highly shareable or sensational disinformation. As disinformation spreads more aggressively, it also triggers faster counter-responses and a quicker rise in user skepticism.

4.6   Model Fitting and Parameter Estimation

To capture the dynamics of disinformation and anti-disinformation spread, precise parameter estimation is vital for predictive accuracy and effective intervention design. We adopted the *Non-Linear Least Squares Method (NLSM)* to estimate model parameters by minimizing the sum of squared errors (SSE) between observed data and model predictions. The error formula is defined as

$$\text{SSE} = \sum_{i=1}^{n} (y_i - f(x_i; \theta))^2$$

where y_i are observations, $f(x_i; \theta)$ are model outputs, and θ denotes the parameter vector.

This process tailors the model to platform-specific data, enabling strategic disinformation and anti-disinformation spread control. Figures in Fig. 6 illustrate how well the model fits observed disinformation and anti-disinformation data across different topics and platforms. In Fig. 4 a disinformation tweets show a sigmoidal growth pattern typical in social contagion, while Fig. 4 b anti-disinformation tweets exhibit a more linear and steady rise. We found anti-disinformation efforts tended to respond more consistently but perhaps less virally than disinformation. Figures 4 c and 4 d show two dynamics of disinformation exchange from different ideological groups. These figures exhibit more complex waves in disinformation propagation. And the last Figs. 4e and 4 f for the Taiwan election on TikTok have low error values, reflecting the effectiveness of model calibration even on short-video platforms.

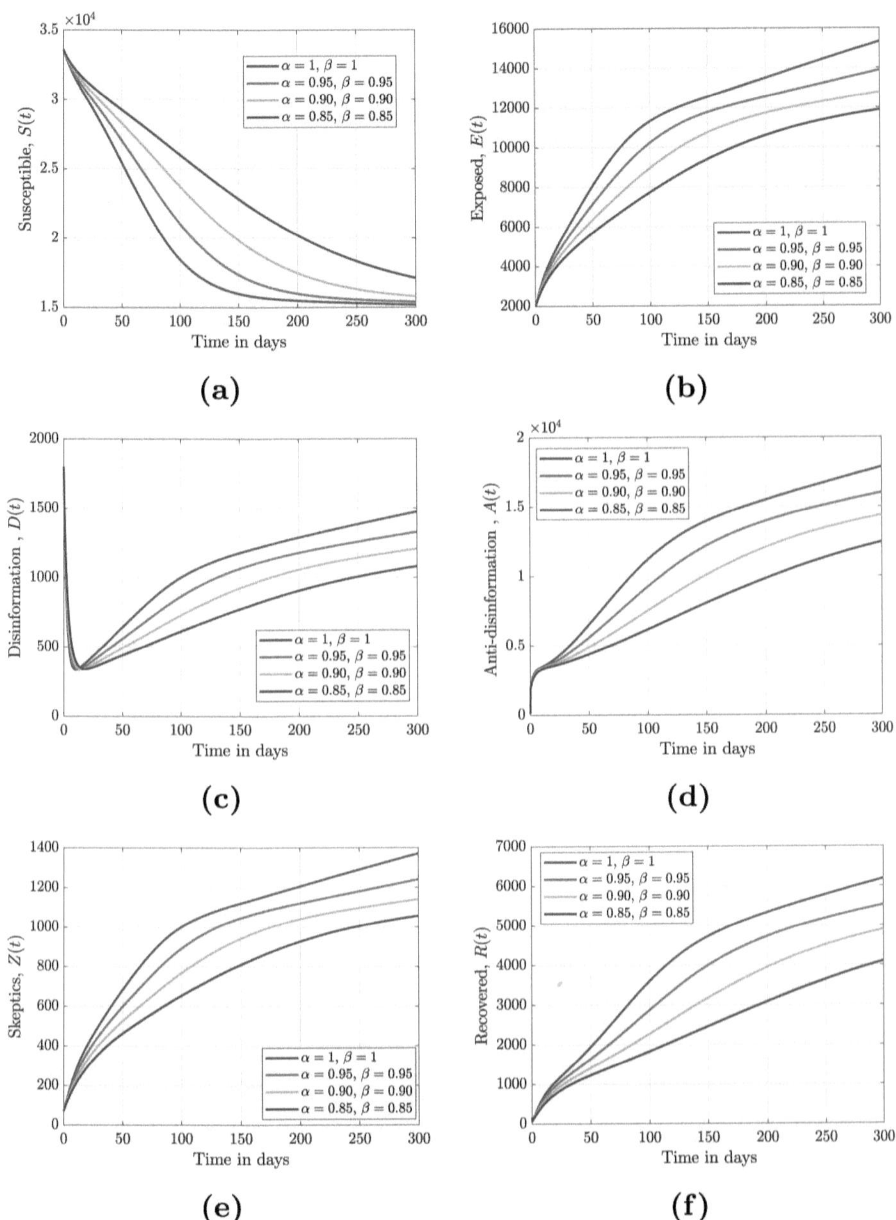

Fig. 4. Numerical trajectories of $SEIQR$ model under the Caputo fractal-fractional operator.

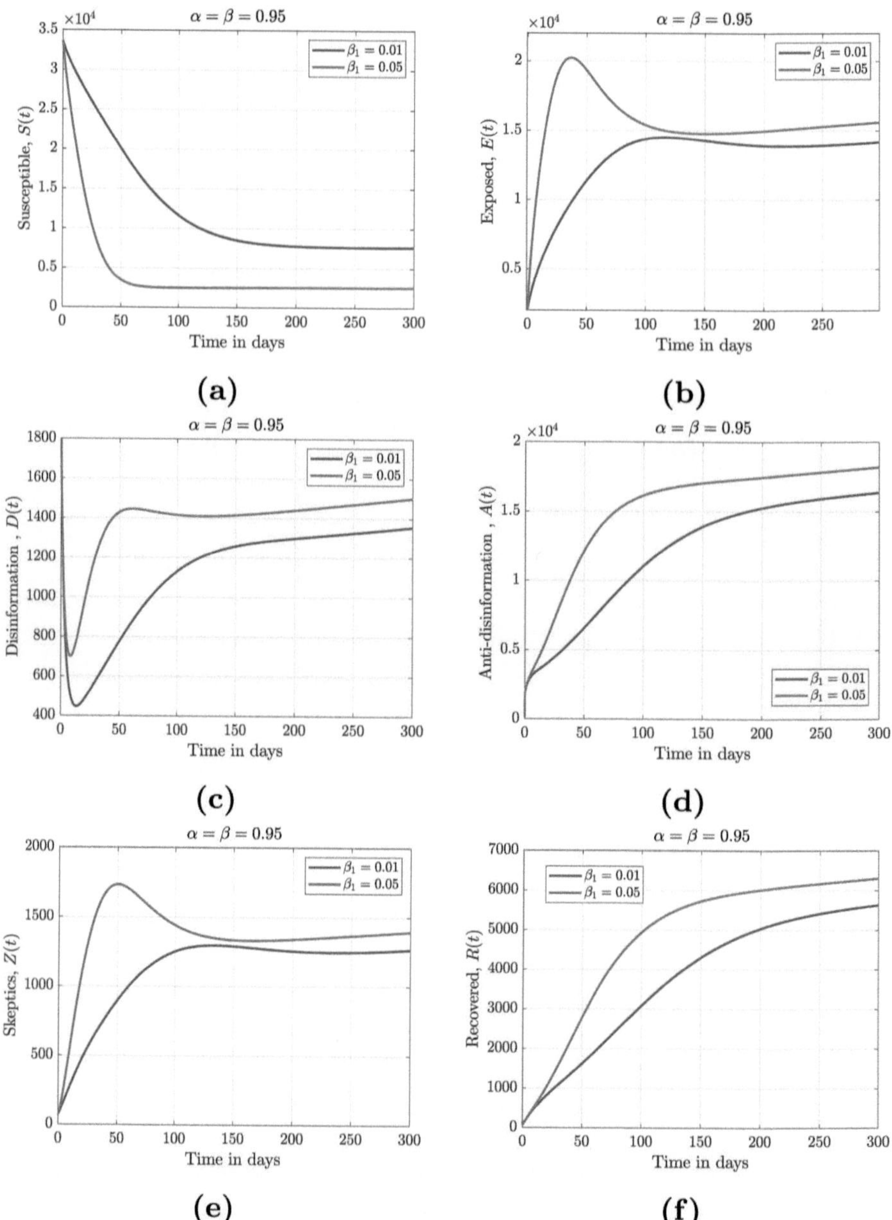

Fig. 5. Numerical trajectories of $SEDAZR$ model under the Caputo fractal-fractional operator with order and dimension ($\alpha = \beta = 0.95$) when one varies the rate of transmission.

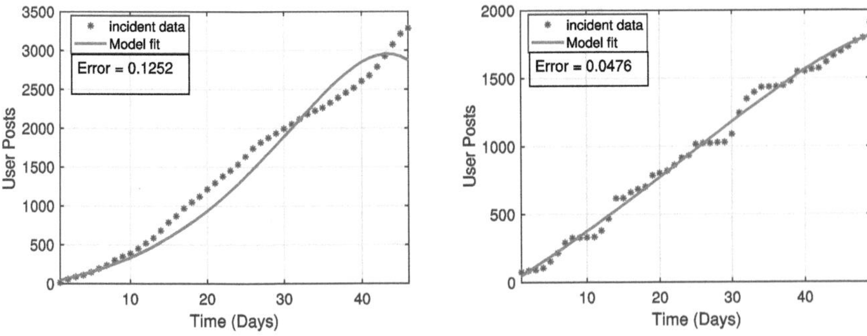

(a) Model fitting for users sharing disinformation tweets about
COVID-19 vaccine

(b) Model fitting for users sharing
Anti-disinformation tweets about
COVID-19 vaccine

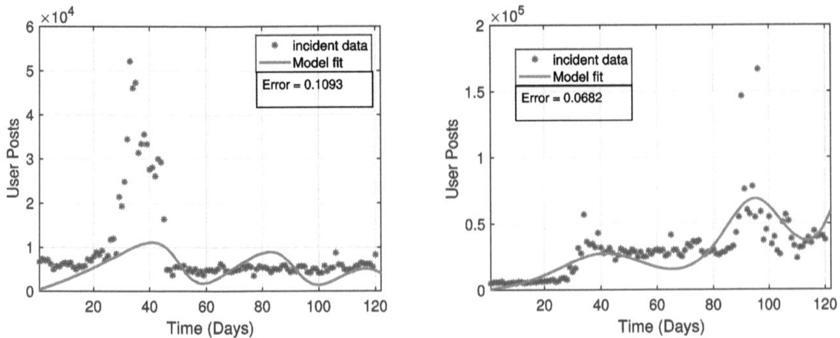

(c) Model fitting for users sharing
disinformation about Ukraine/Rus-
sia war on Telegram (Pro-Ukraine)

(d) Model fitting for users sharing
disinformation about Ukraine/Rus-
sia war on Telegram (Pro-Russia)

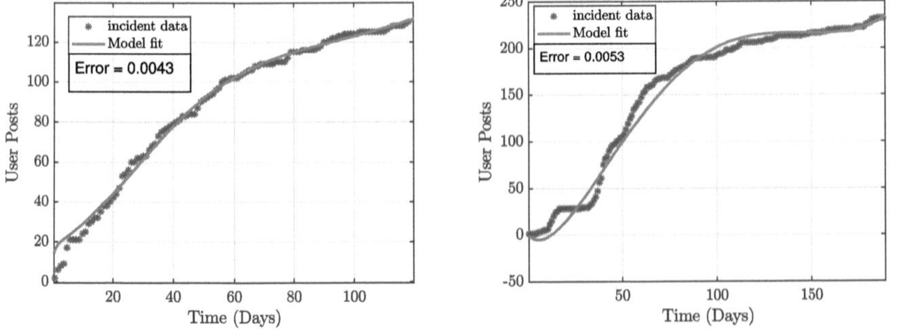

(e) Model fitting for users sharing disinformation content related
to Taiwan's election campaign on
TikTok

(f) Model fitting for users sharing
anti-disinformation content related
to Taiwan's election campaign on
TikTok.

Fig. 6. The $SEDAZR$ model fitted to disinformation and anti-disinformation posts on different platform.

5   Conclusion and Future Works

This study introduces a novel SEDAZR epidemiological model, enhanced with fractal-fractional operators, to understand the intertwined dynamics of disinformation and anti-disinformation campaigns on social media platforms. Through a rigorous framework incorporating data from Twitter, Telegram, and TikTok, the model successfully captures the temporal evolution and memory-dependent behaviors of users engaging with misleading or corrective narratives.

Key findings include the derivation of the basic reproduction number $\mathcal{R}_0$, which quantifies the spread potential of disinformation, and its sensitivity to key transmission and recovery parameters. The Ulam-Hyers stability and existence-uniqueness analysis affirm the model's robustness under perturbations. Numerical simulations demonstrate that both memory effects and transmission rates play crucial roles in shaping the spread dynamics. Model fitting across real-world case studies revealed strong alignment with empirical data, underscoring the model's applicability for platform-specific interventions.

Looking forward, future work will explore adaptive control strategies leveraging real-time data to dynamically adjust platform responses. Integration with agent-based modeling and reinforcement learning could enable scenario testing for disinformation mitigation policies. Additionally, extending the model to multi-platform interaction networks and incorporating user demographic and behavioral heterogeneity will offer more granular insights for combating the evolving landscape of digital disinformation.

Acknowledgements. This research is funded in part by the U.S. National Science Foundation (OIA-1946391, OIA-1920920), U.S. Office of the Under Secretary of Defense for Research and Engineering (FA9550-22-1-0332), U.S. Army Research Office (W911NF-23-1-0011, W911NF-24-1-0078, W911NF-25-1-0147), U.S. Office of Naval Research (N00014-21-1-2121, N00014-21-1-2765, N00014-22-1-2318), U.S. Air Force Research Laboratory, U.S. Defense Advanced Research Projects Agency, the Australian Department of Defense Strategic Policy Grants Program, Arkansas Research Alliance, the Jerry L. Maulden/Entergy Endowment, and the Donaghey Foundation at the University of Arkansas at Little Rock. Any opinions, findings, and conclusions or recommendations expressed in this material are those of the authors and do not necessarily reflect the views of the funding organizations. The researchers gratefully acknowledge the support.

References

1. Cinelli, M., Quattrociocchi, W., Galeazzi, A., et al.: The COVID-19 social media infodemic. Sci. Rep. **10**, 16598 (2020)
2. Wang, Y., et al.: Systematic literature review on the spread of health-related disinformation on social media. Soc. Sci. Med. **240**, 112552 (2019)
3. Cinelli, M., et al.: The echo chamber effect on social media. Proc. National Academy Sci. **118**(9) (2021)

4. Roth, Y., Achuthan, K.: Algorithmic amplification and the limits of content moderation. Brookings Institution TechStream (2021)
5. Nguyen, T.T., et al.: Echo chambers and information spread on social media: a case study on Telegram during geopolitical crises
6. Velásquez, N., et al.: Hate multiverse spreads malicious COVID-19 content online beyond individual platforms. Sci. Rep. **11**, 1–13 (2021)
7. Wilson, S.L., Wiysonge, C.: Social media and vaccine hesitancy. BMJ Glob. Health **5**(10), e004206 (2020)
8. Ballard, A.O., et al.: Stop the steal: tracking the rise of election disinformation narratives. Brookings Inst. (2021)
9. Vosoughi, S., et al.: The spread of true and false news online. Science **359**(6380), 1146–1151 (2018)
10. Wardle, C., Derakhshan, H.: Information disorder: toward an interdisciplinary framework for research and policy making. Council of Europe report, DGI(2017)09 (2017)
11. MediaWise: Helping people of all ages identify disinformation online. The Poynter Institute
12. United Nations: #ThinkBeforeYouShare Campaign
13. Twitter Transparency Center: Political content policy updates (2022)
14. Shu, K., Sliva, A., et al.: Fake news detection on social media: a data mining perspective. ACM SIGKDD Explorations Newsl **19**(1), 22–36 (2017)
15. Wang, L., Chen, X., et al.: Epidemic spreading on complex networks with general degree and weight distributions. Sci. Rep. **9**, 12520 (2019)
16. Tambuscio, M., et al.: Fact-checking effect on viral hoaxes: a model of disinformation spread in social networks. In: Proceedings of the 24th International Conference on World Wide Web (WWW) (2015)
17. Baleanu, D., et al.: On a fractional-order SIR epidemic model with Atangana-Baleanu derivatives. Chaos, Solitons Fractals **117**, 409–417 (2019)
18. Khan, M.A., et al.: A new fractal–fractional SEIR model with non-singular kernel: application to COVID-19 data. Results Phys. **21**, 103817 (2021)

From Inclusion to Contention: Analyzing DEI and "Woke" Narratives on Reddit

Marcelo Sartori Locatelli[1,3](✉), Arthur S. da Costa[2], Victor Thome[1], Marisa Vasconcelos[1], and Virgilio Almeida[1]

[1] Universidade Federal de Minas Gerais, 31270-901 Belo Horizonte, Brazil
`{locatellimarcelo,victor.thome,marisavasconcelos,virgilio}@dcc.ufmg.br`
[2] Universidade Estadual de Campinas, 13083–970 Campinas, Brazil
`atcosta@recod.unicamp.br`
[3] Max Planck Institute for Security and Privacy (MPISP), 44799 Bochum, Germany

Abstract. Diversity, Equity, and Inclusion (DEI) policies have recently become extremely controversial, with many companies vowing to end their support. This has led to mixed reactions online. This was intensified by the ongoing "woke" vs "anti-woke" culture war. Both groups defend and consume content that aligns with their ideologies. In this context, understanding the discourse surrounding these issues online is essential, as such movements have the potential to lead to real-world harm. For this reason, we conduct a large-scale study around the DEI and "woke" discussion on the Reddit platform from 2020–2024, finding that it has grown significantly during the studied period, spreading across a large variety of seemingly unrelated topics. Finally, we note that the discourse has become increasingly polarized, with a growing trend of toxicity and negative sentiments, coupled with changes in the meaning of the terms "woke" and DEI on the platform. These findings have important implications for public policy related to social issues.

Keywords: Culture War · Woke · Social Media · Toxicity · Topic Analysis

1 Introduction

Over the past decade, Diversity, Equity, and Inclusion (DEI) policies have been implemented with the goal of ensuring equal opportunities, fostering unbiased organizational practices, and cultivating a sense of belonging within institutions [17]. Despite evidence suggesting that such policies can be beneficial to overall company performance and innovation [13], DEI has become a highly controversial topic. The adoption of such policies has faced resistance from members of socially advantaged groups, who may perceive them as threatening their access to opportunities or being forced to adapt to unfamiliar values and expectations [15,29].

This kind of discourse has closely intertwined with the rise of the anti-"woke" movement, which intensified during the lead-up to the 2024 U.S. Presidential Election. DEI initiatives became prominent targets of Donald Trump's anti-'woke' stance during and after his campaign[1].

Originally a slang term for awareness of social injustice, "woke" has since been co-opted as a catch-all for progressive or leftist ideologies, including DEI [34]. The polarization between "woke" and anti-"woke" ideologies has contributed to what many describe as a *culture war* [4,8,32], marked by ideological clashes, incivility, and a deepening "us-versus-them" mentality.

These dynamics are particularly visible on social media platforms. Conspiracy theories such as the so-called "woke agenda" have proliferated across different domains (e.g., video games [20]), often fueling radicalization, harassment, and hate speech. Reddit plays a central role in this ecosystem. Its support for long-form posts, structured subreddit communities, and community-driven moderation enables close observation of how controversial discussions evolve organically over time. Moreover, Reddit has shown real-world influence: the 2021 U.S. Capitol invasion was, partially, organized through alt-right Reddit communities [22]. Given its significance, it is essential to investigate not only *what* is discussed on Reddit, but also *how* it is discussed, especially when it comes to politically charged terms like "woke" and "DEI".

In light of these developments, this paper examines how the meanings and uses of terms like "woke" and "DEI" have changed over time on Reddit, and what these shifts reveal about broader social and political trends. In particular, "woke" appears to have shifted in meaning around 2020, from promoting ideas of social justice and equality to becoming a pejorative label associated with toxic discourse and political radicalization [30]. Reddit serves as a compelling case study for analyzing this transformation, given its well-documented role in hosting and fostering radical and conspiratorial communities [19].

To that end, this paper explores the evolution of "woke" and DEI-related discourse on Reddit from 2020 to 2024. In particular, we address the following research questions:

- **RQ1:** How was the discourse around DEI policies and "woke" amplified and transformed over time?
- **RQ2:** To what extent has the tone around the DEI and woke discussion changed over time on Reddit?
- **RQ3:** What kinds of topics and themes are associated with DEI and "woke" on Reddit?

This paper contributes to ongoing debates about the social-political impact of online platforms. It provides empirical evidence on how online discourse around social justice, specifically DEI and "woke", has evolved in both tone and toxicity. We show how digital spaces can influence, sometimes distort, and even radicalize these conversations. These findings have important implications for content

---

[1] https://www.theguardian.com/commentisfree/2025/mar/26/donald-trump-war-on-woke-science-diversity.

moderation, platform governance, and the development of public policies that address online radicalization and foster healthier discussions about social issues.

2   Related Work

2.1   Computational Approaches to Discourse Analysis

Recent methodological advances have enabled increasingly sophisticated analyses of large-scale social media discourse. Topic modeling approaches [3] have long been applied to identify thematic patterns in discussions of controversial social issues. More recently, neural network-based methods, such as BERTopic [11] and automatic hate speech detection techniques [31], have enabled more nuanced semantic analyses of the short, context-dependent texts typical of social media platforms. These techniques allow researchers to capture subtle shifts in meaning and tone over time.

By leveraging such tools, researchers have tackled challenging problems in computational social science. For instance, Locatelli *et al.* [21] identified highly politicized topics on YouTube, while Magno *et al.* [23] used word embeddings to infer political and social biases in online behavior, showing strong correlations between online discourse and offline cultural values such as religiosity.

These works highlight the utility of computational methods for tracking the evolution of politically charged language, around topics like DEI and "woke", particularly on platforms like Reddit, where decentralized moderation leads to highly heterogeneous discourse norms across communities.

2.2   Radicalization on Social Media

Social media ecosystems often foster ideological polarization through phenomena such as echo chambers [5] and filter bubbles [6], which reinforce in-group narratives. This kind of environment can contribute to a gradual process of radicalization, as observed by Ribeiro et al. [28] on YouTube, where recommendation systems tend to push users toward increasingly extreme content. On Reddit, Klein *et al.* [19] show that changes in language use can serve as early indicators of conspiratorial thinking and ideological shifts. These shifts are often accompanied by semantic shifts, where users progressively adopt and reshape the meanings of specific terms to fit emergent ideologies and group identities.

For example, Assenmacher *et al.* [2] show how the term "bot" evolves from referring to an AI or automated system to being associated with trolls or political actors, and eventually becomes a dehumanizing label used as an insult. A similar shift can be observed in the terms related to DEI and "woke" discourses, which have gradually evolved from promoting public good to becoming focal points in a ongoing culture war, where opposing viewpoints are often de-legitimized [4].

Despite growing attention to these trends in public discourse, including extensive media coverage in the U.S. and around the world, few studies have focused specifically on tracing how the meanings of DEI and "woke" have changed over time in large-scale social media data. One exception is Gomez *et al.* [10], who show how terms like "woke" and "cancel" have become mainstays for criticizing ads that fail to meet user expectations. Another example is Letzi *et al.* [20], who present a case study of the *r/thelastofus2* subreddit, evidencing how political agendas and marketing failures can radicalize online communities, especially when users perceive their values as under threat, such as the "war on woke". They report evidence of harassment and hate speech as outcomes of this radicalization.

Our work builds on and extends these previous studies by analyzing Reddit as a whole, rather than focusing on isolated communities or specific events. To the best of our knowledge, this is the first large-scale study to investigate the broader dynamics of DEI and "woke" discourses across Reddit platform.

3   Methodology

This section describes our dataset and the methods used to analyze the data.

3.1   Reddit Data

We collected all Reddit comments posted between 2020 and 2024 using the Pushshift Data Dumps, available via Academic Torrents [33]. To identify content relevant to our study, we applied a keyword-based filter to extract all comments containing the terms "Woke" or "DEI". Since these terms can appear in contexts unrelated to the culture wars or political debates–e.g., *dei* is common in Italian, Portuguese, and Latin, and *woke* is frequently used as a verb (e.g., "woke up")–we implemented two additional filtering steps. First, we used a fastText language classifier [18] , a tool for identifying the language of text, to ensure that only English-language comments were retained. Next, we employed part-of-speech (POS) tagging [12] to filter out instances where "woke" was used as a verb (e.g., 'woke up'). These filtering steps aimed to isolate the use of these terms in the cultural and political sense relevant for our analysis. For each selected comment, we also collected the associated Reddit post.

Our final dataset comprises approximately 1.47 million comments containing the term "woke" and over 400,000 containing "DEI". About 10,000 comments contain both terms. These comments were posted by 675,000 and 211,000 unique users, across 890,188 and 202,918 unique Reddit posts, respectively, spanning 30,115 subreddits.

3.2   Semantic Shift of Terms Over Time

Word embeddings capture semantic relationships by modeling the proximity between terms in a vector space. Inspired by Garg *et al.* work [9], we track the evolution of the meanings of "DEI" and "woke" to identify when these terms began acquiring more politicized or controversial connotations. For that, we trained a separate Word2Vec model for each semester of data using Gensim's implementation[2], with the CBOW architecture and negative sampling. For each

---

[2] https://radimrehurek.com/gensim/models/word2vec.html.

period, we retrieved the top terms closest to "DEI" and "woke" using cosine similarity. To improve robustness, we trained five models per time slice with different random seeds and only retained words consistently appearing across all five models, following the procedure described in [2].

3.3 Sentiment and Toxicity Analysis

To assess how "DEI" and "woke" are emotionally and morally framed, we analyzed both sentiment (i.e., positive or negative) and the presence of hate or discriminatory language (i.e., toxicity). For sentiment analysis, we employed VADER [14], a rule-based model optimized for social media texts. For toxicity detection, we applied a RoBERTa model fine-tuned for multiclass hate speech classification [1], which assigns each comment to one of the following classes: sexism, racism, disability, sexual orientation, religion, other, or not hate[3].

3.4 Topic Modeling with BERTopic

To uncover the main themes associated with "DEI" and "woke" on Reddit, we applied topic modeling using BERTopic [11], which combines transformer-based embeddings with clustering techniques to generate interpretable topics.

We first encoded each comment using Sentence-BERT [27]. Sentence-BERT is a model designed to capture semantic content in short texts, making it particularly effective for analyzing Reddit comments. We then applied UMAP for dimensionality reduction, followed by HDBSCAN to cluster the resulting embeddings into semantically coherent groups.

4 Reddit Discussions of "DEI" and "Woke": Key Trends

In this section, we present the main findings of our analysis of Reddit discussions involving the terms "DEI" and "woke" between 2020 and 2024. We first describe the volume and distribution of relevant comments in the broader context of Reddit activity, followed by an analysis of the terms' semantic evolution, sentiment trends, and dominant conversation topics.

4.1 Presence of "DEI" and "Woke"

Reddit has experienced substantial growth in recent years, reporting 213 million daily users in 2022 and reaching 379 million by the end of 2024. In 2023, Reddit users generated 2.8 billion comments across 469 million posts[4]. This expansion has amplified discussions around "woke" and "DEI", both of which have gained increasing visibility since 2020.

Figure 1 illustrates the growth in the frequency of these terms in Reddit comments over time. Both have seen a significant rise in usage, with mentions

---

[3] https://huggingface.co/cardiffnlp/twitter-roberta-base-hate-multiclass-latest.
[4] https://backlinko.com/reddit-users.

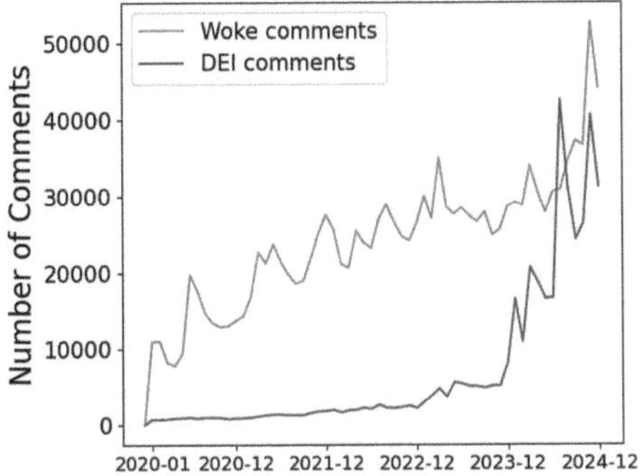

Fig. 1. Frequency of "woke" and "DEI" in Reddit comments from 2020 to 2024.

of "DEI" more than quadrupling from early 2023 to the end of 2024. Albeit less dramatic, usage of "woke" has also significantly increased, particularly during 2024. This surge may be partially attributed to the anti-DEI discourse promoted during Donald Trump's campaign [16]. Importantly, this trend cannot be explained solely by Reddit's overall growth, as the total number of comments posted annually has remained relatively stable (see footnote 7).

Table 1 presents the 15 subreddits with the highest number of comments mentioning either "woke" or "DEI". Together, these communities account for approximately 18% of all such comments. Although many of the subreddits are difficult to categorize under a single theme, most focus on gaming, political discussions, political memes, or political and cultural figures. A few subreddits present clear ideological leanings, for instance, *r/Conservative* and *r/JoeRogan* align with right-wing perspectives, whereas *r/stupidpol* and *r/Gamingcirclejerk* tend to reflect left-leaning or liberal viewpoints. Others, such as *r/AskReddit*, *r/politics*, and *r/PoliticalCompassMemes*, have more ideologically diverse or ambiguous user bases, requiring closer contextual interpretation. This distribution suggests that conversations about "woke" and "DEI" are not confined to ideologically homogeneous spaces, but are instead dispersed across a wide range of Reddit communities.

Table 1. Top 15 subreddits by number of comments mentioning "woke" or "DEI".

Rank, Subreddit, Term frequency								
1	r/KotakuInAction	37,803	6	r/Gamingcirclejerk	25,373	11	r/conspiracy	14,553
2	r/politics	33,604	7	r/facepalm	24,174	12	r/JoeRogan	13,582
3	r/AskReddit	33,384	8	r/neoliberal	22,863	13	r/JordanPeterson	13,488
4	r/Conservative	26,943	9	r/stupidpol	21,528	14	r/Asmongold	12,751
5	r/PoliticalCompassMemes	26,194	10	r/WhitePeopleTwitter	20,903	15	r/samharris	12,259

Table 2. Top 15 words closest to "DEI" in the embedding space over time (2020–2024). Over the years, an increasing number of these terms reflect negative or culture war-related connotations[7] (highlighted in red), while the presence of positive or descriptive associations (in blue) remains relatively stable. Notably, the term "woke" emerges as semantically close to "DEI" in the second half of 2022, making a shift in the discourse as the two terms become increasingly mixed.

Period	Words
2020-01 – 2020-06	really, literally, work, also, one, way, something, think, another, things, like, newsweek, still, actually, even
2020-07 – 2020-12	one, thing, also, really, like, actually, everything, probably, gt, different, still, never, something, good, always
2021-01 – 2021-06	really, think, company, manager, good, always, team, school, actually, definitely, sometimes, one, ok, thing, bad
2021-07 – 2021-12	diversity, one, maybe, really, anyway, actual, actually, also, company, larger, whole, hr, place, fair, well
2022-01 – 2022-06	diversity, actually, company, one, really, good, also, new, basically, shitty, workplace, usually, magnum, hr, performative
2022-07 – 2022-12	diversity, really, hr, also, company, work, honestly, woke, salary, performative, university, specific, leadership, rxx, however
2023-01 – 2023-06	diversity, hr, mandatory, antiracism, leadership, inclusivity, bloated, woke, wasteful, ideological, outreach, actually, company, diverse, marketing
2023-07 – 2023-12	diversity, hr, woke, actually, implemented, pr, diverse, company, performative, hiring, corporate, exclusionary, equity, corporations, companies
2024-01 – 2024-06	diversity, inclusivity, esg, corporate, woke, defection, sbi, superfluous, hr, dinapoli, aa, reaffirms, wokeness, inclusion, disney
2024-07 – 2024-12	diversity, inclusivity, woke, rbl, sbi, sweetbabyinc, mcdaniels, tokenism, performative, wokeness, grady, esg, natalism, theee, lspd

4.2 Semantic Evolution of "Woke" and "DEI"

To explore how the meanings of the terms "DEI" and "woke" evolved over time on Reddit, we analyzed their semantic contexts using word embeddings trained on data from each semester between 2020 and 2024. Table 2 shows the top 15 terms closest to "DEI" in the embedding space for each period. Words in blue are classified as descriptive or positive, while those in red are negative or associated with criticism and polarization.

Table 3. Top 15 words closest to "woke" in the embedding space over time (2020–2024). Early associations (2020) reveal a consistent link to negative and critical terms, suggesting cultural critique related to 'cancel culture' and the 'social justice warriors' (SJWs). As time progressed, the number of political terms increased (left-leaning terms highlighted in blue, right-leaning in red), suggesting the growing politicization of "woke-ness".

Period	Words
2020-01 − 2020-06	pc, sjw, insufferable, annoying, progressive, popular, cancel, trendy, pretentious, hardcore, dumb, obnoxious, pious, cringy, retarded
2020-07 − 2020-12	pc, sjw, progressive, regressive, crazy, cancel, annoying, irritating, hysterical, pretentious, hypocritical, lefty, wokie, retarded, popular
2021-01 − 2021-06	pc, sjw, progressive, cancel, radical, annoying, braindead, leftist, crazy, gullible, hysterical, rightoid, performative, hypocritical, wokescold
2021-07 − 2021-12	pc, sjw, progressive, cancel, leftist, crazy, insufferable, obnoxious, butthurt, liberal, radlib, trendy, vaxer, braindead, maga
2022-01 − 2022-06	pc, sjw, leftist, progressive, reactionary, radical, cancel, annoying, hysterical, pandering, lib, liberal, sjws, mainstream, nowadays
2022-07 − 2022-12	pc, sjw, progressive, leftist, antiwoke, rightwing, pretentious, stupid, annoying, cancel, reactionary, liberal, radical, crazy, mainstream
2023-01 − 2023-06	pc, sjw, progressive, liberal, wokeness, leftist, antiwoke, radical, cancel, nowadays, stupid, reactionary, chickenshit, regressive, dumb
2023-07 − 2023-12	pc, sjw, leftist, progressive, liberal, wokeness, pandering, braindead, radical, stupid, reactionary, nowadays, reeee, crazy, cancel
2024-01 − 2024-06	sjw, progressive, wokeness, pc, antiwoke, leftist, reactionary, stupid, liberal, radical, dei, annoying, wokism, cancel, racist
2024-07 − 2024-12	sjw, pc, wokeness, dei, progressive, stupid, vaxxer, antiwoke, crazy, semitic, vaxxers, natalism, feminazi, annoying, vaxx

In the early stages (2020–2021), the terms surrounding "DEI" were largely generic or neutral—words like *really*, *also*, *one*, and *thing* dominated, suggesting an ambiguous or emotionally neutral context. Starting in mid-2021, we observe the emergence of terms more explicitly linked to workplace settings, such as *company*, *manager*, *hr*, and *team*. This indicates that "DEI" discussions increasingly occurred in professional or organizational contexts. By early 2022, a noticeable shift emerges: terms with negative or culture war-related connotations, like *per-*

formative, *shitty*, and eventually *woke* itself, begin to appear. From this point on, "woke" becomes one of the terms most closely associated with "DEI", revealing a convergence likely shaped by the growing political and cultural polarization.

This trend intensifies through 2023 and 2024, with increasingly critical terms such as *bloated, wasteful, superfluous, tokenism*, and *exclusionary* becoming more frequent. However, positive associations like *diversity, inclusivity*, and *equity* persist, revealing a semantic tension in which "DEI" is simultaneously framed in idealistic and critical terms.

A similar trend is visible for the term "woke", as shown in Table 3. However, unlike "DEI", "woke" has been consistently associated with negative and critical terms since 2020, including *crazy* and *annoying*. Still, the broader semantic field around "woke" has shifted in meaningfully over time. In fact, during 2020, although predominantly negative, the associated terms reflect critiques of *cancel culture* [25] and the so-called "Social Justice Warriors" [26], with less direct political engagement. Terms like *insufferable, annoying*, and *cancel* signal early cultural criticisms that align with broader debates about political correctness. These critiques, however, remain inherently political, reflecting societal divisions and ideological fault lines [35].

From 2021 onward, and more clearly throughout 2022, the semantic field surrounding "woke" incorporates more politically charged terms. A noticeable shift begins mid-2021, with terms like *leftist* and *wokescold* gaining prominence, indicating the growing politicization of "woke". By this stage, the term is used not only pejoratively, but also as a marker in ideological debates. This trend intensifies from late 2022 through 2024, with the emergence of both left-leaning labels (e.g., *progressive, lib, leftist*) and right-leaning ones (e.g., *antiwoke, maga, rightwing*). The coexistence of these opposing labels suggests that "woke" has become a central term in polarized political discussions, especially within the culture war. In the most recent period (2024-01 to 2024-06), terms like *racist* emerge among the closest associations, reflecting intensified debates on racial justice and the growing conflation of "woke" discourse with accusations of racism or performative activism [24].

Interestingly, the top terms associated with both "woke" and "DEI" reveal the multifaceted and diffuse nature of the culture war discourse. This discourse spans a range of seemingly unrelated topics from video games (*sweetbabyinc*) to politics (*liberal, rightwing*), feminism (*feminazi*), racism (*racist*), religion (*semitic*), and public health (*vaxxer*). Understanding how this discourse is structured is crucial for identifying and mitigating the potential harms it may generate. Moreover, the wide thematic range of these associations indicates that the culture war is no longer confined to specific online niches, but has become pervasive across the entire platform, as further evidenced by the high number of unique subreddits where these terms appear (Sect. 3.1).

These analyses suggest that while "DEI" initially appeared in more neutral or administrative contexts, and "woke" once referred to social awareness, both terms have gradually acquired more ideological and critical meanings. This semantic shift reflects broader social and political tensions present in online discussions.

4.3   Emotions and Hostility in Reddit Discussions

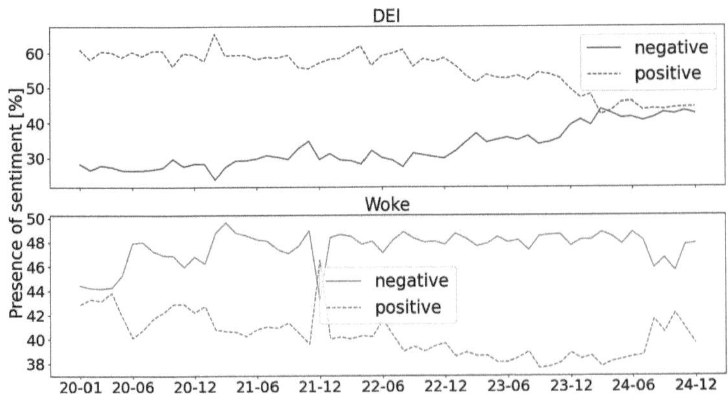

Fig. 2. Sentiment presence for "woke" and "DEI" comments over time.

Alongside the semantic analysis, trends in sentiment and hostility provide valuable insights into how "woke" and "DEI" are socially perceived. Figure 2 shows the evolution of sentiment in comments mentioning these terms. As early as 2020, "DEI" was predominantly associated with positive sentiment, while "woke" already carried negative connotations. Over time, positive sentiment declined for both terms. By 2024, "DEI" had approached neutrality, while "woke" had become increasingly negatively charged.

Hostility toward both terms follows a similar trajectory. Figure 3 shows the presence of different types of hate speech in comments. On average, hateful content accounts for about 1% of all comments analyzed per month. For "DEI", the rise in hostility aligns with the growth in comment volume and negative sentiment. A spike in sexist language in the second half of 2020 stands out and may be related to changes in policies or public criticism of DEI initiatives, potentially influenced by statements from political figures like Donald Trump during his administration[8].

Toxicity in discussions surrounding "woke" reflects overall sentiment trends, starting at already high levels and continuing to rise over time. For both terms, hostile comments are primarily concentrated in two categories: sexism and racism. This suggests that discussions involving these terms are often embedded in broader debates around identity politics and social justice.

These patterns complement the semantic shifts described in Sect. 4.2. In particular, the decline in positive sentiment toward "DEI" corresponds with its transformation into a controversial and even vilified concept, reaching peak hostility in 2024. In contrast, "woke" has maintained mostly negative sentiment since 2020, with growing opposition over time. Combined with previous analyses of

---

[8] https://www.npr.org/2020/09/17/914127266.

co-occurring terms and contexts, these findings suggest that "woke" and "DEI" have increasingly been weaponized, not just as descriptive terms, but as emotionally and ideologically charged labels used to discredit individuals, actions, or institutions.

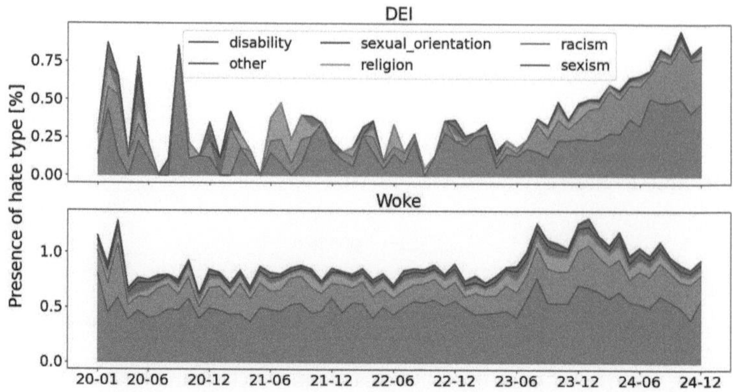

Fig. 3. Types of hate speech present in "woke" and "DEI" comments over time.

4.4 Key Themes in "Woke" and "DEI" Debates

(a) UMAP projection of topic clusters from Reddit posts mentioning "DEI".

(b) UMAP projection of topic clusters from Reddit posts mentioning "woke".

Fig. 4. UMAP projection of Reddit topic clusters for "DEI" and "woke".

As seen in Sect. 4.1, discussions around "DEI" and "woke" are widespread on Reddit and span multiple ideological perspectives. Topic analysis helps identify the dominant themes associated with these terms, allowing us to quantify their diversity and breadth of usage. Based on semantic similarity, we manually grouped related topics into "semantic bubbles" that aggregate the overall meanings of thematically connected clusters. Figures 4 a and 4 b show reduced embeddings generated by BERTopic, using posts that mention "DEI" and "woke", respectively. A total of 164 topics were identified for "DEI" and 301 for "woke".

In the "DEI" figure, a group of topics in the lower-left corner relates to Latin and Italy contexts, illustrating how the term "DEI" may appear in other languages or in unrelated religious discourses. Nearby, discussions about tourism in Italy also emerge. This is the only data segment without any political connotation, and it represents a small portion of our dataset (approximately 5%).

The remaining clusters highlight the diverse environments where "DEI" discourse permeates. Notably, the original use of "DEI" to denote inclusion-focused hiring policies appears in the top-right cluster. More recent topics, aligned with the semantic shifts discussed in Sect. 4.2, are reflected in other areas. For instance, the Entertainment cluster captures 2024 trends that frame "DEI" negatively in video games and television. One highlighted case is Dragon Age: The Veilguard, which faced criticism from the gaming community, accusing the game of being "woke" and overly "DEI"[9]. This reinforces previous findings that "DEI" has become a subclass of "woke" and often serves as a negative label. This intercession in the Entertainment domain is also visible in the "woke" clusters, with overlapping references to companies such as Ubisoft and Marvel.

The "woke" clusters follow a pattern similar to those observed for "DEI", with discussions centered on entertainment, social media, and politics, highlighting how deeply embedded the term has become in public discourse. Political topics are consistent across both terms, with frequent mentions of figures like Trump, Kamala Harris, and Elon Musk, reflecting how "woke" and "DEI" have both acquired political connotations. However, discussions involving "woke" cover a wider range of specific issues, such as *Roe v. Wade* and the *Joe Rogan* podcast. This is likely due to the term's broader and longer-standing usage on the platform.

Additionally, near the center of Fig. 4 b, we observe instances of "woke" used as a verb rather than an adjective, which falls outside the scope of our analysis. This represents a small portion of noise in our dataset (less than 1%).

5   Conclusion

During the 2024 American election, the culture war surrounding "DEI" policies and the "woke"/ anti-"woke" movements were brought to the forefront, fueled by then-candidate and now President Trump's vows to end "wokeness", in contrast to the more favorable views by Biden and Kamala Harris. This issue served as yet another point of division between Republicans and Democrats. However, it did not emerge from nowhere, as the topic had already been gaining traction on social media, influencing a wide range of communities, from those centered on politics to those focused on memes.

To better understand how the "woke" culture war has taken shape, we analyzed discussions around "woke" and "DEI" on Reddit from 2020 to 2024. We

---

[9] https://knowyourmeme.com/memes/events/dragon-age-the-veilguard-reviews-controversy.

found that mentions of these terms increased rapidly over the years, becoming two and five times more frequent by the end of the period, respectively, far surpassing Reddit's overall growth. Furthermore, the tone of the discourse has shifted, with both terms increasingly associated with negative and political connotations, especially after 2022. This shift was accompanied by a rise in negativity and toxicity – particularly racism and sexism – suggesting that these topics have become more controversial and polarized. Our findings highlight some of the potential harms of online discussions as they become politicized.

Gaming subreddits offer a compelling example of how culture wars can emerge in seemingly non-political spaces. Echoing the *Gamergate* scandal [7], discussions across various subreddits reveal a persistent tug-of-war between groups resistant to change and those advocating for greater inclusion. With each new game perceived as "woke" or anti-"woke", design choices are often met with criticism, sometimes grounded, but frequently radicalized, as seen by the controversies surrounding "The Last of Us 2" [20] and, more recently, "Dragon Age: The Veilguard".

Although we explored the broad landscape of the "woke" culture war on Reddit, this work focuses mostly on the linguistic and discursive aspects of the phenomenon. Understanding how users begin engaging in such debates and which communities are more prone to radicalization remain important directions for future research.

Limitations. While our study provides a analysis of DEI and "woke" discourse on Reddit, there are some limitations that must be acknowledged. Our reliance on keywords,"DEI" and "woke", for data collection risks both over- and under-inclusion. While we attempt to mitigate some of that by using part-of-speech tagging to reduce noise, it is still possible that relevant content was omitted or that non-political uses were included, especially in edge cases. By focusing on Reddit, we neglect to explore the discourse on other platforms which could be significantly different depending on demographic factors, moderation, etc.

Acknowledgement. This work was partially funded by CNPq, CAPES, FAPEMIG, and IAIA - INCT on AI. We appreciate Recod.AI for providing computational and physical infrastructure.

References

1. Antypas, D., Camacho-Collados, J.: Robust hate speech detection in social media: a cross-dataset empirical evaluation (2023)
2. Assenmacher, D., Fröhling, L., Wagner, C.: You are a bot!-studying the development of bot accusations on twitter. In: Proc. of the ICWSM., vol. 18, pp. 113–125 (2024)
3. Blei, D.M., Ng, A.Y., Jordan, M.I.: Latent dirichlet allocation. J. Mach. Learn.: Res. **3**(Jan), 993–1022 (2003)
4. Cammaerts, B.: The abnormalisation of social justice: the 'anti-woke culture war'discourse in the UK. Discourse Soc. **33**(6), 730–743 (2022)

5. Cinelli, M., De Francisci Morales, G., Galeazzi, A., Quattrociocchi, W., Starnini, M.: The echo chamber effect on social media. PNAS **118**(9), e2023301118 (2021)

6. Conover, M., Ratkiewicz, J., Francisco, M., Gonçalves, B., Menczer, F., Flammini, A.: Political polarization on twitter. In: Proc. of the ICWSM. vol. 5, pp. 89–96 (2011)

7. Dewey, C.: The only guide to gamergate you will ever need to read. The Washington Post **14** (2014)

8. Duffy, B., Gottfried, G., May, G., Hewlett, K., Skinner, G.: Woke vs anti-woke? culture war divisions and politics (2023)

9. Garg, N., Schiebinger, L., Jurafsky, D., Zou, J.: Word embeddings quantify 100 years of gender and ethnic stereotypes. PNAS **115**(16), E3635–E3644 (2018)

10. Gomez-Mejia, G.: Fail, clickbait, cringe, cancel, woke": vernacular criticisms of digital advertising in social media platforms. In: Social Computing and Social Media. Participation, User Experience, Consumer Experience, and Applications of Social Computing, pp. 309–324. Springer (2020)

11. Grootendorst, M.: Bertopic: neural topic modeling with a class-based tf-idf procedure. arXiv preprint arXiv:2203.05794 (2022)

12. Honnibal, M., Montani, I., Van Landeghem, S., Boyd, A., et al.: Spacy: industrial-strength natural language processing in python (2020)

13. Hunt, V., Layton, D., Prince, S., et al.: Diversity matters. McKinsey & Company **1**(1), 15–29 (2015)

14. Hutto, C., Gilbert, E.: Vader: a parsimonious rule-based model for sentiment analysis of social media text. In: Proc. of the ICWSM. vol. 8, pp. 216–225 (2014)

15. Iyer, A.: Understanding advantaged groups' opposition to diversity, equity, and inclusion (DEI) policies: the role of perceived threat. Soc. Personality Psychol. Compass **16**(5), e12666 (2022)

16. Jessica, G.: Trump vows to crush 'anti-white' racism, DEI if he wins 2024 election. USA Today (2024). https://www.usatoday.com/story/money/2024/05/01/donald-trump-anti-white-racism-dei/73528246007/, Accessed 18 Apr 2025

17. Jora, R.B., Sodhi, K.K., Mittal, P., Saxena, P.: Role of artificial intelligence (AI) in meeting diversity, equality and inclusion (DEI) goals. In: ICACCS 2022. vol. 1, pp. 1687–1690. IEEE (2022)

18. Joulin, A., Grave, E., Bojanowski, P., Mikolov, T.: Bag of tricks for efficient text classification. arXiv preprint arXiv:1607.01759 (2016)

19. Klein, C., Clutton, P., Dunn, A.G.: Pathways to conspiracy: the social and linguistic precursors of involvement in reddit's conspiracy theory forum. PLoS ONE **14**(11), e0225098 (2019)

20. Letizi, R., Norman, C.: "you took that from me": conspiracism and online harassment in the alt-fandom of the last of us part ii. Games Cul. **19**(4), 513–534 (2024)

21. Locatelli, M.S., et al.: Topic shifts as a proxy for assessing politicization in social media. In: Proc. of the ICWSM. **18**, 972–984 (2024)

22. Lytvynenko, J., Hensley-Clancy, M.: The rioters who took over the capitol have been planning online in the open for weeks. https://www.buzzfeednews.com/article/janelytvynenko/trump-rioters-planned-online (2021)

23. Magno, G., Almeida, V.: Measuring international online human values with word embeddings. ACM Trans. Web (TWEB) **16**(2), 1–38 (2021)

24. Marshall, P.L., Wilson, J.: Toward a discourse on the threat of performative wokeness to justice agendas in education. Urban Educ. **60**(2), 404–433 (2025)

25. Ng, E.: No grand pronouncements here...: reflections on cancel culture and digital media participation. Television & New Media **21**(6), 621–627 (2020)

26. Ohlheiser, A.: Why'social justice warrior,'a gamergate insult, is now a dictionary entry. The Washington Post (2015)
27. Reimers, N., Gurevych, I.: Sentence-bert: sentence embeddings using siamese bert-networks. In: Proc. of the EMNLP. Assoc. Comput. Linguistics (2019). https://arxiv.org/abs/1908.10084
28. Ribeiro, M.H., Ottoni, R., West, R., Almeida, V.A., Meira, W., Jr.: Auditing radicalization pathways on youtube. In: Proc. of the ACM FAT, pp. 131–141 (2020)
29. Rios, K., Sosa, N., Osborn, H.: An experimental approach to intergroup threat theory: manipulations, moderators, and consequences of realistic vs. symbolic threat. European Rev. Soc. Psychol. **29**(1), 212–255 (2018)
30. Rose, S.: How the word 'woke' was weaponised by the right. https://www.theguardian.com/society/shortcuts/2020/jan/21/how-the-word-woke-was-weaponised-by-the-right (2020), Accessed 11 Apr2025
31. Schmidt, A., Wiegand, M.: A survey on hate speech detection using natural language processing. In: Proceedings of the Fifth International Workshop on Natural Language Processing for Social Media, pp. 1–10 (2017)
32. Steel, J.: Free speech,"cancel culture" and the "war on woke." In: The Routledge Companion to Freedom of Expression and Censorship, pp. 232–244. Routledge (2023)
33. stuck_in_the_matrix, Watchful1, R.: Reddit comments/submissions 2005-06 to 2024-12 (2025), https://www.reddit.com/r/pushshift/comments/1i4mlqu/dump_files_from_200506_to_202412/
34. Thomason, B., Opie, T., Livingston, B., Sitzmann, T.: "woke" diversity strategies: Science or sensationalism? Acad. Manag. Perspect. **37**(2), 193–201 (2023)
35. Álvarez Trigo, L.: Cancel culture: the phenomenon, online communities and open letters. PopMeC Res. Blog (2020). https://popmec.hypotheses.org/3041, iSSN 2660-8839

CommTox: Contextually-Aware Community Perceived Toxicity Classification

Ayan Chowdhury, Rhett Hanscom[✉], Tamara Lehman, Qin Lv,
and Shivakant Mishra

University of Colorado, Boulder, CO 80309, USA
Rhett.Hanscom@Colorado.edu
https://www.colorado.edu/center/demtech/

Abstract. CommTox, a community perceived toxicity classifier, leverages machine learning and historical behavioral data in order to assign a score for the perceived toxicity within a community. Building contextual awareness on top of Perspective API, CommTox brings highly flexible and adaptable context-aware toxicity classification to developers. CommTox is deployed across YouTube, and evaluates perceived toxicity across a number of online communities. Perceived toxicity is community-specific and incorporates historical community behavior into the decision making. Results indicate that while community reception of comments offers a fair amount of accuracy when predicting perceived toxicity, the most effective models need to include some level of text-dependent features, such as word-embeddings. The goal of CommTox is to provide a standardized metric from which comparisons free of bias can be drawn for varying communities.

Keywords: Toxicity · hate-speech · censorship · machine learning

1 Introduction

Toxicity classification has long challenged researchers due to the inherently subjective and context-dependent nature of toxic language. Traditional systems often treat comments in isolation, ignoring conversational issues or community context [1,4,9,21,35]. This is further complicated by annotator bias [5], demographic variance in speech perception, and platform-specific manifestations of toxicity [6]. Without standardized definitions, many studies develop individual classification criteria, limiting cross-comparison.

Most social media platforms (SMPs) assess toxicity at the comment level using natural language processing (NLP), but few incorporate user behavior or community norms [10]. While the Perspective API offers a scalable context-free

---

A. Chowdhury and R. Hanscom—The first two listed authors contributed equally to this work.

A. An et al. (Eds.): ASONAM 2025, LNCS 16323, pp. 279–288, 2026.
https://doi.org/10.1007/978-3-032-13821-7_23

solution, it has notable limitations including a lack of contextual awareness and susceptibility to adversarial inputs [11,13].

In this work, we propose CommTox, a contextually-aware toxicity classifier that augments Perspective API scores with community behavior data. Rather than focusing solely on how a comment is written, CommTox examines how it is received, capturing subtle signals of *perceived toxicity*. This enables measurement of three key indicators: (1) alignment between predicted toxicity and community judgment, (2) the resilience of communities to toxicity, and (3) broader trends in toxic discourse.

Despite an expanding body of literature, standardized tools for analyzing toxicity at the community level remain scarce [22–26]. As a result, researchers must develop custom tools, which hinder reproducibility and scalability. This gap is even more pronounced for general users, who lack tools to assess toxicity patterns in their online spaces without technical expertise.

Comment-level toxicity detection is now commonplace, but it fails to capture the nuances of community interaction. Not all negative comments are toxic, for instance rudeness can exist with productive discourse depending on context [7]. A deeper understanding of how communities engage with content enables better classification of toxicity, detection of effective de-escalation tactics, and the identification of resilient communities.

We define *toxicity resilience* as a community's ability to transform toxic content (as flagged by Perspective) into constructive dialogue. For example, minority groups often reclaim slurs as terms of empowerment [27], and while Perspective may flag these as toxic, the community may not perceive them as such. CommTox captures these discrepancies by considering response patterns rather than relying solely on content.

Prior work has shown the value of advanced machine learning models in toxicity classification. Zaheri *et al.* found that LSTMs outperformed traditional classifiers in identifying harmful content [32]. Udhayakumar *et al.* demonstrated the effectiveness of logistic regression when enhanced with context-aware recommendations [4]. Anuchitanukul *et al.* highlighted how conversational structure influences toxicity perceptions [10]. Beyond individual comments, several studies have explored user and community dynamics. Mall *et al.* classified users based on long-term toxic behavior, aiding moderation [33], while Almerekhi *et al.* investigated how Reddit users shift into toxicity across communities [34]. Despite these advances, few models are tailored to visually oriented platforms like YouTube, and fewer still offer transferable frameworks that quantify how toxicity is perceived across diverse communities.

CommTox bridges this gap by combining NLP-based toxicity scores with features derived from community reception, allowing for scalable and context-aware moderation across platforms. It also opens the door to implementing preemptive interventions when communities approach tipping points.

2   Methodology

To assign context-free toxicity scores, CommTox builds on the Perspective API developed by Jigsaw and Google [11]. This machine learning tool scores user-generated content across attributes such as *toxicity, severe_toxicity, identity_attack, insult, profanity,* and *threat.* While widely adopted for moderation on platforms like Reddit and The New York Times, its use as a foundation for community-aware models remains underexplored [11]. Experimental attributes such as *flirtation* and *sexually_explicit* were omitted due to instability (Fig. 1).

Example Comment	'No one was involved in an insurrection. You people on the left can't think for yourselves, bunch of useful idiots.'	
Perspective Attributes	**Attributes Defined by Perspective**	**Perspective Scores For Example Comment**
Toxicity	A rude, disrespectful, or unreasonable comment that is likely to make people leave a discussion.	0.8540474
Severe Toxicity	A very hateful, aggressive, disrespectful comment or otherwise very likely to make a user leave a discussion or give up on sharing their perspective.	0.0484574
Identity Attack	Negative or hateful comments targeting someone because of their identity.	0.1823592
Insult	Insulting, inflammatory, or negative comment towards a person or a group of people.	0.8722597
Profanity	Swear words, curse words, or other obscene or profane language.	0.4044591
Threat	Describes an intention to inflict pain, injury, or violence against an individual or group.	0.0097739
Flirtation	Contains references to sexual acts, body parts, or other lewd content.	0.1771561
Sexually Explicit	Pickup lines, complimenting appearance, subtle sexual innuendos, etc.	0.0356222

Fig. 1. Example of Perspective API scores alongside attribute definitions [11].

Perspective scores range from 0 to 1, with thresholds between 0.7 and 0.9 typically used to flag toxicity. We lower this cutoff to 0.65 to better capture borderline cases that often trigger community responses. However, Perspective's limitations, including a lack of contextual awareness, annotator bias, and vulnerability to adversarial inputs, necessitate additional behavioral modeling [1,5,8,12,13].

CommTox evaluates perceived toxicity using YouTube data from May through September 2024. We collected comments from trending videos across five content categories: Politics, Sports, Music, Movies, and Technology. Topics were identified using `pytrends` [37] and categorized via GPT-4o [38]. Additional search terms were generated when categories lacked sufficient coverage. This approach has been shown effective at similar tasks surrounding human-like text generation [36]. Video IDs were retrieved using the YouTube Data API, and only recent content (past six weeks) was scraped to ensure relevance.

Communities were defined as sets of comments on videos belonging to playlists aligned with the five categories. After removing duplicates, we filtered non-English comments, applied standard preprocessing (e.g., lemmatization, stopword removal), and converted emojis to text to preserve sentimental nuances. Toxicity labels were generated using Perspective, and threads (nested sequences of comments and replies forming a distinct conversations both separate from and apart of the larger discourse on a video) were further categorized based on reply behavior.

Finally, comments above the toxicity threshold with replies were examined for response patterns. Toxic comments without replies were ignored as community reception would be difficult to infer using only the comment itself. CommTox labels a thread as toxic if replies also score highly, and resilient if replies are predominantly non-toxic. These interaction patterns form the behavioral context that informs our classifier.

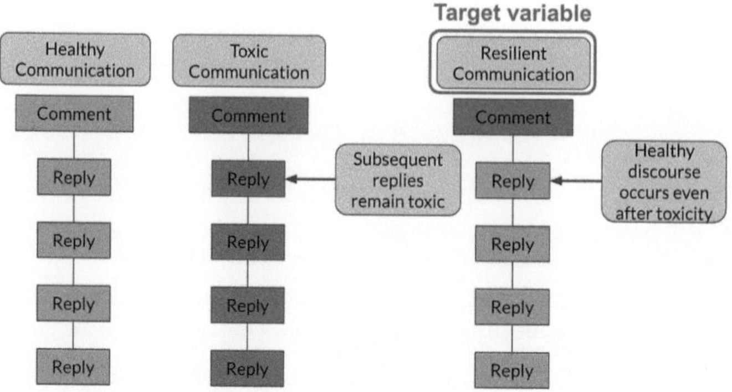

Fig. 2. Community behavior patterns: **Healthy**, **Toxic**, and **Resilient**. Red indicates Perspective-flagged toxicity; green indicates low toxicity. Blue circles mark classifier targets.

3   The CommTox Classifier

Perceived toxicity, or how online communities receive comments labeled as toxic by systems such as the Perspective API, is modeled and assessed though use of the Random Forest (RF) within CommTox. Unlike context-free classification, CommTox integrates user responses, enabling fine-grained detection of community-specific norms and *toxicity resilience.*

A comment is labeled as perceived toxic if (1) its Perspective toxicity score is ≥ 0.65, (2) it has at least one reply, and (3) $\geq 30\%$ of those replies are also toxic. Conversely, resilient communication occurs when replies remain largely non-toxic.

3.1   Model Architecture

CommTox employs a Random Forest classifier composed of decision trees trained with bootstrapped samples and random feature subsets [2,14]. This approach reduces overfitting and improves generalizability. Each tree votes independently, and predictions are aggregated via majority vote. Feature importance is extracted post-training to assess which variables drive predictions [15].

3.2   Feature Sets

CommTox integrates three categories of features: (1) **CFT**: Context-free Perspective API scores [11], (2) **WEF**: Word embeddings from Google's Word2Vec, averaged per comment [3], (3) **Non-WEF**: Eleven engineered linguistic and interactional features: 1. toxic word count (sourced from an open-access Carnegie Mellon lexicon [16]) , 2. punctuation count, 3. longest toxic word run, 4. total word count, 5. unique word count, 6. uppercase word count, 7. exclamation count, 8. question mark count, 9. emoji count, 10. unique emoji count, and 11. log-transformed like count. Together, these features capture both textual signals and engagement-driven context across platforms.

3.3   Model Variants

We evaluate two model configurations:

1. **CFT + Non-WEF**: Baseline numeric model with 80% accuracy.
2. **CFT + WEF**: In addition to previous features, adds embeddings and TF-IDF, improving performance to 83%.

To address class imbalance, we apply SMOTE [20], and augment training data via synonym substitution [18]. Community-specific classifiers are trained by splitting data per content domain (e.g., Politics, Sports), capturing interaction nuances in each community separately.

3.4   Context-Free vs. Perceived Toxicity

Context-free toxicity (CFT) offers standardized, scalable tagging but ignores discourse structure, speaker identity, or cultural re-appropriation (such as reclaimed slurs [27]). Perceived toxicity accounts for community reception: comments flagged as toxic by Perspective but received positively may be misclassified. CommTox bridges this gap by incorporating community behavior.

Communities also differ in *toxicity resilience*, or their ability to de-escalate toxic threads. High-resilience communities respond to toxicity with civility, while low-resilience groups may amplify it. CommTox quantifies these dynamics via reply-chain analysis.

3.5   Model Training

We focus training on top-level comments (not replies), since these are more visible within SMPs. Figure 2 shows three reply-chain patterns:

1. **Healthy**: Non-toxic comment followed by non-toxic replies.
2. **Toxic**: Toxic comment triggers toxic replies.
3. **Resilient**: Toxic comment receives non-toxic replies.

CommTox classifies comment threads into these categories based on Perspective scores and reply behavior.

3.6   Model Optimization

We use GridSearchCV to optimize RF hyperparameters (tree depth, estimators, etc.) [19]. Each model is trained and evaluated using an 80/20 temporal split (early data for training, later data for testing). Separate models are fine-tuned for each community to better capture domain-specific language and behavioral patterns. For each community, we produce a complete feature set by combining the TF-IDF vectorized text data with additional numerical features and embeddings.

4   Results and Discussion

CommTox is evaluated using data from the 14 oldest days for training and the rest for testing. Two model variants are compared: *CFT + Non-WEF* and *CFT + WEF*. Figure 3 shows that the WEF model consistently outperforms the non-WEF model across communities. Accuracy and F1 scores (Fig. 3a) are higher for the WEF model, and ROC curves (Figs. 3b, 3d) show AUC scores of 0.94 and 0.97, respectively. Figure 3c shows variation in baseline toxicity across domains.

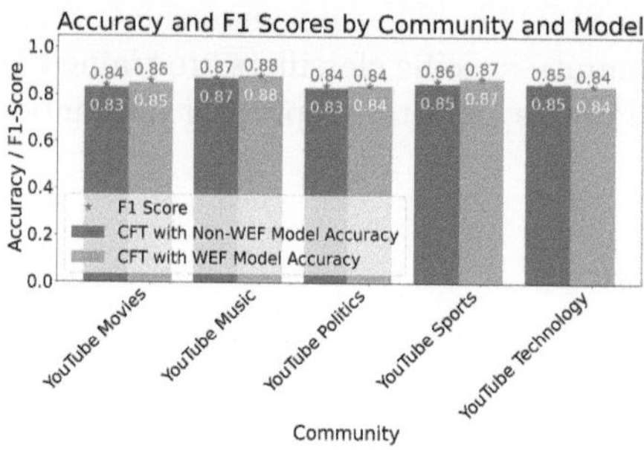

(a) Accuracy and F1-scores for CommTox models.

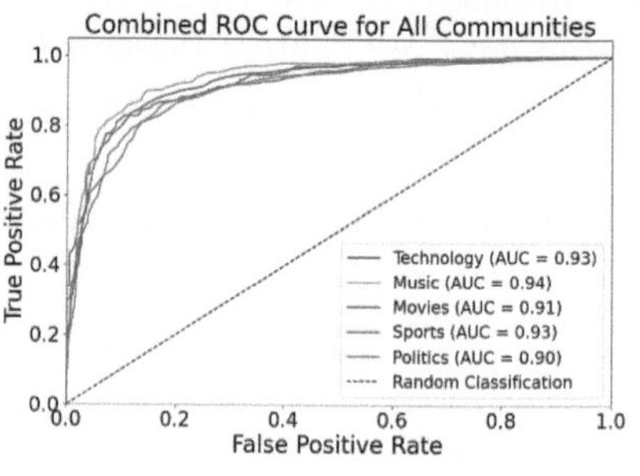

(b) AUC for *CFT + Non-WEF*.

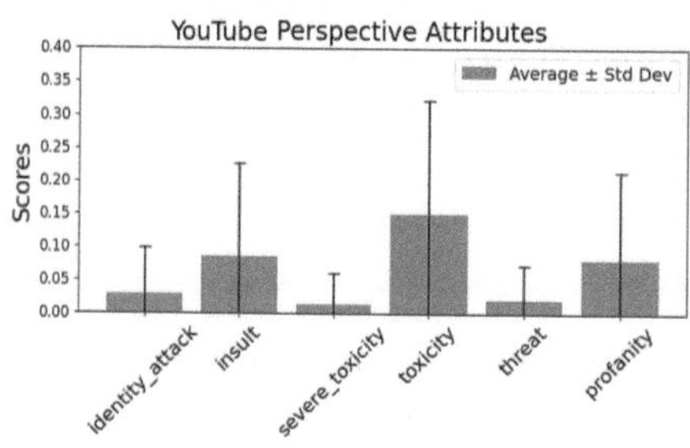

(c) CFT variation across YouTube communities.

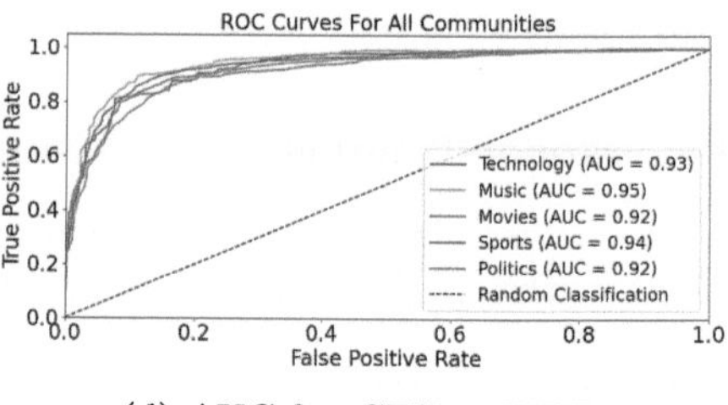

(d) AUC for *CFT + WEF*.

Fig. 3. Model performance metrics across communities.

4.1   Community Toxicity Resilience

To assess community response patterns, we analyzed reply chains for head comments with high CFT scores (≥ 0.65). A thread is labeled *perceived toxic* if at least one reply is also toxic; otherwise, it is *perceived non-toxic*. Figures 4a and 4b summarize results across five communities.

Community	Total Comments	Total Toxic	Perceived Toxic	Perceived Non-Toxic
Sports	198,620	1,210 (0.61%)	53 (0.03%)	198,567 (99.97%)
Music	53,684	467 (0.87%)	32 (0.06%)	53,652 (99.94%)
Movies	88,098	777 (0.88%)	46 (0.05%)	88,052 (99.95%)
Technology	49,038	194 (0.40%)	5 (0.01%)	49,033 (99.99%)
Politics	125,575	911 (0.73%)	65 (0.05%)	125,510 (99.95%)

(a) Toxicity chain metrics: Non-WEF model.

Community	Total Comments	Total Toxic	Perceived Toxic	Perceived Non-Toxic
Sports	198,620	26,860 (13.52%)	6,899 (3.47%)	191,721 (96.53%)
Music	53,684	7,236 (13.48%)	2,132 (3.97%)	51,552 (96.03%)
Movies	88,098	12,185 (13.83%)	3,452 (3.92%)	84,646 (96.08%)
Technology	49,038	5,933 (12.10%)	1,757 (3.58%)	47,281 (96.42%)
Politics	125,575	18,539 (14.76%)	5,484 (4.37%)	120,091 (95.63%)

(b) Toxicity chain metrics: WEF model.

Fig. 4. Reply-chain analysis of perceived toxicity across communities.

While the WEF model detects more toxic comments (e.g., 13.5% in Sports), over 95% of these threads do not escalate—indicating strong community resilience. The Non-WEF model detects fewer cases but shows even higher non-escalation rates (99.9%). In 1,327 conflicting cases, the WEF model flagged comments as toxic but found replies remained non-toxic in 88% of cases, reinforcing the need for contextual interpretation.

4.2   Implications and Limitations

Despite variations in baseline toxicity, most communities demonstrate de-escalatory behavior. For example, in Politics (our most toxic community) 14.8% of comments are flagged, but only 4.4% of threads become perceived toxic. This suggests moderation efforts should focus not only on detection but also on fostering resilience.

CommTox highlights the benefits of integrating community response into toxicity classification. Behavior-aware models outperform content-only approaches in both sensitivity and interpretability. However, reliance on Perspective API introduces limitations: annotator bias, poor slang handling, and adversarial vulnerabilities [5,8]. Pre-trained Word2Vec embeddings may also miss platform-specific language nuances. Data coverage can vary by topic due to API rate limits and user activity imbalance.

4.3   Conclusion

CommTox offers a context-aware framework for assessing toxicity by incorporating both linguistic features and community response. By distinguishing between context-free toxicity and perceived toxicity, it identifies not just harmful content but also the community's ability to de-escalate. Our findings underscore the importance of feature-rich, behaviorally grounded models for moderation, particularly on visually oriented platforms such as YouTube. CommTox is generalizable across SMPs and provides a scalable metric for comparing toxicity and resilience across communities.

References

1. Kumar, D., et al.: Designing toxic content classification for a diversity of perspectives. SOUPS (2021)
2. Altman, N., Krzywinski, M.: Ensemble methods: bagging and random forests. Nat. Methods **14**(10), 933–935 (2017)
3. Hugging Face, fse: word2vec-google-news-300 (2025)
4. Udhayakumar, S., Nancy, J.S., UmaNandhini, D, Ashwin, P, Ganesh, R.: Context aware text classification and recommendation model for toxic comments using logistic regression. In: ICBDCC 2019 (2021)
5. Sap, M., Swayamdipta, S., Vianna, L., Zhou, X., Choi, Y., Smith, N.A.: Annotators with attitudes: how annotator beliefs and identities bias toxic language detection. In: Conference of the North American Chapter of the Association for Computational Linguistics: Human Language Technologies (2022)
6. Singh, A.K., Ghafouri, V., Such, J., Suarez-Tangil, G.: Differences in the toxic language of cross-platform communities. In: Proceedings of the International AAAI Conference on Web and Social Media (2024)
7. Sheth, A., Shalin, V.L., Kursuncu, U.: Defining and detecting toxicity on social media: context and knowledge are key. Neurocomputing (2022)
8. Rieder, B., Skop, Y.: Studying the technical, normative, and organizational structure of Perspective API. Big Data Soc. **8** (2021)
9. Eke, C.I., Norman, A.A., Shuib, L.: Context-based feature technique for sarcasm identification in benchmark datasets using deep learning and BERT model. IEEE Access **9** (2021)
10. Anuchitanukul, A., Ive, J., Specia, L.: Revisiting contextual toxicity detection in conversations. ACM J. Data Inf. Qual. (2022)
11. Google Jigsaw: Perspective API Documentation (2025)
12. Hosseini, H., Kannan, S., Zhang, B., Poovendran, R.: Deceiving google's perspective api built for detecting toxic comments arXiv:1702.08138 (2017)

13. Jain, E., et al.: Adversarial text generation for google's perspective API. In: CSCI (2018)
14. Ali, J., Khan, R., Ahmad, N., Maqsood, I.: Random forests and decision trees. IJCSI (2012)
15. Archer, K.J., Kimes, R.V.: Empirical characterization of random forest variable importance measures. Comput. Stat. Data Anal. (2008)
16. von Ahn, L.: List of Bad Words (2025). cs.cmu.edu/ biglou/resources
17. Ramos, J.: Using tf-idf to determine word relevance in document queries. In: Instructional Conference on Machine Learning, vol. 242, no. 1, pp. 29–48 (2003)
18. Shorten, C., Khoshgoftaar, T.M., Furht, B.: Text data augmentation for deep learning. J. Big Data 8(1), 101 (2021)
19. Scikit-Learn Developers: Grid Search - Scikit Documentation (2025)
20. Chawla, N.V., Bowyer, K.W., Hall, L.O., Kegelmeyer, W.P.: SMOTE: synthetic minority over-sampling technique. J. Artif. Intell. Res. (2002)
21. Dadvar, M., Trieschnigg, D., Ordelman, R., De Jong, F.: Improving cyberbullying detection with user context. In: ECIR (2013)
22. Wang, W., Feng, F., Nie, L., Chua, T.-S.: User-controllable recommendation against filter bubbles. In: SIGIR Conference on Research and Development in Information Retrieval (2022)
23. Salminen, J., et al.: Developing an online hate classifier for multiple social media platforms. Hum.-Centric Comput. (2020)
24. Saveski, M., Roy, B., Roy, D.: The structure of toxic conversations on Twitter. In: Proceedings of the Web Conference (2021)
25. Rupapara, V., et al.: Impact of SMOTE on imbalanced text features for toxic comments classification using RVVC model. IEEE Access (2021)
26. Akuma, S., Lubem, T., Adom, I.T.: Comparing Bag of Words and TF-IDF with different models for hate speech detection from live tweets. Int. J. Inf. Technol. (2022)
27. Worthen, M.G.F.: Queer identities in the 21st century: reclamation and stigma. Curr. Opin. Psychol. (2023)
28. Madhu, H., Satapara, S., Modha, S., Mandl, T., Majumder, P.: Detecting offensive speech in conversational code-mixed dialogue on social media: a contextual dataset and benchmark experiments. Expert Syst. Appl. (2023)
29. Reimers, N., Gurevych, I.: Sentence-BERT: sentence embeddings using siamese BERT-networks. In: Empirical Methods in Natural Language Processing and the International Joint Conference on Natural Language Processing (2019)
30. Hochreiter, S., Schmidhuber, J.: Long short-term memory. Neural Comput. 9(8), 1735–1780 (1997)
31. Devlin, J., Chang, M.-W., Lee, K., Toutanova, K.: BERT: pre-training of deep bidirectional transformers for language understanding. In: Computational Linguistics: Human Language Technologies (2019)
32. Zaheri, S., Leath, J., Stroud, D.: Toxic comment classification. SMU Data Sci. Rev. (2020)
33. Mall, R., Nagpal, M., Salminen, J., Almerekhi, H., Jung, S.-G., Jansen, B.J.: Four types of toxic people. In: Nordic Conference on Human-Computer Interaction (2020)
34. Almerekhi, H., Kwak, H., Jansen, B.J.: Investigating toxicity changes of cross-community redditors from 2 billion posts and comments. PeerJ Comput. Sci. (2022)
35. Pavlopoulos, J., Sorensen, J., Dixon, L., Thain, N., Androutsopoulos, I.: Toxicity detection: does context really matter?. In: Annual Meeting of the Association for Computational Linguistics, pp. 4296–4305 (2020)

36. Orrù, G., Biancofiore, F., Qian, W., Ji, Y., Sapienza, A., Cambria, E.: Human or not? Inf. Fusion (2023)
37. Hogue, J.: pytrends: Pseudo API for Google Trends. GitHub repository. https://github.com/GeneralMills/pytrends. Accessed 8 July 2025
38. OpenAI. GPT-4o Technical Report. OpenAI (2024). https://openai.com/research/gpt-4o

A Consent-Driven Model for Reducing Echo Chambers in Social Media

Naomi Korem, Tammar Shrot, and Hadassa Daltrophe[✉]

Shamoon College of Engineering, 84 Jabotinsky St., 77245 Ashdod, Israel
{naomiko,tammash,hadasda1}@sce.ac.il

Abstract. Echo chambers in social media pose a growing threat to democratic discourse. Unlike other approaches that address this challenge by imposing obligations on the platforms or through regulatory measures that violate users' rights, our proposal preserves user autonomy by allowing them to decide whether to explore opinions outside their echo chamber. This paper investigates whether a regulation applied only to users who have granted *explicit consent* can promote balanced information flow across polarized communities throughout the network. We propose a general model that captures how information spreads on social media. The model accounts for users' friends, opinions, and message virality. We conduct simulations with varying parameters over real-world data to analyze the model's behavior. Our results show that even targeting a small fraction of consenting users can significantly enhance cross-group message reach (without overstepping user entitlements). This work underscores the potential for a consent-driven regulation to foster healthier public dialogue.

Keywords: Social Network · Regulation · Personalization Algorithms · Polarization · Privacy Preserving

1 Introduction

Polarization in contemporary societies has become increasingly pronounced, with stark divisions emerging along political, social, and cultural lines [9]. A key contributor to this trend is the role played by social media platforms, particularly through their personalization (a.k.a. recommendation) algorithms [10]. These algorithms are designed to maximize users' engagement by presenting content that aligns with their individual preferences. This often results in the creation of "echo chambers", where users are predominantly exposed to views that mirror their own or discredit opposing views. In such settings, beliefs are amplified [4] through repeated communication within a closed network, insulated from outside perspectives or rebuttal [3]. Such environments can undermine informed democratic discourse. Moreover, members of an echo chamber tend to develop feelings like hate, distrust and contempt towards people who don't share their views, those that exist outside their echo chamber [6]. In recent years, echo

A. An et al. (Eds.): ASONAM 2025, LNCS 16323, pp. 289–296, 2026.
https://doi.org/10.1007/978-3-032-13821-7_24

chambers have been observed across various social networks [4]. While their precise role remains debated [5], various studies suggest that the existence of echo chambers contributes to social polarization [8].

These concerns point to the need for some form of regulation. One possible solution is to manipulate personalization algorithms to recommend potentially relevant and diverse friends from outside the users' echo chamber [12]. However, this solution requires the consent of social media platforms such as *Meta* or *X*, a consent that would be difficult to achieve or enforce. Alternatively, regulation could occur externally, without access to platform internals, but this too poses challenges: even if such a regulation has good reasons, there is also an important reason against it. After all, When the state decides for us that we can no longer consume only opinions similar to our own, it is compromising our *autonomy* to decide for ourselves. Autonomy is generally taken to be a central value of liberalism, and we all tend to get quite nervous when our autonomy is threatened.

In this paper, we propose a regulation that takes seriously the notion of autonomy. We take inspiration from, and base our research upon, a recent study [2] that explores the question of whether regulation can reduce the echo chamber effect, given a general information-spreading model that captures the essence of a social media, friends-based, information-spreading process. In this study, a crucial criterion for any such regulation is a commitment to respecting user privacy. Specifically, regulatory functions cannot access or use user opinions. We investigate whether improved exposure to diverse opinions can be achieved by allowing users to voluntarily renounce their privacy and grant access to their opinions. Such users reflect people in the real world who wish to escape their echo chamber, and therefore give the regulator access to their opinion. Their autonomy is, therefore, respected. We study how this voluntary disclosure affects exposure across the network.

Main Contribution. We propose a regulatory framework for social media platforms that utilizes a consent-based mechanism to respect user autonomy. To support this approach, we develop a network-based spreading model that integrates user consent into the regulatory intervention process. Additionally, we define an objective function for echo chamber mitigation that explicitly considers the network's structural topology. Finally, we validate the effectiveness of our proposed model through extensive simulations on real-world social network data. Specifically, we simulate message spreading over several models of network spreading, while also examining the effects of the parameter values.

2   Social-Media Spreading Model

We present a simplified model for information propagation in a social-media network. The framework captures user interactions, platform behavior, and regulatory mechanisms. Our presentation is based on [2], where full technical details and extensions can be found.

We model a social network as a tuple $N = (G, c, s)$, where $G = (V, E)$ is an undirected graph, V denotes the set of users, and $E \subseteq V \times V$

represents social connections. Each user $v \in V$ is assigned an opinion via a coloring function $c : V \to \{\texttt{red}, \texttt{blue}\}$. Additionally, a response function $s : V \to \{\texttt{inactive}, \texttt{react}, \texttt{ignore}\}$ specifies each user's reaction to a message. All users begin in the neutral state $\texttt{inactive}$, and upon receiving a message, may transition to either $\texttt{react}$ or $\texttt{ignore}$. The transition is monotonic: once a user changes state, the response cannot be reverted. A message originates from a $\texttt{red}$ user v with $s(v) = \texttt{react}$ at time $t = 0$. The process unfolds in discrete time steps.

Let $\mathcal{A}_t = L_t \cup I_t$ be the set of users who have reacted by time t, with L_t and I_t denoting users who have $\texttt{react}$-ed or $\texttt{ignore}$-ed the message, respectively. The evolution $\mathcal{P}_t = \langle \mathcal{A}_0, \ldots, \mathcal{A}_t \rangle$ defines the *spreading sequence*. To model the spreading behavior, we define the *social media spreading function*, $\mathcal{F}_M$, the *user response function*, $\mathcal{F}_U$, and the *regulation spreading function*, $\mathcal{F}_R$. The specific implementations of $\mathcal{F}_M$, $\mathcal{F}_U$, and $\mathcal{F}_R$ are left abstract to allow for various theoretical and empirical investigations. We can now formally describe the evolution of a generic social media spreading process.

Definition 1 (Social Media Spreading Process). *A social media spreading process is defined by a 5-tuple $\langle v, N, \mathcal{F}_M, \mathcal{F}_R, \mathcal{F}_U \rangle$ where the initial message originates from user v in network N. The process unfolds in rounds indexed by t, generating the spreading sequence $\mathcal{P}_t$ using the following steps:*

1. ***Message Sharing:*** *At the end of time t, any user who responded with $\texttt{react}$ shares the message. At $t = 0$, the originator v sets $s(v) = \texttt{react}$ and shares the message.*
2. ***Social Media Choice:*** *The platform selects a candidate inbox set M_{t+1} of inactive users to receive the message at time $t + 1$, using $\mathcal{F}_M(N, \mathcal{P}_t, v)$.*
3. ***Regulation Choice:*** *A regulatory mechanism selects the final inbox set $Q_{t+1} = \mathcal{F}_R(N, M_{t+1})$, potentially extending the platform's selection. In the case of passive regulation, $\mathcal{F}_R = \emptyset_R$ and $Q_{t+1} = M_{t+1}$.*
4. ***User Response:*** *Each user $u \in Q_{t+1}$ receives the message in their inbox and updates their status via $s(u) = \mathcal{F}_U(N, \mathcal{P}_t, v)$. Then:*

$$L_{t+1} = L_t \cup \{u \mid u \in Q_{t+1}, s(u) = \texttt{react}\}, I_{t+1} = I_t \cup \{u \mid u \in Q_{t+1}, s(u) = \texttt{ignore}\}.$$

Hence, $\mathcal{A}_{t+1} = L_{t+1} \cup I_{t+1}$.
5. ***Repeat or Stop:*** *If new users $\texttt{react}$ the message ($L_{t+1} \neq L_t$), the process continues to the next round. Otherwise, it terminates.*

This framework outlines a general and extensible model for opinion spreading in social networks. In the next sections, we present concrete instantiations of $\mathcal{F}_M$, $\mathcal{F}_U$, and $\mathcal{F}_R$ to explore fundamental behaviors under different policies.

2.1   Modeling Social Media Spreading Function, $\mathcal{F}_M$

Social media platforms employ complex proprietary algorithms to determine which content is displayed in the user feed. These algorithms may consider message content, user interaction history, and other contextual factors. However, in this work, we focus specifically on the echo chamber and thus adopt a simplified yet principled model of message propagation. We use the following assumptions:

- A message is only propagated by users who previously chose to `react`.
- A message shared by a user v is eligible to be seen only by v's neighbors.
- A message shared at time t may appear only in the feed of users who are `inactive` at time t, and only for the next round $(t+1)$.
- The decision to deliver the message to each neighbor is made independently of other neighbors.

Let us define $p, q \in [0,1]$ as two probabilities controlling how likely a user is to receive the message based on opinion similarity. The probability that an `inactive` node $u \in \bar{\mathcal{A}}_t$, who is a neighbor of a newly active user v, is chosen to receive the message in round $t+1$ is given by:

$$\delta(v,u) = \begin{cases} 0 & (v,u) \neq E \\ p & (v,u) \in E \text{ AND } c(u) = c(v) \\ q & (v,u) \in E \text{ AND } c(u) \neq c(v) \end{cases}$$

This defines the **spreading probability** from v to u based on their connection and opinion similarity.

Definition 2 (social media spreading function). *The function $\mathcal{F}_M(N, \mathcal{P}_t, v)$ defines the candidate inbox set for round $t+1$, denoted by M_{t+1}. This set is generated as follows: for every edge $(v,u) \in E$ such that $v \in L_t \setminus L_{t-1}$ and $u \in \bar{\mathcal{A}}_t$, node u is included in M_{t+1} independently with probability $\delta(v,u)$.*

To explore the impact of social media algorithms on echo chambers, we consider the following specific configurations of the parameters p and q:

1. **Uniform spreading ($p = 1, q = 1$):** The message is forwarded to *all* inactive neighbors of newly active users, regardless of color.
2. **p-homophily ($p \geq \frac{1}{2}$, $q = 1-p$):** The message is more likely to be forwarded to neighbors with the same opinion as the sender. This models homophilic behavior, where users with similar views are preferentially exposed to shared content.

2.2   Modeling User Response Function, $\mathcal{F}_U$

When a user receives a new message in their inbox (i.e., feed), how will they react to it? What will cause them to `react` to the message or `ignore` it? Obviously, this is a non-transparent, complex process that is hard to model exactly.

There are several factors that are known to influence the number of *likes* a post receives. These include the identity of the people doing the liking [11], and its existing *like* count [7]. First, when a `react` comes from friends, familiar people, or people with similar opinions to ours, they carry greater social proof and elicit more subsequent `reacts` from others, strengthening relational bonds and encouraging further engagement. Second, posts that already have more `reacts` tend to attract disproportionately more new `reacts`—a "rich-get-richer" effect—whereby early popularity begets further popularity.

Hence, for the sake of tractability, we assume that a user's reaction is determined by three factors: (i) the user u opinion (modeled by its color $c(u)$), (ii) the identity of the sender, v, specifically whether the sender is a neighbor and their associated opinion (i.e., $c(v), c(u)$), and (iii) the cumulative number of users who have `react`-ed to the message up to time t.

Recall that the color of the message is fixed to `red`, therefore, the color-dependent function $g(u)$ provides high probability for a `red` user to `react` to a message:
$$g(u) = \begin{cases} 1 & c(u) = \texttt{red} \\ -1 & \text{otherwise} \end{cases}$$

The friendship function $f(v, u)$ reflects the influence of the sender v identity and adjacency with user u;
$$f(v, u) = \begin{cases} -1 & (v, u) \neq E \\ 0 & (v, u) \in E \text{ AND } c(u) \neq c(v) \\ 1 & (v, u) \in E \text{ AND } c(u) = c(v) \end{cases}$$

Finally, recall that n is the number of users in the network N, and $|L_t|$ is the number of users who response with `react`, the virality-function $h(L_t, n)$ models the impact of the social proof: $h(L_t, n) = |L_t|/n$. These three factors underlie the modeling of the *user reaction function*, denoted by $\mathcal{F}_U(N, \mathcal{P}_t, v)$.

Definition 3 (User reaction function, $\mathcal{F}_U$). *Let $|L_t|$ denote the number of users who have responded with* `react` *up to time t. Given a message recipient u and a sender v, the user reaction function $\mathcal{F}_U(N, \mathcal{P}_t, v)$ determines whether user u responded with* `react` *or* `ignore` *to the message, according to the following probabilistic rule:*
$$s(u) = \mathcal{F}_U(N, \mathcal{P}_t, v) = \begin{cases} \texttt{react} & \text{with probability } \sigma\left(h(L_t, n) \cdot (\alpha g(u) + \beta f(v, u))\right) \\ \texttt{ignore} & \text{otherwise} \end{cases}$$
where $\sigma(x) = \frac{1}{1+e^{-x-1/2}}$ is the sigmoid function, modeling the stochastic nature of the response, and α, β are weight parameters that modulate the relative influence of g and f.

2.3   Modeling the Consent-Driven Regulation Function, $\mathcal{F}_R$

The proposed regulatory mechanism is based on an opt-in principle: Only users who have explicitly consented to regulation are subject to intervention. This group of consenting users is referred to as the *opt-in set*, denoted by Q.

Consent may arise from various motivations, for instance, a willingness to be exposed to diverse perspectives or an awareness (enabled through transparency mechanisms) that the user is currently embedded within an ideological echo chamber. For the purposes of this model, all members of Q must hold the `blue` opinion, as the message being distributed in the system is of opinion `red`.

The regulation mechanism selectively intervenes for users in $Q \subseteq V_{\texttt{blue}}$ (the set of `blue` users) by potentially exposing them to content that challenges their existing opinion. This is achieved by injecting additional `red`-content into their feed, beyond what they would receive through the normal spreading function.

Definition 4 (Consent-Driven Function $\mathcal{F}_R$). *Given a set of opt-in users $Q \subseteq V_{\texttt{blue}}$, a candidate message recipient set $M_t \subseteq V$, and a regulation parameter $\rho \in [0,1]$, The regulation function at time t, denoted by $\mathcal{F}_R(M_t, Q, \rho)$, is computed as: $\mathcal{F}_R = M_t \cup Q_t$, where $Q_t \subseteq Q$ is a set of* inactive *users selected uniformly at random from the set Q, and $|Q_t| = \lceil \rho \cdot |M_t| \rceil$.*

3   Results

Experimental Setup. To evaluate the influence of the Consent-Driven Regulation mechanism on the spreading dynamics, a series of simulations were carried out on the *Bloggers*[52,48] graph. This network comprises 1222 nodes and 16,717 edges, representing the largest connected component of a weblog network centered on U.S. political discourse in 2005 [1]. Each node corresponds to a user whose political affiliation is classified as either conservative or liberal, with 636 users (52%) labeled as `red` and 586 users (48%) as `blue`. The graph structure includes 7841 `red` edges and 7301 `blue` edges, which denote intra-group connections, as well as 1575 inter-group (cross-party) edges.

The spreading process is initiated by selecting a `red` user uniformly at random and updating their status to `react`. The spreading then proceeds according to the dynamics defined in Definition 1, using the following parameters:

(i) **Spreading function:** $\mathcal{F}_M$ with parameter settings $(p = 1, q = 0)$ and $(p = 0.9, q = 0.1)$.

(ii) **User Response function:** $\mathcal{F}_U$ with parameter setting $(\alpha = 0.7, \beta = 0.3)$.

(iii) **Consent-Driven Regulation Function:** $\mathcal{F}_R$ parameterized by ρ, which denotes the relative fraction of additional users from the opt-in set who received the message. The values considered are $\rho \in \{0, 0.001, 0.01, 0.1\}$.

Once the spreading process terminates, we record the distribution of user responses (`react` or `ignore`) among those who were exposed to the message. Each configuration is simulated 1000 times, and the results are averaged to obtain the expected number of reactions.

Reference Point for Echo Chamber Reduction Evaluation. In addressing the challenge of mitigating the echo chamber phenomenon in social media, a fundamental question arises: what form of message distribution would constitute a meaningful step toward reducing ideological segregation in the network? We propose that the design of the objective function should take into account the *original topology* of the network. Specifically, we suggest a reference point in which a message originating in the `red` community is spreading uniformly across both `red` and `blue` neighbors of each node, without regulatory intervention. This objective, captured by the "Uniform spreading" model (see Sect. 2.1), serves as a natural reference point for evaluating the effects of any regulatory mechanism.

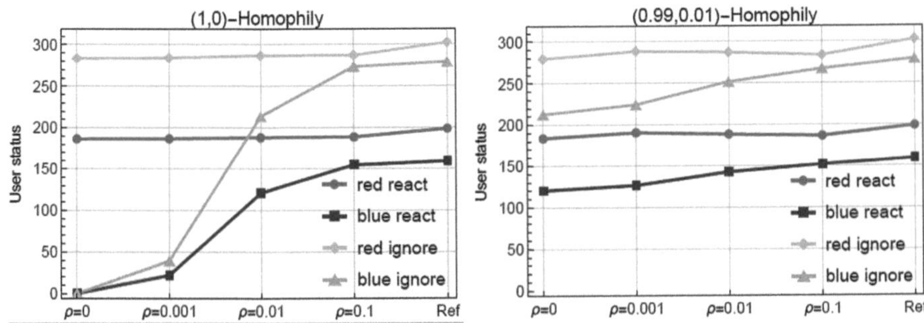

Fig. 1. Consent-Driven Regulation intervention (ρ) under two homophily settings: pure homophily ($p = 1, q = 0$) (left) and relaxed homophily ($p = 0.99, q = 0.01$) (right).

Experimental Output. Figure 1 shows the aggregated results. The rightmost value ('Ref') represents the reference scenario, where each user shares the message uniformly with all neighbors, without homophily or regulation.

The left plot in Fig. 1 shows a pure homophily spreading function. When $\rho = 0$ (i.e., passive regulation), a **red** user spreads the message *only* to other **red** users. Hence, we can see that only **red** users got the message, which led to only **red** response in the population. As expected, increasing the regulation intervention by ρ, allows **blue** users to receive the message. However, even a minimal regulatory adjustment ($\rho = 0.001$) results in a substantial increase in both blue exposure and reactivity, demonstrating the high sensitivity of the network to small interventions. Similar results are observed even when the social media spreading mechanism is less strictly homophilic, for instance, under parameter settings such as ($p = 0.999, q = 0.001$).

The right plot in Fig. 1 illustrates a spreading mechanism with a 1% tolerance for differing opinions, resulting in a less homogeneous echoing effect even in the absence of regulation (i.e., $\rho = 0$). Introducing the Consent-Driven Regulation mechanism progressively guides the system toward the desired distribution, as indicated by the reference point.

Notably, in both scenarios, our results show that even targeting a small fraction of consenting users can significantly enhance cross-group message reach. Furthermore, in both scenarios, the red group's reactivity remains largely unchanged across all levels of regulation.

4   Discussion

The results demonstrate that regulatory intervention mitigates the echo chamber effect by expanding message reach within the **blue** bubble. Notably, even regulation with only 1% additional users per phase, yields a substantial improvement in cross-group exposure. Moreover, the number of **blue** recipients far exceeds those chosen by the regulator, who are a negligible subset. These findings show that lightweight regulatory mechanisms can reduce polarization, even under strong homophily (e.g., $p = 0.999$, $q = 0.001$). Small interventions ($\sim 1\%$) achieve significant diversity in exposure. Thus, effective platform regulation need not involve sweeping algorithmic changes. Importantly, our results offer practical guidance for social media platforms and policymakers. Injecting messages into a small fraction of unreached consenting users can significantly improve exposure diversity. The regulation can be implemented flexibly, allowing users to opt-out and thus preserving user consent while improving balance. From a policy standpoint, our finding support digital regulation frameworks like the EU Digital Services Act Regulation improves exposure diversity without affecting **red** group exposure, suggesting that public–interest interventions can be both effective and minimally invasive. While the model captures key dynamics of polarization, its simplicity limits real-world applicability. Future work could explore alternative spreading and user reaction functions.

References

1. Adamic, L.A., Glance, N.: The political blogosphere and the 2004 US election: divided they blog. In: Proceedings of the 3rd international workshop on Link discovery, pp. 36–43 (2005)
2. Avin, C., Daltrophe, H., Lotker, Z.: On the impossibility of breaking the echo chamber effect in social media using regulation. Sci. Rep. **14**(1), 1107 (2024)
3. Baumann, F., Lorenz-Spreen, P., Sokolov, I.M., Starnini, M.: Modeling echo chambers and polarization dynamics in social networks. Phys. Rev. Lett. **124**(4), 048301 (2020)
4. Cinelli, M., Morales, G.D.F., Galeazzi, A., Quattrociocchi, W., Starnini, M.: The echo chamber effect on social media. Proc. National Acad. Sci. **118**(9) (2021)
5. Haidt, J., Bail, C.: (ongoing) social media and political dysfunction: a collaborative review. New York university (2022). https://tinyurl.com/PoliticalDysfunctionReview, unpublished manuscript
6. Iyengar, S., Lelkes, Y., Levendusky, M., Malhotra, N., Westwood, S.J.: The origins and consequences of affective polarization in the United States. Annu. Rev. Polit. Sci. **22**(1), 129–146 (2019)
7. Muchnik, L., Aral, S., Taylor, S.J.: Social influence bias: a randomized experiment. Science **341**(6146), 647–651 (2013)
8. Settle, J.E.: Frenemies: how social media polarizes America. Cambridge University Press (2018)
9. Silver, L.: Most across 19 countries see strong partisan conflicts in their society, especially in South Korea and the US. Pew Research Center (2022)
10. Stinson, C.: Algorithms are not neutral: bias in collaborative filtering. AI Ethics **2**(4), 763–770 (2022)
11. Stsiampkouskaya, K., Joinson, A., Piwek, L.: To like or not to like? an experimental study on relational closeness, social grooming, reciprocity, and emotions in social media liking. J. Comput. Mediat. Commun. **28**(2), zmac036 (2023)
12. Tommasel, A., Rodriguez, J.M., Godoy, D.: I want to break free! recommending friends from outside the echo chamber. In: Proceedings of the 15th ACM Conference on Recommender Systems, pp. 23–33 (2021)

Modeling Toxicity Propagation in Social Networks with Weighted Focal Structure Analysis and Monte Carlo Epidemic Models

Tope Christopher Falade[1] and Nitin Agarwal[1,2]($\boxtimes$)

[1] COSMOS Research Center, University of Arkansas at Little Rock, Little Rock, USA
{tcfalade,nxagarwal}@ualr.edu
[2] International Computer Science Institute, Berkeley, USA

Abstract. Traditional online toxicity analysis focuses on individual users, overlooking structural dynamics within online communities. We propose the Weighted Focal Structure Analysis (WFSA) algorithm to identify focal toxic structures (FTSs): densely interconnected node groups that intensify toxic discourse. WFSA demonstrates significant gains in detecting toxic influence structures, validated using F1 scores and standard metrics. We apply SIR, SEIR, and SEIZ models with 1,500 Monte Carlo simulations to assess toxicity propagation by FTSs versus influential toxic individuals (ITIs). Results show FTSs significantly outperform highly central individuals in propagating toxicity across network topologies. SEIZ achieves the lowest macro-error, confirming predictive robustness. Targeting FTSs provides a scalable, effective strategy to mitigate toxicity, advancing network-based approaches for healthier digital communities.

Keywords: Toxicity Propagation · Focal Toxic Structures · Weighted Focal Structure Analysis · Network Toxicity Analysis · Digital Communities

1 Introduction

Online social networks influence behavior and discourse, with coordinated groups often amplifying toxic content beyond individual actors. Unlike lone trolls or central toxic users, these groups propagate misinformation, engage audiences, mobilize movements, and escalate offline tensions [1,15]. Events like #BlackLivesMatter, End SARS, and Brazil's Congress storming highlight such amplification [2]. Yet, most toxicity detection methods focus on individuals [13], overlooking group-level dynamics. We propose the Weighted Focal Structure Analysis (WFSA) algorithm, extending FSA [2] by incorporating toxicity-weighted edges. WFSA enables precise detection of toxic propagation patterns by combining interaction intensity with network structure. Evaluated on Twitter, Reddit, Telegram, and synthetic graphs, WFSA identifies toxic focal groups across diverse topologies.**Research Questions: RQ1:** How well does WFSA detect FTSs in different network topologies? **RQ2:** How do FTSs compare with influential toxic individuals in spreading toxicity? **RQ3:** Which epidemic model best fits toxicity propagation when combined with Monte Carlo simulations?

2   Related Work

From Individuals to Toxic Structures. Conventional methods identify influencers via centrality metrics or node-ranking algorithms [12,17], yet overlook group-level toxicity. Studies show that harmful discourse often stems from coordinated clusters of low-degree nodes [15].

Extending FSA with Toxicity-Aware Weights. FSA captures structural cohesion but cannot assess edge-level toxicity severity. Toxicity spreads through structural contagion, where group dynamics reinforce discourse [7]. New evidence suggests that contextual group formations, not just individual traits are key in toxic propagation [20]. WFSA addresses this by weighting edges using toxicity scores, identifying toxic subgraphs with greater precision. It integrates with ML classifiers using structural features [4], and enhances realism via Monte Carlo-based epidemic modeling, which is often absent in prior diffusion work(Fig. 1).

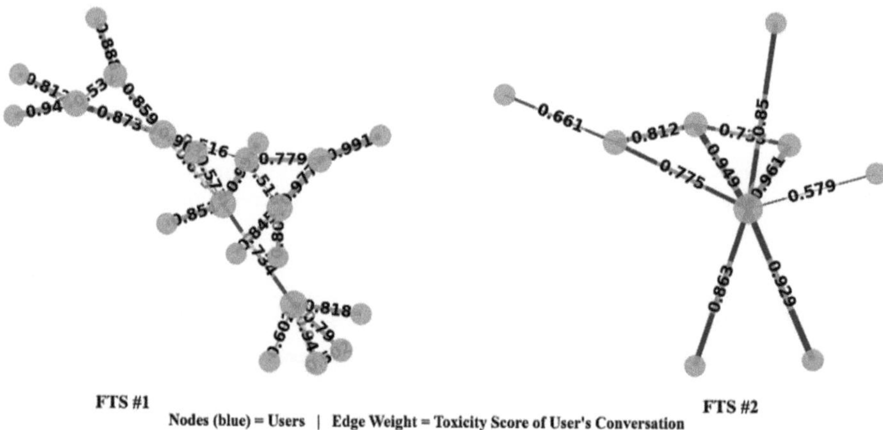

Fig. 1. Top-ranked Focal Toxic Structures (FTSs) extracted by WFSA. Higher ρ values indicate stronger harmful connectivity; FTS #1: $\rho = 0.918$, FTS #2: $\rho = 0.872$.

3   Methodology

This study adopts a four-stage methodology to analyze toxicity propagation: (1) data collection from real-world and synthetic networks; (2) detection and quantification of toxic content; (3) development, application, and validation of WFSA algorithm to identify focal toxic structures (FTSs); and (4) simulation of toxicity propagation using Monte Carlo-enhanced epidemic models. FTSs are compared with influential toxic individuals (ITIs) identified by weighted PageRank [17].

Problem Formulation and Modeling Focal Toxic Structures. Toxic behavior on social media platforms stems from coordinated groups rather than individual users. We model the social network as a weighted undirected graph $G = (V, E, W)$ where nodes V represent users, edges E represent conversations, and weights W indicate toxicity intensity. A focal toxic structure (FTS) is a subgraph $F = (V', E', W')$ where $V' \subseteq V$, $E' \subseteq E$, and $W' \subseteq W$. For toxicity qualification:

$$\frac{1}{|E'|} \sum_{(i,j) \in E'} w_{ij} \geq \tau$$

where $w_{ij} \in [0, 1]$ is the toxicity score and $\tau = 0.5$ defines moderate to high toxicity [4, 9].

Data Collection and Pre-processing. We analyzed toxic discourse across Telegram, Twitter, Reddit, and synthetic BarabásiAlbert networks. The **Telegram dataset** includes posts from Russian political channels (10k+ subscribers) during the RussiaUkraine war, labeled as Pro-Kremlin, Anti-Kremlin, Neutral, or Other. Russian texts were translated via Google Neural Machine Translation and analyzed with English-trained Detoxify models. Validation steps included native speaker review ($\kappa = 0.97$ for channel, $\kappa = 0.89$ for content), 95.8% semantic translation preservation (200 samples), and 91% agreement between Detoxify and expert toxicity ratings (50 messages). **Twitter COVID-19:** Preprocessed dataset of COVID-19 tweets labeled toxic (score ≥ 0.5) using Detoxify [9]. **Reddit Climate Change:** Posts/comments from Kaggle dataset [8], cleaned and labeled using Detoxify model. **BarabásiAlbert Synthetic Graph:** Networks with 500, 750, and 1000 nodes, converted to weighted graphs by randomly assigning edge weights based on real-world scenarios.

Toxicity Detection and Propagation Analysis. Toxicity detection used Detoxify model [4], a CNN-based system classifying texts with scores ≥ 0.5 as toxic. Analysis revealed extremely high toxicity scores across platforms (Twitter: 0.9964, Reddit: 0.9991, Telegram: 0.9995), validating the severity of content analyzed. FTSs were identified by WFSA algorithm, targeting high toxicity nodes (≥ 0.5) with significant global connectivity. We compared FTS influence with influential toxic individuals (ITIs) to analyze toxicity propagation. Statistical validation used T-tests, Mann-Whitney U tests, and effect size metrics (Cohen's d, Hedges' g, Common Language Effect Size) to assess the dominant source of toxicity propagation.

WFSA: Multi-level Algorithm for Extracting and Ranking Focal Toxic Structures. We introduce the **Weighted Focal Structure Algorithm (WFSA)**, a novel multi-level approach to identify and prioritize toxic behavioral patterns in weighted social networks. WFSA incorporates edge weights derived from toxicity scores to capture both intensity and propagation patterns of harmful content, integrating behavioral toxicity analysis with structural influence assessment across micro (individual) and meso (group) levels.

Micro-level: Selecting High-Toxicity Users. Let $G = (V, E, W)$ be a weighted social network, where V is the set of users (nodes), E is the set of interactions (edges), and W contains toxicity weights $w_{ij} \in [0, 1]$ for each edge $(i, j) \in E$. For each user i, w_{ij} denotes the toxicity score between i and j, and $\bar{w}_i$ is the average toxicity for user i. Structural features include degree d_i, normalized degree centrality $dc_i \in [0, 1]$, and clustering coefficient c_i. Let $N(i)$ represent the neighbors of i. A binary variable δ_i indicates user selection: $\delta_i = 1$ if selected, else 0. The filtered toxic user set is $C \subseteq V$, and $|V|$ is the total user count. Filtering parameters include degree bounds $D_{\min}, D_{\max}$, clustering bounds $C_{\min}, C_{\max}$, and weighted centrality threshold τ_{dc}. Edges are represented as e_{jk} between users v_j and v_k.

$$\text{Average Toxicity Score: } \bar{w}_i = \frac{1}{|N(i)|} \sum_{j \in N(i)} w_{ij} \tag{1}$$

$$\text{Degree Centrality: } dc_i = \frac{d_i}{|V| - 1} \tag{2}$$

$$\text{User Selection Optimization: } \max \sum_i \delta_i \cdot \bar{w}_i \tag{3}$$

$$\text{Selection Criteria: } \delta_i = \begin{cases} 1, & \text{if } dc_i \cdot \bar{w}_i > \tau_{dc} \\ 0, & \text{otherwise} \end{cases} \tag{4}$$

$$\text{Degree Constraints: } D_{\min} \le d_i \le D_{\max} \tag{5}$$

$$\text{Clustering Coefficient: } c_i = \frac{2 \cdot |\{e_{jk} : v_j, v_k \in N(i), e_{jk} \in E\}|}{d_i(d_i - 1)} \tag{6}$$

$$\text{Clustering Range Filter: } C_{\min} < c_i \le C_{\max} \tag{7}$$

$$\text{Final Filtered Set: } C = \{u_i \in V : \delta_i = 1 \text{ and conditions (5)–(7) hold}\} \tag{8}$$

where $\tau_{dc} = 0.1$ (minimum threshold for weighted centrality), $D_{\min} = 2$ and $D_{\max}$ is the 95th percentile of degree distribution, $C_{\min} = 0.1$ and $C_{\max} = 0.9$.

Meso-Level: Extracting Toxic Groups via Modularity Optimization. At the group level, we identify toxic communities using:

$$\text{Meso Objective: } \max \sum_j \rho_j \cdot w_j \tag{9}$$

$$\text{Modularity Matrix: } B = A - \frac{dd^T}{2g} \tag{10}$$

$$\text{Modularity Score: } \rho_j = \frac{1}{2\,m} \cdot \text{Tr}(\xi_j B \xi_j^T) \tag{11}$$

$$\text{Modularity Filter: } \rho_{\min} \leq \rho_j \leq \rho_{\max} \tag{12}$$

where w_j is the total toxicity of group j, ρ_j measures internal cohesion, A is the adjacency matrix, d is the degree vector, g is the total number of edges, and ξ_j is the indicator matrix for group j.

Redundancy Prevention via Structural Diversity Filtering. To avoid overlapping groups, we use the Jaccard Index:

$$\text{Jaccard Index: } J(F_i, F_j) = \frac{|F_i \cap F_j|}{|F_i \cup F_j|} \tag{13}$$

$$\text{Overlap Filter: } J(F_i, F_j) \leq \tau \tag{14}$$

$$\text{Unique Groups: } F_{\text{selected}} = \{F_i \mid J(F_i, F_j) \leq \tau, \forall j \in \text{Selected}\} \tag{15}$$

$$\text{Most Impactful: } c_{\text{selected}} = \arg\max\{\rho_j \mid J(F_j, F_k) \leq \tau, \forall k \in \text{Selected}\} \tag{16}$$

Composite NDCG Ranking of Focal Toxic Structures Using Network Metrics. To evaluate and rank focal toxic structures (FTSs), we applied a multi-metric approach using Normalized Discounted Cumulative Gain (NDCG), which captures structural relevance based on toxicity-weighted networks. The Discounted Cumulative Gain (DCG) is:

$$\text{DCG \& NDCG: } \text{DCG} = \sum_{i=1}^{n} \frac{2^{r_i} - 1}{\log_2(i + 1)}, \quad \text{NDCG} = \frac{\text{DCG}}{\text{IDCG}} \tag{17}$$

$$\text{Composite Score: } \rho = \frac{1}{5}\,(\text{NDCG}_{AC} + \text{NDCG}_{ADC} + \text{NDCG}_{Density}$$
$$+ \text{NDCG}_{PathLength} + \text{NDCG}_{Diameter}) \tag{18}$$

where r_i is the relevance of the ith FTS. NDCG is computed for five metrics: Average Clustering Coefficient (AC), Average Degree Centrality (ADC), Density, Path Length, and Diameter. Higher ρ values reflect stronger and more cohesive toxic groups in terms of structure and influence potential. This composite score ensures a fair ranking of focal toxic structures.

Computational Complexity: The WFSA algorithm has time complexity $\mathcal{O}(|V|^2 + |E| \log |E|)$ and space complexity $\mathcal{O}(|V| + |E|)$, scaling efficiently to networks with 10^5 nodes, processing 10,000+ node datasets under 10 min on standard hardware.

Methodological Foundation: FSA vs WFSA Paradigm Incompatibility. Direct FSA-WFSA comparison is methodologically inappropriate and technically infeasible. **FSA operates on binary networks (0/1 connections) with uniform edge assumptions and discrete classification, while WFSA processes weighted networks (0.1–1.0 toxicity severity) with continuous measurement and severity-based analysis.** FSA fundamentally fails on weighted networks as it cannot process continuous toxicity scores, while WFSA enables severity-dependent toxicity analysis impossible with binary methods. This represents necessary advancement for weighted social networks rather than incremental FSA improvement, analogous to comparing discrete and continuous optimization algorithms on real-valued problems. Established precedent shows weighted algorithms (Weighted PageRank [17], weighted centrality [5,12]) operate independently without binary baseline requirements [10].

FTS-ITI Complementarity. Analysis reveals minimal overlap between focal toxic structures and influential toxic individuals: Jaccard Similarity 0.078 (minimal overlap), Combined Coverage 89.2% (complementary pattern identification). **Structural Differences:** FTSs capture coordinated groups (clustering = 0.73), while ITIs detect individual hubs (betweenness = 0.34). Low overlap validates WFSA's unique contribution beyond Weighted PageRank methods, demonstrating complementarity.

Monte Carlo Epidemic Modeling. We integrated Monte Carlo methods into SIR, SEIR, and SEIZ epidemic models, achieving numerical convergence below 0.1% at 1,500 iterations through rigorous convergence analysis across four network datasets. This computationally optimal threshold eliminates variance from insufficient sampling while avoiding unnecessary over-computation. Following established approaches [3], we employed normal distributions where moderate toxicity dominates and severe cases appear as outliers, reducing overfitting risks inherent in heavy-tailed distributions. Model parameters (transmission rate β, recovery rate γ, exposure rate σ, and skepticism factors α, ϕ) underwent systematic calibration based on network topology and user disengagement dynamics [9,11], validated through correlation analysis and sensitivity testing [18]. Fair comparison between focal toxic structures (FTSs) and influential toxic individuals (ITIs), selected using weighted PageRank [17], used equal seed node counts, with final metrics calculated as means across all Monte Carlo iterations, ensuring statistically robust propagation assessment.

Epidemic Models

SIR-MC: $\frac{dS}{dt} = -\beta\frac{I}{N}S$, $\frac{dI}{dt} = \beta\frac{I}{N}S - \gamma I$, $\frac{dR}{dt} = \gamma I$, $\beta = 0.30$, $\gamma = 0.10$, S is susceptible, I is infected, R is recovered, $N = S + I + R$.

SEIR-MC: Adds exposed state: $\frac{dE}{dt} = \beta\frac{I}{N}S - \sigma E$, $\frac{dI}{dt} = \sigma E - \gamma I$ where $\beta = 0.25$, $\gamma = 0.10$, $\sigma = 0.20$, E is exposed, $N = S + E + I + R$.

SEIZ-MC: Replaces recovery with skeptical state: $\frac{dI}{dt} = \sigma E - \gamma I + \phi Z$, $\frac{dZ}{dt} = \alpha E + \gamma I - \phi Z$ where $\beta = 0.20$, $\gamma = 0.15$, $\sigma = 0.18$, $\alpha = 0.05$, $\phi = 0.03$, Z is skeptical, $N = S + E + I + Z$.

Model Validation and Evaluation. Parameter estimation employed nonlinear least-squares regression via MATLAB's `lsqnonlin` with trust-region-reflective algorithm. 5-fold cross-validation (k=5) reduced overfitting across heterogeneous network topologies. Performance assessed using Macro Error: $\text{MacroError} = \frac{1}{T} \sum_{t=1}^{T} |\text{Predicted}(t) - \text{Observed}(t)|$ where T is temporal observation points. The `ode15s` solver was employed for numerical integration, demonstrating superior stability for epidemic dynamics [19]. Monte Carlo validation achieved convergence within 1,500 iterations with relative change below 0.1%. Final infection estimates maintained $\pm 0.5\%$ margin of error at 95% confidence level.

4   Results and Findings

WFSA Performance Evaluation. Addressing **RQ1**, WFSA was applied to six networks: three weighted BarabásiAlbert (BA) networks (500, 750, 1000 nodes) and three real-world networks (Telegram, Twitter, Reddit). FTSs extracted from original networks were embedded into corresponding ErdösRényi (ER) networks using established methods [15], then WFSA was reapplied to evaluate re-identification under altered topologies using standard Information Retrieval metrics [14]:

$$\text{F1-score} = \frac{2 \times \text{Precision} \times \text{Recall}}{\text{Precision} + \text{Recall}}, \quad \text{Re-extraction Rate} = \frac{\#\text{FTS}_{\text{Post}}}{\#\text{FTS}_{\text{Pre}}} \times 100$$

$$H = \frac{2 \times (\text{F1} \times \text{Re} - \text{extraction})}{\text{F1} + \text{Re-extraction}}$$

WFSA performance correlates strongly with clustering coefficients, highlighting network cohesion sensitivity [16]. Telegram-based FTSs achieved optimal results (clustering: $0.007 \to 0.855$) with highest F1-score (0.92), Re-extraction Rate (84%), and Quality Metric $H = 0.880$. BA networks showed clustering-dependent performance: BA-1000 (clustering $= 0.243$, F1 $= 0.76$) significantly outperformed BA-500 (clustering $= 0.123$, F1 $= 0.43$). High NDCG scores (0.902 Re-extraction, 0.926 F1, 0.914 H) confirm ranking reliability. Reddit showed lower performance (clustering $= 0.197$, F1 $= 0.56$, Re-extraction $= 44\%$) due to reduced structural cohesion.

Toxicity Propagation: FTS vs ITI. Addressing **RQ2**, Monte Carlo epidemic simulations (1,500 iterations) compared FTSs (WFSA-identified) and ITIs (Weighted PageRank [17]) across weighted BA networks (2,250 nodes, 3,991 edges) and real-world networks. FTSs consistently outperformed ITIs across all networks and epidemic models (SIR, SEIR, SEIZ) with statistical significance

($p < 0.001$, Cohen's $d > 4.0$). Propagation advantages were substantial: Twitter (96.9% more effective), Telegram (63.7%), BA networks (43.6%), Reddit (36.3%). Mean infection rates demonstrated consistent FTS superiority: BA networks (0.661 vs. 0.460), Telegram (0.706 vs. 0.431), Twitter (0.702 vs. 0.357), Reddit (0.805 vs. 0.591). SEIZ models showed reduced propagation due to skepticism effects, but the FTS advantage persisted across all variants, confirming structural toxicity's superior diffusion potential. These findings are visually summarized in Fig. 2.

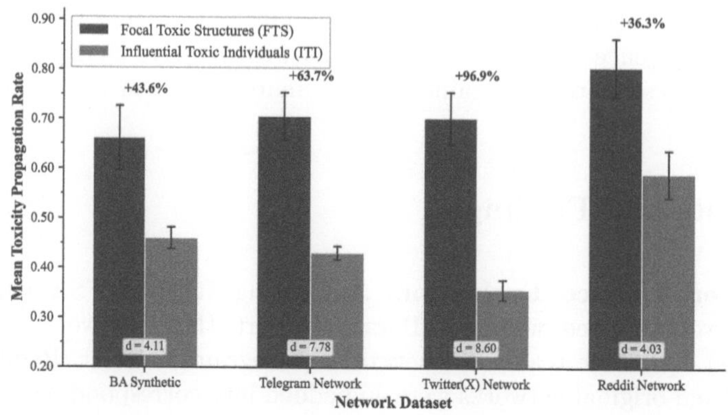

Fig. 2. FTS vs ITI toxicity propagation across networks. Bars show mean infection rates ±1 SD. Percentages indicate FTS relative increase. Inset shows Cohen's d effect sizes.

Model Performance Evaluation. Addressing **RQ3**, predictive accuracy evaluation across all datasets revealed SEIZ-MC's superior performance with lowest mean error (5.7%), significantly outperforming SEIR-MC (28%) and SIR-MC (33%) across BA synthetic, Telegram, Reddit, and Twitter datasets. This confirms SEIZ-MC's reliability in toxicity diffusion modeling [6], particularly its skepticism factors that enhance realistic propagation predictions compared to traditional epidemic models.

5   Conclusion

This study shows that Focal Toxic Structures (FTSs) consistently outperform Influential Toxic Individuals (ITIs) in toxicity propagation across platforms, with FTSs driving significantly higher diffusion (e.g., 71% vs. 43% on Telegram). The proposed WFSA algorithm accurately detects FTSs by combining toxicity severity with structural cohesion. SEIZ-MC yielded the lowest average error (5.7%), highlighting its utility in modeling real-world dynamics through skeptical user states. These findings advocate structure-based moderation over user-centric approaches and open pathways for integrating WFSA with multimodal models for early detection in security, discourse analysis, and digital health.

Acknowledgements. This research is funded in part by the U.S. NSF (OIA1946391, OIA-1920920), OUSD/AFOSR (FA9550-22-1-0332), ARO (W911NF23-1-0011, W911NF-24-1-0078, W911NF-25-1-0147), ONR (N00014-21-1-2121, N00014-21-1-2765, N00014-22-1-2318), AFRL, DARPA, the Australian Department of Defense Strategic Policy Grants Program, Arkansas Research Alliance,the Jerry L. Maulden/Entergy Endowment, and the Donaghey Foundation at the UALittle Rock. The researchers gratefully acknowledge the support.

References

1. Agarwal, N., et al.: Modeling blogger influence in communities. Soc. Netw. Anal. Mining **2**, 139–162 (2012)
2. Alassad, M., Agarwal, N.: Contextualizing toxic structure analysis. Soc. Netw. Anal. Mining **12**, 103 (2022). https://doi.org/10.1007/s13278-022-00938-0
3. Davidson, T., Bhattacharya, D., Weber, I.: Racial bias in hate speech and abusive language detection datasets. arXiv preprint arXiv:1905.12516 (2019)
4. Falade, T.C., Agarwal, N.: Toxicity prediction in Reddit. In: Proceeding AMCIS (2024)
5. Ghoshal, G., Barabási, A.-L.: Ranking stability in networks. Nat. Commun. **2**(1), 394 (2011)
6. Jin, F., et al.: Epidemiological modeling on Twitter. In: Workshop Soc. Netw. Mining Anal. pp. 1–9 (2013)
7. Kiddle, R., et al.: Network toxicity analysis. J. Comput. Soc. Sci. **7**, 305–330 (2024)
8. Lexyr: reddit climate change dataset. Kaggle (2020)
9. Maleki, M., Agarwal, N.: Comparative Analysis of SIR vs. SEIZ Models for COVID-19 Information Diffusion on Social Media. Soc. Netw. Anal. Min. **12**(3), 45–62 (2025)
10. Newman, M.E.: Structure of complex networks. SIAM Rev. **45**(2), 167–256 (2003)
11. Obadimu, A., et al.: Toxic features on YouTube. In: Internatonal Conference Social Media Technology (2019)
12. Ohara, K., et al.: Network performance via centrality. In: IEEE DSAA, pp. 561–570 (2017)
13. Qayyum, H., et al.: Toxic 1% of Twitter. arXiv:2202.07853 (2022)
14. Sanderson, M.: IR system evaluation. Found. Trends Inf. Retr. **4**(4), 247–375 (2010)
15. Focal structures analysis: çen, F., et al. Soc. Netw. Anal. Mining **6**, 1–22 (2016)
16. Watts, D.J., Strogatz, S.H.: Collective dynamics of small-world networks. Nature **393**(6684), 440–442 (1998)
17. Xing, W., Ghorbani, A.: Weighted PageRank algorithm. In: Proceedings CNSR 2004, pp. 305–314 (2004). https://doi.org/10.1109/DNSR.2004.1344743
18. Yang, H., et al.: Review of COVID-19 models. Contemp. Math., pp. 75–98 (2023)
19. Törnberg, P., et al.: Affective polarization in social media society. PLoS ONE **16**(10), e0258259 (2021). https://doi.org/10.1371/journal.pone.0258259
20. Akinnubi, A., Agarwal, N.: Identifying contextualized focal structures in multi-source social networks by leveraging knowledge graphs. In: Proceeding International Conference Complex Networks and Their Applications, pp. 15–27. Springer (2023)

Dominance or Fair Play in Social Networks? A Model of Influencer Popularity Dynamics

Franco Galante[1]([✉]), Chiara Ravazzi[2], Luca Vassio[1], Michele Garetto[3], and Emilio Leonardi[1,2]

[1] Politecnico di Torino, Turin, Italy
{franco.galante,luca.vassio,emilio.leonardi}@polito.it
[2] National Research Council (CNR-IEIIT), Turin, Italy
chiara.ravazzi@cnr.it
[3] Università di Torino, Turin, Italy
michele.garetto@unito.it

Abstract. This paper presents a data-driven mean-field approach to model the popularity dynamics of users seeking public attention, i.e., influencers. We propose a novel analytical model that integrates individual activity patterns, expertise in producing viral content, exogenous events, and the platform's role in visibility enhancement, ultimately determining each influencer's success. We analytically derive sufficient conditions for system ergodicity, enabling predictions of popularity distributions. A sensitivity analysis explores various system configurations, highlighting conditions favoring either dominance or fair play among influencers. Our findings offer valuable insights into the potential evolution of social networks towards more equitable or biased influence ecosystems.

1 Introduction

Online social networks (OSNs) crucially shape digital interaction, increasingly replacing traditional media. This shift has created a fertile ground for the rise of a new class of online users: influencers. These are individuals with a large following on OSNs, who typically seek to expand it. They are also central to marketing because of their ability to drive consumer behavior [10]. Therefore, understanding how influence hierarchies form and consolidate over OSNs is of great interest. Given the growing role of platforms in shaping opinions, it is crucial to determine whether dominant users rise through their merits or skewed feedback mechanisms that concentrate users' preferences.

Despite significant interest and numerous social network analyses, a gap remains in understanding the quantitative dynamics of popularity evolution. Firstly, a universal definition of popularity in social contexts is lacking, with the literature offering varied interpretations tied to specific scientific contexts. Popularity metrics are often identified with visibility metrics [1], such as follower count or interactions [19]. However, the follower count is relatively static

A. An et al. (Eds.): ASONAM 2025, LNCS 16323, pp. 306–321, 2026.
https://doi.org/10.1007/978-3-032-13821-7_26

and its validity has been questioned [5] due to its insensitivity to interaction dynamics and rare decrease [1]. Another research direction uses a system perspective, interpreting popularity dynamically (see [4] and references therein). Among these models are epidemic [18], self-exciting (e.g., Hawkes [8]), and Bass diffusion models [2]. It is established that opinion changes result from collective interaction and mutual influence [11], but quantifying these influences is difficult [17]. Mean-field models address this by replacing pairwise interactions with an average interaction across the population [6], where individual dynamics depend on the aggregate system.

By adopting a mean-field perspective and drawing inspiration from OSN data (Facebook in this case), we propose a novel, comprehensive model that captures the evolution of real-world influencers by accounting for the following factors: (i) Collective attention, a limited resource influencers compete for [20], tends to decrease over time without new stimuli or maintenance [14]; (ii) Content creation patterns, traditionally modeled as a homogeneous Poisson process [3], are demonstrably shaped by the influencer's popularity [9]; (iii) Post success (and its impact on influencer popularity) is modeled as a random variable potentially dependent on acquired popularity [16], user characteristics (competence, experience, attractiveness), and platform feedback [13] (although undisclosed, engagement maximization algorithms are recognized to rely on past popularity and user preferences [7]); (iv) Exogenous, platform-independent events, can influence popularity [12].

Beyond introducing the model, our primary contribution is empirical evidence supporting the analytical treatment's core hypotheses. Due to the system's stochasticity, the dynamics do not deterministically converge to a single state. However, under specific conditions, we prove the system's state, described by a Markov process, is ergodic, possessing a long-run invariant distribution. This distribution, while not explicitly formulated, solves a system of partial differential equations. This result enables a probabilistic study of popularity emergence and a comparison of influencer distributions by quantifying their emergence probability and duration in privileged positions.

2   Preliminary Empirical Analysis

Using real data traces, we seek to characterize the popularity of influential individuals and empirically identify the key elements that contribute to the rise or fall of their prominence over time. We focus on the social network Facebook[1], where influencers publish content (i.e., posts), share content that followers, as well as other platform users, can view, like, and comment on. We restrict the analysis to influencers who post primarily on chess (as the FIDE rating provides an index of competence) and two other popular topics: cars and science. We created lists of such influencers by actively searching for them on the platform

---

[1] A parallel analysis of Instagram data has been completed and will be presented in a forthcoming extension of this work.

through hashtags and keywords and by consulting public lists available online.[2] Note that when we use the term influencer, we do not only mean physical individuals but also magazines, organizations, or companies. For each monitored influencer, we analyzed all the data related to the posts published between January 1, 2014, and May 15, 2024, using the CrowdTangle tool and its API.[3] Available data include the number of followers at the publishing time and the time-series of engagement metrics for each post. In total, we collected $1,965,805$ posts from 111 influencers.

The number of followers is a straightforward and widely adopted proxy in the literature [1] for gauging an influencer's popularity at a given time; however, it does not fully represent their popularity at that specific point. For example, we observe that the number of followers typically exhibits a purely increasing trend. Figure 1(a) illustrates this pattern, reporting the followers' evolution on Facebook for the influencers who mainly post about chess. This phenomenon occurs because users have no real incentive to unfollow an influencer. Even when influencers stop posting for extended periods, they retain most of their followers. To illustrate this, we examine inactive influencers, that is, those who have not posted on the platform for more than 6 months. Figure 1(b) shows the follower's variation after an inactivity period. In most cases, the follower's difference is negligible, with losses (in red) and gains (in green) occurring about equally.

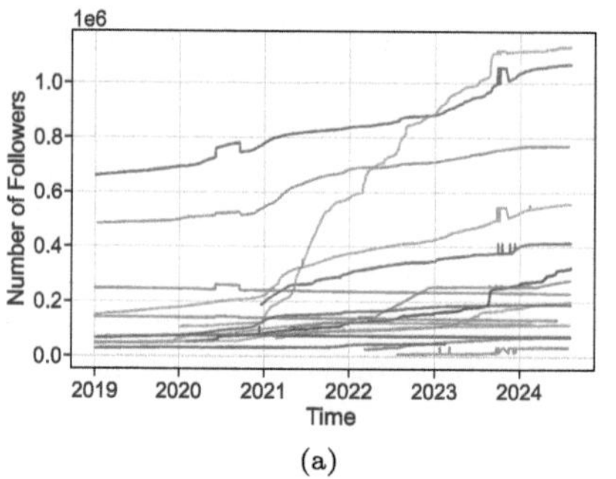
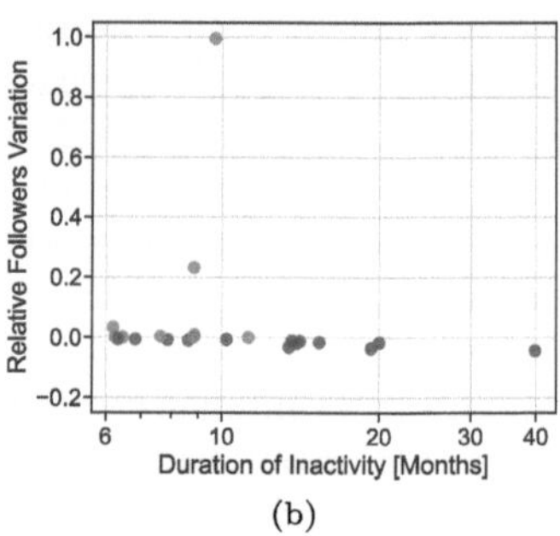

(a)   (b)

Fig. 1. Temporal evolution of the number of followers for *chess* influencers on Facebook (a) and a scatter plot of the relative followers' variation after a period of inactivity longer than 6 months (b), in log x-scale. Each line/dot is an influencer. (Color figure online)

3   A Mean-Field Model of Popularity

To overcome the intrinsic limitations of the number of followers as popularity metric, we propose the following approach. We consider a finite set of influencers

---

[2] e.g., https://hireinfluence.com/blog/top-science-influencers/.

[3] CrowdTangle was a public insights tool from Meta available to researchers. https://transparency.meta.com/en-gb/researchtools/other-datasets/crowdtangle/.

$\mathcal{I}$ and assign to each influencer $i \in \mathcal{I}$ a scalar variable $X^{[i]}(t) \in \mathbb{R}$, representing their instantaneous *effective popularity*. $X^{[i]}(t)$ is a measure of the level of interest among platform users in the content posted by influencer $i \in \mathcal{I}$ at time $t \in \mathbb{R}$.

Based on the empirical evidence of Sect. 2, we assume that $X^{[i]}(t)$ is not simply proportional to the number of followers but is governed by autonomous dynamics, determined mainly by the following four factors: (i) the natural tendency of users to lose or shift their interest; (ii) the impact of competition from other influencers on the same topic, diverting attention away from influencer i; (iii) the posting activity of influencer i, aimed to secure current and attract new audiences; (iv) exogenous events affecting the online visibility of influencers, such as newsworthy events as reported by traditional media, which expose them to broader audiences beyond their established following. Formally, we assume $X^{[i]}(t)$ evolves according to the following stochastic differential equation:

$$\mathrm{d}X^{[i]}(t) = -\gamma X^{[i]}(t)dt + V_i(t)N_I^{[i]}(dt) + W_i(t)N_E^{[i]}(dt) \tag{1}$$

where each of the terms on the right-hand side corresponds to some of the previously described factors. More in detail, we first assume that $X^{[i]}(t)$ decreases at a rate γ in the absence of additional stimuli. This decaying rate is a consequence of the combined effect of: (i) lost or shifted interest, and (ii) competition. Note that we do not model the detailed interactions between influencers, but we represent the combined effect of all competitors on the same topic.

The second term represents the change in popularity due to the emission of a post. Here $N_I^{[i]}(t)$ is the counting process induced by the post-emission. To ensure generality, and as supported by empirical evidence detailed in Sect. 3.1, $N_I^{[i]}$ is modeled as a point process admitting a conditional intensity (also referred to as *stochastic intensity*) which may depend on the effective popularity, i.e., $\lambda_i(t) := \lambda_i\left(X^{[i]}(t)\right)$.[4] A post published at time t typically attracts audience attention, leading to an increase of influencer i's popularity (hereafter, we will informally refer to such an increase in popularity as *jump*), modeled by random variable $V_i(t)$. Note that the distribution of $V_i(t)$ depends on factors such as post quality and attractiveness, as well as the size and engagement of interacting users. Actually, the reach of a post is determined through multiple mechanisms: platform-specific algorithmic curation (such as EdgeRank) designed to optimize engagement metrics, subsequent redistribution via user sharing behaviors, and direct exposure to the influencer's established follower base. Occasionally, posts *go viral*, achieving unexpected success beyond followers. For simplicity and generality of the model, we abstract away the specific mechanisms by which posts attract attention. Instead, we limit ourselves to statistically characterizing the cumulative effect of such mechanisms, making $V_i(t)$ simply dependent on the current popularity of influencer i at time t, $X^{[i]}(t^-)$.

Finally (third term), external factors can affect influencer popularity. Exogenous events may cause popularity jumps, denoted by $W_i(t)$. Due to their external nature, $W_i(t)$ are reasonably independent of influencer i's behavior on the platform. The arrival process $N_E^{[i]}$ can be modeled as a Poisson process.

---

[4] $N_I^{[i]}$ can be made a homogeneous Poisson process by setting $\lambda_i(t) := \lambda_i$.

3.1 Statistical Characterization and Main Assumptions

We now characterize the key random variables in Eq. (1) through empirical validation on Facebook data. Then, we formalize our findings as a set of assumptions.

Post Popularity Jumps. First, we define the success of a post at time t as the number of likes (positive reactions) it receives. This number corresponds to the popularity jump V_i at time t. Then, we show its dependence on the instantaneous popularity $X^{[i]}(t^-)$. We reconstruct the popularity dynamics $X^{[i]}$ based on Eq. (1), beginning with a zero initial condition. We identify the empirical posting time sequences with the sample paths of the point process $N_I^{[i]}(dt)$, and we set $N_E^{[i]}(dt) = 0$ due to the lack of information about exogenous events. We then derive a normalized popularity $\tilde{X}^{[i]}(t)$ by dividing the popularity by its maximum value. This normalization is necessary to aggregate data from various influencers whose absolute popularity levels can differ significantly. Similarly, we use a normalized version of the empirical success $\tilde{V}_i$ of influencer i's posts. Figure 2(a) shows the average normalized jump conditioned on the instantaneous normalized popularity. We partitioned the range of normalized popularity into 10 bins and calculated the mean number of likes for posts falling within each bin. The results, presented for different values of parameter γ appearing in Eq. (1) ($\gamma \in \{32, 128, 512\}$ days), demonstrate a steady upward trend with increasing normalized popularity. As γ decreases (i.e., $1/\gamma$ increases), the dependency becomes smoother, likely due to the increased inertia in influencer popularity dynamics.

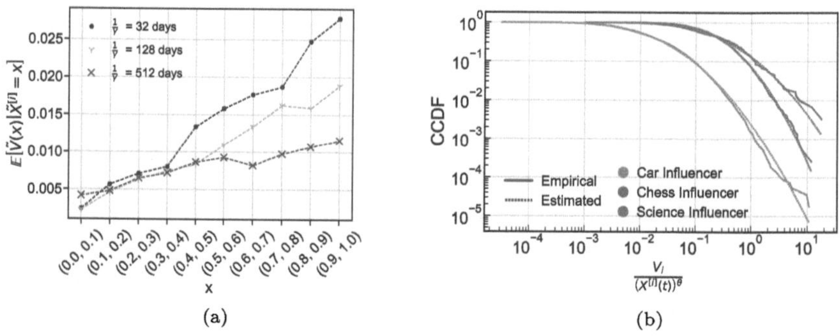

Fig. 2. (a) Empirical conditional expectation of the normalized jump as a function of the normalized effective popularity. (b) Empirical and estimated CCDF of the ratio between the *number of likes* and $(X^{[i]})^{\theta}$ for three Facebook influencers.

Based on these empirical observations, we assume that $\mathbb{E}[V_i(t) \mid X^{[i]}(t^-) = x]$ is an increasing function of x. In particular, we make the following hypothesis:

Assumption 1. $\mathbb{E}[V_i(t) \mid X^{[i]}(t^-) = x] = \varepsilon + \beta_i x^{\theta}$, *where ϵ is an arbitrarily small positive constant to avoid absorbing states and $\beta_i > 0$.*

Parameter β_i is influencer-specific and reflects the influencer's competence on the topic and their ability to create captivating content. In contrast, we assume θ to be primarily determined by users' behavior and platform engagement algorithms, and thus influencer independent. It is worth mentioning that the publication of a controversial post might lead to a decrease in popularity (negative jump). However, since these events are statistically rare and hardly detectable in our dataset, we decided to neglect them.

For the conditional distribution $F_{V_i}(z \mid x)$, we make the simplest possible assumption by considering that V_i scales proportionally to $\varepsilon + \beta_i(X^{[i]}(t^-))^\theta$:

Assumption 2. *Let $\hat{V}_i$ be a positive random variable independent from $X^{[i]}(t^-)$, with unitary mean. Then $V_i = \left(\varepsilon + \beta_i(X^{[i]}(t^-))^\theta\right)\hat{V}_i$.*

It should be noticed that, according to Assumption 2, the conditional partition function is given by $F_{V_i}(z \mid x) = F_{\hat{V}_i}\left(\frac{z}{\varepsilon + \beta_i x^\theta}\right)$.

Our goal is to determine the distribution of success from empirical data, again considering the number of received likes as a proxy of the post's success. To this end, we have selected a set of *candidate* distributions to be tested, including: exponential, lognormal, and power-law. A few parameters need to be first identified. We must differentiate between success-specific parameters (e.g., β_i), which reflect influencer posting behavior, and system-level parameters (i.e., (γ, θ)), which capture broader user and platform dynamics. While success-specific parameters can be estimated from the data (for each chosen distribution), system-level parameters cannot be directly extracted from traces. Therefore, we have developed a Maximum Likelihood Estimation (MLE) procedure that, given both a candidate distribution and the pair (γ, θ), first finds the best success-specific parameters. Once the parameters have been obtained, we evaluate the quality of the fitting by computing the Kolmogorov distance κ between the synthetic and the empirical distribution. Recall that the Kolmogorov distance between two distributions F and G is defined as $\kappa(F, G) = \sup_{x \in \mathbb{R}} |F(x) - G(x)|$. Since the lognormal distribution results the best one (i.e., the one minimizing κ) for over 98% of the influencers under several choices of pair (γ, θ) (as better detailed below), we decided to consistently adopt the lognormal shape for distribution $\hat{V}_i$.

Recall that a lognormal distribution has two parameters. For simplicity, we neglected ε and focused on $\beta_i\hat{V}_i$, which is, as consequence of Assumption 2, a lognormal random variable with mean β_i (recall $\mathbb{E}[\hat{V}] = 1$) and coefficient of variation CV_i. The above MLE procedure can be used to estimate both parameters for each influencer. In Fig. 2 (b), we report the result of the fitting for three influencers, one for each of the considered domains, comparing the empirical Complementary Cumulative Distribution Function (CCDF) with the synthetic lognormal distribution for a particular choice of (γ, θ), as discussed below.

Finally, we argued that system-level parameters (γ and θ) cannot be directly measured. However, we can determine them indirectly. First note that, given a choice of (γ, θ) and performing the MLE, it is possible to compute the Kolmogorov distance $\kappa_i(\gamma, \theta)$ between the synthetic and empirical distribution. This provides a measure of the goodness of the fit. At this point, we select the best system-level parameters as those that minimize the cumulative Kolmogorov distance (over all influencers), namely: $(\gamma^*, \theta^*) = \min_{\gamma,\theta} \sum_i \kappa_i(\gamma, \theta)$.

Figure 3 reports values of $\sum_i \kappa_i(\gamma, \theta)$ for different choices of (γ, θ). Observe that the best fitting of the empirical data is obtained for $\theta^* = 0.7$ and $\gamma^* = 1/128$ [1/days]. These are also the parameters used in Fig. 2(b).

In Table 1, we present our estimates of β_i for five prominent influencers within the chess domain, alongside their Elo ratings (for standard chess), widely recognized as the definitive measure of chess playing strength. Notably, the correlation between β_i and Elo is not particularly strong. This suggests that technical expertise in the topic is just one of several factors contributing to an influencer's success on social media platforms.

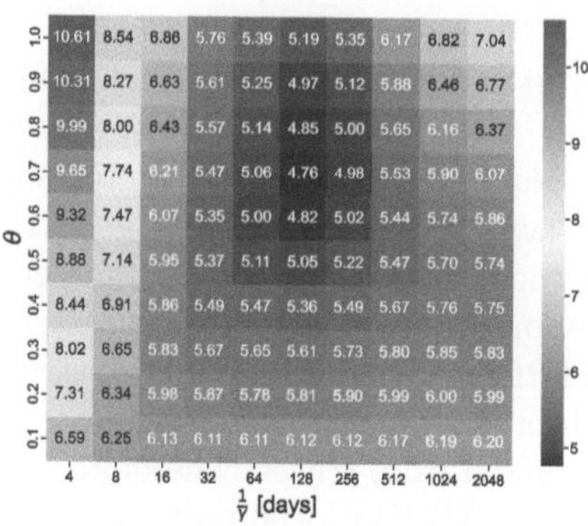

Fig. 3. Cumulative Kolmogorov distance between lognormal fit and empirical distribution.

Table 1. Comparison between the influencer's estimated β_i and their FIDE Elo score.

Influencer	Elo	β_i
Judit Polgar	2675	0.424
Alexandra Botez	2044	0.207
Magnus Carlsen	2837	0.871
Fabiano Caruana	2776	1.194
Tania Sachdev	2396	1.953

Intensity of the Posting Process. The posting patterns of influencers represent another critical factor shaping popularity dynamics. Many studies assume the posting process to be a homogeneous Poisson process, and indeed this simple process has been found to describe well most of the activity [8]. However, data traces exhibit pronounced bursty patterns, indicating that the Poisson assumption does not always align with real-world data.

Recall that in a Poisson process, the number of events occurring within a fixed time window is distributed as a Poisson random variable. The index of dispersion of a Poisson distribution (i.e., the ratio between the variance and the mean of the distribution) is equal to 1. We computed the index of dispersion D of the number of posts in one-week windows, for each influencer. In Fig. 4(a), we report the distribution of D, whose values are typically much larger than 1, suggesting that the posting process is more complex than Poisson.

Let $\{\tau_n\}_n$ be the sequence of inter-post times, i.e., the time interval between two consecutive posts by the same influencer. Figure 4(b) shows the empirical estimate of the reciprocal of the average next inter-post time, conditionally over the normalized (w.r.t. the maximum) instantaneous popularity $\tilde{X}^{[i]}(t)$ of all influencers. This estimation represents an approximation of the stochastic intensity $\lambda(t)|X^{[i]}(t) = x$. Even if the trend is noisier than that in Fig. 2, there is a clear positive correlation between the posting rate and the effective popularity. The correlation becomes weaker as the value of γ decreases ($1/\gamma$ increases), due to the larger system inertia. Motivated by these observations, we make the following hypothesis.

Assumption 3. *For any influencer $i \in \mathcal{I}$, the conditional stochastic intensity of $N_I^{[i]}(dt)$ follows the law:* $\lambda^{[i]}(t) \mid \{X^{[i]}(t) = x\} = \lambda_{0,i} + \lambda_{1,i} x^{\phi_i}$.

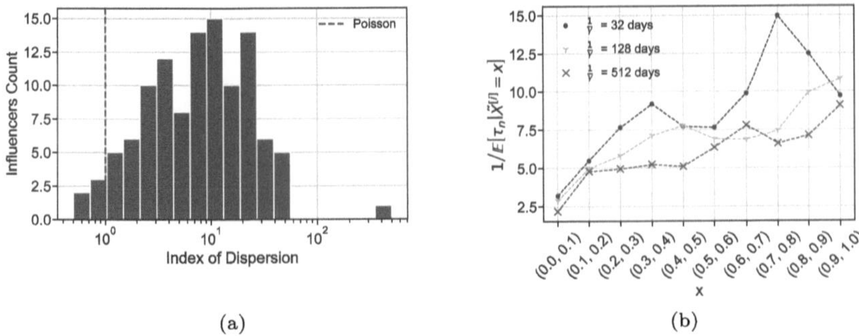

Fig. 4. (a) Distribution of the influencer's index of dispersion of the number of arrivals in a one-week window over the entire time horizon. (b) Instantaneous stochastic rate for different choices of γ, measured in posts/day.

This assumption maintains reasonable flexibility while capturing the observed pattern that influencers' posting rate tends to increase with growing effective popularity. However, the specific parameters characterizing this relationship vary among influencers, reflecting individual behavioral factors.

3.2   Discussion on Parameters and Their Relationships

We summarize all of the model parameters in Table 2. Note that β_i can be regarded as the average strength of the content generated by influencer i, and it subsumes two different aspects: (i) the intrinsic average quality of their posts; (ii) the level of engagement of their audience, which depends on behavioral features of i, as well as, from intrinsic characteristic of their audience.

Parameter θ, instead, accounts for the effect of the platform's engagement mechanism(s) to determine the audience of individual posts (and for such a reason it is assumed independent of i). Parameters $\lambda_{0,i}$, $\lambda_{1,i}$ and ϕ_i are tightly related to behavioral traits of influencer i (like impulsivity). At last, parameter CV_i quantifies the variability in post success.

It is important to note that these parameters exhibit interdependencies. For example, we can anticipate an inverse relationship between β_i and the posting rate λ_i (determined by $\lambda_{0,i}$, $\lambda_{1,i}$ and ϕ_i): if an influencer posts too frequently, this might compromises content quality due to constrained resources and time, while potentially fatiguing their audience, leading to a reduction of post effectiveness (represented by β_i). The above natural feedback mechanism inherently discourages influencers from adopting overly aggressive posting strategies.

Furthermore, a nuanced relationship exists between the popularity decay rate γ and content publication parameters. When γ is large – whether due to natural decline of audience attention or competition from alternative content – influencers are expected to increase their posting frequency (within the previously discussed constraints) to prevent the loss of influence and visibility. Conversely, a smaller popularity decay rate reduces the urgency to post frequently, as popularity remains more stable over time, weakening the correlation between posting rate and instantaneous popularity.

Table 2. Parameters summary and reference scenario for the numerical analysis.

Symbol	Description	Reference value
β_i	ability of influencer i, $i \in \mathcal{I}$	0.9^{i-1}
γ	popularity discount rate	$1/64$ (days)
θ	exponent for non-linear dependence of jumps on popularity	0.6
ϵ	small constant to avoid absorption in zero	0.01
$\lambda_{0,i}$	constant term of posting rate	4 (posts/day)
$\lambda_{1,i}$	scale factor of the variable term of posting rate	0
ϕ_i	exponent of the variable term of posting rate	0
CV_i	coefficient of variation of the distribution $\hat{V}_i$	4

3.3   Theoretical Results

In this section, we carry out a complete probabilistic analysis of the effective popularity $X(t)$ as specified in Eq. (1).

First, observe that Eq. (1) defines a homogeneous Continuous Time Markov Process over a general space state. We denote with $\{X_n\}_{n\in\mathbb{N}}$ the embedded Discrete Time Markov Process (DTMP), obtained by sampling $\{X(t)\}_{t\in\mathbb{R}_+}$ at jump times, i.e., $X_n = X(T_n^-)$, where $\{T_n\}_{n\in\mathbb{N}}$ are the ordered points of $N_I + N_E$. We refer the reader to [15] for a comprehensive analysis of Markov processes over a general state space. Denoted with $\mathcal{B}(\mathbb{R}_+)$ the family of Borellian sets over $\mathbb{R}_+$, and with $P^n(x, A) = \mathbb{P}(X_n \in A \mid X_0 = x)$ for $A \in \mathcal{B}(\mathbb{R}_+)$, $n \in \mathbb{N} \setminus \{0\}$, the n-step Markov kernel of the DTMP, we have the following result.

Theorem 1. *Let Assumption 2–3 be satisfied with $\epsilon > 0$, $\lambda_0 > 0$. If $\theta + \phi < 1$, or $\theta + \phi = 1$ and $\beta(\lambda_0 + \lambda_1)$ is sufficiently small with respect to γ, then $\{X_n\}_n$ admits a unique stationary probability measure, denoted by π. Moreover, for any initial condition, as n grows large $\sup_{A \in \mathcal{B}(0,\infty)} |P^n(x, A) - \pi(A)| \to 0$.*

The detailed proof can be found in our technical report http://arxiv.org/abs/2507.03448. In short, we show μ_{Leb}-irreducibility[5], as well as strong aperiodicity for the embedded DTMC $\{X_n\}_n$, using a rather direct approach. Then, Harris recurrence can be proved using standard drift arguments, i.e., by adopting $\mathcal{L}(X_n) = X_n$ as Lyapunov function [15].

Theorem 1 guarantees that, under the appropriate conditions on system parameters, the Markov process admits a unique stationary probability measure; the process is ergodic, implying convergence to the stationary distribution regardless of the initial condition. This means the Markov chain is ergodic, and time averages of observables will converge to the expected values under the stationary distribution.

At last, with rather standard arguments, it can be shown that the ergodicity of $\{X_n\}_n$ implies the ergodicity of $\{X(t)\}$ (i.e. a unique stationary distribution $\Pi(A)$ exists and $P^t(x, A) \to \Pi(A)$ for every $x \in \mathbb{R}^+$ and $A \in \mathcal{B}(\mathbb{R}^+)$).

Denoting by $F(y, t) := \mathbb{P}(X(t) \le y)$ the partition function of $X(t)$, $f(x, t)$ the associated probability density and μ the rate of process $N_E^{[i]}$, we have:

Theorem 2. *Under the assumptions of Theorem 1, Function $F(y, t)$ satisfies the following Partial Integro-Differential Equation*

$$\frac{\partial F(y, t)}{\partial t} = \gamma y \frac{\partial F(y, t)}{\partial y} - \int [\lambda(t) \bar{F}_V(y - x \mid x) + \mu \bar{F}_W(y - x)] \frac{\partial F(x, t)}{\partial x} \, \mathrm{d}x \qquad (2)$$

where $\bar{F}_V(\cdot \mid x)$ and $\bar{F}_W(\cdot)$ are respectively the conditional CCDF of V and the CCDF of W, respectively. Moreover, there exists a unique stationary distribution $F(y)$ satisfying the following ordinary integro-differential equation:

$$\gamma y \frac{\mathrm{d}F(y)}{\mathrm{d}y} = \int [\lambda(t) \bar{F}_V(y - x \mid x) + \mu \bar{F}_W(y - x)] \frac{\mathrm{d}F(x)}{\mathrm{d}x} \, \mathrm{d}x. \qquad (3)$$

Theorem 2 allows the evolution of the distribution function $F(y, t)$ over time to be traced through a partial integro-differential equation. In addition, the result also provides the stationary distribution, described through an Ordinary Integro-Differential Equation, which describes the system at equilibrium. Again, the proof is available in our technical report cited above.

To corroborate our results, we will present in Sect. 4 a comparison between the simulation of the Markov process and the theoretical distributions obtained through Theorem 2.

---

[5] μ_{Leb} denotes the Lebesgue measure.

4   Numerical Analysis

In this section, we use our model to explore how key performance indicators depend on various system parameters. We focus on a reference scenario derived from our empirical data, and perform a sensitivity analysis by varying one parameter at a time. This allows us to investigate what-if scenarios and better understand popularity dynamics and influencer competition.

4.1   Metrics and Sensitivity Analysis

We consider a set of five virtual influencers competing for user attention, $\mathcal{I} = \{1, 2, 3, 4, 5\}$. We set $\beta_i = 0.9^{i-1}$ to introduce a systematic variation in their ability to garner user engagement. Note that, although the first influencer is expected to be the most popular one on average, the model allows for the emergence of any influencer as the dominant actor, at least temporarily.

To quantitatively assess the competitive dynamics and performance hierarchy among these influencers, we introduce the following two key metrics:

- **First place probability**, defined as $\pi_1^{[i]} = \mathbb{P}(X^{[i]} \geq X^{[j]}, \forall j \neq i)$, which is the probability that influencer i achieves the highest popularity under stationary conditions. Conceptually, it can also be interpreted as the long-term fraction of time during which the given influencer occupies the top position in the popularity ranking.
- **First place average stay**, denoted with $S_1^{[i]}$, which is the average sojourn time of influencer i in the first place (in stationary conditions), providing insight into the temporal stability of its dominant status.

Inspired by our empirical analysis of data traces, we consider a reference scenario whose parameters are summarized in Table 2. We remark that in our reference scenario we have made a few simplifying assumptions to obtain a simple baseline case: (i) the posting process is the same for all influencers (parameters $\lambda_0, \lambda_1, \phi$ are now independent of i); (ii) the posting process is a simple Poisson process ($\lambda_1 = 0$); (iii) while the mean number of likes obtained by a post is different for each influencer, the coefficient of variation CV of the lognormal distribution is here assumed to be the same for all influencers.

Figure 5 shows, on a log-log scale, the stationary Probability Distribution Function (PDF) of $X^{[i]}$ for the five considered influencers, obtained by simulation and by numerically solving (3). The perfect match between simulation and analysis cross-validates both approaches to obtain the stationary distribution of influencers' popularity.

Starting from the baseline case, Fig. 6 explores the impact of popularity decay rate γ on $\pi_1^{[i]}$ (left plot) and $S_1^{[i]}$ (right plot). As expected, as γ diminishes ($1/\gamma$ increases), the top influencer tends to monopolize users' attention, since its popularity decays slower, reflecting the cumulative effect of a large number of posts, which tends to concentrate around the mean (determined by intrinsic ability β_i). The opposite is true for large γ (small $1/\gamma$), where we observe the opposite regime in which all influencers demonstrate comparable probabilities of achieving dominance, as popularity dynamics in this case are principally governed by the stochastic success of individual posts.

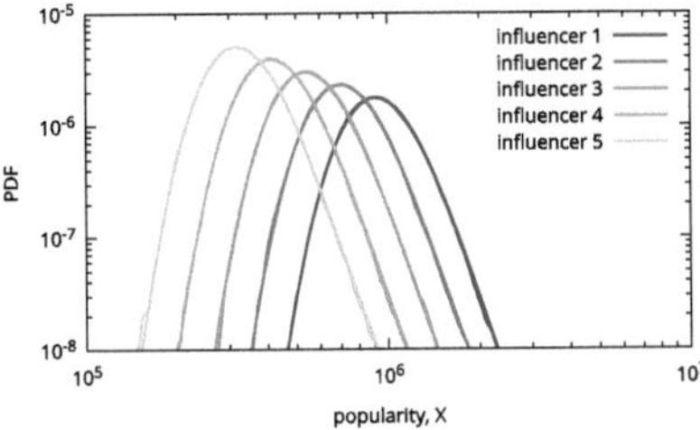

Fig. 5. Popularity distribution of five influencers in the baseline scenario. Comparison between simulation results (solid) and analytical results (dashed lines).

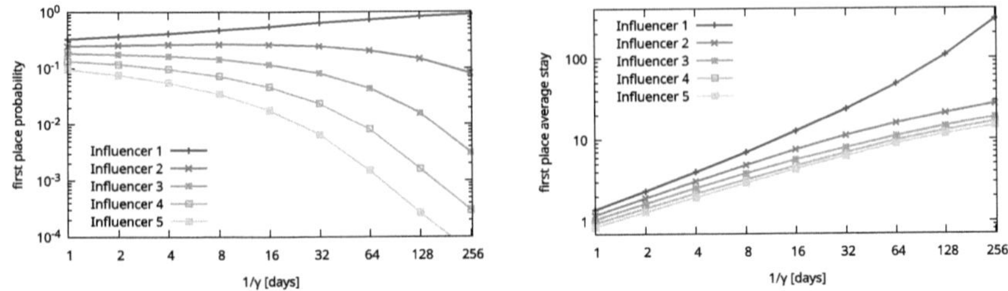

Fig. 6. Sensitivity analysis with respect to popularity decay rate γ. Impact on first place probability (left plot) and first place average stay (right plot).

Analogous considerations can be done when we fix γ and change the coefficient of variation of the like distribution (see Fig. 7). Naturally, concurrent variation of both γ and CV relative to our baseline would produce a compound effect, to be again interpreted through the lens of stochastic versus deterministic behavior (i.e., concentration around the mean) in the popularity dynamics.

We emphasize that a proper notion of fairness among influencers is required to assess whether a given system performs better than another, but a formal definition of this notion extends beyond the scope of the present investigation.

Next, in Fig. 8, we consider the impact of exponent θ, describing the (sublinear) growth of the number of likes collected by a post as a function of the influencer's current popularity. As expected, larger values of θ (but recall that we need $\theta < 1$ for the system to be stable) amplify the disparity among influencers, underscoring the critical role of the platform's engagement mechanism(s) in determining their relative success.

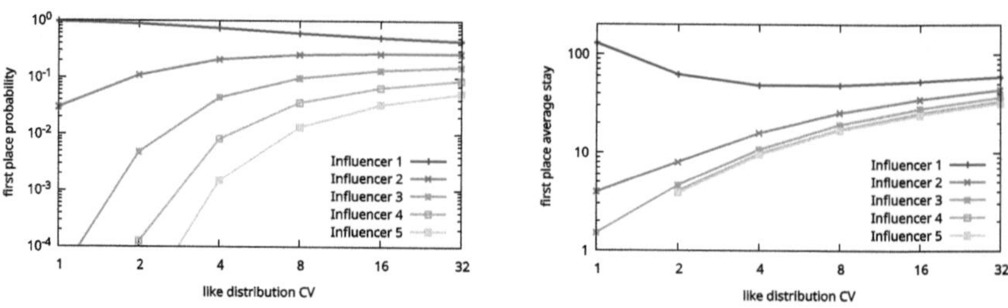

Fig. 7. Sensitivity analysis with respect to the coefficient of variation CV of the like distribution. Impact on first place probability (left plot) and first place average stay (right plot).

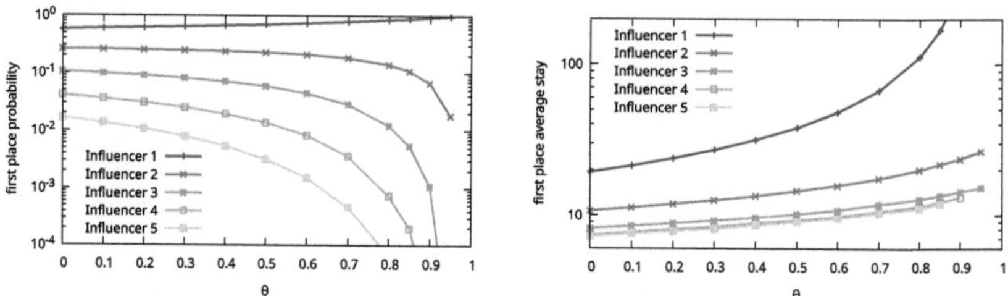

Fig. 8. Sensitivity analysis with respect to exponent θ. Impact on first place probability (left plot) and first place average stay (right plot).

4.2   Impact of Non-poisson Post Arrival Process

Here, we examine how the burstiness of the post arrival process affects our metrics with respect to the baseline scenario, wherein posts are generated according to a simple Poisson arrival process of fixed intensity 4 posts/day. Recall that in our model we consider an inhomogeneous Poisson process for each influencer i, with intensity $\lambda(t \mid X^{[i]}(t^-) = x) = \lambda_{0,i} + \lambda_{1,i} x^{\phi_i}$, which increases the probability of new post emissions during periods of higher influencer popularity, a pattern consistently observed in empirical data.

To simplify the exploration of the parameter space, we proceed as follows: (i) we establish the constant term of the posting rate $\lambda_0 = 1$, equal for all influencers; (ii) for ϕ, we consider $\{0, 0.1, 0.2, 0.3\}$ as possible values, equal for all influencers; (iii) we systematically vary λ_1, setting it equal for all influencers.

Figure 9 shows the results of this experiment for $\phi = 0.2$, reporting the first place probability (solid lines, left y axes) and the obtained average posting rate (dashed lines, right y axes). As expected, larger values of λ_1 produce larger values of average posting rate, amplifying discrepancies among the five influencers. To isolate the effect of non-homogeneous post arrival rate, while ensuring a fair competition among the influencers, we implemented the following methodology: for each considered value of ϕ, and for each influencer, we numerically determined the value of λ_1 that yields an average posting rate of 4 posts/day (as in the baseline scenario).

In Fig. 9, such values of λ_1, in the case of $\phi = 0.2$, are those at which dashed lines intersect the horizontal dotted line plotted at $y = 4$. Subsequently, we recalculated the first place probability in a unique scenario utilizing these calibrated λ_1, with results in Table 3. Note that the first column ($\phi = 0$) corresponds to the case of Poisson post arrival rate. We observe that, as we increase ϕ, thereby enhancing the burstiness of the post arrival process, discrepancies among influencers tend to reduce.

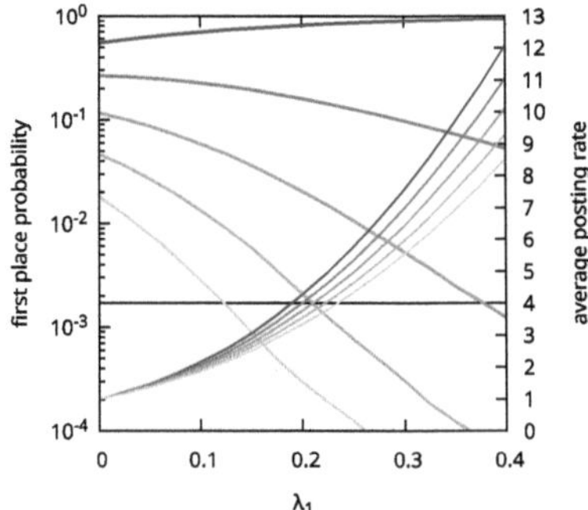

Fig. 9. Sensitivity analysis with respect to λ_1, for fixed $\lambda_0 = 1$, $\phi = 0.2$.

Table 3. First place probability with adapted λ_1, so that the average posting rate is constant (4 posts/day) for all influencers.

Influencer	$\phi = 0$	$\phi = 0.1$	$\phi = 0.2$	$\phi = 0.3$
1	0.738	0.701	0.651	0.597
2	0.208	0.226	0.253	0.264
3	0.045	0.058	0.073	0.099
4	0.008	0.012	0.019	0.032
5	0.002	0.002	0.004	0.009

5   Discussion and Concluding Remarks

Our work combines theoretical modeling of popularity dynamics with empirical data from Facebook, providing insights into the complex interaction of factors like individual activity, popularity decay, content attractiveness, and the platform's role in content visibility. Besides deriving ergodicity conditions, we conducted a sensitivity analysis to explore the impact of system parameters on possible outcomes.

In principle, an ideal system should provide each influencer with a fair opportunity to gain attention, commensurate with their intrinsic merit. In this context, one should aim to avoid two problematic extremes: (i) a situation in which the most attractive influencer monopolizes attention, leaving too little visibility for others; and (ii) a condition in which influencers are roughly equally likely to gain primacy, irrespective of their intrinsic merit or capabilities. Fairness, therefore, involves not only fostering an environment of discussion and information exchange in which each influencer has a chance to gain public attention commensurate with merit, but also ensuring that the attention amplification induced by recommendation systems and platform algorithms does not distort competition. Finding an optimal balance between the above two extremes involves complex ethical, technological, sociological, and political issues that are beyond the scope of this analysis. However, the proposed model, by offering a quantitative tool for examining how various factors influence the considered metrics, allows one to explore "what-if" scenarios, yielding valuable insights into popularity dynamics and competitive processes within online social networks.

Subsequent research will extend the analysis to other platforms, develop a framework for influencer competition, and explore control strategies to foster equity in competitive environments.

Acknowledgments. This research has been partially supported by the European Union – Next Generation EU by the Spoke 1 "FutureHPC & BigData" of ICSC - Centro Nazionale di Ricerca in High-Performance-Computing, Big Data and Quantum Computing and by Mission 4, Component 1, under the PRIN project TECHIE: "A control and network-based approach for fostering the adoption of new technologies in the ecological transition" Cod. 2022KPHA24 CUP Master: D53D23001320006, CUP: B53D23002760006.

Disclosure of Interests. Authors do not have any competing interests to declare.

References

1. Bakshy, E., Hofman, J.M., Mason, W.A., Watts, D.J.: Everyone's an influencer: quantifying influence on twitter. In: ACM WSDM 2011, New York, NY, USA (2011)
2. Bass, F.M.: A new product growth for model consumer durables. Manage. Sci. **15**(5), 215–227 (1969)
3. Bessi, A.: On the statistical properties of viral misinformation in online social media. XXPhys. A **469**, 459–470 (2017)
4. Castaldo, M.: Attention dynamics on YouTube: conceptual models, temporal analysisof engagement metrics, fake views. Theses, Université Grenoble Alpes (2022)
5. Cha, M., Haddadi, H., Benevenuto, F., Gummadi, K.: Measuring user influence in twitter: the million follower fallacy. In: Proceedings of the International AAAI Conference on Web and Social Media, vol. 4, no. 1, pp. 10–17 (2010)
6. Collet, F., Pra, P.D., Sartori, E.: A simple mean field model for social interactions: dynamics, fluctuations, criticality. J. Stat. Phys. **139**(5) (2010)
7. Covington, P., Adams, J., Sargin, E.: Deep neural networks for youtube recommendations. In: Proceedings of the 10th ACM Conference on Recommender Systems (2016)
8. Crane, R., Sornette, D.: Robust dynamic classes revealed by measuring the response function of a social system. Proc. Natl. Acad. Sci. **105**(41), 15649–15653 (2008)
9. De Choudhury, M.: Modeling and predicting group activity over time in online social media. In: Proceedings of the 20th ACM Conference on Hypertext and Hypermedia, HT 2009, New York, NY, USA, pp. 349–350 (2009)
10. Doshi, R., Ramesh, A., Rao, S.: Modeling influencer marketing campaigns in social networks. IEEE Trans. Comput. Soc. Syst. **10**(1), 322–334 (2023)
11. Friedkin, N., Johnsen, E.: Social influence networks and opinion change. Adv. Group Process. **16** (1999)
12. Hilgartner, S., Bosk, C.L.: The rise and fall of social problems: a public arenas model. Am. J. Sociol. **94**(7), 53–78 (1988)

13. Jiang, R., Chiappa, S., Lattimore, T., György, A., Kohli, P.: Degenerate feedback loops in recommender systems. In: Proceedings of the 2019 AAAI/ACM Conference on AI, Ethics, and Society, AIES 2019, pp. 383–390 (2019)
14. Lorenz-Spreen, P., Mønsted, B.M., Høvel, P., Lehmann, S.: Accelerating dynamics of collective attention. Nat. Commun. **10**(1), 1759 (2019)
15. Meyn, S.P., Tweedie, R.L.: Markov chains and stochastic stability. Communications and Control Engineering, 1993 edn. Springer, London (2012)
16. Muchnik, L., Aral, S., Taylor, S.: Social influence bias: a randomized experiment. Science **341**(6146), 647–651 (2013)
17. Ravazzi, C., Dabbene, F., Lagoa, C., Proskurnikov, A.V.: Learning hidden influences in large-scale dynamical social networks: a data-driven sparsity-based approach. IEEE Control Syst. Mag. **41**(5), 61–103 (2021)
18. Richier, C., Altman, E., Elazouzi, R., Jimenez, T., Linares, G., Portilla, Y.: Bio-inspired models for characterizing youtube viewcout. In: ASONAM (2014)
19. Vassio, L., Garetto, M., Leonardi, E., Chiasserini, C.F.: Mining and modelling temporal dynamics of followers' engagement on online social networks. Soc. Netw. Anal. Min. **12**(1), 96 (2022)
20. Weng, L., Flammini, A., Vespignani, A., Menczer, F.: Competition among memes in a world with limited attention. Sci. Rep. **2**(1), 335 (2012)

Justice for the Disadvantaged: A Study of Public Reactions on Indian Supreme Court Judgments

Soumilya De[1(✉)], Soumyajit Datta[2], Koustav Rudra[3], Saptarshi Ghosh[3], Ashiqur KhudaBuksh[2], and Kripabandhu Ghosh[1]

[1] Indian Institute of Science Education and Research, Kolkata, India
soumilya.de.scholar@gmail.com
[2] Rochester Institute of Technology, Rochester, NY, USA
[3] Indian Institute of Technology, Kharagpur, India

Abstract. The judgments of a country's apex court on socially pertinent issues often invite a wide spectrum of public reactions reflecting a range of polarities. In this paper, we examine public reactions to three landmark judgments of the Indian Supreme Court – *Triple Talaq* (on Islamic divorce), *Sect. 377* (focused on the criminalization of homosexual activity), and *Sabarimala Temple* (on restricting the entry of women and girls of reproductive age into a Hindu temple) – involving disadvantaged groups such as women and sexual minorities. To our knowledge, this is the first-ever work that investigates social web discourse pivoting landmark rulings for disadvantaged groups in India. We first annotate a substantial novel dataset of 23,418 comments, partially annotated through LLM-human partnership, particularly enriched by the participation of disadvantaged groups in the annotation process. Our analyses reveal that not all verdicts receive comparable support or criticism – civic receptivity considerably varies across verdicts, with the ban on instant Triple Talaq receiving overwhelming support. (Note that the authors express *no* opinion on the verdicts of the honorable Supreme Court of India, and limit the study to analyzing *anonymous* public discourse. Some of the contents in this paper can be disturbing and deemed offensive.)

Keywords: disadvantaged groups · landmark verdicts · civic receptivity

1 Introduction

In 1829, Raja Ram Mohun Roy, a pioneering social reformer in India, submitted a petition to abolish '*Sati*' – a retrograde social practice of self-immolation of the widow on the funeral pyre of her husband [32]. Roy had a modest 300 signatories indicating their support in his petition. In contrast, the petition was challenged by a counter-petition that had more than 3,300 signatures [12]. Legal reforms for disadvantaged groups have seldom been smooth sailing and often faced resistance as they challenged religious beliefs and societal norms.[1]

---

[1] The Problems of Marginalized Groups in India; Living with Dignity: Sexual Orientation and Gender Identity-Based Human Rights Violations in India.

How does modern society react to watershed court judgments championing the rights of the disadvantaged? In this paper, via substantial datasets of 23,418 comments in total from 872 relevant YouTube videos, we analyze civic engagement with three recent major judgements of the Indian Supreme Court (INSC) favoring rights for disadvantaged groups: (1) abolishing the practice of instant Triple Talaq, (2) writing down of Sect. 377 focused on queer population, and (3) allowing entry of menstruating women into Sabarimala Temple (detailed in Sect. 1.1).

Several prior works have explored civic engagement as a stance detection problem on contemporary social issues ranging from gun control/right to the #metoo movement [16–19, 29]. Notable works [24, 31, 34, 35, 39] in computational law in India revolve around legal documents. However, barring a few recent computational social science studies that examined gender and in-group biases in court proceedings [2, 14], civic reaction to important court rulings in India through the lens of the social web is rather underexplored. Table 1 indicates that social web discourse around controversial court rulings can present an effective instrument to gauge civic receptivity, especially if the decisions affect women and sexual minorities.

Our work introduces a novel aspect of stance detection where social media intersects with legal discourse. Unlike traditional stance detection datasets / approaches which have *three* classes (favor, against and neutral), we consider an additional dimension by distinguishing between direct and indirect references to the judiciary for both favor and criticism, and consider *five* classes. People often express their opinions through allusions circumventing the use of definitive keywords related to the judiciary or the verdict, necessitating the granularity and adding to the complexity of the task.

Our Contributions: We make the following contributions in this paper:

- *Social:* Via a substantial corpus of 23,418 YouTube comments on 872 relevant YouTube videos, we analyze civic engagement with three major recent Supreme Court rulings in India. To our knowledge, this is the *first paper* that investigates social web discourse around watershed court rulings championing women and sexual minorities. Our analyses reveal that not all verdicts receive comparable support or criticism – civic receptivity considerably varies across verdicts, with the ban on triple talaq receiving overwhelming support.
- *Resource:* We release a novel dataset[2] of 23,418 social web posts (anonymized) with an annotated stance on the three verdicts. One of the annotators of our datasets self-identifies as a member of the queer community. Our work thus contributes to the growing literature of participatory AI [7, 10, 20, 27, 41], where disadvantaged stakeholders take prominent roles in the curation of the datasets and AI systems.
- *Methodological:* We leverage state-of-the-art NLP methods, customized for the novel task of *automatic* public stance detection toward Supreme Court verdicts. We address class imbalance by leveraging an LLM-assisted approach

---

[2] https://github.com/khorg0sh/Justice-for-the-Disadvantaged..

Table 1. Example comments per class. The first four classes capture stance relevant to the verdicts.

Classes	Triple Talaq	Section 377	Sabarimala
Direct Critic	Such a shameless verdict ...	The greatest disaster. Shame on the judgment. Don't understand what these judges are sitting for??	"Notions of rationality cannot be invoked in matters of religion" SC should not interfere in religious matters
Indirect Critic	whatever they said everything is correct. don't interfere in religions matter.	Destruction of Indian society has started itself. Results shall be coming soon..	A temple is not a picnic spot
Indirect Favor	great relief to Muslim sisters as they were used, exposed, and disposed like tissue	*Finally, I am not a criminal by the law !* But an equal citizen of this great nation!	if a God punishes his followers just bcoz women want to worship him in his temple, he is not worthy to be a God
Direct Favor	Landmark judgement by honorable Supreme Court. Wish all Muslim women good luck! Justice for all!	This is the good decision taken by Supreme Court ... Bcoz Fundamental right are equal for all.	I always love to see the supremacy of the Constitution over all
Undetermined	When penguins defends sharks	Wow happy to know different opinions ,	it is situated in the Periyar Tiger Reserve

that augments new instances without compromising the organic nature of user-generated comments. Although our work considers three Indian Supreme Court judgments, the pipeline adopted can be deployed for other such rulings in India and other countries to gauge public reaction to controversial judgments.

1.1 Background

The Supreme Court of India has a history of delivering reformative judgments that drive social progress while balancing the sensitivities of a pluralistic society.

- *Instant Triple Talaq:* In 2016, Shayara Bano filed a writ petition in the Supreme Court of India when her marital status was altered in an instant from *married* to *divorced* through *Talaq-e-Biddat* or instantaneous Triple Talaq. A year later, the apex court described the pronouncement of divorce through successive utterances of Talaq as *manifestly arbitrary* and instituted a ban on it.[3] The 2017 verdict is seen as a notable attempt to grant justice to a historically oppressed gender practicing a specific religion [47] (approximately, 7% of the Indian population are Muslim women). In 2019, following the verdict, a bill was passed legislatively making the practice a criminal offense [4].

- ***Sect. 377:*** Pronounced under "Unnatural Offenses", Sect. 377 of the Indian Penal Code (instituted in 1860 during the British rule) stated that *whoever voluntarily has carnal intercourse against the order of nature with any man, woman or animal* may face *imprisonment for life*. It has been claimed that throughout its history, the section, with no explicit mention of sexuality, served as a tool for harassing and intimidating sexual minorities [33, 42].

  In the absence of comprehensive data, and based on global prevalence estimates, the queer population of India is conservatively approximated to be at least 10% of the population, amounting to around 140 million. In a longed-for moment of respite for the huge queer population, the Indian Supreme Court in September 2018 ruled that consensual sexual activities among adults are no longer a criminal activity and partially read down Sect. 377 with a note *"History owes an apology to the members of this community"*. The sexual identities earlier associated with deviant behavior and offense now received recognition. The verdict has paved the way for further discussions on advancing LGBTQ+ rights in India – legalization of same-sex marriage,[4] right to adoption for LGBTQ+ couples,[5] and enactment of anti-discrimination laws.[6]

- ***Sabarimala Temple:*** Does an *exception placed on women because of biological differences violate the Constitution*? The Indian Supreme Court in the Sabarimala verdict passed in 2018 responded, stating that such exceptions are violative of the *Right to Equality* of women and perpetuate gender-based discrimination [3]. The temple of Lord Ayyappa at Sabarimala adhered to a practice believed to be a tradition [40] that prohibited entry of women of menstruating age (10–50). The justification for the ban is that Lord Ayyappa is said to be celibate (Britannica). In a 4:1 majority 2018 verdict, the apex court lifted the ban, citing that *the menstrual status of a woman cannot be a valid constitutional basis to deny her the dignity of being and the autonomy of personhood*. This verdict is seen as another attempt at ensuring gender equality within the purview of existing religious practices through legal alterations.

What binds these three verdicts? The *Right to Equality*. Article 14,[7] states that *The State shall not deny to any person equality before the law or the equal protection of the laws*. Across the cases, *discrimination* is a recurring theme

---

[3] Triple Talaq Explained.
[4] Same Sex Marriages in India.
[5] Why LGBTQIA+ couples should be allowed to adopt.
[6] India's LGBTQIA+ community notches legal wins but still faces societal hurdles.
[7] Indian Kanoon: Article 14.

where *equality* is a challenged prospect and the verdicts uphold the rights of the historically disadvantaged groups.

For the rest of this paper, we indicate these verdicts by italicizing them: *Triple Talaq* denotes the verdict that abolished instant Triple Talaq by law; *Sabarimala* denotes the verdict allowing entry of women into Sabarimala temple; and *Sect. 377* represents the verdict writing down Sect. 377.

2   Data Collection

To analyze the public discourse on the three aforementioned landmark judgments, we first construct the datasets from YouTube[8] comments on relevant videos. To our knowledge, the datasets are the first of its kind with a novel set of classes. In what follows, we describe our dataset curation steps.

2.1   Data Collection

Our choice of social web platform (YouTube) is guided by (1) *YouTube's popularity in India*: As of 2024, YouTube has the highest user base in India, 462 million out of 820 million active internet users. (2) *Presence of relevant discourse*: Following a court ruling, various news agencies usually upload a variety of videos on YouTube covering the judgment. These videos, often presenting contrasting opinions, become focal points for discussion through comments. (3) *Ease of API access*: YouTube provides publicly available and free API access. *Each* dataset is prepared through the following steps :

1. **Keywords for search**: We curate keywords consisting of two components, the case name (e.g. *Sabarimala Temple*) and a supporting term from the set {*judgment, verdict, Supreme Court judgment, Supreme Court verdict*} trailing it. Therefore, per judgment we have four keywords to iterate over.

2. **API Search**: An API search is conducted on each keyword to **extract *relevant* (API parameter) videos**. The union of the video IDs is taken for further processing.

3. **Timeline-based filtration**: We observe a substantial number of videos are posted promptly following the verdict, but the initial enthusiasm gradually dies down. Hence, we consider only the videos posted in the first three months from the date of the verdict.

4. **Retrieval of comments**: The filtered video IDs are now processed to **retrieve comments** under each one of them, with associated details such as number of likes and replies. Note that we do *not* collect any user identities of the users who posted the comments.

Language of comments. The retrieved comments are in English and various Indian languages such as Hindi, Bangla, Malayalam, Telugu, etc. We consider only the lingua franca, i.e., English, mainly due to annotator unavailability for other Indian languages and potential region-specific bias in opinions in considering only select languages. To **identify and extract English comments**, we use Google Translator API version 4.0.0rc1. Table 2 reports the numbers.

---

[8] www.youtube.com.

Table 2. The total number of comments collected vs the number of comments with English as the identified language

Dataset	Total Comments	Comments in English
Triple Talaq	25,335	11,071
Sect. 377	9,141	5,350
Sabarimala	12,740	6,997

2.2   Class Definitions

On a subset of comments on individual verdicts, we first follow an *Open Coding* [25] approach and observe the following two broad comment patterns:

- **Direct:** References the judiciary *directly* using related terms such as 'Supreme Court', 'verdict', 'judgment', 'judges', etc. The keyword(s) used in the comment is the indicative factor. Identification of such comments requires no prior knowledge about the judgments.
- **Indirect:** Alludes to the judgment or the judiciary *indirectly* in no immediate judiciary-related term, and only suggests a stance. Such comments come with varied degrees of subjectivity where familiarity with the verdict and contemporary socio-political context is necessary (see examples in Table 1).

For instance, "shame on the judges" is a *Direct* comment where the categorization can immediately be based on the keyword "judges". In contrast, the comment "a temple is not a picnic spot" does *not* use any judiciary-related term and as per understanding of the verdicts, the comment refers to the Sabarimala temple, therefore, it is an example of *Indirect* comment.

Besides *Direct/Indirect*, the polarity is captured as:

- **Favor:** the stance expressed is of approval towards the verdict
- **Critic:** the stance expressed is of disapproval towards the verdict

Accordingly, we formulate the following classes based on the above-mentioned dimensions (see examples in Table 1):

1. **Direct Critic**: expresses criticism with direct reference to the judiciary.
2. **Indirect Critic**: criticism with *no* direct reference.
3. **Direct favor**: expresses approval with direct reference to the judiciary.
4. **Indirect favor**: approval with *no* direct reference.
5. **Undetermined / Others**

The first four classes reflect a clear stance regarding the verdicts while the fifth class *Undetermined/Others* considers samples where either the stance is unclear or there is no established relevance to the judgment. As an example, "Wow happy to know different opinions" bears no stance around the verdict, it merely expresses delight in observing a spectrum of opinions.

Candidates for Annotation: Consistent with prior literature around non-native English-speaking populations [36], we observe that a considerable portion of the collection exhibits spelling and grammatical disfluencies, consequently making the expression of the stance ambiguous. In our work, the expressiveness of a comment is assumed to be determined by public understanding of the comment that, in turn, is indicated by *engagement* in terms of likes and replies. Comments with a degree of engagement, as per our observation, are coherent and offer more clarity on the stance.

The engagement is quantified taking into account the number of likes and replies on each comment. We leverage the sum of the counts (of likes and replies) to arrange the comments in descending order. To obtain the set to annotate, we consider the 75 percentile value (Q3) as the threshold and retrieve only the comments with higher engagement (see Table 3 for the number of such comments), while the rest of the collection remains unlabeled.

Table 3. Number of candidate comments for annotation. L and R represent the number of likes and replies respectively. E.g., *Section 377* has 1,146 comments with L+R>4.0

Verdict	Q3 of L+R	# of comments
Sabarimala	1.0	1,655
Sect. 377	4.0	1,146
Triple Talaq	1.0	2,350
Total	–	5,151

Table 4. The initial class distributions (Before) are enhanced to obtain comparatively less imbalanced datasets (After).

Classes	Triple Talaq		Section 377		Sabarimala	
	Before	After	Before	After	Before	After
Direct Critic	12 (0.51%)	17 (0.68%)	30 (2.62%)	80 (5.01%)	107 (6.47%)	221 (11.81%)
Indirect Critic	95 (4.04%)	155 (6.24%)	193 (16.84%)	488 (20.58%)	466 (34.51%)	466 (24.91%)
Direct favor	84 (3.57%)	151 (6.08%)	130 (11.34%)	235 (14.72%)	42 (2.54%)	80 (4.28%)
Indirect favor	407 (17.31%)	407 (16.39%)	348 (30.37%)	348 (21.80%)	101 (7.45%)	165 (8.82%)
Undetermined	1752 (74.55%)	1752 (70.60%)	445 (38.83%)	445 (27.88%)	939 (56.74%)	939 (50.19%)

Annotation: The annotation process involved three annotators who are fluent in English and use of Youtube.[9] The initial annotation was done by two annotators where one annotator is a self-identified queer person, and the other identifies as a cisgender female. The senior annotator (the tie-breaker) identifies as cisgender male. Prior literature has considered several approaches for disagreement

---

[9] To be noted, given the offensive nature of several comments, the annotators were cautioned about potential sensitivity.

resolution – e.g., majority voting [9,48] or third objective instance [15]. In our work, accounting for the participation of the disadvantaged groups, we resolve the disagreements with a priority placed on the perspective of the annotator from the concerned disadvantaged group (e.g., our queer annotator for Sect. 377), in *Indirect* vs *Undetermined* where the majority of disagreement occurs. In case of a disagreement around the polarity, we use *third objective instance* and involve the third annotator. We observe considerable agreement in the annotation process (Cohen's κ 0.73).

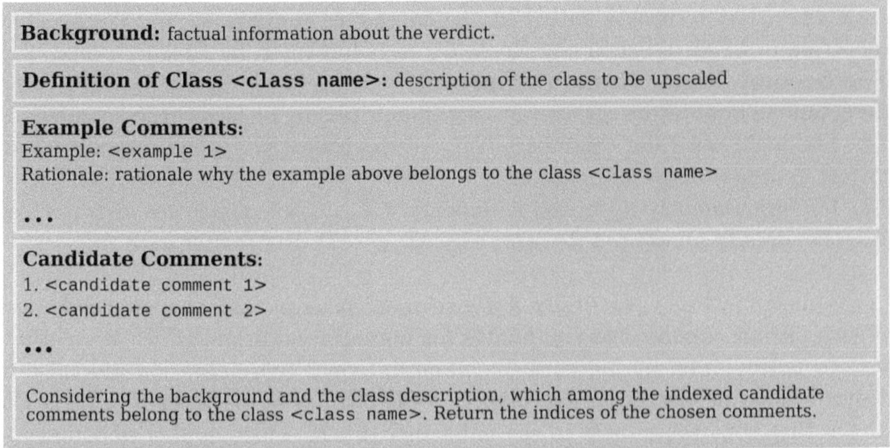

Fig. 1. The five-segment prompt contains a total of ten examples with rationales for an individual minority class and five candidates per comment in the minority class.

2.3   Mitigating Imbalance in the Dataset

Table 4 shows that the class *Undetermined* consumes a significant share from each dataset while several classes with notably low numbers of comments lead to considerable imbalance in the datasets. To address this imbalance, we utilize an LLM-assisted approach that supplements the set of underrepresented classes with fresh user-generated comments, where the minimum requirement of *additional* annotator involvement is deferred to the final stage. While LLM-assisted annotation has been extensively studied as an alternative to human annotators [21,26,38], recent lines of work have also recommended caution [43]. Here, LLM is utilized to address *only* the imbalance in the datasets with the primary goal of minimizing human efforts.

We follow a two-stage approach for each dataset $\mathcal{D}$, where the first stage involves LLM and the second stage involves the human annotators.

The First Stage: LLM.

In the first stage, LLM receives through prompt (Fig. 1) a set of potential additions and returns a subset to undergo human review (second stage). The steps are as follows:

1. Identify the classes to be supplemented with new comments, $\mathcal{M}$.

2. For each $m \in \mathcal{M}$, do

2.1. For each comment c_m in the class m, do

2.1.1. Identify *five* nearest neighbours (using the embedding space[10]) of the comment, c_{mn}, from the unlabelled portion of the dataset.

2.1.2. Pass the comments c_{mn} in the prompt (Fig. 1 provides the structure) as candidates for the LLM to choose from as relevant to the class m.

2.1.3 The LLM returns a subset of the candidate comments, $c_{llm} \subseteq c_{mn}$. The collection of LLM-returned comments for m is indicated by C_{llm}

The Second Stage: Human Approval.

Here, human annotators review (and not annotate) the LLM-returned comments.

2.2. The LLM-returned comments C_{llm} are reviewed by human annotators for correct comment-class association.

2.3. The unanimously approved comments, $C_{approved} \in C_{llm}$, are incorporated into the already annotated dataset, $C_{approved} \to \mathcal{D}$. Repeat for each m.

As shown in Fig. 1, we utilize a *five* segment prompt with nearest neighbours of each anchor comment as candidates for potential addition, which were otherwise to be reviewed by humans. To maintain equal representation among *four* stance-indicating classes not considering *Undetermined*, we choose to upscale the classes that contribute most to the imbalance due to a low number of comments – for *Triple Talaq* and *Sect. 377*: Direct Critic, Indirect Critic, Direct Favor; for *Sabarimala*: Direct Critic, Direct Favor, Indirect Favor. To deploy the approach described above, we utilize the Gemini-Pro 1.5 LLM for its ability of contextual grounding [46]. In the attempt to minimize manual efforts, utilization of LLM reduces the total number of neighbours to be reviewed by the human annotators in the second stage down by 42.46% in *Triple Talaq*, 28.4% in *Section 377* and 46.41% in *Sabarimala*. LLM here reduces the efforts since *only* LLM-returned comments are only *reviewed* in the second stage.

Table 4 shows the previous and revised distributions, produced by the two-stage approach. After the deployment of the approach, there is a noticeable difference in the distributions. While *Triple Talaq* has, although low in number but mostly positive comments reflecting majority support for the change, the *Sabarimala* verdict finds more criticism. Therefore, the number of critic comments in *Triple Talaq* is substantially low and for *Sabarimala* the exact opposite is true. *Section 377* however shows the approach can be effective if each class has an adequate number of comments in the unlabelled portion of the dataset.

While a manual inspection of the class distributions in Table 4 suggests that our approach has reduced class imbalance, in what follows, we provide a quantitative analysis of imbalance. Following a similar approach as Ansari *et al.* [1], we

---

[10] We generate the embeddings using Google's embedding model `embedding-004`.

formalize a quantifiable measure of class imbalance. Consider a dataset $\mathcal{D}$ with k classes denoted by $\mathcal{C}_1, \mathcal{C}_2, \ldots, \mathcal{C}_k$. Consider $\mathcal{C}_i$ represents l_i instances in $\mathcal{D}$.

We first construct the probability vector $\mathbf{l}$:

$$\left[\frac{l_1}{\sum_{i=1}^{k} l_i}, \frac{l_2}{\sum_{i=1}^{k} l_i}, \ldots, \frac{l_k}{\sum_{i=1}^{k} l_i} \right] \tag{1}$$

In simple words, the j-th element of this probability vector $\mathbf{l}$ denotes the fraction of class $\mathcal{C}_j$ instances in $\mathcal{D}$.

For $\mathcal{D}$, we define the imbalance as the KL divergence between this probability vector and a uniform discrete probability vector with k elements.

$$imbalance(\mathcal{D}) = KL(\mathbf{l}, [\tfrac{1}{k}, \tfrac{1}{k}, \ldots, \tfrac{1}{k}]) \tag{2}$$

$imbalance(\mathcal{D})$ measures how far the class distribution of $\mathcal{D}$ is from a uniform discrete distribution, i.e., a perfectly balanced scenario where each class has equal representation in the dataset. If $\mathcal{D}$ is perfectly balanced, $imbalance(\mathcal{D})$ will be 0. A higher value of this measure indicates greater imbalance. As shown in Table 6, among the three datasets, *Triple Talaq* exhibits the highest imbalance value, suggesting the most uneven distribution. We further observe considerable reduction in imbalance after employing our human-LLM collaborative approach.

Table 5. Classifier perfomrance on our datasets. Zero-shot models (`Llama3.1` and `Gemini-1.5`) are indicated with a subscript *zero*. For each dataset, the best classifier performance is highlighted.

	Triple Talaq		Section 377		Sabarimala	
	Accuracy	mac-F1-Score	Accuracy	mac-F1-Score	Accuracy	mac-F1-Score
Mistral (Mistral-7B-Instruct-v0.3)	77.23±1.50	65.76±2.19	84.68±0.83	85.43±0.94	79.79±0.64	78.92±0.81
Llama3 (Llama-3.1-8B-Instruct)	80.67±0.90	68.67±3.99	83.13±0.81	84.34±0.53	77.26±1.58	76.34±1.33
DeepSeek (DeepSeek-R1-Distill-Llama-8B)	75.36±2.73	59.62±2.69	80.21±1.37	80.97±1.42	73.24±1.92	69.55±2.06
SVM (Google Embeddings)	79.17±1.55	65.19±5.69	82.21±2.76	82.00±2.55	75.28±2.19	68.27±3.29
NB (Google Embeddings)	72.88±3.21	59.35±7.44	78.49±2.82	79.5±3.41	71.33±1.75	67.76±2.06
BERT-Base-Uncased	70.32±3.66	57.54±4.73	75.60±1.47	76.83±1.61	70.44±2.84	65.83±2.91
DistilBERT	71.26±2.79	53.23±2.10	74.50±2.68	75.86±1.94	70.17±2.88	66.56±2.71
RoBERTa	72.69±3.49	55.24±5.00	75.40±1.36	76.96±1.20	70.69±2.11	65.96±1.89
Gemini$_{zero}$	67.28±1.02	55.92±1.36	77.97±3.15	73.00±3.86	71.39±3.16	71.52±0.96
Llama3.1-8B$_{zero}$	48.81±0.61	44.05±0.56	70.26±3.43	71.57±2.62	63.89±4.05	65.96±3.40

3   Results and Analyses

3.1   Stance Classifier Performance

We consider three well-known open large language models fine-tuned on our datasets: `Llama3` [13]; `Mistral` [23]; and `Deepseek` [5]. In addition, following prior literature in stance classifiers (e.g., [22,28,37,45]), we consider Support Vector Machine (SVM) [8]; Naive Bayes (NB) [6], and three `BERT`-based models

Table 6. Dataset imbalance as computed using Eq. 2. A higher value indicates greater imbalance. The *before* column lists the imbalance in individual datasets before we employed our human-LLM collaboration pipeline to address imbalance. The *after* column lists the imbalance in individual classes after we addressed class imbalance as described in Sect. 2.3. We observe that for all datasets, our approach has considerably reduced class imbalance.

Dataset	Before	After	Change in imabalance
Sabarimala	0.49	0.32	−0.17
Sect. 377	0.24	0.13	−0.11
Triple Talaq	0.79	0.69	−0.10

(BERT [11]; DistilBERT [44]; and RoBERTa [30]). We use 70:30 train/test splits and for each model. Refer to Supplemental Information (SI) for training details.

Following standard machine learning practices for evaluating classifiers on imbalanced datasets [6], we use the macro-F1 score as our primary performance evaluation metric. In addition, in Table 5, we report model accuracy on individual datasets. As shown in Table 5, we observe that (1) fine-tuned models perform considerably better than the zero-shot models; and (2) compared to all other baselines Mistral and LLaMA 3.1 perform the best with Mistral achieving best performance on two datasets (*Sect. 377* and *Sabarimala*) and LLaMA 3.1 achieving best performance on the remaining one (*Triple Talaq*). Across all three datasets, the best performance is achieved on *Section 377*. We note that, this dataset has the lowest imbalance as shown in Table 6.

Error Analysis: We observe that the models mostly struggled with distinguishing between indirect stances (favor or critic) and undetermined. Upon manual inspection, we observe a recurring theme. There were instances where the models could not understand nuanced cultural contexts. For instance, the comment *As usual Chee News* is a wordplay on Zee News (the news outlet) and the Hindi word **Chee** which is used to express disgust. The model classified this example as undetermined while the annotators labeled it as indirect critic. Similarly, the comment *Congrats to those who wanted to see INDIA like AMERICA ..* was annotated as Indirect Critic while the models predicted it as Undetermined. For a sizable conservative population in India, America (and the West in general) is looked down upon as a country with a highly visible queer population, which conservative Indians believe has destroyed the cultural fabric there. SI contains a detailed exposition of error analysis with confusion matrices.

3.2   Discourse Around the Verdicts

The best-performing model per verdict is run on the unlabeled portion of the corresponding dataset Table 7 summarizes the distributions of comments in the wild according to the model. We first note that not all verdicts received a similar share of support or criticism – civic receptivity considerably varied

Table 7. Distributions of the remaining i.e. unlabelled comments on deployment of the best models.

Classes	Triple Talaq	Sect. 377	Sabarimala
Direct Critic	0.19%	2.64%	4.23%
Indirect Critic	3.94%	21.02%	33.5%
Direct Favor	3.11%	4.59%	1.41%
Indirect Favor	17.79%	14.60%	4.59%
Undetermined	74.95%	57.11%	56.21%

Table 8. Comments indicating a favorable stance found in the wild. Refer to SI for more such comments.

Triple Talaq
▶ Brought tears, even I am also victim of triple talaq, I am an well educated gal alhmdlh but cudn't raise my voice against injustice fr which I regrate myself, I just want to be like u strong enough to fight against sch evils
Section 377
▶ My goodness, we finally got the freedom to live, 24 years of struggle and i cant stop crying Congrats India
Sabarimala
▶ Sati pratha was also a tradition and what if it wasn't stopped then would people still doubt that it is our thousand year old culture and no one has right to interfere? I am completely aware about the tradition and culture with sabarimala but this is 21st century and suppression of any human being Wether men or women needs to be stopped...

across different judgments. Among all three verdicts, *Sabarimala* received minimal support while *Triple Talaq* received the maximum support (see, Fig. 2). The overwhelming support for *Triple Talaq* aligns with the fact that more than 1 million Muslims in India signed a petition to abolish Triple Talaq. Table 8 shows an example comment in which the author self-identifies as a victim of this law.

As highlighted already, our dataset is annotated by a self-identified queer person from India. Before homosexuality was decriminalized in India, being openly gay in India was an uphill task. Beyond many comments reiterating *love is love*, we observe a rare humanization of a particularly invisible community in India

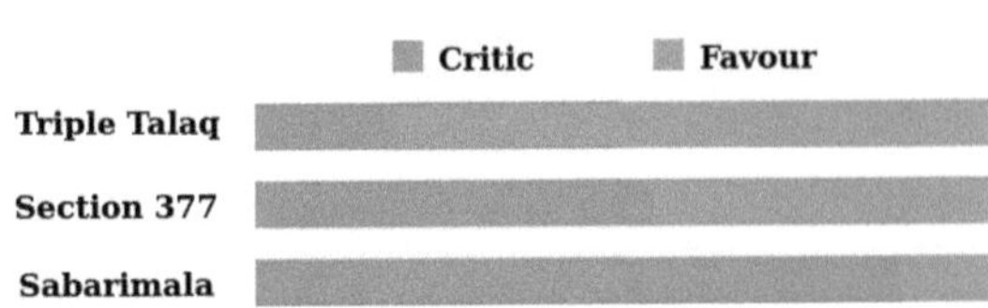

Fig. 2. Distributions of the unlabelled comments indicate the tilt in polarity is overwhelmingly negative for *Sabarimala* and positive for *Triple Talaq* while for *Sect. 377* it is comparatively balanced.

where several queer people voiced support in the first person in the comments section. Finally, in the discourse around *Sabarimala*, we notice several comments drawing parallel with this landmark judgment with the abolishment of Sati by Raja Ram Mohun Roy in 1829. Table 8 lists example comments.

4 Conclusion

In the study, we consider three landmark judgments of the Indian Supreme Court that encompass two major aspects of Indian society – gender and religion and, additionally, sexual identity, in alignment with the Sustainable Development Goal of achieving equality. We observe that verdicts around disadvantaged groups receive varied responses from the public, with the ban on instantaneous *Triple Talaq* receiving a major upvote and the entry of menstruating women at Sabarimala being highly criticized. We look forward to considering comments in other languages especially regional Indian languages and extending our study to other jurisdictions.

Limitations of the Study

For the study, we consider a single platform (YouTube) and a monolingual setup – only English, which constitutes around 50% of the collection (Table 2). Due to annotator unavailability, our work does not consider regional languages. However, the verdicts triggered widespread pan-India discussions which were mostly held in English. India's demography provides a high degree of varied opinions, which we believe provides substantial sample for an empirical study. The identified limitations highlight an opportunity for future research to include multilingual data across multiple platforms for a more holistic analysis.

Acknowledgement. Koustav Rudra is a recipient of the DST-INSPIRE Faculty Fellowship (DST/ INSPIRE/04/2021/003055 in the year 2021 under Engineering Sciences) We acknowledge the annotators who helped us in developing the dataset.

Ethical Statement. We have used only public data on the Web, collected using the publicly available YouTube API. We did not collect any user identities or user-details during the data collection process. The LLMs used may contain inherent biases. We have compensated the annotators commensurate with their efforts, and the annotators were informed of the purpose of their annotations. Given the sensitive nature of the data, we have anonymized the texts of the comments in our datasets.

References

1. Ansari, M.A., Sidhpura, J., Mandal, V.K., Khudabukhsh, A.R.: Quantifying the transience of social web datasets. In: ASONAM, pp. 286–293 (2023)
2. Ash, E., et al.: In-group bias in the Indian judiciary: evidence from 5 million criminal cases. Tech. rep, Center for Global Development (2023)

3. Ayesha, J.: Sabarimala verdict: a watershed moment in the history of affirmative action (2020)
4. BBC: Triple talaq: India criminalises Muslim 'instant divorce' (2019). www.bbc.com/news/world-asia-india-49160818
5. Bi, X., et al.: Deepseek LLM: scaling open-source language models with longtermism. arXiv preprint arXiv:2401.02954 (2024)
6. Bishop, C.M.: Pattern Recognition and Machine Learning (Information Science and Statistics). Springer-Verlag, Berlin, Heidelberg (2006)
7. Bondi, E., Xu, L., Acosta-Navas, D., Killian, J.A.: Envisioning communities: a participatory approach towards AI for social good. In: AIES 2021, pp. 425–436 (2021)
8. Boser, B.E., Guyon, I.M., Vapnik, V.N.: A training algorithm for optimal margin classifiers. In: Proceedings of the Fifth Annual Workshop on Computational Learning Theory, pp. 144–152 (1992)
9. Davidson, T., Warmsley, D., Macy, M., Weber, I.: Automated hate speech detection and the problem of offensive language. In: ICWSM 2017, pp. 512–515 (2017)
10. Delgado, F., Barocas, S., Levy, K.: An uncommon task: participatory design in legal AI. CSCW **6**(CSCW1), 1–23 (2022)
11. Devlin, J., Chang, M.W., Lee, K., Toutanova, K.: BERT: pre-training of deep bidirectional transformers for language understanding. In: NAACL: HLT, pp. 4171–4186. ACL (2019). https://aclanthology.org/N19-1423
12. Dodwell, H.: The Cambridge history of the British empire, vol. 5. CUP Archive (1932)
13. Dubey, A., et al.: The llama 3 herd of models. arXiv preprint arXiv:2407.21783 (2024)
14. Dutta, S., Srivastava, P., Solunke, V., Nath, S., KhudaBukhsh, A.R.: Disentangling societal inequality from model biases: gender inequality in divorce court proceedings. In: IJCAI 2023, pp. 5959–5967 (2023)
15. Gao, L., Huang, R.: Detecting online hate speech using context aware models. arXiv preprint arXiv:1710.07395 (2017)
16. Gautam, A., Mathur, P., Gosangi, R., Mahata, D., Sawhney, R., Shah, R.R.: # metooma: multi-aspect annotations of tweets related to the metoo movement. In: ICWSM, pp. 209–216 (2020)
17. Glandt, K., Khanal, S., Li, Y., Caragea, D., Caragea, C.: Stance detection in covid-19 tweets. In: ACL-IJNLP 2021. vol. 1 (2021)
18. Grasso, F., Locci, S., Siragusa, G., Caro, L.D.: Ecoverse: an annotated twitter dataset for eco-relevance classification, environmental impact analysis, and stance detection (2024). https://api.semanticscholar.org/CorpusID:269004840
19. Gyawali, N., et al.: Gunstance: stance detection for gun control and gun regulation. In: ACL **2024**, 12027–12044 (2024)
20. Harrington, C., Erete, S., Piper, A.M.: Deconstructing community-based collaborative design: towards more equitable participatory design engagements. CSCW **3**(CSCW), 1–25 (2019)
21. He, X., et al.: AnnoLLM: making large language models to be better crowdsourced annotators. In: NAACL: HLT (Volume 6: Industry Track), pp. 165–190. ACL (2024). https://aclanthology.org/2024.naacl-industry.15/
22. He, Z., Mokhberian, N., Lerman, K.: Infusing knowledge from wikipedia to enhance stance detection. arXiv preprint arXiv:2204.03839 (2022)
23. Jiang, A.Q., et al.: Mistral 7b. arXiv preprint arXiv:2310.06825 (2023)

24. Joshi, A., Paul, S., Sharma, A., Goyal, P., Ghosh, S., Modi, A.: IL-TUR: benchmark for indian legal text understanding and reasoning. In: ACL 2024, pp. 11460–11499 (2024)

25. Khandkar, S.H.: Open coding. University of Calgary **23**, 2009 (2009)

26. Kholodna, N., Julka, S., Khodadadi, M., Gumus, M.N., Granitzer, M.: Llms in the loop: Leveraging large language model annotations for active learning in low-resource languages. In: ECML PKDD 2024, pp. 397–412. Springer-Verlag, Berlin, Heidelberg (2024). https://doi.org/10.1007/978-3-031-70381-2_25

27. Khorramrouz, A., Dutta, S., KhudaBukhsh, A.R.: For women, life, freedom: a participatory AI-based social web analysis of a watershed moment in iran's gender struggles. In: IJCAI 2023, pp. 6013–6021 (2023)

28. Lan, X., Gao, C., Jin, D., Li, Y.: Stance detection with collaborative role-infused llm-based agents. In: ICWSM. **18**, 891–903 (2024)

29. Li, Y., Zhang, Y.: Pro-woman, anti-man? identifying gender bias in stance detection. In: Findings of ACL 2024, pp. 3229–3236 (2024)

30. Liu, Y., et al.: Roberta: a robustly optimized bert pretraining approach (2019). https://arxiv.org/abs/1907.11692

31. Malik, V., et al.: ILDC for CJPE: indian legal documents corpus for court judgment prediction and explanation. In: ACL/IJCNLP 2021, pp. 4046–4062 (2021)

32. Mani, L.: Contentious traditions: the debate on sati in colonial India. Univ of California Press (1998)

33. Mitra, D.: History's apology: Sexuality and the 377 supreme court decision in India. Epicenter, Harvard University (2018)

34. Nigam, S.K., Patnaik, B.D., Mishra, S., Shallum, N., Ghosh, K., Bhattacharya, A.: NYAYAANUMANA and INLEGALLLAMA: the largest Indian legal judgment prediction dataset and specialized language model for enhanced decision analysis. In: COLING 2025, pp. 11135–11160. ACL (2025). https://aclanthology.org/2025.coling-main.738/

35. Nigam, S.K., Sharma, A., Khanna, D., Shallum, N., Ghosh, K., Bhattacharya, A.: Legal judgment reimagined: predex and the rise of intelligent AI interpretation in Indian courts. In: Findings of ACL, pp. 4296–4315 (2024)

36. Palakodety, S., KhudaBukhsh, A.R., Carbonell, J.G.: Hope speech detection: a computational analysis of the voice of peace. In: ECAI 2020, pp. 1881–1889 (2020)

37. Palakodety, S., KhudaBukhsh, A.R., Carbonell, J.G.: Voice for the voiceless: active sampling to detect comments supporting the rohingyas. AAAI **34**(01), 454–462 (2020)

38. Pangakis, N., Wolken, S., Fasching, N.: Automated annotation with generative AI requires validation. ArXiv abs/2306.00176 (2023). https://api.semanticscholar.org/CorpusID:259000016

39. Paul, S., Bhatt, R., Goyal, P., Ghosh, S.: Legal statute identification: a case study using state-of-the-art datasets and methods. In: SIGIR 2024, pp. 2231–2240. ACM (2024)

40. PTI: British era survey report says Sabarimala ban existed 200 years ago. The Week (2018)

41. QueerInAI, O.O., et al.: Queer in AI: a case study in community-led participatory AI. In: FAccT 2023, pp. 1882–1895. ACM (2023). https://doi.org/10.1145/3593013.3594134

42. Rao, R.: Out of time: the queer politics of postcoloniality. Oxford University Press, pp. 7–9 (2020)

43. Reiss, M.V.: Testing the reliability of ChatGPT for text annotation and classification: a cautionary remark. ArXiv abs/2304.11085 (2023). https://api.semanticscholar.org/CorpusID:258291402
44. Sanh, V., Debut, L., Chaumond, J., Wolf, T.: DistilBERT, a distilled version of BERT: smaller, faster, cheaper and lighter (2020)
45. Siddiqua, U.A., Chy, A.N., Aono, M.: Stance detection on microblog focusing on syntactic tree representation. In: DMBD 2018, pp. 478–490. Springer (2018)
46. Team, G Gemini: Gemini 1.5: Unlocking multimodal understanding across millions of tokens of context. https://google/GeminiV1-5 (2024)
47. The Economist: recent court rulings in India suggest justice is improving (2017)
48. Wiegand, M., Ruppenhofer, J., Kleinbauer, T.: Detection of abusive language: the problem of biased datasets. In: NAACL-HLT 2019, pp. 602–608 (2019)

In Bad Faith: Assessing Discussion Quality on Social Media

Celia Chen[1]([✉]) [iD], Alex Leitch[1] [iD], William Jordan Conway[1], Eric Cotugno[1], Emily Klein[2], Rajesh Kumar Gnanasekaran[1], Kristin Buckstad Hamilton[1], Casi Sherman[1], Celia Sterrn[1], Logan C. Stevens[1], Rebecca Zarrella[1], and Jennifer Golbeck[1] [iD]

[1] University of Maryland, College Park, MD 20740, USA
{clichen,jgolbeck}@umd.edu
[2] University of Albany, Albany, NY 12227, USA

Abstract. The quality of a user's social media experience is determined both by the content they see and by the quality of the conversation and interaction around it. In this paper, we look at replies to tweets from mainstream media outlets and official government agencies and assess if they are good faith, engaging honestly and constructively with the original post, or bad faith, attacking the author or derailing the conversation. We assess automated approaches that may help in making this determination and then show that within our dataset of replies to mainstream media outlets and government agencies, bad faith interactions constitute 68.3% of all replies we studied, suggesting potential concerns about the quality of discourse in these specific conversational contexts. This is particularly true from verified accounts, where 91.7% of replies were bad faith. Given that verified accounts are algorithmically amplified, we discuss the implications of our work for understanding the user experience on social media.

Keywords: Social Media · Discussion Quality · Computational Social Science · Content Analysis

1 Introduction

Social media is an important source of news and information, with half of Americans getting news from social platforms [1]. The sources, accuracy, and amplification of social media content is important, as is the conversation around that content – the thing that makes it social. Online cultures can be engaged, curious, and organized around sharing high-quality and high-value information, or they can be unhealthy, riddled with harassment, bad faith engagement, and hate speech.

In this paper, we propose a definition and set of criteria for differentiating good and bad faith interactions on social media as a way of measuring one aspect of an online environment's conversational health. Using a codebook built on those criteria, we code a set of replies on popular tweets from mainstream media outlets and official US government accounts. This dataset forms the basis for addressing two main.

A. An et al. (Eds.): ASONAM 2025, LNCS 16323, pp. 338–345, 2026.
https://doi.org/10.1007/978-3-032-13821-7_28

research questions:

RQ1: Can automated techniques accurately assess whether a social media reply is in good or bad faith?

RQ2: What is the state of good vs. bad faith interactions on Twitter/X.

RQ2a: How does verified status relate to good and bad faith interaction on Twitter/X?

For RQ1, we analyze if LLMs, particularly ChatGPT, can read a tweet and reply and accurately label that reply as good or bad faith. Our results show for the dataset studied here, ChatGPT performs at the same level as a human coder, suggesting it may be.appropriate for automatically labeling data at scale.

We use both the human-labeled data and a larger set annotated by ChatGPT to.

further assess the alignment between human and automated coding, and also to assess the state of discourse on Twitter/X. Our results suggest the vast majority of replies on the types of posts we studied are in bad faith and that replies from Twitter/X's Verified.accounts engage in bad faith at a significantly higher rate than unverified accounts.

We emphasize that our findings are specifically applicable to the context of direct replies to high-profile mainstream media and government accounts with substantial.engagement (over 100 comments). While this represents a window into public.discourse with authoritative information sources, we acknowledge the limitations in generalizing these findings to the entirety of Twitter/X conversations or to other social media platforms.

2 Related Work and Methodology

2.1 Related Work

Previous work has examined conversation quality through various lenses, including natural language processing of online comments [2] and network analysis of how.

incivility spreads within social graphs [3]. Platform features and design choices.

influence discussion quality, with research showing that certain network affordances can improve discussion quality [4], while the effectiveness of moderation techniques varies across platforms [5]. Network effects also play a role, with studies finding that small groups of users can influence overall discourse quality [6], creating patterns that affect how views spread over time [7].

2.2 Theoretical Foundations and Opereational Definition

Drawing on philosophical work from Sartre [8] and Johannesen [9] and recent.

frameworks from Roberts-Miller [10] and Craig [11], we developed criteria for.

distinguishing good and bad faith interactions. Bad faith engagement is characterized by "cynical consciousness" and willful denial of truth [8], while good faith embodies authenticity, self-awareness, and commitment to seeking understanding [9].

We acknowledge that classifying interactions into a binary framework represents a simplification of communicative behaviors that exist along a spectrum. Our coding framework focuses on identifying predominant characteristics to determine whether.

interactions primarily advance or hinder meaningful discourse.

Bad faith comments demonstrate: dismissal of evidence without substantive engagement; strategic derailment through topic shifting; pseudo-engagement that prevents meaningful dialogue; personal attacks and ad hominem arguments; deliberate misrepresentation of facts; inflammatory or derogatory language; and speculative accusations without evidence.

Good faith comments exhibit: direct engagement with the original topic; evidence-based reasoning; constructive disagreement or criticism; genuine questions seeking clarification; recognition of issue complexity; respectful tone; and willingness to consider alternative viewpoints.

2.3 Data Collection

Twitter/X was selected as a site for this study as it offers a robust collection of fixed, short-format texts in English. This baseline offers good generalizability for posts based in anglophone countries, and mobility to non-X platforms with comparable content formatting, such as Threads or BlueSky.

We collected tweets from mainstream media accounts (NBC News, CBS News, CNN, Washington Post, New York Times, Wall Street Journal, Associated Press, Reuters) based on their presence in Pew studies [12], and official US government accounts from a federal directory. For each account, we used Twitter/X's advanced search to select all 2024 posts with at least 100 comments, ensuring strong engagement within the established Twitter/X ecosystem.

In total, 601 posts met our criteria: 441 from mainstream media (led by NBC News with 198 posts, CBS News with 121) and 160 from 26 government agencies (led by State Department with 50 posts, NASA with 21). We collected 52,469 total replies, of which 31,283 were unique.

Twitter/X's Terms of Use prohibit the public release of this data, but researchers who want access can email jgolbeck@umd.edu to request a copy.

2.4 Coding Process

We randomly selected 400 tweet-reply pairs for human coding. Two coders independently labeled each reply, with a third coder resolving disagreements through majority vote. This established our ground truth dataset.

After human coding, ChatGPT-4 independently labeled each reply using a prompt incorporating our codebook criteria:

"I'm going to ask you whether a reply to a tweet is a good faith engagement. Here are the characteristics of good vs. bad faith engagements:

Characteristics of bad faith comments: Dismissal of data – when factual data is presented and ignored or waved off; Generalization – broad unsupported statements; Lack of engagement of non-constructive engagement with the original post –conflating issues, derailing the conversation, switching topics, changing focus, deflection, irrelevant comments; Lack of depth, simple solutions offered to complex problems; Tone or language that is sarcastic / dismissive / aggressive / threatening / conspiratorial / derogatory; Personal attacks, ad hominem attacks, and personal criticism; Provocation; Misinformation or misrepresentation of facts; Speculative accusation.

Characteristics of good faith comments: Acknowledgement of the issue; Engaged with / relevant to the original topic; Reasoned agreement or evidence-based disagreement; Constructive Argument / Criticism / Inquiry; Solution-oriented or strategic comments; Tone that is respectful / positive / playful / non-inflammatory; Encourages further interaction; Constructive speculation; Concern for accuracy.

Now consider this tweet from < ACCOUNT >: < ORIGINAL TWEET TEXT >.

A user replies: < REPLY TEXT >

Using the criteria above, is the reply a good faith interaction with the original? Please answer in one word, yes or no".

Examples of good faith interaction include the following:

National Park Service: Living your life to the fullest does not have to involve selfies with bison.

Reply: Ya really should not have to tweet this, yet here we are.

NBC News: Analysis by Philip Bump: Why would a news organization pay someone to lie to viewers?

Reply: Good question. I'm glad the journalists and NBC News hosts are speaking out against the hiring of Ronna McDaniel. She actually participated in the attempt to.

overthrow the free, fair & most secure election in the U.S. She belongs in jail, not normalized on NBC.

Examples of bad faith interactions are:

CBS News: JPMorgan Chase CEO Jamie Dimon says he worries geopolitical events and U.S. political polarization "may very well be creating risks that could eclipse anything since World War II."

Reply: Risks? Like illegal immigration, rigged elections, sideshows on freeways and violent criminals walking with no bail? Doesn't sound risky at all.

NASA: LIVE: A new spacecraft is launching with crew for the first time! @NASA_Astronauts Butch Wilmore and Suni Williams are scheduled to lift off on @BoeingSpace 's #Starliner Crew Flight Test, riding aboard a @ULALaunch Atlas V rocket, at 12:25pm ET (1625 UTC).

Reply: So so old. Are they able to move around on their own? You better send a nurse just in case they forget what they are doing. Now I see why the other countries mock us.

3   Results

3.1   Coding Accuracy Assessment

Of 400 tweet-reply pairs, 397 were coded (3 dropped for non-English content). Human coders agreed 87.7% of the time (Cohen's $\kappa = 0.64$). ChatGPT achieved 89.0% agreement with final human labels ($\kappa = 0.75$). For good faith detection, ChatGPT achieved 84.43% precision and 81.75% recall. For bad faith detection, precision was 91.64% and recall was 92.98%.

Table 1. Confusion Matrix of ChatGPT vs. Human Coding for Good and Bad Faith Replies.

		Human	
		Good	Bad
ChatGPT	Good	103	19
	Bad	23	252

The moderate human inter-rater reliability ($\kappa = 0.64$) highlights the inherent.

challenge in assessing good and bad faith interactions, as noted in theoretical work [10,11]. ChatGPT's strong performance against human ground truth suggests LLMs can reliably identify these patterns.

3.2 Good and Bad Faith Interactions on Twitter/X

In our human-coded sample ($N = 397$), 31.7% of replies were good faith. There were stark differences between account types: media accounts received 20.8% good faith replies versus government accounts' 39.7%.

Verification status showed significant patterns. Among unverified accounts ($N = 246$), 37.8% of replies were good faith. For verified accounts ($N = 151$), only 21.9% were good faith. ChatGPT labeling showed similar distributions with no significant differences ($p = 0.76$ overall, $p = 0.67$ for verified, $p = 0.92$ for unverified).

Using ChatGPT to label all 31,283 replies revealed: 24.9% good faith overall, but only 18.7% from verified users versus 28.5% from unverified users. Verified accounts produced 81.3% bad faith interactions compared to 71.5% from unverified accounts.

3.3 Algorithmic Amplification Patterns

Verified status strongly influences reply ranking. The correlation between rank and.

percentage of verified account tweets at that rank is $r = -0.85$, indicating verified accounts dominate top-ranked positions. Average reply rank differs significantly ($p < 0.001$): 32.8 for verified accounts versus 59.8 for unverified accounts.

While we found no significant correlation between rank and good faith percentage ($r = 0.18$), the combination of verified accounts' higher bad faith rates and their.

algorithmic amplification raises concerns about discourse quality in highly visible reply positions.

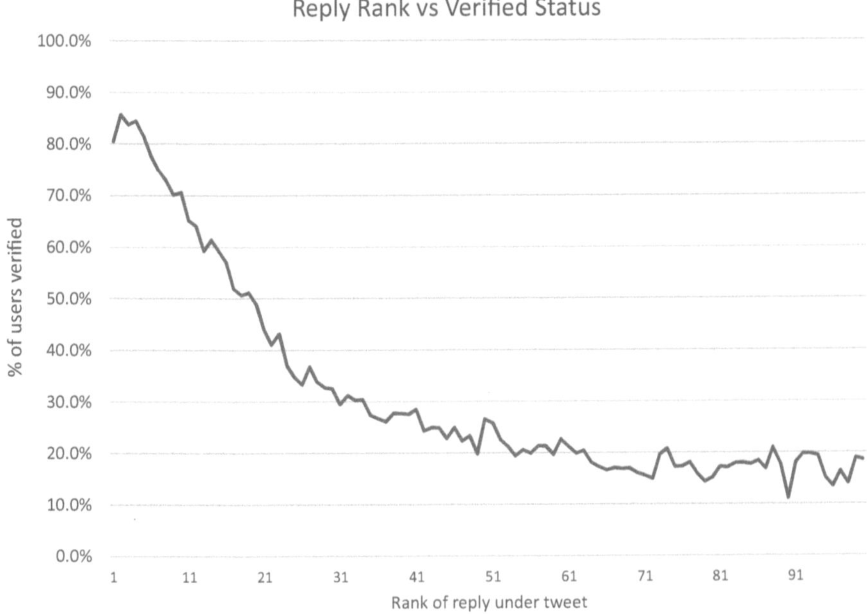

Fig. 1. Percentage of Verified Users by Reply Rank.

4 Discussion

4.1 Discussion Quality in High-Visibility Contexts

Within our specific sample of high-engagement posts from mainstream media and.government accounts, bad faith interactions dominate (68.3% overall). This pattern is pronounced for verified accounts (81.3% bad faith), which are algorithmically.amplified to prominent positions. While these findings cannot be generalized to all Twitter/X conversations, they suggest concerning patterns in how users engage with authoritative information sources that serve important democratic functions.

The high rate of bad faith interactions from verified accounts may reflect the.parasocial nature of engagement on Twitter/X, where replies often function as.performances for one's own followers rather than genuine dialogue attempts [13].

Strategic harassment of high-visibility targets can increase the attacker's own visibility within the platform ecosystem, creating perverse incentives for bad faith engagement.

4.2 Platform Design Implications

Our findings suggest Twitter/X's algorithmic amplification may inadvertently reward inflammatory content by prioritizing verified accounts that show higher rates of bad faith engagement. If platforms prioritized conversational health, they could consider reply quality as a ranking factor. Given that LLMs can identify good/bad faith replies with accuracy comparable to human coders, such interventions are technically feasible.

The tensions between platform business models and conversational health present significant challenges. Many social media platforms operate on engagement metrics that may conflict with discourse quality [14]. Interventions to improve conversational health must contend with these economic realities, potentially requiring metrics that better align platform success with user wellbeing rather than raw engagement numbers.

4.3 Limitations and Future Work

Our focus on direct replies to mainstream media and government accounts provides insight into engagement with authoritative sources but limits generalizability. The.
binary classification of good versus bad faith represents a necessary simplification of complex communicative behaviors. Future work should examine whether similar.
patterns appear in other conversational contexts and explore more nuanced.
categorization schemes.
The moderate human inter-rater reliability also suggests that determining faith can be subtle and context-dependent, indicating potential benefits from more detailed.
coding frameworks that capture different types or degrees of bad faith engagement.

5 Conclusion

We developed a framework for identifying good and bad faith interactions on social media and demonstrated that ChatGPT can label English-language replies with accuracy comparable to human coders. Within our studied sample of high-engagement posts from mainstream media and government accounts, 68.3% of replies were bad faith, with verified accounts showing particularly high rates (81.3%).
While these findings are specific to our sample context, they raise concerns about discourse quality around authoritative information sources. The combination of high bad faith rates from verified accounts and their algorithmic amplification suggests.
platform design choices may inadvertently undermine conversational health.
Future work should examine scalable approaches to improving online discourse quality while considering the complex relationships between platform economics, user behavior, and democratic engagement. By advancing understanding of good faith.
interactions and developing ethical ways to promote them, we can work toward creating more constructive digital public spaces.

References

1. Liedke, J., Wang, L.: News Platform Fact Sheet. Pew Research Center 2024. Retrieved from https://www.pewresearch.org/journalism/fact-sheet/news-platform-fact-sheet/
2. Qiu, X., Oliveira, D.F.M., Sahami Shirazi, A., Flammini, A., Menczer, F.: Limited individual attention and online virality of low-quality information. Nat. Hum. Behav. 1(7), 0132 (2017)
3. Cheng, J., Danescu-Niculescu-Mizil, C., Leskovec, J., Bernstein, M.: Anyone can become a troll: causes of trolling behavior in online discussions. In: Proceedings of the 2017 ACM Conference on Computer Supported Cooperative Work and Social Computing, pp. 1217–1230. New York: Association for Computing Machinery 2017

4. Jaidka, K., Zhou, A., Lelkes, Y., Egelhofer, J. L., Lecheler, S.: Beyond anonymity: network affordances, under deindividuation, improve social media discussion quality. J. Comput. Med. Commun. **27**(1), zmab019 (2022)
5. Jhaver, S., Ghoshal, S., Bruckman, A., Gilbert, E.: Online harassment and content moderation: the case of blocklists. ACM Trans. Comput. Hum. Int. **25**(2), 1–33 (2018)
6. Berry, G., Taylor, S. J.: Discussion quality diffuses in the digital public square. In: Proceedings of the 26th International Conference on World Wide Web, pp. 1371–1380 (2017). New York: Association for Computing Machinery
7. Vargo, C.J., Hopp, T.: Socioeconomic status, social capital, and partisan polarity as predictors of political incivility on Twitter: a congressional district-level analysis. Soc. Sci. Comput. Rev. **38**(1), 10–32 (2020)
8. Santoni, R.E.: Bad Faith, Good Faith, and Authenticity in Sartre's Early Philosophy. Temple University Press, Philadelphia (2016)
9. Johannesen, R.L.: Ethics in Human Communication. Waveland Press, Long Grove, IL (1995)
10. Roberts-Miller, P.: Fanatical Schemes: Proslavery Rhetoric and the Tragedy of Consensus. University of Alabama Press, Tuscaloosa, AL (2009)
11. Craig, R.: Rhetorical Closure. Rhetor. Soc. Q. **47**(4), 313–334 (2017)
12. Shearer, E., Mitchell, A.: Broad Agreement in US–Even Among Partisans–on Which News Outlets Are Part of the 'Mainstream Media'. Pew Research Center (2021)
13. Marwick, A. E., boyd, D.: To see and be seen: celebrity practice on Twitter. Convergence **17**(2), 139–158 2011. https://doi.org/10.1177/1354856510394539
14. Zuboff, S.: The Age of Surveillance Capitalism: The Fight for a Human Future at the New Frontier of Power. Public Affairs, New York (2019)

Fair2Vec: Learning Fair and Topic-Aware Representations for Influencer Recommendation

Arpan Dam[1(✉)], Sayan Pathak[2], and Bivas Mitra[1]

[1] IIT Kharagpur, Kharagpur 721302, India
`arpand@kgpian.iitkgp.ac.in` , `bivas@cse.iitkgp.ac.in`
[2] Microsoft AI and Research, Washington, USA
`sayanpa@microsoft.com`

Abstract. Balancing influence maximization with demographic fairness remains a critical challenge in recommendation systems. Existing methods either ignore topic-sensitive fairness or rely on heuristic approximations that lack scalability. We propose *Fair2Vec*, a novel framework to jointly recommend (1) top-k influencers, (2) top-r topics, and (3) ensure the influenced population's demographic distribution aligns with the broader topic-specific community. *Fair2Vec* leverages topic-aware embeddings to model influence dynamics and fairness constraints, eliminating error-prone multi-hop computations. By restructuring networks as bipartite graphs, it reduces time complexity compared to state-of-the-art heuristics. Experiments on *Meetup*, *Yelp*, and *DBLP* datasets demonstrate *Fair2Vec's* superiority: it achieves higher fairness and greater influenced populations than baselines. Our work bridges the gap between scalable influence maximization and topic-aware fairness in recommendations, offering actionable insights for platforms aiming to foster inclusive engagement while preserving relevance to user interests.

Keywords: Influence · Fairness · Embedding · Topic · Social networks

1 Introduction

Influence Maximization (IM) [1] aims to identify a small set of individuals who can maximize the spread of influence in a network. Traditional IM models assume a uniform influence across all topics, but [2] introduced topic-aware IM, showing that influence varies depending on the topic. For example, on LinkedIn, a professional known for insightful posts on data science and analytics may have a large following and spark wide discussions in tech circles, yet may not resonate as strongly with audiences interested in topics like HR practices, personal branding, or early-career guidance. This underscores the necessity of topic-aware influence maximization (*TAIM*), where both influencers and the topics they dominate must be jointly optimized.

The need for fairness in Topic-Aware Influence Maximization (*TAIM*) grows critical when addressing demographic disparities in topic engagement. Prior work [3,4] proposes recommending influencers such that the influenced population's sensitive attribute distribution (e.g., gender ratio) matches the entire population's distribution. However, in *TAIM*, topics often exhibit distinct demographic skews. On platforms like LinkedIn, interest in topics such as leadership, entrepreneurship often sees greater participation from male professionals, while discussions around work-life balance, wellness, or diversity in the workplace tend to engage more female users. For instance, if posts on diversity and inclusion naturally attract 80% female engagement, then strictly enforcing a balanced gender ratio (say, equal fraction of male & female) while recommending such content could result in targeting disinterested male audiences, thereby reducing interaction quality and content relevance. In contrast, aligning recommendations with topic-specific audience distributions (e.g., 80 : 20) ensures authenticity, relevance, and a more inclusive approach that honors genuine interests. Failing to proportionately represent female audiences in topics where they are naturally more engaged (e.g., work-life balance) leads to knowledge access inequality, where underrepresented groups receive less exposure to meaningful, career-enhancing content. This can limit professional growth, reduce visibility in key domains, and reinforce existing inequities within the platform's ecosystem. Promoting fairness in *TAIM* through topic-aware strategies helps bridge such divides and fosters a more equitable professional community.

Prior *TAIM* methods [2,5] assume fixed topics and ignore demographic fairness within influenced populations, whereas fairness-aware IM frameworks [3,4,6] neglect topic-specific fairness. Two additional limitations hinder current approaches: *Heuristic Inefficiency:* Several methods [2] estimate influence probabilities using arbitrary heuristics or noisy historical interaction logs, leading to unreliable outcomes. Furthermore, as network depth increases, computing influence spread across multiple hops becomes computationally intractable [5], severely limiting scalability. To address these issues, recent works [7,8] have represented influence relationships using embeddings. Embedding-based methods offer key advantages: for instance, if an influencer u impacts v indirectly through multiple hops, their embeddings can estimate the probability of influence with higher accuracy and lower computational costs. Moreover, embeddings can effectively quantify the influence of individuals who exert similar levels of influence among their respective followers. However, existing embedding-based methods do not incorporate fairness considerations. Though adversarial methods [9,10] merge fairness with embeddings, they assume topic-invariant influence, ignoring how an influencer's efficacy varies across topics like *Sports* versus *Art*. This gap underscores the need for a novel approach that simultaneously optimizes influence spread and ensures fairness across recommended topics.

In this paper, we propose *Fair2Vec*, a method that computes topic-wise embeddings for influencers and followers to recommend: (i) the top-k influential members I_k, and (ii) the top-r influence topics T_r, ensuring that I_k is both highly effective for T_r and fair with respect to sensitive attributes (e.g., gender) across the influenced population for each $t \in T_r$. *Fair2Vec* comprises three main components. First, we identify potential influencers and compute a *topic-wise fairness score*, measuring how closely the sensitive attribute distribution in their influenced population matches that of the broader topic-specific audience. Second, we introduce a *multi-task embedding model* to learn topic-wise embeddings, where the fairness score acts as a penalty that limits each influencer's impact, thereby guiding influence allocation. These embeddings are used to estimate influence probabilities, eliminating reliance on heuristic assumptions. Finally, we construct a *bipartite graph* where edge weights capture both influence probability and fairness. We then solve an optimization problem to recommend I_k and T_r that maximize influence while enforcing fairness constraints per topic. By embedding fairness directly into the learning process and avoiding multi-hop computations, *Fair2Vec* offers both scalability and stronger fairness guarantees than prior methods. We evaluate *Fair2Vec* on three real-world datasets—*Meetup* (event-based), *Yelp* (location-based), and *DBLP* (citation network)—demonstrating superior influence spread and fairness over baselines.

2   Related work

Influence maximization: [1] introduced the problem of influence maximization where the author proposed 2 greedy algorithm (i) Independent cascade and (ii) Linear threshold to find the influence spread. After this, many algorithms like [11] are developed to reduce the time complexity. But all this algorithm depends on a diffusion graph with edges weighted on a power of influence; this influence power is found by either using historical logs or by making simple assumptions. These algorithms do not consider the impact of unfairness on the influenced population and also did not capture the effect of topics on influence maximization.

Topical Influence in Social Networks: This section discusses work on identifying topical influencers in social networks. Studies such as [2], and [12] address influence propagation given input topics (queries), aiming to find topic-specific influencers. [5] and [13] focus on finding the top-k influencers and the best r influence tags for platforms like *Meetup* and *Yelp*. Notably, these studies do not consider fairness and treat all influencers equally.

Fair Influence Maximization: Several works have integrated fairness into influence maximization. Tsang et al. [3] introduced fairness in resource allocation, inspiring fairness-aware models. Techniques include integer programming [4], welfare optimization [6], and reinforcement learning [14]. Adversarial [9] and clustering-based methods face challenges with multi-attribute fairness. Lin et al. [15] adapted the RRS algorithm for fair seed selection. Deep learning with historical cascades [16] and concave fairness frameworks [17] struggle with dynamic environments. Community-based strategies [18] enhance fairness but rely on rigid structures. Optimization approaches like multi-objective models [19] improve fairness but increase computational cost. Hypergraph [20] and counterfactual graph-based methods [21] offer alternatives, though they require careful tuning. These approaches underscore the trade-off between fairness, scalability, and adaptability.

3   Motivation Study and Problem Statement

First, we introduce all the datasets, then we conduct some pilot studies to highlight the limitations of potential influencers identified using the standard algorithm [22], and finally, we describe the problem statement.

3.1   Dataset

In this paper, we introduce three different social network dataset namely *Meetup* (EBSN), *Yelp* (LBSN), and *DBLP* (citation network). *Meetup* is a popular event based social networking (EBSN) portal that facilitates hosting events in various localities around the world [22]. *Meetup* groups are organized into 33 official categories e.g., *Career and Business, Technology* that define their general focus. Each group hosts events on specific topics, such as *Accounting* or *Drawing*, which reflect the interests of both the group and its members. Upon joining, members select tags or topics that reflect their personal interests. These topics help personalize recommendations and connect members with relevant communities and events. Meetup event attendees are users who responded "Yes" to the event RSVP, as indicated by their RSVP status ("Yes", "No", or "Maybe"). In this paper, we focus on groups in Chicago under the 'Career and Business' category (767 groups, avg. 83 events). *Yelp* is a location-based social network where users post reviews about restaurants. Each review is associated with specific cuisines (e.g., 'Chinese', 'Pizza'), which we treat as topics. Our analysis focuses on 267 restaurants in San Francisco, comprising approximately 1.9 million reviews. The network includes around 13,000 users and 53 distinct cuisine-based topics. *DBLP* is an academic citation network where topics correspond to research keywords (e.g., 'Information Flow', 'Security'), extracted from paper metadata. To infer the gender of citing authors, we use the first author's name from each citing paper, applying probabilistic methods based on the SSA baby name dataset and the Gender API. The dataset consists of approximately 95 topics and 900 authors.

3.2   Motivation and Pilot Study

This section presents the datasets and a pilot study motivating our fairness-aware approach. A member u_i is labeled a potential influencer if another member u_j RSVPs to the same event within five hours of u_i's RSVP.[1] If this pattern occurs for at least four events, u_i is said to influence u_j on the associated event topics t_e. In this case, we assign u_i the *influence topic* t_e and denote the influence relationship as $u_i \xrightarrow{t_e} u_j$. The set of all such potential influencers is denoted by

---

[1] We follow the empirically validated threshold used in [22].

U_N. For each $u_i \in U_N$, we define their *direct followers* as $F_i = \bigcup_j u_j$, where $u_i \Rightarrow F_i$ implies that u_i has influenced all users in F_i. The size of this set, $|F_i|$, quantifies the *influence capacity* of u_i. Here in the pilot study, we consider the number of direct followers as influence capacity, however, in the developed methodology, we implement a standard procedure to compute the influenced population (direct and indirect).

First, we handpick top-20 potential influential members $U_N(N = 20)$ of *Meetup* for the category *Career and Business* in *Chicago* city based on their influence capacity and highlight their limitations as influential members.

(a) Capacity of the Influential Member Varies Across Event Topics: We analyze a potential influencer $u_i \in U_N$ attending events of a *Meetup* group G_i, which hosts topics like {'Women Profession', 'IT', 'Fundraising', 'Investing'}. Figure 1 ashows the event topics t_e (x-axis) attended by u_i. The blue bar represents the fraction of u_i's followers $f_i \in F_i$ attending each event ($u_i \xrightarrow{t_e} f_i$), while the green bar shows the fraction of event attendees who are u_i's followers. This can be observed that event topics like 'IT' and 'Fundraising' attract significantly more followers than 'Women Profession' and 'Investing' (p-value < 0.05, two-sided t-test). This suggests that the effectiveness of an influencer can vary across topics, emphasizing the need to identify the most suitable event topics while detecting influential members in *Meetup*.

(b) Fairness of the influential member varies across event topics: We analyzed a potential influential member u with two influence topics: *Accounting* and *Entrepreneurship*. To assess gender fairness, we compared the gender distribution of u's followers for each topic with that of the broader *Meetup* population in Chicago, based on event attendance. As shown in Fig. 1 b, the distribution for *Accounting* aligns closely with the population, indicating fairness. However, for *Entrepreneurship*, only 0.19% of u's followers were female, compared to 0.34% in the general population—revealing gender bias. This underscores the importance of evaluating fairness on a topic-by-topic basis to understand an influential user's reach.

(c) Bias in Event Attendance are Detrimental for Groups: Our pilot study reveals that the underrepresentation or overrepresentation of any gender becomes detrimental for the *Meetup* groups. In Fig. 1 c, we plot the performance of the *Meetup* group (as event attendance and group size) with respect to fraction of female attendees across events hosted by those respective *Meetup* groups. We observe that the event attendance and group size drop as female (or male) presence is marginalized (around 10%) in those respective *Meetup* events. This clearly indicates that if event attendance is dominated by one gender, it can make other gender feel unwelcome, reduce interest in the event, and eventually lead to a decline in group performance.

(d) Strict Enforcement of Fairness is Detrimental for Influence Capacity: We conduct a study to determine the optimal proportion of females (or males) in an influencer's follower population to maximize influence capacity. We select six female-biased topics (e.g., *Beauty Products, Fashion*) where roughly

70% of interested users are female and cluster influencers by their female follower fractions (10%–90%). Figure 1d plots the average influence capacity (y-axis) against the fraction of females present as their followers (x-axis). We repeat this for several male-biased topics (female interest $\approx$ 40%). In both cases, influence capacity peaks when the follower gender ratio is close to the fraction of females interested in those topics (say, 70% or 40%). Notably, enforcing equal gender balance can reduce influence, as it introduces disengaged participants. This may stem from the fact that bringing more men into female-oriented topics can result in disengaged participants, reducing overall influence.

3.3   Problem Statement

Consider a *Meetup* group G located in city $\mathcal{C} \in C$. Objective of this paper is to develop *Fair2Vec*, which recommends top-k of influential members I_k, who may influence the *Meetup* members, in city $\mathcal{C}$ to attend the events hosted by the group G to make them popular. For each recommended influencer member $I_i \in I_k$, we also recommend top-r topics T_r which are most effective for I_i to influence her followers to attend the *Meetup* events. Importantly, *Fair2Vec* ensures gender fairness among the influenced population. Precisely, for each recommended topic $T_i \in T_r$, the gender distribution of the influenced population must closely match the corresponding distribution in the *Meetup* population interested in topic T_i.

This framework extends naturally to other platforms. For example, in *Yelp*, Fair2Vec recommends top reviewers (influencers) and top cuisines (topics) to attract customers to restaurants, while ensuring the gender distribution of influenced customers aligns with the demographic composition of users interested in each cuisine. Similarly, in *DBLP*, it recommends top authors (influencers) and research areas (topics) to promote citation influence, ensuring that the gender ratio of authors citing the recommended researchers matches the inherent demographic distribution of each research topic (e.g., male/female ratios in research topic 'Security').

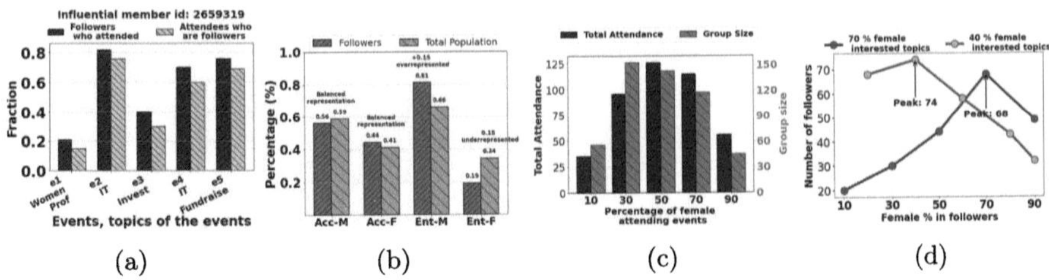

(a)   (b)   (c)   (d)

Fig. 1. (a) Capacity of influential member varies across various topics (b) Gender representation in topic *Entrepreneurship* and *Accounting*. Males are overrepresented in *Entrepreneurship* (Ent), while *Accounting* (Acc) shows balanced representation. (c) Impact of Declining Female Participation on Group Dynamics. (d) Influence peaks when the gender ratio in the followers aligns with the topic's natural audience (e.g., 70% female).

The crux of *Fair2Vec* relies on the correct learning of the influence intensity that one influential member exerts on her direct and indirect followers. We aim to first represent the influence capacity of an influencer with the help of an embedding, which keeps both her topic awareness and gender fairness in consideration. Similarly, we model the susceptibility of a member to influence through an embedding that reflects their likelihood of being influenced by others. This formulation is applied across multiple real-world datasets, including *Meetup*, *Yelp*, and *DBLP*, each representing distinct types of networks. Finally, these two embeddings—one for the influencer and one for the follower—are used together to compute the overall influence intensity that an influencer exerts on both her direct and indirect followers.

4 Development of *Fair2Vec*

In this section, we describe the development of *Fair2Vec*[2]. While the framework generalizes across platforms, we detail its implementation for *Meetup* below, with analogous steps applicable to other datasets like *Yelp* or *DBLP*.

4.1 Identifying Group Aligned Potential Influencers

First, we identify all the event topics T_G that are aligned with *Meetup* group G. For that, we extract all the past hosted events E_G of G, and from each event's textual description, we extract the most relevant keywords using *YAKE* [23]. We populate T_G with the top 20 most frequently occurring keywords of events $E_G{}^3$.

Next, we identify all the group aligned potential influencers U_C, who influences other *Meetup* members via group aligned topics T_G. For that, first we identify all the potential influencers U_N following the procedure explained in Sect. 3.2, and then find the subset of potential influencers ($U_C \subseteq U_N$), who influence other *Meetup* members exclusively on topics $t_j \in T_G$ that align with the group G's interest. For each potential influencer $u_i \in U_C$, the influence context A_{u_i} includes all members influenced by u_i on a specific topic t_j, encompassing both direct followers F_{u_i} and indirect (multi-hop) followers. For example, if u_1 influences u_2 on the topic *IOT*, and u_2 subsequently influences u_3 on the same topic, then influence context of u_1 becomes $A_{u_1} = \{u_2, u_3\}$. The size of A_{u_i} quantifies u_i's influence capacity on topic t_j.

---

[2] Our code is publicly available at https://github.com/ArpanDam/fair-influence-embedding.

[3] We also include few additional topics from other events, which are semantically close to T_G.

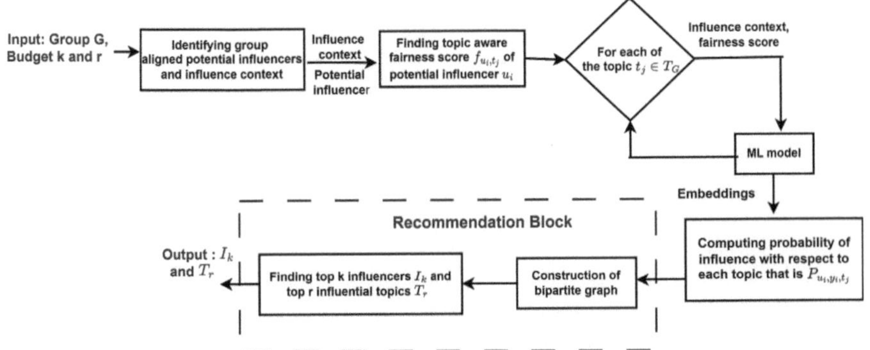

Fig. 2. Flowchart of *Fair2Vec*.

4.2 Estimating Fairness of a Potential Influencer

As discussed in Sect. 3.2, fairness of a influencer with respect to a sensitive attribute (say, gender) may vary significantly across different topics. Fairness of an influencer u_i is measured observing the fairness ratio $\mathcal{F}_j$ across various sensitive attributes j. We define fairness ratio $\mathcal{F}_j$ as the ratio between the fraction of a sensitive attribute j (say female) present in the influence context of u_i for topic t_j (say, V_j), and the fraction of the same sensitive attribute j (say female) present in overall Meetup population interested in topic t_j (say, E_j). For a perfectly fair influencer u_i, one should observe $\mathcal{F}_i = \frac{V_j}{E_j} = \mathcal{F}_j = \frac{V_i}{E_i}$ for various sensitive attributes i (say male), j (say female) etc. [3]. Higher diversity in the fairness ratio $\mathcal{F}_j \ \forall j$ points to an unfair influencer u_i. Hence to quantify fairness of a influencer u_i, we compute the standard deviation σ and the mean μ of the fairness ratios $\mathcal{F}_j$ across various sensitive attributes j and then derive the coefficient of variation $D_{u_i} = \frac{\sigma}{\mu}$, which measures the degree of unfairness of u_i. Subsequently, we define the normalized fairness score $f_{u_i} = \frac{2}{1+\exp(D_{u_i})}$ of u_i, where fairness score closer to 1 indicates a fair influencer, while a lower score suggests greater unfairness. For each group-aligned influencer u_i, we obtain a fairness score vector f_{u_i,t_j}, where each element represents the fairness score of u_i for a specific influence topic $t_j \in T_G$.

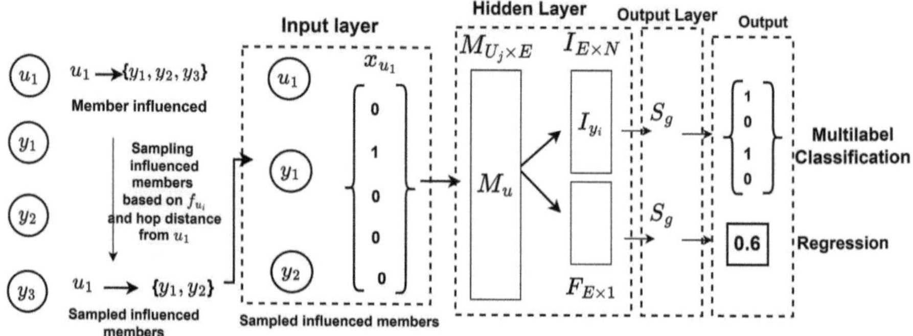

Fig. 3. Multitask neural network to find embedding where u_1 is a potential influencer. u_1 is influencing $\{y_1, y_2, y_3\}$, f_{u_1} is 0.6 which is the fairness score of u_1. Influenced members are sampled based on f_{u_1} and the model has to predict the sampled influenced users and f_{u_1}.

4.3 Learning Fairness Aware Influencer Embeddings

In this section, we implement a multi-task neural network model (see Fig. 3) to learn the capacity of an influential member $u_i \in U_C$ to fairly influence the members in her influence context A_{u_i}. We represent the influence capacity of u_i with the help of embedding M_{u_i}. The key idea of this MTL model is to penalize an unfair influencer u_i by downsampling her influence context based on its topic aware fairness score f_{u_i,t_j}. Precisely, given an influencer u_i with *influence topic* t_j, her influence context is downsampled to $A^s_{u_i}$ by selecting $|A_{u_i}| \times f_{u_i,t_j}$ nodes from its influence context $|A_{u_i}|$. We prioritize retaining the followers who are closer in hop distance to u_i, as they are more likely to be directly influenced. The probability of retaining a node $y \in A^s_{u_i}$ in the sampled influence context $A^s_{u_i}$ is determined by its hop distance from u_i, with farther nodes being more likely to be removed. This ensures that the fairness score acts as a penalty for an unfair influencer while preserving strong direct and near-indirect influence relationships. The proposed MTL model simultaneously conducts two separate tasks: (a) given a potential influential member u_i, the model predicts its direct and indirect influenced members (sampled influence context $A^s_{u_i}$), and (b) estimates the fairness score (f_{u_i,t_j}) of u_i. Here, estimating the fairness score is a regression task, whereas predicting the influenced members is a multi-label classification task.

4.3.1 Model Construction

We train the multi-task learning (MTL) model for each group-aligned topic $t_j \in T_G$, designed to process two inputs: (1) pairs of influential nodes and their sampled influence contexts and (2) fairness scores. For a topic t_j, let $A^s_{u_i} = \{y_1, y_2, \ldots, y_m\}$ represents the (down)sampled influence context of influencer u_i. The first input is encoded as $X^i = \{(x_{u_i}, x_{A^s_{u_i}})\}$, where $x_{u_i} \in \mathbb{R}^{|U_j|}$ is a one-hot vector for u_i, $|U_j|$ denotes the number of topic-specific influencers, and $x_{A_{u_i}^s} \in \mathbb{R}^N$ encodes the downsampled influenced context $A_{u_i}^s$) of size N. The second input, $X^c = \{(x_{u_i}, f_{u_i,t_j})\}$, pairs u_i with its fairness score f_{u_i,t_j}. The MTL architecture (Fig. 3) consists of a shared embedding layer $\mathbf{M} \in \mathbb{R}^{|U_j| \times E}$ with embedding dimension[4] $E = 50$, where $M_{u_i} = x_{u_i}\mathbf{M}$ generates influencer embeddings. Task-specific layers include $\mathbf{I} \in \mathbb{R}^{E \times N}$ for influence prediction (yielding embeddings I_{y_i} for influenced members y_i) and $F \in \mathbb{R}^{E \times 1}$ for fairness score estimation, enabling joint optimization of influence spread and demographic fairness through shared representations.

Loss Function: To predict the influenced members $A_{u_i}^s = \{y_1, y_2, \ldots, y_m\}$, we apply the sigmoid activation function S_g at the output layer. Since this is a multi-label classification task, we use the binary cross-entropy loss function L_e. For estimating the fairness score, we employ the Mean Squared Error (MSE) loss function L_m. The total loss L that we aim to minimize is the sum of both components $L = L_e + L_m$.

Estimating Fair Influence Capacity: Let u_i be a potential influencer with an associated influence topic t_j. If u_i influences the member y_i to participate in events related to t_j, we apply a sigmoid transformation on the dot product of M_{u_i} and I_{y_i} to compute p_{u_i,y_i,t_j}. This value represents the capacity of u_i to influence y_i through the topic t_j.

$$p_{u_i,y_i,t_j} = S_g(M_{u_i}I_{y_i}) \tag{1}$$

For each of the topics $t_j \in T_G$ we train the MTL model and compute the capacity of influence p_{u_i,y_{u_i},t_j} for all $u_i \in U_C$, where y_{u_i} is the influence context of u_i with influence topic t_j. The training is conducted for each of the topics $t_j \in T_G$. The training time is $|T_G| \times |W| \times N$ where $|T_G|$ is the number of group-aligned topics, W is the average number of sampled members influenced per topic, and N is the total number of members in *Meetup*.

4.4   Influencer Recommendation

Finally, leveraging the influence capacity of influencers, we recommend top k fair influencers and their respective top r influence topics. First, we construct a weighted bipartite graph.

(a) Construction of Bipartite Graph: We construct an attributed bipartite graph $G(U_C, A_{u_i}, E)$, where the first partition contains the group aligned potential influencers U_C, and the second partition contains the influence contexts A_{u_i}. E denotes the directed links from potential influencers $u_i \in U_C$ to its respective followers A_{u_i}. Each link of this graph contains two different attributes: (i) The influence topic t_j, through which influential member u_i influences y_i to attend an event on topic t_j. (ii) the probability p_{u_i,y_i,t_j}, representing the capacity of an

---

[4] Embedding size empirically set to 50.

influencer u_i to influence the member y_i on topic t_j (from Eq. (1)). A potential influencer of the first partition may appear as a follower in the second partition.

(b) Recommending Top k Influencers and Top r Influential Topics: We employ the Independent Cascade (IC) [1] on each potential influencer $u_i \in U_C$ of the first partition to obtain the influenced population $\widehat{A}_i$. Our framework ensures fairness by integrating fairness scores directly into the influence capacity p_{u_i,y_i,t_j} of the bipartite graph. We greedily select the top-k influencers I_k based on the influenced population $\widehat{A}_i$, prioritizing those with both high influence potential and fair audience alignment. Unfair influencers receive lower capacity due to their topic-specific fairness penalties f_{u_i,t_j}, reducing their likelihood of being selected. Once I_k is selected, we find the influenced population using IC, then we analyse the edges from I_k to the influenced population and greedily select the top-r influence topics T_r that maximise the influenced population. The final output consists of the top-k fair influencers I_k, their top-r influence topics T_r, and the total influenced population $\widehat{A}_{k,r}$.

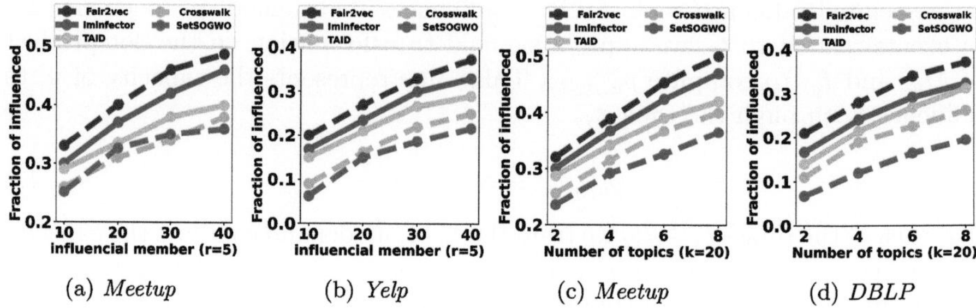

Fig. 4. (a) - (d) shows the effectiveness of I_k in terms of fraction of influenced.

Time Complexity: Selecting the top-k influencers using the greedy Independent Cascade (IC) model takes $\mathcal{O}(k \cdot |U_C| \cdot m)$ time, where $|U_C|$ is the number of group-aligned influencers and m is the number of edges. Identifying the top-r topics adds $\mathcal{O}(k \cdot m)$, but as $|U_C| \gg 1$, the total simplifies to $\mathcal{O}(k \cdot |U_C| \cdot m)$. This offers notable efficiency over traditional multi-hop methods by focusing only on direct, fairness-adjusted influence pathways, ensuring scalability.

5   Performance Evaluation

In this section, we evaluate the performance of *Fair2Vec* from various perspectives.

5.1 Overall Evaluation of *Fair2Vec*

(a) Fair2Vec Optimizes the Influenced Population: In Fig 4, we plot the fraction of influenced population $\widehat{A}_{k,r}$ of the recommended top-k influencers I_k. For the sake of brevity and to avoid repetition, we present results for only a subset of the datasets. Figure 4a and 4b shows that for *Meetup* and *Yelp*, *Fair2Vec* outperforms the baselines in terms of the fraction of influenced population. The limitation of *SetSOGWO* and *TAID* stems from their inability to properly capture the influence capacity of the influencers, which are computed from the historical logs only, thus producing poor-quality influencers. On the other hand, Fair IM algorithm like *Crosswalk* does not explicitly capture topic-specific efficiency of the influencers, leading to suboptimal performance. Fig 4c and 4d show that *Fair2Vec* is effective for recommending the top r topics that maximize the influence spread in *Meetup* and *DBLP* datasets.

(b) Fair2Vec Maintains Fairness: In Fig 5a, we show the extent of fair gender distribution of influenced population $\widehat{A}_{k,r}$ for the proposed *Fair2Vec* against the various baseline algorithms. We demonstrate fairness with the help of (i) utility gap and (ii) L1 norm. Figure 5a and 5b show that *Fair2Vec* exhibits a better fairness score compared to all the baseline algorithms. The low performance of *SetSOGWO* is because *SetSOGWO* assigns influence probabilities using historical logs and overlooks topic-specific fairness, resulting in poor demographic balance in topic-wise influence. As to the embedding-based method, *Crosswalk*, the algorithm for selecting the influencers is clustering based, and it fails to properly capture the fairness aspect of the influencers.

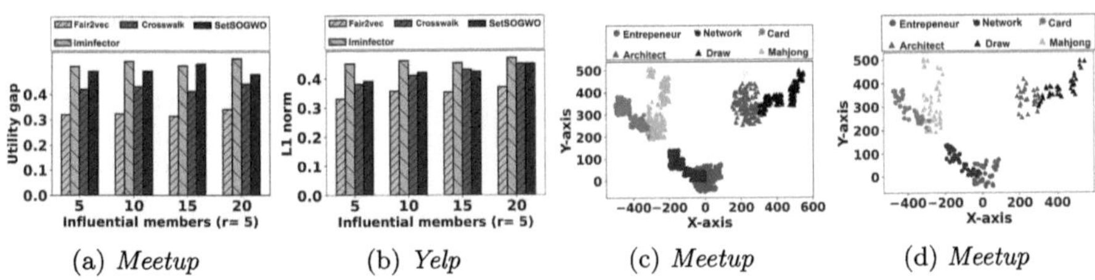

(a) *Meetup*   (b) *Yelp*   (c) *Meetup*   (d) *Meetup*

Fig. 5. (a) (b) Figure showing *Fair2Vec* has lower utility gap and L1 norm for *Meetup* and *Yelp*, hence better fairness. (c) Different embeddings for influencers (*Meetup*) for different topics. Similar topics have embeddings close to one another and dissimilar topics have embeddings far apart. (d) Different embeddings of the same influencers for different topics.

5.2 Embedding Quality of *Fair2Vec*

(a) Capturing Topic: *Fair2Vec* learns embeddings for influencers exclusively for different topics, hence for each topic, an influencer gets an unique embedding.

Figure 5c shows the embeddings of influencers (*Meetup*) for six different topics. It is evident from Fig. 5c that for similar topics (e.g., 'Drawing' and 'Architecture'), influencer embeddings become close to each other, while for dissimilar topics (e.g., 'Drawing' and 'Networking'), influencers remain farther apart in the embedding space. This is important to note that a single influencer may have different embeddings for different topics. To illustrate this, we have taken 47 influencers common to all six topics and plotted their embeddings. Figure 5d shows that the same influencers have different embeddings for different topics.

(b) Capturing Fairness: Next, we evaluate the embedding quality in the context of fairness. We classify 624 *Meetup* influencers on the same recommended topic 'Advertising' into highly fair ($f_{u_i} > 0.8$), moderate ($0.2 < f_{u_i} < 0.8$), and poorly fair ($f_{u_i} < 0.2$) categories based on their fairness score. Figure 6a plots the embeddings of these 624 influencers. We observe that *Fair2Vec* successfully discriminates these 624 influencers based on their individual fairness in the embedding space.

(c) Capturing Influence Capacity: Finally, we evaluate the embeddings in the context of influence capacity. We classify 624 *Meetup* influencers into highly, moderately, and poorly influential categories, and plot the embeddings of all these influencers in Fig. 6 b. We observe that *Fair2Vec* effectively discriminates these three class of influencers in the embedding space, though some overlap occurs due to the fairness-influence trade-off.

5.3   Justifying Fairness Score of *Fair2Vec*

We conduct an experiment to justify the fairness score introduced in Sect. 4.2. In place of topic specific computation of fairness ratio $\mathcal{F}_i$ and fairness score (f_{u_i,t_j}) for topic t_j, we compute the fairness score (f_{u_i,t_j}) based on the overall (male & female) population present in Meetup. Hence, we (re)define fairness ratio F_j as the ratio between the fraction of a sensitive attribute j (say female)

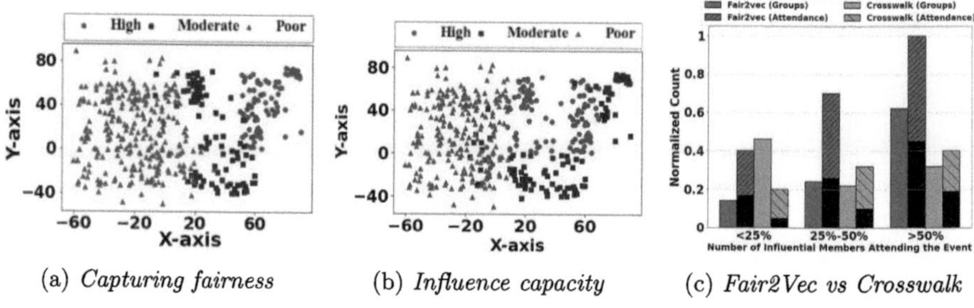

(a) *Capturing fairness*   (b) *Influence capacity*   (c) *Fair2Vec vs Crosswalk*

Fig. 6. (a)(b) Embeddings of influential members of *Meetup* for the topic *Advertising*: *Fair2Vec* shows good clustering in terms of fairness and influence spread. **(c)** Normalized group and event attendance comparison between *Fair2Vec* and *Crosswalk*, showing stronger influencer impact and follower engagement for *Fair2Vec*.

present in the influence context of u_i, vis-e-vis the fraction of the same sensitive attribute j (say female) present in overall *Meetup* population, *irrespective of any topical interest*. Based on this fairness score, we implement a variation of *Fair2Vec* as *Fair2VecNT*. Figure 7c shows that *Fair2Vec* consistently outperforms *Fair2VecNT* in terms of influenced population on the *Meetup* and *Yelp* datasets (with the number of topics fixed at 5). This is because *Fair2VecNT* attempts to influence *Meetup* members of a specific gender (say male), who may not be interested in the given topic, leading to reduced influence coverage. Interestingly, Fig. 7d reveals that *Fair2VecNT* achieves higher fairness by enforcing a uniform gender ratio across all topics. Study shows that the overall population in Meetup consists of 60% males and 40% females. *Fair2VecNT* ensures that this ratio is reflected in the influenced population, even for topics like *Beauty Product*, which may naturally skew towards females. While this promotes global gender balance, it risks misaligning with topic-specific audience dynamics.

5.4   Efficiency of *Fair2Vec* in Practice

To demonstrate the practical effectiveness of *Fair2Vec*, we handpick 50 *Meetup* groups and run *Fair2Vec* and *Crosswalk* on 80% of the data (2015–2021) to recommend the top-20 influencers (I_k) with 5 topics. We then test whether these influencers attract their followers to events during 2021–2022. Figure 6c shows that *Fair2Vec*'s influencers attended more relevant events and drove significantly higher attendance ($p < 0.05$), with shaded bars showing follower impact. Among six common influencers, topics uniquely recommended by *Fair2Vec* attracted $1.8\times$ more users than those of *Crosswalk*. Finally, *Fair2Vec* achieves better fairness (utility gap: 0.36 vs. 0.54), confirming its ability to maximize both influence and demographic balance.

5.5   Running Time of *Fair2Vec*

In Fig. 7a, we compare the training time of *Fair2Vec* and *TAID* on the *Yelp* dataset, keeping the number of influencers and topics fixed at 10 and 5, respectively. The results show that *Fair2Vec* outperforms *TAID* in terms of time efficiency. Figure 7b further demonstrates scalability by varying the number of recommended influencers k (x-axis) while fixing topics at 5. As number of influencers increase, the time required for *TAID* grows significantly faster compared to *Fair2Vec*. This is primarily because *TAID* rely on indirect link traversal whereas *Fair2Vec* reconstructs the network as a bipartite graph, which removes indirect edges and focuses solely on direct influence pathways, eliminating redundant computations.

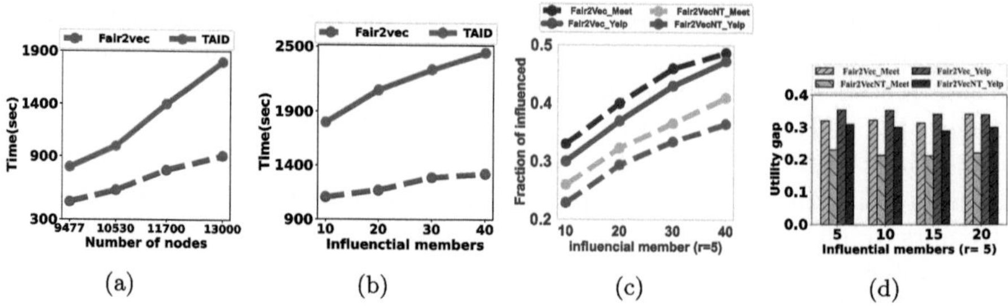

Fig. 7. (a) Training time: *Fair2Vec* vs *TAID* for *Yelp*. (b) Recommendation Time: *Fair2Vec* vs *TAID* for *Yelp* (c) (d) Comparison of *Fair2Vec* with *Fair2VecNT*.

6   Experimental setup

6.1   Performance metrics

Here, we find out the top k fair influencers I_k and top r influence topics T_r and then evaluate the performance of the influencers and topics based on two criteria: (1) Fraction of influenced population and (2) Fair presence of the influenced population across various topics.

Fraction of influenced population: For a *Meetup* group or *Yelp* restaurant, we compute the fraction of users influenced by I_k using the Independent Cascade (IC) model [1]. For *Meetup*, this reflects event attendance; for *Yelp*, restaurant visits. Results are averaged across all groups/restaurants in the same category to ensure robustness.

Measuring fairness: To quantify fairness across recommended topics, we use two metrics: **(a) L1 Norm:** L1 norm [4] measures the absolute disparity in influence distribution across sensitive attributes. It is computed as: $\sum_s |p_s - \bar{p}|$ where p_s is the fraction of influenced members from a particular sensitive attribute (e.g., gender), and $\bar{p}$ is the overall influenced fraction. **(b) Utility Gap:** Utility gap [6] measures the highest difference of expected influenced population between a pair of sensitive attributes. To compute the utility gap across recommended topics (e.g., t_1 and t_2), we calculate the utility gap within each topic separately and average the utility gap across all recommended topics. The final utility gap is averaged over all $t \in T_r$. Lower values of *L1 norm* and *utility gap* ensure better fairness.

Alignment of influenced population: We measure how well the influenced population's interests align with the service providers focus (e.g., a *Meetup* group's past events). We represent the providers interest as the average of embeddings from their historical events (e.g., 'hiking', 'tech talks') and the influenced users interests as the average of embeddings from events they attended. The alignment is computed via cosine similarity between these embeddings, with higher values indicating stronger relevance.

6.2   Evaluation methodology

We divide the dataset into training and testing data based on their time of occurrence. For example, in *Meetup*, the groups existed from the time period 2015 to 2022. We split the lifetime of *Meetup* into two halves, considering [2015 to 2021] as training and [2021 to 2022] as testing periods. We apply MTL on the training data to learn topic-wise influence capacities between influencers and followers. Using this, we construct a bipartite graph on the test data and identify the top-k influencers. For *Yelp*, we similarly divide the dataset based on the timing of reviews. We consider the period from 2017 to 2020 as the training set and 2020 to 2022 as the testing set. For the *DBLP* dataset, we utilized citation information, specifically the year in which author A cited a paper authored by B. The training data spans the period from 2000 to 2010, while the testing data covers the years 2010 to 2013.

6.3   Baseline algorithm

We implement the following baselines to compare the performance of our proposed algorithm. **(a)** *TAID* [5] Here, the authors have proposed a heuristics approach to find top k influencers and top r topics. **(b)** *Iminfector* [7] Here, the author has proposed a Multi-task learning model to find embeddings of influencers and subsequently find top k, influential members. *TAID* and *Iminfector* process doesn't consider fairness while recommending influential users.**(c)** *Set-SOGWO*: It is a single-objective version of SetMOGWO, which is developed based on gray wolf optimization. Here the objective is to find fair influencers while maximizing the fairness [3]. Here, we assign the probability of influence based on historical logs. **(d)** *Crosswalk* [10]: It is a random walk-based graph representation method, which enhances fairness by re-weighting the edges between nodes from different groups. We initialize the edge weights based on the in-out degree. Since these baselines mentioned above do not recommend topics, we adopt these models by finding top k influencers and then greedily selecting the r topics that give the highest influence spread from the k influencers.

7   Conclusion

We introduce *Fair2Vec*, a novel framework for recommending fair influencers and topics with demographic parity in influence spread. Unlike traditional influence maximization (IM) methods, *Fair2Vec* incorporates fairness directly into the influencer selection process. It computes fairness scores based on demographic influence (e.g., male and female) and uses a multi-task learning model to predict both influence reach and fairness. A fairness-aware downsampling method penalizes unfair influencers. Topic-specific embeddings for influencers and followers help estimate influence probabilities, forming a weighted bipartite graph. We then greedily select the top k influencers and r topics. Experiments on real-world datasets (*Meetup, Yelp, DBLP*) demonstrate that *Fair2Vec* outperforms baselines in both influence spread and fairness.

References

1. Kempe, D., Kleinberg, J., Tardos, É.: Maximizing the spread of influence through a social network. In: ACM SIGKDD (2003)
2. Barbieri, N., Bonchi, F., Manco, G.: Topic-aware social influence propagation models. KAIS (2013)
3. Tsang, A., Wilder, B., Rice, E., Tambe, M., Zick, Y.: Group-fairness in influence maximization. IJCAI (2019)
4. Farnad, G., Babaki, B., Gendreau, M.: A unifying framework for fairness-aware influence maximization. In: WWW (2020)
5. Dam, A., Kumar, S., Bhattacharjee, D., Pathak, S., Mitra, B.: Topic aware influential member detection in meetup. In: ACM/SAC (2023)
6. Rahmattalabi, A., et al.: Fair influence maximization: a welfare optimization approach. In: Proceedings of the AAAI Conference on Artificial Intelligence(2021)
7. Panagopoulos, G., Malliaros, F.D., Vazirgiannis, M.: Multi-task learning for influence estimation and maximization. TKDE (2020)
8. Panagopoulos, G., Malliaros, F.D., Vazirgianis, M.: Influence maximization using influence and susceptibility embeddings. In: ICWSM (2020)
9. Khajehnejad, M., Rezaei, A.A., Babaei, M., Hoffmann, J., Jalili, M., Weller, A.: Adversarial graph embeddings for fair influence maximization over social networks. IJCAI (2020)
10. Khajehnejad, A., Khajehnejad, M., Babaei, M., Gummadi, K.P., Weller, A., Mirzasoleiman, B.: Crosswalk: Fairness-enhanced node representation learning. In: AAAI (2022)
11. Goyal, A., Lu, W., Lakshmanan, L.V.: Celf++ optimizing the greedy algorithm for influence maximization in social networks. In: WWW (2011)
12. Chen, S., Fan, J., Li, G., Feng, J., Tan, K.l., Tang, J.: Online topic-aware influence maximization. VLDB (2015)
13. Ke, X., Khan, A., Cong, G.: Finding seeds and relevant tags jointly: for targeted influence maximization in social networks. In: SIGMOD (2018)
14. Yang, S., et al.: Balanced influence maximization in social networks based on deep reinforcement learning. Neural Netw. (2024)
15. Lin, M., et al.: Fair influence maximization in large-scale social networks based on attribute-aware reverse influence sampling. J. Artif. Intell. Res. (2023)
16. Feng, Y., Patel, A., Cautis, B., Vahabi, H.: Influence maximization with fairness at scale (extended version). ACM SIGKDD (2023)
17. Wang, Z., Zhao, J., Sun, C., Rui, X., Yu, P.S.: A general concave fairness framework for influence maximization based on poverty reward. TKDD (2024)
18. Nguyen, B.N.T., Pham, P.N., Le, V.V., Snášel, V.: Influence maximization under fairness budget distribution in online social networks. Mathematics (2022)
19. Chowdhary, S., De Pasquale, G., Lanzetti, N., Stoica, A.A., Dorfler, F.: Fairness in social influence maximization via optimal transport. NeurIPS (2024)
20. Xie, J., Zhang, S.S., Liu, C., Zhan, X.X.: Fair influence maximization in hypergraphs. In: Proceedings of the Third International Workshop on Social and Metaverse Computing, Sensing and Networking, pp. 8–14 (2024)
21. Chen, W., et al.: Fairgap: Fairness-aware recommendation via generating counterfactual graph. ACM TOIS (2024)
22. Bhowmick, A.K., Pramanik, S., Pathak, S., Mitra, B.: On the splitting dynamics of meetup social groups. In: ICWSM (2020)
23. Campos, R., Mangaravite, V., Pasquali, A., Jorge, A., Nunes, C., Jatowt, A.: Yake! keyword extraction from single documents using multiple local features. Information Sciences (2020)

Duplicating Deceit: Inauthentic Behavior Among Indian Misinformation Duplicators on X/Twitter

Ashfaq Ali Shafin[(✉)] and Bogdan Carbunar

Florida International University, Miami, FL 33199, USA
`shafinashfaqali21@gmail.com, carbunar@fiu.edu`

Abstract. This paper investigates inauthentic duplication on social media, where multiple accounts share identical misinformation tweets. Leveraging a dataset of misinformation verified by AltNews, an Indian fact-checking organization, we analyze over 12 million posts from 5,493 accounts known to have duplicated such content. Contrary to common assumptions that bots are primarily responsible for spreading false information, fewer than 1% of these accounts exhibit bot-like behavior. We present TweeXster, a framework for detecting and analyzing duplication campaigns, revealing clusters of accounts involved in repeated and sometimes revived dissemination of false or abusive content.

Keywords: Content Duplication Detection · Inauthentic Duplication · Misinformation Campaigns · Toxic Content · Social Media Manipulation

1 Introduction

Social media enables rapid and anonymous sharing of information. While these features encourage open communication, they are also often exploited by malicious actors to spread misinformation and abuse [8,19]. Such manipulation is particularly common during elections and public health crises, when public opinion is most vulnerable [25]. Coordinated campaigns often use deceptive tactics that include content duplication, to amplify harmful narratives and lend them false credibility. Detecting and understanding these efforts is critical for countering their impact [24,26].

To support fact-checking efforts, this paper investigates inauthentic opinion manipulation on X/Twitter, with a focus on identifying candidate content for verification through patterns of duplication. We aim to characterize the actors involved in duplication campaigns and evaluate the predictive value of past behaviors. Specifically, we address the following research questions:

- **RQ1:** What kinds of accounts post duplicate misinformation on X/Twitter? What inauthentic behaviors do such accounts exhibit?

© The Author(s), under exclusive license to Springer Nature Switzerland AG 2026
A. An et al. (Eds.): ASONAM 2025, LNCS 16323, pp. 363–371, 2026.
https://doi.org/10.1007/978-3-032-13821-7_30

- **RQ2**: Is past involvement in content duplication a predictor of future duplication activities? Can such accounts help identify newly promoted inauthentic content?

We tackle these questions by focusing on post duplication behaviors, where multiple accounts share identical content. To uncover relevant content and associated accounts, we first collected and analyzed misinformation verified by AltNews [1], a prominent Indian fact-checking platform. We identified 5,493 accounts that duplicated AltNews-verified misinformation on Twitter prior to its rebranding as X. In 2023, we collected over 12 million posts from these accounts. Our findings reveal that fewer than 1% misinformation-duplicator accounts exhibit bot-like behavior [2], while approximately 4% are Twitter-verified.

We introduce TweeXster, a framework to study posting activities and analyze content duplication campaigns. TweeXster uncovered inauthentic behaviors including (1) clusters of accounts frequently duplicating content, (2) content repetition and misinformation revival, and (3) campaigns promoting toxic content and specious news sources. Past duplication involvement predicts future activities for both misinformation and abusive speech. Key contributions:

- Demonstrate majority of misinformation-disseminating accounts are controlled by real users, not bots [§ 4].
- Introduce TweeXster framework for identifying and studying content duplication campaigns [§ 5.1].
- Provide evidence that AltNews misinformation duplicators persist in duplicating behaviors and inauthentic content dissemination [§5.2, §5.3].

2   Related Work

Political Use of X/Twitter in India. The political use of X/Twitter in India has been extensively studied, revealing highly polarized networks driven by partisanship. Masud and Charaborty [14] analyze posts from the 2022 Indian assembly elections, showing how platforms serve as arenas for self-promotion and political critique. This aligns with Neyazi et al. [16], who found Twitter networks polarized by party affiliations and campaign engagement, and Dash et al. [10], who demonstrated that polarized influencers receive higher engagement during political crises, highlighting partisanship's crucial role in platform dynamics.

Misinformation Campaigns and Bots. Misinformation campaigns have become a global challenge, with actors using social media to manipulate public opinion and interfere in democratic processes. Research on Russian disinformation efforts [15,27] has shown targeting of electoral processes in the US, UK, and Germany, while in India, campaigns often target religious groups and political opponents [20]. Although previous studies identify malicious social bots as key amplifiers of misinformation [9,23] our findings reveal significant misinformation duplicator accounts are operated by real users rather than bots.

3   Data Collection

Fact-Checked Misinformation. We collected misinformation reports verified by AltNews [1], a leading Indian fact-checking organization. We collected 433 reports published between April, 2020 and April, 2022, labeled as follows: politics (237), religion (72), news (62), society (44), media (17), and technology (1).

Misinformation Duplicator Accounts. We extracted 622 tweets directly linked in AltNews reports as examples of misinformation. Using Twitter search functionality, we identified an additional 6,431 tweets duplicating these 433 instances. We collected metadata for 7,053 tweets, posted by 5,747 unique accounts. We collected additional metadata about these accounts, including profile details and follower/friend counts. We excluded accounts that were (1) suspended or deleted, (2) private, or (3) actively debunking the misinformation. After filtering, we retained 5,493 *duplicator accounts*.

Tweets of Duplicator Accounts. In February 2023, we used the Twitter API to collect up to the latest 3,200 tweets for each of the 5,493 duplicators, yielding over 12.7 million tweets. After removing retweets, we obtained 6,879,220 original tweets. To reduce noise, we filtered out posts (1) not written in Hindi or English and (2) containing fewer than four unique words [12]. The final dataset, which we refer to as **Dup'23**, consists of 5,070,548 tweets.

Specious News Websites. We curated a comprehensive list of 1,166 specious websites, collected from prior work [11,13] and Indian fact-checking organizations [1,3,4], all of which are known to publish fabricated or misleading content, to verify the presence of these websites among the tweets in the Dup'23 dataset.

4   Duplicator Account Classification

We collected user profile data from the duplicator accounts prior to Elon Musk's acquisition of Twitter. Using the BotometerX API [2], we identified 44 duplicator accounts as bots, with both their Complete Automation Probability (CAP) and Raw Bot Score (RBS) exceeding 0.9, to prioritize precision and minimize false positives. The CAP score represents the probability that an account with a given RBS score or higher is automated. Thus, only 0.8% of the 5,493 active accounts exhibited bot-like behavior. Additionally, 213 accounts were verified by Twitter before the introduction of subscription-based verification on X. Our analysis excludes accounts verified through X's paid subscription service. Notably, all Twitter-verified accounts had CAP and RBS scores below 0.9. Consequently, the dataset includes 5,236 *regular* misinformation duplicator accounts, neither bots nor verified. We analyzed political discourse by leveraging the NivaDuck database [18] to identify Indian political accounts.

5   TweeXster Framework

5.1   Identifying Clusters of Similar Posts

To determine if accounts that duplicated AltNews-reported misinformation continue duplicating other content, we identify duplicate tweets in Dup'23 (§ 3). Since duplicate tweets are not always identical (containing different URLs or other changes), we describe our process for identifying clusters of similar tweets.

Tweet Embeddings. We preprocessed tweet text (removing URLs, mentions, etc.), then used SBert with siamese and triplet network architectures to generate embeddings for Dup'23 tweets with more than 4 unique words to reduce noise [12]. We employed the paraphrase multilingual MiniLM-L12-v2 transformer model [22] supporting 50+ languages (including English and Hindi). SBert produces 384-dimensional vectors with values between -1 and 1, yielding minimum Euclidean distance of 0 and maximum distance of ≈ 39.19.

Clustering Tweet Embeddings. We used DBSCAN clustering with maximum Euclidean distance of 1, chosen for its ability to identify arbitrary-shaped clusters without pre-specifying cluster count, which is valuable for detecting duplicate tweets where campaign numbers are unknown. To determine the distance threshold, we applied DBSCAN to 7,053 manually identified duplicate misinformation tweets from AltNews, varying distance from 0.1 to 2. A distance threshold of 1 produced 427 clusters, closely aligning with the 433 misinformation reports from AltNews. Of 7,053 misinformation tweets, 7,044 were correctly labeled with only 9 misclassified due to identical tweets in different contexts. Density-based algorithms without explicit distance thresholds (e.g., HDBSCAN) proved less effective, producing clusters with substantial non-duplicate content by grouping tweets based on semantic similarity rather than the strict textual duplication required for identifying exact or near-identical duplicates.

In Dup'23, we identified 172,589 clusters containing 514,958 tweets from 4,938 accounts, with 3,357 clusters having ≥ 10 duplicates and the largest containing 398 duplicates. Clusters averaged 2.98 tweets (SD=3.01). While many clusters appear small, this reflects our limited account subset. Manual searches of 100 randomly-selected small campaigns found >25 duplicates per campaign still available on X/Twitter from accounts outside our dataset, suggesting these campaigns represent only the tip of the iceberg of content duplication activities.

To verify cluster consistency, we calculated the cosine similarity between the tweet embeddings within the identified clusters. The lowest observed cosine similarity across all campaigns is 0.91, and the average similarity is 0.99. This indicates a high degree of similarity across all identified clusters, confirming that the campaigns contain near-identical text. Furthermore, we manually analyzed 200 randomly selected clusters to assess their consistency and found that all clusters consisted of duplicate posts, with no anomalies observed.

Table 1 compares TweeXster with two Ratcliff/Obershelp pattern matching (ROPM) [21] baselines: ROPM-10 and ROPM-100. ROPM sorts tweets chronologically and compares each to the next 10 or 100 tweets. ROPM-10 is commonly used for coordinated inauthentic behavior (CIB) detection [17,25]. ROPM-10 and ROPM-100 identify 42,820 and 172,635 duplicate tweets across 2,613 and 4,348 accounts, respectively. TweeXster identifies 514,958 duplicate tweets across 4,938 accounts, yielding 1,295,785 tweet pairs and 736,147 account pairs. These results demonstrate TweeXster captures broader and denser duplication networks than ROPM-based methods, suggesting improved sensitivity for detecting coordinated behaviors.

Table 1. Comparison of duplicate tweets detected by ROPM and our approach.

Method	#Tweets	#Pairs	#Accs
ROPM-10	42,820	25,934	2,613
ROPM-100	172,635	147,555	4,348
Ours	514,958	1,295,785	4,938

5.2 Inauthentic Duplication Behaviors

We identified 8,118 pairs of accounts that duplicated at least 10 tweets. These pairs involved 1,366 unique accounts, which we refer to as *super-duplicator*. Only three accounts were flagged as bots, while 86 were verified by Twitter. Furthermore, 163 accounts had political affiliations [18], which categorizes accounts based on public declarations and interaction patterns. 79 political accounts were affiliated with the Bharatiya Janata Party (BJP) and 73 with the Indian National Congress (INC), reflecting the two dominant political parties in India.

To understand the structure of duplication behavior, we applied the Louvain community detection algorithm [7] to the graph formed by these account pairs. In this graph, nodes represent accounts and edges indicate that the connected accounts duplicated at least 10 tweets in common. The algorithm identified 62 communities with a modularity score of 0.74, suggesting strong intra-community ties and sparse inter-community connections.

The majority of the accounts (85.6%) belonged to the top nine communities, each containing at least 10 accounts. Figure 1 shows these communities, where node size reflects the degree (number of duplication partners). Based on annotations from NivaDuck, six of the largest communities predominantly included BJP-affiliated accounts (shades of red), while two others were largely composed of INC-affiliated accounts (shades of green). One community (blue) did not display any clear political affiliation. Importantly, no single community contained a mix

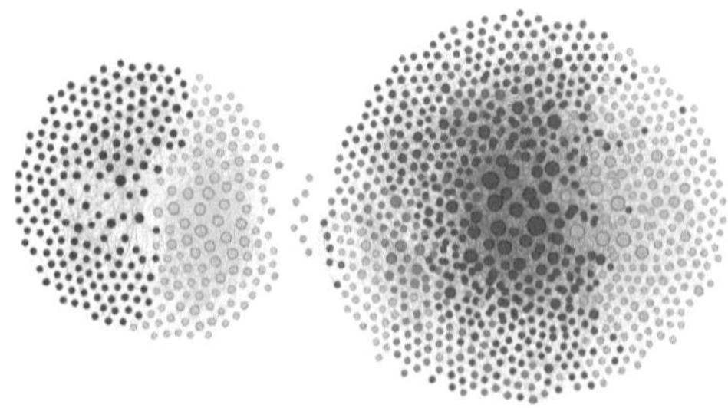

Fig. 1. Communities of accounts duplicating content. Nodes represent users connected by edges if they duplicated at least 10 posts in common. Node sizes indicate connection degrees. 1,169 accounts (85.6% of 1,366 total) belong to only 9 clusters.

of opposing political affiliations, suggesting alignment in duplication behavior within ideological groups.

5.3   Patterns of Inauthentic Content

In the following, we examine the inauthentic methods employed by misinformation duplicators, focusing on patterns of manipulation observed across content dissemination and platform use.

Detecting New Misinformation . We compiled 20 keywords indicating controversial subjects (e.g., Russia-Ukraine War, Trump, Putin, Biden, Rahul Gandhi, Narendra Modi, Kashmir files, boycott, Adani, Hindutva) or abusive speech against religious minorities/political parties (e.g., bulldozer, stone pelters, love jihad). In the Dup'23 dataset, 79,703 tweets from 32,900 clusters contained at least one keyword. We selected the five longest-active clusters for each keyword, then two researchers independently fact-checked tweets from these 200 clusters using Alt News methodology [5] (Cohen's Kappa k=0.62, indicating moderate agreement). We identified 53 clusters containing misinformation unreported by AltNews and 34 additional clusters with abusive speech. The misinformation clusters contained 209 tweets with 128,658 likes and 65,998 retweets, including false claims about a Pfizer VP arrest, US troops discarding medals, UN Kashmir status changes, and Israeli death sentences for rapists. An example of a tweet containing false information identified through manual fact-checking:

"VP of Pfizer arrested after leaked documents show only 12% vaccine efficacy and severe side effects. Thanking our govt Pfizer was not allowed in India"

Duplicated Toxic Content.
We analyzed the tweet content using Google's Perspective API [6], which provides probabilistic scores across multiple toxicity dimensions including identity attacks, threats, profanity, insults, and general toxicity. Tweets receiving scores above 0.5 on any dimension were classified accordingly. Since all the posts in a cluster are near duplicates, we used the Perspective API to retrieve scores for a randomly selected post from each cluster in the Dup'23 (§ 5.1). Table 2 shows the numbers of clusters with toxicity values over 0.5, including the number of clusters associated with BJP and INC accounts. An example toxic tweet identified by the Perspective API:

Table 2. Breakdown of toxic duplicate clusters across labels and political parties.

Label	# Clusters	# BJP	# INC
Toxicity	4,013	2,782	639
Severe Toxicity	1,088	840	107
Identity Attack	4,226	3,276	453
Threat	1,454	1,072	179
Insult	5,391	3,800	776
Profanity	931	642	173

"CHINA must be dragged into International Court and stripped of its VETO power in the UN. 'Crime against humanity'. COVID-19 is a Chinese Virus. "

Specious News Websites. In the Dup'23 set, 41,421 tweets contained at least one URL pointing to a specious website (see § 3), and 4,249 duplication clusters have tweets with such links. Of the 1,366 super-duplicator accounts, 531 posted at least one tweet with a URL to a specious site, in the Dup'23 dataset, and were responsible for posting 12,822 of the tweets linking to such sites. Accounts affiliated with BJP communities posted 12,440 tweets whereas INC-affiliated accounts only posted 343 tweets. Figure 2 shows the timeline of the number of tweets posted by the super-duplicator accounts, that contain links to specious websites, between January 1 and February 15, 2023. During the first six weeks of 2023, these accounts posted a total of 3,245 tweets linking to a specious site, averaging over 72 tweets per day.

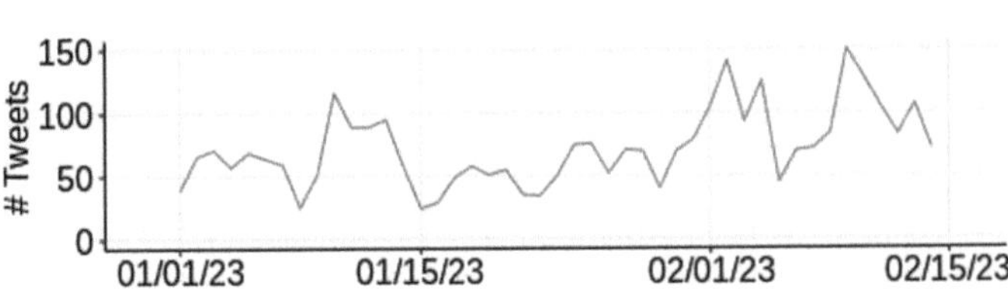

Fig. 2. Timeline of posting of tweets containing links to specious websites during January 1, 2023 to February 15, 2023.

6 Conclusions

We analyzed over five thousand X/Twitter accounts duplicating misinformation verified by AltNews using our TweeXster framework, detecting over half a million duplicate tweets and identifying clusters of coordinated inauthentic behavior including sustained misinformation campaigns, toxic discourse, and amplification via specious websites. Remarkably, fewer than 1% of duplicators were bots, with verified and politically affiliated accounts serving as primary content originators. Our analysis demonstrates that content duplication behavior is both persistent and predictive: accounts sharing past misinformation exhibit significantly higher likelihood of promoting future false content. These findings suggest leveraging historical duplication patterns could enhance fact-checking prioritization, platform moderation, and early campaign detection, offering practical applications for combating online misinformation ecosystems.

Acknowledgement. This work was supported in part through NSF awards 2321649 and 2114911. We thank Dr. Lotzi Bölöni for early discussions.

References

1. AltNews. https://www.altnews.in/
2. BotometerX. https://botometer.osome.iu.edu/
3. DFRAC: Digital Forensics, Research and Analytics Center. https://www.fdfrac.org/en/
4. Factly. https://www.factly.in/
5. Methodology for fact checking. https://www.altnews.in/methodology-for-fact-checking/
6. Perspective. https://www.perspectiveapi.com/
7. Blondel, V.D., Guillaume, J.L., Lambiotte, R., Lefebvre, E.: Fast unfolding of communities in large networks. J. Stat. Mech. Theory Exp. (2008)
8. Cinelli, M., De Francisci Morales, G., Galeazzi, A., Quattrociocchi, W., Starnini, M.: The echo chamber effect on social media. Proc. Natl. Acad. Sci. **118**(9) (2021)
9. Cresci, S., Petrocchi, M., Spognardi, A., Tognazzi, S.: Better safe than sorry: an adversarial approach to improve social bot detection. In: Proceedings of the 10th ACM Conference on Web Science (2019)
10. Dash, S., Mishra, D., Shekhawat, G., Pal, J.: Divided we rule: influencer polarization on twitter during political crises in India. Proceedings of the International AAAI Conference on Web and Social Media (2022)
11. Hanley, H.W., Kumar, D., Durumeric, Z.: Specious sites: tracking the spread and sway of spurious news stories at scale. In: Proceedings of the IEEE Symposium on Security and Privacy (2024)
12. Luceri, L., Pantè, V., Burghardt, K., Ferrara, E.: Unmasking the web of deceit: uncovering coordinated activity to expose information operations on twitter. In: Proceedings of the ACM Web Conference 2024 (2024)
13. Machado, G., Alaphilippe, A., Adamczyk, R., Grégoire, A.: Indian chronicles: deep dive into a 15-year operation targeting the eu and un to serve indian interests (2020). https://www.disinfo.eu/publications/indian-chronicles-deep-dive-into-a-15-year-operation-targeting-the-eu-and-un-to-serve-indian-interests/
14. Masud, S., Charaborty, T.: Political mud slandering and power dynamics during Indian assembly elections. Soc. Netw. Anal. Min. **13**(1), 108 (2023)
15. Narayanan, V., Howard, P.N., Kollanyi, B., Elswah, M.: Russian involvement and junk news during brexit. In: The Computational Propaganda Project. Algorithms, Automation and Digital Politics (2017)
16. Neyazi, T.A., Kumar, A., Semetko, H.A.: Campaigns, digital media, and mobilization in India. Int. J. Press/Politics **21**(3) (2016)
17. Pacheco, D., Flammini, A., Menczer, F.: Unveiling coordinated groups behind white helmets disinformation. In: Companion Proceedings of the Web Conference (2020)
18. Panda, A., et al.: Nivaduck - a scalable pipeline to build a database of political twitter handles for India and the United States. In: International Conference on Social Media and Society (2020)
19. Pierri, F., Luceri, L., Jindal, N., Ferrara, E.: Propaganda and misinformation on facebook and twitter during the Russian invasion of Ukraine. In: Proceedings of the 15th ACM Web Science Conference 2023 (2023)
20. Rajadesingan, A., Panda, A., Pal, J.: Leader or party? personalization in twitter political campaigns during the 2019 Indian elections. In: International Conference on Social Media and Society (2020)

21. Ratcliff, J.W., Metzener, D.E.: Pattern-matching: the gestalt approach. Dr. Dobb's J. **13**(7), 46 (1988)
22. Reimers, N., Gurevych, I.: Making monolingual sentence embeddings multilingual using knowledge distillation. In: Proceedings of the 2020 Conference on Empirical Methods in Natural Language Processing (2020)
23. Shao, C., Ciampaglia, G.L., Varol, O., Yang, K.C., Flammini, A., Menczer, F.: The spread of low-credibility content by social bots. Nat. Commun. **9**(1), 1–9 (2018)
24. Torres-Lugo, C., Yang, K.C., Menczer, F.: The manufacture of partisan echo chambers by follow train abuse on twitter. In: Proceedings of the International AAAI Conference on Web and Social Media (2022)
25. Vishnuprasad, P.S., Nogara, G., Cardoso, F., Cresci, S., Giordano, S., Luceri, L.: Tracking fringe and coordinated activity on twitter leading up to the us capitol attack. In: Proceedings of the International AAAI Conference on Web and Social Media (2024)
26. Vosoughi, S., Roy, D., Aral, S.: The spread of true and false news online. Science **359**(6380) (2018)
27. Zannettou, S., Caulfield, T., Bradlyn, B., De Cristofaro, E., Stringhini, G., Blackburn, J.: Characterizing the use of images in state-sponsored information warfare operations by Russian trolls on twitter. In: Proceedings of the International AAAI Conference on Web and Social Media (2020)

Weak Links in LinkedIn: Enhancing Fake Profile Detection in the Age of LLMs

Apoorva Gulati[1], Rajesh Kumar[2(✉)], Vinti Agarwal[1], and Aditya Sharma[1]

[1] BITS Pilani, Pilani, India
{f20210934,vinti.agarwal,p20200470}@pilani.bits-pilani.ac.in
[2] Bucknell University, Lewisburg, USA
rajesh.kumar@bucknell.edu

Abstract. Large Language Models (LLMs) have made it easier to create realistic fake profiles on platforms like LinkedIn. This poses a significant risk for text-based fake profile detectors. In this study, we evaluate the robustness of existing detectors against LLM-generated profiles. While highly effective in detecting manually created fake profiles (False Accept Rate: $6 - 7\%$), the existing detectors fail to identify GPT-generated profiles (False Accept Rate: $42 - 52\%$). We propose GPT-assisted adversarial training as a countermeasure, restoring the False Accept Rate to between $1 - 7\%$ without impacting the False Reject Rates ($0.5 - 2\%$). Ablation studies revealed that detectors trained on combined numerical and textual embeddings exhibit the highest robustness, followed by those using numerical-only embeddings, and lastly those using textual-only embeddings. Complementary analysis on the ability of prompt-based GPT-4Turbo and human evaluators affirms the need for robust automated detectors such as the one proposed in this study.

Keywords: Fake Profile Detection · LLMs · Adversarial Training · LinkedIn

1 Introduction

Online professional networks, such as LinkedIn, play a crucial role in professional interactions, hosting over 1.15 billion active users and generating significant economic activity [1]. However, such platforms face growing threats from fake profiles used for phishing, misinformation, and recruitment fraud [2,3]. Recent advances in Large Language Models (LLMs), particularly GPT-3.5 and GPT-4, have simplified the creation of highly realistic fake profiles, posing a significant threat to the existing detectors [4,5]. Between 2021 and 2022, the number of fake profiles on LinkedIn nearly doubled [5]. Prompt-based evaluations of humans and GPT-4 achieved modest detection accuracy (F1 Human: 59%, F1 GPT-zero shot: 71%, F1 GPT-few shot: 86%, see Sect. 4.3). Existing detection approaches, such as Section and Subsection Tag Embeddings (SSTE) proposed in [4], perform well (F1~96%) against manually created fake profiles but fail sharply (F1~ 68%) against LLM-generated profiles.

A. An et al. (Eds.): ASONAM 2025, LNCS 16323, pp. 372–382, 2026.
https://doi.org/10.1007/978-3-032-13821-7_31

To address these challenges systematically, we pose and address q_1 How vulnerable are current detection methods to profiles generated by advanced LLMs? q_2 Can adversarial training with LLM-generated profiles enhance detection robustness? q_3 How does the effectiveness of our proposed detection methods compare to human evaluators and GPT-4?

Our primary contributions are as follows. ① We implement a series of robust fake profile detection systems using textual, numerical, and fused features, incorporating Section Tag Embeddings (STE), Section and Sub-Section Tag Embeddings (SSTE), along with PCA-based dimensionality reduction. The best setup outperformed prior methods on genuine and manual fake profiles [6]. ② We augment the existing dataset with 600 fake profiles that we generated using GPT-4-Turbo with carefully crafted prompts. These synthetic profiles closely mimic legitimate users, as verified by similarity metrics, and used for creating attack vectors. ③ We demonstrate that existing detectors fail against LLM-generated profiles (FAR: $42-52\%$) and proposed GPT-assisted adversarial training, which restored FAR to $1-7\%$ without compromising the legitimate user classification. ④ We also benchmark detection capabilities of human annotators and GPT-4, confirming the need for ML-based automated detectors. ⑤ Finally, we conducted ablation studies revealing text embeddings alone are fragile under LLM attack, whereas numerical profile features remain sturdier; their fusion yields the most robust detector.

The remainder of this paper is structured as follows: Sect. 2 reviews related literature, Sect. 3 describes materials and methods, Sect. 4 reports and discusses results, Sect. 5 limitations and future research directions, and Sect. 6 concludes.

2 Related Work

Research on fake profile detection spans numerical, graph-based, behavioral, and textual methods. Early efforts used correlation-based analysis of profile attributes. For instance, Adikari et al. [3] achieved 87.34% accuracy on LinkedIn profiles; however, their approach relied on historical data and assumed attribute consistency, which are limitations when handling cold-start accounts. Graph-based models, such as SybilBelief [7], SybilEdge [8], and SybilFlyover [9], leverage network topology and user connectivity, often achieving AUCs above 0.9. However, they require relational metadata (e.g., connections, followers), *limiting their applicability for newly created or minimally active profiles*. Early stylometric techniques relied on N-grams and writing patterns [10]. The LLM-assited fake profile detection problem is similar to LLM-assisted cheating detection [11,12]. Recent keystroke dynamics-based approaches [13,14] achieve a detection accuracy close to 95%. Using activity-based features such as post frequency and follower-following ratios, Alnagi et al. [15] employed XGBoost with SHAP-based interpretability, achieving 94% precision on Instagram and 91% on Twitter.

Ayoobi et al. [4] proposed Section and Subsection Tag Embeddings (SSTE), reaching 95% accuracy on genuine and manually crafted fake LinkedIn profiles. However, their performance drops sharply (to $71--76\%$ accuracy) against

GPT-generated profiles, revealing a growing vulnerability. Our work differs from Ayoobi et al. [4] and focuses on (1) investigating the robustness of baseline detectors (trained on genuine and manually created fake profiles) against profiles generated by GPT3.5 and GPT4Turbo, (2) assessing the power of GPT3.5, GPT4Turbo, and GPT3.5+GPT4Turbo-assisted adversarial training, and (3) evaluating the performance of Human and GPT-based evaluators systematically.

3   Materials and Methods

3.1   Augmenting Existing Dataset

We augment the dataset presented by Ayoobi et al. [4] by adding 600 GPT-4-generated profiles (GPT4Ps), resulting in $4,200$ profiles: $1,800$ legitimate LinkedIn profiles (LLPs), 600 manually crafted fakes (FLPs), $1,200$ GPT-3.5-generated profiles (GPT3.5Ps), and 600 GPT4Ps. GPT3.5Ps were created using zero-shot prompting from both LLP and FLP templates. GPT4Ps were created using few-shot prompting with curated LLP exemplars and GPT-4 Turbo. All profiles adhere to LinkedIn's structure, featuring fields for name, location, education, work history, skills, recommendations, and summary. Prompts and similarity-based quality validation details are provided on a dedicated webpage [16].

3.2   Feature Extraction

Each profile was cleaned and parsed: malformed records were corrected, composite entries split, and essential fields (Name, Experience, Education, Location) verified. We extracted 17 numerical features that capture profile structure, including the count of jobs, education entries, skills, recommendations, followers, and connections.

For textual features, we tested six encoders: BERT [17], RoBERTa [18], DeBERTa-v3 [19], ModernBERT [20], Flair [21], and GloVe [22]. PCA was applied to reduce embeddings to 150 dimensions from 786, improving robustness by eliminating low-ranked components [23,24]. We selected RoBERTa, Modern-BERT, DeBERTa, and Flair for further analysis.

We simplify the original Section and Subsection Tag Embeddings (SSTE) [4] to Section Tag Embeddings (STE), aggregating each section's text (e.g., Education) as a single unit, and computed as $F = \frac{1}{N} \sum_{j=1}^{N} \left(E_j - \mathrm{Em}(\mathrm{Tag}_j) \right)$, where E_j is the embedding of the j-th section's text, $\mathrm{Em}(\mathrm{Tag}_j)$ is the embedding of its tag, and N is the total number of sections. Text-embeddings were concatenated with 17 normalized numerical features, yielding a 167-dimensional profile vector.

3.3   Choice of Classifiers and Hyperparameter Tuning

We used six classifiers: Logistic Regression, Random Forest, SVM, KNN, XGBoost [25], and CatBoost [26], reflecting standard choices in prior work [4].

XGBoost and CatBoost consistently performed best and were selected for full evaluation.

Hyperparameters were tuned using Bayesian Optimization (BO) [27, 28] and Genetic Algorithms (GA) [29]. BO used 30 trials on a validation split, followed by 20 trials with five-fold cross-validation. GA used 50 individuals over three generations, followed by two fine-tuned generations. All experiments were run on an NVIDIA A100 40GB GPU. Embedding and preprocessing consumed ~ 100 GPU hours; hyperparameter tuning and cross-validation added ~ 50 GPU hours. More details are provided in our GitHub repository [6].

3.4   Training and Evaluation Scenarios

We trained models on LLP vs FLP as a baseline, and introduced three attack and three adversarial training scenarios using GPT3.5Ps, GPT4Ps, or both. Each model was evaluated on all four profile types (LLPs, FLPs, GPT3.5Ps, and GPT4Ps) (Table 1). Classifiers were trained using STE embeddings from RoBERTa, DeBERTa, ModernBERT, and Flair with XGBoost and CatBoost.

Table 1. Training and test splits across scenarios. Left: training data composition. Right: test sets for robustness evaluation.

	Train set					Test/Attack set			
Train scenario	LLPs	FLPs	GPT3.5Ps	GPT4Ps	Test scenario	LLPs	FLPs	GPT3.5Ps	GPT4Ps
Baseline	1260	420	–	–	Baseline	540	180	–	–
GPT3.5 Retrain	1260	420	840	-	GPT3.5 Attack	540	180	360	–
GPT4 Retrain	1260	420	–	420	GPT4 Attack	540	180	–	180
GPT3.5+4 Retrain	1260	420	840	420	Combined Attack	540	180	360	180

Models were evaluated using F1 score, false accept rate (FAR; fake $\rightarrow$ legitimate), and false reject rate (FRR; legitimate $\rightarrow$ fake). The effectiveness of the attack and countermeasure was measured by changes in FAR under adversarial conditions and after retraining. Calibration was assessed using reliability curves [30], which compare predicted probabilities to empirical frequencies; the diagonal indicating perfect calibration. Brier score [31] was also computed as a scalar measure of calibration, where lower values indicate more reliable confidence estimates, critical for minimizing overconfident mis-classification of LLM-generated profiles.

3.5   Human and GPT-4 Evaluation

We benchmarked human and GPT-4 detectors on the same inputs: Name, Location, Education, Experience, Skills, Connections, Followers, Summary, and derived statistics. GPT-4 was tested on 360 profiles (180 real, 180 fake) using the OpenAI API with zero-shot (single input) and few-shot (3 random labeled examples) prompting. Profiles labeled fake included both FLPs and LLM-generated profiles. More details are included in the GitHub repository [6].

Thirty human evaluators classified 15 profiles each (5 LLPs, 5 FLPs, 5 LLM-generated) through a structured web portal [32]. For each profile description presented, they selected one of three labels: legitimate, manual fake, or LLM fake. We collected a total of 450 responses (15 profiles × 30 participants). Results were binarized (fake vs legitimate) to enable comparison with classifier and GPT-4 performance.

4   Results and Discussion

4.1   Feature and Classifier Selection

PCA analysis (Fig. 1, Left) shows that the top 150 components captured 93.6 − 98.9% of variance across encoders, with negligible gains beyond this point. Consequently, we fixed 150 components for RoBERTa, DeBERTa, ModernBERT, and Flair.

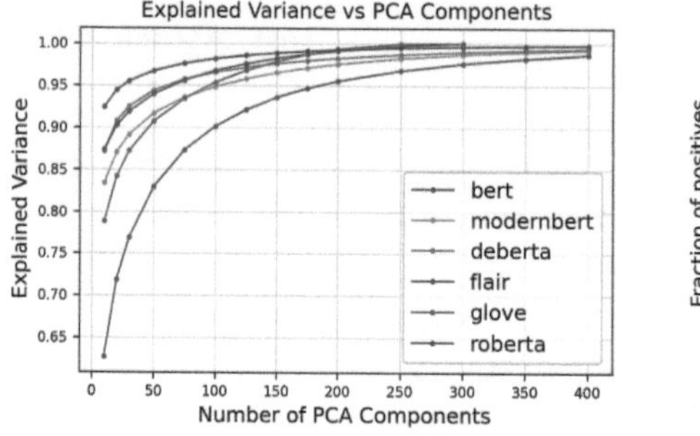

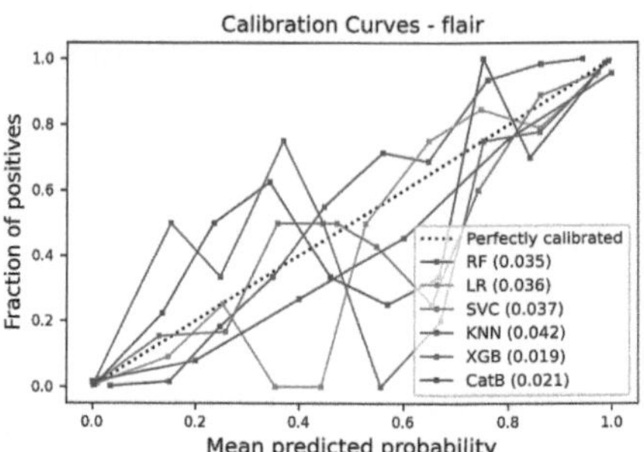

Fig. 1. (Left) PCA variance curves highlight that Flair and RoBERTa achieve faster variance saturation, suggesting higher intrinsic dimensional efficiency compared to BERT and GloVe. (Right) Flair-based calibration curves show boosting classifiers (XGBoost, CatBoost) align most closely with ideal calibration, as reflected in their low Brier scores; other models exhibit under- or overconfidence, particularly in mid-range probabilities.

Classifier calibration using Flair embeddings (Fig. 1, Right) showed that boosting models—CatBoost (0.021) and XGBoost (0.019)—achieved the lowest Brier scores, outperforming Logistic Regression (0.036), Random Forest (0.035), and KNN (0.042). XGBoost was slightly overconfident in the mid-range (0.5 − 0.7), while CatBoost maintained better reliability in high-confidence regions (0.7 − 1.0), which is critical for minimizing false accept rates. These calibration properties motivated the selection of CatBoost and XGBoost as our primary classifiers for further analysis [33].

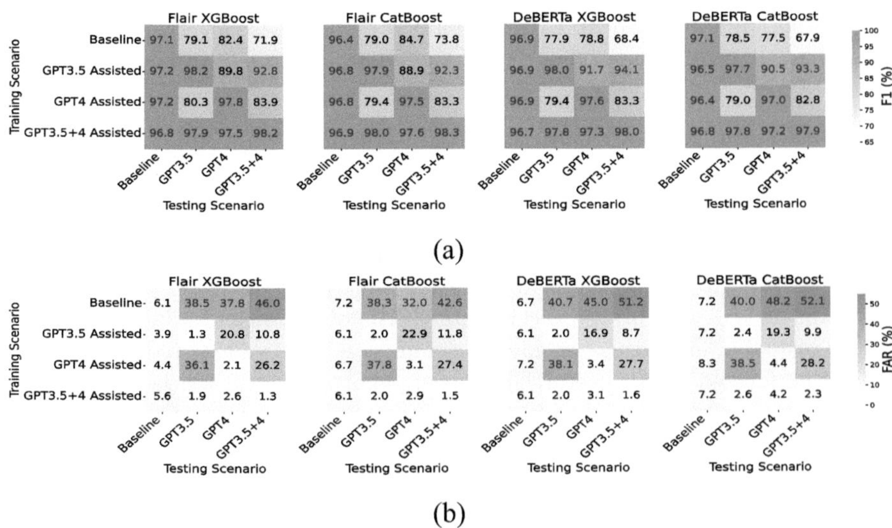

Fig. 2. Performance of STE-based models with Flair and DeBERTa embeddings across different training and testing scenarios. (a) F1 show performance degradation under GPT-generated profile attacks, particularly in the baseline setting. (b) False Accept Rates (FAR) highlight model vulnerability to GPT3.5 and GPT4 profiles, with FARs exceeding 50% in the worst case. Adversarial training—especially with combined GPT3.5+4P data—restores detection performance, yielding consistently high F1 scores and low FARs. Flair and DeBERTa results are shown; all classifiers and embeddings are included in the full evaluation (visit GitHub [6]).

4.2 Performance Under Baseline and Adversarial Scenarios

Figure 2 summarizes model performance across training and testing scenarios.

Baseline performance: Our STE-based models using Flair and DeBERTa embeddings outperformed prior work by [4], achieving F1 scores of $96.39\% - 97.08\%$, compared to their reported $87.78\% - 94.28\%$ (STE) and $95.00\% - 96.33\%$ (SSTE).

Vulnerability to GPT-generated profiles: On GPT3.5+4P attacks, F1 scores dropped to $67.88\% - 73.82\%$, and FARs rose to 52.1% (DeBERTa+CatBoost), indicating over half of sophisticated fake profiles were misclassified as legitimate. This degradation aligns with high textual similarity between GPT-generated and real profiles (mean: 88.9%, range: $64.2\% - 99.4\%$).

Adversarial training: GPT3.5-assisted training improved F1 to $97.83\% - 98.15\%$ and cut FARs on GPT3.5Ps to as low as 1.3%, but remained vulnerable to GPT4Ps (FARs: $16.9\% - 19.3\%$). GPT4-assisted training reversed this—F1 up to 97.84% and FARs on GPT4Ps down to $\sim 2\%$, but showed limited generalization to GPT3.5Ps. In contrast, training on the combined GPT3.5+4P dataset yielded strong generalization across all attacks, with FARs between 1.34% and 2.6% and F1 scores consistently above 97.5%. Flair+XGBoost achieved the best overall performance (F1 $= 98.2\%$, FAR $= 1.34\%$ on combined attacks). Across all adversarial training settings, FRRs remained stable (1.48%–2.41%), confirming no significant compromise on correctly classifying legitimate profiles.

4.3 LLM and Human Benchmarking Results

Figure 3 compares the performance of human evaluators and GPT-4 on the task of LinkedIn fake profile detection. Human evaluators showed limited effectiveness, particularly on GPT-generated profiles, with a three-class accuracy of only 31.4% on this category. Aggregated into a binary classification task, their F1 score was 58.9%, with a false accept rate (FAR) of 38.7% and a false reject rate (FRR) of 46.6%, indicating considerable confusion between real and fake profiles. GPT-4 performed better overall. In the zero-shot setting, it reached an F1score of 71.3% but misclassified 43.9% of fake profiles. With few-shot prompting, its performance improved substantially, achieving perfect accuracy on legitimate profiles and reducing the FAR on fakes to 25.0%, raising the F1 score to 85.7%. However, both approaches fall short of our adversarially trained models, which consistently achieve F1 scores above 97.5% and FARs below 2% across all LLM-generated profile scenarios.

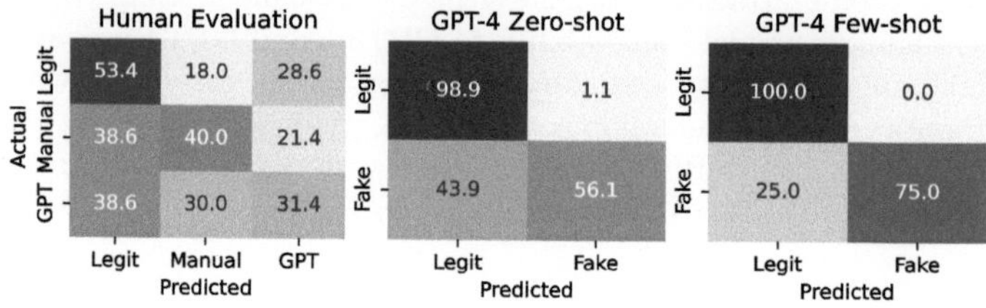

Fig. 3. Confusion matrices comparing human and GPT-4 performance on LinkedIn fake profile detection. Left: Human annotators ($n = 30$) show moderate accuracy on legitimate profiles but perform poorly on fake ones, particularly GPT-generated cases. Middle: GPT-4 (zero-shot) detects legitimate profiles with high accuracy (98.9%) but misclassifies nearly half of fake profiles. Right: Few-shot prompting improves GPT-4's fake detection to 75.0% while maintaining 100% accuracy on legitimate profiles.

4.4 Model Robustness Indicator

To assess the link between model calibration and robustness to adversarial inputs, we computed Pearson correlations between Brier scores [31] and false accept rates (FAR) across encoders and classifiers. Results show a consistent positive correlation: models with lower Brier scores—indicating better-calibrated confidence estimates—tended to exhibit lower FARs against LLM-generated fake profiles. DeBERTa embeddings showed particularly strong correlations (Pearson $r > 0.96$, $p < 0.001$), with CatBoost yielding the highest observed coefficients ($r \approx 0.978$–0.979). Flair embeddings demonstrated slightly weaker but still significant correlations ($r = 0.809$–0.972, $p < 0.001$). Adversarial training improved both calibration and robustness. For instance, DeBERTa with CatBoost reduced its Brier score from 0.135 to 0.063 and its FAR from 52.15% to 2.78% after GPT3.5+4P-assisted training. These findings support prior evidence that well-calibrated models with sharper decision boundaries are more resistant to high-quality adversarial content [34,35].

4.5 Ablation Study

Contributions of the text and numerical embedding (baseline and attack). To assess the contribution of different feature modalities, we compared models trained using only STE embeddings (150 dimensions) versus only numerical features (17 dimensions). Under baseline conditions, both configurations performed comparably: STE achieved F1 scores of 95.19% (CatBoost) and 96.23% (XGBoost), while numerical features reached 95.56% and 95.04%, respectively.

Under adversarial attack, STE-based models experienced substantial performance degradation. F1 scores fell to 67.1%–77.17% (GPT3.5Ps), 75.16%–81.41% (GPT4Ps), and 57.49%–71.63% (combined). In contrast, models using only numerical features exhibited greater robustness, with F1 scores consistently in the range of 78.67%–80.63% across attack types.

These results suggest that while textual features are effective against manually constructed fakes, they are more susceptible to LLM-generated attacks. Numerical features, although lower in dimensionality, appear to capture structural patterns that generalize more effectively in adversarial contexts. This complementarity underscores the benefit of combining both feature types for robust detection.

Text vs. numerical features (post-adversarial training). Feature types also responded differently to adversarial training. Using only STE embeddings, GPT4P-assisted training reduced FARs to 2.59%–8.33% (GPT3.5Ps) and 3.12%–8.33% (GPT4Ps), indicating improved generalization across LLM variants.

In contrast, models using numerical features demonstrated asymmetric gains. For the full 167-dimensional feature set, GPT4P-assisted training substantially reduced FARs for GPT4Ps but had a limited impact on GPT3.5Ps. For example, Flair+XGBoost: FAR dropped from 38.52% to 36.11%. A similar trend was observed when using only numerical features: GPT3.5P-assisted training improved F1 scores from 78.67%–79.21% to 82.55%–84.08% on GPT3.5Ps, whereas GPT4P-assisted training led to a larger jump for GPT4Ps (up to 96.75%).

These findings suggest that textual features tend to generalize more effectively across model variants and adversarial scenarios, whereas numerical features seem to encode generation-specific artifacts. Moreover, the compact 17-dimensional numerical representation offers a lightweight alternative for detection in resource-constrained settings.

5   Limitations and Future Research Directions

While our approach achieves low FARs (1.34%–2.28%) through STE-based features, PCA, and adversarial training under both adversarial and non-adversarial environments, several limitations remain. First, the evaluation is restricted to English-language LinkedIn profiles and should be extended to languages other than English. The method's applicability to other platforms or multilingual contexts has not been tested. Second, embedding extraction relies on a fixed set of LLM-based encoders (e.g., DeBERTa, RoBERTa), which may affect stability as model architectures evolve. Third, both the creation of fake profiles for generating attack vectors and adversarial training used models from the same LLM family (OpenAI GPT). The system needs to be evaluated against a wide variety of advanced LLMs. Fourth, the current experiments should be expanded to include legitimate profiles created by legitimate people who utilized LLMs for creating and polishing their profiles.

6   Conclusion

Existing LinkedIn fake profile detectors perform well on manually created profiles (F1 > 95%) but fail on GPT3.5 and GPT4-generated ones, with F1 dropping to 67.88% and false accept rates (FAR) exceeding 52%. Human annotators (F1 = 58.9%) and general-purpose LLMs (F1 = 85.7%) also underperform in this setting. Targeted adversarial training using GPT-generated profiles restored F1 to 98.2% and reduced FAR to 1.34%, with minimal impact on legitimate profile rejection (FRR < 2.5%). Flair embeddings with XGBoost gave the most consistent results. Ablation experiments revealed that textual features degrade sharply under attack, while numerical features remain more robust. Their combination yields better generalization across model variants and input conditions. These findings support the need for task-specific retraining to maintain robustness against high-quality synthetic profiles generated with the help of LLMs.

References

1. DemandSage. Linkedin statistics 2025: Active users data (worldwide) (2024). https://www.demandsage.com/linkedin-statistics/
2. Cao, Q., Sirivianos, M., Yang, X., Pregueiro, T.: Aiding the detection of fake accounts in large scale social online services. In: NSDI (2012)
3. Adikari, S., Dutta, K.: Identifying fake profiles in linkedin (2020). https://arxiv.org/abs/2006.01381
4. Ayoobi, N., Shahriar, S., Mukherjee, A.: The looming threat of fake and llm-generated linkedin profiles: challenges and opportunities for detection and prevention. In: ACM HT '23 (2023)
5. Strandell, J.: Fake accounts are getting way more common on linkedin (data) (2024). https://besedo.com/blog/linkedin-fake-accounts/
6. Gulati, A., Kumar, R., Agarwal, V.: Linkedin fake profile detection (2024). https://github.com/apoorva106/linkedin_fake_profile_detection

7. Gong, N.Z., Frank, M., Mittal, P.: Sybilbelief: a semi-supervised learning approach for structure-based sybil detection. IEEE TIFS **9**, 976–987 (2014)

8. Breuer, A., Eilat, R., Weinsberg, U.: Friend or faux: graph-based early detection of fake accounts on social networks. In: ACM-WWW (2020)

9. Li, S., Yang, J.: Sybilflyover: Heterogeneous graph-based fake account detection model on social networks. Knowl.-Based Syst. **258**, 110038 (2022)

10. Barbon, S., Igawa, R.A., Bogaz Zarpelão, B.: Authorship verification applied to detection of compromised accounts on online social networks: a continuous approach. Multimedia Tools Appl. **76**, 3213–3233 (2016)

11. Kundu, D., et al.: Keystroke dynamics against academic dishonesty in the age of llms. In: IEEE-IJCB (2024)

12. Roh, D., Kumar, R., Ngo, A.: Llm-assisted cheating detection in Korean language via keystrokes. In: IEEE-IJCB (2025)

13. Kuruvilla, A., Daley, R., Kumar, R.: Spotting fake profiles in social networks via keystroke dynamics. In: IEEE-CCNC (2024)

14. Bhattasali, T., Saeed, K.: Typing Pattern Analysis for Fake Profile Detection in Social Media (2021)

15. Alnagi, E., Ahmad, A., Al-Haija, Q.A., Aref, A.: Unmasking fake social network accounts with explainable intelligence. IJACSA **15**, 1–7 (2024)

16. https://sites.google.com/view/weaklinksinlinkedin

17. Devlin, J., Chang, M.-W., et al.: BERT: pre-training of deep bidirectional transformers for language understanding. ACL (2019)

18. Liu, Y., et al.: Roberta: a robustly optimized bert pretraining approach. In: ICLR (2020)

19. He, P., Liu, X., Gao, J., Chen, W.: Deberta: decoding-enhanced bert with disentangled attention. In: ICLR (2021)

20. Warner, B., et al.: Smarter, better, faster, longer: A modern bidirectional encoder for fast, memory efficient, and long context finetuning and inference. arXiv:2412.13663 (2024)

21. Akbik, A., Blythe, D., Vollgraf, R.: Contextual string embeddings for sequence labeling. In: NAACL-HLT 2018 (2018)

22. Pennington, J., Socher, R., Manning, C.D.: Glove: global vectors for word representation. In: EMNLP (2014)

23. Bhagoji, A.N., Cullina, D., Sitawarin, C., Mittal, P.: Enhancing robustness of machine learning systems via data transformations (2017). https://arxiv.org/abs/1704.02654

24. Demontis, A., Melis, M.: Why do adversarial attacks transfer? Explaining transferability of evasion and poisoning attacks. In: USENIX Security (2019)

25. Chen, T., Guestrin, C.: Xgboost: a scalable tree boosting system. In: SIGKDD (2016)

26. Prokhorenkova, L., Gusev, G.: Catboost: unbiased boosting with categorical features. In: NeurIPS (2018)

27. Snoek, J., Larochelle, H., Adams, R.P.: Practical bayesian optimization of machine learning algorithms (2012)

28. Bergstra, J., Bardenet, R.: Algorithms for hyper-parameter optimization. In: NeurIPS (2011)

29. Young, S.R., Rose, D.C.: Optimizing deep learning hyperparameters through an evolutionary algorithm. In: MLHPC. ACM (2015)

30. Pavlovic, M.: Understanding model calibration – a gentle introduction and visual exploration of calibration and the expected calibration error (2025)

31. Brier, G.W.: Verification of forecasts expressed in terms of probability. Monthly Weather Rev. (1950)
32. https://editor.p5js.org/anonymous_icwsm/full/N2Ait_Cwo (2025)
33. Kasneci, G., Kasneci, E.: Enriching tabular data with contextual llm embeddings: a comprehensive ablation study for ensemble classifiers (2024)
34. Qin, Y., Wang, X., Beutel, A., Chi, E.H.: Improving calibration through the relationship with adversarial robustness. In: NeurIPS (2020)
35. Emde, C., Pinto, F., Lukasiewicz, T., Torr, P.H., Bibi, A.: Towards certification of uncertainty calibration under adversarial attacks. In: ICLR (2025)

Handling Publication Imbalance for Effective Community Detection in Scholarly Networks

Md Asaduzzaman Noor$^{(\boxtimes)}$ [ID], John Sheppard [ID], and Jason Clark [ID]

Montana State University, Bozeman, MT 59717, USA
`{mdasaduzzamannoor,john.sheppard,jaclark}@montana.edu`

Abstract. Finding potential research collaborators is a challenging task, especially in today's fast-growing, interdisciplinary research landscape. While traditional methods rely on observable ties like co-authorships and citations, we focus solely on publication content to build a topic-based research network using BERTopic with a fine-tuned SciB-ERT model that connects and recommends researchers across disciplines based on shared topical interests. A key challenge we address is publication imbalance, where some researchers publish much more than others, often across several topics. Without careful handling, their less frequent interests are hidden under dominant topics, limiting the network's ability to capture their full research scope. To tackle this, we introduce a cloning strategy that clusters a researcher's publications and treats each cluster as a separate node. This allows researchers to belong to multiple communities, improving the detection of interdisciplinary links. Evaluation shows that the cloned network leads to more meaningful communities and uncovers broader collaboration opportunities.

Keywords: Community detection · Collaboration recommendation · Topic-based scholarly network · BERTopic · Social network analysis

1 Introduction

Research collaboration plays a crucial role in advancing scientific discovery, often leading to impactful and interdisciplinary outcomes. As the volume of scholarly publications grows, recommending meaningful collaborations has become increasingly challenging. Most existing approaches rely on observable relationships, such as co-authorship or citation networks, which tend to reinforce known connections and overlook opportunities based on shared topical interests.

We argue that topical similarity, derived from publication content, is a powerful relation for identifying potential collaborations. Researchers working on similar themes may never have co-authored a paper or even be aware of each other's work. By focusing on what researchers publish, we can uncover hidden connections and recommend more diverse collaborations beyond disciplinary lines.

© The Author(s), under exclusive license to Springer Nature Switzerland AG 2026
A. An et al. (Eds.): ASONAM 2025, LNCS 16323, pp. 383–390, 2026.
https://doi.org/10.1007/978-3-032-13821-7_32

While prior work has used publication data, most focus narrowly on ranking candidates with limited interpretability. In contrast, social network analysis (SNA) offers a broader view, revealing how researchers are organized, highlighting influential nodes, and providing community-driven insights through network structures.

In this work, we construct a scholarly network based on topic similarity, using publication titles and abstracts to group researchers by shared research themes. Building on our prior work [11,12], we now address the challenge of publication imbalance. High-output researchers often work across multiple topics, but their less frequent interests are overshadowed by dominant ones, limiting the network's ability to detect meaningful connections.

To address this, we introduce a cloning strategy that clusters a researcher's publications into distinct topical groups, creating multiple "clones" that participate in different communities. This improves the detection of diverse and interdisciplinary collaborations.

Our key contributions are as follows. We introduce a cloning-based strategy to address publication imbalance and improve community detection in topic-based research networks. Using BERTopic on publication titles and abstracts, we build a researcher similarity matrix that captures diverse research interests. We empirically show that our approach uncovers more meaningful collaboration opportunities.

2   Related Work

One key goal of researcher social network analysis is to recommend potential collaborators. Most existing work relies on direct relationships, such as co-authorship or citation links, to suggest collaborators or identify communities. While effective, these methods often overlook the topical diversity of individual researchers, limiting connections based on shared research interests.

Earlier studies framed collaboration recommendation as a link prediction problem on co-authorship networks [1,8]. Hybrid approaches combined direct links with content features to improve recommendations [6,15,16], but still depend on existing connections and tend to reinforce them rather than discover new interdisciplinary links.

Content-based methods rely solely on publication data to suggest collaborations. For example, Liang et al. [7] used LDA topic vectors for cross-disciplinary recommendations, and Kong et al. [5] modeled evolving interests with time-weighted topic distributions. However, these approaches focus on document similarity and top-k recommendations, often lacking interpretability.

Integrating social network analysis with content data offers a more transparent and structural view, highlighting researcher clusters, topic distributions, and key participants through community detection.

Our work builds a topic-based researcher network while explicitly addressing publication count imbalance to enable fairer and more meaningful community detection. To our knowledge, this is the first study to tackle this issue in topic-based community detection for research collaboration.

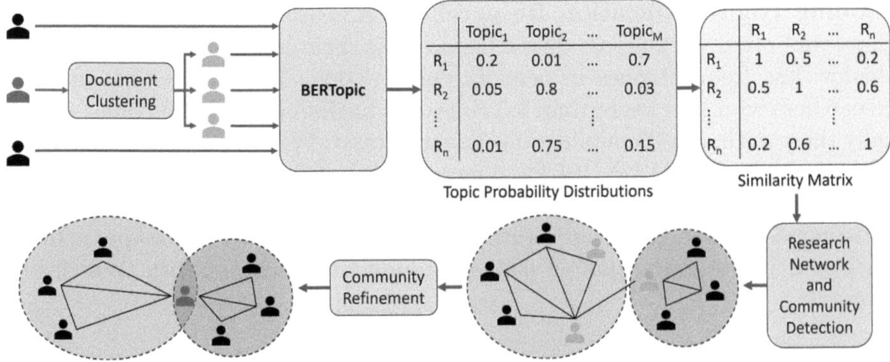

Fig. 1. Overview of the proposed methodology.

3   Dataset

To build the researcher dataset, we used Montana State University's (MSU) current faculty list and retrieved their publication history using OpenAlex [14], an open-source API for accessing scholarly metadata. We collected publication titles, abstracts, and author IDs from 2004 to 2025 for papers affiliated with MSU faculty. In total, we extracted metadata for 9,768 publications. To ensure meaningful topic distributions for our network construction, we excluded researchers with fewer than five publications. This resulted in a final dataset of 296 faculty members, with a maximum of 190 publications for a single researcher and mean and median publication counts of 33 and 22, respectively.

The publication count distribution across researchers is heavily right-skewed: a small number of researchers publish significantly more than others. This imbalance highlights the need to address publication count disparities for effective community detection.

4   Methodology

Our proposed method (Fig. 1) consists of several steps: training a topic model, cloning high-publication researchers, computing topic similarity, building the research network, detecting communities, and refining the structure.

Topic Modeling. We train a BERTopic model [4] on publication titles and abstracts from all researchers to extract topic distributions. To improve domain relevance, we fine-tune the sentence transformer using Masked Language Modeling (MLM) [3] on our corpus, enabling the model to better capture the context of scientific text specific to our dataset. The trained model produces topic-word distributions and document-topic probabilities that are used in the subsequent steps.

Cloning High-Publication Researchers. Researchers with a high publication count often work across diverse topics, but their dominant themes can overshadow less frequent ones in network construction. To address this, we clone researchers who have more than 1.5 times the median publication count, specifically those with over 33 publications in our dataset. We cluster their publications by first applying UMAP [10] for dimensionality reduction, followed by HDBSCAN [9] for document grouping. Each resulting cluster forms a "clone" that corresponds to a thematic area within the broader research landscape, allowing the researcher to participate in multiple communities aligned with their diverse interests.

Computing Topic Similarity. For each researcher or clone, we aggregate the topic probabilities of their publications to obtain a single topic distribution that represents their research focus. We then compute pairwise similarities using Jensen-Shannon Divergence (JSD), where lower divergence values indicate stronger topical alignment. This process results in a topic similarity matrix that captures the topical relationships between all researchers and their clones.

Constructing the Research Network. We construct a fully connected weighted graph using the similarity matrix as the adjacency matrix, where edge weights reflect topic similarity between researchers. To focus the network on meaningful connections, we prune edges with weights below a selected threshold, removing weaker links and highlighting more substantial topic alignments.

Community Detection. Communities are identified using the Nested Hierarchical Louvain (NH-Louvain) algorithm [13], which detects researcher groups at multiple levels of granularity. The hierarchical structure uncovered by this method naturally aligns with how research topics are organized, ranging from broad disciplines to more specific subfields.

Refining Community Structure. Since clones of the same researcher may appear multiple times within a single community, we refine the community structure by merging clones that belong to the same group. This ensures that each researcher is uniquely represented within a community while still preserving multi-community membership if their clones appear in different communities.

Experimental Design and Hyperparameter Tuning. We fine-tuned the sentence embeddings using MLM with 15% token masking over 40 epochs, starting from the `allenai/scibert_scivocab_uncased` model [2]. This fine-tuning step helped the model adapt to our research domain and improved the coherence of the extracted topics. For dimensionality reduction in BERTopic, we used UMAP with `n_neighbors = 15`, `n_components = 5`, and `min_dist = 0.0`, which preserved local document relationships in a low-dimensional space. Topic clustering was performed using HDBSCAN with `min_cluster_size = 8`

Table 1. Summary statistics of the researchers with clones

Total Number of Researchers	296
High-Impact Researchers (More than 33 Papers)	96
Researchers with Clones	68
Max clones for a researcher	10
Median clones per researcher	3

and `min_samples = 4`, which produced 445 distinct topics after training the fine-tuned model.

To create clones, we clustered each high-output researcher's publications using the same fine-tuned sentence embeddings. We applied HDBSCAN with `min_cluster_size = 10` and `min_samples = 5` to form clone groups that captured diverse topical areas within an individual's work. For the class-based TF-IDF representation, we applied standard NLP preprocessing steps, including stopword removal, digit and punctuation filtering, and lemmatization, to ensure cleaner topic representations. Hyperparameters throughout the pipeline were selected through random search, with a focus on finding interpretable and stable clusters rather than pursuing exhaustive optimization.

5 Results and Discussion

We begin by evaluating whether cloning improves community detection, especially for high-impact researchers. Although our method is unsupervised and lacks ground truth, we provide both quantitative and qualitative analyses to assess its impact. Table 1 summarizes the cloning outcomes. Of the 296 researchers in our dataset, 96 were classified as high-impact with more than 33 publications. Among them, 68 researchers formed multiple publication clusters via HDBSCAN, while the rest formed either a single cluster or were classified as outliers. The maximum number of clones for a researcher was 10, the median number of clones was 3, and the median publication count among clones was 23, which closely aligns with the original median of 22 before cloning.

We compared edge weight distributions before and after cloning, as shown in Fig. 2. After applying the community refinement step to the cloned network, we observed reduced skew and increased mean and median edge weights, suggesting that topic similarity between researchers became more pronounced.

Figure 3 shows the mean edge weights of cloned researchers before and after cloning. For all cloned researchers, mean edge weights increased, indicating that cloning better captured their diverse research topics.

For community detection, we pruned edges until the network reached a density of 0.1. This threshold retains only strong connections, which helps uncover more meaningful and well-separated community structures. We used the NH-Louvain algorithm with a minimum community size of 30, balancing granularity and interpretability. The final network had 30 communities, with sizes ranging

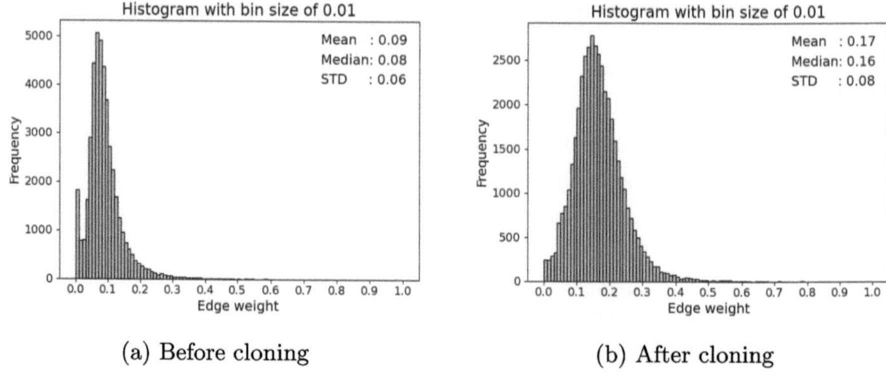

(a) Before cloning

(b) After cloning

Fig. 2. Distribution of edge weights before and after cloning.

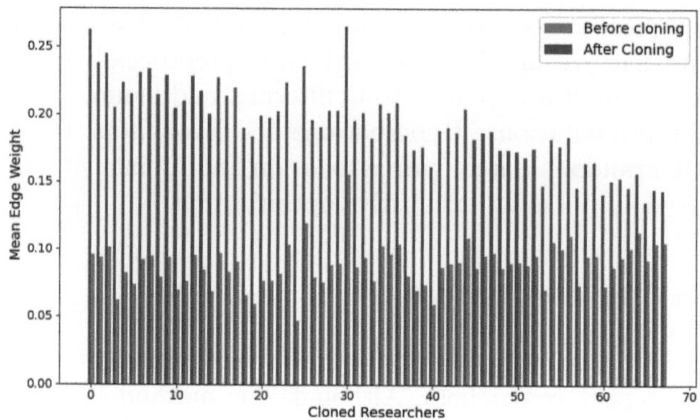

Fig. 3. Mean edge weights of cloned researchers before and after cloning.

from 2 to 28 researchers (mean 11.2), and an average community density of 0.64, indicating strong internal connectivity.

We also observed overlapping community memberships. In total, 29 researchers belonged to more than one community after the refinement step, confirming that cloning helped reveal diverse topical affiliations. Most overlapping researchers appeared in two communities, with the maximum being four.

Figure 4 shows an example subnetwork where researchers 74, 228, 394, and 454 belong to multiple communities. Researcher 74 appears in all three communities, while others overlap between two.

Figure 5 provides a wordcloud example for overlapping researcher 454. The pre-cloning wordcloud (left) shows a mixture of topics, while the two clones (middle and right) show distinct topical focuses, allowing them to be placed in different communities.

Although our method was not explicitly designed for overlapping community detection, cloning naturally enabled multiple memberships. This opens the possibility of using our approach for detecting overlapping communities in text-based

Fig. 4. Example of overlapping communities. Dashed circles indicate overlapping researchers.

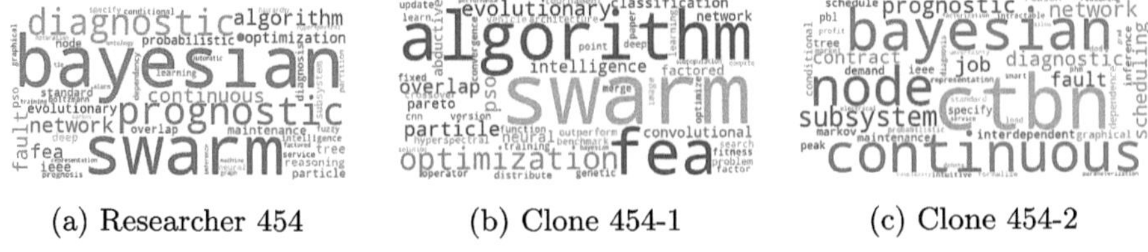

(a) Researcher 454   (b) Clone 454-1   (c) Clone 454-2

Fig. 5. Wordclouds showing top 50 words for Researcher 454 and its two clones.

networks. Future work should also explore broader datasets, stronger baselines, sensitivity analyses on key thresholds, and scalability assessments to further validate and generalize the approach.

6 Conclusion

In this paper, we presented an approach exploring topic-based networks for identifying research communities and enabling diverse collaboration recommendations. Using BERTopic and a fine-tuned SciBERT model, we built a topic similarity network capturing connections across disciplines. To address publication imbalance, we introduced a cloning strategy that clusters publications, highlighting less common research areas otherwise overshadowed. This approach allows researchers to belong to multiple communities, better reflecting their full research scope and supporting interdisciplinary recommendations. Our evaluation shows that the cloned network improves both community coherence and the diversity of potential collaborations.

Acknowledgments. This paper is based on work supported, in part, by NSF EPSCoR Cooperative Agreement OIA-2242802. Any opinions, findings, and conclusions or recommendations expressed in this material are those of the author(s) and do not necessarily reflect the views of the National Science Foundation.

References

1. Backstrom, L., Leskovec, J.: Supervised random walks: predicting and recommending links in social networks. In: Proceedings of the Fourth ACM International Conference on Web Search and Data Mining, pp. 635–644 (2011)
2. Beltagy, I., Lo, K., Cohan, A.: SciBERT: a pretrained language model for scientific text. In: Proceedings of the 2019 Conference on Empirical Methods in Natural Language Processing and the 9th International Joint Conference on Natural Language Processing (EMNLP-IJCNLP), pp. 3615–3620 (2019)
3. Devlin, J., Chang, M.W., Lee, K., Toutanova, K.: Bert: pre-training of deep bidirectional transformers for language understanding. arXiv preprint arXiv:1810.04805 (2019)
4. Grootendorst, M.: Bertopic: neural topic modeling with a class-based tf-idf procedure. arXiv preprint arXiv:2203.05794 (2022)
5. Kong, X., Jiang, H., Wang, W., Bekele, T.M., Xu, Z., Wang, M.: Exploring dynamic research interest and academic influence for scientific collaborator recommendation. Scientometrics 113, 369–385 (2017)
6. Kong, X., Jiang, H., Yang, Z., Xu, Z., Xia, F., Tolba, A.: Exploiting publication contents and collaboration networks for collaborator recommendation. Public Libr. Sci. 11(2), e0148492 (2016)
7. Liang, W., Zhou, X., Huang, S., Hu, C., Jin, Q.: Recommendation for cross-disciplinary collaboration based on potential research field discovery. In: 2017 Fifth International Conference on Advanced Cloud and Big Data (CBD), pp. 349–354 (2017)
8. Liben-Nowell, D., Kleinberg, J.: The link prediction problem for social networks. In: Proceedings of the Twelfth International Conference on Information and Knowledge Management, pp. 556–559 (2003)
9. McInnes, L., Healy, J., Astels, S.: hdbscan: hierarchical density based clustering. J. Open Source Softw. 2(11), 205 (2017)
10. McInnes, L., Healy, J., Saul, N., Großberger, L.: Umap: uniform manifold approximation and projection. J. Open Source Softw. 3(29), 861 (2018)
11. Noor, M.A., Clark, J.A., Sheppard, J.W.: Scholarnodes: applying content-based filtering to recommend interdisciplinary communities within scholarly social networks. In: Proceedings of the 47th International ACM SIGIR Conference on Research and Development in Information Retrieval, pp. 2791–2795 (2024)
12. Noor, M.A., Sheppard, J., Clark, J.: Finding potential research collaborations from social networks derived from topic models. In: 10th International Conference on Behavioural and Social Computing, pp. 1–7 (2023)
13. Noor, M.A., Sheppard, J.W., A. Clark, J.: Identifying hierarchical community structures in content-based scholarly social networks. In: 2024 International Conference on Machine Learning and Applications (ICMLA), pp. 440–447 (2024)
14. Priem, J., Piwowar, H., Orr, R.: Openalex: a fully-open index of scholarly works, authors, venues, institutions, and concepts. arXiv preprint arXiv:2205.01833 (2022)
15. Yang, C., Sun, J., Ma, J., Zhang, S., Wang, G., Hua, Z.: Scientific collaborator recommendation in heterogeneous bibliographic networks. In: 2015 48th Hawaii International Conference on System Sciences, pp. 552–561 (2015)
16. Zhou, X., Liang, W., Wang, K.I.K., Huang, R., Jin, Q.: Academic influence aware and multidimensional network analysis for research collaboration navigation based on scholarly big data. IEEE Trans. Emerg. Top. Comput. 9(1), 246–257 (2021)

Author Index

MIX
Papier aus verantwortungsvollen Quellen
Paper from responsible sources
FSC® C105338

If you have any concerns about our products,
you can contact us on
ProductSafety@springernature.com

In case Publisher is established outside the EU,
the EU authorized representative is:
**Springer Nature Customer Service Center GmbH
Europaplatz 3, 69115 Heidelberg, Germany**

Printed by Libri Plureos GmbH
in Hamburg, Germany